THE OXFORD HANDBO

WITCHCRAFT IN EARLY MODERN EUROPE AND COLONIAL AMERICA

'a worthwhile contribution to the literature which all concerned with early modern witchcraft will consult with profit'

Michael Hunter, *History Today*

'it abounds with fresh details and perspectives'

Ronald Hutton, *The Journal of Ecclesiastical History*

The essays in this *Handbook*, written by leading scholars working in the rapidly developing field of witchcraft studies, explore the historical literature regarding witch beliefs and witch trials in Europe and colonial America between the early fifteenth and early eighteenth centuries. During these years witches were thought to be evil people who used magical power to inflict physical harm or misfortune on their neighbours. Witches were also believed to have made pacts with the devil and sometimes to have worshipped him at nocturnal assemblies known as sabbaths. These beliefs provided the basis for defining witchcraft as a secular and ecclesiastical crime and prosecuting tens of thousands of women and men for this offence. The trials resulted in as many as fifty thousand executions.

These essays study the rise and fall of witchcraft prosecutions in the various kingdoms and territories of Europe and in English, Spanish, and Portuguese colonies in the Americas. They also relate these prosecutions to the Catholic and Protestant reformations, the introduction of new forms of criminal procedure, medical and scientific thought, the process of state-building, profound social and economic change, early modern patterns of gender relations, and the wave of demonic possessions that occurred in Europe at the same time. The essays survey the current state of knowledge in the field, explore the academic controversies that have arisen regarding witch beliefs and witch trials, propose new ways of studying the subject, and identify areas for future research.

Brian P. Levack is John E. Green Regents Professor in History at the University of Texas at Austin.

THE OXFORD HANDBOOK OF

WITCHCRAFT IN EARLY MODERN EUROPE AND COLONIAL AMERICA

Edited by
BRIAN P. LEVACK

OXFORD
UNIVERSITY PRESS

OXFORD
UNIVERSITY PRESS

Great Clarendon Street, Oxford OX2 6DP
United Kingdom

Oxford University Press is a department of the University of Oxford.
It furthers the University's objective of excellence in research, scholarship,
and education by publishing worldwide. Oxford is a registered trade mark of
Oxford University Press in the UK and in certain other countries

First published 2013
First published in paperback 2014

Impression: 1

Published in the United States of America by Oxford University Press
198 Madison Avenue, New York, NY 10016, United States of America

British Library Cataloguing in Publication Data

Data available

ISBN 978–0–19–957816–0 (Hbk.)
ISBN 978–0–19–872363–9 (Pbk.)

TABLE OF CONTENTS

PART I WITCH BELIEFS

PART II WITCHCRAFT PROSECUTIONS

PART III THEMES OF WITCHCRAFT RESEARCH

LIST OF TABLES

Notes on Contributors

Edward Bever is Professor of History at the State University of New York College at Old Westbury. He earned his Ph.D. from Princeton University in 1983 with a dissertation titled 'Witchcraft in Early Modern Wuerttemberg'. He has published numerous articles and entries on witchcraft and magic in early modern Europe, and in 2008 published *The Realities of Witchcraft and Popular Magic in Early Modern Europe: Culture, Cognition, and Everyday Life*. He is currently co-editing a volume of papers, *Magic and the Modern*, and his most recent article is 'Current Trends in the Application of Cognitive Science to Magic' in *Magic, Ritual, and Witchcraft* (2012).

Willem de Blécourt is an historical anthropologist and Honorary Research Fellow at the Huizinga Institute and the Meertens Institute, both in Amsterdam. He is co-author of *Witchcraft and Magic in Europe: The Twentieth Century* (1999) and co-editor of a number of books on the history of witchcraft and medical history, the latest being a volume on shapeshifting. His book, *Tales of Magic, Tales in Print: On the Genealogy of Fairy Tales and the Brothers Grimm*, appeared in 2012. Among his many articles are 'The Return of the Sabbat' in *Palgrave Advances in Witchcraft Historiography* (2007) and 'A Journey to Hell: Reconsidering the Livonian "Werewolf"' in *Magic, Ritual and Witchcraft* (2007). He is co-editor of the book series, *Historical Studies in Witchcraft and Magic*.

Robin Briggs is Emeritus Senior Research Fellow, All Souls College, Oxford, and a Fellow of the British Academy. His publications include *Early Modern France, 1560–1715* (1977), *Communities of Belief: Social and Cultural Tensions in Early Modern France* (1989), *Witches and Neighbours: The Social and Cultural Context of European Witchcraft* (1996), and *The Witches of Lorraine* (Oxford, 2007). His website of *Lorraine Witchcraft Trials*, including abstracts of some 400 Lorraine trials, is available at <http://www.history.ox.ac.uk/staff/robinbriggs>.

Hans Peter Broedel is an Associate Professor of History at the University of North Dakota, and received his Ph.D. from the University of Washington. He is the author of *The* Malleus Maleficarum *and the Construction of Witchcraft: Theology and Popular Belief* (2003), and has published articles on witches, late medieval apparitions, and early modern natural history. His current research investigates credulity and scepticism in early modern attitudes towards fantastic animals.

Johannes Dillinger studied history, Catholic theology, and educational theory at Tübingen University, Trier University, and the University of East Anglia. Dillinger is currently senior lecturer in early modern history at Oxford Brookes University. His Ph.D. thesis, 'Böse Leute', won the Friedrich Spee Award for Outstanding Contributions to the History of Witchcraft in 1999 and was translated into English as *"Evil People": A Comparative Study of Witch Hunts in Swabian Austria and the Electorate of Trier* (2009). Dillinger has published several works on witchcraft and magic, including two monographs on treasure hunting, as well as books and articles on constitutional history and political crime.

Oscar Di Simplicio, former lecturer of modern history at the University of Florence, lives in Siena. He has written extensively on the history of witchcraft, and his publications include *Inquisizione stregoneria medicina. Siena e il suo stato, 1580–1721* (2000) and *Autunno della stregoneria. Maleficio e magia nell'Italia moderna* (2005). He has contributed to *The Encyclopedia of Witchcraft* (2006) and to *Witchcraft and Masculinity in Early Modern Europe* (2009). He is the author of *Luxuria. Eros e violenza nel Seicento* (2011), in which he has sketched a neuropsychological approach to the study of witchcraft cognition. He will deal with this subject in depth in his forthcoming book, *Dentro la stregoneria*.

Peter Elmer, after seventeen years as a lecturer at the Open University in the UK, in September 2012 began a five year post as a Wellcome Trust funded Senior Research Fellow at the University of Exeter, engaged on a project aiming to create a database of all men and women engaged in medical practice in England, Ireland, and Wales between about 1500 and 1715. The prosopographical nature of this research will form the basis of a major new appraisal of the place of medicine in early modern British society.

Sarah Ferber is Associate Professor of History at the University of Wollongong. She is the author of *Demonic Possession and Exorcism in Early Modern France* (2004). She contributed several entries to the *Encyclopedia of Witchcraft* (2006), and an essay on gender and demonic possession appeared in Alison Rowlands (ed.), *Witchcraft and Masculinities in Early Modern Europe* (2009). Sarah participated with Robin Briggs, Moshe Sluhovsky, and Denis Crouzet in a French docudrama *L'énergumène* (ed. Jean Loïc Portron, 2010), on the life of the demoniac Marthe Brossier.

Iris Gareis received her Ph.D. from the University of Munich in 1987 and a Habilitation from Goethe-University, Frankfurt in 1999. She has taught at several German universities and in San Juan, Argentina. Currently she is extraordinary professor of Anthropology at Goethe-University, Frankfurt and interim professor of Latin American and Southwest-European History at Erfurt University. She is co-editor of the series 'Hexenforschung' (Witchcraft Research, Bielefeld) and author of numerous articles on witchcraft and related subjects, especially in the Hispanic and Lusophone world. Research interests include popular belief systems and cultures of knowledge, as well as gender and transculturation.

Malcolm Gaskill is Professor of Early Modern History at the University of East Anglia. Educated at Cambridge University, he has taught at five UK universities and is a Fellow of the Royal Historical Society. He is the author of numerous studies relating to witchcraft, including four books: *Crime and Mentalities in Early Modern England* (2000), *Hellish Nell: Last of Britain's Witches* (2001), *Witchfinders: a Seventeenth-Century English Tragedy* (2005), and *Witchcraft: A Very Short* Introduction (2010). His latest work is a study of culture and mentality in seventeenth-century America, culminating in the Salem witch-trials, to be published in 2013.

Richard Godbeer is Professor of History at the University of Miami. He is author of *The Devil's Dominion: Magic and Religion in Early New England* (1992), *Sexual Revolution in Early America* (2002), *Escaping Salem: The Other Witch Hunt of 1692* (2005), *The Overflowing of Friendship: Love between Men and the Creation of the American Republic* (2009), and *The Salem Witch Hunt: A Brief History with Documents* (2011).

Julian Goodare is Reader in History, University of Edinburgh. His books include *State and Society in Early Modern Scotland* (1999), *The Government of Scotland, 1560–1625* (2004), *The Scottish Witch-Hunt in Context* (Manchester, 2002) (as editor), and *Witchcraft and Belief in Early Modern Scotland* (2008) (as co-editor with Lauren Martin and Joyce Miller). He is currently writing *The European Witch-Hunt* for Routledge. He was Director of the Survey of Scottish Witchcraft, which went online in 2003.

Rune Blix Hagen is an Associate Professor of History in the Department of History and Religious Studies in the Faculty of Humanities, Social Sciences and Education, at the University of Tromsø. His fields of research include the persecution of alleged witches in Arctic Norway, 1590–1695 and the relationship between shamanism and witchcraft. He has also written books and articles on early modern mentalities, historiography, and the discovery and exploration of the extreme north during the sixteenth and seventeenth centuries.

Tamar Herzig is a senior lecturer in early modern history at Tel Aviv University, Israel, and the author of *Savonarola's Women: Visions and Reform in Renaissance Italy* (2008). Her articles on fifteenth and sixteenth-century Italian inquisitors and demonologists were published in the *Sixteenth Century Journal*, *Journal of Early Modern History* and *Magic, Ritual, and Witchcraft*, and she also contributed entries to the *Encyclopedia of Witchcraft* (2006) and to the *Dizionario Storico dell'Inquisizione*. Her latest book is *Christ Transformed into a Virgin Woman: Lucia Brocadelli, Heinrich Institoris and the Defense of Faith* (2013).

Richard Kieckhefer teaches at Northwestern University, in the departments of Religious Studies and History. He works on the religious culture of late medieval Europe, including the history of witchcraft and magic. His publications in this area include

European Witch Trials: Their Foundations in Popular and Learned Culture (1976), *Magic in the Middle Ages* (1989), and *Forbidden Rites: A Necromancer's Handbook of the Fifteenth Century* (1997). He also has a long-standing interest in the history of church-building as it relates to late medieval religion and society.

Valerie Kivelson is Professor of History and Arthur F. Thurnau Professor at the University of Michigan in Ann Arbor. Her newest work, *Desperate Magic: The Moral Economy of Witchcraft in Seventeenth Century Russia* will be published in 2013. She is the author of *Cartographies of Tsardom: The Land and Its Meanings in Seventeenth-Century Russia* (2006) and *Autocracy in the Provinces: Russian Political Culture and the Gentry in the Seventeenth Century* (1997), and co-editor of several volumes, including, with Joan Neuberger, *Picturing Russia: Explorations in Visual Culture* (2008).

Ildikó Sz. Kristóf is Senior Research Fellow in the Institute of Ethnology of the Hungarian Academy of Sciences, Budapest. She holds her Ph.D. from the Hungarian Academy of Sciences (1994). Her doctoral thesis, 'The Social and Cultural Foundation of Witch-Hunting in the City of Debrecen and Bihar County between the Sixteenth and the Eighteenth Centuries', was published in Hungarian in 1998. Her research interests include the social and cultural history of witch-hunting, the history of early modern communication (orality, writing, and printing), and currently the history of the science of anthropology (the reception and appropriation of non-European indigenous peoples, especially American Indians in Eastern Europe/Hungary).

Brian P. Levack is the John E. Green Regents Professor in History at the University of Texas at Austin. He has published widely on English and Scottish legal history and the history of witchcraft prosecutions. His publications on witchcraft include *The Witch-Hunt in Early Modern Europe* (3rd edn, 2006) and *Witch-Hunting in Scotland: Law, Politics and Religion* (2008). He is co-author of *Witchcraft and Magic in Europe: The Eighteenth and Nineteenth Centuries* (1999) and the editor of *The Witchcraft Source-book* (2004). His most recent book is *The Devil Within: Possession and Exorcism in the Christian West* (2013).

William Monter, Professor Emeritus of History at Northwestern University, has published often on this subject since 1971 and contributed numerous articles to Richard Golden, ed., *Encyclopedia of Witchcraft: The Western Tradition* (2006). His most recent book is *The Bewitched Duchy: Lorraine and Its Dukes, 1477–1737* (2007). He serves on the editorial board of *Magic, Ritual and Witchcraft*.

Michael Ostling has taught at the University of Toronto, Wilfrid Laurier University, and Central Michigan University. He is the author of *Between the Devil and the Host: Imagining Witchcraft in Early Modern Poland* (2011). As a postdoctoral fellow at the Centre for the History of European Discourses at the University of Queensland, Ostling is currently undertaking research on the intermingling of beliefs related to fairies, goblins, and devils.

Diane Purkiss is Fellow and Tutor in English at Keble College, Oxford. She has published widely on witchcraft in history and literature, and on the English Civil War, Milton and Marvell. Her next book will be entitled *Shakespeare and the Supernatural*, and she is also working on a history of food and taste.

Thomas Robisheaux is the Fred W. Schaffer Professor of History at Duke University in Durham, North Carolina. He is author of *Rural Society and the Search for Order in Early Modern Germany* (1989) and *The Last Witch of Langenburg: Murder in a German Village* (2009). His research interests include the social and cultural history of early modern Germany, the history of magic, religion, and science in the Western world to the present day and micro-historical approaches to history.

Alison Rowlands took a BA in history at St Hilda's College, Oxford and a Ph.D. in early modern German history under the supervision of Bob Scribner at Clare College, Cambridge. She has taught early modern history at the University of Essex since 1992. Her main areas of research interest are early modern witchcraft and witch-trials; women and gender; and the history of Rothenburg ob der Tauber. Key publications include *Witchcraft Narratives in Germany: Rothenburg, 1561–1652* (2003), 'Witchcraft and Old Women in Early Modern Germany', *Past & Present* (2001), and (ed.) *Witchcraft and Masculinities in Early Modern Europe* (2009).

Walter Stephens is the Charles S. Singleton Professor of Italian Studies at Johns Hopkins University. He is the author of *Giants in Those Days: Folklore, Ancient History, and Nationalism* (1989), *Demon Lovers: Witchcraft, Sex, and the Crisis of Belief* (2002), and co-editor of *The Body in Early Modern Italy* (Baltimore, 2010). His articles on witchcraft and demonology appear in *Encyclopedia of Witchcraft: The Western Tradition* (Santa Barbara, 2006), *The Encyclopedia of Religion* (2nd edn, Detroit, 2005), *A Cultural History of Sexuality in the Renaissance* (2011), and other reference works.

Hans de Waardt lectures on early modern cultural history at VU University in Amsterdam, where he also acts as coordinator of a masters course on the history of medicine. His research focuses on the history of witchcraft, on medical history, and on the history of science and humanism in the early modern Low Countries. In 1991 he published *Toverij en samenleving: Holland 1500–1800* (*Sorcery and Society: Holland 1500–1800*), and in 2005 *Mending Minds: A Cultural History of Dutch Academic Psychiatry*. Currently he is preparing an intellectual biography of Johan Wier, the Dutch physician who in 1563 published his plea against the witchcraft prosecutions, *De praestigiis daemonum* (*On the Illusions of Demons*).

Gary K. Waite is a Professor of medieval and early-modern History at the University of New Brunswick, Fredericton, Canada. His research on the Reformation and the witchhunts has resulted in several articles and two books: *Heresy, Magic, and Witchcraft in Early Modern Europe* (2003) and *Eradicating the Devil's Minions: Anabaptists and Witches in Reformation Europe* (2007). He is currently pursuing research on the intersecting themes of spiritualism and beliefs about Jews and Muslims in seventeenth-century Europe.

Gerhild Scholz Williams is the Barbara Schaps Thomas and David M. Thomas Professor in the Humanities in Arts and Sciences, Vice Provost, and Associate Vice Chancellor at Washington University in St Louis. She has written books and articles on German and French medieval and early modern literature and culture, including *Ways of Knowing in Early Modern Germany: Johannes Praetorius as a Witness to his Time* (2006), *On the Inconstancy of Witches: Pierre de Lancre's* Tableau de l'inconstance des mauvais anges et demons (1612) (2006), and *Defining Dominion: The Discourses of Magic and Witchcraft in Early Modern France and Germany* (1995).

Charles Zika is Professorial Fellow in the School of Historical and Philosophical Studies at the University of Melbourne, and Chief Investigator in the Australian Research Council Centre of Excellence in the History of the Emotions (Europe 1100–1800). He is a Fellow of the Australian Academy of the Humanities and in 2010–11 was resident fellow at the Institute of Advanced Studies, Lichtenberg-Kolleg, University of Goettingen. His publications have focused on the religious and visual culture of early modern Germany, and his most recent book is *The Appearance of Witchcraft: Print and Visual Culture in Sixteenth-Century Europe* (2007).

INTRODUCTION

BRIAN P. LEVACK

THE scholarly study of the history of witchcraft, which began with the publication of Wilhelm Soldan's study of witch trials in the mid-nineteenth century, continues to grow at a furious pace and shows no signs of abating. One reason for the proliferation of witchcraft studies, especially in the past few decades, has been the interdisciplinary nature of the field. Historians continue to form the nucleus of witchcraft scholarship, but anthropologists, folklorists, literary scholars, sociologists, art historians, and psychologists, as well as scholars working in the interdisciplinary fields of religious studies and gender studies, have also made notable contributions to the field.

Among the many signs of the health and fertility of witchcraft studies are the plethora of local and regional studies in the regions where witches were prosecuted; numerous collections of scholarly essays;[1] the publication of a six-volume history of witchcraft and magic in Europe from ancient times to the present;[2] an authoritative four-volume encyclopedia of witchcraft with entries by scholars from twenty-eight countries;[3] the publication of modern scholarly editions of early modern treatises on witchcraft and demonology;[4] a six-volume edition of English pamphlets and

---

[1] Two of the most influential such anthologies are Bengt Ankarloo and Gustav Henningsen, eds, *Early Modern European Witchcraft: Centres and Peripheries* (Oxford, 1991) and Jonathan Barry, Marianne Hester, and Gareth Roberts, eds, *Witchcraft in Early Modern Europe: Studies in Culture and Belief* (Cambridge, 1996).

[2] Bengt Ankarloo and Stuart Clark, eds, *Witchcraft and Magic in Europe*, 6 vols (London, 1999–2002).

[3] Richard Golden, ed., *Encyclopedia of Witchcraft: The Western Tradition*, 4 vols (Santa Barbara, CA, 2006).

[4] *Witches, Devil, and Doctors in the Renaissance: Johann Weyer*, De praestigiis daemonum, ed. George Mora (Binghamton, NY, 1991) ; Henricus Institoris, *Malleus Maleficarum*, ed. and tr. Christopher S. MacKay, 2 vols (Cambridge, 2006); Jean Bodin, *On the Demon-Mania of Witches*, tr. Randy A. Scott, ed. Jonathan L. Pearl (Toronto, 2001); Friedrich Spee von Langenfeld, *Cautio Criminalis, or a Book on Witch Trials*, tr. Marcus Hellyer (Charlottesville, VA, 2003); *On the Inconstancy of Witches: Pierre de Lancre's* Tableau de l'inconstance des mauvais anges et demons *(1612)*, ed. Gerhild Scholz Williams

demonological treatises spanning the years 1520–1736;[5] the publication of anthologies of primary sources;[6] and the establishment of national witchcraft research projects in Scotland, Germany, Norway, Hungary, and Poland. A journal devoted exclusively to magic and witchcraft, *Magic, Ritual, and Witchcraft*, commenced publication in 2006, while an internet listserv, *Hexenforschung*, produces daily postings, mostly in German but with a good number in English.[7] One sign that the field of witchcraft studies has come of age has been the publication of a book devoted entirely to witchcraft historiography.[8] Reviews of the literature of witchcraft have also appeared from time to time.[9]

The purpose of this volume is threefold. The first is to summarize the current state of knowledge in the field. The contributors have done this in such a way as to make their presentations useful both to those already familiar with the topic and those who are coming to it for the first time. The second objective is to identify the most important historical literature that has been produced on the subject, to discuss the different ways scholars have approached the subject, and comment on the controversies to which the subject has given rise. The titles listed as Further Reading in each chapter are intended to identify the most significant works in the field, with a preference for works in English, while the notes provide suggestions for those who might wish to conduct further research. The third objective is to propose new ways of looking at the topic or suggest avenues for further research.

The chapters in this volume are grouped in three sections. The first part, which includes Chapters 1–8, focuses on witch beliefs—the ideas of both educated elites and illiterate villagers and townspeople regarding the identity, powers, and activities of those people known as witches. The second part, spanning Chapters 9–24, deals with witchcraft prosecutions—the formal accusation, trial, and punishment of those suspected of perpetrating the crime of witchcraft. The chapters in this second section are organized geographically, although the first chapter deals with the origins of trials for diabolical witchcraft in France, Switzerland, and Italy and concludes with a study of the decline and end of witch-hunting throughout Europe and in European settlements in the Americas. The third part addresses some of the thematic issues that scholars have explored in studying the subject. These deal with the relationship between

(Tempe, AZ, 2006); Martín Del Rio, *Investigations into Magic*, ed. P. G. Maxwell-Stuart (Manchester, 2000).

[5] James Sharpe, Marion Gibson, Malcolm Gaskill, and Peter Elmer, eds, *English Witchcraft, 1560–1736*, 6 vols (London, 2003).

[6] Alan Kors and Edward Peters, eds, *European Witchcraft 400–1700* (2nd edn, Philadelphia, PA, 2003); Marion Gibson, ed., *Witchcraft and Society in England and America, 1550–1750* (Ithaca, NY, 2003); Brian P. Levack, ed., *The Witchcraft Sourcebook* (London, 2004).

[7] hexenforschung@listserv.dfn.de.

[8] Jonathan Barry and Owen Davies, eds, *Palgrave Advances in Witchcraft Historiography* (Basingstoke, 2007).

[9] For two reviews of witchcraft literature that have appeared since 2000 see Brian P. Levack, 'Themes of Recent Witchcraft Research', *ARV: Nordic Yearbook of Folklore*, 62 (2006), 7–31; Malcolm Gaskill, 'The Pursuit of Reality: Recent Research into the History of Witchcraft', *Historical Journal*, 51 (2008), 1069–88.

witch-hunting and some of the main developments in early modern European history. They include the Catholic and Protestant Reformations, the development of science and medicine, economic and social change, the growth of the modern state, the introduction of new systems of criminal procedure, changing gender roles, and the increase in the number of demonic possessions.

It is, of course, impossible to separate the trials themselves from the beliefs upon which prosecutions were based. The beliefs of judges or inquisitors who conducted the trials and those of the witches' neighbours who initially suspected and accused them had a direct bearing on the judicial case against the accused. At the same time, the formal sentencing of witches, the public reading of their confessions at the time and place of execution, and the publication of accounts of their misdeeds and trials promoted or reaffirmed the witch beliefs of judges and witnesses alike. Evidence gained from the trials was also incorporated into demonological treatises, especially those written by judges or inquisitors, and those treatises in turn contributed to the diffusion of witch beliefs to a wider audience, especially after these works became available in print.

The witch beliefs that inspired the trials and were enshrined in the demonological literature were far from homogeneous. There was little consensus regarding the identity of a typical witch or the powers she or he possessed. Reference to the development of a cumulative or composite concept of witchcraft—a notion that originated in the work of the German scholar Joseph Hansen at the beginning of the twentieth century—is useful in identifying the full complement of diabolical and magical activities that witches were believed to perform, but there were very few trials in which the witches were actually accused of all the elements included in this concept.[10] The most salient feature of that concept, the alleged nocturnal assemblies of witches, often referred to as the witches' sabbath (sabbat in French), was itself a composite of many different notions of both popular and learned origin that admitted countless variations in different parts of Europe. Like many other alleged activities of witches, references to the collective worship of the devil did not appear in the judicial record of even a majority of witchcraft prosecutions. Other witch beliefs, such as the magical practices that witches were engaged in, the different relationships between witches and the demons that were believed to be the source of their power, the personal characteristics of witches, and the nature of their relationships with their communities, varied from place to place. There was no one stereotype of the European witch, and even within specific localities witches did not conform to a single social profile. There was broad agreement that witches were individuals who could cause harm, misfortune, or evil by some sort of preternatural or occult means, but even that broad definition

---

[10] Joseph Hansen, *Zauberwahn, Inquisition und Hexenprozeß im Mittelalter, und die Entstehung der großen Hexenverfolgung* (Munich, 1900). For a late twentieth-century account of the gradual but by no means linear accumulation of the different elements of this concept of witchcraft see Norman Cohn, *Europe's Inner Demons: The Demonization of Christians in Medieval Christendom* (rev. edn, Chicago, 1993).

excludes so-called good or white witches, who performed a variety of beneficent functions by occult means.

The absence of any clear sense of the identity of witches was reflected in the many different ways in which the crime of witchcraft was defined. Most of the early modern authors who discussed witchcraft claimed that it involved both the practice of harmful magic (*maleficium*) and a subservient relationship with the devil, with whom the witch was believed to have formed a pact that enabled her, among other things, to exercise magical powers. But different jurisdictions chose to emphasize one dimension of the witch's crime to the exclusion of the other, and the judicial record reflects those differences. On the one hand, many witchcraft prosecutions throughout Europe enumerated the alleged *maleficia* of accused witches but made no reference to the relationship between the accused and the devil. On the other hand, large clusters of witches who were tried for having made pacts with the devil and worshipping him at the witches' sabbath were never specifically charged with performing acts of magical harm. This latter situation prevailed mainly in so-called chain-reaction witch-hunts, in which confessing witches, subjected to or threatened with additional torture, named their alleged accomplices. All these offenders were referred to as witches. The reason for the very broad, imprecise definition of witchcraft is that it was a composite crime that allowed lay and ecclesiastical, local and central judicial authorities to prosecute individuals for engaging in those activities which represented the greatest perceived threat to religious orthodoxy, political stability, or the social order.

One of the main impediments to establishing a precise definition of witchcraft was its ambivalent relationship to magic. Although the charges against witches usually included the practice of maleficent magic, magic could also be prosecuted as a separate crime in many jurisdictions. Most languages had different words for the two offences, as in German, where *Zauberei* could be distinguished from *Hexerei*. One reason for the ambivalent relationship between witchcraft and magic was that the practice of ritual magic in the late Middle Ages had a formative influence in defining the crime of witchcraft in the early modern period.[11] The central witch belief of the pact with the devil, for example, developed mainly within the context of the condemnation of ritual magic. In a certain sense the male, educated ritual magician was transformed into the illiterate female witch in the early fifteenth century. After this transformation occurred, however, those suspected of practising magic might still be prosecuted as magicians rather than witches. Towards the end of the period of the witch trials, the incorporation of magic into witchcraft was reversed, as the composite crime of witchcraft broke down into its various components. As authorities became increasingly reluctant to prosecute people for making pacts with the devil or gathering at the sabbath, they continued to prosecute them for performing magical acts. In this connection it is noteworthy that in the early eighteenth century, the Saxon jurist Christian Thomasius titled his critique of witchcraft prosecutions *De crimine magiae*.

---

[11] See Edward Peters, *The Magician, the Witch and the Law* (Philadelphia, PA, 1978).

The ambivalent relationship between witchcraft and other offences was also appar-ent when judicial and ecclesiastical authorities emphasized the spiritual or heretical nature of the crime. The distinction between witchcraft and other heresies emerged in the context of efforts by inquisitors to identify and prosecute Waldensians in the early fifteenth century, and notions drawn from dualist heresies further influenced the representation of the witches' sabbath. In early witchcraft trials, however, witchcraft was viewed as a new religious offence that resembled other medieval heresies in some respects but not others. Witches were heretics, apostates, and antinomians whose activities differed from those of others who had allegedly abandoned their faith or denied some of the basic articles of the Christian faith. In Catholic lands witches could also be distinguished from Protestant 'heretics', while in Protestant territories they could be distinguished from Anabaptists or members of other radical sects. But towards the end of the period of the trials, when the concept of witchcraft began to break down and courts stopped hearing witchcraft cases, prosecutions of individuals who might earlier have been tried for witchcraft were sometimes not identified as such but prosecuted only for blasphemy, sacrilege, or even making pacts with the devil.

The problem of defining the crime of witchcraft with any consistency or precision is only one difficulty when making sensible estimates of the number of prosecutions and executions during the early modern period. Historians have never taken seriously the claim, first advanced by an eighteenth-century anticlerical lawyer, that nine million witches were executed during the early modern period. This implausible claim, based on a crude extrapolation of the number of executions in one German town, nonetheless found favour among a small group of modern popular writers in the twentieth century who, for ideological reasons, wished to make the death toll from witchcraft prosecu-tions greater than that of the Holocaust.[12] Nor have modern historians accepted uncritically the inflated claims of early modern judges who boasted about how many witches they had executed or the size of the imagined armies of witches that rulers feared were threatening their domains or all of Christendom.[13] Nevertheless, until scholars began to scour local and regional archives in search of evidence of witchcraft trials and executions, the estimates of the number of witchcraft executions tended to be high. Since then, these estimates have tended to be significantly lower. In some cases, however, the discovery of previously unknown records has led scholars to make modest upward estimates of the number of witches in some jurisdictions.

This research has resulted in a broad agreement that approximately 100,000 individ-uals in Europe and colonial America were prosecuted for witchcraft between 1400

---

[12] See Robin Briggs, 'Number of Witches', *Encyclopedia of Witchcraft*, iii, 839–41; Diane Purkiss, *The Witch in History: Early Modern and Twentieth-Century Representations* (London, 1996), 7–29.

[13] The Burgundian judge and demonologist Henri Boguet speculated that there were 300,000 witches in France alone, and more than 1,800,000 in all of Europe at the beginning of the seventeenth century. Henry Boguet, *An Examen of Witches*, tr. E. Allen Ashwin (London, 1929), p. xxxii.

and 1775, and that the number of executions did not greatly exceed 50,000.[14] These estimates, therefore, have also forced a reconsideration of the once common assumption that the great majority of those witches who were brought to trial were executed. Archival research has revealed that as many as 75 per cent of witches who were prosecuted in some jurisdictions escaped with their lives. Restraint in the administration of torture and the reversal of sentences on appeal help to explain why so many accused witches avoided the stake or the gallows. Those witches whose lives were spared were not, however, treated kindly. A sizeable number of them received non-capital sentences, which might have included corporal punishment, imprisonment, or banishment. These punishments took a physical and emotional toll, and banishment was often considered a fate worse than death. Those who were acquitted or otherwise set free, sometimes after successfully withstanding torture, did not fare much better. Shunned by their neighbours, who had in most cases been the first to suspect and accuse them, they lived in fear of physical assault and lynching by villagers who were convinced that the cause of justice had not been served.

Lower estimates of the number of trials and executions have not reduced the importance of witchcraft in early modern European society. For one thing, the number of trials does not reflect the number of those who were accused but never brought to trial. That number included villagers and townspeople whom confessing witches named as accomplices but who were not tried. It also included the numbers who were in prison awaiting trial when higher authorities decided to stop the trials. Many others were suspected of being witches but were never formally charged, while still others lived in fear of such accusations. The prevalence of witch beliefs in all levels of society made witchcraft a more significant dimension of European society and culture than the number of trials might suggest.

The extensive archival work undertaken in recent years has also made possible more precise comparisons between witch-hunting in different countries and regions. It should come as no surprise that roughly half of all European witchcraft executions took place within the boundaries of the Holy Roman Empire—mainly because of the weakness of imperial judicial control over the smaller territories and the absence of an effective appellate structure within the empire. For this reason it has become customary to refer to Germany, or more precisely the lands within the Holy Roman Empire, as the heartland of the witch-hunt.[15] This region included the predominantly French-speaking duchy of Lorraine, although most of the territories within the empire were German-speaking. By comparison, all other European countries, with the exception of some of the Swiss cantons, showed relative restraint in prosecuting and executing witches. Even in Germany there were wide discrepancies in the geography of

---

[14] For estimates of the number of executions in the various European states and territories and a calculation of their intensity based on the size of the population see Wolfgang Behringer, *Witches and Witch-Hunts: A Global History* (Cambridge, 2004), 149–51.

[15] H. C. Erik Midelfort, 'Heartland of the Witch-Craze: Central and Northern Europe', *History Today*, 31 (1981), 27–31.

witch-hunting. Some of the worst hunts occurred within small ecclesiastical territories, such as Ellwangen, Würzburg, and Bamberg. By comparison there were very few executions in some of the imperial free cities, such as Rothenburg ob der Tauber.[16] A comparative study of Electoral Trier and Swabian Austria also reveals striking differences in the relative intensity of witch-hunting in German-speaking lands.[17]

Research in judicial records has led to a major reconsideration of the claim that witchcraft accusations on the European continent usually came 'from above' (i.e. that they originated in charges introduced by judicial officials), whereas those in England, where officers of the common law courts could not initiate prosecutions, came 'from below' (i.e. that they originated in charges made by the witches' neighbours). It is true that some members of ruling elites on the Continent deliberately initiated witch-hunts in their territories, either because they genuinely believed that witches were threatening to destroy the social order or, more cynically, because they wanted to use the prosecutions to legitimize their own tenuous rule or distract their subjects from other, more pressing concerns. The use of the inquisitorial system of criminal procedure on the Continent, which allowed judges to arrest and prosecute suspects without formal accusations by their neighbours, also made it appear that the courts were taking the initiative in such witch-hunts. But except when the accused witches were themselves members of ruling or educated elites, the courts did not initiate prosecutions without first receiving a complaint or accusation that arose from the lower ranks of society. Even when courts proceeded *ex officio* rather than waiting for an accusation or denunciation from the people in the witch's community, they had to rely on widespread rumour or mere suspicion that certain individuals were reputed to be witches. In that sense all witchcraft prosecutions of non-elites came from below.

Successful witchcraft prosecutions usually required the cooperation of the witches' neighbours, who made the original accusations and testified against the accused in court, and the judicial elites, who conducted the trials and in most cases determined their outcome. Witchcraft historians have traditionally distinguished between the witch beliefs of the educated and those of the illiterate or minimally educated. There is a measure of truth in that distinction. The illiterate, for the most part, thought of witches as evil people who caused misfortunes by magical means, whereas educated elites, especially those trained in theology and law, were more concerned with the demonic, and therefore religious, dimension of the witches' crime. The distinction between popular and learned culture, however, was never ironclad. Most villagers and townspeople believed in the existence of the devil and the possibility that he could have commerce with human beings. During early modern witch-hunts a process of cultural negotiation and exchange took place between the illiterate, on the one hand, and those who were educated, on the other. Sermons preached at the times of the trials provided

---

[16] Alison Rowlands, 'Imperial Free Cities', *Encyclopedia of Witchcraft*, ii, 540–4.

[17] Johannes Dillinger, *'Evil People': A Comparative Study of Witch-Hunts in Swabian Austria and the Electorate of Trier*, tr. Laura Stokes (Charlottesville, VA, 2009).

one means of instructing the broader population in the diabolical dimension of witchcraft, but the trials themselves proved to be even more instrumental in this cultural exchange.[18] The interrogation of witnesses and the use of torture and other forms of judicial pressure to extract confessions from witches imposed learned notions of witchcraft on villagers who had little or no knowledge of theology or demonology, while the reference to popular beliefs regarding magic and the world of spirits, often embodied in folkloric traditions, led to the assimilation of the demonological ideas of inquisitors. One body of popular beliefs that worked its way into learned demonology was local lore concerning the alleged gathering of witches, including the identification of the mythical sites where witches were believed to assemble, such as Blåkulla in Sweden or Blocksberg in Germany.

Most witchcraft historians now agree that popular and learned notions of witchcraft informed each other at various times and in different ways. Some notions of witchcraft that demonologists cited from classical Greek and Roman literature were themselves the product of learned commentaries on popular beliefs, such as the characteristics of the mythological witch figures Diana and Hecate, the metamorphoses of witches in the works of Ovid and Apuleius, and the description of bacchanalian orgies in ancient times that contributed to the origin of the idea of the witches' sabbath. The belief of some demonologists and judges that witches could fly provides one of the best examples of the interaction between popular beliefs, some of which had a history stretching back into ancient and medieval times, and demonological ideas anchored in scholastic theology regarding the power of the devil to move people and objects through the air.

Popular witch beliefs in the early modern period command greater interest and respect among historians today than they did in the early and mid-twentieth century. It is no longer possible, or certainly not advisable, for historians to dismiss the beliefs of the uneducated as mere 'peasant superstition', as one historian did in the 1960s.[19] Anthropological studies of witchcraft and other beliefs in non-Western societies have also led historians to understand that popular notions of witchcraft had their own internal coherence. The same can be said of the ideas of theologians and judges, which historians in the liberal, rational tradition have likewise dismissed as 'irrational', but which also followed their own internal logic. Whatever its perceived shortcomings, scholastic theology cannot be labelled as irrational. Nor can demonology be readily dismissed as unscientific or incompatible with a rational view of the natural world.[20]

---

[18] David Hall, ed., *Witch-hunting in Seventeenth-Century New England* (Boston, MA, 1991), 9; Gustav Henningsen, 'The Papers of Alonso de Salazar Frias', *Temenos*, 5 (1969), 105.

[19] H. R. Trevor-Roper, *The European Witch-Craze of the Sixteenth and Seventeenth Centuries and Other Essays* (New York, 1969).

[20] Stuart Clark, *Thinking with Demons: The Idea of Witchcraft in Early Modern Europe* (Oxford, 1997), 151–78.

The attention that historians have given to early modern treatises on witchcraft has also made it difficult to sustain the traditional polarity between a large body of credulous works that endorsed the reality of witchcraft and those of a small band of sceptics who called them into question. A simple distinction between believers and non-believers can no longer be maintained. On the one hand, even the most ardent promoters of witchcraft theory entertained at least some doubts regarding the reality of the crime, and very few of them accepted all the beliefs contained in the composite notion of witchcraft. On the other hand, many of those contemporaries who have won fame among historians as sceptics did not deny that witches existed or that the devil could exercise power in the world. Instead they chose to deny specific aspects of the witches' alleged crime, such as their ability to fly, transform themselves into beasts, or copulate with demons. Belief in the existence of witchcraft was also common among men often identified in the literature as judicial sceptics—judges and other men trained in the law, who came to the realization that the crime of witchcraft, while possible, could not be proved at law. Instead of subscribing to the traditional distinction between believers and sceptics, witchcraft historians now agree that there were different types and degrees of belief regarding witchcraft, and that there were elements of belief and disbelief in the works of all demonologists. The same can be said of the witch beliefs of the less educated members of society, who tended not to subscribe to the beliefs of demonologists regarding the relationships between witches and demons.

Historians do not agree on the exact chronological boundaries of the early modern period of European history, but for many it stretched from about 1400, just before trials for witchcraft began, and 1750, when most of them had come to an end. Witch beliefs have a much longer history, extending back into classical antiquity and forward into the modern period, and for that reason the 'history of witchcraft' covers a much broader chronological span than the period of the trials. But the reason for restricting this volume to the early modern period is that the overwhelming majority of trials and all the large panics took place during these years. Nevertheless, the prosecution of individuals identified variously as sorcerers, practitioners of magic, or 'witches' occurred in Europe before 1400, while the lynching of witches, that is, their illegal murder to satisfy the demands of popular justice, has continued to the present day, especially in Africa and Asia.

The witchcraft prosecutions discussed in Part II of this volume include those held in Russia, which straddled the boundaries between Europe and Asia, and others that took place outside Europe in English, Spanish, and Portuguese colonies in the New World. This book also includes a separate chapter on the multilingual Rhine-Moselle border-lands, which witnessed some of the most intense witch-hunting in all of Europe. The assignment of a single chapter to the Iberian Peninsula is based on the many similar-ities between witch beliefs and witchcraft prosecutions in the Spanish kingdoms and Portugal. Similar considerations informed the decision to deal with all five Nordic countries in a single chapter. There is no separate chapter on Switzerland, whose cultural and linguistic diversity makes the history of witchcraft prosecutions in its cantons difficult to treat as a unit, but fifteenth-century trials in francophone Switzer-land receive coverage in other chapters.[21]

In preparing this volume, no effort was made to impose uniformity in approach or interpretation, and the chapters reflect that diversity. This is how it should be in a field as complex and controversial as that of witchcraft studies. Indeed, differences of approach and interpretation help make the history of early modern European witch-craft challenging, vital, and exciting.

---

[21] For francophone Switzerland see E. William Monter, *Witchcraft in France and Switzerland: The Borderlands during the Reformation* (Ithaca, NY, 1976). On German-speaking areas see Guido Bader, *Die Hexenprozesse in der Schweiz* (Affoltern, 1945).

PART I

WITCH BELIEFS

CHAPTER 1

MAGIC AND ITS HAZARDS IN THE LATE MEDIEVAL WEST

RICHARD KIECKHEFER

UNTIL the late twentieth century, work on the history of magic has been less interpretive than work on witchcraft. Witch trials have been studied as a series of events whose origins, patterns, and termination lend themselves to historical analysis. Gender bias, the impact of the Reformation, and links with judicial control and state formation have been traced and debated. Theological and legal writings on witchcraft have been examined as both sparks to prosecution and reflections on trials, and their place in intellectual history has occupied a significant place in the historiography. Magic, however, has remained relatively uninterpreted, except when it enters major currents of cultural history through the writings of figures such as the Renaissance mages. Recently, however, the history of magic has been enlivened by several intersecting strands of historical enquiry.

First, attention has focused on ritual magic and the conjuring of angels. Two collections of articles edited by Claire Fanger, *Conjuring Spirits* and *Invoking Angels*, have contributed to this trend, as has an issue of the *Mélanges de l'École Française de Rome*.[1] The phenomenon of angel magic has long been known, and in particular its cultivation by John Dee. We now have a much fuller sense of its development and significance. It problematizes distinctions between magic and religion, being manifestly

---

[1] Claire Fanger, ed., *Conjuring Spirits: Texts and Traditions of Medieval Ritual Magic* (Stroud, 1998), and *Invoking Angels: Theurgic Ideas and Practices, Thirteenth to Sixteenth Centuries* (University Park, PA, 2012); Henri Bresc and Benoît Grévin, eds, 'Les Anges et la magie au Moyen Âge: Actes da la table ronde, Nanterre, 8–9 décembre 2000', *Mélanges de l'École Française de Rome, Moyen Âge*, 114 (2002), 589–890.

religious in its forms and theological assumptions and not entirely distinct even in its aims. It also problematizes the definition and typology of magic: writers from the thirteenth century onwards were familiar with the notions of 'demonic magic' that relied on demons' aid and 'natural magic' that exploited occult virtues within nature, but angel magic eludes this dichotomy and makes clear that the conceptual map used in medieval and early modern literature on magic did not correspond to the territory it was meant to survey.

Secondly, the link between magic and science has been studied with greater precision. In his encyclopedic *History of Magic and Experimental Science* (1923–58) Lynn Thorndike meant to show connections between magic and science, and while his work remains a gold mine of information and an invaluable guide to the manuscripts, historical analysis was not his strong suit. Frances Yates situated magic and the occult within the scientific traditions of early modern Europe.[2] But it is the recent work of Nicolas Weill-Parot, Jean-Patrice Boudet, and others that has given us a more deeply grounded sense of astral magic as a point of connection between magic and the science of astrology, and an appreciation of the historical contexts for that link.[3]

Thirdly, important work has been done on magic and cultural exchange. The importance of Arabic writings translated into Latin in the twelfth century has long been known; Charles Burnett has made this transmission his life's study and has given us a deeper understanding of the process. Less explored until very recently is the connection between Christian and Jewish magic. Michael Swartz, Gideon Bohak, and others have opened the history of Jewish magic to historical understanding, and Katelyn Mesler has begun, with unparalleled knowledge of the sources on both sides, to show precisely how Jewish and Christian magic came into contact.[4]

Fourthly, magic and the history of books has become an important area for study. Benedek Láng has done work in Hungary, Bohemia, and Poland, showing how manuscript culture in those lands promoted the study and practice of magic. Frank Klaassen has done much the same for England, and Sophie Page has examined the magical tradition in English monastic manuscripts.[5] My edition and analysis of a manual of necromancy from fifteenth-century Germany has explored how a miscellany

  [2] Lynn Thorndike, *The History of Magic and Experimental Science*, 8 vols (New York, 1923–58); Frances A. Yates, *The Occult Philosophy in the Elizabethan Age* (London, 1979).

  [3] Nicolas Weill-Parot, *Les 'images astrologiques' au moyen âge et à la renaissance: spéculations intellectuelles et pratiques magiques (XIIᵉ–XVᵉ siècle)* (Paris, 2002); Jean-Patrice Boudet, *Entre science et nigromance: astrologie, divination et magie dans l'occident médiéval, XIIᵉ–XVᵉ siècle* (Paris, 2006).

  [4] Charles Burnett, *Magic and Divination in the Middle Ages: Texts and Techniques in the Islamic and Christian Worlds* (Aldershot, 1996); Michael D. Swartz, *Scholastic Magic: Ritual and Revelation in Early Jewish Mysticism* (Princeton, 1996); Gideon Bohak, *Ancient Jewish Magic* (Cambridge, 2008); Katelyn Mesler, 'The *Liber iuratus Honorii* and the Christian Reception of Angel Magic', in Fanger, *Invoking Angels*, 113–50.

  [5] Benedek Láng, *Unlocked Books: Manuscripts of Learned Magic in the Medieval Libraries of Central Europe* (University Park, PA, 2008).

was compiled and how its contents help us understand not only the practice of magic and fantasies about magic but the conception of the book of magic as itself a numinous object.[6]

Fifthly, historians have discussed the ways magic was tolerated and absorbed within Christian practice. Keith Thomas went so far as to speak of 'the magic of the medieval Church', while Eamon Duffy has called attention to a 'sense of defiance in the face of relentless enemies' as an 'insistent and striking feature' of prayers in late medieval books of hours, often taking the form of exorcisms and adjurations, and the fact that such prayers were used by Christians at all social levels. For Valerie Flint, accommodation of magic within Christianity was a conscious policy of tolerant churchmen in the early Middle Ages.[7] These writers have made clear the difficulty of distinguishing in the concrete between orthopraxy on the one hand, magic and superstition on the other. What remains important is that writers on magic insisted there was a distinction, and crossing the line was a serious offence, a flirtation with demonic aid, even if, for an outsider, the line seems invisible.[8]

All these developments accentuate the ways magic grew out of or was integrated into later medieval culture. Even the work on angel magic brings ritual magic into relationship with other rituals and devotional practices. Important and valuable as these trends are, they turn our attention away from those aspects of magic that link it with witchcraft and the witch trials. People were brought to trial most often not for conjuring angels or using astral talismans in medicine, but for attempting other types of magic. This chapter complements recent literature by focusing on what it was about magic that made it not just suspect but threatening.

In modern usage the terms 'magic' and 'magical' have largely positive connotation that would have seemed odd and mysterious to most medieval writers. The *magoi* of antiquity who made their way into the Mediterranean world were thought of as sinister characters, often charlatans. Early Christian writers were sure that the 'magical arts' had been imparted by demons, probably worked through demonic agency, and proved to be illusions worked either by demons or by the magicians themselves. Centuries later, in the high and late Middle Ages, space was carved out for the notion of 'natural magic', which worked by manipulating 'occult virtues' within the natural order. This allowed a new way of conceiving magic: it could be defined as the exploitation either of demonic power or of occult powers in nature. Still, the positive or at least neutral category of natural magic remained shadowy and disputed. Practising magicians took over the traditions of magic borrowed from Arabic sources in the twelfth and following centuries, or elaborated forms of angel magic in the thirteenth century, or claimed

---

[6] Richard Kieckhefer, *Forbidden Rites: A Necromancer's Manual of the Fifteenth Century* (Stroud, 1998).

[7] Keith Thomas, *Religion and the Decline of Magic* (London, 1971), 25–50; Eamon Duffy, *The Stripping of the Altars: Traditional Religion in England, c.1400–c.1580* (2nd edn, New Haven, CT, 2005), 266–87; Valerie I. J. Flint, *The Rise of Magic in Early Medieval Europe* (Princeton, 1991).

[8] Richard Kieckhefer, 'The Specific Rationality of Medieval Magic', *American Historical Review*, 99 (1994), 813–36.

Neoplatonic or Hermetic grounding for their magical systems in the later fifteenth century, representing all these as valid and honourable traditions, but they had to argue their views in the face of considerable scepticism. The vernacular terms that served as approximate equivalents to *magica* or *ars magica*—*wicchecraft* in Middle English, *sorcellerie* in French, *zauberei* in German—were if anything more emphatically pejorative. Mere superstition was perhaps less powerful and thus less evil than these, but scarcely more respectable. Magic might become alluring in courtly literature, but even there its practitioners were seldom depicted as reliable.[9]

While the concept of magic always held the potential for arousing suspicion, however, the practice of magic did not uniformly elicit censure or lead to prosecution. Certain forms of healing, blessing, and protecting that might be categorized as magic might alternatively be accommodated within licit or at least tolerated systems of practice so long as they were free of overtly demonic or pagan elements, in which case they were licit but not thought of as magic.[10] Invoking demonic or pagan spirits meant courting censure and prosecution, and so too did the exercise of magic for clearly antisocial purposes: harm to humans or animals, manipulation of affections, arousing inclement weather, and the like. Even so, practices of this sort came under judicial scrutiny only under circumstances that are difficult to define with precision. When people were brought to trial, we often learn that they had reputations for practising magic that extended back for many years. Why was it that, after long impunity, the accused were now brought to court? A zealous inquisitor, a town exerting judicial authority over a newly expanded rural territory, a town council eager to regulate moral conduct in the name of public order—any of these factors could result in prosecution for magic that would otherwise pass beneath the judicial radar. But the word *could* is important here. None of these factors, alone or even jointly, became an infallible predictor of judicial rigour, setting loose inexorable forces of persecution or springing the iron trap of inevitability.

This chapter, then, will examine the various forms of magic known in medieval Europe, focusing on those features that made it suspect and led to censure, prohibition, and especially prosecution. It will suggest connections or, in some instances, disconnections between the *prescriptive* texts of the magicians themselves, the *proscriptive* text of their opponents, and the *descriptive* literature (including judicial records) that claims to recount actual instances of magical activity. It will deal not simply with beliefs or with trials, but with the link between the two: the patterns of behaviour and perception that made it likely for magic to fall under suspicion and for the magician to be brought to trial.

---

[9] Lynn Thorndike, 'Some Medieval Conceptions of Magic', *The Monist*, 25 (1915), 107–39.

[10] On this point see Flint, *The Rise of Magic*, and Kieckhefer, 'The Specific Rationality of Medieval Magic'.

1.1 FACTORS TENDING TO RENDER MAGIC SUSPECT

Clearly a necessary precondition for judicial action was a judicial authority eager to solicit allegations of criminal magic, or at least willing to receive and act on such information. Townspeople and villagers who had long harboured grudges against their neighbours, fearing that they were muttering dark curses, bewitching cattle, inflicting illness on children, and so forth might be delighted to learn of a nearby judge willing to hear them out and bring satisfaction. The municipalities of late medieval Europe often adapted elements of inquisitorial procedure that could be applied to a wide range of crimes but proved especially useful for prosecuting the secret crimes of magic: they were willing to dispense with the old requirements of accusatory justice (in which the victim brought charges and took responsibility for establishing their truth), and were willing to apply torture and other forms of judicial coercion to secure confessions and convictions. Increasingly attentive to matters of public morality, municipalities and other jurisdictions, secular and ecclesiastical, often applied judicial solutions to perceived problems such as blasphemy and sodomy.[11] The penalty for such offences was often banishment, because the authorities were less interested in solving the problem than in removing it from their boundaries, but capital punishment for illicit magic had long been known and was increasingly common.

It is tempting, then, to begin explaining trials for sorcery by looking for zealous persecuting jurisdictions. The trial records from Nuremberg are instructive, because they illustrate, but at the same time problematize, this development.[12] In the late fifteenth century the town council requested and received from Heinrich Kramer a vernacular adaptation of his counsel in the *Malleus maleficarum* for prosecution of witches,[13] and over several decades the council had shown itself increasingly willing to hear accusations of sorcery: milk-theft, love magic, and other such offences. Yet the punishments were relatively lenient (usually banishment, sometimes branding, or public exposure on the stocks), and exoneration was frequent. Even as recorded accusations grew more frequent in the fifteenth century, so did acquittal. A jurisdiction might be willing to investigate charges of illicit magic, but suspects still came before the authorities only when circumstances had rendered them vulnerable to accusation. Several factors tended to catch the wary eye of the potential accuser.

The first of these was *a specialist–client relationship*. Not all magic required the services of a specialist, and in principle there was no reason why do-it-yourself magic

---

[11] Laura Patricia Stokes, *Demons of Urban Reform: Early European Witch Trials and Criminal Justice, 1430–1530* (New York, 2011).

[12] Hartmut H. Kunstmann, *Zauberwahn und Hexenprozess in der Reichsstadt Nürnberg* (Nuremberg, 1970).

[13] Rudolf Endres, 'Heinrich Institoris, sein Hexenhammer und der Nürnberger Rat', in Peter Segl, ed., *Der Hexenhammer: Entstehung und Umfeld des* Malleus maleficarum *von 1487* (Cologne, 1988), 195–216.

should seem less threatening, but cases in which a client engaged a specialist practitioner occur often in the trial records, probably at a disproportionate rate. Any time the number of people involved in magic increased, there was more likelihood that one member of the group would leak information about its activities. Either the client or the magician could turn informer when it became clear that the specialist's services were ineffective, or when, for other reasons, the relationship soured. Specialists would call attention to themselves not only by their repeated involvement in magic but by the very notoriety required to attract clients. The magical specialist often had a variety of magical means at her disposal: she might use herbs, conjurations, incantation of unclean spirits, or imitative magic that involved cutting an egg and giving one half to a dog, the other to a cat, to cause disaffection. She might be equally versatile in the purposes she served. The same practitioner could exercise love magic but also healing potions, or magic intended to transfer a disease from one person to another. A specialist might one day use magic to harm clients' adversaries, and the next recite exorcisms to cast out demons. Reputation for all these occult arts was grounded largely in a kind of persuasive but hazardous showmanship that could no doubt be adapted easily to a variety of circumstances.

A second factor that could arouse suspicion was simply *possessing a book of magic*. In some instances this was the main or even the only incriminating circumstance. Owning a book of magical experiments implied a level of both expertise and commitment that the more casual use of orally transmitted formulas did not so clearly suggest. More than other objects, books contain explicit detail about magical practice, and when they fell into the hands of authorities they could be powerfully incriminating. A book of magic could also point to a circle of fellow magicians to whom it could be lent for use and for copying. Inquisitors and other judges sometimes seized books of magic and took them as evidence of misconduct. A monk accused of owning 'books of experiments' might protest that he held it merely out of curiosity and never actually used it. A book of rituals could easily appear to have numinous power, whether sacred or sinister. We have surviving rituals for the consecration of a magical book.

One French magician confessed to owning books of magic that he deemed 'good and holy', perhaps in part because he had consecrated them. Stories about books of magical experiments sometimes recall the tale of the sorcerer's apprentice, which stems from the second-century writer Lucian of Samosata, and is echoed both in later literature and in the experience of magicians. When a young man of Norway went to study in Paris, his master went out one day leaving his book of magic on view; when the student began reading the book he inadvertently caused a raging storm, which was quelled only when the master returned and realized what had happened.[14]

Various types of magical books have survived: systematic or unsystematic books of recipes (which tend to focus on the ingredients to be used), books of experiments

---

[14] Daniel Ogden, *In Search of the Sorcerer's Apprentice: The Traditional Tales of Lucian's Lover of Lies* (Swansea, 2007); Stephen A. Mitchell, *Witchcraft and Magic in the Nordic Middle Ages* (Philadelphia, PA, 2010), 46.

(which may give more detail for the rituals to be performed), and treatises on magic such as those translated from the Arabic in the twelfth and following centuries, or those by Renaissance mages of the fifteenth and sixteenth centuries. The Arabic compilation that was translated into Latin in the thirteenth century as *Picatrix* is a rich source of experiments in which the operator is advised how to use rituals, magical substances, and engraved symbols to exploit astral powers for magical effect; it survives in manuscripts chiefly from the fifteenth century. Important as all these materials are, they give a skewed understanding of the field if read in isolation from those anonymous compilations of recipes and experiments, or compilations of medical counsel and household management that included magical recipes and experiments alongside non-magical material. While less interesting for the study of magical theory, these practical compendia are surely more representative of the sources most widely available to practitioners of magic. Many such books were destroyed by authorities or discarded at the death of the owner by heirs who had little use for them. Nicholas Eymericus tells of the book burning that he carried out as inquisitor in the mid-fourteenth century, which included the destruction of a weighty book on the invocation of demons.[15]

A third factor that could draw critical attention was *the public disclosure of deeply private activities*. Usually this meant the articulation of a public threat that implied a private curse. It may seem clear to us that the threat was a trigger for autosuggestion, and doubtless that mechanism was always possible, but contemporaries who credited accusations of sorcery assumed it was effective because covert operation gave effect to the overt threat. The witnesses to the menacing words sometimes insisted that ill effects followed quickly. Barbara Selachin at Innsbruck was said to have threatened a couple that they would become lame and would have to creep out of their house on all fours, and *immediately* they began to experience a strange swelling. The same defendant quarrelled with another woman over apparently petty insults; on one occasion walking by the woman in public, spitting on the ground, and calling out, 'You are not worthy that I should look at you!' When she threatened that her adversary's health and possessions would be ruined, the woman became ill the next day and remained so at the time of the trial.[16] In cases of this sort the borders are obscured: it seems as if the threat *is* the curse, and the curse *is* the effective cause of bewitchment. Even so, the public expression of malice gave rise to the question of what else the malefactor was doing in the privacy of her chamber.

The *role of gender* in making magic seem threatening is a complex issue.[17] Necromancy and the more complicated forms of astral magic were primarily exercised by

---

[15] Nicholas Eymericus, *Directorium inquisitorum*, ed. Franciscus Pegna (Venice, 1595), pt. 2, qu. 28, pp. 316–17.

[16] Hartmann Ammann, 'Der Innsbrucker Hexenprozeß von 1485', *Zeitschrift des Ferdinandeums für Tirol und Vorarlberg*, 34 (1890), 55–7.

[17] Elspeth Whitney, 'International Trends: The Witch "She"/the Historian "He": Gender and the Historiography of the European Witch-hunts', *Journal of Women's History*, 7 (1995), 77–101; Katherine Park, 'Medicine and Magic: The Healing Arts', in Judith C. Brown and Robert C. Davis, eds, *Gender and Society in Renaissance Italy* (London, 1998), 129–49; Heidi Breuer, *Crafting the Witch: Gendering Magic in Medieval and Early Modern England* (New York, 2009); Tamar Herzig, 'Flies, Heretics, and the

clergy, which is to say males with some degree of learning in Latin and familiarity with ritual practices. Most other types of magic were, in principle, available to anyone, and surely practised by men as well as women, but the trial records do suggest that women were more liable to prosecution. Thus, trials for sorcery in late medieval Germany featured mostly women as defendants: winning the affection of a married man, making a former lover impotent, and so forth. In such cases the magic was typically used by women to gain power or advantage over men, which surely gave it much of its threatening character.

Women were even more threatening when they joined forces, as they seem often to have done. The association of two or more women called itself to people's attention by their coming and going, and when any one of them fell under suspicion the others might also. Association of a small cluster did not amount to a conspiracy, but it did raise the question of whether women were banding together in the exercise of their magic arts, and perhaps made it easier to fantasize about broader networks of sorceresses that did verge on conspiracy. The association was often a kind of apprenticeship. When Heinrich Kramer carried out extensive prosecution at Innsbruck in 1485, one common charge was that a woman who practised bewitchment taught it to younger women.[18] These apprentice relationships seem to have occurred less often when the accused were male, or at least they are less often recorded.

While Kramer believed midwives were especially prone to the use of magic, and there are some cases of midwives being prosecuted, they do not seem to have been exceptionally vulnerable to suspicion; indeed, given the frequency of stillbirth and death in childbirth, it is perhaps surprising that midwives did not fall under suspicion of sorcery more often. A factor surely more likely to make women more vulnerable to accusation and conviction was a reputation for sexual immorality. A woman tried at Nuremberg in 1503, who had been notorious for years, for having associated with disreputable characters and having several children by various fathers outside marriage, was the sort on whom suspicion readily fell.[19]

The one common element in all the factors that made magic dangerous to its practitioners was the risk of disclosure. A disgruntled, repentant, or simply garrulous client could compromise the secrecy of magic. A book left out by mistake and seen by the wrong person, a public threat that implied private action, an unsavoury set of relationships could all call attention to magical practice which, under safer circumstances, might have gone undetected and unpunished. Secular prosecution presupposed a leak of some sort, and even inquisitorial trials were based on information disclosed, usually by neighbours who had got wind of what was happening behind closed doors. Magic, of its nature, entailed elements of secrecy. When it came to light, the disclosure must have evoked a sense of breakthrough into a world of darkness in

Gendering of Witchcraft', *Magic, Ritual, and Witchcraft*, 5 (2010), 51–80; Lara Apps and Andrew Gow, *Male Witches in Early Modern Europe* (Manchester, 2003).

[18] Ammann, 'Der Innsbrucker Hexenprozeß', 13–14, 18–20.
[19] Kunstmann, *Zauberwahn und Hexenprozess*, 35.

which schemes and contacts, which had lain hidden and might before have been imagined dimly, could now be imagined far more vividly and persuasively.

Yet disclosure was not the only difficulty; the deeper issue was the secrecy that resisted disclosure. Secrecy implied sinister intent, undetermined means, and the unfairness of a surprise attack—three elements which, even if they do not strictly define maleficent magic, still characterize it and go far towards explaining why it was feared. Secrecy betokened that will to harm which preys on the anxieties of neighbours.

1.2 HOMOLOGIES BETWEEN BENEFICENT AND MALEFICENT MAGIC: BODILY HARM TO HUMANS

Much magic was unambiguously intended to cause harm. The prescriptive literature occasionally gives experiments for that purpose: one can find procedures in *Picatrix* and related text for destroying an enemy or a city, for putting a person into a deathlike sleep, and for other forms of magical attack.

In the judicial records the means for causing bodily harm and death are often composite, and they may involve invocation of spirits, but usually this element is subordinated to others. First and most basically, a person could be given magical poison, which is often vaguely specified, no doubt because once ingested its contents could not be determined.[20] Secondly, harm could be caused by contagion, which meant placing noxious objects and substances beneath a threshold, under a pillow, or in a person's garments.[21] Bodies of noxious animals like mice could also be wrapped in a bundle and placed beneath a threshold. Thirdly, imitative magic—including image magic—could be used for harm. Burning a candle could be meant to kill a man: as the candle was consumed, so would the victim be.[22] But imitation could involve rituals far more complex than this, combining the mimetic action with incantations or conjurations.[23] Fourthly, a victim could be cursed. Three women at Innsbruck were

---

[20] Franck Collard, '"Veneficiis vel maleficiis": réflexion sur les relations entre le crime de poison et la sorcellerie dans l'Occident médiéval', *Le Moyen Age: Revue d'histoire et de philologie*, 109 (2003), 9–57; Franck Collard, *The Crime of Poison in the Middle Ages*, tr. Deborah Nelson-Campbell (Westport, CT, 2008). For an example, see Ammann, 'Der Innsbrucker Hexenprozeß', 20–1.

[21] Ugolino Nicolini, 'La stregoneria a Perugia e in Umbria nel Medioevo: con i testi di sette processi a Perugia e uno a Bologna', *Bollettino della Deputazione di storia patria per l'Umbria*, 84 (1987), app. 1–6, pp. 58–63.

[22] W. H. Hale, ed., *A Series of Precedents and Proceedings in Criminal Causes, Extending from the Year 1475 to 1640, Extracted from Act-Books of Ecclesiastical Courts in the Diocese of London, Illustrative of the Discipline of the Church of England* (London, 1847), 20.

[23] Gene A. Brucker, 'Sorcery in Early Renaissance Florence', *Studies in the Renaissance*, 10 (1963), 13–16, 22–3; Gene A. Brucker, ed., *The Society of Renaissance Florence: A Documentary Study* (New York, 1971), 361–6.

said to have uttered a curse against a victim to the effect that he should have as much pain in his head as Mary had in her genitals when she gave birth to Jesus.[24]

While magic could be meant for harm, however, the problem was exacerbated: not only did the same individuals often have expertise in both healing and harming, but the techniques for healing and for harming resembled each other so closely that an observer might well be confused and deem it safest to suspect foul play even when the purpose was benign. The means for harm were largely homologous with the means for healing and promoting health. Magical poisons were negative versions of medicines ingested for health. Maleficent substances that worked by contagion were analogous to medicinal ligatures and suspensions, that is, objects affixed to the body or worn around the neck. Beneficent counterparts to harmful image magic may seem less obvious, but the procedures for causing harm sometimes could be reversed by digging up the buried image, removing the needle, washing the figure in clean water, and so forth, which is to say that healing operations carried out on the image could take effect on the person represented, just as harmful operations did. As for curses, they were the negative counterpart to charms and blessings. The curse at Innsbruck cited above involved a reference to a narrative of Mary's childbirth. Charms and blessings, too, could begin with *historiolae* referring to sacred or apocryphal narrative: just as Peter was cured of a toothache, so should the patient be.[25]

1.3 THE MAGIC FORCE OF EMOTION: EROTIC MAGIC

If bodily harm was morally and legally problematic for straightforward and obvious reasons, magic to manipulate people's emotions was objectionable for a variety of reasons, some less obvious than others.

In the prescriptive literature of the magicians one finds rather often advice on how to curry favour with others. Carrying specified characters in one's left hand can ensure a favour from any person. The SATOR-AREPO square written on virgin parchment with the blood of a white dove would win favour in the sight of all. If two people quarrel, a friend should seek two lizards, put them in pot and cook them, then take the powder that remains after cooking and sew it up in clothes of the quarrellers, and at once their enmity will turn to friendship.[26] Most of this counsel seems harmless from a distance of several centuries, and it seems to have aroused little opposition at the time under most circumstances. If magic could engender friendship, however, it could also promote

[24] Ammann, 'Der Innsbrucker Hexenprozeß', 13.

[25] Richard Kieckhefer, *Magic in the Middle Ages* (2nd edn, Cambridge, 2000), 153–6; 56–94, esp. 81–2.

[26] Bodleian Library, Oxford, MS Wood empt. 18, fol. 32r; Bodleian Library, MS e Mus. 219, fol. 186v.

enmity: potions and imitative rituals could be used to separate a husband and wife or a parent and child.[27]

The most complicated incidents of emotional coercion emerged in cases of erotic magic. This was probably the area in which there was closest correspondence among the various sources: prescriptive, proscriptive, and descriptive. In principle, erotic magic could be used to persuade or coerce sexual consent (sex-inducing magic), to foster or restore an intimate and enduring relationship (love magic), or to heighten the pleasure of sexual partners (sex-enhancing magic), and examples of all these varieties could be cited. Most threatening was sex-inducing magic, but love magic could also, paradoxically, be seen as sinister, even when used to restore affection between spouses.[28] Discussion of all these types can be found in prescriptive, proscriptive, and descriptive texts.

Erotic magic seems to have been—probably more than any other form, except perhaps medicinal magic—a specialty exercised on behalf of clients, at least judging from the court records. Potions, charms and adjurations, image magic, and contagious magic could all be brought into service. A specialist at Lucca made a wax image on behalf of a client and stuck pins into it, uttered conjurations and adjurations over it, and cast it into a fire while saying an incantation to the effect that her client's lover should burn with love for the client, just as the wax burned in the fire.[29] Erotic magic was typically meant to be coercive, often violently so. Images were pierced to cause severe pain in the person afflicted until she yielded; they might be accompanied by incantations specifying that she should not sleep or wake, lie down or walk until she burns with love for the magician or the client. In these cases the will to dominate and the will to harm are inseparably linked.

The trial of Gabrina degli Albeti illustrates further ways erotic magic might be threatening. When women asked how to regain their husbands' affections (in one case inducing the husband to set aside his concubine), Gabrina gave them elaborate procedures for that end.[30] One might think there was no harm in such marital therapy, but coercion through clandestine means was suspect even within marriage. She is also supposed to have instructed a woman to take a 'chrism' that she gave her, anoint her own mouth, then kiss her husband to make him love her greatly. The record notes that the oil was not in fact a sacred chrism, as she pretended, but plain oil. Although

---

[27] Nicolini, 'La stregoneria a Perugia', app. 1–8, pp. 66–73; Christine Meek, 'Men, Women and Magic: Some Cases from Late Medieval Lucca', in Christine Meek, ed., *Women in Renaissance and Early Modern Europe* (Dublin, 2000), 51–6; Domenico Mammoli, *The Record of the Trial and Condemnation of a Witch, Matteuccia di Francesco, at Todi, 20 March 1428* (Rome, 1972), 19.

[28] Richard Kieckhefer, 'Erotic Magic in Medieval Europe', in Joyce Salisbury, ed., *Sex in the Middle Ages: A Book of Essays* (New York, 1991), 30–55; Jörg Rogge, 'Gefängnis, Flucht und Liebeszauber: Ursachen und Verlaufsformen von Geschlechterkonflikten im hohen Adel des deutschen Reiches im späten Mittelalter', *Zeitschrift für historische Forschung*, 28 (2001), 487–511.

[29] Meek, 'Men, Women and Magic', 62; see also Mammoli, *The Record of the Trial*, 20.

[30] Aldo Cerlini, 'Una strega reggiana e il suo processo', *Studi storici*, 15 (1906), 64.

Gabrina herself knew the oil was not chrism, nonetheless she sinned by causing the client, who believed the oil to be sacred, to commit this serious sin.

Whatever the ethics of the intended use, magical manipulation of affection was dangerous because, like a powerful hallucinogen, it could go awry and leave a person demented. A man seeking an affair with a married woman named Antonia consulted Caterina di Giorgio for her help; she gave him magical substances to place beneath the lintel of the married couple. The intent was that Antonia should despise her husband and fall in love with the client; the effect, however, was to drive Antonia helplessly mad. In one case the madness was intended. A woman wishing to bind her husband's will and put him into a stupor so she could carry on an affair used techniques ranging from the simple to the moderately complex. What actually succeeded in driving him mad, however, was a plant that she mixed in with several of his meals.[31]

Magic could be used for anti-erotic as well as erotic ends, and magically induced impotence was a matter of particular importance, much discussed by theologians, canon lawyers, and physicians. Catherine Rider has recently explored the role of magical impotence as a point of contact among these faculties within the academic world.[32] A man could become impotent in relations with a particular woman, or with all women other than oneself. One time-honoured technique was to extinguish and break a blessed candle while reciting an incantation; as an extra touch, the ceremony could be done at a crossroad, and the broken candle deposited there.

1.4 TAMPERING WITH THE ORDER OF NATURE: HARM TO ANIMALS AND WEATHER MAGIC

Wall paintings in the churches of Scandinavia and some parts of Germany show witches taking milk or producing butter with the aid of demons.[33] There are parallel cases where demons aid in brewing or spinning; at Ågerup in Denmark two demons stand by a spinning woman, labelled as a 'bad woman'. More often the demons aid in churning butter (as at Västra Vemmerlöv in Sweden), or in pilfering milk from people's cows. In all these cases the witch is self-interested and intent on gaining advantage, sometimes by theft from a neighbour.

The difference between sheer malevolence and self-interest is not always clear. It remains doubtful, for example, when a cow is found to be bewitched so that it gives little or no milk. Has the animal simply been rendered incapable, or is the milk being spirited away and used by the witch? Sorcerers who came to the attention of the

---

[31] Nicolini, 'La stregoneria a Perugia', 46.

[32] Catherine Rider, *Magic and Impotence in the Middle Ages* (Oxford, 2006).

[33] Jens Chr. V. Johansen, 'Hexen auf mittelalterlichen Wandmalereien: Zur Genese der Hexenprozesse in Dänemark', in Andreas Blauert, ed., *Ketzer, Zauberer, Hexen: Die Anfänge der europäischen Hexenverfolgungen* (Frankfurt am Main, 1990), 217–40.

authorities at Nuremberg in 1477 were said to steal milk from their neighbours by means of sorcery.[34] But at Lucerne around 1480 the situation was different when a woman was accused of causing cows to give blood rather than milk, resulting in the death of cows, horses, and geese.[35] In cases of this sort there is no suggestion of self-interest; the bewitchment is meant to harm the livestock and its owners, with no corresponding gain.

Those accused of harm to livestock are often the same ones thought to engage in weather magic. The woman at Lucerne who was judged guilty of bewitching animals was believed also to cause inclement weather. When witches were tried at Ravensburg in 1484, there had been severe rain and hail, and two women confessed that they had caused hail and storms, and had inflicted harm on humans and cattle, over many years.[36]

The two forms of magic, bewitchment of animals and creating inclement weather, are what one would expect in an agrarian setting, and their ascription to the same sorceresses is not surprising. But the association goes somewhat deeper than this: the utter dependence of village society on the forces of nature gives it a vulnerability that is brought into focus by the presence of a fellow villager thought to have exceptional power to affect what others cannot regulate, to manipulate the elements in a way that only God should be able to do. The sinister force of the magicians, their will to harm, is here heightened by its extension beyond the human sphere into the very order of nature. No doubt attacking livestock and attacking the crops of the fields was a further way of attacking human enemies, but the scope of malevolence extended more widely, into spheres where humans were not expected to have such power.

1.4.1 Ambiguous Spirits: Angel Magic and Necromancy (Nigromancy)

In later medieval parlance the term 'necromancy' came to mean overtly demonic magic, although it sometimes could be used broadly as an unspecific pejorative term for magic. It was usually spelled 'nigromancy' or 'nygromancy', which could be translated as 'black magic' or 'black divination', and some historians prefer to observe that spelling. Yet for later medieval writers 'necromancy' and 'nigromancy' were not clearly distinct phenomena: the spellings could be used interchangeably, and even a writer who spoke of 'nigromancy' could identify it with the magical art that an earlier writer like Isidore of Seville had called 'necromancy'. The blurring of boundaries is

[34] Kunstmann, *Zauberwahn und Hexenprozess*, 30–1.

[35] E. Hoffmann-Krayer, 'Luzerner Akten zum Hexen- und Zauberwesen', *Schweizerisches Archiv für Volkskunde*, 3 (1899), 81–6.

[36] Andreas Schmauder, ed., *Frühe Hexenverfolgung in Ravensburg und am Bodensee* (Konstanz, 2001); see also Joseph Hansen, ed., *Quellen und Untersuchungen zur Geschichte des Hexenwahns und der Hexenverfolgung im Mittelalter* (Bonn, 1901; repr. Hildesheim, 1963), 589–90.

itself important. A necromancer might intend to conjure the dead, but from an orthodox perspective the spirit who appeared was actually an imposter, a demon pretending to be the deceased.[37] The further complicating factor is that many magicians in later medieval Europe conjured angels, and from an orthodox viewpoint these too were likely to be demon imposters. The distinction of spirits (*discretio spirituum*) was never easy.

Full-fledged necromancy was formally analogous to exorcism; indeed, the words 'conjuration' and 'exorcism' were themselves interchangeable, both referring to a formal command. The conjurer summoning a demon, like the exorcist dispelling one, was typically a cleric ordained at least to the minor orders, one of which was that of exorcist. The rituals required knowledge of Latin and of ritual forms; a necromantic experiment might, for example, tell the magician to recite the Psalm *Miserere*, assuming he would know what that was. While in most trials involving full-fledged necromancy the practitioners were clerics, their clients were often laymen.[38] Gilles de Rais, tried in 1440, was himself an aristocrat and soldier, but he engaged the services of more than one clerical necromancer, and these conjurers seem to have duped him into believing in their ability to summon demons to help him recover his fortunes through the art of alchemy.[39]

Exorcistic formulas to command the demons provided the core of necromancy, but made use of ritual paraphernalia and observances often shared with other forms of magic, and to some extent assimilated necromancy to those other types. These could involve a wax or metal image meant to represent the victim, rituals at astrologically determined times, and magic circles traced on the ground as a further means of gaining power over the spirits (and then seen also, especially in orthodox writings, as a protection against these spirits and their wiles).

Necromancy could be used for a range of purposes: constraining the thoughts or affections of victims, arousing love or hatred, driving people mad, creating illusions such as a banquet or a flying horse, or divining the future or secret affairs.[40] Trial records suggest that necromancy could be meant also for killing, sometimes for political assassination, although in these cases it is difficult to determine how far the conjurations were conceived as the effective techniques and how far the magicians were relying on other techniques such as image magic or magic potions. In any case, even when necromancy appeared to be purely entertaining, as when it was supposed to conjure an illusory banquet with entertainment, it tapped the resources of a malevolent demonic will. It might or might not express a will to harm on the magician's part, but it

---

[37] E.g. Johann Hartlieb, *Das Buch aller verbotenen Künste, des Aberglaubens und der Zauberei*, c. 28, ed. and tr. Falk Eisermann und Eckhard Graf (Ahlerstedt, 1989), 40–1, notes that Isidore uses the term 'Nigramancia' broadly. On this point see, however, Boudet, *Entre science et nigromance*, 92–4.

[38] Kieckhefer, *Magic in the Middle Ages*, 153–6; Kieckhefer, *Forbidden Rites*, 12–13 (note the reference to lay conjuring in n. 31).

[39] Reginald Hyatte, tr. with intro., *Laughter for the Devil: The Trials of Gilles de Rais, Companion-in-Arms of Joan of Arc (1440)* (Rutherford, NJ, 1984).

[40] Kieckhefer, *Forbidden Rites*, 25–6.

explicitly called upon malign spirits whose will to harm had to be held in precarious check by a battery of spiritual forces. The necromancer realized that his art was risky, and, calling upon the aid of all things sacred, he commanded the demon to come in a non-threatening form. Caesarius of Heisterbach and other preachers gave voice to fears that must have seemed reasonable: the necromancer who took one false step and left the protective confines of the magic circle would instantly be carried off to perdition in hell.[41]

Perhaps more numerous than necromancers were the magicians who saw themselves as conjuring unfallen or neutral angels: spirits who took neither side in Satan's rebellion against God, or the offspring of demons, or spirits who had turned to harm by their location in the sublunary world. When Jehan de Bar made a detailed confession of his magic in 1398, he admitted that in his books were 'several errors against our faith, such as to say that some devils are good and benign, some are powerful and all-knowing, some are neither in hell nor in heaven, and that good angels have revealed such sciences, and that the holy prophets and others performed miracles and proclaimed their prophecies by such arts'.[42] The good character of the angels was particularly doubtful when the magic was meant for harm. One book of ostensibly angelic magic tells how to poison a person's drink, how to afflict a bodily member, even how to kill a person, by means of magic worked largely through the invocation of spirits, astral or otherwise, although the invocation is combined with image magic that might elsewhere be thought efficacious in itself.[43]

Somewhat as astrology and other occult sciences could be set forth in simplified form for the laity, so could necromancy, and in its more popular forms the conjuring of demons was less exclusively the preserve of clergy.[44] There is evidence for this spillover effect in prescriptive texts: medieval lapidaries, for example, told of the diadochos stone, which enabled its bearer to gain command of 'what devil of hell thou wilt', without harm, and which served also to animate dead bodies.[45] In the trial literature there are cases of lay practitioners whose magic resembled clerical necromancy at least in its use of demonic images, magic circles, and conjurations. Three laymen tried before the Court of King's Bench in 1331 were alleged to have used a book of magic circles, characters, and formulas, alongside image magic, and were found performing a ceremony inside their magic circle.[46] Nor was it only men who could mimic clerical

---

[41] Kieckhefer, *Magic in the Middle Ages*, 172–5.

[42] J. R. Veenstra, *Magic and Divination at the Courts of Burgundy and France: Text and Context of Laurens Pignon's* Contre les devineurs *(1411)* (Leiden, 1998), 351–5.

[43] Juris G. Lidaka, 'The Book of Angels, Rings, Characters and Images of the Planets attributed to Osbern Bokenham', in Claire Fanger, ed., *Conjuring Spirits: Texts and Traditions of Medieval Ritual Magic* (Stroud, 1998), 32–75.

[44] Boudet, *Entre science et nigromance*, 383–93; the point is made already in Kieckhefer, *Forbidden Rites*.

[45] Joan Evans and Mary S. Serjeantson, eds, *English Mediaeval Lapidaries* (London, 1933), 84.

[46] Sayles, *Select Cases*, 53–7; see also Thomas Favent, *Historia siue narracio de modo et forma mirabilis Parliamenti*, ed. May McKisack, Camden Miscellany, 14 (London, 1926), 18.

necromancy. In a trial at Wolfsberg in 1493, three women were said to have pierced and buried a wax image of a victim. Each woman had her own devil, with the folkloric names Welland Dreistain, Tillian, and Pfabennswanz, and they baptized the image in the name of this unholy trinity.[47]

Still, when it was clergy who practised necromancy and related arts, their doing so no doubt aroused a sense of betrayal among those who had trusted them, not entirely unlike the reaction when clerical sex abuse is disclosed. Late medieval Christians may not always have had high expectations for their clergy, but clerical necromancy was by definition a turning of the sacred towards transgressive ends, and the desecration was a betrayal of trust that cannot have been taken lightly.

1.5 DIVINATION AS A NON-VICTIMLESS CRIME: DETECTION OF THEFT AND BEWITCHMENT

If fear of necromancy manifestly expresses anxiety about the ultimate harmful will, divination might seem to lie at the opposite end of the spectrum, a purely innocuous and in no way obviously malevolent activity. From the moralist's perspective, this was its greatest danger. What seemed harmless was, for that reason, all the more harmful. The diviner might seem a simpleton, a mountebank, sometimes a useful resource, in any event rarely malevolent, but if his art required demonic aid it still involved a will to harm. The perceived threat of divination was not unlike that of the Ouija board, an apparently innocent pastime with the potential to become threatening if it leads to sinister revelations. Yet the analogy is imperfect, because even when the revelations were not themselves dark the powers behind them were, because it involved communication with demons. The flight and calls of birds had no inherent power to predict the future, but a demon could use such means to respond to the enquiries of a diviner, and because demons had long experience and keen powers of observation they could surmise with fair accuracy what the future might hold. From that perspective divination was not at the opposite end of the spectrum from necromancy—rather, it was itself a form of necromancy, whether subtly or unsubtly calling on demons for their aid.

Divination sought information. When Isidore of Seville discussed magic, most of the categories he cited were modes of divination: foretelling the future by observing signs in the natural order or performing experiments to determine what would occur.[48]

---

[47] Fritz Byloff, ed., *Volkskundliches aus Strafprozessen der osterreichischen Alpenländer, mit besonderer Berücksichtigung der Zauberei- und Hexenprozesse 1455 bis 1850* (Berlin and Leipzig, 1929), 12–13, no. 14.

[48] Isidore of Seville, *The Etymologies*, bk. 8, ch. 9, tr. Stephen A. Barney, W. J. Lewis, J. A. Beach, and Oliver Berghof (Cambridge, 2006), 181–3; Isidoro di Siviglia, *Etimologie o origini*, ed. Angelo Valastro Canale (Turin, 2004), i, 662–70 (Latin), 663–71 (Italian).

Sometimes these entailed passive observation: the flight or calls of birds could foretell the future, as could dreams or thunderbolts, if one only knew how to interpret them. In other cases divination was experimental, meaning that the diviner had to perform some operation to gain the information required. The experiment might be mechanical, involving perhaps the rolling of dice and the consultation of elaborate charts. It might also be spiritual: scrying with a polished or otherwise luminous surface was meant to induce visions, which might be merely hypnotic but might be taken as apparitions of malign spirits, at which point it clearly became threatening. In any case, John of Salisbury reported that the boys who were made to cooperate in such experiments were psychologically abused and often bore unfortunate consequences through life.[49]

Johannes Hartlieb's *Book of All Forbidden Arts* (1456) explains the workings of seven magical arts, and apart from the first ('nigromancy') they are all divinatory: geomancy (divination by earth) involves casting lots on a board on which figures and points have been inscribed; hydromancy (divination by water) entails the discernment of images on water, sometimes with the service of a boy medium; aeromancy (divination by air) includes the observation of birds, signs in the heavens, and the motion of objects suspended in air; pyromancy (divination by fire) involves the observation of fire and scrying with shiny surfaces; chiromancy, or palmistry, is associated in part with Gypsies; spatulamancy involves the observation of animal bones thought to change their appearance in response to questions. Hartlieb repeatedly warns that these arts are hazardous to the soul of the practitioner; clearly he himself had learned a great deal about them all, and historians have debated how far he was a practitioner or meant to instruct his reader in the practice (however, he does not actually give enough information to carry out the experiments he describes).[50]

Apart from the risk of consorting with demons, divination became most obviously problematic when it was used to detect thieves and other malefactors, the danger being false accusation. No doubt the diviners often knew which individuals in a community might plausibly be charged with crime, which means their art could be a moderately subtle application of a social stereotype. A resident of Coventry was robbed of forty pounds and consulted diviners, who identified a local pauper as the thief, and in 1480 the town council at Nuremberg had Hans Pressel arrested for using sorcery to recover lost objects or determine where they were hidden.[51]

If divination to identify a thief was risky business, so too was divination to identify a witch, and this seems to have been a frequent prelude to formal proceedings. Heinrich Kramer's trial at Innsbruck affords insight into the informal modes of dealing with sorcery that went on before the inquisitor's arrival. Among the options open to the victim was consulting a diviner who might confirm that the affliction was caused

   [49] Kieckhefer, *Magic in the Middle Ages*, 151.
   [50] Hartlieb, *Das Buch aller verbotenen Künste*; Frank Fürbeth, *Johannes Hartlieb: Untersuchungen zu Leben und Werk* (Tübingen, 1992).
   [51] C. Trice Martin, 'Clerical Life in the Fifteenth Century, as Illustrated by Proceedings in the Court of Chancery', *Archaeologia*, 60 (1907), 371–2, 377–8; Kunstmann, *Zauberwahn und Hexenprozess*, 31–3.

by bewitchment, might identify the perpetrator, and might tell where the source of magical contagion was located. Thus, when Hans Portner's wife was bewitched, a trip to a diviner suggested searching for a bundle of noxious substances which, when found and burned, cured the victim's condition.[52]

A case at Angermünd in 1499 sheds valuable light on the informal proceedings that might precede formal prosecution but might also become part of the formal legal action. One Adolf Schlingerstock fell ill, and his cows began to give too little milk. When he tried using drugs, they did not prove to be much good. And so he concluded his cattle were bewitched, and a Master Conrad Steinbrecher confirmed this opinion, evidently through divination. Schlingerstock then brought charges against two women, Bilien Neckels and her daughter Irmgen Neckels. To reinforce his accusation he produced a letter from Conrad Steinbrecher, and Steinbrecher himself then went and said he wished to investigate the two women, but when he did so, giving a truth-inducing drink and questioning the daughter 'according to the gift given him by God', he found her innocent, and he then said he believed her mother too was innocent. The women were tortured, but the finding of innocence remained unshaken.[53]

1.6 DEMONIZATION OF THE MAGICIAN

Whether the defendants were accused of conjuring demons or not, trial records and other texts referring to magic are often saturated with the rhetoric of demonization. Echoing early Christian writers, John XXII spoke of magical procedures as 'the arts of demons, arisen from the pestiferous society of men and wicked angels'.[54] Destruction of the vines around Metz was caused by 'the diabolical art of sorcerers and sorceresses' or by 'the art of the devil'.[55] In Italy perhaps more than elsewhere, those practising magic of various sorts were said to have been inspired by the devil, instigated by a diabolical spirit, given over to diabolical arts and works, acting with diabolical intent, 'inspired by a diabolical spirit and not having God before her eyes'.[56] One was said to be a 'wretched, diabolical, and accursed woman', acting 'at the instigation of the devil' and 'on diabolical instruction', mindless of her eternal salvation; she had before her eyes not God but rather the enemy of humankind.[57] Another invoked the Trinity, the Virgin, and Saint Peter to cure people, but even in these apparently pious acts she was 'inspired by a diabolical spirit'.[58] Counsel on restoring a husband's affection was 'diabolical'

---

[52] Ammann, 'Der Innsbrucker Hexenprozeß', 44–6; cf. 48–9.

[53] Emil Pauls, 'Zauberwesen und Hexenwahn am Niederrhein', *Beiträge zur Geschichte des Niederrheins: Jahrbuch des Düsseldorfer Geschichts-Vereins*, 13 (1898), 211, 239–40.

[54] Hansen, *Quellen*, 2–4.

[55] Hansen, *Quellen*, 565–6.

[56] Cerlini, 'Una strega reggiana e il suo processo', 67; Nicolini, 'La stregoneria a Perugia', 32, 47–8, 60.

[57] Nicolini, 'La stregoneria a Perugia', 52–3, 55, 57.

[58] Mammoli, *The Record of the Trial*, 11–12.

instruction.[59] When Giacomo della Marca preached about sorcery to a congregation, he said if they did not believe what he had to say on the subject they should just go and look at the face of some enchantress, and they would see that her face itself seems diabolical because the devil always dwells within her—and this was his cue to tell of the trial and burning of a sorceress.[60]

This rhetoric is found in cases that have nothing to do with necromancy, let alone conspiratorial witchcraft. Magic per se, even in forms that might seem innocent to an observer outside the culture, could be viewed as inherently diabolical because it was taught by demons, instigated by demons, and made possible through the agency of demons. Such rhetoric gives voice to profound anxiety about magic as the expression of a will to harm, and it descries behind that will a yet more sinister urge towards gratuitous evil, evil for its own sake, which is the chief mark of the demonic. This chapter has attempted to survey some of the reasons for that anxiety. More accurately, perhaps, it has sought to show how anxieties which, in other cultures, might be articulated differently, perhaps in racial terms, came into focus in the denunciation, accusation, and conviction of people feared for the practice of a magic that could not be tolerated in late medieval society.

FURTHER READING

Bailey, Michael D., 'The Meanings of Magic', *Magic, Ritual, and Witchcraft*, 1 (2006), 1–23.

Bailey, Michael D., *Magic and Superstition in Europe: A Concise History from Antiquity to the Present* (Lanham, MD, 2007).

Bailey, Michael D., 'The Age of Magicians: Periodization in the History of European Magic', *Magic, Ritual, and Witchcraft*, 3 (2008), 3–28.

Bremmer, Jan N. and Veenstra, Jan R., eds, *The Metamorphosis of Magic from Late Antiquity to the Early Modern Period* (Leuven, 2002).

Jolly, Karen, Raudvere, Catharine, and Peters, Edward, *Witchcraft and Magic in Europe: The Middle Ages*, ed. Bengt Ankarloo and Stuart Clark (London, 2001).

Kieckhefer, Richard, *Magic in the Middle Ages* (new edn, Cambridge, 2000).

Klaniczay, Gábor and Pócs, Éva, eds, *Communicating with the Spirits: Christian Demonology and Popular Mythology* (Budapest, 2005).

Maxwell-Stuart, P. G., *The Occult in Medieval Europe* (New York, 2005).

Skemer, Don C., *Binding Words: Textual Amulets in the Middle Ages* (University Park, PA, 2006).

Thorndike, Lynn, *The History of Magic and Experimental Science*, 8 vols (New York, 1923–58).

Wilson, Stephen W., *Magical Universe: Everyday Ritual and Magic in Pre-Modern Europe* (London, 2001).

---

[59] Cerlini, 'Una strega reggiana e il suo processo', 64.

[60] Nicolini, 'La stregoneria a Perugia', 50–1.

CHAPTER 2

··

FIFTEENTH-CENTURY
WITCH BELIEFS

··

HANS PETER BROEDEL

IN 1437 Pope Eugenius IV addressed a warning to 'all inquisitors of heretical depravity' that Satan had so bewitched some Christians, that they 'sacrifice to demons, adore them . . . do homage to them, and make with them a written agreement or another kind of pact through which, by a single word, touch, or sign, they may perform whatever evil deeds and sorcery they wish . . .'[1] He then directed that all such accomplices of the devil should be prosecuted and punished, with the assistance of secular and episcopal authorities as necessary. The inquisitors were apparently unable to carry out this papal directive fully, since four years later, in a scathing denunciation of the anti-Pope Felix V (previously Amadeus VIII, the Duke of Savoy), Eugenius charged that heretical sorcerers commonly called *stregule* or *Waldenses* were still both numerous and tolerated in his rival's homeland.[2] Eugenius' writings, like those of many of his contemporaries, convey both the sect's danger and its novelty. This was not traditional heresy—the pope knew full well that those he called *Waldenses* were utterly unlike traditional Waldensians—and these heretics did not practise traditional sorts of magic. This was instead a recent innovation, a new sect under the personal tutelage of the devil, whose adherents worshipped him directly in return for maleficent magical powers.

The overwhelming consensus of modern historians is that the pope was fundamentally mistaken: his sorcerous diabolic sect existed only in the imaginations of a few like-minded men. Nonetheless, this mental construct, which we call witchcraft, proved to be enormously influential, and became the operative principle behind the prosecution of perhaps 100,000 alleged witches over the next three hundred years. Yet the pope was

[1] Alan Charles Kors and Edward Peters, eds, *Witchcraft in Europe, 400–1700: A Documentary History* (Philadelphia, PA, 2001), 154–5.

[2] Kors and Peters, *Witchcraft in Europe*, 154.

right about one thing: this was a new idea in the early fifteenth century, and to explain why witches and witchcraft appeared at just this time and place, taking the particular forms they did, remain basic problems in the historiography of European witchcraft.

Over a century ago the German archivist Joseph Hansen took a brilliant stab at a solution: he argued that diabolic witchcraft, as Pope Eugenius and others conceived it, was a synthetic 'collective concept' (*Kollektivbegriff*), the result of a fusion of ideas associated with heresy and magic in the minds of educated men.[3] The witches' pact with the devil, and their nocturnal conclave, the sabbath, provided focal points around which this assimilation occurred, but other motifs—flight, animal transformation, and sexual relations with demons—were borrowed from other traditions as well. The culmination of this process was a composite that scholars have variously dubbed the 'fully developed', 'cumulative', or 'elaborated' concept of witchcraft, and it remains the paradigmatic concept of historical scholarship. Recent research, however, has revealed its limitations. Late nineteenth-century German idealism strongly influenced Hansen's approach to intellectual history. In particular, he found witchcraft such a strikingly powerful concept, and one so apt to the late medieval conceptual world, that it developed inexorably and seemingly of its own accord towards a single stable form, which, once perfected, achieved a kind of real existence independent of specific social and intellectual contexts.[4] For this reason, Hansen and his followers tend to treat their conception of the late medieval witch as a kind of supra-historical analytical category; however, as H. C. Erik Midelfort, among others, has observed, some of Hansen's criteria are plainly arbitrary.[5] Why, for example, when a great many apparently flightless witches were burned, should magical flight be a necessary part of the witch stereotype? Richard Kieckhefer points out the still more basic problem that there was never a single monolithic late medieval conception of witchcraft, but rather 'multiple mythologies', that varied distinctly over time and space.[6] Italian witches, Swiss witches, and French witches were conceived in different terms, and hence, Kieckhefer notes, functioned differently within their various social contexts. Fixation upon a single paradigm and the unwarranted assumption that witchcraft evolved along a single path, has also led to misleading arguments about whether one set of ideas or another made a more essential contribution to the witch's final form. Yet the evidence shows, much as one would expect, that understandings of witchcraft varied broadly depending upon personal experience, and that consensus about the nature of witchcraft developed only slowly. In sum, then, although late medieval conceptions of witchcraft are still best understood as composites, the evidence requires a more nuanced view of their diversity, construction, and development.

---

[3] Joseph Hansen, *Zauberwahn, Inquisition und Hexenprozess im Mittelalter* (1900, repr. Munich, 1964), 35–6.

[4] Hajo Holborn, 'The History of Ideas', *American Historical Review*, 73 (1968), 683–95.

[5] H. C. Erik Midelfort, 'Witchcraft and Religion in Sixteenth Century Germany: The Formation and Consequences of Orthodoxy', *Archive for Reformation History*, 62 (1971), 268.

[6] Richard Kieckhefer, 'Mythologies of Witchcraft in the Fifteenth Century', *Magic, Ritual, and Witchcraft*, 1 (2006), 80.

2.1 Magic, *Maleficium*, and Late Medieval Witchcraft

Central to discussions of European witchcraft at any time is the perception of *maleficium*, of magical harm. Prior to the modern era, most Europeans took the reality of magic for granted.[7] They were therefore ready to consider the possibility of sorcery (by which here and elsewhere I mean simply harmful magic) when an injury's circumstances suggested human agency but also seemed to defy natural explanation. In such cases, a variety of practitioners, both clerical and lay, stood ready to provide necessary countermeasures; but should these fail, and should more direct action seem unpalatable, the injured party could pursue the matter in court. Nonetheless, evidence suggests that prosecutions for *maleficia* were likely few in number until the fourteenth century—a testament either to the efficacy of local remedies or to the indifference of local magistrates—when then they began to increase in frequency. By the fifteenth century, trials were common in Italy and Switzerland, while the rest of Europe experienced scattered but increasing numbers of prosecutions.[8]

Historians have proposed several explanations for this apparent upsurge in sorcery trials. As many have noted, the people of the late Middle Ages had no shortage of things to worry about, and generalized anxiety associated with war, pestilence, famine, and religious turmoil may have led to increasing fears of the devil's occult powers, and to a search for his more tangible human counterparts.[9] More concretely, Wolfgang Behringer notes that in the Alpine regions of Central Europe, prosecutions for sorcery and witchcraft were particularly common in the early fifteenth century, as were previously unusual accusations of weather magic.[10] Growing fear of *maleficia* in these regions, he argues, reflected extraordinarily extreme weather that modern climate science associates with the onset of the 'Little Ice Age'. Yet, although suspicions of sorcery may have reflected the intensity of local anxieties, variations in judicial procedures also determined whether prosecutions for harmful sorcery would be encouraged or suppressed in a given region.[11] In general, in those jurisdictions where the plaintiff initiated legal action with a formal, public accusation, where the accused was compensated for unproven allegations, where torture was not applied, and where courts operated

---

[7] Stephen Wilson, *The Magical Universe: Everyday Ritual and Magic in Pre-Modern Europe* (London, 2000); Edward Bever, *The Realities of Witchcraft and Popular Magic in Early Modern Europe: Culture, Cognition, and Everyday Life* (Basingstoke, 2008).

[8] Richard Kieckhefer, *European Witch Trials: Their Foundation in Popular and Learned Culture, 1300–1500* (London, 1976), 18–23.

[9] Robert Thurston, *The Witch Hunts: A History of Witch Persecutions in Europe and North America* (Harlow, 2007), 25–64.

[10] Wolfgang Behringer, 'Climatic Change and Witch-Hunting: The Impact of the Little Ice Age on Mentalities', *Climatic Change*, 43 (1999), 335–51.

[11] Brian P. Levack, *The Witch-hunt in Early Modern Europe* (3rd edn, Harlow, 2006), 74–108.

under close supervision, rates of conviction for both magic and witchcraft were low. Under such conditions, we can reasonably suppose that many supposed sorcerers stayed out of court simply because bringing an accusation entailed considerable risk, with little likelihood of conviction. On the other hand, where Roman law and inquisitorial procedure prevailed, where denunciations were secret and carried no risk, and where torture was freely applied, the numbers of prosecutions and convictions were often much higher. This useful contrast unquestionably helps to explain the intensity of persecution in many places, but unfortunately not everywhere: early and severe persecutions of witches and sorcerers often occurred in regions characterized by a confusing jumble of overlapping jurisdictions, courts, magistrates, and procedures.[12] Harmful magic was in places prosecuted aggressively even where local juries and traditional 'accusatorial procedures' remained the rule, while some inquisitorial courts seem to have lazily ignored the presence of witches and sorcerers in their midst. On the whole, recent investigations of the social and legal contexts of late medieval sorcery and witchcraft trials emphasize that particular local conditions determined patterns of prosecution in ways unsuitable to the formation of broad causal claims, since although sustained prosecutions were contingent upon the support of local leaders, the reasons for that support varied widely from place to place.[13]

Yet if it remains difficult to explain why sorcery should have been prosecuted more vigorously in the fifteenth century, the links between sorcery and diabolic witchcraft are reasonably clear. For most people, including most magical practitioners, magic seems to have depended variously upon the power of God, the saints, or more ambivalent spirits, or on the intrinsic properties of material things, words, performances, or magicians themselves.[14] For the clerical elite, on the contrary, it was obvious that spells and charms lacked the innate power to accomplish what the magician intended: a wax image could not really cause a man to burn with love, a knotted string could not really cause impotence, regardless of how elaborate the magician's accompanying performance. Some clerics therefore identified such practices as empty superstitions, which could do no physical harm despite their manifest spiritual danger. But by the late Middle Ages such scepticism was rare. Instead, churchmen argued that magic involved a kind of occult communication, in which demons secretly carried out desired effects in response to magicians' performances, in order to lead them deeper into sin. This theoretical arrangement, technically termed an 'implicit pact', had originally provided scholastic theologians with a conceptual model through which they could accept and explain the apparent efficacy of superstitions. By the fifteenth

---

[12] Brian P. Levack, 'Crime and the Law', in Jonathan Barry and Owen Davies, eds, *Witchcraft Historiography* (Basingstoke, 2007), 149–51.

[13] Compare, for example, the political contexts of two sets of Alpine trials in Georg Modestin, *Le diable chez l'évêque: chasse aux sorciers dans le diocèse de Lausanne (vers 1460)* (Lausanne, 1999), and Niklaus Schatzmann, *Verdorrende Bäume und Brote wie Kuhfladen: Hexenprozesse in der Leventina 1431–1459 und die Anfänge der Hexenverfolgung auf der Alpensüdseite* (Zurich, 2003).

[14] Richard Kieckhefer, *Magic in the Middle Ages* (Cambridge, 1989), 56–94; Bever, *The Realities of Witchcraft*, 271–335.

century, however, this theory had begun to influence pastoral practice, as theologians sought to convince the laity that a host of useful and seemingly benign superstitions actually entailed commerce with Satan.[15] This stress on the fundamentally diabolic nature of all magic, which one sees in the writings of men such as Jean Gerson (d.1429) and Johannes Nider (d.1438), blurred the distinction between the implicit pact, in which practitioners were entirely ignorant of the role of demons, and the explicit, in which magicians actively sought their aid. After all, once one has been told that magic necessarily entails demonic assistance, any future occult experiment would be tantamount to a knowing invocation of the devil.

2.2 The Identification of Sorcery with Diabolic Heresy

From the clerical perspective, actively summoning a demon to work magic was heresy, rather than simple superstition, and hence a matter for an inquisition. This understanding of magic had crystallized during the thirteenth and fourteenth centuries in scholastic and inquisitorial considerations of the demonic underpinnings of the text-based magic of learned magicians. By 1400, however, some commentators within the Church viewed folk magic in similar terms. Michael Bailey, following Kieckhefer, argues that the inability of educated clerics to understand allegations of popular sorcery, except through the lens provided by their theoretical understanding of learned magic, led directly to the diabolization of *maleficium* and the invention of satanic witchcraft.[16] As evidence, he points to Johannes Nider's account of a string of witch trials that occurred around 1400 in the Swiss mountains near Bern.[17] Nider relates that a local magistrate's investigation of widespread *maleficia*, including sterility, weather magic, and the sorcerous theft of crops, uncovered an extensive conspiracy of satanic devil worshippers, who met regularly to perform blasphemous rites involving infanticide and ritual cannibalism, and who in return received magical powers. Nider, a Dominican reformer and theologian, included these tales in a moralizing didactic treatise called the *Formicarius* (The Ant Hill), which he wrote around 1437 while attending the Council of Basel. Bailey's analysis suggests that stories of the diabolic sabbath buzzing around the Council strongly coloured Nider's interpretation of the dark events of forty years earlier. For Nider, traditional village *maleficia*—stories of

---

[15] Euan Cameron, *Enchanted Europe: Superstition, Reason, and Religion, 1250–1750* (Oxford, 2010), 108–9.

[16] Michael Bailey, 'From Sorcery to Witchcraft: Clerical Conceptions of Magic in the Later Middle Ages', *Speculum*, 76 (2001), 960–90.

[17] Kieckhefer, *European Witch Trials*, 78–82; Michael Bailey, *Battling Demons: Witchcraft, Heresy, and Reform in the Late Middle Ages* (University Park, PA, 2003), 37–45; see also Arno Borst, 'The Origins of the Witch-Craze in the Alps', in *Medieval Worlds*, tr. Eric Hansen (Chicago, 1992), 101–22.

which remain distinctly embedded in his text—were indistinguishable from learned diabolic necromancy, and so evoked associations with current tales of the satanic cult. Such witches made perfect sense within Nider's millenarian worldview, both as an example of the awful consequences of sin, and 'as yet another battalion in the diabolic army that threatened the reform of the world'.[18]

Nider's interpretation of witchcraft was grounded in quite particular intellectual and geographic contexts, and so somewhat different explanations must be sought to understand why people from different backgrounds attest to generally similar concerns. Further contemporary evidence for widespread witch beliefs comes from the small Italian hill town of Todi, where the notorious 'witch' Matteuccia Francisci was executed in 1428.[19] Matteuccia was a well-known folk healer and magician, who specialized in providing magical remedies, along with counselling for battered wives. Her business must have made her enemies, because a large number of people, 'honest and truthful citizens', denounced her to the authorities, accusing her of assorted magical practices. Towards the end of her trial record, however, a series of shocking confessions suddenly replaces the litany of conventional accusations: Matteuccia admits that she went with other witches to meet Lucifer; that she flew through the air on the back of a demonic goat; and that she smeared herself with bat blood and sucked the blood from babies. Richard Kieckhefer plausibly attributes this shift to the aggressive intervention of learned magistrates, eager to make the trial conform to their own notions of witchcraft, probably through the free use of torture.

These magistrates did not produce these charges out of thin air: Matteuccia's trial and condemnation almost certainly reflect the views of another reform-minded cleric, the Franciscan Bernardino of Siena (d.1444), who preached in Todi before large crowds two years earlier. Although the subjects of these sermons have not survived, we know that the details of Matteuccia's confession, even down to meeting the devil by a walnut tree in Benevento, parallel exactly those in sermons the friar preached elsewhere Further, while Bernardino was in Todi the town council altered their laws on the friar's suggestion, prescribing death by fire for 'enchanters and spell makers', and those who 'conjure up devils'.[20] Given that the persecution of witches was a well-established component of Bernardino's reforming programme, it seems likely that his preaching led many people in Todi to see Matteuccia's magic in a far more sinister light, and provided the magistrates with the conceptual template necessary to transform her from superstitious wise woman to child-murdering, devil-worshipping witch. Within broad limits, witchcraft fitted into Bernardino's apocalyptic, spiritually charged mental universe much as it did into Nider's, but Bernardino's witch was far less a product of

---

[18] Bailey, *Battling Demons*, 117.
[19] Kieckhefer, *European Witch Trials*, 73; William Monter, 'Todi, Witch of (1428)', in Richard M. Golden, ed., *The Encyclopedia of Witchcraft: The Western Tradition* (Santa Barbara, CA, 2006), iv, 1125–6; Franco Mormando, *The Preacher's Demons: Bernardino of Siena and the Social Underworld of Early Renaissance Italy* (Chicago, 1999), 72–80.
[20] Mormando, *The Preacher's Demons*, 73.

scholastic theology, and much more a reflection of Italian folk beliefs. Both Nider's *exempla* and Bernardino's sermons illustrate how late medieval authors could transform the familiar image of the magical practitioner into the witch, through the creative use of motifs borrowed from such familiar but disparate categories as folklore and heresy.

The notion of a heretical sect of devil worshippers was as much a fantasy of the medieval imagination as satanic witches themselves. Yet the charge of outright demonolatry, and with it a number of ancillary abominations—infanticide, cannibalism, and incestuous orgies—had been levelled against heretics for hundreds of years.[21] The Cathars, perhaps because of their dualist beliefs and unconventional practices, had been especially liable to accusations of this sort, but eventually even pious Waldensians were alleged to engage in obscene nocturnal demonic rites. Kathrin Utz Tremp has meticulously documented this gradual 'diabolization of heresy' and the corresponding 'hereticization' of magic, which she sees as two aspects of a gradual, uneven, but extremely widespread assimilation of mental categories in late medieval Europe.[22] Her research demonstrates that where early witch prosecutions were most intense, in the Alpine regions of Switzerland, Savoy, southern France, and northern Italy, heresy trials were the driving force behind this syncretic evolution of witch beliefs, and conceptions of diabolized heresy, not sorcery, played the most significant role in the development of the witch.

2.3 THE FIRST TRIALS OF DIABOLIC WITCHES IN THE ALPS

The witch trials in the western Alps were an outgrowth of the sustained persecution of Waldensian heretics that began in the late fourteenth century. The region was ripe for such a campaign: there were substantial numbers of Waldensians, members of families who had fled to the mountains to escape earlier persecutions; the preaching of Vincent Ferrar (d.1419) was spreading apocalyptic fervour and fears; and local authorities in this politically fractured region were quite willing to extend their reach into local affairs through the persecution of dangerous deviants.[23] Inquisitors duly found Waldensians, but they also discovered others who, it was said, worshipped Lucifer directly, engaged in promiscuous orgies, and sacrificed children. Then, in 1409, Pope Alexander V responded

---

[21] Jeffrey Burton Russell, *Witchcraft in the Middle Ages* (Ithaca, NY, 1972), 101–98; Norman Cohn, *Europe's Inner Demons* (rev. edn, Chicago, 1993), 75–8.

[22] Kathrin Utz Tremp, *Von der Häresie zur Hexerie: 'Wirkliche' und imaginäre Sekten im Spätmittelalter* (Hanover, 2008), 384.

[23] Gabriel Audisio, *The Waldensian Dissent: Persecution and Survival, c.1170–c.1570*, tr. Claire Davison (Cambridge, 1999), 62–3. See also, Laura Stokes, 'Prelude: Early Witch-Hunting in Germany and Switzerland', *Magic, Ritual, and Witchcraft*, 4 (2009), 54–61.

to a report from Ponce Feugeyron, an inquisitor working in the Duchy of Savoy, urging him to prosecute Christians and Jews belonging to 'new sects', that taught 'hidden doctrines', and practiced 'forbidden arts', including sorcery, magic, and summoning demons.[24] The pope's letter takes the form of a rescript, and so directly reflects the local inquisitor's thinking: it stresses that this activity is something new, and that it constitutes an organized heretical sect of sorcerers. The pope failed to mention devil worship and its assorted trappings, however—an omission repeated in 1418 and 1434, when later popes renewed Feugeyron's authority. Yet the combination of sorcery, heresy, and occult conspiracy constitutes an important step in the development of witch beliefs, as does the inquisitor's sweeping papal mandate.[25]

While Feugeyron was making life miserable for suspected heretics in the Savoy, other members of these 'new sects' were tried and executed in the nearby Swiss Valais. The chronicler, Hans Fründ, who records these events in some detail, relates that in 1428 the region was infested with sorcerers—over 700 in all—who used diabolical magic to cause death, injury, sterility, and impotence.[26] They could also metamorphose into wolves, fly on magic chairs, and enter storehouses and larders at night to feast and drink, a crime which must have been difficult to detect, since they entered invisibly and magically restored all they consumed prior to leaving. At certain times, they gathered in 'schools' to do homage to an 'evil spirit', and to consume the flesh of children. According to Fründ, over 200 of these noxious cultists were eventually burned. From any perspective, these are curious creatures, sharing many characteristics with other witches and sorcerers, but with a particular flavour all their own. Fründ ties their *maleficia* to nocturnal meetings with a spirit, but never mentions demons or the devil; nor do these heretics exactly worship their leader, but instead give him tribute in the form of sheep or oats; finally, these heretics enjoy many of the same powers as fairies or bogies, powers in which many churchmen would find it hard to believe. The singularity of Fründ's witches and the ferocity with which they were pursued over the course of many years demonstrates that the 'cumulative' witch was not necessary for large-scale persecution; far more important seems to have been the fear of a massive anti-social conspiracy—which needed to be suppressed through concerted efforts—and the liberal use of torture as the preferred tool of suppression.

Fründ explains that these trials began in the French-speaking Lower Valais, a region under the authority of the Duke of Savoy, whose territories as a whole seem to have served as a vital nexus for the early dissemination of ideas about diabolic witchcraft and its persecution.[27] Despite the claims of Pope Eugenius to the contrary, Duke Amadeus VIII

[24] Kors and Peters, *Witchcraft in Europe*, 152–3.

[25] Martine Ostorero, 'Itinéraire d'un inquisiteur gâté: Ponce Feugeyron, les juifs et le sabbat des sorciers', *Médiévals*, 43 (2002), 103–18.

[26] Katherin Utz Tremp and Catherine Chène, 'Hans Fründ', in Martine Ostorero, Agostino Paravicini Bagliani, and Kathrin Utz Tremp, eds, *L'imaginaire du sabbat* (Lausanne, 1999), 21–51.

[27] Martine Ostorero, 'Savoy, Duchy of', in *Encyclopedia of Witchcraft*, ii, 1006–8; Chantal Ammann-Doubliez, 'La Première Chasse aux Sorciers en Valais (1428–1436?)', in Ostorero et al., eds, *L'imaginaire du sabbat*, 63–98.

consistently supported efforts to rid his lands of the scourge of witches and sorcerers, perhaps in part due to fears stemming from the alleged attempts of a Jewish sorcerer and physician to do him magical harm. *Maleficia* directed against a sovereign prince constituted *lèse majesté*, a crime far greater than run-of-the-village sorcery, and this overtly political threat, when placed in the context of a widespread and well-organized diabolic conspiracy, goes far to explain the enthusiasm with which Duke Amadeus and other leaders supported the persecution of witches. The duke's personal experience may also help to explain why the emerging construct of witchcraft within his domains incorporated distinctive elements derived from contemporary anti-Semitic discourse, such as the accusation that witches spread disease through the use of poison powders that they obtained at diabolic *synagoga*. Ponce Feugeyron, the leader of the Savoyard Inquisition, was also a zealous persecutor of the Jews, however, and no further explanation may be necessary. Feugeyron's influence over the development and spread of the concept of witches should not be underestimated, since, during his lengthy tenure, he appears to have fostered the growth of a kind of professional inquisitorial community committed to the eradication of diabolic witches. Ulric de Torrenté, the inquisitor who presided over early witch trials in the Lower Valais, was one of Feugeyron's colleagues.

The Savoyard connection is also present in a lengthy series of trials in neighbouring Fribourg in the diocese of Lausanne. Here, the Inquisition of the prince-bishop had been ferreting out fairly familiar Waldensian heretics since the late fourteenth century, but around 1430, and once again under the influence of Ulric de Torrenté, some Waldensians were also accused of attending 'synagogues' and of possessing magical powers.[28] Kathrin Utz Tremp notes that rural villagers seemingly denounced one woman simply because she was said to practise sorcery; but while the tribunal heard the case, and concluded that she had indeed caused *maleficia*, she was eventually released because there was no accompanying evidence of overt heresy or demonolatry.[29] A dozen years later, however, the same woman was again arrested for sorcery, which this time the Inquisition took for direct evidence of diabolism, and she was consigned to the stake. In Fribourg, then, we can trace in some detail the gradual shift of persecution from Waldensian heretics, to Waldensians imagined to worship Satan and practise sorcery, to diabolic witches detected solely through their reputations for causing magical harm. Yet despite this evidentiary importance, *maleficia* does not play a central role in their trials. Instead, coercive interrogation and torture produced confessions that emphasized the witches' personal relationships with the devil, their demonolatry and the obscene kiss, and their denial of God and desecration of holy objects. The diabolic 'synagogue' provided an appropriately horrific setting for this systematic rejection of social norms, accompanied by an array of motifs derived from anti-heretical polemic, including the promiscuous orgy, infanticide, and cannibalism.

---

[28] Andreas Blauert, *Frühe Hexenverfolgungen: Ketzer-, Zauberei- und Hexenprozesse des 15. Jahrhunderts* (Hamburg, 1989), 27, 37–43; Utz Tremp, *Von der Häresie zur Hexerie*, 441, 465–523.

[29] Utz Tremp, *Von der Häresie zur Hexerie*, 502–9, 528–9.

These confessions reflect a conception of witchcraft framed in terms of contemporary notions of diabolic heresy, shared among the inquisitors of Lausanne, and forcibly imposed upon the victims of their trials.[30] This evolutionary assimilation of sorcerers into heretics is apparent in the very word for witches in the French-speaking Alps—*Vaudois*, that is, Waldensians—a linguistic idiosyncrasy that is particularly striking given that, almost everywhere else, the word 'witch' derived from a rich stock of vernacular terms for 'sorcerer'.[31]

At present, there is no broadly synthetic analysis of the development of witch beliefs in Alpine Europe during the crucial years from 1410–40, but plainly by the 1430s new conceptions of diabolic witchcraft were taking shape in a parallel series of trials in the western Alps. The most uniform articulations of witchcraft, and those most obviously dependent upon heretical motifs, emerged under the watchful gaze of inquisitions, and probably owe much to a few dedicated inquisitors. Secular magistrates in Switzerland and the Dauphiné accepted the basic structures of diabolic witchcraft as the underpinnings of their prosecutions, but tended to conceive of witchcraft more flexibly and with greater attention to traditional secular narratives.[32] The collective significance of these trials awaits further study, but it is possible to make three preliminary observations. First, early Alpine persecutions revealed witches who made their pacts with the devil face-to-face, and offered him worship directly, as did imagined Luciferian heretics. For these witches, the diabolic pact was nothing like the theoretical construct of words and actions developed by scholastic theologians, but a formal contract, necessarily involving apostasy of the most flagrant kind. The critical locus of this personal encounter between witch and demon was the sabbath, a colourful description of which—scripted to a greater or lesser degree—became one of the hallmarks of a witch's confession. Second, in these trials authorities, for the first time, sought sustained, large-scale prosecutions of witches, indicating that the fear of witchcraft had evolved beyond the personal dynamics of insult, threat, and harm of local sorcery, into a generalized danger to Christian society. Otherwise, witchcraft persecution responded to a broad range of anxieties and agendas, including fears of *maleficia* and anti-social conspiracy, clerical apocalypticism and reformist goals, local jurisdictional claims, and state-building agendas. Thus, motives varied widely, but this—and the emerging consensus that persecution was necessary—suggests the conceptual utility of diabolic witchcraft in late medieval Europe. Third, despite substantial local variations, experts recognized family resemblances between witches that revealed them all to be manifestations of a single massive pan-European heretical conspiracy. This perception of identity enabled witch experts to translate their core beliefs across geographic, cultural, and linguistic frontiers, and find their fears validated almost everywhere.

[30] Kieckhefer, 'Mythologies of Witchcraft', 84–6.

[31] E. William Monter, *Witchcraft in France and Switzerland: The Borderlands during the Reformation* (Ithaca, NY, 1976), 22.

[32] Pierette Parvay, 'Claude Tholosan', in Ostorero, et al., eds, *L'imaginaire du sabbat*, 355–437.

2.4 THE DIFFUSION OF WITCH MYTHOLOGIES

Precisely how this regionally specific conception of diabolic witchcraft spread across Europe is still being worked out, but all evidence points to the Council of Basel (1431–49) as an initial point of dissemination.[33] Through an unfortunate coincidence, the Council brought clerical representatives from all corners of Europe to Switzerland at precisely the moment when the persecution of heretics was giving way to the persecution of witches. Local inquisitors, such as Feugeyron, were in attendance, and given the contemporary interest in heresy and sorcery, and the roles of magic and spirits in the recent trial of Joan of Arc, considerable discussion of the locally ubiquitous 'new sect' of witches was inevitable. Informal and undocumented conversations were probably the most significant avenues of diffusion, but several of the earliest and most influential witch treatises also have clear connections to the Council. Johannes Nider acquired his extensive knowledge of witchcraft at Basel, and used this information as the basis of his treatment of the subject in the *Formicarius*.[34] The discussion of witchcraft in Martin Le Franc's *Le champion des dames* (The Defender of Ladies), although part of a lengthy and intentionally amusing romance, probably also derives from his experiences at Basel as secretary to Duke Amadeus VIII. Nicholas Jacquier, author of the *Flagellum haereticorum fascinariorum* (Scourge of Heretical Enchanters) was part of a large inquisitorial contingent at Basel, and his work reflects views typical of Feugeyron and de Torrenté. The anonymous treatise, *Errores Gazariorum* (Errors of the Gazarii) probably comes closest, however, to capturing intact the particularly Savoyard mythology of witches.[35] The earliest version of the manuscript was written in the Val d'Aoste, in Savoyard territory in northern Italy around 1437, and both Feugeyron and de Torrenté have been nominated as the possible author.[36] Regardless, the author was working for the bishop, Georges de Saluces, who seems to have acquired his interest in witchcraft while at Basel, where he could have easily met either inquisitor, both of whom he would later employ; further, both known versions of the treatise were found with other documents pertaining to the Council.[37] All of which substantiates the thesis that through Basel, a regional preoccupation with witches became a European concern.

Over the next several decades, outside the confines of the western Alps, the concept of the witch remained extremely fluid, while generalized fears of witches grew.

---

[33] Michael Bailey and Edward Peters, 'A Sabbat of Demonologists: Basel, 1431–1440', *The Historian*, 65 (2003), 1375–95.

[34] Bailey, *Battling Demons*, 96–7.

[35] Kathrin Utz Tremp and Martine Ostorero, '*Errores Gazariorum*', in Ostorero, et al., eds, *L'imaginaire du sabbat*, 269–99.

[36] Ostorero, 'Itinéraire d'un inquisiteur gâté: Ponce Feugeyron', 115–16; Wolfgang Behringer, *Witches and Witch-Hunts: A Global History* (Cambridge, 2004), 65.

[37] Peters and Bailey, 'A Sabbat of Demonologists', 1388–9.

Reformers within the Church portrayed witches with a broad brush as the enemies of Christian society, in whom heresy, sorcery, and frightening motifs drawn from folklore converged. In the 1450s, in churches from Slovenia to the Denmark, paintings of flying witches reinforced this pastoral message, possibly as part of a widespread 'anti-witch campaign'.[38] Trials of witches in both civil and clerical courts increased at the same time, although the precise charges levied against them varied widely. In most regions, emerging witchcraft mythologies were increasingly grounded in notions associated with *maleficia* rather than heresy, in large part because the motifs of diabolic witchcraft were easily grafted onto sorcery trials, and because mechanisms were already in place to identify likely sorcerers.[39] As Utz Tremp remarks, even in the Alps, 'the heretical tradition receded in favour of the magical tradition, which would have been more apparent and more important in village society'.[40] The paradigm of the diabolic heretic-witch, the *Vaudois*, remained strongly viable only in eastern France and northwards through the territories of the Duke of Burgundy, where close-knit ecclesiastical communities kept the concept alive, and where trials focusing on the wider social dangers of diabolic heresy served regional political agendas. Even here, however, without careful oversight, the pressures of local social contexts and traditions quickly eroded the detailed contours developed in Lausanne and Savoy. The result, Kieckhefer writes, was 'a highly fluid mythology, in which no two trials resemble each other very closely; sporadic, rather than sustained persecution, in which the victims may be disreputable women but may also be respected theologians, because the imported and fragmented mythology is accompanied by no criteria at all for its application'.[41]

As an example, those accused of *vaulderie* in a series of trials in Arras in 1460 included a nobleman and wealthy, respected citizens, alongside artists, eccentrics, and prostitutes. This social diversity reflected the view of the clerics responsible, the Dominican inquisitor Nicholas Jacquier among them, that these witches were but a small part of a massive satanic conspiracy, involving 'a third of Christendom and more', in which even bishops and cardinals were implicated.[42] After torture and false promises of mercy, the accused confessed to devil worship, infanticide, and every sexual sin their judges could imagine, but in Arras, unlike Savoy and the Alps, there was no strong local consensus that the accused were truly social deviants, either heretics or sorcerers. Indeed, Franck Mercier argues that the prosecutions of Arras responded more to friction between political elites, who found the trials a useful venue for cooperative and competitive display, and to personal jealousies and agendas, than to widespread fears of witchcraft.[43] The trials therefore generated almost immediate

---

[38] Behringer, *Witch-hunts*, 69.

[39] Bever, *The Realities of Witchcraft*, 40–60.

[40] Kathrin Utz Tremp, 'Heresy', in *Encyclopedia of Witchcraft*, ii, 487.

[41] Kieckhefer, 'Mythologies of Witchcraft', 102.

[42] Jacques du Clercq, *Mémoires*, in P. G. Maxwell-Stuart, ed. and tr., *The Occult in Medieval Europe, 500–1500: A Documentary History* (Basingstoke, 2005), 122–9.

[43] Franck Mercier, *La Vauderie d'Arras: Une chasse aux sorcières à l'Automne du Moyen Âge* (Rennes, 2006), 139–62 and *passim*.

opposition, and ultimately not even the warning from the Dean of Arras that anyone who protested would be arrested as a witch could stifle all complaints, some of which persuaded Philip the Good, Duke of Burgundy (d.1467), that it would be politically expedient to bring the trials to an end.

The ultimate failure of the persecutions at Arras was not exceptional. Opposition to witch trials came from the family and friends of alleged witches and from rival elites, suspicious of ulterior motives. The growing influence of believers also served to mobilize more conservative and sceptical clerics, who objected to the new mythologies of witchcraft on pastoral and theological grounds. Nicholas of Cusa (d.1464), an ardent reformer and yet another participant at the Council of Basel, was one of many who felt the outlandish claim that witches flew through the air at night to attend the diabolic revels of the sabbath contradicted the ruling of the canon *Episcopi*: that such things happened only in the imagination. In his sermons he admonished his auditors not to persecute 'decrepit and delirious' old women, because they were not witches, and their bizarre dreams harmed none but themselves.[44] In a similar vein, his contemporary, the Bishop of Cuenca insisted that night-flying witches as a species were simply imaginary, and that 'to believe the contrary is to be lacking in common sense'.[45]

2.5 THE *MALLEUS MALEFICARUM* AND THE LEARNED DISCOURSE OF WITCHCRAFT

In the absence of solid empirical evidence, scholastic tradition, textual authority, and an epistemological stance deeply suspicious of outward appearances combined to make the diabolic witch cult hard to swallow.[46] Yet empirical evidence in the form of confessions and abundant eyewitness testimony was exactly what witch trials seemed to provide, forcing some otherwise sceptical authors to construct carefully parsed witch mythologies that tried to distinguish the real from the imaginary. Nider, for example, denied that witches flew through the air and vacillated about whether demons appeared visibly to witches, but believed in the devil's cult and the reality of *maleficia*.[47] The Franciscan Alphonso de Spina was both more systematic and more confusing when he tackled witches in the final book of his *Fortalitium Fidei* (Fortress of Faith, c.1460): he claimed that *bruxae* were heretics and apostates who took potions to induce a deep

---

[44] Hans Peter Broedel, *The Malleus Maleficarum and the Construction of Witchcraft: Theology and Popular Belief* (Manchester, 2003), 109.

[45] Julio Caro Baroja, *The World of the Witches*, tr. O. N. V. Glendinning (Chicago, 1964), 278.

[46] Gábor Klaniczay, 'The Process of Trance, Heavenly and Diabolic Apparitions in Johannes Nider's *Formicarius*', *Collegium Budapest Discussion Paper Series*, 65 (2003), 37–40.

[47] Klaniczay, 'The Process of Trance', 20–3.

stupor. Then the devil 'takes the figure and fancies of each of them and carries these to the places they desire, while their bodies remain invisible and insensible...'[48] The witches attended the sabbath and did their evil deeds through the intermediary of demons, who later reunited their imaginations with their bodies. In this way, Spina maintained the reality of the diabolic cult and the culpability of the witches (who were justly burned for heresy when they were caught), but still claimed that it was all a diabolic illusion. Less ambivalent writers, however, mounted a full-throated defence of the complete reality of witchcraft. Nicholas Jacquier, for example, argued that only the bodily presence of witches at the sabbath could explain their subsequent post-coital exhaustion.[49] Like a number of other witch believers, Jacquier also claimed that the antiquity of the canon *Episcopi* meant that it could hardly apply to such recent abominations as the modern sect of witches.

A large number of late medieval texts dealt with problems associated with witches, and they can give the misleading impression of a unified, coherent debate. Yet, in fact, coherent dialogue is almost completely absent, because theorists created idiosyncratic interpretations of witchcraft founded upon their own experience and not upon the work of other witchcraft 'experts'. Working from the common, but sometimes thin, substrate of late medieval education, authors built their witches from materials immediately to hand, fitting together the evidence of trials, testimony, and folklore in patterns that their own 'mental tool-kit' determined.[50] Yet no one seems to have found this diversity of form and substance particularly troubling, since all writers acknowledged that at bottom they were dealing with a single phenomenon. Instead, the questions that divided authors were the relevance of the canon *Episcopi* and the essential reality of witchcraft, and the related problem of whether witchcraft could be dissected into its component parts, or must be accepted or rejected as an integrated and indivisible whole.

These are the issues that in 1486 led Heinrich Kramer (d.1505; Latinized as Henricus Institoris) to write the most infamous of all late medieval witch treatises, the *Malleus maleficarum* (*The Hammer of Witches*).[51] The previous year, Kramer had arrived in the Tyrolean town of Innsbruck armed with a mandate from Pope Innocent VIII to prosecute the witches infesting Germany and more than two decades of inquisitorial experience.[52] Kramer discovered a town rife with witchcraft, and, with the assistance of

[48] Henry Charles Lea, *Materials Toward a History of Witchcraft*, ed. Arthur C. Howland, 3 vols (New York, 1957), i, 285–92.

[49] Lea, *Materials Toward a History of Witchcraft*, i, 276–85.

[50] Martine Ostorero, 'The Concept of the Witches' Sabbath in the Alpine Region (1430–1440): Text and Context', in Gábor Klaniczay and Éva Pócs, eds, *Witchcraft Mythologies and Persecutions* (Budapest, 2008), 19.

[51] Henricus Institoris, *Malleus Maleficarum*, ed. and tr. Christopher Mackay, 2 vols (Cambridge, 2006); Heinrich Kramer, *Der Hexenhammer*, ed. and tr. Wolfgang Behringer, Günter Jerouschek, and Werner Tschacher (Munich, 2000).

[52] Eric Wilson, 'Institoris at Innsbruck: Heinrich Institoris, the *Summis Desiderantes* and the Brixen Witch-Trial of 1485', in Bob Scribner and Trevor Johnson, eds, *Popular Religion in Germany and Central Europe 1400–1800* (New York, 1996), 87–100.

the local authorities, he rounded up suspects and commenced their trial. At this point, however, his carefully laid plans went awry: his thuggish tactics, legal misconduct, and procedural errors inspired numerous protests, destroying the fragile consensus upon which successful witch prosecutions depended. More fundamentally, local officials, led by the bishop, Georg Golser, lacked Kramer's wholly integrated understanding of witchcraft: they did not agree that *maleficia* invariably implied satanic heresy, and they certainly did not share his view that witchcraft necessarily entailed sexual relations with demons. The trials were ended, the suspects released, and, after some initial resistance, Kramer (whom the irate bishop described in private correspondence as 'really deranged') was unceremoniously expelled from the diocese.

The *Malleus maleficarum* was Kramer's response to this shabby treatment, a vindication of his views, a refutation of his critics, and a guide for theologians, preachers, and witch-hunters. This was a massive treatise, hurriedly written in less than a year, and consequently poorly organized and often poorly written. In most respects, indeed, the *Malleus* is just a bad book, but its reputation is not entirely undeserved: Kramer's was the first witch treatise to benefit from printing, and so was available in large numbers and circulated widely. The papal bull that prefaced the text predisposed readers to take its contents seriously, as did a writ of approval from the faculty of Cologne, and the impressive qualifications of its co-author, the distinguished Dominican reformer, Jacob Sprenger. Granted, Sprenger may have contributed nothing to the book save his name—and that unknowingly—and the faculty's approbation may have been at least in part a forgery, but to most late medieval readers the *Malleus'* credentials must have seemed impeccable.[53] As a result, the *Malleus* achieved far more lasting influence than other fifteenth-century witch treatises, was reprinted many times, and in the following century provided an authoritative reference for witch believers, including Sylvester Prierias, Jean Bodin, and Martin Del Rio, and for critics, such as Johann Weyer.[54]

For this reason, the characteristics of the *Malleus'* witch have particular importance. Like most other witch theorists, Kramer defined witchcraft in broadly theoretical terms as a particularly awful kind of heresy. Witches had confessed to him that they gave themselves to Satan body and soul, and slavishly carried out his commands. Perhaps surprisingly, though, Kramer placed comparatively little emphasis upon the sabbath: in his experience witches sometimes were carried bodily to the festivities by invisible demons, sometimes attended merely in spirit, and sometimes skipped the proceedings entirely. Instead, the crucial relationship for Kramer was the intimate personal connection between witch and demon, a bond sealed through sexual intercourse. Witches inhabited a world in which demons were seemingly omnipresent, acting as their masters, servants, advisors, suitors, and lovers. For the rest of humanity, however,

---

[53] See Christopher Mackay, 'Introduction', in Institoris, *Malleus Maleficarum*, i, 103–41, contra Wolfgang Behringer, 'Das unheilvollste Buch der Weltliteratur', in Kramer, *Der Hexenhammer*, 27–40.
[54] Mackay, 'Introduction', in Institoris, *Malleus Maleficarum*, i, 170–1; Broedel, *Malleus Maleficarum*, 6–8.

the matter was completely different: demons were invisible, almost undetectable, and worked their will only through their partners, the witches.[55] In practice, witches in the *Malleus* revealed themselves solely through magical harm, which they alone had the power to inflict. This absolute identity between witches and *maleficium* enabled Kramer to mobilize the perceived empirical basis for sorcery on behalf of witches; for example, he refutes scepticism inspired by the canon *Episcopi*, writing 'who is so stupid that he would on these grounds affirm that all acts of sorcery and harm committed by sorcerers are figments of fantasy and imagination, when the opposite is clear to every-one's senses . . . ?'[56] Similarly, because witches in the *Malleus* were identified precisely with village sorcerers, they could be readily identified through their evil reputations or through local discourses that determined the human agency behind otherwise inexplic-able ill fortune.

Kramer thus rejected the arguments of earlier treatises that anyone at all could be a witch, or that all magic implied witchcraft. Instead, the witch of the *Malleus* was defined clearly as poor, uneducated, frequently unmarried, sexually rapacious, usually old and barren, and with a quarrelsome reputation. In particular, too, she was a woman, a point that Kramer hammers home repeatedly throughout his text. Generally speaking, this was not an original claim: in most regions, pervasive cultural stereotypes led women to be accused of sorcery more often than men, although perhaps women were indeed prone to settle scores through magic.[57] To the extent, then, that witchcraft was linked to *maleficia*, women were logically suspect, and eventually in both popular and learned imaginations typically female sorceresses were conflated with malevolent female spirits out of folklore to create monstrous and distinctly feminine witches. Of course, alterna-tive mythologies implied different sets of gender dynamics. In early trials in Lausanne, for example, ecclesiastical judges imposed a witch mythology heavily dependent upon the stereotypes of diabolic heresy, but, since women were not especially implicated in heretical cults, men outnumbered women among the accused.[58] Yet by the late fifteenth century, most theorists agreed that, based on the evidence, witchcraft was largely a crime perpetrated by women. Their view coincided nicely with the well-established claim that the mental and spiritual weakness of women made them prone to supersti-tion, and, from Nider onwards, witch theorists explained women's predilection for witchcraft in this way.[59] In this respect, Kramer was exceptional only in his unique claims that witches were virtually always women, and that witchcraft was an expression of female lust, the sign of which was heterosexual demonic intercourse.

[55] Broedel, *Malleus Maleficarum*, 40–60.

[56] Institoris, *Malleus Maleficarum*, ii, 253.

[57] Clive Holmes, 'Women: Witnesses and Witches', *Past & Present*, 140 (1993), 45–78; Bever, *The Realities of Witchcraft*, 47–60.

[58] Monter, *Witchcraft in France and Switzerland*, 23–4; Susanna Burghartz, 'The Equation of Women and Witches: A Case Study of Witchcraft Trials in Lucerne and Lausanne in the Fifteenth and Sixteenth Centuries', in Richard J. Evans, ed., *The German Underworld* (London, 1988), 57–74.

[59] Michael Bailey, 'The Feminization of Magic and the Emerging Idea of the Female Witch in the Late Middle Ages', *Essays in Medieval Studies*, 19 (2002), 120–34.

In an ingenious essay, Tamar Herzig observes that this extremely feminized construction of witchcraft in the *Malleus* can be understood as one aspect of a larger conceptual dichotomy in Kramer's thinking.[60] Herzig argues that, unlike virtually every other witch writer of his day, Kramer separated witchcraft and conventional heresy into two complementary but entirely distinct categories. The sects of 'Waldensians' were largely made up of men who spread false doctrines; the modern heresy of witches, on the other hand, was composed of women who performed black magic directly at the devil's instigation. Both groups were part of a single diabolic conspiracy, but while heretics posed terrible dangers to Christian souls, witches inflicted physical harm on Christendom; and while a male heresiarch led conventional cults, demons personally supervised witches. Hence, although the spiritual crimes of 'Waldensians' made them the legitimate prey of the Inquisition, witches caused injuries that could be justly punished in secular courts. This 'gendered division of labor' avoided conflating heretics, who in most places were not suspected of sorcery, with witches, who were precisely the people who were.[61] Herzig notes that by the sixteenth century, writers and magistrates had overwhelmingly accepted this division, albeit without comment, so that most of those executed for heresy over the next two hundred years were men, while most of those condemned as witches were women.

2.6 CONCLUSION

Fuelled by widespread plagues, terrible weather, wars, and millenarian fervour, the prosecution of witches continued in many parts of Europe through the early sixteenth century.[62] During this time, through treatises such as the *Malleus*, and through personal and professional contacts, witch mythologies providing explanatory paradigms for misfortune circulated among an interested intellectual and political elite. Heinrich Kramer promoted the spread of his own distinctive brand of witchcraft in Italy through a network of Dominican and inquisitorial colleagues with such success that the *Malleus* became 'the focal point of the Italian debate over witch-hunting'.[63] Through printed tracts, the discourse of witchcraft had for the first time acquired a distinct textual basis, an awareness of which promoted a degree of uniformity within

---

[60] Tamar Herzig, 'Flies, Heretics, and the Gendering of Witchcraft', *Magic, Ritual, and Witchcraft*, 5 (2010), 51–80.

[61] But see Wolfgang Behringer, 'How Waldensians Became Witches: Heretics and their Journey to the Other World', in Gábor Klaniczay and Éva Pócs, eds, *Communicating with the Spirits* (Budapest, 2005), 155–92.

[62] Behringer, *Witches and Witch-Hunts*, 77.

[63] Tamar Herzig, 'Bridging North and South: Inquisitorial Networks and Witchcraft Theory on the Eve of the Reformation', *Journal of Early Modern History*, 12 (2008), 361–82, esp. 361; see also Michael Tavuzzi, *Renaissance Inquisitors: Dominican Inquisitors and Inquisitorial Districts in Northern Italy, 1474–1527* (Leiden, 2007).

European witch mythologies. Although significant local variations remained between witches, by 1500 authors and magistrates seem to have found these insignificant in comparison with the accepted essential core of witchcraft: the satanic cult of sorcerers. This was a concept flexible enough to accommodate such bizarre elaborations as magical flight, metamorphosis, familiar spirits, and night-time 'games', while retaining its menace and explanatory power. Even unbelievers accepted the basic terms of witchcraft, so that while earlier writers had expressed their doubts through careful attempts to reconcile competing evidence in highly individual constructions of witchcraft, later sceptics such as Johann Weyer or Samuel de Cassini attacked the notion of diabolic witchcraft wholesale. Thus, although the pace of witchcraft prosecutions would slacken after 1520, the imaginative construct of witchcraft that was worked out in late medieval courtrooms and treatises would endure.

FURTHER READING

Bagliani, Agostino Paravicini and Utz Tremp, Kathrin, eds, *L'imaginaire du sabbat* (Lausanne, 1999).

Bailey, Michael, *Battling Demons: Witchcraft, Heresy, and Reform in the Late Middle Ages* (University Park, PA, 2003).

Behringer, Wolfgang, *Witches and Witch-Hunts: A Global History* (Cambridge, 2004).

Broedel, Hans Peter, *The 'Malleus Maleficarum' and the Construction of Witchcraft: Theology and Popular Belief* (Manchester, 2003).

Cohn, Norman, *Europe's Inner Demons: The Demonization of Christians in Medieval Christendom* (rev. edn, Chicago, 1993).

Golden, Richard M., ed., *The Encyclopedia of Witchcraft: The Western Tradition*, 4 vols (Santa Barbara, CA, 2006).

Institoris, Henricus, *Malleus Maleficarum*, ed. and tr. Christopher Mackay, 2 vols (Cambridge, 2006).

Kieckhefer, Richard, *European Witch Trials: Their Foundation in Popular and Learned Culture, 1300–1500* (London, 1976).

Levack, Brian P., *The Witch-Hunt in Early Modern Europe* (3rd edn, Harlow, 2006).

Mormando, Franco, *The Preacher's Demons: Bernardino of Siena and the Social Underworld of Early Renaissance Italy* (Chicago, 1999).

Stokes, Laura Patricia, *Demons of Urban Reform: Early European Witch Trials and Criminal Justice, 1430–1530* (New York, 2011).

Utz Tremp, Kathrin, *Von der Häresie zur Hexerie: 'Wirkliche' und imaginäre Sekten im Spätmittelalter* (Hanover, 2008).

CHAPTER 3

....

POPULAR WITCH BELIEFS AND MAGICAL PRACTICES

....

EDWARD BEVER

TRADITIONALLY, historians of early modern witchcraft have focused more on the beliefs and practices of Europe's cultural and political elites than on those of ordinary peasants and townspeople.[1] They have done so partly because the sources of information about elite culture are more accessible than the sources for popular culture, and partly because historians have generally been more interested in why the witch-hunts took place and how they related to other aspects of European history than in witchcraft itself. They have, however, always recognized that popular culture played a role in the hunts by providing an assortment of activities attributed to witches that were incorporated into demonological treatises, and by generating at least some accusations and influencing the content of some confessions. Furthermore, some historians have looked beyond the trials to study these beliefs and practices on their own terms, as part of a widespread system of ideas and activities concerning magical forces and beings.[2] In the last generation there has been particular interest in this system as a source of insight not only into the roots of the trials, but also into popular culture as a whole, ordinary people's *mentalities*, and the fabric of their everyday lives.

3.1 THE CURRENT STATE OF KNOWLEDGE
....

Historians of witchcraft now generally acknowledge that while official concern about a diabolic conspiracy played a key role in the virulent witch-hunts in early modern

---

[1] Raisa Maria Toivo, 'The Witch-Craze as Holocaust', in Jonathan Barry and Owen Davies, eds, *Palgrave Advances in Witchcraft Historiography* (Basingstoke, 2007), 97–8.

[2] Christina Tuczay, 'The Nineteenth Century: Medievalism and Witchcraft', in Barry and Davies, eds, *Witchcraft Historiography*, 53–5, 59–60.

Europe, most trials started from accusations manifesting popular apprehensions concerning harmful magic.[3] Furthermore, while demonology drew some elements from literary traditions stretching back to antiquity, most of the attributes it ascribed to witches came from popular magical traditions.[4] These traditions exhibited enormous diversity in detail across Europe, but nonetheless shared basic features with each other and with witchcraft fears found in other agricultural societies worldwide, in both classical and Germanic culture, and throughout medieval Europe: a belief in occult, or hidden, forces and ethereal conscious entities that influence the visible material world; an array of words, rituals, and objects employed to harness or defend against them; a set of practitioners who specialized in interacting with them; and a conviction that some people utilized them to injure others. Specific elements that made their way from popular beliefs into learned demonology included the idea that some people flew at night to afflict neighbours or participate in activities with other magical humans and spirits; the ascription of the ability to fly to the use of magical salves or potions; the locations where witches' gatherings were supposed to take place, like the Blocksberg in northern Germany, the Heuberg in Swabia, and the walnut tree of Benevento; animal metamorphosis; and most of the mechanisms by which people were thought to inflict injury.

3.1.1 The 'Magical Universe' in Popular Culture

Important as historians' heightened awareness of the role of popular traditions in the witch-hunts is, even more so is their growing recognition of the limited place of witchcraft and witch trials in the total constellation of early modern Europeans' magical beliefs and practices.[5] The 'magical universe', as Stephen Wilson has dubbed it, was an embracing reality for the entire population of early modern Europe. The conscious, or at least responsive, occult dimension touched on all aspects of human life, they believed, from the broadest structures of the universe, through the natural and social orders, to the mundane aspects of daily life. This understanding mixed official Christianity, Christianized magical traditions, and a few beliefs and practices unconnected to the dominant religion.

Official Christianity supplied the authorized understanding of broad cosmological issues and the major rituals mediating human interaction with the spirit world during life-stage transitions, the yearly cycle, and the periodic spiritual cleansing of confession and communion. It also provided a comprehensive guide to the morally correct conduct critical for eternal salvation, along with some coping mechanisms for afflictions attributed

---

[3] Walter Rummel, 'Popular Persecution', in Richard M. Golden, ed., *Encyclopedia of Witchcraft: The Western Tradition*, 4 vols (Santa Barbara, CA, 2006), iii, 917.

[4] Edward Bever, *The Realities of Witchcraft and Popular Magic in Early Modern Europe* (Basingstoke, 2008), 67–8, 94–7, 151–3, 215.

[5] Stephen Wilson, *The Magical Universe* (London, 2000), pp. xvii–xviii, 48–9, 467–8.

to occult as well as material forces in this life. However, while official Christianity formally had a dominant (in theory, exclusive) place in early modern European culture, in practice most people had a relatively limited understanding of and participation in it, although both undoubtedly increased significantly from 1500 to 1800.[6]

As a corollary of official Christianity's limited penetration of popular consciousness, popular magical traditions played a substantial role in most people's lives. In many cases they played at least as great a role as formal Christianity, although most of these traditions were at least superficially Christianized. In general, they focused on practical solutions to life-problems, particularly those involving health, fertility, and prosperity, rather than on cosmological issues or the moral requirements of salvation. These traditions included both Christian prayers, rituals, and materials appropriated for mundane purposes, and customary beliefs and practices, presumably of pagan origin, that had been Christianized over the centuries, perhaps to avoid reprimand in this world or the next, but perhaps also because Christian elements were assumed to add or ensure spiritual power. The traditions ranged from local practices undertaken in tandem with official ceremonies marking life-stage transitions and the yearly cycle (which themselves had often been superimposed over older ritual observances), to customary rituals used to ward off dangers and effect cures.

The smattering of non-Christianized elements included beliefs about ghosts, monsters, and local spirits; rituals, stories, and experiences involving interactions with such spirits; and incantations and rituals that appear to have assumed, but did not reference any specific, spiritual power. In some cases these elements may have been religiously based traditions that were de-Christianized at some point, but most were not 'survivals' but rather evolutionary developments of pre-Christian beliefs and practices. In many cases, like that of ghosts, which Christian doctrine did not accommodate, people simply ignored the question of their relationship to the dominant religion. In some cases, like that of the Italian magical fertility warriors known as *benandanti*, the traditions were thought to be consistent with, although separate from, the dominant religion. In still others, like some fairies in Britain, the spirits were held to be overtly hostile to Christianity.[7]

3.1.2 Popular Witch Beliefs

Within this magical universe, witchcraft, the ability of certain people to cause harm through occult channels, was just one of many perceived sources of supernatural danger. A vast number involved a failure to observe traditional strictures and imperatives governing important activities, which could bring misfortune either because God

---

[6] Robert Muchembled, *Popular Culture and Elite Culture in France 1400–1750* (Baton Rouge, LA, 1985), 221–3.

[7] Bever, *Realities of Witchcraft*, 179.

or some other governing spirit felt thereby offended, or through a relatively mechanical process in which an occult process was clearly assumed but not specified.[8] In many other cases, misfortune was attributed to disembodied spirits that were thought to hover at the edge of the human world, waiting to swoop in during moments of vulnerability. Belief in the power of malevolent people to project their malice magically was widespread and long-standing, but its importance relative to other sources of misfortune, the frequency with which it was suspected, the magnitude of the power it was thought to carry, the mechanisms thought to underlie it, and the responses thought appropriate to it varied considerably from place to place and over time.

In some cases witchcraft was perceived to be a vague, generalized threat. The 'night witch' in particular was a distant, mysterious figure, almost indistinguishable from other ethereal menaces thought to fly through the dark to afflict victims chosen because they were vulnerable or out of sheer malice.[9] More commonly, though, witchcraft was believed to involve a personalized attack, motivated by some specific enmity. The root might be a cold calculation of interest in some rivalry, but more often it was thought to stem from an emotional animus. Envy was one emotion held to be an important stimulus to witchcraft, but the most common was anger, generally stemming from some perceived wrong done to the witch by the person whose misfortune she was thought to have caused.[10]

In theory almost anyone could be suspected of witchcraft, but in practice certain types of people were particularly likely to be. One such group was specialized magical practitioners, 'cunning folk', whose activities performing beneficent magic—healing rituals, identification of thieves, love magic, and the like—were thought to involve techniques and powers that could be used for malign purposes as well. Another such group was women, particularly quarrelsome or disreputable elderly women, for in most parts of Europe they were held to be particularly prone to *malefic* magic. This association was so strong that relatives of such women were often also suspected of witchcraft, since it was commonly held to run in families. Fear of cunning 'sorcerer witches' or cantankerous 'neighbourhood [or village] witches' was found in most early modern communities.[11] To quote a Danish proverb, 'Every village has its witch, and every parish has its cunning-man.'[12]

The distinction between 'sorcerer witches' and 'village witches' is neater in theory than it was in practice, but it parallels a significant distinction in the presumed sources of power available to witches: the deliberate use of rituals to cause harm, or what anthropologists call 'sorcery', versus an innate ability to project malice, which they call 'witchcraft'.[13] This distinction, too, is neater in theory than it was in practice, for a

---

[8] Wilson, *Magical Universe*, esp. pp. xvii–xxiv, 467.

[9] Éva Pócs, *Between the Living and the Dead* (Budapest, 1999), 11.

[10] Keith Thomas, *Religion and the Decline of Magic* (London, 1971), 509.

[11] Pócs, *Between the Living and the Dead*, 10.

[12] Joan Rockwell, 'Animals and Witchcraft in Danish Popular Culture', in J. R. Porter and W. M. S. Russell, eds, *Animals in Folklore* (Ipswich, 1978), 95.

[13] Max Marwick, *Witchcraft and Sorcery* (Harmondsworth, 1970), 12–13.

sorcerer might be thought to possess both an innate ability and a knowledge of rituals, while a malevolent woman might be assumed to use rituals to supplement an inherent power. Furthermore, people often did not try to specify how a suspected witch had inflicted harm. Nevertheless, the distinction is found in many cultures, and early modern Europeans seem to have understood it well. More specifically, sorcery involved incantations, ritual curses, symbolic gestures, magically potent objects, and potions, which were often used surreptitiously, such as a spell recited or a 'puppet' (what we would call a 'voodoo doll') mutilated in private, a bone hidden under a threshold, or poison mixed in a gift of food. Witchcraft, in this typology, involved spontaneous acts like threats, impulsive curses, scowls, piercing glances (the 'evil eye'), gestures, and physical contact (touch or blows), or even just malicious thoughts. Most of the acts associated with witchcraft were thus overt, although thoughts, like most sorcery, were covert. In both cases, though, it was assumed that animus could be masked by a false friendliness.

There were a variety of occult mechanisms by which witches' attacks were supposed to work. 'Night witches' were thought to 'press' people in their beds (what folklorists call 'Old Hag' experiences), devour the souls of babies in their cribs, abduct adults while they slept, and harass people by appearing in spectral form.[14] Human witches might do the same, or might dispatch other spirits by summoning them through ritual invocation or by keeping them as 'familiars'. Witches were often thought to be able to change into animals, or to employ small animals to conduct reconnaissance and execute attacks. People believed that witches could cause injury by mishandling objects that symbolized or were connected to their target (like 'puppets' and nail clippings), or by secreting magically potent objects on their target's property. More directly, they were thought to inflict harm via curses, gestures, the evil eye, breath, physical contact, or poisons. Not all these beliefs were current in all parts of Europe at all times, but most of them were known in many different places, and virtually every local culture included some of them. Similarly, not every form of attack was considered equally likely. Fear of the more exotic actions-at-a-distance may have contributed to the general sense that anyone could be afflicted at any time, but actual accusations tended to involve the more prosaic forms of attack, entailing face-to-face confrontations or physical proximity.[15]

Just as witches were thought to attack in a wide variety of ways, they were also thought to inflict a wide variety of misfortunes. These included some generalized calamities like hailstorms and other forms of bad weather, but more often involved afflictions to one person in particular.[16] Some involved disruption of economic activities or domestic processes like brewing beer or churning butter, and bad luck and

[14] David Hufford, *The Terror that Comes in the Night* (Philadelphia, PA, 1982); Richard Kieckhefer, 'Avenging the Blood of Children', in Alberto Ferrerio, ed., *The Devil, Heresy, and Witchcraft in the Middle Ages* (Leiden, 1998); Pócs, *Between the Living and the Dead*, 73–85.

[15] Éva Labouvie, 'Hexenspuk und Hexenabwehr', in Richard van Dühlman, ed., *Hexenwahn: Magie und Imagination von 16–20 Jahrhundert* (Frankfurt, 1993), 83.

[16] Thomas, *Religion and the Decline of Magic*, 436–7; Robin Briggs, *Witches and Neighbours* (London, 1996), 63.

accidents were also sometimes blamed on witches, but by far the most common form of injury was illness or death suffered by adults, their children, or their domestic animals. Certain ailments, like impotence in men, infertility in women, and lack of milk in cows, were particularly associated with witchcraft, but many different illnesses might be ascribed to it. Witches were only infrequently blamed for epidemic diseases, and diseases with clear and well-known symptoms were less likely to be blamed on them than ones whose etiology was unclear. Conversely, witchcraft was particularly likely to be suspected when a disease came on unusually swiftly, lingered unusually long, could not be diagnosed clearly, or presented some other unusual symptoms. In addition, witchcraft was indicated if the onset of the disease followed some interpersonal interaction, especially if the interaction was hostile, the symptoms seemed linked symbolically (like loss of use in a limb that had been touched), or if misfortune had been explicitly threatened.

3.1.3 Countermeasures against Witchcraft

Since witchcraft was just one of many occult sources of harm that threatened early modern Europeans, it was also just one of many that they tried to counteract. While some countermeasures were specific to witchcraft, most were part of a generalized arsenal of defensive techniques. These countermeasures can be divided into two basic types: passive and active. Passive countermeasures were means of avoiding injury in the first place, while active countermeasures were ways of counteracting a specific attack once it was thought to have occurred.

The most basic passive countermeasure was avoidance. This might mean staying in at an astrologically unfavourable time or on an unlucky calendar day, detouring around a reputed witch's house, or not attending an event at which she would be present.[17] Passive countermeasures also included defensive measures like painting protective symbols on buildings or secreting 'witch bottles' in their walls or under thresholds to deter or trap ethereal intruders; wearing amulets (including both crosses and religious medallions and magically potent profane objects); and saying prayers (official supplications for protection), charms (non-religious incantations), or blessings (Christianized charms). Passive countermeasures also included maintaining good relations with other members of the community to minimize antagonisms that might lead to a magical attack while maximizing communal support if one appeared to occur.

Active countermeasures involved a range of actions thought to neutralize magical attacks. At one extreme, these included simply treating the manifest injury. They also included prayer and other religious ceremonies to mobilize spiritual defences. Both

---

remedies and prayers were employed against maladies that were understood to be purely natural or due to impersonal magical forces, but bewitchment had a special set of countermeasures that reflected its assumed origin in another person's malice. To begin with, whether the source of the malady was witchcraft would be determined through gut feeling, logical deduction, or magical divination. Next, the witch would be identified using the same means. These steps could be undertaken by the victim or her family, but 'cunning folk' frequently offered 'un-witching' as one of the magical services they provided, and they would often be consulted if witchcraft was suspected.

Once witchcraft was confirmed and the witch identified, several possible counter-measures could be employed. One was to appeal to the witch to remove the spell out of compassion or fear of retribution, or because her need to exert power would be satisfied by the appeal. Such supplication could easily merge into the next strategy, appease-ment, if the appeal was accompanied by an apology for any wrong that might have motivated the attack. Appeasement could also take the form of a gift, and a reputation as a witch could therefore be the basis of a veritable 'protection racket'.[18]

If the 'victim' did not want to beg or bribe, or the 'witch' proved impervious, the afflicted person could choose to strike back by using magical, physical, or social means. Magic rituals and materials could be used in an attempt to suppress or break the spell, or transfer it somewhere else. The latter technique could be used to transfer the spell back onto the witch herself, either to get revenge while getting rid of it or to compel her to end it. Like divination, counter-magic could be done privately, but it was also one of the services provided by cunning folk.

Physical violence could be threatened and, if that didn't work, used to compel a witch to take back a spell. This tactic was mostly employed by young or middle-aged men, although it was not very common. In contrast, witches 'victims' frequently mobilized social support. This could involve shunning, mob violence, or legal proceed-ings. Shunning could unfold spontaneously—when members of the community adopted the strategy of avoidance—or be deliberately instigated by a cunning person. Mob violence was more likely deliberate since it required some degree of coordination, while judicial prosecutions, though they might begin with an informal investigation into a rumour, proceeded deliberately once the legal machinery went into operation.

3.1.4 Witchcraft and the Devil in Popular Culture

The devil was a familiar figure in popular culture throughout the Middle Ages, but played a more limited role in the world, and especially in witchcraft, than learned demonologists ascribed to him. To begin with, while most people understood his official status as the chief evil spirit, in practice he was just one of a number of malevolent spiritual forces. Other possibilities included ghosts or the spirits of the

---

[18] John Swain, 'Witchcraft, Economy and Society in the Forest of Pendle', in Robert Poole, ed., *The Lancashire Witches* (Manchester, 2002), 83.

dead; fairies or similar supernatural beings; other local spirits, often identified with specific places or situations; classical or Germanic gods like Diana, Holda or Wotan; lesser demons; and hostile magicians and witches.[19] The Church held all of these to be subordinate to the devil in a rigid hierarchy, but the people talked of them as relatively autonomous. Fairies in popular culture were essentially independent. They had no place in Christianity, and they were neither good nor evil, but instead sometimes helpful and sometimes destructive. Witches, too, were thought of as independent agents, and while popular consciousness of their connection with the devil grew over the early modern period as a result of clerical instruction, the fact that it dwindled once the elite stopped preaching about witchcraft suggests that the diabolical nature of witchcraft never put down very firm roots among the people.

Not only did popular culture neglect the devil's role as the prince of evil, but it also limited his powers. There were certainly references to him as the ultimate source of temptation and distress, a looming presence that exerted a pervasive influence on the world, but there were many depictions of him as a human-scale figure who sauntered around the countryside sweet-talking women and offering to trade favours in this world for one's soul after death. He was often encountered at crossroads; some held that he could be driven away by salt; blacksmiths were thought to have a special relationship with him in many local traditions; and some thought he was likely to be incarnated as a hare.[20] He could be resisted and even outsmarted, in which case he could end up looking rather comical.

In most cases his powers were taken more seriously, as capable of inflicting real harm on individuals and entire communities, but in general he worked through natural processes rather than flaunting his supernatural powers like some horror-film monster. He was often held responsible for bad weather, particularly violent storms, and he liked to disrupt childbirth because it presented the opportunity to snatch the baby's soul before it was baptized. He was not, however, held responsible for swapping babies with 'changelings'; fairies were blamed for that activity.[21] He was often blamed for illness. His connection with magic was ambiguous. Church doctrine held him responsible for all magic, whatever its purpose, and some popular spells invoked him directly. The great majority of spells, however, including many intended to harm or manipulate others, made no reference to him. Ironically, he could be invoked in love magic, while harmful spells might well appeal to God if the person who cast the spell felt that he was avenging a wrong.[22] Over the course of the early modern period the devil's direct role in harmful magic undoubtedly increased, a paradoxical result of the dissemination of

---

[19] Wolfgang Behringer, *Shaman of Oberstdorf: Chonrad Stoekhlin and the Phantoms of the Night*, tr. H. C. Erik Midelfort (Charlottesville, VA, 1998), 29.

[20] Wilson, *Magical Universe*, 456, 421–2, 417.

[21] Wilson, *Magical Universe*, 210–11.

[22] Ruth Martin, *Witchcraft and the Inquisition in Venice* (Oxford, 1989), 207; Angelica Bachman, 'Allerhand gottloses abgöttisches Werckhn: Glaube—Aberglaube—Zauberei. Magie in der dörflichen Gesellschaft Württembergs des 17. und 18. Jahrhunderts', in Johannes Dillinger, ed., *Zauberer—Selbstmörder—Schatzsucher* (Trier, 2003), 68–9.

learned demonology. Whether his role in popular spells declined along with the idea that witches were members of a diabolic sect once the elite abandoned this idea is unclear.

3.2 HISTORIOGRAPHICAL ISSUES AND CONTROVERSIES

3.2.1 Elite versus Popular Culture

The most basic historiographical controversy regarding popular witch beliefs concerns the very existence of a set of popular beliefs distinct from those of the elite. The discussion is connected to a larger debate in early modern history about the broad distinction made between elite and popular culture, which is rooted in the notion of a 'great tradition' of the literate elite separate from the 'little tradition' of the illiterate masses. This debate explicitly entered historical discussions of witchcraft in the writings of Richard Kieckhefer and Norman Cohn.[23] Kieckhefer himself raised the question of whether popular and elite witch beliefs could meaningfully be distinguished. To some extent the distinction is a victim of its own success, for not only these works, but the divergent directions taken by Erik Midelfort's study of theology and legal practice in south-western Germany and Alan Macfarlane's anthropologically inspired study of communal dynamics behind witch accusations in England supported the concept so strongly that it quickly became a shared assumption among historians.[24] Used uncritically, it could imply that the two traditions were essentially separate, only connected through sermons and trials, with most of the influence passing downwards. The recognition that members of the elite participated in 'popular' culture in their everyday lives, that demonologists drew heavily on stories they heard from common people, and that 'popular culture', including magical beliefs, had absorbed innumerable 'elite' influences over the course of centuries, therefore serves as a salutary corrective. Kieckhefer, for example, developed the concept of a 'common tradition' in a later survey of medieval magic. Nevertheless, as he pointed out in his original work, the literate elite 'could resurrect . . . ideas that had lain dormant for centuries' and 'maintain contact with centers . . . remote from their own countries', centres that cultivated common ideas in common institutions, the Church, and universities, even while participating in the culture of the illiterate classes, who had direct contact only with

---

[23] Marko Nenonen, 'Culture Wars: State, Religion, and Popular Culture', in Barry and Davies, eds, *Witchcraft Historiography*, 119, 112; Richard Kieckhefer, *European Witch Trials: Their Foundations in Learned and Popular Culture* (London, 1976), ix; Norman Cohn, *Europe's Inner Demons* (New York, 1975), 251–2, 255.

[24] H. C. Erik Midelfort, *Witch Hunting in Southwestern Germany* (Stanford, CA, 1972); Alan Macfarlane, *Witchcraft in Tudor and Stuart England* (London, 1970).

their own local traditions.[25] Therefore, the distinction between the two cultures, or perhaps more properly 'subcultures', continues to be used, although at best with as much attention to the interplay as to the differences between them.

A related issue concerns the cohesiveness implied by the phrase 'popular culture', which gives a misleading impression of uniformity to a phenomenon that was incredibly multifaceted. Early modern popular culture was divided along linguistic, regional, and even local lines, and, within any locality, along lines of occupation, tenancy or citizenship, wealth, and even age and gender. Consequently, there was, as Peter Burke has observed, not one but 'many popular cultures or many varieties of popular culture', and what we call popular culture was often only 'the culture of the most visible of the people'.[26] Popular witch beliefs and magical practices were a prime example of the broad diversity and richness found across Europe, as Wilson's encyclopedic *Magical Universe* conveys. Wilson argues, however, that early modern Europe was 'a specific cultural area' based on a persistent and pervasive socio-economic structure, and the different magical traditions had commonalities of purpose, practice, and even underlying principle that gave an overarching unity to their innumerable particular forms.[27] These included witchcraft, which had some broad common features at the popular level across large areas and over many centuries that make it meaningful to talk about popular witch beliefs and magical practices as a unit, even while acknowledging that the common framework had a different face and unique features in practically every village and town.

Another historiographical dispute concerning the relationship between elite and popular culture involves their respective contributions to the demonological ideas that informed the persecutions. A strong tradition rooted in the Romantic movement of the early nineteenth century emphasized the role of popular beliefs in early modern witchcraft. However, the rise of academic history under the influence of Ranke later in the century led to the ascendancy of a 'rationalist' tradition that 'considered witchcraft a mere chimera' foisted on the populace by fanatic clerics, with any popular elements merely 'the mental rubbish of peasant credulity and feminine hysteria'.[28] The German historians Wilhelm Soldan and Joseph Hansen, and the Americans George Lincoln Burr and H. C. Lea, played prominent roles in establishing this tradition as 'the orthodoxy in witchcraft studies'.

This orthodoxy was challenged in the 1920s by Dame Margaret Murray's theory that the trials were directed at members of an ancient fertility cult that had survived underground since pagan times. Murray's theory was rooted in the early anthropologist Sir James Frazer's notion that vestiges of a universal prehistoric fertility religion

---

[25] Richard Kieckhefer, *Magic in the Middle Ages* (2nd edn, Cambridge, 2000), 56–7; Kieckhefer, *Witch Trials*, 4.

[26] Nenonen, 'Culture Wars', 119.

[27] Wilson, *Magical Universe*, xxx, xxviii.

[28] Tuczay, 'Nineteenth Century', 56–9; Hugh Trevor-Roper, *The European Witch-Craze of the Sixteenth and Seventeenth Centuries and Other Essays* (New York, 1969), 116.

survived among the peasantry.[29] Murray's work was highly influential, and her entry on witchcraft in the *Encyclopedia Britannica* was not replaced until 1968, but historians discredited her theory by demonstrating that it was based on a selective and credulous reading of limited source materials. Cohn, who put the final nails in its coffin, reiterated the rationalists' emphasis on the learned roots of the early modern stereotype and the elite's decisive role in the prosecutions.[30]

Nevertheless, even Cohn acknowledged the popular origins of concern about *malefic magic*, and the fact that the division between popular fears of *maleficium* and elite preoccupation with diabolism has become a common assumption in witchcraft studies. Cohn also recognized the popular origin of the belief that witches could fly. Even before Cohn's book appeared, Carlo Ginzburg had published a study of self-styled fertility warriors in northern Italy who said they went out at night on specific evenings to gatherings of compatriots, who battled witches for the success of the harvest.[31] This study gave evidence of at least one instance of a popular tradition with strong elements related to diabolism, and Ginzburg was also able to show how the self-conception of these fertility warriors was gradually diabolized under inquisitorial pressure. Subsequent studies have shown similar beliefs and processes in other parts of Europe, so while it is clear that elite culture supplied some of the specific elements, the consistency, and the moral meaning of the supposed diabolic conspiracy, it is equally clear that many of its individual elements, and even the overall structure of recruitment, flight to meetings in a spirit realm, and return with magical powers were drawn from popular sources.[32]

In the end, the whole issue seems somewhat overblown since it is clear that popular beliefs and elite theories were in constant interaction, with the elite learning of popular traditions, integrating and developing them, and returning them back into popular culture, which integrated and developed them in turn, in a continuous cycle. The most important contributions of the elite side of this interaction were the insistence that all magical activities evinced allegiance to the devil and hence membership in his conspiracy, and a 'ratchet' mechanism whereby individual elements drawn from various sources across Europe were permanently incorporated into this unified construct which then flowed back to different localities to help structure the confessions that seemed to prove its reality.

The 'acculturation thesis' proposed by Robert Muchembled provoked another historiographical controversy centring on the relationship between elite and popular culture. Drawing on an old anthropological theory about the way dominant cultures impose themselves on subordinate ones, Muchembled argued that the witch trials were an outgrowth of the elite's attempt to acculturate the masses by suppressing disorderly,

---

[29] Tuczay, 'Nineteenth Century', 59–60; Juliette Wood, 'The Reality of Witch Cults Reasserted: Fertility and Satanism', in Barry and Davies, eds, *Witchcraft Historiography*, 70–5.

[30] Cohn, *Europe's Inner Demons*, xi–xii, 239.

[31] Carlo Ginzbeurg, *The Night Battles: Witchcraft and Agrarian Cults in the Sixteenth and Seventeenth Centuries*, tr. John and Anne Tedeschi (Baltimore, MD, 1983), ix.

[32] Bever, *Realities of Witchcraft*, 186–9, 434–7.

only loosely Christianized, local traditions as part of the process of building modern states—a process which local authorities and communal leaders either resisted or assisted ambivalently.[33] Since this theory dovetailed with a broader interest among early modernists in social discipline and confessionalization—complementary processes sponsored by the secular and clerical elites—it won quick acceptance as a key explanation of the trials.

Muchembled's thesis also aroused strong opposition, partly because anthropologists had rejected 'acculturation' in favour of more 'assimilationist' models, and partly because it did not fit certain aspects of the European situation well. First, local authorities or leading commoners were often most enthusiastic about hunting witches, while strong central governments often acted to restrain them. Second, many of the policies that seemed designed to discipline the masses served more to reform the behaviour of the elite. In response to these criticisms, Muchembled revised and qualified his theory in a series of books, although a recent survey of the debate concludes that ironically, 'even if he overemphasizes the repressive nature of the state and religious machinery, his viewpoint is to some extent shared by most scholars'.[34]

One other criticism of the acculturation thesis has been the assertion that the tenacious survival of many local traditions, and subversive adaptations of many reforms, make the disciplinary effort 'look like a heroic failure rather than the history of a brutal success'.[35] This point ties in directly with the last historiographical issue involving the relationship between popular and elite culture, which is the end of the trials and the decline of magic. The traditional view was that the end of the trials reflected the beginnings of the Enlightenment in elite culture, and was followed by the steady decline of magical beliefs as Enlightenment thought diffused into popular culture, until magic more or less disappeared. More recently, studies of popular witch beliefs and magical practices from the eighteenth to the twentieth century have shown that while elite culture may have rejected the occult, many people in towns and cities as well as the countryside continued to fear witches and practise magic. Consequently, the whole concept of the 'decline of magic' has given way to a corrective emphasis on the survival of traditional forms in popular culture well into the twentieth century.[36]

Even more recently, however, this new consensus has been challenged by the argument that while traditional notions may have exaggerated the decline of magic, witchcraft beliefs and magical practices were in fact increasingly marginalized in European culture as a whole from the Enlightenment through the twentieth century. Not only were they discredited in elite culture, which became the culture of an ever increasing portion of the population as the educated urban middle class grew, but also

---

[33] Robin Briggs, 'Acculturation Thesis', in *Encyclopedia of Witchcraft*, i, 2–3; Nenonen, 'Culture Wars', 110–13, 115–17.
[34] Nenonen, 'Culture Wars', 110.
[35] Briggs, 'Acculturation Thesis', 3.
[36] Owen Davies and Willem de Blécourt, eds, *Beyond the Witch Trials* and *Witchcraft Continued* (Manchester, 2004).

they steadily diminished in rural popular culture as well.[37] Furthermore, this marginalization was directly related to repressive efforts by Church and state, as Muchembled argued. The process started with the witch trials, which mortally threatened anyone who practised magic or manifested apparently magical powers, and continued afterwards as magical beliefs and practices were ridiculed as backward and foolish, still denounced as sinful, and prosecuted as fraud. In 1500 beneficent magical practices were conducted routinely and relatively openly, and the belief that some people practised *malefic* magic was widespread. By 1900, these practices and beliefs were much less common, and were increasingly furtive and defensive in the face of persistent cultural and occasional legal harassment. While magic did not disappear from Western culture, there is no denying that it did decline drastically, and while the elite's three-century campaign of repression was not the only cause, it clearly played a significant role.

3.2.2 The Sociology of Suspects

The social characteristics of individuals accused of witchcraft is actually one area in which there is considerable consensus. The traditional image and historical studies agree that the great majority were female, a 'solid majority' were over fifty, they 'were often described as sharp-tongued, bad-tempered, and quarrelsome', and they tended to be from the lower levels of the settled community. Female healers were particularly vulnerable to accusations 'of using their magical arts for maleficent purposes'.[38]

However, since this composite image is based on general tendencies, the existence of minorities within each category—men, young people, nice people, well-to-do people, and destitute vagrants—has made generalizations seeking to explain the characteristics of the majority vulnerable to counter-examples drawn from the minority and criticisms that the explanations fail to account sufficiently for the minorities. Thus, the fact that some suspects were not quarrelsome or reputed magicians has been used to call into question explanations involving typical suspects' personalities or behaviours.[39] In the case of socio-economic status, the existence of minorities above and below the level of most suspects has led to some overly narrow explanatory schemes that obscure more than they illuminate. Investigations into the important minority of child suspects, in contrast, has yielded insights into how children absorbed witchcraft beliefs and used them to express their feelings about their lives and to exert power in the adult world.[40]

---

[37] Bever, *Realities of Witchcraft*, ch. 8, esp. 424–30.

[38] Brian P. Levack, *The Witch-Hunt in Early Modern Europe* (2nd edn, Harlow, 1995), 133, 139, 141, 149, 152.

[39] Alison Rowlands, 'Witchcraft and Old Women in Early Modern Germany', *Past & Present*, 173 (2001), 52–7.

[40] Robert Walinski-Kiehl, 'The Devil's Children: Child Witch-Trials in Early Modern Germany', *Continuity and Change*, 11 (1996), 171–89; Lyndal Roper, '"Evil Imaginings and Fantasies": Child-Witches and the End of the Witch Craze', *Past & Present*, 167 (2000), 107–39.

Male witches have also become the object of specialized study, with some dispute about the extent to which they were caught up because they were related to female suspects (and thus were incidental to a female-centred process); because they engaged in male-oriented occupations that made them suspect (particularly 'cunning men', but also blacksmiths, executioners, and vagrants); or because the witch stereotype detached gender roles from biology, essentially feminizing males suspected of witchcraft.[41]

A more pointed debate has taken place recently on the question of age. Earlier discussions of witchcraft that focused on this factor have been challenged not only on the basis of the existence of younger suspects, but also because of the typical lag of years, or even decades, between first suspicions and formal accusations, leading to the contention that age has been strongly overemphasized.[42] One of the historians thus criticized, however, has renewed and expanded her original thesis that old women aroused particular hostility because of their physical signs of infertility, arguing that it was at the time of arrest that the role of 'witch' crystallized. Another, who related witch-like behaviours to the climacteric, countered that since many suspects were considerably older than fifty at the time of arrest, the problematic behaviours actually date back to that age, while in other cases, the behaviour patterns in question may have begun earlier in life, but became critically problematic during that transition.

While the association of women and witchcraft has not been challenged in as pointed a way, historical understanding of its relationship to popular culture has changed significantly in the last generation. The traditional rationalist view was that misogynist demonologists originated the focus on women, and more recently feminists have interpreted the trials as part of the imposition of patriarchy. However, research has shown that the earliest trials involved more men than women, and studies of later trials have shown that many accusations against women came from other women.[43] Furthermore, women had been associated with witchcraft in popular culture since antiquity, and demonologists generally did not express particularly strong levels of misogyny. The gendering of the early modern witch stereotype was not imposed from above, but reflected popular beliefs. The trials did effectively punish women who exhibited aggressiveness and promiscuity that men disapproved of, but so, too, did many other women. The key players were not high officials, but ordinary people, and they brought the charges as a way of dealing with a magical threat that they felt came especially, though not exclusively, from women.

---

[41] Laura Apps and Andrew Gow, *Male Witches in Early Modern Europe* (Manchester, 2003).

[42] Rowlands, 'Witchcraft and Old Women', 78–9; Lyndal Roper, *Witch Craze: Terror and Fantasy in Baroque Germany* (New Haven, CT, 2004), 160–4; Bever, *Realities of Witchcraft*, 57, 60.

[43] Arno Borst, *Medieval Worlds: Barbarians, Heretics and Artists in the Middle Ages* (Cambridge, 1991), 302; Bever, *Realities of Witchcraft*, 47; Edward Bever, 'Witchcraft, Female Aggression, and Power in the Early Modern Community', *Journal of Social History*, 35 (2002), 957; Stuart Clark, *Thinking with Demons: The Idea of Witchcraft in Early Modern Europe* (Oxford, 1997), 115.

3.2.3 The Sources of Popular Witch Beliefs and Accusations

Historians have developed four main lines of analysis to explain the sources of popular witch beliefs and accusations: social–psychological, structural–functionalist, cultural–linguistic, and realist.

The social–psychological approach treats witch beliefs as some sort of collective psychopathology or cognitive malfunction. The original 'rationalist' tradition considered witch beliefs to be a mixture of the peasantry's age-old susceptibility to 'primitive' magical thinking and the more recent absorption of diabolism into melancholic women's fantasies. Later interpretations went beyond these crude class and gender prejudices to explain belief in the power of *malefic* magic as a way of accounting for otherwise inexplicable misfortune, as a form of projection in which people who felt guilty about an offence they had committed projected the guilt onto the person who made them feel that way, or as a result of hostility the 'witch' aroused for some less direct but common psychological reason: that old women embodied infertility and decay, or that they evoked people's childish anger towards their mothers, who could never satisfy all of their infantile desires.[44]

Structural–functionalist interpretations generally incorporate one or more of the social psychological explanations above into a theory of social scapegoating in which other, 'real' social tensions were sublimated into witchcraft suspicions. Beyond providing satisfying explanations for misfortune and relief from various psychological tensions related to the suspect, accusations in this view both manifested lines of social strain and set boundaries for acceptable behaviours. Originally developed by anthropologists, this approach was introduced by Alan Macfarlane and Keith Thomas in the 1970s into the historical discussion. It won rapid acceptance partly because it related the witch trials to the larger contemporary movement to study history 'from below', and partly because it related the trials to larger socio-economic developments in early modern Europe. Specifically, Macfarlane and Thomas pointed to the breakdown of traditional communal society under the pressure of rising individualistic capitalism as the reason the kinds of situations that typically led to accusations increased. Their archetypal 'charity-denial model' involved a villager who accused a poor old woman of witchcraft after he denied her request for charity, she went away muttering angrily, and shortly thereafter some misfortune befell his household. While the historians recognized that many other conflicts led to accusations, their approach highlighted accusations' roots in the dynamics of local communities, and explained both the rise of prosecutions and their decline as functions of economic developments that first sundered communities and then alleviated distress through innovations like poor relief and insurance. This approach was weakened by Macfarlane's own conclusion in a later work—that English individualism developed long before the early modern period—undercutting both the guilt-reversal mechanism posited to be the psychological process

---

[44] Deborah Willis, *Malevolent Nurture* (Ithaca, NY, 1995), 45.

behind accusations, and the link between village tensions and sweeping historical change. Nevertheless, the 'charity-denial' scenario remains a powerful exemplar of the circumstances in which witchcraft accusations might arise.[45]

Cultural–linguistic explanations seek to account for witch beliefs in terms of their place in the total matrix of beliefs that made up the culture and the structural imperatives of language and narrative that shape thought. While this approach is rooted in the intellectual history of the demonology, it has been applied to popular culture as well. It is characterized by two radically different methodologies from previous approaches. First, it adopts anthropology's stance of cultural relativism, in this case a neutrality about the objective reality not only of magical powers (which structural–functionalists and post-rationalist social–psychological interpreters also do), but also of the behaviour and practices ascribed to witches. It neither affirms nor denies if anyone actually did, or experienced, the things contained in the beliefs, but instead asserts that the only historical 'reality' that can be legitimately investigated is the beliefs themselves. Second, since there is no 'reality' beyond the historical record to be discerned or explained, this approach concentrates on 'exploring patterns of meaning rather than causal relationships' by deconstructing not only the documents as texts, but also the beliefs and actions they describe 'as expressions of beliefs, values, and fantasies . . . ideological and cultural' resources, and symbols and metaphors.[46] Thus, for example, witch cases have been used to analyse 'the workings of sex, gender, and honour in the daily experiences of women'. To the extent that explanations are advanced, they are made in terms of the workings of language, in particular narrative, so that trial records are examined not as windows into some separate reality, but as the place where reality was constructed, with the governing principal the 'story-types . . . formally required for judicial procedures . . . to work'. Witchcraft was a discourse, in other words, a way of talking about, and thus organizing, relationships and experiences. 'The truth about witchcraft—its reality,' according to Stuart Clark, the most notable advocate of this approach, 'was created rather than reflected by the judicial process', demonological treatises, legal tracts, pamphlet reports, sermons, gossip and rumour, and even interior mentation. By this logic, the source of witch beliefs—the popular beliefs during the early modern period as well as the learned demonology—was simply the contingent development of European culture over the centuries, the shifting pattern of intertextual references that gave and revised their meanings, while the source of specific accusations was their power to provide an acceptable narrative structure for important issues in people's lives.

The fourth, 'realist' approach starts from historians' traditional assumption that there was an objective reality in the past, independent of what was said and written

[45] Alan Macfarlane, 'The Origins of English Individualism: Some Surprises', *Theory and Society*, 6 (1978), 269; James Sharpe, 'Macfarlane, Alan', in *Encyclopedia of Witchcraft*, iii, 687; David Hall, 'Witchcraft and the Limits of Interpretation', *New England Quarterly*, 58 (1985), 258.

[46] Stuart Clark, ed., *Languages of Witchcraft: Narrative, Ideology and Meaning in Early Modern Culture* (Basingstoke, 2001), 6–16.

about it, that can be partially reconstructed from the record; this view sees determining the extent to which the beliefs and accusations in the historical record reflected things people actually did and experienced as critical to a full understanding of early modern witchcraft. This approach includes what have traditionally been called romantic inter- pretations, from the nineteenth-century folkloric ones through to Murray's (a tradition that can be termed 'romantic realism'), more recent studies that have examined archival evidence of actual practices in popular culture that suggest the continuance of pre-Christian shamanistic traditions connected to the idea of the sabbath ('cultural realism'), and, most recently, attempts to assess the reality of both *malefic* and diabolic elements in light of what has been termed the 'cognitive revolution' in the human sciences ('cognitive realism').[47] The various strands of this tradition point to the evidence that a variety of beliefs about witchcraft referenced actual practices, behav- iours, and experiences. First of all, the undisputed activities of beneficent magical practitioners were explicitly diabolized and prosecuted, sometimes as outright witch- craft and more often as lesser offences that nonetheless served the devil's purpose by drawing people into magic. Second, there is ample evidence that some people did employ magic rituals and substances in order to inflict harm on their personal enemies, while others habitually manifested spontaneous aggressive behaviours associated with witchcraft in interpersonal confrontations. Third, there is also substantial evidence that some people experienced contact with spirits as disembodied voices or fully formed, three-dimensional figures, which they understood to be angels, traditional non-Christian spirits like fairies or familiars, or the devil himself. Similarly, some people experienced magical flight while in trance states, in which they flew to gather- ings with other magical people and spirits, and made merry or did battle.

The idea that these latter spiritual experiences represent survivals of pre-Christian shamanism is currently in dispute. Advocates point to: 1) shamanic cultures on the northern and eastern edges of the European cultural area, 2) clearly shamanic practi- tioners in parts of Eastern Europe, 3) experiences reminiscent of shamanism in other parts of Europe, and 4) shamanic elements in folklore scattered throughout the region. In response, critics point out the thinness of the evidence in the last case, the substantial differences from shamanism in the third, the fragmentary correspondences in the second, and the location of the practitioners mentioned in the first point outside the European cultural zone. A way out of this impasse is suggested by cognitive realism, which defines shamanism not in anthropological but in neurocognitive terms: as the exploitation of human neurobiological potentials rather than a cultural tradition.[48] In this view, experiences of contact with spirits and magical flight are perceptual manifest- ations of altered cognitive processing that can happen spontaneously, or can be deliber- ately induced. Thus, manipulating the nervous system and altering consciousness

---

[47] Carlo Ginzburg, *Night Battles* and *Ecstasies: Deciphering the Witches' Sabbath* (New York, 1991); Behringer, *Shaman of Oberstdorf*; Emma Wilby, *Cunning Folk and Familiar Spirits* (Brighton, 2009); Bever, *Realities of Witchcraft*.
[48] Bever, *Realities of Witchcraft*, 194–212.

enables access to knowledge and abilities that are not available in normal waking consciousness. And since a substantial proportion of magic involves activities that manipulate the practitioner's own or other people's nervous systems to help or to harm via the connections between emotional states, bodily functions, and interpersonal relations, this definition of shamanism suggests a new way of understanding magic and witchcraft as well.

The realist interpretation does not suggest that the demonology's diabolic conspiracy existed or that the victims of the witch-hunts deserved their fate. What it does suggest is that while witch-hunts may best be understood in terms of some socio-cultural-psychological pathology, witch beliefs can only be fully understood in light of their reference to reality.

3.2.4 New Directions for Research

First of all, there is still much work to be done in applying the cultural–linguistic approach to explore the meaning of witch beliefs in popular culture. This approach has yielded rich rewards over the past generation, and continued work will be useful for further exploring the meaning of the beliefs in their own right, for further illuminating related aspects of the larger culture, and for helping with the traditional historical task of identifying the biases in the sources in order to better get at the reality they reflect.

Secondly, further exploration of actual practices and experiences is needed. What people actually did and what they actually experienced need to be more clearly demarcated from what they merely believed and talked about. Furthermore, what they experienced needs to be related to emerging insights into human cognition to better understand why and how they felt, saw, and heard the things that made up their encounters with the spirit world.

Thirdly, the efficacy of various forms of magic, including *maleficium*, needs to be further investigated in light of new developments in cognitive, medical, and related sciences. Historians have been working on the basis of the assumptions of the Enlightenment since the Enlightenment, and advances in our understanding of how interpersonal relations, ideas and emotions, perceptions, cognition, and bodily functions influence each other need to be incorporated into historical understanding.

Fourth, the evolution of popular beliefs about and practices related to witchcraft from the late Middle Ages to the modern period needs to be delineated, especially in relationship to the elite's changing theories and legal practices.

Finally, the evolution of scepticism about popular elements in witchcraft needs to be explored. Before the period of the trials, no one doubted that some people practised harmful magic, experienced encounters with spirits, and went on trips to the spirit world. The only questions were how much was real and whether the people involved were inspired, culpable, or crazy. During the course of the trials, it became clear that large numbers of people innocent of any of these activities were being victimized through unfounded accusations and tortured confessions, a realization that played a key role in ending the persecutions. By the late seventeenth century, commentators were beginning to note that while witches had existed in the recent past, they were no longer to be found.[49] By the nineteenth century, it had become possible to argue that witches had never really existed, that even self-styled ones were the product, rather than the source, of demonology. By the late twentieth century the very existence of reality beyond the documentary record had been called into question, so that it had become theoretically impossible to ask, let alone verify, if there had ever really been witches by any definition at all. How we got here from there will make a fascinating study in the social construction of reality.

Further Reading

Behringer, Wolfgang, *Shaman of Oberstdorf: Chonrad Stoekhlin and the Phantoms of the Night*, tr. H. C. Erik Midelfort (Charlottesville, VA, 1998).

Bever, Edward, *The Realities of Witchcraft and Popular Magic in Early Modern Europe* (Basingstoke, 2008).

Briggs, Robin, *Witches and Neighbours: The Social and Cultural Context of European Witchcraft* (Harmondsworth, 1996).

Burke, Peter, *Popular Culture in Early Modern Europe* (3rd edn, Farnham, 2009).

Clark, Stuart, 'Witchcraft and Magic in Early Modern Culture', in Bengt Ankarloo and Stuart Clark, eds, *Witchcraft and Magic in Europe: The Period of the Witch Trials* (London, 2002), 97–169.

Davies, Owen, *Cunning-Folk* (London, 2003).

Ginzburg, Carlo, *Night Battles: Witchcraft and Agrarian Cults in the Sixteenth and Seventeenth Centuries* (New York, 1985).

Kieckhefer, Richard, *Magic in the Middle Ages* (2nd edn, Cambridge, 2000).

Klaniczay, Gábor, *The Uses of Supernatural Power* (Princeton, 1990).

MacFarlane, Alan, *Witchcraft in Tudor and Stuart England: A Regional and Comparative Study* (London, 1970).

Martin, Ruth, *Witchcraft and the Inquisition in Venice 1550–1650* (Oxford, 1989).

Muchembled, Robert, *Popular Culture and Elite Culture in France 1400–1750* (Baton Rouge, LA, 1985).

Pócs, Éva, *Between the Living and the Dead: A Perspective on Witches and Seers in the Early Modern Age* (Budapest, 1999).

Thomas, Keith, *Religion and the Decline of Magic* (London, 1971).

Wilby, Emma, *Cunning Folk and Familiar Spirits* (Brighton, 2009).

Wilson, Stephen, *The Magical Universe: Everyday Ritual and Magic in Early Modern Europe* (London, 2000).

---

[49] Edward Bever, 'Witchcraft Prosecutions and the Decline of Magic', *Journal of Interdisciplinary History*, 40 (2009), 280.

CHAPTER 4

....

DEMONOLOGIES[1]

....

GERHILD SCHOLZ WILLIAMS

WRITTEN by learned physicians, jurists, and theologians, demonologies (or 'witchcraft theories' as Walter Stephens and Stuart Clark call them[2]) are compendious tracts that examine all aspects of the interactions alleged to take place between Satan and his demons (or fallen angels) and human beings, in particular women accused of being witches.[3] Employed as aids in the identification and prosecution of witches, demonologies examine the history and theology as well as the legal and medical implications and consequences of such interactions.[4] They constitute an early modern literary genre: the rational, that is, the scientific, legal, and theological exploration of a phenomenon that appears to the modern reader anything but rational or scientific. Moreover, the witch was not only a learned preoccupation. Popular belief saw the witch, male or female, either positively as a person with special talents and knowledge who could heal, foretell the future, or cast spells. Negatively, this same person could be accused of practising evil by uttering destructive curses that caused impotence, inflicted illness, conjured weather, and destroyed harvests. Worse still, the witch's glance or evil eye was

---

[1] Parts of this chapter have appeared in Gerhild Scholz Williams, 'Demonologies: Writing About Magic and Witchcraft', in Max Reinhart, ed., *Early Modern German Literature 1350–1700* (Rochester, 2007), 45, 141. Used with permission.

[2] Walter Stephens, *Demon Lovers: Witchcraft, Sex, and the Crisis of Belief* (Chicago, 2002), 323. Stephens rejects the terms 'demonologists' and 'demonologies', which I will employ for reasons of practicality and efficacy; Walter Rummel and Rita Voltmer, *Hexen und Hexenverfolgung in der Frühen Neuzeit* (Darmstadt, 2008).

[3] Among them Jean Bodin, Peter Binsfeld, Pierre de Lancre, Johann Weyer, Richard Baxter, James VI of Scotland, William Perkins, Reginald Scott, Andrea Alciati, Martin Del Rio, and many others.

[4] For an exhaustive bibliography on 'demonic manifestations and sorcery from the Middle Ages to this day' see Jean-Pierre Coumont, ed., *Demonology and Witchcraft: An Annotated Bibliography with Related Works on Magic, Medicine, Superstition, Etc.* (Brussels, 2004). For a selection of currently available electronic resources pertaining to demonology and witch research see H. C. Erik Midelfort, 'Witchcraft', in David M. Whitford, ed., *Reformation and Early Modern Europe: A Guide to Research* (Kirksville, MO, 2008), 348.

believed to affect the judgement of magistrates who sat in trial over the accused. And it was, in large part, these trials that brought popular imaginings about witches into learned demonologies.

The genre evolved over a long period of time, with the first reports of devil worship appearing in the 1430s.[5] Over the course of several centuries, works such as *Flagellum maleficorum* (Lashing Those Who Commit Evil Deeds, c.1462), *Quaestio de Strigis* (An Investigation of Witches, c.1470), *Malleus maleficarum* (*The Hammer of Witches*, 1487), *De praestigiis daemonum* (On the Illusions of Demons, 1563), or *De Betoverde Weereld* (The Bewitched World, 1691/3) were published, read, and quoted in subsequent demonologies, witch tracts, sermons, broadsheets, witch trials, and laws pertaining to the practice of witchcraft. According to Stephens, witchcraft theorists developed ways of systematically describing ideas about the relationships between humans and demons—the central source of evidence being the testimony of witches on trial: 'Witchcraft persecution was a complex phenomenon, but the motives of its defenders were comprehensible, familiar, and rational.'[6] To add intellectual and legal substance to their arguments, witchcraft theorists made use of theological and philosophical sources, trial records, and manuals produced for and by magistrates charged with prosecuting suspected witches. For the most part, demonologists accepted that demons were real and that they engaged in sexual congress with humans, specifically with women. Moreover, scholars and lay people alike accepted as a theological and scientific truth the idea that demons had the ability to take on the shape and appearance of humans to the point that they could not be distinguished from human beings by any observer, be it husband, friend, or family member.

While the production and consumption of demonologies was vigorous from the 1430s to the 1700s, twentieth-century historians and literary scholars have, until recently, shown relatively little interest in them. Assessing the state of research on demonology as of 1977, Sydney Anglo concluded that, more often than not, demonologies had been neglected, or worse, rejected as aberrant musings of otherwise reasonable men. Analyses of the structure, arguments, language, interrelations, and reception of these texts had been dismissed as unessential and uninteresting.[7] Rather than examining these texts as cultural documents in their own right, Stuart Clark, whose *Thinking with Demons* (1997) takes pride of place as the most comprehensive review to date of the great variety of demonological materials, notes that earlier critics had tended to focus on 'the social and institutional configurations of witch hunting, together with the patterns of prosecutions in various European regions and the local circumstances that produce them'.[8] Clark's work, on the other hand, along with that of his cohorts,

[5] Stuart Clark, 'Demonology', in Richard M. Golden, ed., *Encyclopedia of Witchcraft: The Western Tradition* (Santa Barbara, CA, 2006), 259–63.

[6] Walter Stephens, *Demon Lovers: Witchcraft, Sex, and the Crisis of Belief* (Chicago, 2002), 9.

[7] Sydney Anglo, 'Evident Authority and Authoritative Evidence: The *Malleus Maleficarum*', in Sydney Anglo, ed., *The Damned Art: Essays in the Literature of Witchcraft* (London, 1977), 2.

[8] Stuart Clark, *Thinking with Demons: The Idea of Witchcraft in Early Modern Europe* (Oxford, 1997), vii.

has greatly clarified how central demonologies were in the times in which they were produced, widely translated, and cited as authoritative sources on issues relating to witchcraft all across Europe. Indeed, closer examination of these publications makes it clear that, during the early modern period, demonology and its counterpart, angelology or the study of angels, constituted a fundamental aspect of Christian cosmology and thus an integral part of the contemporary study and practice of theology, law, medicine, and science. No matter what their professional specialization or perspective on the prosecution of witches, the majority of scholars accepted as basic the premise that demons and witches existed, and that they could and did inflict harm on humankind.[9]

The witch was usually an older woman who was past childbearing age; it was only in a distinct minority of cases that the witch was a man. She was purported to enter into a contract with Satan, fly to the sabbath, engage in sexual contact with Satan, his demons, and all other participants in the devilish celebration, and subsequently visit misfortune and illness on her neighbours by conjuring ill weather, destroying harvests, impacting human fertility, and causing the illness and death of children. Her evil deeds were believed to be perpetrated by curses, touch, or simply by a glance. The witch acquired her evil powers, her magic words, at the sabbath, from other witches, or else simply as a product of her pact with Satan. Her prosecution was widespread in early modern Europe, although countries and regions differed in the degree of presumed infestation. With the conquest of the Americas, the witch phenomenon also migrated across the Atlantic.[10] The association of travel reports with witch writings and discussions of witches flying to the sabbath appeared in Gianfrancesco Pico's *Strix* (1523) and Bartolomeo Spina's *Inquiry into Witches* (1523), whose most cited source was the *Malleus maleficarum*. Like many other witchcraft theorists, both of these authors insisted that the only way to prove the existence of witchcraft was by the testimony offered by witnesses in court. In much the same way, the French demonologist Pierre de Lancre (1612) made extensive use of court records to prove the reality of the assemblies of the witches whom he prosecuted in the French Basque country.

4.1 DEMONOLOGY AND MAGIC

In order to understand why learned men spent considerable intellectual effort, time, and money writing and publishing on witches and witchcraft, it is important to be familiar with early modern magical practices and beliefs. These had emerged from a

---

[9] Stephens, *Demon Lovers*; Armando Maggi, *In the Company of Demons: Unnatural Beings, Love, and Identity in the Italian Renaissance* (Chicago, 2006).

[10] Richard Godbeer, *The Devil's Dominion: Magic and Religion in Early New England* (Cambridge, 1992).

variety of pre-Christian, non-Christian, biblical, patristic, and medieval sources.[11] Theology, cosmology, and natural philosophy were agreed on the nature of the cosmos and mankind's place in it as well as on the existential danger implicit in wishing to exert control over both. The association between the order of the universe and magical words and numbers and, conversely, the conviction that the improper and illicit use of magical discourses signalled transgression and disorder, made magical and occult practices and their knowledge at all times a perilous privilege, as much feared as sought after. With the help of magical languages, secret rituals, hidden powers, and contracts with the occult, the aspiring practitioner could unlock the secrets of the universe.[12] Pierre de Lancre, for example, anguished over his inability to enter into and understand the secret demonic language exchanged among witches. Similarly, early modern exorcists struggled with the challenge of finding the language with which to excise evil from human beings held in the clutches of Satan.[13] The inherent contradiction for both the learned and unlearned between the simultaneous necessities of knowledge and secrecy regarding their practice of demonology and magic led to the relentless pursuit of those presumed to be in illicit possession of secrets: namely, people accused of being witches. In the hands of the witch, magic was thought to change from a divine science into a 'semantic of deceit', a 'rhetoric of seduction'.[14] To keep their access licit, the practitioners of white magic often vigorously prosecuted witches, fearing that their (generally) uneducated counterparts would access knowledge only to visit misfortune on those around them by seeking control over people, animals, weather, the stars, and social order and institutions.[15]

As an intellectual and cultural language, magic and the discourse of witches lent expression to the extraordinary, to the occult, and to the satanic. Demonic magic was accepted as a form of religion, albeit a perverted one that distorted the tenets of Christian theology and religious practice. Serving Satan instead of God, the practitioners invoked demons in their efforts to perform *maleficia* (evil deeds) and gain access to illicit knowledge. Thus, demonology and magic were always about keeping secrets: the learned magician shared his knowledge only with other magicians. Similarly, the witch kept company with her own kind, whose ranks she strove to increase by bringing others, preferably young children, to Satan. How to deal with children who consorted

---

[11] Alan Charles Kors and Edward Peters, eds, *Witchcraft in Europe, 400–1700: A Documentary History* (Philadelphia, PA, 2001).

[12] Stuart Clark, ed., *Languages of Witchcraft: Narrative, Ideology and Meaning in Early Modern Culture* (Basingstoke, 2001).

[13] Armando Maggi, *Satan's Rhetoric: A Study of Renaissance Demonology* (Chicago, 2001).

[14] Gabriele Schwab, 'Seduced by Witches: Nathaniel Hawthorne's *The Scarlet Letter* in the Context of New England Witchcraft Fiction', in Dianne Hunter, ed., *Seduction and Theory: Readings of Gender, Representation, and Rhetoric* (Urbana, IL, 1989), 172.

[15] The Indo-European *magh* means 'to be able to', 'to help'; *maghti* (power) = *Macht* (might). The Sanskrit *magha* also means 'power', 'strength', 'wealth'. Thus magic, considered formally, stands for an ability or a power to execute certain actions. See B. P. Copenhaver, 'Natural Magic, Hermeticism, and Occultism in Early Modern Science', in David C. Lindberg and Robert S. Westman, eds, *Reappraisals of the Scientific Revolution* (Cambridge, 1990), 216–301.

with the devil was the topic of the anonymous and widely read tract *Newer Tractat von der verführten Kinder Zauberey* (New Treatise on Children Led Astray by Magic, 1629).[16] By the time this treatise was published, the idea that mothers led their children to Satan (especially their daughters) and that whole families swore allegiance to the devil had become commonplace.

Generally speaking, accusations of demonological practices, that is, the performance of malevolent magic or witchcraft, were levelled in 'areas of ambiguous social relations', where festering neighbourly envy, hatreds, and the fear of illness and misfortune combined with destructive results.[17] Moreover, Protestant reformers, while vigorously opposing the intercessional power of saints, were loath to let go of Satan and his minions as tools for social discipline and the affirmation of the faith.[18] In fact, demonological beliefs significantly contributed to the persecution of Anabaptist believers and Amerindian natives.[19]

4.2 DEMONOLOGY AND THE WITCH

Any discussion of early modern demonology inevitably turns to the association of demonology with witchcraft and the witch. Witch-like creatures had been feared since antiquity: Homer's Circe changed Ulysses' companions into swine; bloodsucking creatures called *lamia* or *striga* appear in the writings of Horace and Ovid. The Old Testament (Exod. 22:18; Lev. 20:6) threatens punishments and levels invectives against witches. ('Thou shalt not suffer a witch to live.') The Latin Middle Ages speak of a *malefica* or *venefica* as a woman who inflicts evil (*maleficium*) on people, animals, and crops, while the early medieval canon *Episcopi* (c.900) tells of women who fly about at night in the company of the goddess Diana.[20] In the thirteenth century, the subject of demonology was addressed in detail by Thomas Aquinas in his *Summa Theologiae* (Summa of Theology, 1265–74), which reviewed *maleficium* (harmful magic) in the context of impotence inflicted by evil spells. Basing his assumptions on his reading of St Augustine, Aquinas supported the idea that sexual relations between demons and humans were possible, although conception of human children after sex with demons

---

[16] Wolfgang Schilling, *Newer Tractat von der verführten Kindr Zauberey* (Cologne, 1629); Lyndal Roper, *Witch Craze: Terror and Fantasy in Baroque Germany* (New Haven, CT, 2004), 204–22.

[17] Robin Briggs, *Witches and Neighbours: The Social and Cultural Context of European Witchcraft* (Harmondsworth, 1998).

[18] Nathan Johnstone, *The Devil and Demonism in Early Modern England* (Cambridge, 2006), 1–26.

[19] Gary K. Waite, *Eradicating the Devil's Minions: Anabaptists and Witches in Reformation Europe, 1525–1600* (Toronto, 2008); Gerhild Scholz Williams, *Defining Dominion: The Discourses of Magic and Witchcraft in Early Modern France and Germany* (Ann Arbor, MI, 1995), 141–5.

[20] The canon, believed to have been issued by the Council of Ancyra (314), was probably no older than the ninth century. It denied the reality of night-rides with Diana. The women who believed in such an experience were considered to be victims of satanic delusions.

was not. Aquinas rejected the idea that witches could fly, while insisting that harmful magic perpetrated either by demons or witches was only possible with God's permission.[21]

Entering into a pact with Satan, the witch was said to have renounced, consciously and voluntarily, the Christian faith, the blessings of baptism, and, thus, salvation. Consequently, witchcraft became associated with heresy and apostasy, although witchcraft was considered more deadly than either crime, as the witch not only endangered her/his own soul, but, more significantly, through her/his evil doings (*maleficia*) also threatened the well-being of the Christian community. By the late Middle Ages the practice of witchcraft (understood as the misuse of Church rituals, violation of the sacraments, and sexual congress with demons) became an offence punishable by both secular and canon law. By 1484 the image of the witch as a night-flying, sexually voracious creature, devoted to her lord Satan and engaged in all manner of evil doings, had been firmly established. It would persist until the late eighteenth century. In December of 1484, the papal bull by Innocent VIII, *Summis desiderantes affectibus*, authorized two inquisitors, the Dominican friars Heinrich Kramer (Institoris) and Jacob Sprenger, to identify, imprison, and prosecute the witches who allegedly plagued south-western Germany and parts of Austria. In response to his experiences, Kramer produced a compendious tract, the *Malleus maleficarum*, describing how to identify and prosecute witches most effectively. This tract became enshrined as the most popular model for demonological writings, evolving into one of the central texts of the European witchcraft prosecutions.[22] Some thirty editions were published between 1486 and 1669. As the most important and persistently popular handbook on the witch phenomenon, the *Malleus* described why women were most prone to become witches, and how they should be identified and prosecuted. It is interesting to note that, in spite of its enduring authority throughout the sixteenth and seventeenth centuries in matters of the legalities associated with prosecuting the witch, the *Malleus* did not mention one of the very important and most lethal aspects of the witch image, namely her propensity to fly to and celebrate orgies at the witches' sabbath. Still, the impact of the text's intensely misogynist message—that women were especially prone to fall victim to the wiles of Satan because of their weak character and their voracious sexual appetite—was far-reaching. Already, by the mid-fifteenth century, the numbers of women executed for alleged witch crimes in south-eastern France, Switzerland, and southwestern Germany had increased significantly. Trials began in Europe around 1430 and ended around 1780, with the years between 1560 and 1630 seeing the most vigorous persecutions.

[21] Geoffrey Scarre, *Witchcraft and Magic in Sixteenth and Seventeenth Century Europe* (Atlantic Highlands, [1987] 2000), 14.

[22] Wolfgang Behringer and Günter Jerouschek, eds, *Heinrich Kramer (Institoris): Der Hexenhammer: Kommentierte Übersetzung* (2nd edn, Munich, 2001); P. G. Maxwell-Stuart, ed., *The Malleus Maleficarum: Selected, Translated, and Annotated* (Manchester, 2007).

However, even early on, during the last quarter of the fifteenth century, moderating voices were raised contesting witch beliefs and arguing against the reality and efficacy of demonic power attributed to women, calling them an illusion. Such was a tract written in opposition to the *Malleus* by Ulrich Molitor, a jurist from Constance. The *De lamiis et phitonicis mulieribus* (1489), translated into German as *Von Unholden und Hexen* (On Demons and Witches),[23] was published in ten editions after 1490. According to Molitor, it was only by permission of God that witches were able to make weather, inflict illness or impotence, fly to the sabbath, or procreate with demons, as only God could bestow whatever power Satan falsely claimed as his own. The woodcuts used to adorn Molitor's tract, illustrating various illusionary witch activities, would influence the iconography of demonologies throughout the early modern period. Beyond the woodcuts in Molitor's work, the visual representations of witches and the eroticism of their activities went mainstream with the representations by Albrecht Dürer and Hans Baldung Grien.[24] The depiction of the nude witch with or without her demon lover (or familiar) significantly influenced later illustrations of the preparations for the sabbath (including putting ointment on the nude body), and travel to it.[25]

4.3 DEMONOLOGIES

Resulting in part from the learned and legal preoccupation with magic and witchcraft, demonologists across Europe produced many printed books, records, tracts, and sermons exploring the reality of demons as a scientific, religious, social, and theological phenomenon, usually with reference to the witch phenomenon.[26] Johannes Nider's *Formicarius* (The Anthill, 1437) is frequently cited in the *Malleus*.[27] Equally widely read were Geiler von Kaysersberg's *Emeis* (1508), and Ulrich Tengler's *Der neü Layenspiegel* (The New Mirror for Lay People, 1511). While the Catholic Church, in concert with the lay authorities, played an important role in the evolution of demonologies, the onset of the Reformation did not significantly change the witch debate. Martin Luther's convictions and teachings about the reality of evil in the form of Satan and his demons formed the basis of Protestant demonology. While he dismissed the witches' sabbath as an illusion, Luther was convinced that sexual intercourse with the devil was possible and

[23] Ulrich Molitor, 'Von Hexen und Unholden', in Abraham Sauer, ed., *Theatrum de veneficis* (Frankfurt, 1586), 70–96.
[24] Linda C. Hults, *The Witch as Muse: Art, Gender, and Power in Early Modern Europe* (Philadelphia, PA, 2005).
[25] Kors and Peters, eds, *Witchcraft in Europe*, 35–7.
[26] David Meder, *Acht Hexenpredigten* (Leipzig, 1605).
[27] Michael D. Bailey, *Battling Demons: Witchcraft, Heresy, and Reform in the Late Middle Ages* (Philadelphia, PA, 2003).

that witches entered into a pact with the devil and practised *maleficia*.[28] He also believed that changelings (*Wechselbälger*) could result from women's intercourse with Satan. He specifically and vigorously condemned the witch's apostasy as the most serious crime against God and the Christian faith. Luther's thinking on demons inspired two contrasting strands of Protestant reaction to the witch phenomenon. On the one hand, there emerged the call for severe punishment for those who entered into commerce with the demon; on the other, his advice on moderation and faith in the healing power of prayer was also heeded.

Insisting on severe punishment, three later writers emphasized the sinful nature of *maleficia* and the God-given duty of the magistrates to eradicate its practise and punish its practitioners. These were the Marburg attorney Abraham Saur in *Eine kurtze/treuwe Warnung...ob auch zu dieser unser Zeit unter uns Christen/Hexen/Zauberer und Unholden vorhanden* (A Short and Candid Warning...that even in our day there are witches, magicians, and devils living among us, 1582); the Württemberg theologian Paul Frisius in *Von dess Teuffels Nebelkappen* (The Devil's Hoodwink, 1583); and Samuel Meigerius, pastor at Nortorf, in *De panurgia lamiarum, sagarum, strigum ac veneficarum* (On the Evil of Sorceresses, Magicians, Hags, and Witches, 1587). The Lutheran pastor Ludwig Milichius, in *Der Zauber-Teuffel* (The Magic Devil, 1563), had advanced similar arguments emphasizing the duty of godly government to prosecute and execute the witch.

Others expressed a more moderate attitude. While not denying the grave culpability of demonological contacts, they tended to recommend prayer, religious instruction, and church discipline in the hope that these actions would effect a spiritual change and return the witch to the faith. These men—among them the Danish Lutheran theologian Niels Hemmingsen, who wrote *Assertiones contra magicum incantationem* (Declaration Against the Magical Incantation, 1569) and *Admonitio de superstitionibus magicis vitandis* (Advice for Avoiding Magical Superstitions, 1575)—were sharply critical of the often relentless insistence expressed by the populace and some judges to prosecute and execute. The debate about the efficacy of the trial by water for the purpose of identifying witches belongs within this context. The suspected witch would be thrown into the water, hands and feet tied. If she floated, her rejection by the sanctified water marked her as a witch, since it revealed the satanic lightness she had assumed upon entering into a pact with Satan. If she sank she was proven innocent, since her uncorrupted human substance made her heavier than water. Towards the end of the sixteenth century, the ordeal by water was vigorously and widely discussed among demonologists, specifically jurists and physicians. In 1583 the Marburg natural philosopher and physician Wilhelm Adolph Schreiber (Scribonius) published *De examine et purgatione sagarum per aquam frigidam epistola* (Epistle on the Examination and Trying of Witches by Cold Water, 1583), which certified the procedure as legally and

---

[28] Martin Luther, 'D. Martinus Lutherus im Buch/Das Colloquia oder Tischgespräch genannt wirdt. Capit. 24. von Zauberey/Teuffelsgespenst/Und Hexerey/Campsionibus und Wechselkindern', in Abraham Sawr, ed., *Theatrum de veneficis* (Frankfurt, 1586).

theologically sound. A forceful rejection of Scribonius' thesis was advanced by Hermann Neuwalt, professor of medicine at the University of Helmstedt, in his *Exegesis purgationis sive examinis sagarum super aquam frigidam* (Exegesis on the Trial or Examination of Witches by Cold Water, 1584). As the first tract devoted exclusively to the question of the efficacy of trial by water, Neuwalt's *Exegesis* was widely discussed and frequently printed. The debate between the two demonologists was subsequently included in the collection of seventeen demonological tracts in German, the *Theatrum de veneficis* (Theatre of Sorcerers, 1586).

Demonological writings significantly influenced one of the rare fictional accounts of demonic interactions, the *Historia von D. Johann Fausten* (History of Dr Johann Faust, 1587) and its sequel, the *Wagnerbuch* (1593). Both works deserve mention in the context of demonologies.[29] The story of a scholar's pact with the devil and his destruction twenty-four years later (for Faust's pupil, Wagner, the time was significantly shorter) became commonplace in European literature. Faust was the son of a peasant and student at the University of Wittenberg before his inappropriate curiosity about the universe and the nature of the divine compelled him to turn to the black arts and to conjure Satan. He entered into a pact with Satan, signing the contract with his own blood. Once the agreement was reached, he was joined by a devil-familiar, Mephistopheles, who instructed him in the occult sciences. At the end of the period agreed to in the pact, Faust's punishment was not to be burned, but rather to be torn limb from limb. His autobiography was discovered by his pupils after his death: 'They found Faust's story recorded and written by him'. The story of his life and death was told by his student and assistant, Christoph Wagner, who, like his mentor, pledged allegiance to the devil in exchange for a life of plenty. He became the protagonist of a sequel, his very own story or *Wagnerbuch* (1593).[30]

While most demonologists agreed on the severity of the crime of witchcraft, at no point in time, not even at the height of the prosecutions, did all demonologists agree on the nature of the witch (aside from the central notion that most witches were women). The physician at the court of Cleve, Johann Weyer, saw her as an old, demented woman in need of spiritual support and medical help rather than criminal prosecution. He developed this thesis in detail in the tract *De praestigiis daemonum* (On the Deceptions of Devils, 1663).[31] By arguing that the moral weakness of women made them easy prey to Satan's temptations, Weyer started one of the most vigorous and enduring controversies surrounding demonology and the witch in the early modern period. He insisted that women were neither helped nor healed by torture or burning, but that they rather needed the healing power of prayer, religious instruction, medical

---

[29] Stephan Fuessel and Hans Joachim Kreutzer, eds, *Historia von D. Faustus: Text des Druckes von 1587*, vol. 1516 (Stuttgart, 1988); David Wootton, ed., *Doctor Faustus with the English Faustbook/ Christopher Marlow* (Indianapolis, IN, 2005).

[30] Günther Mahal, ed., *Das Wagnerbuch von 1593*, 2 vols (Tübingen, 2010).

[31] *Witches, Devils, and Doctors in the Renaissance: Johann Weyer*, De praestigiis daemonum, ed. George Mora (Binghamton, NY, 1991).

intervention, and meditative isolation. By contrast, in *De la démonomanie des sorciers* (On the Diabolical Madness of Witches, 1580), the French jurist and theorist of the absolutist state, Jean Bodin, made a vigorous case for witch persecutions. He launched a vitriolic polemic against Weyer's theses, arguing that it played down the profoundly sinful nature of the witch's crime. Translated into German by Johann Fischart as *Vom aussgelasnen wütigen Teuffelsheer* (On the Wild and Furious Host of Demons, 1581), Bodin's tract became canonical in demonological literature.[32] Along with the work of Flemish–Spanish Jesuit Martin Del Rio, *Disquisitionum magicarum libri sex* (Six Books of Disquisitions on Witches, 1599–1600), it was cited as authoritative by demonologists into the early eighteenth century. Del Rio's teacher at the College of Clermont in Paris was the Spanish Jesuit and demonologist Juan Maldonado (*Traicté des anges et démons*, 1605), whose passionate writings against witches deeply influenced not only Del Rio, but also his student de Lancre, who frequently quoted Maldonado's writings.

Though most vigorously condemned by his contemporary demonologists, Johann Weyer was not alone in his doubts about women being witches and capable of exercising satanic powers. Equally unconvinced was the English author Reginald Scot, whose *Discoverie of Witchcraft* (1584) showed him to be strongly critical of both the *Malleus maleficarum* and Jean Bodin's *Démonomanie*. The hostility directed at Scot by both Catholic and Protestant demonologists was no less vitriolic than Bodin's diatribes against Johann Weyer. Moreover, James VI of Scotland, author of *Daemonologie* (1597) and a firm believer in the power and danger of the witch, strongly rebuked Scot and the views he had put forth in the *Discoverie*. James VI's rejection of Scot's scepticism was later supported by William Perkins in his *Discourse of the Damned Art of Witchcraft* (1608). As a Protestant, however, Perkins was more critical of witchcraft as an act of apostasy, as a denial of the Christian faith through the pledge of allegiance to Satan, than of any real acts of magic perpetrated by the witch.

Very influential for later demonological writings for and against the belief in the witch's satanic powers were a number of Italian scholars, one of which was Bartolomeo della Spina. An inquisitor during the time of the witch trials at Modena, della Spina wrote three short witch tracts in 1523, which appeared as a collected edition in 1576, titled *Quaestio de strigibus una cum tractatu de praeminentia sacrae theologiae et quadruplici Apologia de Lamiis contra Ponzinibium* (An Investigation on Witches with a Treatise on the Supremacy of Sacred Theology and a Fourfold Defense from Ponzinibio's on Witches). In his inquisitorial work, della Spina significantly relied on the *Malleus maleficarum*. He insisted that witches did indeed fly to the sabbath in person and that this was not, as others had claimed, an illusion.

Yet another widely influential demonologist was the Tuscan native Paolo Grillando, who gained fame with his *Tractatus de hereticis et sortilegiis eorumque poenis* (Treatise on Heretics and Sorcerers and their Punishments, 1524). His description of the witches' sabbath influenced later tracts on the topic to such an extent that his work was

---

[32] Jean Bodin, *De la démonomanie des sorciers* (Paris, 1580; repr. Hildesheim, 1988); Bodin, *Vom aussgelasnen wütigen Teuffelsheer* (1591), tr. Johann Fischart (Graz, 1973).

published in 1615, together with the *Malleus maleficarum*, as a legal handbook. Grillando's work was cited by de Lancre, Del Rio, and another Italian demonologist, Francesco-Maria Guazzo (*Compendium Maleficarum* [A Summary of Witches, 1608]) who witnessed witch trials in Milan. Guazzo penned his *Compendium* in response to witch-burnings in 1599 and 1603. Equally energetic in his persecution of the witch was Carlo Borromeo, who vigorously pursued not only witches but also Protestants. His *De Superstitionibus* (Of Superstitions, 1576) asserted that all magic and witchcraft constituted a serious threat against Christian order and needed to be rooted out. Two other Italians, however, Pietro Pomponazzi (*De naturalium effectuum causis, sive de incantationibus* [On the Causes of Natural Effects, or of Incantations], 1556) and the lawyer Andrea Alciati (*Parergon iuris* [On the Accessory of Jurisprudence, 1544]), expressed serious reservations about the efficacy of demonic action and witchcraft, convictions that later strengthened Reginald Scot in his rejection of satanic powers. In the same way, Johann Weyer employed many of Alciati's arguments, namely that the witch was delusional and should be treated by physicians, not persecuted by jurists.

Among the German demonologists with somewhat equivocating views of the witch we have to mention the Rostock jurist Johann Georg Godelmann. He distinguishes in his *Disputatio de magis, veneficis et lamiis* (Disputation on Magicians, Sorceresses, and Witches, 1592) among pacts that lead to real *maleficium*, those that do not, and those where the crimes are mere illusions. Misgivings about witch trials were also voiced by the Lemgo pastor Jodocus Hocker (or, Hieronymus Höcker) in *Der Teufel selbs* (The Devil Himself, 1568); the pastor and theologian Hermann Hamelmann in *Eine Predigt zu Gandersheim ... wider die Beschwerer ... Zeuberer/Nachweiser/und Segner* (A Sermon at Gandersheim Against Conjurers ... Magicians, Seers, and Prognosticators, 1572); the Bremen physician Johann Ewich in *De sagarum quas vulgo venificas appellant* (On Magicians, Which Are Commonly Called Witches, 1584); the Heidelberg University professor of Greek and mathematics, Herman Witekind (Augustin Lerchheimer von Steinfelden) in *Christlich Bedencken und Erinnerung von Zauberey* (Christian Admonition and Warning about the Practise of Magic, 1585);[33] the Frankfurt jurist Johann Fichart, in *Consilia* (Judgements, 1590); and the Zurich theologian Ludwig Lavater, in *De spectris, lemuribus et maguis* (On Spectres, Ghosts, and Magicians, 1580). The Heidelberg theologian Anton Praetorius (Johann Scultetus) wrote one of the most widely read and discussed tracts, the *Gründliche[r] Bericht von Zauberey und Zauberern* (Elementary Report on Magic and Magicians, 1598).[34] While Praetorius did not doubt the reality of satanic influence over humanity, he spoke out forcefully both in general against the treatment of women suspected of being witches and in particular against the use of torture as an instrument to elicit confessions.

As noted, Catholic demonologists did not differ much from their Protestant counterparts in their basic beliefs concerning witches. Even so, it is a matter of record that

---

[33] Frank Baron, ed., *Herman Witekinds Christlich Bedencken und die Entstehung des Faustbuchs von 1587* (Berlin, 2009).

[34] Hartmut Hegeler, *Anton Praetorius, Kämpfer gegen Hexenprozesse und Folter* (Unna, 2002).

some of the most intense prosecutions of witches took place in the archbishoprics of Trier and Cologne, and in the Catholic cities of Würzburg, Bamberg, Eichstädt, Augsburg, Fulda, and Breslau. With some two thousand recorded cases, the prosecutions in the territories of Cologne and Westphalia represented the zenith of witch-burnings. Among those who advanced the most authoritative and influential Catholic views on witches were the Trier bishop and jurist Peter Binsfeld in *Tractatus de confessionibus maleficorum et sagarum* (Treatise on the Confessions of Witches and Magicians, 1589), the Jesuit Martin Del Rio in *Disquisitionum magicarum libri sex* (Six Books of Disquisitions on Witches, 1599), and the French jurist Henri Boguet, who, in his *Discours des sorciers* (Discourse on Witches, 1602), reported the prosecutions in Franche-Comté. Also influential beyond the borders of France was the *Daemonolatria* (Demonolatry, 1595) by Nicolas Remy, *procureur général* of the duchy of Lorraine,[35] and Pierre Crespet's tract *Deux livres de la hayne de Sathan et malins Esprits contre l'homme* (Two Books on the Hatred of Satan and Evil Spirits Against Mankind, 1590). Crespet vigorously inveighed against Protestantism—which he considered a satanic heresy—much as Pierre de Lancre would do a few years later.

Significantly influenced by the demonologists mentioned, and many more, was Pierre de Lancre, jurist at the court of Henry IV, who wrote at length about his witch-hunting expedition to the Basque region of the French Pyrenees in 1609.[36] While de Lancre was absolutely convinced of the reality of the witch and her danger to the state, his vigorously argued legal tract can also be read as an ethnological exploration of the Labourt region and its Basque inhabitants. Moreover, de Lancre constructed one of the most vivid descriptions of the witches' sabbath, including the image of children being presented with toads in velvet suits, to be guarded while their parents amused themselves with the unspeakable pleasures of the sabbath feast.[37] On the basis of trial testimony, de Lancre believed that the witches' sabbath was ongoing but visible only to the witches themselves; that the Basque witch flew over the oceans causing storms and sinking ships; and that she made harvests wither. Few demonologists blended popular and learned witch beliefs as effectively as did de Lancre. Moreover, he firmly believed witches to be a threat to the body politic, offering a detailed argument as to why secular magistrates and the government had to move with firmness and vigour against the menace witches posed. He reviewed in detail the role and importance of the translator in conveying the experiences of the Basque witches to the French-speaking magistrates. And he also expressed intense anxiety that important information might get lost if the translator was not expert in the Basque language or, worse, if he mistranslated witness testimony in order to protect the witch against prosecution.

[35] Nicolas Remy, *Demonolatry*, tr. E. A. Ashwin and ed. Montague Summers (London, 1930).

[36] Pierre de Lancre, *On the Inconstancy of Witches: Pierre de Lancre's Tableau de l'inconstance des mauvais angese et demons (1612)*, ed. Gerhild Scholz Williams (Tempe, AZ, 2005).

[37] De Lancre, *On the Inconstancy of Witches*, 399–401.

The fact that, relatively late in the century, the Flemish Reformed pastor and demonologist Bartholomäus Anhorn still based his demonology, entitled *Magiologia* (On Magic, 1674), to a significant degree on both the *Malleus* and on Del Rio's *Disquisitiones*, confirms that the differences between Catholics and Protestants regarding the remedies believed to be efficacious against witchcraft were only a matter of degree.[38] Both meant to empower the authorities to seek out witches and bring them to justice. Furthermore, the Catholic Church remained committed to exorcisms and to other sacramental and ritualistic remedies when seeking help for the witch. While Protestants prosecuted with comparable vigour, these therapies against satanic power were not available to them.[39]

Leading Catholic voices against witchcraft prosecutions include the Jesuit Friedrich von Spee in *Cautio Criminalis oder Rechtliches Bedencken wegen der Hexenprozesse* (Precautions in Criminal Matters, or juridical caution concerning witch trials, 1631) and Adam Tanner, theologian at Ingolstadt, in *Tractatus theologicus de processu adversus crimina excepta, ac speciatim adversus crimen venefici* (Treatise on the Trying of Exceptional Crimes, particularly the crime of witchcraft, 1629). While not denying the reality of Satan and his minions in his *Cautio Criminalis*, Spee, one of the great stylists of the Baroque period, composed a forceful critique of trial procedures in cases of witchcraft, specifically of the practise of torture. The Lutheran theologian from Erfurt, Matthäus Meyfart, in *Christliche erinnerung [. . .] wie das abschewliche Laster der Hexerey mit Ernst auszurotten* (Christian Admonition [. . .] on seriously extinguishing the abominable sin of witchcraft, 1666), also raised his voice in defence of the woman accused of being a witch. To the tracts against the torture and burning of the witch must be added Hermann Löher's *Hochnötige unterthanige wemütige Klage der frommen Unschültigen* (The Sad Complaint of the Faithful Innocents, 1676), which contained a number of subsequently popular illustrations of the treatment and plight of the witch. In 1668, when the Leipzig author Johannes Praetorius published his tract *Blockes-Berges Verrichtung* (Witches' Actions at the Blockberg), the number of tracts devoted to Satan, the witch, and her demonic proclivities had grown to about sixty sources, many of them well-known tracts. Praetorius' list constituted a cross section of all that was written up to this time about demons and witches.[40]

Demonologies also influenced less scholarly writings on witches and demons, such Johann Greater's *Hexen oder Unholden Predigten* (Sermons on Witches and Devils, 1599), David Meder's *Acht Hexenpredigten* (Eight Sermons on Witches, 1605), or

[38] Ursula Bigler-Brunold, ed., *Teufelsmacht und Hexenwerk: Lehrmeinungen und Exempel in der 'Magiologia' des Bartholomäus Anhorn (1616–1700)* (Chur, 2003).
[39] Keith Thomas, *Religion and the Decline of Magic: Studies in Popular Beliefs in Sixteenth and Seventeenth Century England* (London, 1971).
[40] Johannes Praetorius, *Blockes-Berges Verrichtung, oder, ausführlicher geographischer Bericht von den hohen trefflich alt- und berühmten Blockes-Berge; Ingleichen von der Hexenfahrt, und Zauber-Sabbathe* (Leipzig, 1668; repr. Aldershot, 2006), 142–4.

Joachim Zehner's *Fünf Predigten von den Hexen* (Five Sermons on Witches, 1613). Moreover, many pamphlets about witch trials and executions were in constant circulation, contributing to an extensive public reception of the elaborated witch image. Collections of demonologies, sermons, and discussions of controversial issues relating to witchcraft were read in all quarters of Europe. Most well known among these collections were the *Theatrum diabolorum* (Theatre of Demons) of 1569 and the already mentioned *Theatrum de veneficis* of 1586. In 1569, the Frankfurt am Main printer Sigmund Feyerabend gathered twenty devil tracts into a folio volume, the *Theatrum diabolorum*. Following this first folio edition, Feyerabend produced a second and third edition in 1575 and 1587/8, respectively.[41] Individual devils were assigned to specific sinful behaviours falling into three thematic groups: moral sins and evil habits (drinking, fashion, cursing, gambling, hunting, stinginess, sloth, arrogance, dancing, flattery, lying, swearing, and melancholy); matrimony and family; and demonology and church life, concerning the use of black magic in relation to salvation.

In turn, the tracts that make up the later *Theatrum de veneficis* covered the whole spectrum of reactions to the witch phenomenon, including severe condemnation as espoused by the Genevan pastor Lambert Daneau in *Dialogus de veneficiis* (A Dialogue with Witches, 1564) and the pastor Jacob Vallick in *Von Zäuberern/ Hexen/und Unholden* (On Magicians, Witches, and Demons). Writers who doubted the witch's ability to commit the acts with which he/she had been charged are also represented. This conviction was forcefully expressed by Hermann Witekind in *Bedencken von Zauberey/woher was/und wie vielfältig sie sey, etc.* (Admonition on the Practise of Magic: where it comes from and how widespread it is, etc., 1585) and Johannes Fischart in *Etliche Bedencken und Rathschläge* (Some Reservations and Advice, 1590).

Several years later, in the early eighteenth century, the work by Leipzig jurist and philosopher Christian Thomasius, *De crimine magiae* (On the Crime of Magic, 1701), also expressed criticism regarding superstition and unjust prosecution of those already weakened by old age and social marginalization. Finally, the *De Betoverde Weereld* (The Bewitched World, 1691/3) by the Dutch Calvinist pastor Balthasar Bekker (1634–1698) moved beyond assessments critical of witch trials to outright denial of Satan's power over people and material things. While dissertations about the efficacy of demons and their dalliances with humans beings continued to be written and defended—renewed interest in the occult surfaced as late as the nineteenth century—the era of the broadly accepted and influential demonology, be it in support of or against the prosecution of witches, had come to an end at last by the mid-nineteenth century.

---

[41] Ria Stambaugh, ed., *Teufelbücher in Auswahl*, 5 vols (Berlin, 1970–80); Heinrich Grimm, 'Die deutschen "Teufelbücher" des 16. Jahrhunderts: Ihre Rolle im Buchwesen und ihre Bedeutung', *Archiv für die Geschichte des Buchwesens*, 2 (1960), 513–70.

FURTHER READING

Baron, Frank, ed., *Herman Witekinds Christlich Bedencken und die Entstehung des Faustbuchs von 1587* (Berlin, 2009).

Clark, Stuart, *Thinking with Demons: The Idea of Witchcraft in Early Modern Europe* (Oxford, 1997).

Coumont, Jean-Pierre, ed., *Demonology and Witchcraft: An Annotated Bibliography with Related Works on Magic, Medicine, Superstition, Etc.* (Brussels, 2004).

Hults, Linda C., *The Witch as Muse: Art, Gender, and Power in Early Modern Europe* (Philadelphia, PA, 2005).

Johnstone, Nathan, *The Devil and Demonism in Early Modern England* (Cambridge, 2006).

Mackay, Christopher S., ed., *Malleus Maleficarum*, 2 vols (Cambridge, 2006).

Maggi, Armando, *In the Company of Demons: Unnatural Beings, Love, and Identity in the Italian Renaissance* (Chicago, 2006).

Maxwell-Stuart, P. G., ed., *The Malleus Maleficarum: Selected, Translated, and Annotated* (Manchester, 2007).

Redden, Andrew, *Diabolism in Colonial Peru, 1500–1750* (London, 2008).

Roper, Lyndal, *Witch Craze: Terror and Fantasy in Baroque Germany* (New Haven, CT, 2004).

Stephens, Walter, *Demon Lovers: Witchcraft, Sex, and the Crisis of Belief* (Chicago, 2002).

Waite, Gary K., *Eradicating the Devil's Minions: Anabaptists and Witches in Reformation Europe, 1525–1600* (Toronto, 2008).

Williams, Gerhild Scholz, *Defining Dominion: The Discourses of Magic and Witchcraft in Early Modern France and Germany* (Ann Arbor, MI, 1995).

Williams, Gerhild Scholz, ed., *On the Inconstancy of Witches: Pierre De Lancre's Tableau de l'inconstance des mauvais anges et demons (1612)*, (Tempe, AZ, 2005).

Wootton, David, ed., *Doctor Faustus with the English Faustbook/Christopher Marlow* (Indianapolis, IN, 2005).

CHAPTER 5

···

SABBATH STORIES:
TOWARDS A NEW HISTORY
OF WITCHES' ASSEMBLIES

···

WILLEM DE BLÉCOURT

THE witches' sabbath (also spelled 'sabbat')[1] is generally regarded as the cultural precondition of most large witch-hunts. If the notion of an individual act of bewitchment came to imply an individual pact with the devil and thus a token of apostasy, a congregation of witches hinted at something far worse: an organized but clandestine sect aiming to overthrow Christendom. At least this was the view of early modern demonologists. On the whole witchcraft historians concur and refer to witchcraft as a 'super crime', a gigantic conspiracy against the Christian community by a 'plague of witches'.[2] In early modern European practice the idea of the sabbath led prosecuting authorities to extend the search for witches from the suspect in custody to a much larger group of accomplices. The usual method was to ask the suspect under torture who else had participated in the sabbath or, as it was sometimes called, 'the dance'. The success of a judicial investigation could be measured by the number of named accomplices.

At the outset it is useful to discern two kinds of witches' sabbaths: that of historians and that of the historical actors. The two are, of course, not completely unrelated, and ultimately the picture painted by historians should represent the contemporary concept fairly accurately. So far, the complexity of the subject has prevented this. Ever since Joseph Hansen referred to the 'cumulative concept' of witchcraft, its sabbath core was combined with bewitchments (*maleficia* from the theorists' perspective), the pact with

---

[1] Some historians prefer the originally French *sabbat* to distinguish between the meeting of witches and the day of worship ('sabbath') in Christian and Jewish religions.

[2] Walter Rummel and Rita Voltmer, *Hexen und Hexenverfolgung in der Frühen Neuzeit* (Darmstadt, 2008), 18; P. G. Maxwell-Stuart, *Witchcraft: A History* (Stroud, 2004), 73.

the devil, and the witch's flight; this whole edifice was thought to have been current throughout Europe from the late Middle Ages to the eighteenth century. Yet it took decades, possibly centuries, to develop: different elements occurred in different forms and some were conspicuously absent at times. When, for instance, the witches' mode of transport to the gathering was incorporated, it obviously mattered whether they flew or walked, since the former enabled a much larger attendance. Flight was the aspect most heatedly discussed and doubted. Another element, the witch's metamorphosis into an animal 'was never fully integrated' into the larger picture; it was not essential for securing a conviction and related more to the individual rather than the collective image of the witch.[3] As a way of thinking about witchcraft, the 'cumulative concept' thus carries its own limitations, especially when it obscures local developments.

The sabbath itself was never a unified, coherent construct either. When presented in general terms it easily verged on the extreme in the writings of demonologists and historians alike. Thus Carlo Ginzburg started his book on the 'roots' of the sabbath with the following description:

> Male and female witches met at night, generally in solitary places, in fields or on mountains. Sometimes, having anointed their bodies, they flew, arriving astride poles or broomsticks; sometimes they arrived on the back of animals, or transformed into animals themselves. Those who came for the first time had to renounce the Christian faith, desecrate the sacrament and offer homage to the devil, who was present in human or (most often) animal or semi-animal form. There would follow banquets, dancing, sexual orgies. Before returning home the female and male witches received evil ointments made from children's fat and other ingredients.[4]

Although this summary appears to contain all the major elements of the sabbath, it is in fact a late twentieth-century construction. The element of cannibalism is missing, and it includes shapeshifting, which, although extremely rare in sixteenth- and seventeenth-century sabbath descriptions, suited Ginzburg's theory. The gender of the participants was not always simply 'male and female'; the markedly different numbers of men and women prosecuted in specific times and places depended ultimately on trial dynamics. The testimony of individual witches, moreover, often introduced details of activities at the sabbath that did not conform to either Ginzburg's or any other general description of these assemblies. Judicial questionnaires were used in a procedural system that included torture, but they imposed only a certain measure of uniformity on the witches' answers. Demonological compilations were abstracts by their very nature, and were rarely concerned with the validity of generalizations. This is clearly shown by Jan Ziarnko's 1613 illustration of the sabbath, which was included in Pierre de Lancre's early seventeenth-century defence of witchcraft prosecution in the Labourd. This engraving depicts twelve different scenes of activities at the sabbath, conveniently numbered for reference to the text beneath. Among them are a court scene, with the

---

[3] Brian P. Levack, *The Witch-Hunt in Early Modern Europe* (3rd edn, Harlow, 2006), *passim*.
[4] Carlo Ginzburg, *Ecstasies: Deciphering the Witches' Sabbath* (London 1990), 1.

enthroned devil in the shape of a goat, two scenes with dancing witches, child witches herding toads, a number of flying witches on brooms and a goat, and witches preparing poisons for their bewitchments.

The sabbath may represent the opposite of the Christian state, 'hell on earth', and a 'parody of court'. In that way it may be read as a 'demonic rule of misrule', but even the principle of inversion, so eloquently evoked by Stuart Clark, cannot be taken as completely accurate, for in some regions descriptions of the sabbath reflected rather than subverted social relations. The historian Robin Briggs thus prefers the expression 'partial inversion'.[5] A black mass figured in the famous case (1609–11) of the French priest Louis Gaufridy, together with 'devil worship, sexual orgies, the feeding of the Host to dogs and the eating of young children';[6] its appearance in other trial records, however, was inversely proportional to its renown. In Lorraine, it quite possibly only surfaced in a rare trial record because a twelve-year-old boy was asked leading questions. It is also sharply contrasted with what is to be found in the average witch trial, where the sabbath was much more subdued, that is, reduced to a 'dance', with less stress on devil worship. The historical concept of the sabbath was fragmented and subject to diversity as well as change. Can it then be maintained that there were enough similar features to deduce a common origin and argue that its dissemination occurred mainly through learned channels?

A challenge of the commonplace opinions of the witches' sabbath would ideally be predicated on a careful reading of actual trial records. But, as an overview like this can only be based on secondary material, its conclusions must remain tentative. Furthermore, detailed descriptions of sabbaths, as well as analyses of the ways they were produced, are not as abundant as might be expected from the huge number of early modern witch trials. One of the paradoxes of historical witchcraft studies is that the sabbath—the presumed attendance at which was the most prominent charge against witches—has hardly been pursued as a proper topic of historical research. One reason for this is the focus on social and political history, another, the problematic nature of the major forays into the origins of the sabbath, and yet another the sheer quantity of trial records.

5.1 APPROACHES

The historiography of the sabbath shows a disturbing preoccupation with a search for 'reality' in several forms. A focus on historical roots, whether as a form of matriarchy,

    [5] Robin Briggs, *The Witches of Lorraine* (Oxford, 2007), 146. On inversion see Stuart Clark, *Thinking with Demons: The Idea of Witchcraft in Early Modern Europe* (Oxford, 1997), *passim*.
    [6] Sarah Ferber, *Demonic Possession and Exorcism in Early Modern France* (London, 2004), 80–1; Robert Mandrou, *Magistrats et sorciers en France au XVIIe siècle: Une analyse de psychologie historique* (Paris, 1968), 198–210.

paganistic rite, or shamanistic journey, has to remain hypothetical and does not concern itself with its many manifestations in the trial records of the early modern period.[7] Neither is the opposite approach, a stress on early modern daily life experience very helpful to explain the sabbath's more fantastical features. Certainly, an 'obsession among historians for accentuating the few heretical, diabolical or lewd elements of a testimony' tends to obscure 'the more numerous ordinary details', but the latter are fairly well known and it is debatable whether they contributed to the diffusion of the sabbath concept.[8] Likewise, it is dubious whether the mundane gatherings described in sabbath testimonies can be interpreted as having been 'imbued with or involved rites with magico-religious significance themselves'.[9] After all, most of these 'normal' descriptions seem to refer to ordinary feasts or weddings rather than carnivals or other semi-religious rites within the annual cycle.

To reduce the sabbath to delirium, dreams, or the product of hallucinogens ultimately amounts to abandoning history altogether. Even when specific 'cultural' translations of such experiences are considered, they still fail to take sufficient account of the interplay between local knowledge and theological interpretation, which sometimes defined sabbath accounts as illusions of the devil in the first place. Several authors have wondered whether other 'facts' lurked behind descriptions of the sabbath, especially the sexual encounters that were one of their most prominent features. These theories have remained speculative. In her study of the Gaufridy case, Sarah Ferber remarked that the medical model 'always seems to default to the female victim in the search for pathology' while the exorcists, and, one could add, the prosecutors, are left off the hook.[10] The search for an underlying 'reality' has usually served to obscure the main event in its different contemporary guises.

Some of this discussion was already conducted at the time when opponents of witch trials characterized the sabbath as 'illusion' or 'fantasy'. Opinions of both advocates and opponents oscillated between accepting the sabbath as a dream or reality, while a number of demonologists even managed to take both positions. Walter Stephens observed that their engagement with the activities of demons was 'entwined with the reality of Christian faith', and proof of the devil was logically strengthening it.[11] While the early modern discussion centred on the capacity of the devil to fool the human senses, the present-day view primarily reflects historians' unease assessing the less factual aspects of the past—hence, one may argue, the explanations of witchcraft and, more specifically, witch trials, in terms of social tensions, political power, economic

---

[7] Willem de Blécourt, 'The Return of the Sabbat', in Jonathan Barry and Owen Davies, eds, *Palgrave Advances in Witchcraft Historiography* (Basingstoke, 2007), 125–45.

[8] Jonathan Durrant, *Witchcraft, Gender and Society in Early Modern Germany* (Leiden, 2007), 146.

[9] Edward Bever, *The Realities of Witchcraft and Popular Magic in Early Modern Europe: Culture, Cognition, and Everyday Life* (Basingstoke, 2008), esp. 93–150.

[10] Sarah Ferber, 'The Abuse of History: Identity Politics, Disordered Identity and the "Really Real" in French Cases of Demonic Possession', in Susan Broomhall and Stephanie Tarbin, eds, *Women, Identities and Communities in Early Modern Europe* (Aldershot, 2008), 29–41.

[11] Walter Stephens, *Demon Lovers: Witchcraft, Sex, and the Crisis of Belief* (Chicago, 2002), 22.

hardship, or even unfavourable weather conditions. Earlier attempts to interpret sabbath accounts as references to fertility cults, too, are exemplary of the desire to reduce what dechristianized academics consider fantastic to something more familiar and malleable.

A different approach considers the sabbath as a story; from the comfortable distance of the twenty-first century, it is argued that it is the historical presence ('reality') of the story that is at stake, rather than its interpretation as a reference to social ritual or individual experience. When demonologists took short stories that were adapted to fit a hegemonical witchcraft discourse as independent corroboration of actual meetings, then these stories' reference to some other 'reality' can be bracketed. At the beginning of the seventeenth century the Burgundian judge Henry Boguet remarked, for instance:

> There have even been cases of persons who were not witches, but have, following the example of and at the instigation of witches, rubbed themselves with a certain ointment, and of farmers, who have been transported to as much as a hundred or two hundred leagues from their homes, so that they have had great difficulty in finding their way back again.[12]

This type of story is known among folklorists as 'Following the Witch',[13] and one of its main characteristics is the gendered role division: a man tries to re-enact a witch's movements and finds himself in a gathering of women from which he then has to escape. It is part of a larger complex that can be labelled as intruder legends. Reading such contemporary evidence for the reality of the sabbath primarily as a story has the advantage of avoiding the historical pitfall of substituting theory for proof. It is probably also more historically accurate to deal with the concept of the sabbath on a narrative level, especially within a Christian context where stories, *exempla*, formed the basic tenets of people's worldview. One of the main questions to be asked is: whose story is it? The answer has to be situated in time and space. Once the stories started to function as legitimation of prosecutions, their direct source mattered much more than where they had originated.

Lyndal Roper, who in the late 1980s helped to bring the analysis of trial accounts back on the agenda, asserted that 'the tales of witches' doings were never the creation of demonologists alone. Information about what witches' confessed...constantly fed back into works of demonology', through 'a process of dialogue'. The authorities, according to Roper, 'translated the amorphous fears of the peasants into an organized, exhaustive questionnaire for suspected witches that omitted no element of the witch-craft fantasy'. In her view, 'interrogators knew when a confession was simply a result of torture or its fear', which they would continue until a 'consistent' confession emerged. With a reference to the cultural significance of pain, Roper thus argues away the 'stereotyped products' (including the sabbath) in the mind of the interrogators, their

---

[12] Henry Boguet, *An Examen of Witches*, tr. E. Allen Ashwin (London, 1929), 41.

[13] An international catalogue of the migratory legends is lacking, cf. Reidar Th. Christiansen, *The Migratory Legends* (Helsinki, 1958), no. 3045.

'leading questions', and ultimately the power relations within the torture chamber. She more or less turned the prosecutor into an early modern version of the modern analyst. Although her basic assumption about the origin of the demonological tales appears reasonable, the rest of her approach is hard to follow. The word 'dialogue' obscures the very unequal power relation between suspect and interrogator, and the answers elicited under torture are more accurately understood as desperate responses to counter both the threat of torture and torture itself. The exchange between interrogator and suspect is much better characterized as a 'tragic misunderstanding'. Roper also ignores existing stories, such as those about witches' flight, which, because they were already circula- ting outside the prison, had very little to do with a perspective obtained while experi- encing pain, as she suggests.[14] Briggs has observed that sabbaths were only mentioned in the confessions of witches and were virtually absent in the depositions of witnesses, but Roper prefers to dwell on what she perceives as the symbolic significance of sabbaths and encounters with demons rather than the concepts themselves.

It is well-nigh impossible to escape the model of superimposed sabbath stories and search for the suspects' underlying fears and feelings. The effort nevertheless forces witchcraft historians to take seriously what only a generation earlier had been dis- missed as the ramblings of mad witch-hunters. The frame story of the sabbath was provided by demonologists, who, when they also acted as judges, enriched it with details elicited from their suspects. Local authorities may nevertheless have used it for their own purposes—such as to strengthen their secular or religious power—as the most atrocious witch trials occurred in places where there was no sharp division between the two. Witchcraft theory worked as a discourse in the Foucauldian sense as it absorbed everything in its orbit and remained firmly in the hands of the powerful. Witchcraft accusations and witchcraft prosecution were at times also driven by 'popu- lar' witchcraft discourse, which contained no mention of demons or sabbaths, and focused on the harm done by witches. So far witchcraft studies have not yet given the interplay between the two the attention it deserves.

The struggle to make sense of sabbath stories concentrates on the issue of coherence, which has a considerable history. When, in the late seventeenth century, the Massa- chusetts minister Cotton Mather described the Blåkulla case (see below), he stressed that the 'declarations' of the different participants 'all agreed...with what other Witches, in other places had confessed'. In his view this made the case more convin- cing; he was not interested in how these similarities arose.[15] However, the construction of an all-encompassing picture of the sabbath could still be a frustrating undertaking, as De Lancre discovered. He emphasized the 'inconstancy' of demons and witches, that is, the variability in what one could know about them. From the start the intellectual

[14] Lyndal Roper, *Witch Craze: Terror and Fantasy in Baroque Germany* (New Haven, CT, 2004), 29, 106–7; Roper, 'Witchcraft and Fantasy in Early Modern Germany', in *Oedipus and the Devil* (London, 1994), 199–225. See the review by Rainer Walz in *H-Soz-u-Kult*, 18 December 2007, <http://hsozkult. geschichte.hu-berlin.de/rezensionen/2007-4-223> (accessed 31 August 2012).
[15] Cotton Mather, *The Wonders of the Invisible World* (London, 1862), 168.

sabbath story was compartmentalized, broken up into its constitutive elements, such as devil worship, dancing, cannibalism, and flight. Later historians who showed any interest in the sabbath pursued a similar investigation by, for example, listing all the different names of the devil or the various places where the witches met. This meant that the different elements in the sabbath stories were decontextualized, and potential links between them were lost.

Approaching the sabbath as a series of stories would mean looking at individual narrative events, be it an interrogation in the torture chamber or the reading of a demonological book, or in whatever other circumstance the sabbath had became a conversation topic. It would imply taking account of the power relations between the participants and the ways each particular story was produced and constructed. The combining of elements from separate events, beyond what had already been established at the time, would obfuscate rather than reveal the historical construct. Better to ask questions about the dissemination of particular sabbath stories; providing answers to them is another matter.

5.2 EARLY INSTANCES

A number of different strands contributed to the notion of the witches' sabbath. Witchcraft itself had always been an individual crime, often ascribed to women and, on an everyday-life level, devoid of any association with the devil. The spells and rituals of male magicians, on the other hand, explicitly involved the assistance of demons. None operated in groups. First, demonologists constructed a concept of witchcraft by conflating and demonizing magical practices. The notion of witches' assemblies evolved from the merging of the prosecution of genuine groups of heretics with stories of the so-called 'good people'; certainly the latter provided the intrusion narratives.

Early reports of witches' meetings venerating the devil have turned out to be falsifications.[16] Only the 1324 Irish case of Dame Alice Kyteler contains some elements of the later stereotype, but it was primarily a heresy trial.[17] It is more rewarding to search for predecessors of the witches' sabbath in literary sources. The late thirteenth-century *Roman de la Rose*, among other texts, makes mention of the 'estries' (lamia, elves; sometimes erroneously translated as 'witches' or 'sorcerers') who roam around with Lady Abundance (Abonde, Abondia, Obonde) and the *bones dames* (good women), and who penetrate into people's houses through the smallest of openings.

---

[16] Compare the first edition of Alan C. Kors and Edward M. Peters, eds, *Witchcraft in Europe, 1100–1700* (Philadelphia, PA, 1972) with the second edition of 2001. The fictitious 'witches of Stedlingerland' (1232) on pp. 48–9 of the first edition are also omitted.

[17] Anne Neary, 'The Origins and Character of the Kilkenny Witchcraft Case of 1324', *Proceedings of the Royal Irish Academy*, 83C (1983), 333–50; L. S. Davidson and J. O. Ward, eds, *The Sorcery Trial of Alice Kyteler: A Contemporary Account (1324)* (Binghamton, NY, 1993).

Not only was the *Roman* hugely popular, but its imagery was echoed in a number of other works. That is hardly proof of its earlier dissemination, however, notwithstanding a reference to 'roaming women' in the tenth-century canon *Episcopi*.

It remains uncertain whether these figures should be understood to be spirits or humans, ritualistic or imaginary, fairies, deities, or demons, or some combination of these. The imagery of the 'good women' did, however, provide several characteristics that facilitated their merging with later witchcraft concepts, such as their gender, nightly forays, and second bodies. In all likelihood, the imagery also pertained to the notion of flying, the more so when the 'women' were reported to go out as spirits. The image of the 'good women' as a group was eventually incorporated into that of the witches. In the late thirteenth century the two were still separate: in the equally popular *Legenda Aurea*, for example, St Germain encountered a dish set for the 'good women'; they turned out to be neighbours in spirit form, an early variant of the intruder legend. But when in 1418–19 a German (Alsatian) version of the *Aurea* was written, the spirits were turned into demons.[18] St Germain was also said to have performed the bone miracle on a calf, a feat that likewise occurred at the meetings of the 'good women' around 1400.

At the close of the fourteenth century, Lombardy inquisitors arrested two women who had joined the 'good people' of the society of Oriente, with whom they roamed through houses. 'Her [Oriente's] followers sometimes slaughtered oxen and ate their meat; then they gathered the bones and put them inside the skin of the dead animals. Oriente would then strike the skin with the pommel of her wand, and the oxen were instantly revived; but they were no longer capable of working.'[19] Through this affiliation the two women were able to function as cunning women, and conveyed stories like this to their clients to support their authority. In their search for truth, a number of theologians, Dominicans and Franciscans in particular, took these stories for histories. They then proceeded not only to declare their interpretation of the stories as final, but also forced it onto the people in their care. One of the women confessed that she had made a pact with a spirit named Lucifello, who had taken her to the 'games'. In early 1428, during the trial of another cunning woman, Matteuccia di Francesco of Umbrian Todi, a similar transition occurred. Prompted by the Franciscan Bernardino di Siena, she finally confessed to have been taken by the demon Lucibello to the gathering of witches at the walnut tree of Benevento, where Lucifer held court.[20]

Scholars differ as to how this case fits precisely into the general development of the sabbath concept. Richard Kieckhefer, who initially categorized it as one of the first

---

[18] Hans Peter Broedel, *The Malleus Maleficarum and the Construction of Witchcraft: Theology and Popular Belief* (Manchester, 2003), 101ff.; Christa Agnes Tuczay, *Ekstase im Kontext: Mittelalterliche und neuere Diskurse einer Entgrenzungserfahrung* (Frankfurt, 2009), 413–54.

[19] Ginzburg, *Ecstasies*, 92–3. See Wolfgang Behringer, *Shaman of Oberstdorf: Chonrad Stoeckhlin and the Phantoms of the Night* (Charlottesville, VA, 1998), for further examples.

[20] Domenico Mammoli, *The Record of the Trial and Condemnation of a Witch, Matteuccia di Francesco, at Todi* (Rome, 1972); Franco Mormando, *The Preacher's Demons: Bernardino of Siena and the Social Underworld of Early Renaissance Italy* (Chicago, 1999), 72–7.

examples of what he called 'diabolism', later qualified his opinion by assigning it to a marginal position in terms of imagery, compared with the central fifteenth-century Italian witchcraft 'mythology', which he now situated in Perugia. This 'Umbrian paradigm' consisted of a sharing of regional concepts by inquisitors and populace alike, and remained unaffected by sabbath interpretations. Kieckhefer also deemed the trials in which ladies like Oriente and Abunda figured as 'only incidentally connected with the mainstream of early witch trials'.[21] The popular/elite dichotomy that played a major part in his earlier work has turned into a more intricate model of different local cultures and international derivations. But such subtlety does not have to replace a fundamental difference between theological and inquisitorial interpretations on the one hand, and local or regional concepts on the other. It can leave both the notion and the motion of superimposed 'elite' interpretations untouched. A more complex model does, however, alert the student to matters of communication.

A convincing case has been made for considering the mixture of trials and treatises in the western Alps shortly before and during the years of the Council of Basel (1431–49) as the site where all the different popular and theological approaches converged to produce sabbath imagery dominant enough to extend its influence over the rest of Europe.[22] Initially it was the Vaudois or Waldensian version of the sabbath, as it was elaborated in the *Errores Gazariorum* (The Errors of the Waldensians), that was exported. Satan presided in some animal form, initiates kissed him, and they were given magic potions made from the exhumed bodies of children, which they also consumed. Witches also flew to their meetings on anointed brooms and participated in orgies. The image of these gatherings was very similar to those of heretics, but was augmented with bewitchments such as the magical raising of storms and hail. Later, Johannes Nider's *Formicarius* had more of an impact. He treated the flight as an illusion and did not discuss orgies.

One of the strengths of the Council of Basel was that it produced different emphases by different authors. Lay authors such as Hans Fründ and Claude Tholosan were particularly interested in the political dimension; the Dominican Nider sought to convey moral lessons, and the Franciscan Ponce Feugeyron, who may have been the author of the *Errores*, specialized in writing against heretical ideas. In his *Le champion des dames* Martin Le Franc referred only briefly to witches' assemblies, in an effort to amuse his readers.[23] The exact relationship between the collective concept of the 'good

---

[21] Richard Kieckhefer, 'Mythologies of Witchcraft in the Fifteenth Century', *Magic, Ritual and Witchcraft*, 1 (2006), 79–108.

[22] Michael D. Bailey and Edward Peters, 'A Sabbath of Demonologists: Basel, 1431–1440', *The Historian*, 65 (2003), 1375–96; Wolfgang Behringer, *Witches and Witch Hunts: A Global History* (Cambridge, 2004), 61–9.

[23] Michael Bailey, 'The Medieval Concepts of the Witches' Sabbath', *Exemplaria*, 8 (1996), 419–39; Martine Ostorero, 'The Concept of the Witches' Sabbath in the Alpine Region (1430–1440): Text and Context', in Gábor Klaniczay and Éva Pócs, eds, *Witchcraft Mythologies and Persecutions* (Budapest, 2008), 15–34. See texts in Martine Ostorero, Agostino Paravicini Bagliani, and Kathrin Utz Tremp, eds, *L'imaginaire du sabbat* (Lausanne, 1999).

women' or the 'society of the game', of which several more examples occurred just before the Swiss trials in northern Italy and the adjacent Austrian Alp, is unclear. Witches' meetings as recorded in the context of the Council of Basel await further research, but an exchange of ideas and information between inquisitors no doubt played a role.[24]

None of these early fifteenth-century examples used the word 'sabbath'. Instead authors wrote about the witches' *societas*, or *consilium*, or *ludum*. In the *Errores* the term *synagoga* was applied. Sabbat, then spelled without an 'h', only made its appearance in the mid-fifteenth century in France; it occurred in a 1446 trial, and the term subsequently surfaced in the work of theorists such as Jacquier (writing in 1458) and Mamoris (1462).[25] It became the main word for the witches' gathering in the works of the late sixteenth-century French demonologists, including Bodin, Remy, and Boguet.

There was also little in the directives emerging from the Council of Basil that referred to meetings with a mysterious female entity. Apart from her replacement by the devil, the main reason for this absence was that the 'good people' belonged to the canon *Episcopi* tradition, which declared them to be illusory, a position demonologists were not always eager to refute. But they kept copying texts in which the *ludus bonae societas* figured, as well as the story of the visits to the tree of Benevento, which later found a place in literary texts. In a parallel development, the 'good people' kept being mentioned in the occasional trial against cunning folk.[26]

5.3 INTRUSION STORIES

Sketches of late sixteenth- and seventeenth-century sabbaths are usually based on regional research into trial records. As a result, they vary in more ways than the time and locality of the assemblies. Many French sabbath accounts are linked to cases of demonic possession while demons disguised as monks appear in a Portuguese example, and toads are typical in the Basque Labourd. Within the German-speaking jurisdictions alone, four different, albeit general, forms of sabbath have been indicated. According to the cultural historian Richard van Dülmen, the role of the devil increased in subsequent sabbath descriptions. Alhough still marginal in relation to bewitchments, mid-sixteenth-century sabbath imagery, he argued, involved more women than in the fifteenth century; they apparently received their ointment from the devil, who participated at their feast and flew along with them when they were causing harm. At the beginning of the seventeenth century the demonic pact and sexual relations with the devil had become more prominent, and the sabbath sometimes featured a wedding

---

[24] Niklaus Schatzmann, *Verdorrende Bäume und Brote wie Kuhfladen: Hexenprozesse in der Leventina 1431–1459 und die Anfänge der Hexenverfolgung auf der Alpensüdseite* (Zurich, 2003), 245–8.

[25] Michael D. Bailey, *Magic and Superstition in Europe* (Lanham, MD, 2007), 135.

[26] Behringer, *Shaman of Oberstdorf*, ch. 9.

between witches and their demons. The end of the century finally saw the devil enthroned at the centre of a satanic ritual, complete with a black mass and sexual orgies.[27] Van Dülmen's assessment, however, was based on selected trial accounts, and he represented specific verdicts as paradigmatic texts. Moreover, he largely ignored specific details, such as diabolic baptism, the presence of a musician, a military display, or the presiding of a queen (next to the devil). His choices can therefore be questioned and his conclusions adjusted: instead of a single development there may have been several more or less simultaneous ones. As none of the sixteenth- and seventeenth-century accounts replicated the earlier ones very closely, some sort of change in the imagery must surely have occurred. But more or less coherent narratives only emerged in judicial verdicts, so more attention needs to be paid to their production.

At an earlier stage of a trial there were questions, many questions. In the section about the witches' dance, a list from Sachse-Coburg of 1629 includes questions about length, frequency, and place; whether they ate or drank first, what they ate, how it tasted, how they danced, with whom, in what order, how the light was, who the musicians were. Only after about twenty such questions did interrogators ask whether the witches worshipped the devil. They were then instructed to find out who else was present at the gathering and whether the suspect would recognize them. An enquiry regarding how the witch had arrived at the dance and whether she had flown through the air followed almost as an afterthought.[28] In different jurisdictions the questions and their sequence were probably different, and only the preparatory phase of the interrogation was recorded. In practice there were repetitions, pauses, and renewed sessions, even interlocutory verdicts, which show how answers were coerced, adjusted, and denied. To quote a small but telling example in 1627, Blankenheim:

> Question: How had she arrived at the dance place?
> Answer: The evil one had brought her there on a white goat.
> {After she had been admonished diligently and threatened with strict questions}:
> On what did the evil one carry her?
> Answer: On a black billy goat.[29]

The witch was not allowed to diverge from previous accounts, and her devil could not be white and female. It also needs to be kept in mind that notes of an interrogation and final reports did not have to correspond. A verdict was arrived at the end of a lengthy process that was completely controlled by the interrogators; while a suspect was there to fill in the blanks, it remains doubtful how much she (or he) could add where particular concepts such as the sabbath were concerned. A single 'narrative event' was in itself so complex that the excavation of what it meant for the suspect requires an

---

[27] Richard van Dülmen, 'Die Dienerin des Bösen: Zum Hexenbild in der frühen Neuzeit', *Zeitschrift für historische Forschung*, 18 (1991), 385–98.

[28] Wolfgang Behringer, ed., *Hexen und Hexenprozesse in Deutschland* (Munich, 2000), 259.

[29] Quoted in Elvira Topalovic, 'Konstruierte Wirklichkeit: Ein quellenkritischer Diskurs zur Textorte Verhorprotokol im 17. Jahrhundert', in Katrin Moeller and Burghart Schmidt, eds, *Realität und Mythos: Hexenverfolgung und Rezeptionsgeschichte* (Hamburg, 2003), 56–76.

extremely intricate analysis that has, so far, not been attempted. More straightforward sources for the study of witchcraft in an everyday context do exist, including slander trials and depositions of witnesses in trials against cunning folk. As far as it is known, these hardly contain any accounts of sabbaths or other meetings of witches, and one can only agree with Briggs that notions of the sabbath primarily circulated among the educated, that is, anybody who read demonological tracts, judicial directives, and the resulting trial accounts. To those involved in popular witchcraft discourse the notion of the sabbath may have been familiar, but it remained an external concept.

Demonologists habitually illustrated their arguments with cases. These were either taken from the existing literature or from their own interrogations. Intrusion stories were especially plentiful in the literature, since these narratives stressed the fact that it was not only witches who attended sabbath meetings. These narratives, moreover, were frequently copied. Thus, to give another example, Francesco Guazzo quoted the *Tractatus de hereticis et sortilegiis* (1536) by Paolo Grillando, which contains the story about a husband who asked his wife to take him to the sabbath:

> The husband was taken to the place of the sabbath and saw the games and dances and everything else and finally sat down with the rest at the tables to eat, but finding the food insipid, he asked for salt and, although there was none on the table, kept asking again and again for it, but was not given any until after much importunacy and long waiting. Then he said: 'Praise be to God, for at last the salt has come!' As soon as he had uttered these words the demons immediately departed, and all the rest vanished, and the lights were put out and he remained there alone and naked.

It turned out that the man was in Benevento, a hundred miles from his home, and he had to beg his way back. In another example, taken from a treatise by the judge and demonologist Nicolas Rémy, a man came upon six dancing women and a 'man like a black bull' who was watching them. When he went on his way, they followed them. One of the women would later declare that the man had tried to steal a golden cup from the table.[30] Both these stories circulated widely. The latter story also appeared in Fischart's translation of Bodin, where the cup was described as silver.[31] Yet another type of story was about a man who invited a little cat to his fire, whereupon a multitude of cats emerged and started to dance, while repeating the man's words to their sister.

As a separate study into the demonologists' use of *fabulates* has yet to be undertaken, these examples need to suffice.[32] They cast a special light on the character of demono-logical tracts—which is often presumed to be elite—but I would argue that a possible popular origin needs to be distinguished from their later intellectual use. As examples the stories also acquired a life of their own, which did not necessarily reflect the earlier

[30] Francesco Maria Guazzo, *Compendium maleficarum*, tr. E. Allen Ashwin (London, 1929), Bk. I, ch. 12.

[31] Jean Bodin, *Vom außgelassnen wütigen Teuffelsheer*, tr. Johann Fischart (Strasburg, 1591), Bk. III, ch. 4.

[32] 'At the Witches' Sabbath' has been assigned type number ML 3050 and 'Drinking Cup Stolen from the Fairies' ML 6045. The cat story has remained numberless so far, cf. Christiansen, *Migratory Legends*.

repertoire of their public. Intruder stories provided demonologists with an outsider dimension. While this strengthened their own argument, it gave critics the ammunition to ridicule and denounce them as the ravings of melancholic women. The presence of a detached observer prevented intruder stories from figuring in confessions, unless the third person was turned into a first.

5.4 WAYS OF DISSEMINATION

In 1630 nine-year-old Stine Teipel from Obernkirchen in Sauerland told the court that, after some ointment had been applied under her arm, she had flown to a meeting place of witches, several of whom she had recognized. She had also been on a mountain where the devil had provided everyone with beautiful clothes, as well as beer and wine in barrels of gold. In her mind the sabbath was a sort of dressing-up party in which the villagers acquired higher status and partook in a splendid meal. Belonging herself to one of the poorest families of cotters, the feast represented a kind of *Schlaraffenland* (Land of Cockayne). The dance had lasted two hours, and her partner had had a 'thing' on his body, which he had put in her private parts, but it had not given her any pleasure. Revealing who she had seen at the dance gave her the power over life and death over her fellow villagers. According to witnesses, she had been telling these stories for a year and a half, ever since witch trials had been started in the region. In her case, the authorities seem to have reacted sceptically,[33] but the significance of her statements does not just lie in the people she denounced or in their outcome (she was executed), but in the fact that she must have heard a description of the sabbath, which made her realize its potential as an instrument of power. In that way she resembled many other children at the time of the witchcraft prosecutions. According to Wolfgang Behringer, the number of trials that involved children increased towards the end of the prosecutions,[34] but some also occurred in the sixteenth century, which sent a message to prosecutors that their judicial procedures were failing. Furthermore, although the diabolical aspects of witchcraft did not have a lasting effect on local witchcraft discourses, the largely unsolicited testimonies of children did show that they were mediated and received. How had these youngsters heard the stories?

Particular cases of witchcraft became widely known when they were deemed sensational enough to be written up and distributed in the form of pamphlets. The main account of the Gaufridy case in 1611, for instance, was not only published separately but

---

[33] Alfred Bruns, ed., *Hexen: Gerichtsbarkeit im kurkölnischen Sauerland* (Schmallenberg, 1984), 26–8; see also the analysis of Rainer Decker in the same volume, 91–118.

[34] Wolfgang Behringer, 'Kinderhexenprozesse: Zur Rolle von Kinder in der Geschichte der Hexenverfolgung', *Zeitschrift für historische Forschung*, 16 (1989), 31–47; William Monter, 'Les enfants au sabbat: bilan provisoire', in Nicole Jacques-Chaquin and Maxime Préaud, eds, *Le sabbat des sorciers en Europe: XVᵉ–XVIIIᵉ siècles* (Grenoble, 1993), 383–8. Cf. Kurt Rau, *Augsburger Kinderhexenprozesse 1625–1730* (Vienna, 2006).

was also included in the *Histoires tragiques*, which in the course of the seventeenth century was reprinted a number of times.[35] Translations of the pamphlet appeared in England as well as in the Netherlands. The horrific events they described were not only re-enacted in subsequent French cases, but served as fodder in the propaganda war against Catholicism, and as admonitory example of how not to proceed. In general, the sabbath concept was mediated through a variety of oral and visual conduits, and the different images that emerged through this process informed each other. Apart from the treatises by demonologists, descriptions of witches' gatherings appeared in sermons, such as David Meder's *Hexenpredigten* (Sermons on Witches), which was reprinted three times during the seventeenth century, and was excerpted in a number of works meant for education and entertainment.[36] More specifically, sabbaths became the subject of pamphlets, often illustrated—including *Wahrhafftige und glaubwirdige Zeitung* (1582) and *Unholden Zeitung* (1590)—all of which insisted on the reliability of their reports.[37] *The Wonderfull Discoverie of Witches in the Countie of Lancaster* (1612) was one of the rare instances of an English sabbath account.[38] Furthermore, besides the printed mass-market material, which sometimes included elaborate sabbath images, individual paintings on the theme had come to constitute a special artistic subgenre by the end of the sixteenth century.[39] And, of course, people talked.

Demonologies were the most influential vehicles for disseminating information about the witches' sabbath. They not only informed particular laws and legal decisions, but they were also the major source for painters, preachers, and teachers. The judicial confessions of witches had less of an impact, except when they were included in pamphlets or demonologies. The various media through which information about the sabbath was transmitted appealed to different audiences. In their turn, specific readers selected particular aspects. Lawyers were especially interested in the demonologists' arguments, whereas artists attempted to paint as comprehensive a picture as possible. Preachers, in their turn, found the stories most suitable for their needs. Their individual impact is hard to determine, but it may be possible to draw some preliminary conclusions and, rather than take the complex web of communications for granted, attempt to bring it into sharper focus. Many a confession, for instance, was made public—but would the detailed descriptions of sabbaths stay fresh in people's minds and be reiterated by some of them at the next prosecution? Would it not be more accurate to assume that it was the names of the convicted that were primarily remembered? After all, the available full sabbath accounts were habitually filtered, edited, and adapted to local circumstances. Children prioritized intruder stories but told their own version in the first person, with themselves as the protagonists. Given

---

[35] Marianne Closson, *L'imaginaire démoniaque en France (1550–1650)* (Geneva, 2000), 216.

[36] See Elfriede Moser-Rath, *Predigtmärlein der Barockzeit* (Berlin, 1964).

[37] Ursula-Maria Krah, 'Fiktionalität und Faktizität in frühneuzeitlichen Kleinschriften (Einblattdrucke und Flugschriften)', in Moeller and Schmidt, eds, *Realität und Mythos*, 77–87.

[38] Marion Gibson, *Reading Witchcraft: Stories of Early English Witches* (London, 1999), 51–61.

[39] This especially applied to painters from the Northern and Southern Netherlands, starting with Bartholomaeus Spranger.

their usual subordinate position this often created a special abduction variant. Since they would not have read the demonologies, they were probably inspired by sermons and other religious teaching.[40]

The Swedish Blåkulla trials of 1668–75 (so named after the mythical meeting place, which is essentially the same word as the German Blocksberg), were also driven by children. In Lutheran Sweden the sabbath concept had been hampered by legal restrictions and only evolved in the course of the seventeenth century.[41] Only when a sufficient number of children started to tell stories about their abduction, and were taken seriously by local authorities, could a regional version of a mass trial emerge. In all likelihood, here too the imagery derived from ecclesiastical sources, as the children couched their stories in the vocabulary of religious services, which included weddings and blasphemous baptisms. In their narratives the devil preached and the Bible was used as toilet paper. Typically, the children were also protected by angels.[42]

5.5 RELIGIOUS CONTEXT

It is as illuminating to consider what was *not* transmitted in the diffusion of sabbath concepts as what was conveyed. The image of the sabbath had reached its apotheosis at about 1600, and centred on devil worship, the black mass, and the most repulsive methods of copulation. This, however, means that all those later instances with less developed imagery stand out and are in need of separate explanation. For the time being it appears that prosecuting Protestants were much more hesitant about subscribing to the full picture than witch-hunting Catholics. Protestant sabbaths were 'naturally less elaborate',[43] and Protestant demonologists were more often troubled by the concept of flight than their Catholic counterparts. The former classified the meetings as imaginary more often than not. In some Protestant jurisdictions prosecutors were instructed not to pay attention to the devil's pact and dances. Instead of a possible conspiracy of witches, the stress was laid on the maintenance of Christian discipline and order: dancing, excessive eating and drinking, as well as sexual transgressions were emphasized more than the witch's relationship with the devil.[44]

---

[40] About the role of the Jesuits see Rita Voltmer, 'Die Gesellschaft Jesu und die Hexenkinder', paper presented at AKIH conference, Weingarten, Germany, 21–4 October 2010.

[41] Bengt Ankarloo, 'Sweden: The Mass Burnings (1668–1676)', in Bengt Ankarloo and Gustav Henningsen, eds, *Early Modern European Witchcraft* (Oxford, 1990), 288–94.

[42] Per Sörlin, 'The Blåkulla Story: Absudity and Rationality', *ARV: Nordic Yearbook of Folklore*, 53 (1997), 131–52; Per-Anders Östling, 'Blåkulla Journeys in Swedish Folklore', *ARV: Nordic Yearbook of Folklore*, 62 (2006), 81–122.

[43] Clark, *Thinking with Demons*, 86.

[44] Ingrid Ahrendt-Schulte, 'Die Zauberschen und ihr Trommelschläger: Geschlechtsspezifische Zuschreibungsmuster in lippischen Hexenprozessen', in Dieter R. Bauer, Sönke Lorenz, and Jürgen Michael Schmidt, eds, *Geschlecht, Magie und Hexenverfolgung* (Bielefeld, 2002), 123–31.

In those Protestant countries where severe prosecutions did occasionally occur, the sabbath barely played a role. In England it remained something of an anomaly; there is no trace of it in the mid-seventeenth-century East Anglian witch-hunt. In Scotland, where fairy lore was at hand to be integrated into the popular witchcraft discourse, the witches' gatherings only made it into trial accounts in the late sixteenth century, and not as often as would be expected from the large number of Scottish cases.[45] In Sweden it only came to the fore relatively late and under specific circumstances. In late seventeenth-century Massachusetts, where reports of Swedish sabbaths were circulating, sabbaths did not figure at all in witchcraft prosecutions.

The possible correlation between religion and a weakened sabbath concept only reflects a fragment of a complex process. There were also Catholic regions that show a similarly muted sabbath, with attendance remaining in single figures.[46] Even in some of the German prince-bishoprics where all legal caution had been set aside, mere participation at a dance could offer a sufficient ideological support for executions. While this would indicate that large-scale witch-hunting was perfectly possible without a fully developed notion of the witches' sabbath, it also demands more precise research into the relation between possible reasons for such prosecutions and its underlying stories.

Sabbath imagery provided a frame story where various fragments could be inserted, such as flight, apostasy, feasting, dancing, copulating, and whatever else caught the fancy of the prosecutors. This flexibility may make it expedient to consider several variants of the narrative with different elements and different combinations of elements, as well as, possibly, different patterns of sabbath dissemination. In turn, the sabbath story was itself embedded in larger religious narratives, as it had been since its construction in the early fifteenth century. Religious changes, therefore, were reflected in sabbath stories, as in all probability was the degree of orthodoxy in the communities where such stories arose. It was also balanced by judicial, medical, and political considerations. This, however, is a history still waiting to be written, but when it finally is, it will probably not be necessary to indulge in new forms of speculation.

FURTHER READING

Ahrendt-Schulte, Ingrid, 'Die Zauberschen und ihr Trommelschläger: Geschlechtsspezifische Zuschreibungsmuster in lippischen Hexenprozessen', in Dieter R. Bauer, Sönke Lorenz, and Jürgen Michael Schmidt, eds, *Geschlecht, Magie und Hexenverfolgung* (Bielefeld, 2002), 123–31.

Bailey, Michael, 'The Medieval Concepts of the Witches' Sabbath', *Exemplaria*, 8 (1996), 419–39.

---

[45] Lauren Martin and Joyce Miller, 'Some Findings from the Survey of Scottish Witchcraft', in Julian Goodare, Lauren Marten, and Joyce Miller, eds, *Witchcraft and Belief in Early Modern Scotland* (Basingstoke, 2008), 63–4; Brian P. Levack, *Witch-Hunting in Scotland: Law, Politics and Religion* (London, 2008).

[46] Briggs, *Witches of Lorraine*, 122.

Bailey, Michael D. and Peters, Edward, 'A Sabbath of Demonologists: Basel, 1431–1440', *The Historian*, 65 (2003), 1375–96.

Blécourt, Willem de, 'The Return of the Sabbat', in Jonathan Barry and Owen Davies, eds, *Palgrave Advances in Witchcraft Historiography* (Basingstoke, 2007), 125–45.

Clark, Stuart, 'Dreams: The Epistemology of Sleep', in *Vanities of the Eye: Vision in Early Modern European Culture* (Oxford, 2007).

Dülmen, Richard van, 'Die Dienerin des Bösen: Zum Hexenbild in der frühen Neuzeit', *Zeitschrift für historische Forschung*, 18 (1991), 385–98.

Jacques-Chaquin, Nicole and Préaud, Maxime, eds, *Le sabbat des sorciers en Europe: XVᵉ–XVIIIᵉ siècles* (Grenoble, 1993).

Kieckhefer, Richard, 'Mythologies of Witchcraft in the Fifteenth Century', *Magic, Ritual and Witchcraft*, 1 (2006), 79–108.

Mormando, Franco, *The Preacher's Demons: Bernardino of Siena and the Social Underworld of Early Renaissance Italy* (Chicago, 1999).

Östling, Per-Anders, 'Blåkulla Journeys in Swedish Folklore', *ARV: Nordic Yearbook of Folklore*, 62 (2006), 81–122.

Ostorero, Martine, 'The Concept of the Witches' Sabbath in the Alpine Region (1430–1440): Text and Context', in Gábor Klaniczay and Éva Pócs, eds, *Witchcraft Mythologies and Persecutions* (Budapest, 2008), 15–34.

Ostorero, Martine, Paravicini Bagliani, Agostino, and Utz Tremp, Kathrin, eds, *L'imaginaire du sabbat* (Lausanne, 1999).

Schatzmann, Niklaus, *Verdorrende Bäume und Brote wie Kuhfladen: Hexenprozesse in der Leventina 1431–1459 und die Anfänge der Hexenverfolgung auf der Alpensüdseite* (Zurich, 2003), 245–8.

CHAPTER 6

....

THE SCEPTICAL TRADITION

....

WALTER STEPHENS

DOES witchcraft actually exist? Can it be shown to produce real effects in the external world of people and things, or is it instead an attempt to manipulate imaginary forces and produce effects that are imaginary, unverifiable, or indistinguishable from those produced by natural causes? This is the problem of *scepticism* concerning witchcraft. The question is far from simple, for it has both historical and theoretical dimensions; the latter involve not only the definition of witchcraft itself, but its intersection with other problems that are historical and theoretical, philosophical and theological.

Surveying scepticism about witchcraft requires that we establish the range of meanings for witchcraft. The definition of witchcraft differs extensively from culture to culture, and in medieval and early modern Europe it varied almost as widely from century to century. One reason for variation was the degree to which any culture, subculture, or writer associated witchcraft with other important concepts and movements. At various times, definitions of witchcraft intersected with ideas about demons and the devil, angels, God, the human soul, the sacraments of the Catholic Church, heresy, the nature of disease and infirmity, the efficacy of medicine, meteorology, and, not least, the nature of women and other disempowered people.

Witchcraft, in short, was a problem that involved not only criminology, but also medicine, philosophy, and, above all, religion. Scepticism about its reality was manifested variously by lawyers, physicians, and theologians; these were the three major disciplines of the medieval university, but even the uneducated sometimes expressed scepticism, particularly when they refused official calls to denounce witches in their communities. All these dimensions have in common the fundamental problem of epistemology, that is, how we know what we think we know—the question of proof. Witchcraft and scepticism are concepts that depend vitally on questions of proof and the acquisition of reliable knowledge.

Given these aspects, it is no longer possible to proclaim, as scholars formerly did, that scepticism about witchcraft arose among a few enlightened individuals in the late sixteenth century, particularly Johann Weyer (or Wier, d.1588) and Reginald Scot (d.1599), and triumphed through the progress of knowledge and scientific discovery in the seventeenth and eighteenth centuries. Such a view presupposed that belief in witchcraft was a timeless, universal *superstition* of ignorant people that lingered on (this 'lingering' is the etymology of superstition) until it was rendered untenable by advances in real knowledge. Far from being a 'medieval' concept, the definition of witchcraft as conscious, willing collaboration with demons in order to harm others arose in the early modern period, and many important thinkers of the seventeenth and eighteenth centuries still professed belief in the same forces that witchcraft presupposed. Some of them defended the reality of witchcraft and the necessity of prosecuting and punishing it; others questioned or denied it.

It is equally important to define scepticism in a historically appropriate way. What did it mean to be 'sceptical' about witchcraft? In modern conversation, to say 'I am sceptical about that' is often a way of saying 'I believe that is absolutely untrue'. But scepticism is broader than mere contradiction; it implies at least a preliminary suspension of judgement. On the other hand, scepticism about witchcraft was not necessarily a rigorously philosophical neutrality; nor was it limited to philosophers. Theologians, jurists, and physicians, even the unlettered and semi-literate, could express strong opinions about witchcraft, and there were many shades and degrees of scepticism on the subject. Finally, the question whether expressions of scepticism had discernible effects on the outcome of trials or the overall decline of witch prosecution must be carefully considered.

6.1 SOURCES OF SCEPTICISM

Although the terms for witches in various vernaculars took several decades longer to stabilize, the essential components of witchcraft were in place by about 1460–75, and susceptible to controversy. The definition given by Heinrich Kramer (Institoris) in *The Hammer of Witches* (1486) provides the most useful starting point for examining the sources of scepticism concerning witchcraft. The crime of witchcraft, Kramer declared, requires three things: the devil, the witch, and the permission of God.[1] During antiquity and the earlier Middle Ages, only the witch had received attention in law codes, such as the one decreed by the Langobardic King Rothair about 643. The mechanics of witchcraft were largely undefined: a witch was someone who performed acts of harmful

---

[1] Henricus Institoris, *Malleus Maleficarum*, ed. and tr. Christopher S. Mackay, 2 vols (Cambridge, 2006), ii, 202–10.

magic, but where the power to perform the magic came from was not a subject for discussion.[2]

When scholastic theologians took an interest in this question, the devil and the permission of God became focal points of interest. The twin disciplines of angelology and demonology emerged in the twelfth century, becoming systematic and, as it were, scientific during the thirteenth and fourteenth, while the iconography of demons also evolved rapidly.[3] The massive heretical movements of the twelfth through the early fifteenth centuries, especially Waldensians, Cathars, and Hussites, inspired worried theologians to imagine sordid and frightening encounters between demons and heretics as expressions of these groups' enmity towards God and the established Church. By the early fifteenth century, some descriptions of these heretical gatherings strongly resembled later writings about the activities of witches: parodies of the Sabbath and its sacraments, murder and cannibalism, lewd dancing and orgiastic sex. The profile of the witch evolved into that of a kind of super-heretic, an apostate Christian rather than a merely deluded or ignorant one.

The question whether or why God permitted these activities was important, and by the time Kramer published the *Hammer*, it required a systematic and convincing answer. Although a vast conspiracy of witches seemed to explain the manifold ills of late medieval society, it posed the classic dilemma of theodicy: rather than imagine that God was willing but unable to prevent such evil, it seemed more reasonable to think that he permitted it, for his own righteous, but often inscrutable, reasons.

Each of these essential features of witchcraft was open to doubt from more than one perspective. In general, assertions about witches or witchcraft could be opposed on legal, medical, or theological grounds. Moreover, it was vital to establish whether the objections concerned witches and witchcraft in general, or the status of a single individual or group. To a certain extent, these categories—devil, witch, and divine permission, legal, medical, and theological, and individual or collective—overlap and intermingle, but they allow us to classify the ways in which individuals framed and expressed their scepticism.

6.2 THE SCEPTICAL CONTEXT

Witchcraft, and scepticism about it, both arose in a period—the 1400s—when scepticism as a formal philosophical stance was re-emerging. While it is rarely possible to establish a direct relation between formal scepticism and doubts about witchcraft, and while expressions of scepticism only infrequently determined the outcome of witchcraft trials, recent scholars have recognized more complex and nuanced relations

---

[2] Richard Kieckhefer, *Magic in the Middle Ages* (Cambridge, 1989).
[3] David Keck, *Angels and Angelology in the Middle Ages* (New York, 1998); Walter Stephens, *Demon Lovers: Witchcraft, Sex, and the Crisis of Belief* (Chicago, 2002), 58–81.

among these forces. Even at a very early stage (*c*.1430–75) general discussions of witchcraft often implied fundamental epistemological and ontological questions, both about demons and about God. Such problems were pursued with increasing rigour throughout the early modern period, and frequently intersected with more general discussions of certainty and doubt.

Richard Popkin, a leading historian of sceptical movements, has characterized the period between about 1450 and 1710 as an era of 'sceptical crisis'. Without ever discussing witchcraft,[4] Popkin sees a threefold crisis of doubt running throughout this period. First, a theological crisis over the 'rule of faith', that is, how to determine the criterion of religious knowledge and truth: was it guaranteed by the institutional authority of the Roman Church, by the prophetic illuminations of a Savonarola or, as Luther daringly maintained, by the individual's conviction of truth when reading the Bible? Popkin dates this crisis of faith from the end of the fifteenth century (Savonarola's fatal clash with papal authority, 1494–8), but stirrings about the role of the Bible in faith figured in the Hussite controversies and wars of the late fourteenth to early sixteenth centuries, and had some influence on thinking about witchcraft.[5] Second, Popkin identifies an ongoing 'humanistic crisis of knowledge, . . . doubt engendered by the rediscovery of the great variety of the points of view of ancient thinkers'.[6] Rediscovery and recirculation of important texts by ancient pagan philosophers and historians began well before Petrarch became the publicist for humanist scholarship about 1340,[7] and by the early fifteenth century, the recovery and translation of ancient Greek and Greek-influenced texts such as Diogenes Laertius' *Lives of the Philosophers*, Diodorus of Sicily's *Library of History*, and Lucretius' atomistic *On the Nature of Things* provided often startling revelations about ancient religions and cosmology. This reacquaintance with a pre-Christian past was soon matched by the discovery of a 'New World' in the Americas, which, during the course of the sixteenth century, revealed still another anthropological universe that was vastly different from Christian Europe.[8]

The religious and humanistic upheavals engendered a third crisis, an upheaval in scientific knowledge. It is worth mentioning that, although earlier scholarship erred in crediting the emergence of sceptical scientific methods with ending witchcraft

---

[4] Richard Popkin, *The History of Scepticism from Savonarola to Bayle* (3rd edn, Oxford, 2003), pp. xvii–16. A single mention of witchcraft occurs on p. 184, in a discussion of Glanvill. See also Brian P. Copenhaver and Charles B. Schmitt, *Renaissance Philosophy* (Oxford, 1992), 196–284, and Charles G. Nauert, Jr, *Agrippa and the Crisis of Renaissance Thought* (Urbana, IL, 1965), 194–221.

[5] Michael Bailey, *Battling Demons: Witchcraft, Heresy, and Reform in the Late Middle Ages* (University Park, PA, 2003).

[6] Popkin, *History of Scepticism*, 55.

[7] Ronald G. Witt, *In the Footsteps of the Ancients: The Origins of Humanism from Lovato to Bruni* (Leiden, 2003), 81–229.

[8] Jill Kraye, 'Philologists and Philosophers', in *The Cambridge Companion to Renaissance Humanism* (Cambridge, 1996), 153–6; Anthony Grafton, 'All Coherence Gone', in Anthony Grafton, April Shelford, and Nancy Siraisi, eds, *New Worlds, Ancient Texts: The Power of Tradition and the Shock of Discovery* (Cambridge, MA, 1992), 95–157; Grafton, 'A Bound World: The Scholar's Cosmos', in Grafton, Shelford, and Siraisi, eds, *New Worlds, Ancient Texts*, 11–58.

persecution, the longer-term process that Popkin describes cannot have been irrelevant to the debate, since it occupied the same chronology and included the same disputants. The Aristotelian model of scientific knowledge, which had triumphed in the thirteenth- and fourteenth-century universities, came under attack, first by early humanists in the wake of Petrarch, and subsequently through the formal revaluation of ancient sceptical philosophy. In the meantime, aspects of Aristotle's philosophy were often disputed by both opponents and proponents of 'witchcraft theory', that is, the speculations of learned writers about the crimes of witches and their demonic accomplices.

Popkin argues that the sceptical crisis was deepened on all three fronts by a 'historical accident, that the writings and theories of the [ancient] Greek sceptics were revived at the same time the sceptical crisis arose'.[9] Far from being a footnote in the history of textual scholarship, this revival had consequences for both religion and the development of natural philosophy. The revival of scepticism received encourage-ment from a seemingly unlikely quarter. Savonarola feared the deleterious influence of philosophical inquisitiveness and arrogance on Christian religious certainty. He advo-cated adopting philosophical scepticism to combat philosophical dogmatism, particu-larly the certainties of scholastic Aristotelianism and the speculations inspired by Florentine Neoplatonism. Savonarola's admirer, Gianfrancesco Pico della Mirandola (d.1533), was the first modern philosopher to quote the arguments of the ancient Pyrrhonian sceptic Sextus Empiricus (d. CE 210) extensively.[10] At the same time, Pico was a major theorist of witchcraft, and vehemently defended the prosecution of witches. This apparent paradox, the exploitation of radically sceptical arguments in order to *defend* the reality of witchcraft rather than to attack it, is essential to understanding the context and complexities of scepticism about witchcraft.

But Pico's overt intrusion of philosophical scepticism into witchcraft controversy did not significantly redefine the terms of the pre-existing debate. Stuart Clark observes that, contrary to modern assumptions, 'demonology presupposed doubt', not only because 'it often anticipated the attacks made on it' by sceptics, but equally because even the defences of witchcraft that modern readers find most credulous presuppose a remarkable measure of scepticism.[11] Clark finds a considerable 'lack of real polariza-tion' between the writings of those who denied the reality of witchcraft and those who defended it. 'Precisely because it could embrace a variety of opinions, absorbing and expressing doubt as occasion demanded, demonology proved to be intellectually

---

[9] Popkin, *History of Scepticism*, 16. See Luciano Floridi, 'The Rediscovery and Posthumous Influence of Scepticism', in Richard Bett, ed., *The Cambridge Companion to Ancient Scepticism* (Cambridge, 2010), 267–87.

[10] Charles B. Schmitt, *Gianfrancesco Pico della Mirandola (1469–1533) and his Critique of Aristotle* (The Hague, 1967); Anna De Pace, *La scepsi, il sapere, e l'anima: Dissonanze nella cerchia laurenziana* (Milan, 2002); Gian Mario Cao, *Gianfrancesco Pico as a Reader of Sextus Empiricus: With a Facing Text of Pico's Quotations from Sextus* (Pisa, 2007).

[11] Stuart Clark, *Thinking with Demons: The Idea of Witchcraft in Early Modern Europe* (Oxford, 1997), 195.

resilient.'[12] To approach early modern thinking about witchcraft as if it displayed a dichotomy between superstition and science, as was assumed from the eighteenth century until deep in the twentieth, is a gross oversimplification. Science in the modern sense was not practised. Standards of proof and demonstration (the 'scientific method') were under construction, so the modern distinction between 'natural' or 'scientific' explanations of causality and those that presuppose 'supernatural' causation did not yet exist.

Moreover, as Clark and others have shown, neither witchcraft sceptics nor its defenders would have defined demonology as a science of the *super*natural. Critics and defenders agreed on a number of fundamental propositions. Like human beings and animals, demons and their unfallen brethren, the good angels, had been created by God, and were thus a part of nature (etymologically, those things that are born). Nature was synonymous with creation, thus only the creator was above nature; like humans, demons were constrained by its limitations. All discussants agreed that demons enjoyed vast advantages over humans, since their greater understanding and longer experience of nature allowed them to manipulate its processes dramatically— for instance, by speeding them up so extremely that snakes and other base forms of life could appear to be created instantaneously from nothing. But only God could create life. Likewise, only God could change one species into another. It was even more erroneous to believe that humans performed magical operations with their own powers. (An apparent exception was the 'evil eye', but it too was susceptible to purely natural explanation.) Thus, when magicians and witches seemed to perform *maleficia* (harmful spells) or to change themselves into cats or wolves, a complex illusion (*praestigium*) was in progress.[13] Not only were demons limited to natural processes, but humans were completely powerless to perform such operations without demonic aid.

When witchcraft phenomena could not be easily explained by recourse to natural causes, their causation might be classified as *occult* (that is, hidden or not understood) or *preter*natural (i.e. highly unusual), but it could not properly be called *supernatural*.[14] Because only God could act outside nature, only his miracles were supernatural. When humans seemed to perform miracles through the power of demons, they were merely 'working wonders'—*mira*, not *miracula*. It was therefore not only possible but normal to defend the reality of witchcraft and demons while simultaneously defining their operations as completely natural. Though not 'scientific' in our sense, demonological explanations of occult, wondrous, or preternatural phenomena were based on the forerunner of science, that is, *natural philosophy*.

[12] Clark, *Thinking with Demons*, 203.
[13] Clark, *Thinking with Demons*, 271–5; Stephens, *Demon Lovers*, 300–14.
[14] Clark, *Thinking with Demons*, 151–214.

6.3 Scepticism about Demons

Despite this common ground, the fundamental question whether, in fact, demons existed was at times openly entertained. Here again, moderns may be led astray by our first impulses. Even early defenders of witchcraft reality sometimes questioned the existence of demons explicitly. Writing about 1450, the French Dominican inquisitor Jean Vinet began his treatise by listing ancient thinkers who denied demonic reality, particularly the Jewish Sadducees and the ancient atomist philosophers Democritus, Epicurus, and Lucretius. He then declared that the existence of witchcraft refutes the opinion of some people, whom he declined to name, 'who say that demons do not exist, except in the imagination of the common people'. The ignorant and naive allow their imaginations to run rampant, and therefore 'some figures can appear to the senses exactly as a man has thought of them, and then it is believed that he is seeing demons'. Vinet replied that the existence of demons is not imaginary: it is proved not only by the experiences of witches, but, moreover, by 'the true faith, through which we believe that angels fell from heaven and are now demons'.[15] The same argument was made practically verbatim by other early theorists of witchcraft, notably Heinrich Kramer in *The Hammer of Witches*.[16] The remarkable uniformity is partly due to habits of scholastic argumentation, which began by opposing the proposition to be proved. But uniformity also derives specifically from Thomas Aquinas, whom all these authors were quoting explicitly (as in the *Hammer*) or paraphrasing (as Vinet and others did). Aquinas made this argument on at least three occasions.[17] Nor was Thomas the first to discuss such scepticism. A generation before Aquinas, about 1225, Caesarius of Heisterbach had staged a dialogue between a Cistercian novice and an older monk; the novice professed to believe in good angels on the authority of scripture but desired proof that demons existed, which his teacher provided by recounting the experiences of monks, necromancers, and the possessed.[18]

Such documents show the extent to which, even before the 'invention' of witchcraft, scepticism about demonic reality was recognized as at least a potential problem. Once discussions of witchcraft began, authors occasionally expressed personal doubts about aspects of demonology. Pietro Pomponazzi, a convinced Aristotelian who taught at Padua, quoted Aquinas' admission that some people claim that demons exist only in the imagination of the common people, but maintained that Aristotle himself was the

---

[15] Jean Vinet (Vineti), *Tractatus contra demonum invocatores* (Cologne, c.1487), sig. a3r–a4r. See also Stephens, *Demon Lovers*, 25; Martine Ostorero, 'Vinet, Jean (Vineti, Johannes) (d. ca. 1470)', in Richard M. Golden, ed., *Encyclopedia of Witchcraft: The Western Tradition* (Santa Barbara, CA, 2006), iv, 1169–70. The definitive treatment of Vinet is now Martine Ostorero, *Le Diable au sabbat: Littérature démonologique et sorcellerie (1440–1460)* (Florence, 2011), 79–115, 251–96, 417–50.

[16] Institoris, *Malleus Maleficarum*, ii, 44–5.

[17] Stephens, *Demon Lovers*, 73–9, 318–31.

[18] Caesarius of Heisterbach, *The Dialogue on Miracles*, tr. Henry von Essen Scott and Charles Cooke Swinton Bland, 2 vols (London, 1929), ii, 314–17; Stephens, *Demon Lovers*, 349–52.

foremost of these sceptics. He used precise passages from Aristotle to argue that purely natural causes could explain everything that Christians attributed to the operation of demons. Opposing the reality of demonic *maleficia*, Pomponazzi declared, in *On Magical Spells*, that he would follow 'the way of Nature, without demons, for I consider that [the existence of *maleficia*] can be more easily argued without demons than with, and that if such things can be done by demons, they can also be done without them'.[19] Pomponazzi wrote this in 1520, but since he was already under attack for demonstrating in 1516 that Aristotle provided no support whatsoever for the Christian doctrine of the immortality of the individual human soul, the treatise on natural causes was not printed until 1556, nearly forty years after his death.

Sixteenth-century writers who defended demonic causation were at times disquieted by Aristotle's perceived indifference or hostility to the existence of demons, among them the Neoplatonist philosopher Agostino Steuco (d.1548) and the Aristotelian physician Andrea Cesalpino (d.1603). Since the notion of demonic witchcraft was founded on scholastic (and thus Aristotelian) principles, Aristotle's neglect or inconclusiveness on the issue of demons was worrisome.[20] Johann Weyer, one of the strongest critics of witch-hunting, was nevertheless careful to stipulate that he firmly believed in the real existence of the devil. The entire first book of his *On the Illusions of Demons* (1563), is devoted to a detailed exposition of the devil's history, motives, and misdeeds, and opens with the declaration that 'I totally reject the maxims of Aristotle and the Peripatetics and also of the Sadducees, all of whom contend that demons do not exist in reality'.[21] An appendix, Weyer's *Pseudomonarchia dæmonum* (False Kingdom of Demons), displayed a demonic counterpart to Pseudo-Dionysius' *Celestial Hierarchy* (*c.*600 CE), discussing the principal demons, their hierarchies, and their functions in meticulous detail.

Heinrich Cornelius Agrippa of Nettesheim observed in his *Three Books of Occult Philosophy* (1531–3) that there was a problem with the very definition of demons, to wit, whether they had naturally occurring bodies or were incorporeal and thus forced to confect artificial bodies before interacting with humans.[22] The problem of demonic corporeality had exercised scholastic theologians since the time of Peter Lombard (d.1160). With the major exception of the Byzantine Michael Psellus (d.1078) and sixteenth-century writers who quoted him,[23] Christians believed that even if natural

[19] Pietro Pomponazzi, *De incantationibus*, ed. Vittoria Perrone Compagni (Florence, 2011), 105–6; see also Stephens, *Demon Lovers*, 77–9.

[20] Agostino Steuco, *De perenni philosophia* (1540; repr. New York, 1972), 460–1; Andrea Cesalpino, *Dæmonum investigatio peripatetica, in qua explicatur locus Hippocratis in Progn: 'Si quid divinum in morbis habetur'* (Florence, 1580). See Stephens, *Demon Lovers*, 73–80, 302–8, 346–7.

[21] *Witches, Devils, and Doctors in the Renaissance: Johann Weyer*, De Praestigiis daemonum, ed. George Mora (Binghamton, NY, 1991), 3.

[22] Heinrich Cornelius Agrippa von Nettesheim, *Three Books of Occult Philosophy*, ed. Donald Tyson (St Paul, MN, 2004), 518–20. The first book was begun in 1510.

[23] Walter Stephens, '"*Habeas Corpus*": Demonic Bodies in Ficino, Psellus, and *Malleus maleficarum*', in Julia Hairston and Walter Stephens, eds, *The Body in Early Modern Italy* (Baltimore, MD, 2010), 74–91.

demonic bodies existed, they were too insubstantial to be perceived by ordinary human senses. This opinion, and the complicated processes required for demons to interact bodily with humans, left ample room for scepticism.[24]

In *The Discoverie of Witchcraft* (1584), the English writer Reginald Scot in effect denied the relevance of demons, if not their reality, pronouncing them devoid of physical existence and thus incapable of interaction with humans. Scot's argument had been anticipated by the Italian jurist Ambrogio Vignati about 1468, who declared belief in demonic corporeality 'a bestial error'.[25] Even Marsilio Ficino, who claimed to be convoking good spirits rather than demons, was led by his own partial translation of Psellus' treatise *On the Works of Demons* (1497) into conclusions about demonic bodies and interactions that were eerily similar to those of *The Hammer of Witches*.[26] In his philosophical dialogue *The Messenger* (1580/7), the Italian poet Torquato Tasso imagined himself interrogating a spirit being who failed to convince him that angels and demons (including the spirit himself) were not imaginary. Later authors such as Henry More, Joseph Glanvill, and John Wesley invoked witchcraft as evidence of spirits' reality, illustrating the arguments of Aquinas, Vinet, and other early authors with extensive case studies.[27] John Webster countered with a milder version of Scot's argument that spirits were ultimately irrelevant to human action. As Cartesian ideas of the separation between matter and spirit, and mechanistic and materialist explanations of phenomena took hold in the seventeenth century, Thomas Hobbes, Baruch Spinoza, and other sceptics put the case more forcefully. In his massive *Enchanted World*, Balthasar Bekker argued from biblical evidence for the existence of spirits, yet declared that in a divinely ruled world 'there is no other Magic than that which is in the imagination of men; there are no Phantoms, no Divination, nor any obsession which is from the Devil'.[28]

Disputes over the reality of demons and their interactions with witches evolved from the heavily theological reasoning of Aquinas and Vinet to the intensely empirical and

[24] Stephens, *Demon Lovers*, 58–86.

[25] Ambrogio Vignati [Ambrosius de Vignate], *Tractatus de hæreticis*, 215–27, in Joseph Hansen, ed., *Quellen und Untersuchungen zur Geschichte des Hexenwahns und Hexenverfolgung im Mittelalters* (Bonn, 1901), 219; quoted in Stephens, *Demon Lovers*, 58.

[26] Stephens, '"Habeas Corpus"'.

[27] Torquato Tasso, *Il messaggiero*, in *Dialoghi*, ed. Giovanni Baffetti, 2 vols (Milan, 1998), i, 309–83 ; Henry More, *An Antidote against Atheisme* (London, 1653); Joseph Glanvill, *Sadducismus Triumphatus* (London, 1681); *The Journal of the Rev. John Wesley*, ed. Nehemiah Curnock, 8 vols (London, 1909–16), v, 265, for 1768; cf. v, 375; Stephens, *Demon Lovers*, 366–7.

[28] John Webster, *The Displaying of Supposed Witchcraft* (London, 1677), excerpt in Brian P. Levack, ed., *The Witchcraft Sourcebook* (London, 2004), 307–11; Thomas Hobbes, *Leviathan* (London, 1651), excerpt in Alan Charles Kors and Edward Peters, eds, *Witchcraft in Europe 400–1700: A Documentary History* (2nd edn, Philadelphia, PA, 2001), 419–25; Baruch Spinoza, *God, Man, and His Well-Being* (c.1660), pt. 2, ch. 25, excerpt in Levack, *Witchcraft Sourcebook*, 305–6; Balthasar Bekker, *Le Monde enchanté*, 4 vols (Amsterdam, 1691), in Kors and Peters, eds, *Witchcraft in Europe*, 429–35, quote at 424. See Michaela Valente, 'La critica alla caccia alle streghe da Johann Wier a Balthasar Bekker', in Dinora Corsi and Matteo Duni, eds, *'Non lasciar vivere la malefica': le streghe nei trattati e nei processi (secoli XIV–XVII)* (Florence, 2008), 67–82.

forensic use of medical and legal evidence by later writers. But there was little progress in the arguments: Aquinas had argued explicitly that the experiences of demoniacs and necromancers proved the reality of demons, while Caesarius' examples had already made the case implicitly. Nor was theology ever absent from even the latest and most empirical arguments. Physical evidence on the bodies of accused witches (stigmata or 'devil's marks', 'witches' teats') and even primitive experiments on witches (particularly involving the 'flying ointment') are attested to in sixteenth- and seventeenth-century trials and treatises. Possession and exorcism continued to be invoked explicitly as evidence of demonic reality, in works such as Girolamo Menghi's *Compendium of the Exorcist's Art* (1576).[29]

6.4 Doubts Concerning God's Permission of Evil

Atheism as a personal philosophy was not articulated until the Enlightenment; instead, the charge of atheism was used for centuries to discredit opponents in religious controversies. Polemicists frequently accused their enemies of authoring the infamous *Book of the Three Great Impostors*, which supposedly demonstrated that Moses, Christ, and Mohammed were charlatans and deceivers; Gregory IX brought the imaginary book to prominence during his quarrels with the Emperor Frederick II Hohenstaufen (1220s), and it remained a staple of religious slander until the eighteenth century.[30]

Accusations of atheism became commonplace in the late seventeenth century, but professions of scepticism about witchcraft could provoke such charges long before then. Moreover, as with disbelief in the reality of demons, defenders of witch prosecutions imagined atheism in the abstract as the ultimate consequence of scepticism, well before they began to identify individual opponents as atheists. Vinet began his treatise by linking the real existence of demons to God's existence as a personal being rather than an Aristotelian 'first principle' or impersonal force. Such argumentation derived from scholastic theologians, who, centuries before the spectre of witchcraft emerged, developed proofs of God's existence, thereby posing it as a problem, even when treating it as a merely formal question. The increasing complexity of discussions about God, from Anselm of Canterbury (*Proslogion*, 1078) through nominalism, culminated in the 'learned ignorance' of the negative theology of Nicolas Cusanus (Nicholas of Cusa) (d.1464),

[29] Girolamo Menghi, *Compendio dell'arte essorcistica, et possibilità delle mirabili, et stupende operationi delli demoni et de i malefici* (1576; repr. Genoa, 1987). See Walter Stephens, 'Experiments and Tests', in *Encyclopedia of Witchcraft*, ii, 340–2.

[30] Georges Minois, *The Atheist's Bible: The Most Dangerous Book that Never Existed*, tr. Lys Ann Weiss (Chicago, 2012).

with its doctrines of God as the synthesis of all opposites (*coincidentia oppositorum*) and as Not-other (*non aliud*).[31]

Such concepts, discussed at the highest levels of theology, are ultimately no more abstruse than the arguments concerning divine permission directed at ordinarily literate audiences of curates, preachers, inquisitors, and magistrates, in systematic treatises such as Kramer's *Hammer of Witches*. Kramer may have been right to claim that the more important divine permission became, the harder it was to preach to lay folk.[32] However, all three levels of God-discourse in this period indicate the importance of understanding the divinity's mode of being and his intentions. To have simple faith in God's goodness, omnipotence, and providence was still the highest of virtues, but to supplement that faith by the use of human reasoning—whether Kramer's or Cusanus'—was increasingly seen as desirable. Even to renounce understanding God's being, as Cusanus did, or his gift of free will to humans, as Erasmus did somewhat later,[33] involved a judicious understanding of theological niceties.

Thus, throughout the literature of witchcraft theory, the most pressing question about God involved his permission of human and demonic mischief. Like Kramer, Johann Weyer maintained that:

> God, almighty and merciful though he is, sometimes (in accordance with His plan and our deserts) permits the demon to practice his mocking deceptions and tyranny ... but he still does not indulge him in all matters ... nor does He allow him infinite license ... Otherwise, we would all perish, slain in a single moment by the Devil ... He confines Satan so narrowly within these limits that he can do nothing, even to beasts, without God's assent ...[34]

For other opponents of witchcraft reality, these problems were susceptible to more elementary reasonings. Samuel de Cassini, a Franciscan theologian, simply denied in 1505 that God would allow demons to transport witches for the purpose of harming innocent victims.[35] For some demonologists, the concept that individual or collective misfortunes could be caused by interactions between humans and demons was an affront to God, since it threatened the concept of Providence. Reginald Scot argued thus in his *Discoverie of Witchcraft*. In the *Hammer*, Kramer attributed such squeamishness about God's permission to 'certain [modern] philosophers' (rather than to lay folk), who were 'devastating all of Christendom' by their resistance to witch-hunting. With his customary exaggeration, Kramer declared these unnamed modern philoso-

---

[31] Copenhaver and Schmitt, *Renaissance Philosophy*, 176–84.

[32] Institoris, *Malleus Maleficarum*, ii, 167.

[33] Desiderius Erasmus, *De libero arbitrio diatribe sive collatio* (1524), in E. Gordon Rupp and Philip S. Watson, eds, *Luther and Erasmus: Free Will and Salvation* (Philadelphia, PA, 1969), 33–97.

[34] Weyer, *Witches, Devils, and Doctors*, 81.

[35] Michaela Valente, 'Cassini (Cassinis) Samuel de (*ca.* 1450–post 1510)', in *Encyclopedia of Witchcraft*, i, 173.

phers almost as reprehensible as 'Democritus and the followers of Epicurus', who denied Providence in favour of chance.[36]

The story of Job provided important biblical warrant for defending divine permissiveness towards demons harming innocent or righteous people, since God allowed Satan to test Job's loyalty by reducing him to misery. Weyer noted that 'God ... agreed that Satan should rage against the fortunes and the person of Job, but He commanded him not to harm Job's soul.'[37] (Weyer declined to discuss the deaths of Job's children, however.)

6.5 SCEPTICISM CONCERNING WITCHES

The earliest document relevant to early modern European witchcraft is the canon *Episcopi* (*c.*906); it was the foundation for assertions about the secret nocturnal meetings of people, especially women, with the devil. However, the canon began the history of witchcraft discourse on a profoundly sceptical note. It asserted that women who believed they rode great distances at night on beasts in the company of 'Diana the goddess of the pagans' were simply dreaming, and never left their beds. According to the canon, Satan inspired the women's nocturnal delusions on account of their backsliding from Christian faith into pagan idolatry. This law and its twelfth-century iterations in canon law (Gratian) and philosophy (John of Salisbury) posed a formidable obstacle to early theorists of witchcraft. Since they could not refute the venerable law, they were forced to argue either that modern witches were different from the women of *Episcopi* or that the canon itself did not categorically deny the reality of such experiences.[38]

Two early testimonies by sceptical churchmen indicate that activities resembling the 'cult of Diana' were still being practised, though by individuals rather than groups of women. In the *Formicarius* (Anthill, 1438), one of the earliest documents to mention witch-like activities, Johannes Nider mentioned a woman who boasted to a Dominican friar (possibly around 1380) that she was carried through the air at night with Diana's company. Unable to convince the woman she was deluded, the friar asked to attend, with witnesses, when next she went out. After rubbing herself with an unguent, the woman fell into a deep sleep, perched precariously in a kneading trough that had been placed on a stool. In the excitement of her dream, she fell, injuring her head and waking up. The Dominican then mocked her, convincing her that she was indeed deluded.

---

[36] Institoris, *Malleus Maleficarum*, ii, 167, 168–79.
[37] Weyer, *Witches, Devils, and Doctors*, 82.
[38] Text of the canon *Episcopi* in Kors and Peters, eds, *Witchcraft in Europe*, 60–7; Hugh of St Victor, John of Salisbury, and other medieval quoters of the canon are in Kors and Peters, eds, *Witchcraft in Europe*, 67–78. A compendious history of attempts to refute the canon *Episcopi* is in Ostorero, *Le Diable au sabbat*, 567–732.

A similar anecdote was recounted by Alonso Tostado (d.1455) in his commentary on Genesis. In this case, the woman had boasted to her neighbours of attending nocturnal banquets and sexual orgies, and it was they, rather than the clergy, who witnessed her disabusement. After she fell asleep, they, either fearing she was dead or simply to torment her, beat and burned her rather severely. On waking, her injuries and their testimony convinced her of her mistake.

As in the canon *Episcopi*, the intent of the stories is to demonstrate the unreality of these women's experiences. Both churchmen mention the women's use of presumably hallucinogenic ointments (rather than normal dreaming), and their utterance of incantations. Nider went so far as to call them 'words of witchcraft' (*verba malefica*), and mentioned the intervention (apparently invisible but presumed real) of a demon (*opere demonis*). More strangely still, although Tostado asserts that the woman in his anecdote was deluded, he claims elsewhere in his biblical commentary that many other women, and men as well, undergo such experiences in reality 'when they have completed some abominable superstitious rites and anointings, [and] are taken by demons and transported' bodily to gatherings where 'they offer tribute to the demons, and abandon themselves to libidinous and filthy acts'. Tostado offers early evidence of an argument that would become standard in defences of demonic transportation and the witch's sabbath: just because canon *Episcopi* says certain experiences are imaginary, its scepticism should not be taken to apply to all cases, 'for sometimes this transvection happens in reality'. The canon does not state that women can never be carried by demons, but only that certain women long ago fell into heresy and idolatry by believing that they were following Diana.[39] Tostado's qualification had been foreshadowed by Jacopo Passavanti's *Mirror of True Penitence* (1354): while echoing the language of *Episcopi*, the Dominican preacher claimed that 'there is no doubt' that the devil can transport persons 'by his natural powers', and 'however he wishes, if he is not held back by divine power'.[40] Tostado was followed by Nicolas Jacquier (1458), Jean Vinet (*c*.1450), Giordano da Bergamo (*c*.1470), and Bartolomeo Spina (1523), among many others.[41] Heinrich Kramer asserted in *The Hammer of Witches* that a 'literal reading' of the canon, as if it excluded all possibility of demonic transportation, contradicted 'all the holy doctors' and 'even the teaching of Holy Scripture'.[42] Ulrich Müller (Molitor,

[39] Johannes Nider, *Formicarius* (Cologne, 1480; repr. Graz, 1971), sig. e4r; Alonso Tostado, *Alonsi Thostati Episcopi Abulensis hispani a se edita super genesim commentaria* (Venice, 1507), fol. 125r. On both, see Stephens, *Demon Lovers*, 145–57.

[40] Jacopo Passavanti, *Lo specchio della vera penitenza*, tr. in Kors and Peters, eds, *Witchcraft in Europe*, 105–11; see Stephens, *Demon Lovers*, 132–4.

[41] Nicolas Jacquier, *Flagellum hæreticorum fascinariorum*, in Hansen, ed., *Quellen und Untersuchungen*, 133–45 at 138–9 (excerpt in English in Kors and Peters, eds, *Witchcraft in Europe*, 171–2); Vinet, *Tractatus*, sig. b1r (English trans. in Stephens, *Demon Lovers*, 135–6); Giordano da Bergamo, *Quæstio de strigis*, in Hansen, ed., *Quellen*, 195–200 at 198 (Stephens, *Demon Lovers*, 136–7); Bartolomeo Spina, *Quadruplex apologia contra Ponzinibium*, in *Quæstio de strigibus, una cum tractatu de præeminentia sacræ theologiæ et quadruplici apologia de lamiis contra Ponzinibium* (1523; repr. Rome, 1576), 160–1 (English trans. in Stephens, *Demon Lovers*, 153–4).

[42] Institoris, *Malleus Maleficarum*, ii, 244–54; Stephens, *Demon Lovers*, 140–2.

1489) found himself forced to accept precisely the 'literal reading' that Kramer opposed, but still opined that witches should be punished for their apostasy. Moreover, despite accepting the canon's interpretation, he cited the biblical examples of Habakkuk (Dan. 14:32–8, Vulgate) and Satan's transportation of Jesus to a high mountain (Mt. 4:3–11) as proof that such interactions were not impossible.[43]

In the century between *The Hammer of Witches* (1486) and Jean Bodin's *On the Demon-Mania of Witches* (1580), the most systematic and impressive refutation of arguments against the reality of witchcraft was Gianfrancesco Pico della Mirandola's *Strix* (The Witch, or on the Deceptions of Demons), published in Latin in 1523 and in Italian the following year.[44] In terms of its form, *Strix* is a standard Italian humanist philosophical dialogue in four voices, but its arguments are profoundly anti-humanistic, for it marshals every resource of philosophy, medicine, law, and theology to argue that all aspects of witchcraft are real and literally true. The dramatis personae are three Christian men and a convicted female witch. One of the men, Apistius (the Unbeliever or Sceptic) is a devout Christian who initially argues that the feats attributed to witches are impossible and ridiculous. His friend, Phronimus (the Prudent Man) attempts to convince Apistius that belief in witchcraft is not only compatible with Christian belief but actually necessary to it. During a long walk, Phronimus argues that ancient pagan religion and modern witchcraft are both varieties of demonic imposture based on idolatry. Every aspect of modern witchcraft, no matter how absurd or seemingly impossible, corresponds to some well-attested myth or practice of Greco-Roman paganism, says Phronimus, and to question the reality of witchcraft is thus to doubt the reality of Greece and Rome. In both cases, demons use their powers of illusion to convince gullible humans to believe and perform things that are sinful. Using scholastic terminology, Phronimus concludes that pagan idolatry and modern witchcraft are the same 'in substance', but differ in their 'accidents' (as if he were to argue that Peter and Paul are both men, but differ in their appearance).

Although Phronimus is an erudite humanist and a good Christian, he cannot convince Apistius, who is an equally learned scholar and a more idealistic Christian. At the end of their walk, they encounter the inquisitor Dicastes (Judge), who has been engaged in the trial of Strix, the eponymous witch. Dicastes is confident that with input from himself and from the Witch, Apistius' stubborn disbelief in witchcraft will vanish. The remainder of the dialogue shifts its focus to the Witch's 'expert testimony', and its ratification by the Judge. Having previously confessed everything during her trial, she is now required to give Apistius a second confession of the sort that witches were

---

[43] Ulrich Müller, *De lanijs et phitonicis mulieribus*, in Jörg Mauz, ed., *Ulrich Molitoris: Schriften*, (Konstanz, 1997), 63–132 at 80–3; Stephens, *Demon Lovers*, 139–40.

[44] Jean Bodin, *Démonomanie des sorciers* (partial English trans. in Randy A. Scott, *On the Demon-Mania of Witches* (Toronto, 2001). On Gianfrancesco Pico see Alfredo Perifano, 'Introduction', in Gianfrancesco Pico della Mirandola, *La Sorcière: dialogue en trois livres sur la tromperie des démons*, ed. Alfredo Perifano (Turnhout, 2007), 5–33; Stephens, *Demon Lovers*, 87–99; Stephens, 'Gianfrancesco Pico e la paura dell'immaginazione: dallo scetticismo alla stregoneria', *Rinascimento*, 2nd. ser., 43 (2003), 49–74.

expected to provide publicly when sentenced. Her confessions to infanticide, profanation of the sacraments, sexual promiscuity (including with demons), 'flying', concoction of the witches' ointment, and attendance at the sabbath provoke the wonder and disgust not only of Apistius, but of Phronimus. Analogies that appear profoundly specious to a modern reader are introduced in all seriousness: when Apistius continues to resist belief in witchcraft, Dicastes asks if he has ever seen a dead man resuscitated; of course not. Does he believe it possible? Yes, because it happens in the Gospels. But modern reality is far stranger than anything recounted there, says Dicastes. Does Apistius believe that ships cross the Atlantic to visit a new world? Of course, the sceptic replies; but on whose authority, asks the inquisitor? That of the merchants who say they have made the trip. Has he ever spoken to these merchants? No, 'but I have spoken with people who had heard it with their own ears from men who declared that they had personally made the trip'. Phronimus now springs the trap laid by Dicastes: unless Apistius suspects these people of taking pleasure in lies, he must also believe firmly that demons transport witches to sabbaths and copulate with them, for the men who describe these things are every bit as trustworthy as the merchants and their witnesses. And 'when many people are of the same opinion about something, and speak of it as if with one voice, it cannot seem credible that someone goes on claiming the right to deny it'.[45] On the basis of this proof and a few stories of demons being routed by the Catholic sacraments, Apistius converts and is renamed Pisticus (the Believer).

Pico's *Strix* was cited and quoted in several later treatises. Although its dialogic vehicle is more literary than usual, *Strix* is important for at least three reasons. First, because of its heavy dependence on *The Hammer of Witches*, and high praise of the treatise. Second, because, like the *Hammer* and a number of other witchcraft documents, it was written to defend a controversial witch-hunt. The Italian translation, by the Dominican inquisitor Leandro Alberti, was the first apologetic treatise intended to be read by and preached to the Italian laity.[46] Both the Latin original and Alberti's Italian translation were published before the final three of ten executions for the crime of witchcraft took place in 1525. Third, as Count of Mirandola, Pico himself was strongly implicated in the dynamics of the witch-hunt; although his role is not entirely clear, he either participated in some proceedings or had privileged access to the trial minutes. Albano Biondi plausibly opined that Pico 'did much more than simply lend the secular arm' to the inquisitor. Moreover, Pico's dialogue is closely related on both textual and personal grounds to two better-known Italian treatises from the same years: *On the Wonders of Witch-Sorceresses and Demons* (1521) by Silvestro Mazzolini (Prierias) and

---

[45] Gianfrancesco Pico della Mirandola, *Dialogus in tres libros divisus: Titulus est Strix* (Bologna, 1523), sigs. F2v–3r; see *La Sorcière: dialogue en trois livres sur la tromperie des démons*, ed. Alfredo Perifano (Turnhout, 2007), 94–5; English trans. in Stephens, *Demon Lovers*, 234–5.

[46] Gianfrancesco Pico, *Libro detto Strega, o delle illusioni del demonio* (1524), ed. Albano Biondi (Venice, 1989). A second Italian translation of *Strix* by Turino Turini was printed in 1555 (*La strega, overo de gli inganni de' demoni*, ed. Ida Li Vigni [Genoa, 1988]). A partial modern English trans. of *Strix* by Rod Boroughs is in *The Renaissance in Europe: An Anthology*, ed. Peter Elmer, Nick Webb, and Roberta Wood (New Haven, CT, 2000), 366–94.

the *Inquiry into Witches* (1523) by Mazzolini's pupil Bartolomeo Spina, who commented explicitly on the commonalities of the three texts.[47]

The *Strix* appears to reflect a reversal of Pico's personal opinions about witchcraft between 1500 and 1523. In 1501 he had expressed his distrust of the human imagination in *On the Imagination*, a short work framed as a comment on Aristotle's *De anima* (On the Soul). As an example of the imagination's proclivity to sin, Pico declared that demons 'run riot in the phantasies of men, and of women called witches [*striges*], and most ruinously seize upon their senses'.[48] This view, which derives from the canon *Episcopi*, reappeared in *Strix* as the naive opinion of Apistius the sceptic: although demons inspire and deceive witches, their crimes take place in their imagination rather than in reality.

In the two decades between *On the Imagination* and *Strix*, Pico repudiated Aristotle and devoted himself to the ancient Pyrrhonian sceptic Sextus Empiricus (d.210 CE), with strange results for his views on witchcraft. The study of Sextus was apparently enjoined upon him by Savonarola, who objected to Aristotelian and Neoplatonic philosophers' pretensions to knowledge and claims to harmonize the Christian faith with pagan philosophy. As Savonarola would have wished, Pico's massive *On the Errors of the Pagans and the Truth of Christianity* (1520) employed Sextus' sceptical arguments to discredit pagan philosophy, with special attention to Aristotle. Aristotle's reliance on the senses as the source of knowledge was not simply an inadequate substitute for revelation, it was actively pernicious, said Pico, who intended to discredit 'the Philosopher' in favour of the Bible. The aim of Pico's scepticism was fideistic: not a Pyrrhonian suspension of judgement, so that 'all would be in doubt', but rather so that the reader 'would turn from philosophy as a source of knowledge to . . . the Christian Revelation'.[49]

Pico's adoption of scepticism seems paradoxical to a modern rational sensibility. Rather than reinforce his earlier opinion that witches' confessions to metamorphosis, flying, and demonic encounters were deluded, scepticism served the opposite conclusion, that witchcraft was real and that everything the witches confessed, no matter how absurd, was true. *Strix* argues lucidly and explicitly that belief in the absolute truth value of witchcraft is a necessary correlative of Christian faith. Along the same lines,

---

[47] Pico, *Libro detto Strega*; Silvestro Mazzolini, *Reverendi Patris F. Silvestri Prieriatis . . . De strigimagarum dæmonumque mirandis* (1521; repr. Rome, 1575); Spina, *Quæstio de strigibus*, 91; Stephens, *Demon Lovers*, 87–92.

[48] Gianfrancesco Pico della Mirandola, *De imaginatione*; text and trans. in Harry Caplan, ed., *On the Imagination* (Westport, CT, 1971), 56–7; see Walter Stephens, 'Gianfrancesco Pico e la paura dell'immaginazione: dallo scetticismo alla stregoneria', *Rinascimento*, 2a serie, 43 (2003), 49–74.

[49] Gianfrancesco Pico della Mirandola, *Examen vanitatis doctrinæ gentium et veritatis Christianæ disciplinæ*, ii, 717–1264, in *Joannes Franciscus Picus Mirandulanus opera omnia* (1573; repr. Turin, 1972); see n. 10 above; Popkin, *History of Scepticism*, 20–1. On scepticism and fideism, see Floridi, 'The Rediscovery', 278–82.

John Wesley would baldly assert in 1768 that 'the giving up of [belief in] witchcraft is the giving up of the Bible'.[50]

Philosophical scepticism did not come into its own until after the texts of Sextus were printed, in 1562 and 1569. Thus, Pico's *Errors of the Pagans* had remarkably little influence on philosophers at large, and none that can be detected on witch-hunting. Montaigne gave scepticism real prominence in the 1580s, and his *Essays* (particularly 'On the Lame') provide the most familiar link between Pyrrhonism and witchcraft. But Pico's attitudes towards both scepticism about witchcraft and systematic philosophical scepticism offer an important insight into the mentality of his times. Both *Strix* and *Errors of the Pagans* are quests for stable truth in matters that generated hydra-like doubts, where certainty could not be won without at least acknowledging the difficulties of belief.

Arguments against the reality of witchcraft often focused on the confessions of witches. Reasons for doubting the evidentiary value of confessions could be theological, medical, or legal. Theological arguments were more frequent in defences of witchcraft reality, but some sceptics, such as Scot, declared that attributing human misfortune to demonic and human interaction affronted Divine Providence by diminishing God's power and justice. Medical and juridical objections often went hand in hand. Johann Weyer argued that the preponderance of poor, aged, ignorant, and malnourished women among defendants prosecuted for witchcraft implied that the crimes and demonic interactions they confessed to were attributable to delusions and hallucinations brought on by melancholia, an excess of black bile. Weyer was careful to specify that he did not doubt the reality of witchcraft, but only its relevance to the majority of individual prosecutions.

Reginald Scot, whose *Discoverie of Witchcraft* appeared in the year following Weyer's final redaction (i.e. in 1583), made many of the same arguments about the melancholic delusions of pathetic aged and poor defendants. Unlike Weyer, Scot also denied the possibility of real interaction between humans and demons, contesting the whole premise of demonic witchcraft, as discussed above.

Weyer's and Scot's views on melancholy were not at all new; they had been foreseen and pre-emptively challenged a century and a quarter earlier, by the inquisitor Girolamo Visconti, in two short treatises on witches.[51] According to Visconti, the 'melancholic insanity' diagnosis was already being used about 1460 by sceptics who objected to witch prosecution. The basis for their objection was the canon *Episcopi*, said Visconti, but it was erroneous to judge this heretical 'modern sect' of witches by such outdated evidence: 'I want to prove by [the canon *Episcopi* itself] that this sect is not afflicted by a

[50] Wesley, *Journal*, v, 265.

[51] Martine Ostorero, 'Visconti, Girolamo (Hieronymus Vicecomes) (d. ca. 1478)', in *Encyclopedia of Witchcraft*, iv, 1171–2; Astrid Estuardo Flaction, 'Girolamo Visconti, un témoin du débat sur la réalité de la sorcellerie au XVe siècle en Italie du Nord', in Martine Ostorero, Georg Modestin, and Kathrin Utz Tremp, eds, *Chasses aux sorcières et démonologie: Entre discours et pratiques (XIVᵉ–XVIIᵉ siècles)* (Florence, 2010), 389–403; Ostorero, *Le Diable au sabbat*, 688–93.

melancholic humour that would impede its members' use of reason and their freedom of the will.' If witches are ill and imagine their misdeeds, they cannot be heretics, cannot be punished, and, he argued, we will offend God by refusing to prosecute them and allowing their sect to grow.[52] Visconti's arguments were taken up from the other side by Andrea Alciati (d.1550), who, while admitting that apostasy and infanticide had often occurred, recommended purgatives such as hellebore and peony to restore the sanity of people who confessed to demonic transportation and the sabbath.[53]

Aside from melancholy and senility, sceptics questioned whether the experiences of witches could be hallucinations caused by pharmacological agents. Alonso Tostado introduced the possibility in his story of the 'flying' woman and her neighbours that is discussed above. While Tostado argued for the reality of demonic transportation in other cases, some sceptics found the pharmacological argument a sufficient explanation of all such phenomena.[54]

As Tostado's anecdote suggests, medical argumentation was peculiarly adaptable to sceptical experimentation. Bartolomeo Spina opposed inquisitors' experiments with witches and their ointments on the grounds that the devil could always inspire scepticism in onlookers by such tricks as instantaneously substituting a fictive double for the witch who was being observed, while he whisked her real person away to the sabbath.[55]

Even without invoking medical reasons, jurists could argue that witchcraft prosecution was legally invalid. Writing in 1520, Giovanni Francesco Ponzinibio combined a critique of common people's credulity with outrage over the injustices of inquisitorial practice, and asserted that civil law had the same authority over witchcraft trials as canon law; however, he was violently rebutted by Bartolomeo Spina, who demanded the burning of Ponzinibio's treatise.[56] The practice of torture was increasingly contested in the sixteenth and seventeenth centuries. Even Kramer had admitted that torture was frequently ineffective, making innocents confess while the guilty might resist. A watershed was the *Cautio criminalis* of Friedrich Spee, published in 1631, which

[52] Girolamo Visconti, *Lamiarum sive striarum opusculum* (Milan, 1490), sig. 1v; Stephens, *Demon Lovers*, 137–8.

[53] Andrea Alciati, *Parergon iuris libri* 8.22, in *Opera omnia* (Lyon, 1544), ii, 406–8 (Italian trans. ed. S. Abbiati, 248–53, in S. Abbiati, A. Agnoletto and M.-R. Lazzati, eds, *La stregoneria: Diavoli, streghe, inquisitori dal Trecento al Settecento* (1984; repr. Milan, 1991); Matteo Duni, 'Alciati, Andrea (1492–1550)', in *Encyclopedia of Witchcraft*, i, 29–30.

[54] H. Sidkey, *Witchcraft, Lycanthropy, Drugs, and Disease: An Anthropological Study of the European Witch-Hunts* (New York, 1997).

[55] Spina, *Quæstio de strigibus*, 5, 82–5; this and other experiments are discussed in Stephens, *Demon Lovers*, 159–76, and Stephens, 'Experiments and Tests', in *Encyclopedia of Witchcraft*, ii, 340–2.

[56] Giovanni Francesco Ponzinibio, *De lamiis et excellentia iuris utriusque* (1520), in *Tractatus duo: Unus de sortilegis D. Pauli Grillandi . . . alter de lamiis et excellentia iuris utriusque D. Ioannis Francisci Ponzinibii* (Frankfurt, 1592); Spina, *Tractatus de præeminentia*, 91–2; Spina, *Quadruplex apologia, Apologia prima*, 133–53 (see n. 41 above); brief Italian trans. by Sergio Abbiati in Abbiati, et al., eds, *La stregoneria*, 264–5. See Dries Vanysacker, 'Ponzinibio, Giovanni Francesco/Gianfrancesco (First Half of the Sixteenth Century)', in *Encyclopedia of Witchcraft*, iii, 912–13.

argued against the grossest abuses; Christian Thomasius' important *On the Crime of Magic* (1701) drew on Spee and several other seventeenth-century critiques.[57]

While theological, medical, and legal reasons for opposing witchcraft prosecution could be advanced in general or abstract terms, legal and medical objections were frequently adduced in individual cases: 'Witches exist, but this person is not one.' Given the dangerous theological and legal ramifications of expressing scepticism about witchcraft, it is seldom possible to know whether the first half of the proposition was advanced sincerely.

An increasingly important development in witchcraft controversy was the linking of *maleficium* with molestation by spirits, either from within the victim's person (possession) or from outside (obsession). As with proofs of demonic reality based on these phenomena, alleged proofs of witches' responsibility for molestation could be produced by experimentation. Such tests were also arranged for various other reasons, from demonstrating the reality of the possession to proving the superiority of Catholic exorcism or (for most Protestants) its inefficacy.[58]

6.6 TRAJECTORIES OF SCEPTICISM ABOUT WITCHCRAFT

The concept of demonic witchcraft accumulated within the historical context of overlapping sceptical crises, yet the inherent adaptability of demonological argumentation allowed it to absorb and neutralize objections, since doubt was already integral to its premises. As a result, although individuals often maintained fixed, dogmatic positions on the reality of witchcraft phenomena, consistency was not inevitable. Conversion from one extreme to the other was possible, while vacillation was not unusual. Tales of sceptics who were converted to belief in spirit possession and necromancy had been told in the third person several centuries before the formation of witchcraft concepts, as the examples in Caesarius of Heisterbach show. Putative real-life conversions are frequently mentioned in witchcraft treatises, usually involving eyewitnesses of sabbaths and other wonders. But few conversions were as rationally motivated as the fictional Apistius' in Pico's *Strix*.

---

[57] Edward Peters, *Torture* (New York, 1985). Excerpts from Spee and Thomasius are in Kors and Peters, eds, *Witchcraft in Europe*, 425–9, 444–8.

[58] Stephens, *Demon Lovers*, 145–79; D. P. Walker, *Unclean Spirits: Possession and Exorcism in France and England in the Late Sixteenth Century* (Philadelphia, PA, 1981); Sarah Ferber, *Demonic Possession and Exorcism in Early Modern France* (New York, 2004); Moshe Sluhovsky, *Believe Not Every Spirit: Possession, Mysticism, and Discernment in Early Modern Catholicism* (Chicago, 2007). Martine Ostorero, *Le Diable au sabbat*, 7–8, has shown that Nicolas Jacquier made the connection between possession and *maleficium* as early as 1452.

The opposite trajectory, from belief to scepticism, is dominated by the example of Alonso de Salazar Frías, an inquisitor whose investigations in the first two decades of the 1600s led him to contest over two thousand confessions, both by investigating the circumstantial details of alleged confessions and by testing empirically the effects of witches' ointments. Convinced of widespread delusion among defendants and their abusive treatment by inquisitors, Salazar insisted that the terms of debate move from what the devil was theoretically capable of doing to what demonstrably happened in individual circumstances.[59]

Finally, there is evidence of vacillation throughout the period, particularly in first-person accounts. The poet Tasso is particularly instructive. In his epic poem *Jerusalem Delivered* (1575/81), he mentioned the trysts of witches and demons as a common belief. His own literary theory allowed Tasso license to represent religious concepts as factual without being convinced of their truth. But when his personal religious crisis deepened, his philosophical dialogues followed the trajectory of Gianfrancesco Pico, initially representing witches as delusional (*c*.1580) but later as the sexual partners of incubus demons (1587). More bluntly than Pico's *Strix*, Tasso's philosophical dialogue, *The Messenger*, betrays the author's struggle to convince himself; it reveals an ongoing resistance to scepticism rather than a conversion to serene belief.[60]

While witchcraft controversies took place in an era of sceptical crises, philosophical scepticism cannot be shown to have had an appreciable effect on the decline of witch-hunting. Evidence accumulated since the 1960s shows that reasoned discourse effected far less change than social factors, such as difficulties in obtaining convictions and the emotional exhaustion of participants in the prosecutorial process. As Stuart Clark concludes, 'the incessant raising of questions' about reasons for the decline 'has not yet been matched by the finding of good answers'.[61]

FURTHER READING

Clark, Stuart, *Thinking with Demons: The Idea of Witchcraft in Early Modern Europe* (Oxford, 1997), 151–280.
Duni, Matteo, 'Skepticism', in Richard M. Golden, ed., *Encyclopedia of Witchcraft: The Western Tradition* (Santa Barbara, CA, 2006), 1044–50.

[59] Gustav Henningsen, *The Witches' Advocate: Basque Witchcraft and the Spanish Inquisition* (Reno, NV, 1980); Gustav Henningsen, ed., *The Salazar Documents: Alonso de Salazar Frías and Others on the Basque Witch Persecution* (Leiden, 2004), excerpt in Kors and Peters, eds, *Witchcraft in Europe*, 407–19.

[60] Torquato Tasso, *Gerusalemme liberata*, canto 13, stanzas 4–12, ed. Lanfranco Caretti (Turin, 1979), 297–9; Tasso, *Il messaggiero*, i, 309–83. See Stuart Clark, 'Tasso and the Literature of Witchcraft', in J. Salmons and W. Moretti, eds, *The Renaissance in Ferrara and its European Horizons* (Cardiff, 1984), 3–21; Walter Stephens, 'Tasso and the Witches', *Annali d'Italianistica*, 12 (1994), 181–202; Stephens, 'Tasso, Torquato (1544-1595)', in *Encyclopedia of Witchcraft*, iv, 1108–9.

[61] Clark, *Thinking with Demons*, 683; Brian P. Levack, 'The Decline and End of Witchcraft Prosecutions', in Bengt Ankarloo and Stuart Clark, eds, *Witchcraft and Magic in Europe: The Eighteenth and Nineteenth Centuries* (London, 1999), 3–93.

Floridi, Luciano, 'The Rediscovery and Posthumous Influence of Scepticism', in Richard Bett, ed., *The Cambridge Companion to Ancient Scepticism* (Cambridge, 2010), 267–87.

Flynn, Tom, ed., *The New Encyclopedia of Unbelief*, foreword by Richard Dawkins (Amherst, MA, 2007).

Kors, Alan Charles and Peters, Edward, *Witchcraft in Europe 400–1700: A Documentary History* (2nd edn, Philadelphia, PA, 2001).

Levack, Brian P., 'The Decline and End of Witchcraft Prosecutions', in Bengt Ankarloo and Stuart Clark, eds, *Witchcraft and Magic in Europe: The Eighteenth and Nineteenth Centuries* (London, 1999), 3–93.

Levack, Brian P., ed., *The Witchcraft Sourcebook* (New York and London, 2004).

Levack, Brian P., *The Witch-Hunt in Early Modern Europe* (3rd edn, Harlow, 2006), 253–88.

Ostorero, Martine, *Le Diable au sabbat: Littérature démonologique et sorcellerie (1440–1460)* (Florence, 2011).

Pico della Mirandola, Gianfrancesco, *La Sorcière: dialogue en trois livres sur la tromperie des démons*, ed. Alfredo Perifano (Turnhout, 2007).

Popkin, Richard, *The History of Scepticism: From Savonarola to Bayle* (3rd edn, Oxford, 2003).

Scot, Reginald, *The Discoverie of Witchcraft*, ed. Brinsley Nicholson (1584; repr. London, 1886).

Stephens, Walter, *Demon Lovers: Witchcraft, Sex, and the Crisis of Belief* (Chicago, 2002).

Stephens, Walter, '"Habeas Corpus": Demonic Bodies in Ficino, Psellus, and *Malleus maleficarum*', in Julia L. Hairston and Walter Stephens, eds, *The Body in Early Modern Italy* (Baltimore, MD, 2010), 74–91.

Weyer, Johann, *Witches, Devils, and Doctors in the Renaissance: Johann Weyer, De præstigiis dæmonum*, tr. John Shea and ed. George Mora, Benjamin Kohl, Erik Midelfort, and Helen Baker, foreword by John Weber et al. (Binghamton, NY, 1991).

CHAPTER 7

··

WITCHCRAFT IN EARLY MODERN LITERATURE[1]

··

DIANE PURKISS

WHILE historians plod through court records, writers like to chase shadowy fantasies in all their extreme variants. Although Greek and Latin literature is fitfully in accord with the magical practices that surrounded it, medieval and Renaissance literature tends to select the most vivid aspects of witchcraft for detailed treatment. Only partially informed about the demonological context, only ever hazily aware of the trials it purports to treat, the early modern drama on which this chapter concentrates is of use to the historian of witchcraft because it shows how cultural narratives circulate between high and low—the low as capable of informing the high as vice versa—and how under-studied institutions like the stage play a part in keeping key stories in motion long after theologians cease to promulgate them. All literary representations produced contemporaneously with the principal period of the witch trials are informed by earlier literary texts, particularly classical literature and medieval romances.

Most literary criticism on witchcraft in the past twenty years has focused on well-known dramatic texts such as *Macbeth*, and has tried to measure them against surviving trial records, tending to assume a close correspondence between dramatists and social contexts; the latter is usually still seen as a way of solving problems presented by the former. More detailed work on individual plays has shown that correspondences are often less close than anticipated. Most of the best recent work has approached witches and their representation in terms of gender. Authors, including Jonson, Herrick, and Milton, have been analysed by feminist critics in relation to their representations of gender through witch figures.[2] Most work has been on drama.

[1] I am grateful for the invaluable assistance of Bronwyn Johnston in researching and writing this chapter.

[2] Jacqueline DiSalvo, 'Fear of Flying: Milton on the Boundaries between Witchcraft and Inspiration', *English Literary Renaissance*, 18 (1988), 114–37.

In 1995, Deborah Willis claimed that both well-known dramas and witch trials reflected a preoccupation with the problematic maternal body, a viewpoint which chimed with research by the present writer and with earlier work by Gail Kern Paster on the embarrassments of the body. New historicist feminist work by Karen Newman, Dympna Callaghan, and Frances Dolan has focused on the gender of the witch in texts by Shakespeare and others, examining witch trials alongside playtexts. More recently, Mary Ellen Lamb's work has emphasized the awkward relations between popular culture as a quarry for plots and sensations and the dramatists who disdain it.[3]

7.1 GREEK AND ROMAN WITCHES

One of the most durable historical mistakes is the idea that Christianity was responsible for the fear of witches. Actually, witches were dreaded in the Greek and Roman worlds, and early modern drama draws extensively on its Greek and Roman precursors. Euripides gave the world Medea, whose magical prowess made her capable of raising the dead, but let her kill her own children in revenge for Jason's adultery. In classical literature, it is her knowledge of herbs and medicine that predominates. Her child murder is not even witchcraft; it floats free of the issues of her powers: 'Let there be no weakness now,/no tender memories of their birth, of them as babies:/forget them now, and weep for them after.'[4] Jason's last lines in Seneca's play show the bleakness of Seneca's world: 'testare nullos esse, qua veheris, deos (Bear witness that where you go the gods are not)' (1026–7).[5] But there is no evidence that he is right. Medea flies unharmed to Athens, where she becomes the stepmother of the hero Theseus.[6] In Theocritus' *Idyll II*, the speaker is a woman: 'Be with me, Hecatê, queen of terrors; help me/To make these drugs.'[7] The poem points to fear, the fear of being enslaved. Hecate is queen of terrors here, capable of 'forcing' the lover home to the girl to whom he used to visit three or four times a day. If the magic doesn't bind him, the girl says, 'I'll make him beat at death's door to be let in.' Theocritus' *Idyll II* ('Sorceress') became a model

---

[3] Deborah Willis, *Malevolent Nurture: Witch-hunting and Maternal Power in Early Modern England* (Ithaca, NY, 1995); Gail Kern Paster, *The Body Embarrassed: Drama and the Disciplines of Shame in Early Modern England* (Ithaca, NY, 1993); Dympna Callaghan, Lorraine Helms, and Jyotsna G. Singh, *Wayward Sisters: Shakespeare and Feminist Politics* (New York, 1994); Frances E. Dolan, *Dangerous Familiars: Representations of Domestic Crime in England, 1550–1700* (Ithaca, NY, 1994); Karen Newman, *Fashioning Femininity and English Renaissance Drama* (Chicago, 1991).

[4] Euripides, *Medea*, tr. Robin Robertson (New York, 2009).

[5] *Seneca his tenne Tragedies, translated into Englysh*, tr. J. Heywood (London, 1581), 2.90. See also *The Seventh Tragedie of Seneca, Entitled Medea*, tr. J. Studley (London, 1566); *Seneca: Tragedies*, ed. and tr. Frank Justus Miller (Cambridge, MA, 1917), ii, 807–8. My translation.

[6] See the essays in James Joseph Clauss and Sarah Iles Johnston, eds, *Medea: Essays on Medea in Myth, Literature, Philosophy, and Art* (Princeton, 1997).

[7] Theocritus, *Idylls*, tr. Robert Wells (Manchester, 1988), 60.

for many later witch scenes. However, Theocritus is mild compared with some of the magical papyri, tiny found poems torn by loathing and longing:[8]

> That Theodotis the daughter of Eus may no longer submit to penetration by a man other than me alone, Ammonion, the son of Hermitaris, and that she may apply her thigh to my thigh, her genitals to my genitals, for sex with me for the entire span of her life.[9]

Is this the fear of love itself, often understood in terms of bondage and paralysis in the ancient world? But it is also the fear that love and desire 'correct' a natural gender imbalance, to be restored by the violence of the spells.

7.2 MEDIEVAL WOMEN OF MAGIC

The power of enchantresses to rape powerful men was shown in many medieval romances, where women possessed of magic could overpower even knights who were normally self-possessed, and then use them as love slaves or toys. Morgan le Fay is 'the false sorseres and wycche moste that is now lyvying'.[10] Morgan is 'a great clerke of nygromancye' (1.2), which seems to mean the creation of ensnaring illusions, but implies the need to seize and use the bodies of humans, especially those of the most highly prized knights. Morgan uses 'false crauftis' to trap her lover Accolon and make him attempt to kill Arthur, and she also imprisons Lancelot by putting a spell on him 'that he shall not awake of all this seven owres' (6.3. 256). Necromantic exploitation of captive bodies bleeds into the magical use of dead bodies; a number of medieval romances set out to explore the way in which love makes every dead body into a relic. In Malory's *Morte d'Arthur*, the sorceress Hallewes threatens Lancelot. Hallewes inhabits a chapel, the Chapel Perilous, from which Lancelot must purloin healing relics, a piece of cloth, and a sword. But Hallewes threatens to turn the tables on him by making the knight himself into a relic. She offers to kiss him, and he declines; then she explains that if he had said yes, she would have preserved his dead body so as to be able to kiss and hold it in her arms every day:

> sytthen I may not rejoyse the nother thy body on lyve, I had kepte no more joy in this worlde but to have thy body dede. Then wolde I have bawmed it and sered it, and so to have kepte hit my lyve dayes; and dayly I sholde have clypped the and kissed the.[11]

---

[8] A found poem, like a found object, involves the use of an object which has not been designed for an artistic purpose, but which exists for another purpose and is taken up aesthetically. Found objects may be utilitarian manufactured items, or natural objects.

[9] Daniel Ogden, *Magic, Witchcraft, and Ghosts* (Oxford, 2009), 231.

[10] Thomas Malory, *Morte D'Arthur*, ed. Stephen H. A. Shepherd (New York, 2003), 8.34.

[11] Malory, *Morte D'Arthur*, i, 281.3–20.

Hallewes' desires mark her as a witch, and it is as such that Lancelot replies to her: 'Jesu preserve me frome youre subtyle crauftys!'[12] Such division of the body into potent parts was an apt symbol of civil war, as it may have been for Malory, writing during the grim carnage of the Wars of the Roses—a battle to possess and control bloodlines as fierce and passionate as any erotic magic. As relics themselves became problematic, even necromantic, so necromantic witches became the most obvious model of witchcraft for dramatists trying to interpret what strange old women might be doing in the countryside.

7.3 NECROMANCY AND DRAMA

Rectors in the late Elizabethan Lake District were dismayed to discover among their congregations both magic users and papist sympathizers. A woman named Agnes Watson was reported because she 'kept a dead man's scalp'. The interesting thing about Agnes is that we cannot be certain about her. Was she keeping the scalp because it was a relic of some kind? People did keep particularly sacred items after the Henrician Reformation and well into Charles' reign. Or was Agnes keeping the scalp as a grisly trophy for use in necromancy? The fact that we cannot know is instructive, because it points towards the ideological and cultural overlap between relics on the one hand, and the materials of necromancy on the other. The scalp is an isolated fragment in many senses; it is plainly metonymic, but we do not know anything of the whole from which it is taken, and hence we cannot know the power with which it is invested. Conversely, its grisliness—the fact that it is a *fragment*—points to a link between the dismembering of the dead and iconoclasm, which always troubled equations between the iconoclasts and forces of good. Relics and their powers could be understood as a licensed form of necromancy, one in which fragments of the bodies of the dead are reanimated to curative or sometimes vatic purposes. Witches and icons were linked by Reformers. The Virgin Mary was called 'the witch of Walsingham'. In Latvia, a wooden statue of the Virgin Mary was boisterously swum as a witch; being wood, it failed, and was duly burnt. As iconolatry collapsed into necromancy, the relation between signs and acts or bodies was under threat, and with it the male identity. An iconoclast might wish to render a statue 'dumb', incapable of suggesting story; by breaking it the story too is demolished—and may itself even be the true target of such violence. The witches in *Macbeth* similarly violate bodies by stripping away their stories in the process of fragmentation; in so doing they instruct their culture in the value of iconoclasm.

---

[12] Janet Knepper, 'A Bad Girl Will Love You to Death', in Bonnie Wheeler and Fiona Tolhurst, eds, *On Arthurian Women* (Dallas, TX, 2001), 229–44. See also Geraldine Heng, 'Enchanted Ground: The Feminine Subtext in Malory', in Thelma S. Fenster, ed., *Arthurian Women* (New York, 2000), 97–114. Carlo Ginzburg, *Ecstasies: Deciphering the Witches' Sabbath* (London, 1990), 75.

For Reformers, the dead were grubby; the transi tombs, which had become popular in chantries, may have reinforced the idea that all flesh is grass, but this did not mean that people wanted to see it or be reminded of it. The same nausea aroused by the dead was also stimulated by relics; Robert Bellarmine remarked that 'there is nothing [Protestants] shudder at so much as the veneration of relics'. Their links with filth are apparent when Latimer talked of relics as 'great bullocks' horns, and locks of hair, and filthy rags, gobbets of wood, under the name of parcels of the holy cross'. Samuel Harsnett was similarly sickened by the bits of the English martyrs used in a Jacobean rite of exorcism, 'Campion's thumb put into Fid's mouth...what wonders they wrought with these poor she-devils, how they made them to vomit, screech and quack like geese that had swallowed down a gag?'[13] The association often made by Reformers between relics and the female rituals of childbirth strengthened the sense that there was something messy about the whole business of the religious and powerful body part. The same distaste came to attach itself to the images that had more or less replaced relics as objects of devotion, in part because Counter-Reformation artists like Rubens actively courted an association between the image and the body by an increase in graphic realism, especially in the depiction of martyrs. This included an eroticization of martyrdom that drew attention to the bodiliness of iconolatry. Thomas Cromwell's 1538 proclamation explicitly outlawed 'candles or tapers to images and relics, or kissing or licking the same'. If an image comes to signify a body, it will partake of that body's capacity to horrify and disgust, a fetishism paradoxically increased by the dismemberment of iconoclasm itself. The use of the icon to bring back the dead—as a line to heaven—is uncomfortably close to necromancy. In contemplating this kind of figure with horror, the Reformers were therefore half-consciously teaching their followers to 'read' relics in particular and icons in general as signifiers of necromancy.

All this is visible in *Macbeth*. Using the body parts of various persons who have died before their time, the witches conjure up apparitions, who have true vatic powers but who also mislead. If Shakespeare had to cobble up more elaborate witches than he had originally intended, there is little doubt about where he turned for inspiration: to the classics, and to Lucan's *Pharsalia*. Yet there is an important difference. In Lucan's portrayal of the Thessalian witches, the process of dismemberment is emphasized—the witch bursts nooses with her own mouth, sinks her hands into its eyes, and tugs on the corpse with all her weight when a muscle refuses to come away. In Shakespeare, we never see the witches chopping up bodies. Nor do we see the body parts that go into the cauldron as part of larger wholes, but *as fragments*. And yet they are still metonyms of stories; take the most striking, the 'finger of birth-strangled babe, ditch-delivered by a drab', an intensely condensed story of parish boundary enforcement, infanticide, and exile. It recalls one of London's most prized relics, the finger of one of the Holy Innocents, returned to St Stephen Walbrook in 1553. Holy Innocents' Day was especially controversial with Reformers because of its strong links with misrule in the

13 Eamon Duffy, *The Stripping of the Altars* (New Haven, CT, 2000), 414–15.

custom of electing a choirboy to be a boy bishop.[14] This transgressive rite was one in which children took on adult powers, so it is directly relevant to *Macbeth*'s cauldron scene, in which child apparitions take power over Macbeth, foreshadowing the power taken by Macduff.

This anxiety increased enormously through the Laudian reforms and the opening years of the Civil War, and manifested itself in two kinds of activity, which felt to their practitioners as if they were resolving critical problems: iconoclasm and witch-hunting. The largest single witch-hunt England was ever to know occurred in the winter of 1644–5, when more than one hundred witches were hanged. These prosecutions were part of a particular kind of civil war that only some combatants were fighting. Just as the Second World War became for some Germans (though not for all) a war against the Jews, so the Civil War became for some a war against 'popery', an elastic term that could be given different valencies, but which often centred on misuse of the body or of representations of the body. The witch embodied the misuse of the body, including her own; her familiars licking her body uncannily replicated pilgrims kissing and licking the grimy relics and icons of the pre-Reformation Church, while her use of the body parts or images of the bodies of others in her rituals signified her link to icons. I want to focus on the circulation and reading of one particular atrocity story, which probably originates in literature rather than life, which may well mean Lucan's witch Erictho gave birth to it. The primary link between Erictho and the witches in *Macbeth* is that she rips foetuses from wombs:

> Volnere sic ventris, non qua natura vocabat,/Extrahitur partus calidis ponendus in aris; (through a wound in the belly, not nature's exit/The foetus is extracted to be put on burning altars). (557–60)

Ripping a foetus from its mother's living womb was the *ne plus ultra* of atrocity stories. It began to circulate in the Thirty Years' War, and especially in the Ulster Rising, both conflicts where Protestants could link this action with icons and hence with witchcraft:

> they laid hold on his wife being big with child, and ravished her, then ripped open her womb, and like so many Neros undauntedly viewed natures bed of conception, afterward took her and her Infant and sacrificed in fire their wounded bodies to appease their Immaculate Souls.[15]

This horrible story shows how the image of the baby untimely ripped from its mother had taken root in the early modern imagination. The baby is treated like a relic or icon, transgressively broken up. When Cheapside Cross was torn down, the iconoclasts assailed it by tearing the figure of the infant Jesus from the arms of its mother and smashing it on the ground. Iconoclasm fantasizes about its own heart of darkness. This Erichthonian crime is linked with patrilinearity and the replication of the father in the body of the infant, both because the icon is a threat to that identity, being a false and

---

[14] Ronald Hutton, *Stations of the Sun* (Oxford, 1996), 100ff.
[15] *A Bloody Batell: or the Rebels Overthrow and Protestants victorie* (1641, n.p.).

deceptive replication, and because relics were not true synecdoches, but offered, necromantically, to control those to whom they appeared to offer power. Like the babies torn from their mothers, Macduff represents exactly the power over death that Macbeth—as a soldier—longs to achieve but has been unable to master. Macduff should be an *aoros*, a baby who dies untimely, and he isn't; his mother is presumably the *aoros*, and she may also be *biaiothanatoi*, dead by violence. These were the two classes of dead most likely to be ghosts, and easiest to summon. Macduff still carries some of their power, and this is, in part, the power of prophecy. This also has to do with prophecy and what it means: prophecy is a synecdoche of the future, the fetish of the past; because both prophecy and fetish bend time, one can be used to call up the other.

In *Macbeth*, bringing remnants of corpses together leads to the unnatural birth of a prodigious child, but despite the cauldron's womblike qualities it does not represent the witch's inside. The scene of bodily horror shifts from the battlefield to the woman's reproductive system—or the latter comes to seem an apt metaphor for the former. So an inverted Erictho appears in the birth of monsters in a group of satirical playtexts that feature an Erictho-like figure that combines a problematic relation between inside and outside with the power to prophesy. These *Mistress Parliament* satires were informed by the many monster pamphlets of the Civil War years, which understood the monster as a prodigy. The birth of monsters was linked in a 1645 pamphlet to the presence of witches and papists in the neighbourhood: 'No parts in England have so many witches, none fuller of Papists.' The mother of the monster is described on the title page as 'a Popish gentlewoman', who has icons in her home, 'many popish pictures and crucifixes, and other popish trumpery in which she much delighted' (8). In such stories, the mother is cast as the susceptible victim of the power of art, the believer whose relation to God—and to her husband—is blocked by her too willing apprehension of the idol. The idea of maternal imagination as the dominant force in the creation of monstrosity or defect grew in the seventeenth century, ousting the idea of monsters as a direct warning from God. That substitution—of maternal obstinacy for divine signification— foregrounded the monster precisely as mixed body parts. It reflected an alteration of the site of anxiety from divine to human sovereignty, from icons to their worshippers, from diabolism to witches. Consequently, the monstrous birth narrative offered peculiar opportunities to represent the disorder resulting from a radical break with patriarchalism.

But it is in Milton that we find both Erictho's most natural explorer and the greatest evasions of her implications. Hags abound in the prose, especially in *Apology against a Pamphlet*. Here Milton links together the personified icon with the figure of the witch:

> And she [the Roman Catholic Church] *like a witch*, but with a contrary policy did not take something of theirs that she might still have powers to bewitch them, but for the same intent left something of her own behind her. And that her whorish cunning should prevail to work upon us her deceitful ends . . . We cry out sacriledge and misdevotion against those who in zeal here demolisht the dens and cages of her uncleane wallowings. (942.20, emphasis mine)

Note the logic of cleansing in the last sentence; the iconoclasts are cleaning up after a witch, who is associated with filth. Meanwhile, the icons that are synecdochal of her power operate like body-part fetishes, keeping the past unnaturally alive and resuscitating the dead body of the Catholic past. As fetishes they are themselves unnatural *merely by virtue of being fetishes*, because to be a fetish is to be dirt, to be a body part, to be an object imbued with a cultural power that always threatens unmanageability. It is against the whole idea of the fetish in the realm of the supernatural that Milton and the iconoclasts try to wage war, and the figure of the necromantic witch is ideologically symbolic of and crucial to their endeavours. She symbolizes powerfully the dangers posed by fetishes; they give power, illegitimately, to those who are not entitled to it, such as usurpers, tyrants, and, above all, figures of femininity. As such, her symbolic power can be used to taint the very idea of the religious fetish or icon with terror by linking it, as dead bodies in churches were linked, with decay, death and disease rather than with their management. Milton's version of Martin Bucer's notions of divorce reflect his understanding of the connections between witchcraft, idolatry, and threats to masculinity:

> If the husband can prove the wife to be an adulteress, *a witch*, a murderesse . . . to have *violated sepulchres*, committed sacrelege. (2.462.29, emphasis mine)

The same fecund metaphor of the baby-killing witch came to stage life before *Macbeth*, in John Marston's *Sophonisba*. While Lucan's Erictho is largely useful as a political prophet, Marston's Erictho is largely a vehicle for love magic. However, Marston will not allow Erictho the lavish, terrifying powers allotted to magic in ancient love spells. Like Reginald Scot—and most of the other dramatists—Marston takes the orthodox line that witches' powers are limited or even delusional; 'could thy weak soul imagine/That 'tis within the grasp of heaven or hell/to enforce love?' (5.1.4–6). Erictho can, however, summon storms and earthquakes, like Prospero, and, also like Prospero, she does this through necromancy. The 1604 Witchcraft Act makes the same connection between the dead body and power to control the bodies of the living:

> or take any dead man woman or child out of his her or theire grave or any other place where the dead body resteth, or the skin, bone or any other parte of any dead person.[16]

Initially, Erictho herself claims: 'forsaken graves and tombs, the ghosts forced out/She joys to inhabit' (4.1.100–1). But she is ultimately portrayed as an ineffectual agent of illicit desires.

---

[16] http://www.corvardus.f9.co.uk/religion/wicca/witch1736.htm.

7.4 SHAKESPEARE AND WITCH TRIALS

Say the words 'Shakespeare' and 'witch' in a sentence, and most people will think first of *Macbeth*. There are, however, two Shakespeare plays in which characters are accused of witchcraft, and *Macbeth* is not one of them. In *Othello*, Othello himself stands trial for enchanting Desdemona; her father is certain that only witchcraft could explain her attraction to him:

> Damn'd as thou art, thou hast enchanted her;
> For I'll refer me to all things of sense,
> If she in chains of magic were not bound,
> . . . Run from her guardage to the sooty bosom
> Of such a thing as thou. (1.2)

Othello is forced to defend himself from the charge of witchcraft before the duke: Brabantio repeats, 'She is abused, stol'n from me, and corrupted/By spells and medicines bought of mountebanks' (1.3). Othello's defence seems sound; he has told Desdemona stories of faraway lands, 'Men whose heads/Do grow beneath their shoulders... This only is the witchcraft I have used', to which the duke responds, 'I think this tale would win my daughter too', words of generous acceptance, and when Desdemona says, 'I saw Othello's visage in his mind', all seems settled in a high humanist register. But this is Act I of a five-act play, and by Act III it is hideously clear that the art of telling stories can indeed bring men to harm. Iago's story of Desdemona's adultery, told with the conviction of a born liar, is convincing because it has a prop, the handkerchief. Questioning Desdemona about the loss of this love token, Othello adds his own invention to Iago's, spinning exactly the kind of exotic story that won her in the first place, a story about witchcraft: 'That handkerchief/Did an Egyptian to my mother give;/She was a charmer, and could almost read/The thoughts of people.' By now, Othello is adhering to the very worldview that would have condemned *him*. He and Desdemona are now caught in that world, the same world where love is a terrible, resistless compulsion, a sociopathology, and fantasy.

The plot is reprised in the other play in which a character is actually accused of witchcraft, *The Winter's Tale*. Leontes, as jealous as Othello but without an Iago to provoke and excuse him, brutally rejects his newborn daughter, and accuses his wife's friend Paulina of being a witch as she brings his baby daughter to him; laying down the child, she is greeted with an outburst: 'Out!/A mankind witch! Hence with her, out o' door' and demands: 'Take up the bastard;/Take't up, I say; give't to thy crone.' He also calls her 'a gross hag'. Like the accusation in Othello, this accusation is false. And yet, as in *Othello*, the accusation seems to spread outwards from the word 'witch', which might be the merest insult, to engulf those who seemed innocent. Leontes soon finds himself in a witchlike infanticidal role in his reaction to Perdita:

> If thou refuse ... [to kill the baby]
> The bastard brains with these my proper hands
> Shall I dash out.

Nobody shudders fearfully over Leontes' attempt to command infanticidal murder. Nobody thinks *he* might be a witch. But he is here reprising a character whose every action invites scrutiny for witch beliefs. In the text of *Macbeth* we have before us, Lady Macbeth keeps alluding, not narratively, but metaphorically, to a lost or dead baby, and once, crucially, to a baby she murdered herself:[17]

> I would, while it was smiling in my face,
> Have plucked my nipple from his boneless gums
> And dashed the brains out, had I so sworn
> As you have done to this. (1.7.54–9)

This baby is figured in sensuous materiality. Shakespeare *delays* the violence to allow us to experience an erotic and bodily closeness; Lady Macbeth's resolute 'I would' is followed by an evocation of tenderness that defers the violent end and makes anticipation of it seem worse—'while it was smiling in my face'. Now comes the stroke of real genius; 'Have plucked my nipple from his boneless gums.' Is *this* the act of untender, unmaternal resolution, the refusal of food? Lady Macbeth is, for a second, merely someone who restrains her child's greed for suckling, but then comes the terrific force of 'and dashed the brains out', delayed again and hence given added force by that initial 'and'. 'Dashed' is just the right word; imagine how much 'knocked' would reduce the force of the lines, losing that onomatopoeic sense of splattering that makes 'dashed' so untender. The very senses that made us respond to the baby so tenderly are now turned to a painful bodily awareness of his destruction, as the imaginary baby becomes a kind of martyr.

Lady Macbeth's other long speech is also haunted by the ghost of a dead baby—even if he only dies in story— and is a way of understanding Lady Macbeth's relations to the supernatural. For it is Lady Macbeth, not Macbeth, and not the Weird Sisters, who delivers the only authentic invocation to the powers of darkness in this play to which so much theatrical superstition attaches:

> Come, you spirits
> That tend on mortal thoughts, unsex me here
> and fill me from the crown to the toe topful
> Of direst cruelty. Make thick my blood
> Stop up th' accents and passage to remorse,
> that no compunctious visitings of nature
> Shake my fell purpose, nor keep peace between
> Th'effect and it. Come to my woman's breasts
> And take my milk for gall, your murdering ministers.

---

[17] *Macbeth* is only in the 1623 Folio, which does not render it problem-free.

This speech is usually read as a renunciation of the sexed body. But what does that mean within the context of the play? The witches, of course, are unsexed; their gender is to Banquo problematically indeterminate because they have beards. But what kind of marker are beards in *women*? Beards are markers of old age, when hair begins to grow in places coded as smooth in young women. What Banquo is seeing is a body unsexed by *old age*, and we shall see in a moment that this is how Lady Macbeth marks her body too. Old age brings the functions of the female body to a halt. Lady Macbeth is making the same choice as the so-called fairy witches who gained their powers by giving up babies to the fairies in order to gain occult powers, but making it much more comprehensively. She is wishing for early menopause, and this is why she asks that her blood be made thick. A witch's blood was thought to be so thick with old age, so lacking in fire that it was impossible to extract it, and it was this idea that lay behind the notion that a witch's body could not be pierced by shot or by a pin. Such hardness is inimical to the soft body of the mother. Yet this is the body Lady Macbeth desires for *herself*: a body that is dried and preserved—just as Hallewes wants to do with Lancelot—a body that is a dead end, not capable of multiplying. With her reproductivity denied, her hard body seems inimical to time, not unlike the body of a virgin. Her body now seems static, caught forever at the instant of her crime like that of an inverse martyr. The witch's body is thus like the body of the saint in being the way in which supernatural power transmits itself to other parts of the material world.

Similarly, Lady Macbeth offers to substitute gall for her breast milk. To early modern medicine, breast milk was impure blood from the womb that was made white and pure by the burning fires of maternal love, which also drew it upwards through the body until it reached the breasts.[18] By contrast, the gall which Lady Macbeth substitutes for milk shows that her heart has failed in maternal love and has been filled instead with the poison in which witches are thought to deal. In an era when babies who were not breastfed were far more likely to die than those who were, she imagines herself murdering her child, via the trope of a refusal to feed it. Lady Macbeth's double refusal of breast milk marks her as a witch, too, because witches were beings who stole the milk of animal and human mothers, substituting blood for it. And, furthermore, she imagines herself not only choosing *not* to feed the child, but to feed something else—to feed the familiar spirits she summons. Worse still, these spectral images of infanticide are haunted by the image of the female demons whose breast milk acted as poison to babies, especially the Jewish mother-demon Lilith and the Byzantine Lamashtu.

Through her sacrifice of any real or potential children, her wish to be prematurely ancient and withered, her summoning of familiars, and her story of sensuous child sacrifice, Lady Macbeth is the play's only true witch. In the play's final act, her shocked repetitive washings uncannily and chillingly replicate the many rituals of relic-devotion, although these ritual cleansings are ineffective because nothing can wipe out the stain of murder from her sight, nor its smell. Such blood spots are simple signs

[18] Jacques Guillemeau, *Child-birth, or, The happy deliuerie of women, etc.* (London, 1635).

of witchcraft. A witch mark in England was a demon's suckling place, but it could also be wounds or bruises on waking that the witches could not explain. The devil left a secret mark on those who made a compact with him. Usually the mark took the form of some kind of sign of bodily relations with the devil, but in England it was more usually a sign of perverse nurturance, a misplaced teat from which devils rather than children were fed. The marks on Lady Macbeth's hands tie in her acts with her will to murder children, through half-remembered stories of host-theft and child murder. Just as Lady Macbeth has denied the supernatural power of Duncan's royal body, so that power manifests itself forcibly in her eyes by the reappearance of his blood, just as it did for the infanticidal mothers of popular story and legend. The relic-like power of the blood Lady Macbeth sees and smells on herself has the ability to transcend death and to bring the living into close—too close—apposition with the dead. At the same time, the finger that entered the witch's cauldron as perhaps their most elaborated ingredient is replicated here in Lady Macbeth's telltale hand. Both fingers and hands were relics that were especially fraught with power.[19] The finger relics of the Holy Innocents are echoed in the innocent baby slain by his guilty mother in *Macbeth*. In the same way, arm and hand relics of the great saints are among the most common of the Middle Ages, especially relics of the right hand. Healing miracles were celebrated with models of healed limbs, which reflected similar beliefs to the display of bones of ordinary people in ossuaries, marking a crucial distinction between the recent dead and 'clean bones'.[20]

7. 5 MIDDLETON AND WEBSTER

Reginald Scot was Middleton's main source for his play, *The Witch*. Despite Scot's scepticism, Middleton was the first to truly mine him for the folkloric information he had collected, and in Middleton's hands Scot's book became the grimoire it would be for later generations of cunning folk. In some places Scot is copied out almost without emendation. Middleton put classical myth together with local lore to fashion the comic figure of Hecate. Hecate has a son called Firestone, who serves as the play's clown. She leads a coven of four other witches, Stadlin, Hoppo, Hellwayn, and Prickle. The occult material in *The Witch* occurs in only three scenes: Act I, scene ii, which opens with a nursery chorus of familiars' names, close in tone to the cauldron scene in *Macbeth*: 'There, take this unbaptised brat;/Boil it well; preserve the fat' (18–19). A pantomimic note is struck when a cat enters playing a fiddle (a role likely to be filled by a musician in feline costume), probably an allusion to a local pub: 'the cat and fiddle? An excellent

---

[19] Right hand reliquaries were the most common because the hand mimicked a bishop's blessing gesture. See Thomas P. F. Hoving, 'A Newly Discovered Reliquary of St. Thomas Becket', *Gesta*, 4 (1965), 28–30.

[20] B. Taylor, 'The Hand of St James', *Berkshire Archaeological Journal*, 75 (1994–7), 97–102.

ordinary!' (229). It is very hard to take this seriously; thus, the implication is that no 'birth-strangled babe' should make us over-serious about the grotesqueries of witch scenes in drama. Act III, scene iii of *The Witch* also shows witches armed 'carrying eggs, herbs etc', and using what is by now a kind of identifying witch-speak: 'there was a bat hung at my lips three times/As we came through the woods, and drank her fill./Old Puckle saw her' (7–9). The song 'Come away', which was added to *Macbeth*, is so repetitive—'I come, I come, I come, I come'—as to approximate nonsense. It describes the witches' flight through the air, but this is all but disarmed of any power to alarm by the comic simplicity of the invocation. The night flights of *benandanti*, or of Diana and the furious horde, are scarcely present even as distant memories. The only true chill comes when Hecate explains that they fly so high as to be out of the sound of any ringing bells with their Christian power. When they reappear, armed with image magic, in Act V, scene ii, there is more grotesque oddity to make the audience shiver; like the so-called 'strong bloody violence' with which today's horror audiences must be kept awake, so the play offers timed assaults of aural violence, similarly part-horror and part-comedy: 'Three ounces of the red-haired girl/I killed last midnight' (55). The whole scene is a reprise of the previous cauldron scene, there to delight. It contains the song 'Black spirits', also inserted into *Macbeth*; like the other song, it is like a nursery rhyme: 'Mingle, mingle, mingle, you that mingle may./Titty, Tiffin,/Keep it stiff in;/Firedrake, Puckey/Make it lucky' (61–5).

Middleton's witches are so comic that it is hard to take seriously their troubling role in family affairs. The play works principally to satirize witches and those who use them; the character of 'scrupulous greatness' who uses them is mercilessly mocked for having to do with such uncouth and childish beings. Two things link Middleton's play to Shakespeare's: the songs and the scribe. To take the latter first: the still-extant manuscript of *The Witch* (Bodleian MS Malone 12), a small quarto bundle of 48 leaves, is in the hand of Ralph Crane, the professional scribe who worked for the King's Men, and who prepared several texts for the first Folio of Shakespeare's plays, as well as two of the surviving manuscripts of Middleton's *A Game at Chess*. The manuscript bears Middleton's dedication to Thomas Holmes, which refers to the play as 'ignorantly ill-fated'. This was long taken to mean that the play failed with the audience; now, some critics think that the play was withdrawn for censorship reasons.[21] Parts of *The Witch* were incorporated into the folio text of Shakespeare's *Macbeth*, Act III, scene v, and Act IV, scene i, lines 39–43 and 125–32, and the play also includes two songs, 'Come away, come away' and 'Black spirits', which are also in *Macbeth* (although they are designated in the latter only by their first lines; this strongly implies that they were well known to the company). Gary Taylor actually includes *Macbeth* in his edition of Middleton's plays. Yet Middleton's play is linked to Shakespeare's by more than the references to the absurd songs. What forces the plays into apposition is their tone, especially the clear relation between the 'fright night' style of their cauldron scenes.

[21] A. A. Bromham, 'The Date of *The Witch* and the Essex Divorce Case', *Notes and Queries*, 225 (1980), 149–52.

Such levity and gross-out horror contrast with the much more serious scepticism of John Webster's *The Duchess of Malfi* (1612 or 1613). Witches are not characters in Webster's play; they are part of the sociopathic mental furniture of Ferdinand, the play's murderous, incestuous, and possessive villain. The witch of his diseased imagining is a terrifying seductress of deception: 'they whose faces do belie their hearts/Are witches ere they arrive at twenty years,/Ay, and give the devil suck.' Ferdinand also imagines himself possessed of witchy powers to command tempests: 'Would I could be one,/That I might toss her palace 'bout her ears,/Root up her goodly forests, blast her meads.' His brother the cardinal also entertains wild imaginings: 'men convey'd by witches through the air,/On violent whirlwinds!' Bosola, however, is more sceptical: 'One would suspect it for a shop of witchcraft, to find in it the fat of serpents, spawn of snakes, Jews' spittle, and their young children's ordure.' Ferdinand fears 'power in potions or in charms,/To make us love whether we will or no?', but then expresses utter disbelief in them: 'Do you think that herbs or charms/Can force the will? . . . straight the witch/Swears by equivocation they are in love./The witch-craft lies in her rank blood.' Yet it is Ferdinand who cannot stop talking about witchcraft. This aligns him with the other madmen of jealousy, Othello and Leontes, whose thoughts also tend to love-charming that they themselves reject. All of them press upon the limits of love and desire in talking thus about witches, and this means they are no longer talking about witches at all.

7.6 Cunning Women in Drama

Alongside the malevolent was a different kind of witch, who plied a lucrative trade in magic. Known as *cunning* or *wise women*, their brand of magic was associated with old wives' remedies and herbal lore, matchmaking, love potions, fortune-telling, midwifery, and natural cures for various ailments. They were also called upon to assist in identifying and hunting down black witches or to perform counter-magic. While they appeared different from the more malevolently viewed witches, cunning folk were regarded with suspicion in a strictly Calvinist context, which denounced all magic as either fraudulent or the work of the devil. Alternatively, they were viewed as frauds or 'cozeners', skilled in the art of deceiving gullible clients into thinking they possessed supernatural abilities or had access to occult knowledge. According to Reginald Scot, such people 'take upon them, either for glorie, fame, or gaine, to doo aniething, which God or the divell can doo; either for foretelling of things to come, bewitching of secrets, curing of maladies, or working of miracles' (5).

Cunning folk come close to outnumbering their more malicious sisters in drama, featuring in several popular plays during the 1590s. Between 1589 and 1602 the repertoire of the Lord Admiral's Men featured eight successful plays about magic, including the extraordinarily popular *Wise Man of Westchester*, performed 32 times in just two years, and John Lyly's *Mother Bombie* (1594), whose wise woman dispenses advice on matters of the heart in mystical rhymed verse. Dismissed as an old fool when her clients fail to grasp the true meaning of her words, the accuracy of her insights into the action of the play and the relationships between people is not realized until the end. Thomas Heywood's 1604 play *The Wise Woman of Hogsdon* shows a woman like Mother Bombie, a master manipulator who earns a comfortable living helping people with her fake magical abilities. She is a matchmaker and a midwife, keeps prostitutes, acts as a healer, and claims she can cure the mad. When she first enters, she complains that her reputed skills are in high demand. She lists some of the other practitioners in the area and their specialties:

> You have heard of Mother Nottingham, who, for her time, was pretty well skilled in casting of waters, and after her, Mother Bombie. And then there is one Hatfield in Pepper Alley; he doth pretty well for a thing that's lost. There's another in Coleharbour that's skilled in the planets. Mother Sturton in Golden Lane is for forspeaking. Mother Philips of the Bankside for the weakness of the back, and then there's a very reverend matron on Clerkenwell Green, good at many things. Mistress Mary on the Bankside for 'rectinga figure, and one (what do you call her?) in Westminster, that practiseth the Book and Key, and the Sieve and the Shears. (II.i.19–31)

Heywood's Wise Woman has no supernatural ability. This is revealed by Luce 2,[22] the plucky girl-disguised-as-boy who has come to London to track down her wayward lover. After finding employment as the Wise Woman's servant, Luce 2 discovers the fraud:

> 'Tis strange the ignorant should be thus fooled. What can this witch, this wizard, or old trot do by enchantment, or by magic spell? Such as profess that art should be deep scholars. What reading can this simple woman have? 'Tis palpable gross foolery. (II.i.33–8)

The play works as an exposé: the Wise Woman acquires her 'uncanny' knowledge of her clients by sitting in an unseen closet and listening to Luce 2 interrogate them about their life and the purpose of their visit. She also lures them into answering their own questions or at least providing her with more information on which she can make more plausible predictions. Simple belief in her power is enough; whether or not she can perform magic is irrelevant, as long as the other characters think she can. She resolves plot complications not with natural magic but with natural means, bringing about happy resolutions with her own reputation for wisdom intact. Rather than scorning her, the characters toast her wisdom.

Several other plays with cunning folk, which were performed on the early modern English stage, have not survived, including *Long Meg of Westminster* (1595), *The Witch of Islington* (c.1597), *The White Witch of Westminster*, and Drayton and Munday's *Mother Redcap* (1598). The eponymous cunning woman of the last-named play was a

---

[22] Confusingly, there are two characters named 'Luce', both intending to marry Robin Chartley, 'a wild headed gentleman', as specified in the *Dramatis Personae* (38).

well-known witch figure and the namesake of a London pub. The establishment is referenced in *The Wise Woman of Hogsdon*, as the latter's house is located right next to Mother Redcap's tavern, and Henslowe's 'Enventary tacken of all the properties for my Lord Admeralles men', compiled in 1598, includes 'item j syne for Mother Redcap'. Mother Redcap also appears in Drayton's *Mooncalfe* (1627), alongside Mother Bombie, Mother Howlet, and Gammer Gurton.[23] In this play, the four characters partake in a storytelling session, with each woman employing her wisdom by interpreting the story of another. In *The Merry Wives of Windsor*, Shakespeare refers to another well-known wise woman when Falstaff disguises himself as 'the Witch of Brainford' in order to avoid detection. Jyl or Gillian of Brainford (Brentford) was mentioned often in ballads and literature: Robert Copland made her a figure of fun in *Jyl of Braintfords Testament* (1562), and she is mentioned in Dekker and Webster's *Westward Ho!* (1607) as 'the olde hag Gillian of Brainford'; she was also in the lost play *Friar Fox and Gill of Brentford* (Thomas Downton and Samuel Rowley, 1592–3).

There were also male cunning folk on the early modern stage. Robert Greene's *Friar Bacon and Friar Bungay* (*c.*1592) features the magus Friar Bacon, modelled on the medieval proto-scientist Roger Bacon whose reputation as a necromancer was firmly embedded in Renaissance magic lore. In the play, however, he is treated in a similar fashion to the Wise Woman when Prince Edward asks him for assistance; he is honoured for his ability to fulfil the desires of those who consult him rather than for his magical achievements. *The Merry Devil of Edmonton* also features a magus, Peter Fabel, who, despite being well known for his necromantic activity, resolves the complicated love plot without any supernatural assistance. In *The Wisdom of Dr Dodypoll* of 1600, the eponymous hero does rustle up a real love potion, of which the hero Alberdure then swallows an overdose. His counterpart, the Enchanter, is far more effective in his absolute control of a troupe of fairies. Shakespeare too uses cunning figures in several other works. In a brief moment in *The Comedy of Errors*, Doctor Pinch is called upon to perform a form of counter-magic to exorcise alleged demons from Antipholus of Ephesus. Shakespeare's best-known 'Wise Man' is Friar Lawrence in *Romeo and Juliet*, a cunning man clothed in the guise of a friar. He reveals a Paracelsian understanding of the magical healing properties of nature and the earth: 'O mickle is the powerful grace that lies/in plants, herbs, stones, and their true qualities' (II.iii.15–16). He provides Juliet with the drug that will make her appear dead, and also dispenses the relationship advice usually associated with female cunning folk. Friar Lawrence also speaks in rhyme, a habit usually associated with supernatural characters, including the witches in *Macbeth*. Unlike the Weird Sisters, however, he is unable to predict the tragic conclusion of the play.

While there was a particular emphasis on the distinctions between different types of witches by legal and demonological writers at the time (and subsequently by critics of the period), the distinction between black and white or malevolent and benevolent

---

[23] *Gammer Gurton's Needle* (London, 1553).

witchcraft is rarely a concern of the early modern theatre in its depiction of witches. In fact, as the case of Heywood's *Wise Woman* illustrates, much of the witchcraft on the early modern stage is based on self-definition. People easily confuse the various definitions of 'witchcraft', as Scot points out: 'at this daie it is indifferent to saie in the English toong; she is a witch; or she is a wise woman' (62). Heywood's Wise Woman is called at least fifteen different names for witch, including 'beldam', 'hag', 'wizard', 'enchantress', 'sorceress', 'she-devil', 'Madam Hecate', 'Lady Proserpine', 'Cunning Woman', and 'Mother Midnight'. When encountering her after a trip to Mother Redcap's tavern, the men in the play accuse the old woman of being in league with the devil. When this idea is first put to Luce 1, she denies the Wise Woman's demonic reputations: 'I hold her to be of no such condition' (I.ii.171). The Wise Woman herself is quick to deny any accusations of conjuring, and works hard to establish her reputation as a purveyor of strictly natural magic, even though the other characters freely project their idea of 'witch' onto her. Mother Bombie similarly denies that she is a witch. Falstaff's 'witch' of Brainford is likewise accused of being both a 'Wise Woman' and a 'Witch'.

7.7 THE WITCH OF EDMONTON

Sometimes, such abuse stuck. In Dekker, Ford, and Rowley's *The Witch of Edmonton* (1627) the titular character's identity as a witch is constructed by her neighbours even before she meets the devil. While Old Banks accuses the old woman, Sawyer, of conjuring spirits, his superstitious son Cuddy comes to her for help in obtaining the object of his affections. Cuddy reassures Sawyer that despite her malevolent reputation she is still 'a motherly woman' (II.i.208) and therefore capable of administering some more natural magic.

Thus far we have seen that the exotic, fearsome and many-coloured witch of literature is likely to disappoint the earnest reader of witch trials, and also offer the clients of cunning women unrealistically inflated expectations. The play world of realism exists in order to sort out and analyse the claims of the witches themselves. Keen to argue that Satan is a real presence, they are also aligned with Reginald Scot and other sceptics in the assumption that no bargain with the devil can really yield any supernatural advantages. In *The Witch of Edmonton*, the dramatists are at pains to show that a pact with the devil brings no real power to Elizabeth Sawyer. In line with thinkers like George Gifford and, later, Thomas Ady, the play seeks to deter those seeking such a pact by portraying it as ineffectual. Sawyer is pitiable, poor, not an object of fear or respect, but the butt of bullying, including bullying by the dramatists. By contrast, the more flamboyant *The Witches of Lancashire* of 1634 dramatizes a case in which Charles I and the physician William Harvey intervened successfully on behalf of the accused; the play takes the opposite tack, showing witchcraft from the most credulous and special-effects-driven position possible. Performed by the King's Men at the Globe, it seemed to try to reprise the thunderous comedy of Shakespeare and Middleton in the new genre of city comedy. The outrageous flying feats of the witches were, however, made less credible by the portrayal of the same events in a contemporary puppet show.

7.8 Witches Now?

Fictional witches congregate more thickly now than they did in early modern times, and all scepticism and comedy have vanished. If you have lately leafed through any book in the fantasy section of a bookshop, you are likely to have encountered the neo-pagan midwife witch in a cottage. She has her origins in the neo-pagan movement's efforts to appropriate the history of the witch trials as a myth of martyrdom. Alarmingly, such popular fiction has parted company with the idea that the accused witches had done nothing at all, and suggested instead that they were bursting with scientific and occult prowess. These mixes of fantasy and history have worrying potential to confuse.

And yet we might also need some bad witches, sometimes, because not all of us are nice, not all of the time. There is a mother in *Buffy the Vampire Slayer* who longs for her own youth as a cheerleader and takes over the young, clumsy body of her daughter through witch powers. This correctly locates the awkward boundlessness between daughter and mother while addressing the witch's maternal ferocity—devouring *and* pushing. My own dream witch is by Jane Gardam, just a plain story about a woman whose yard is a little too neat, and whose food is too solid, and who makes you feel sick and sullen without knowing why. This story takes the reader into the actual mental world of those who feared and prosecuted witches, and thus opens up to them a piece of history that others seem eager to close.

FURTHER READING

Butterworth, Philip, *Magic on the Early English Stage* (Cambridge, 2010).

Clauss, James Joseph and Johnston, Sarah Iles, eds, *Medea: Essays on Medea in Myth, Literature, Philosophy, and Art* (Princeton, 1997).

Friesen, Ryan Curti, *Supernatural Fiction in Early Modern Drama and Culture* (Eastbourne, 2009).

Gibson, Marion, *Reading Witchcraft: Stories of Early English Witches* (London, 1999).

Heng, Geraldine, 'Enchanted Ground: The Feminine Subtext in Malory', in Thelma S. Fenster, ed., *Arthurian Women* (London, 2000), 97–114.

Knepper, Janet, 'A Bad Girl Will Love You to Death: Excessive Love in the Stanzaic Morte Arthur and Malory', in Bonnie Wheeler and Fiona Tolhurst, eds, *On Arthurian Women: Essays in Memory of Maureen Fries* (Dallas, TX, 2001), 229–44.

Knutson, Roslyn L. and McInnis, David, eds, 'The Lost Plays Database' (Melbourne, 2009), <http://www.lostplays.org/index.php/Main_Page> (accessed 30 August 2012).

Lamb, Mary Ellen, *The Popular Culture of Shakespeare, Spenser and Jonson* (London, 2006).

Ogden, Daniel, *Magic, Witchcraft, and Ghosts in the Greek and Roman Worlds* (Oxford, 2009).

Paster, Gail Kern, *The Body Embarrassed: Drama and the Disciplines of Shame in Early Modern England* (Ithaca, NY, 1993).

Purkiss, Diane, *The Witch in History: Early Modern and Twentieth-Century Representations* (London, 1996).

Saunders, Corinne, *Magic and the Supernatural in Medieval English Romance* (Cambridge, 2010).

Taylor, Gary, *Thomas Middleton and Early Modern Textual Culture: A Companion to the Collected Works* (Oxford, 2007).

Willis, Deborah, *Malevolent Nurture: Witch-Hunting and Maternal Power in Early Modern England* (Ithaca, NY, 1995).

Willis, Deborah, 'Magic and Witchcraft', in Arthur F. Kinney, ed., *A Companion to Renaissance Drama* (Oxford, 2002), 135–44.

CHAPTER 8

....

IMAGES OF WITCHCRAFT IN EARLY MODERN EUROPE

....

CHARLES ZIKA

THE scholarly study of visual images of witchcraft in early modern Europe began in the 1970s. Previous to this the imagery of witchcraft was regarded as little more than a form of decorative illustration to the history of the European witch-hunt. When it did become the object of more serious attention, as in the case of the French historian of the occult, Émile Grillot de Givry, it was severely limited by the lack of critical and detailed analysis, often ignoring the concerns and the oeuvre of the artists involved, the media employed, the genre within which particular images needed to be understood, and the possible audience, dating, and circulation.[1] A major breakthrough came with the 1973 catalogue to the first exhibition dedicated to the subject of witchcraft, *Les Sorcières*, mounted at the Bibliothèque Nationale by Maxime Préaud, a curator in its Department of Prints. Préaud brought a professional art historian's approach to these images, describing them with respect to artist, medium, size, and content, as well as situating them within broader visual discourses such as infanticide and bacchanal. Clearly influenced by the recent revival of interest in studies of the European witch-hunt by Julio Caro Baroja, Michel de Certeau, Robert Mandrou, and especially Hugh Trevor-Roper, Préaud also related these images to particular witchcraft treatises and the history of judicial prosecution.[2]

It was the German art historian Sigrid Schade, however, who attempted the first major synthesis of witchcraft imagery. In a doctoral dissertation published in 1983,

---

[1] This chapter was completed during a Fellowship at the Institute of Advanced Studies, Lichtenberg-Kolleg, University of Göttingen. For a more detailed consideration of studies prior to the 1970s and of the historiography of witchcraft images in general, see Charles Zika, 'Images and Witchcraft Studies: A Short History', in Marko Nenonen and Raisa Maria Toivo, eds, *Writing Witch-Hunt Histories: Challenging the Paradigm* (forthcoming).

[2] Maxime Préaud, *Les Sorcières* (Paris, 1973). Both Caro Baroja's work of 1964 and Trevor-Roper's of 1968 were published in French translation in 1972.

Schade argued that the witchcraft images of early sixteenth-century artists, such as Albrecht Altdorfer, Albrecht Dürer, Lucas Cranach, and especially Hans Baldung Grien, transformed traditional notions of magic by locating the source of this magic in the eroticism of the female body.[3] Schade's feminist analysis was premised on the notion of a fundamental structural transformation and paradigm shift in the sixteenth century, drawn from social theorists such as Jürgen Habermas, Norbert Elias, and Michel Foucault. It characterized witchcraft images and treatises as masculinist projections of a view of nature that had to be displaced in order to establish a new patriarchal rationalist order. While the imposition of such meta-historical schemas on individual images might seem questionable, Schade's work laid the basis for a far more rigorous study of witchcraft motifs in the work of early sixteenth-century artists, and the manner in which these were deployed or transformed. It also demonstrated how images were often direct responses to structural change, rather than simply illustrations of literary texts, thus showing that the power and meaning of these images had to be sought in the associations created within a complex of visual themes, such as the meaning of nature, representations of the wild horde, the relationship between melancholy and lust, and, most especially, male fears concerning the power of the female body.

Sigrid Schade's work would influence the historiography of witchcraft images over the next two decades, either directly or indirectly, in two important respects: firstly, through a concentration on the work of early sixteenth-century artists and especially that of Hans Baldung; and secondly, through the link created between witchcraft imagery and gender change in European society and culture. These two emphases were already becoming evident at the time Schade was writing, but her work was to provide them with broader theoretical grounding as well as empirical focus. In 1961 Gustav Hartlaub, Professor of Art at the University of Heidelberg, had published the first short monograph dedicated to Baldung's witchcraft images, following a chapter-length study of the subject in 1938 by Gustav Radbruch, a distinguished legal philosopher at the same university.[4] But both studies were quickly overhauled as part of a major re-evaluation of Baldung's oeuvre in German art historical scholarship through the 1960s and 1970s. Major publications of Baldung's graphic and painted works, as well as exhibitions in Karlsruhe in 1959 and in Basel in 1978, transformed Baldung from a pupil of Albrecht Dürer who showed little artistic originality to one of the most creative German artists of the sixteenth century.[5]

---

[3] Sigrid Schade, *Schadenzauber und die Magie des Körpers: Hexenbilder der frühen Neuzeit* (Worms, 1983).

[4] Gustav Radbruch, *Elegantiae Juris Criminalis: sieben Studien zur Geschichte des Strafrechts* (Basel and Leipzig, 1938), 26–37; Gustav Hartlaub, *Hans Baldung Grien: Hexenbilder* (Stuttgart, 1961).

[5] Jan Lauts, ed. (1959). *Hans Baldung Grien: Ausstellung unter dem Protektorat des I.C.O.M., 4 Juli–27 September 1959*, exhibition catalogue, Staatliche Kunsthalle, Karlsruhe; Matthias Mende, *Hans Baldung Grien: das graphische Werk. Vollständiger Bildkatalog der Einzelholzschnitte, Buchillustrationen und Kupferstiche* (Unterschneidheim, 1978); Marianne Bernhard, *Hans Baldung Grien: Handzeichnungen,*

In the Anglophone art historical world Hans Baldung's work underwent the same historical evaluation, and this brought attention to his works on witchcraft. A landmark exhibition was held in 1981 at the National Gallery of Art, Washington, DC, and at the Yale University Art Gallery. As the editors pointed out in their foreword and introduction, the main purpose of the exhibition was to introduce to an American audience a little known but highly creative artist of the early sixteenth century.[6] The catalogue emphasized Baldung's 'extraordinarily fertile imagination', and one aspect of that imagination was 'his vision of women as predatory, powerful and erotic'.[7] The most remarkable form this vision of women took, argued Charles Talbot in one of the three catalogue essays, was Baldung's imagery of witchcraft.

The most important scholar to explore Baldung's witchcraft imagery over the next two decades was another contributor to the 1981 Baldung catalogue, Linda Hults, who at that time had recently completed her doctorate on the relationship between Baldung and Dürer. During the 1980s Hults published three important articles on Baldung: on the 1523 painting traditionally entitled *The Weather Witches*, on the woodcut of *Bewitched Groom* (c.1544), and on the so-called Freiburg drawings, which were pro-duced in that city during 1514–15 while Baldung was working on the high altar in the Münster.[8] The most important insights to emerge from these studies were the ambiguity of Baldung's portrayal of female lust as both attractive and threatening; the importance of subjective fantasy rather than narrative reality as a key to the under-standing of these images; and the need to view Baldung's images as self-referential expressions of personal inventiveness and artistic creativity. As Hults wrote in her study: 'What better opportunity to exhibit the artist's brave excursions into the realm of pure imagination than the phantasmagoric context of witchcraft?'[9]

The concentration in the 1980s and 1990s on the images of Hans Baldung and the new iconography of witchcraft created by Baldung and his early sixteenth-century south German and Swiss contemporaries, was further stimulated and supported by the gradual emergence of feminist issues in witchcraft scholarship. The path-breaking studies of scholars like Carol Karlsen, Lyndal Roper, Deborah Willis, and Diane Purkiss in the late 1980s and 1990s, preceded by the work of Claudia Honegger, Gabrielle Becker, Helmut Brackert, Silvia Bovenschen, and Christina Larner a decade earlier, gradually moved gender, and to some extent sexuality, to the centre of analyses of

Druckgraphik (Munich, 1978); Gert von der Osten, *Hans Baldung Grien: Gemälde und Dokumente* (Berlin, 1983).

   [6] James H. Marrow and Alan Shestack, eds (1981). *Hans Baldung Grien, Prints and Drawings*, exhibition catalogue, National Gallery of Art, Washington, DC, and Yale University Gallery, New Haven, CT.

   [7] Marrow and Shestack, *Hans Baldung Grien*, pp. viii, 4, 19–37.

   [8] Linda Hults, 'Hans Baldung Grien's *Weather Witches* in Frankfurt', *Pantheon*, 40 (1982), 124–30; Hults, 'Baldung's *Bewitched Groom* Revisited: Artistic Temperament, Fantasy and the *Dream of Reason*', *Sixteenth Century Journal*, 15 (1984), 259–79; Hults, 'Baldung and the Witches of Freiburg: the Evidence of Images', *Journal of Interdisciplinary History*, 18 (1987), 249–76.

   [9] Hults, 'Baldung and the Witches of Freiburg', 273.

witchcraft, and this obviously influenced interest in artists like Baldung, for whom gender and sexuality were critical themes.[10] This interest was clearly reflected in studies published by Dale Hoak and Dorinda Neave in English and Lène Dresen-Coenders in Dutch during the 1980s, and in the choice and content of the three articles chosen for reproduction in the important twelve-volume collection of articles on witchcraft, magic, and demonology, edited by Brian Levack in 1992.[11] With very few exceptions, especially in the world of Anglophone scholarship, the visual image of witchcraft in the 1980s and 1990s had become strongly identified with the work of Hans Baldung.[12] The narrow range of images and artists on which much of this literature was based, was matched by an almost total reliance on the *Malleus maleficarum* as the supposed literary source for their iconography.

One early exception to this concentration on the witchcraft images of Baldung was the general book on the witch in northern European art published by the American art historian Jane Davison in 1987.[13] While many scholars would reject some of Davidson's claims, such as the assertion that artists of the early modern period 'were engaged in recording facts about witchcraft',[14] the virtue of her book was that it introduced the English reader in particular to the witchcraft images of Flemish and Dutch artists, such as Pieter Bruegel the Elder, Frans Francken the Younger, David Teniers the Younger, Jacques de Gheyn II, David Ryckaert III, Cornelis Saftleven, and Leonaert Bramer. It also identified commonalities in their iconography and related their work to the content of witchcraft treatises and the prosecution of witches. Meanwhile, Dutch scholars such as Machteld Löwensteyn and Marijke Lucas were expanding knowledge about the variety of witchcraft images produced in the Netherlands in the seventeenth century, while Ursula Härting made the numerous witchcraft scenes created in the

---

[10]   Carol F. Karlsen, *The Devil in the Shape of a Woman: Witchcraft in Colonial New England* (New York, 1989); Lyndal Roper, *Oedipus and the Devil: Witchcraft, Sexuality and Religion in Early Modern Europe* (London, 1994); Deborah Willis, *Malevolent Nurture: Witch-Hunting and Maternal Power in Early Modern England* (Ithaca, NY, 1995); Diane Purkiss, *The Witch in History: Early Modern and Twentieth-century Representations* (London, 1996); Claudia Honegger, *Die Hexen der Neuzeit: Studien zur Sozialgeschichte eines kulturellen Deutungsmusters* (Frankfurt, 1978); Gabriele Becker, Silvia Bovenschen, Helmut Brackert, et al., eds, *Aus der Zeit der Verzweiflung: Zur Genese und Aktualität des Hexenbildes* (Frankfurt, 1977); Christina Larner, *Enemies of God: The Witch-hunt in Scotland* (London, 1983).

[11]   Dale Hoak, 'Witch-hunting and Women in the Art of the Renaissance', *History Today*, 31 (1981), 22–6; Hoak, 'Art, Culture, and Mentality in Renaissance Society: The Meaning of Hans Baldung Grien's "Bewitched Groom" (1544)', *Renaissance Quarterly*, 38 (1985), 488–510; Dorinda Neave, 'The Witch in Early 16th-century German Art', *Women's Art Journal*, 9 (1988), 3–9; Lène Dresen-Coenders, ed., *Saints and She-Devils: Images of Women in the 15th and 16th centuries* (London, 1987). The three articles republished in Brian Levack, ed., *Articles on Witchcraft, Magic and Demonology*, xii: *Witchcraft and Demonology in Art and Literature* (Hamden, CT, 1992), were the two cited above by Hoak, as well as one by Jane Davidson, 'Great Black Goats and Evil Little Women: The Image of the Witch in Sixteenth-Century German Art', 45–61.

[12]   An indication of this was the frequency with which one of Baldung's images was used by publishers on book covers.

[13]   Jane Davidson, *The Witch in Northern European Art, 1470–1750* (Freren, 1987).

[14]   Davidson, *The Witch in Northern European Art*, 97–8.

early seventeenth century by the Flemish artist Frans Francken the Younger far more accessible to a broader readership through a *catalogue raisonné*.[15]

Exhibition catalogues published over the last two decades have done much to broaden our understanding of the visual imagery of witchcraft through space and time.[16] An important early example was the exhibition, 'The World of Witches: Magic and Imagination', organized at the Stadtgalerie in Saarbrücken in 1987 by Richard van Dülmen, Professor of Early Modern History at the University of Saarland, and one of his then doctoral students, Eva Labouvie. Apart from the rich collection of 240 images, organized into five different sections with a short introduction preceding each, the catalogue contained an excellent general overview of witches in pictorial art from the sixteenth to twentieth centuries by Sigrid Schade.[17] As well as sixteenth-century German and seventeenth-century Flemish and Dutch artists, it also considered the work of Italians like Agostino Veneziano and Salvator Rosa, as well as eighteenth-century artists such Claude Gillot and Francisco Goya. Schade presented the different ways witchcraft images reflected and also transformed a traditional imaginative world, and developed her thesis concerning the central role played by masculine phantasies of women in constructing early modern subjectivity and history. She showed how a history of witchcraft imagery needs to relate not only to the history of literary discourses and social practices associated with witchcraft, but also to a more general history of the imagination—for images of witchcraft provide testimony of the imaginative worlds we construct.

Other important catalogues of a similar kind followed. Helfried Valentinitsch, Professor of History at the University of Graz, edited a catalogue in 1987 for an exhibition on witchcraft and sorcery held in the castle complex in Riegersburg, in the Austrian state of Styria.[18] In 1994, an extremely useful catalogue edited by Harald Siebenmorgen appeared in association with an exhibition held in the Badisches Landesmuseum in Karlsruhe in 1994; and the accompanying volume edited by the Tübingen historian, Sönke Lorenz, contained two essays specifically concerned with pictorial

---

[15] Machteld Löwensteyn, 'Helse hebzucht en wereldse wellust: Een iconografische interpretate van enkele heksenvoorstellingen van Jacques de Gheyn II', *Volkskundig Bulletin*, 12 (1986), 241–61; Löwensteyn, 'Peindre le pandémonium païen: images du sabbat des sorcières aux Pays-Bas (1450–1650)', in Nicole Jacques-Chaquin and Maxime Préaud, eds, *Le sabbat des sorciers en Europe (XVe–XVIIIe siècles)* (Grenoble, 1993), 427–37; Marijke S. Lucas, 'Het heksengeloof verbeeld 17de eeuwse voorstellingen in de Nederlanden', *Jaarboek van het Koninklijk Museum voor Schone Kunsten Antwerpen* (1996), 91–140; Ursula Härting, *Frans Francken der Jüngere (1581–1642): die Gemälde mit kritischem Oeuvrekatalog* (Freren, 1989).

[16] I should also mention works that are primarily pictorial collections, such as those edited by Jean-Michel Sallmann, Hans-Jürgen Wolf, and Robert Muchembled. See Zika, 'Images and Witchcraft Studies', at notes 61–3.

[17] Sigrid Schade, 'Kunsthexen—Hexenkünste', in Richard van Dülmen, ed., *Hexenwelten: Magie und Imagination, vom 16.–20. Jahrhundert* (Frankfurt, 1987), 170–218.

[18] Helfried Valentinitsch, ed., *Hexen und Zauberer: Die große Verfolgung—ein europäisches Phänomen in der Steiermark* (Graz, 1987); Valentinitsch, ed. (1987). *Hexen und Zauberer: Katalog der Steirischen Landesausstellung*, exhibition catalogue, Riegersburg, Oststeiermark, Graz.

imagery.[19] In 1990, Rita Voltmer and Franz Irsigler, both historians from the University of Trier and participants in a research project on sorcery and witchcraft trials in the Meuse-Rhine-Moselle region, produced a catalogue for an exhibition entitled 'Incubi Succubi', held in the Musée d'Histoire de la Ville in Luxembourg. And lastly and most importantly, Voltmer and Irsigler, together with Rosemarie Beier-de Haan of the German Historical Museum, Berlin, produced a considerably expanded, and— especially for the visual objects—better documented, version of the Luxembourg catalogue for an exhibition entitled 'Witchcraze', held in the German Historical Museum, Berlin, in 1992. But even in this very fine catalogue, any attempt to systemat- ically analyse these visual 'fantasies' (as they are labelled) and relate them to the mentality of the time (one of the stated aims of the exhibition) seems to have been considered beyond its scope.[20]

Since the early 1990s scholarship on witchcraft images has seen a greater range of witchcraft imagery studied, an increasing sophistication in its analysis, and, most importantly, more concerted attention to how we need to read witchcraft images. The American art historian Patricia Emison, for instance, has provided a detailed and subtle analysis of a large print, probably engraved by Agostino dei Musi (Agostino Veneziano) and usually called *Lo Stregozzo* (The Carcass).[21] Emison has argued that although we need to recognize the centrality of imaginative fantasy for the representa- tion of witchcraft and sexuality in this print, the somewhat puzzling iconographical elements need also to be related to the execution of seven male witches for witchcraft in the north Italian territory of Mirandola in 1522–3. The beautiful young male consorts of a wild female figure enthroned on a giant animal carcass, argues Emison, reflect the male rituals associated with the Mirandola trials and disseminated in the works of the Italian humanist Gianfrancesco Pico.

The 2005 monograph on the Dutch painter and printmaker, Jacques de Gheyn II by the American art historian Claudia Swan has greatly advanced our sophistication in the reading of witchcraft images.[22] Swan's doctoral thesis and earlier articles had explored the contribution of demonology to the discourse concerning the nature of

[19] Harald Siebenmorgen, ed. (1994). *Hexen und Hexenverfolgung im deutschen Südwesten*, exhibition catalogue, Badisches Landesmuseum, Karlsruhe and Ostfildern, Cantz; Wolfgang Schild, 'Hexenglaube, Hexenbegriff und Hexenphantasie', and Harald Sipek, '"Neue Zeitung"—Marginalien zur Flugblatt- und Flugschriftenpublizistik', in Sönke Lorenz, ed., *Hexen und Hexenverfolgung im deutschen Südwesten. Aufsatzband* (Ostfildern, 1994), 11–48, 85–92.

[20] Rita Voltmer and Franz Irsigler, eds, *Incubi Succubi: Hexen und ihre Henker bis heute. Ein historisches Lesebuch zur Ausstellung* (Luxembourg, 2000); Rosemarie Beier-de Haan, Rita Voltmer, and Franz Irsigler, eds (2002). *Hexenwahn: Ängste der Neuzeit*, exhibition catalogue, Deutsches Historisches Museum, Berlin.

[21] Patricia Emison, 'Truth and *bizzarria* in an Engraving of *Lo stregozzo*', Art Bulletin, 81 (1999), 623–36; also Gioconda Albrici, '*Lo Stregozzo* di Agostino Veneziano', Arte Veneta, 36 (1982), 55–61.

[22] Claudia Swan, *Art, Science and Witchcraft in Early Modern Holland: Jacques de Gheyn II (1565–1629)* (Cambridge, 2005).

the imagination.[23] In her later book Swan applies much of this knowledge to de Gheyn and the way his artistic production oscillates between scientific naturalism and imaginative fantasy. She argues that de Gheyn's images of witchcraft were strongly influenced by the contemporary demonological theories of the deluded imagination as elaborated by Johann Weyer, Reginald Scot, and Ambroise Paré, and shows how they become available to a Dutch readership. The continuing interest in witchcraft by de Gheyn, she concludes, was its capacity to exercise the artistic imagination. De Gheyn's witchcraft images represented visual forms of imaginative illusion.

Like these explorations of Italian and Dutch artists, scholarship on Hans Baldung has also become more nuanced and sophisticated over the last two decades. Three important studies have been the catalogue for a 2001 exhibition held in Freiburg and edited by the German art historian, Saskia Durian-Ress; an evaluation of the relationship between early sixteenth-century images of witchcraft and the humanist revival of classical literature by the American art historian, Margaret Sullivan; and an exploration of the precise subject of Baldung's 1515 drawing, traditionally entitled *Witch and Dragon*, by the Vienna art historian, Erwin Pokorny.[24] But it is the challenging 1993 study of the interrelationship between Baldung and his master Dürer by the American art historian Joseph Leo Koerner that has been especially significant. Koerner has attempted to explain the eroticism of Baldung's female witches as 'the male subject's radical Other', expressions of an artistic self-consciousness that offers a 'parodic response' to his master, Albrecht Dürer.[25] Through a psychic narrative of the young disciple who needs to fashion a self that absorbs and destroys the models created by the father, Koerner argues that Baldung's witches aim to overturn and disfigure the beauty of the human form found in Dürer, so as to present the uncontained and fallen self of Baldung. Bodo Brinkmann, a curator at the Städel Museum in Frankfurt, has challenged our reading of Baldung by wholly reassessing the embedded meanings in Baldung's 1523 painting, traditionally called *The Weather Witches*. Rather than a depiction of weather magic, Brinkmann argues, the subject is the dangers of syphilis for those who succumb to the temptations of lust. Whether we accept Brinkmann's

[23] Claudia Swan, 'Jacques de Gheyn II and the Representation of the Natural World in the Netherlands, ca. 1600', Ph.D. dissertation, Columbia University, New York, 1997; Swan, 'The *Preparation for the Sabbath* by Jacques de Gheyn II: The Issue of Inversion', *Print Quarterly*, 16 (1999), 327–39; Swan, 'Eyes Wide Shut: Early Modern Imagination, Demonology and the Visual Arts', *Zeitsprünge. Forschungen zur Frühen Neuzeit*, 7 (2003), 560–81; Swan, 'Diagnosing and Representing Witchcraft: Medico-Philosophical Theories of the Imagination in the Context of Artistic Practice in the Netherlands ca. 1600', in Stefanie Zaun, Daniela Watzke, and Jörn Steigerwald, eds, *Imagination und Sexualität: Pathologien der Einbildungskraft in medizinischen Diskursen der frühen Neuzeit* (Frankfurt, 2004), 59–82.

[24] Saskia Durian-Ress, ed. (2001). *Hans Baldung Grien in Freiburg*, exhibition catalogue, Augustinermuseum, Freiburg im Breisgau; Margaret A. Sullivan, 'The Witches of Dürer and Hans Baldung Grien', *Renaissance Quarterly*, 53 (2000), 332–401; Erwin Pokorny, 'Eine Hexe, die keine ist? Zu Hans Baldung Griens Hexen-Zeichnung in Karlsruhe', *Zeitschrift für Kunstgeschichte*, 71 (2008), 559–66.

[25] Joseph Leo Koerner, *The Moment of Self-portraiture in German Renaissance Art* (Chicago, 1993), 323–62, esp. 318.

reassessment or not, the deeper challenge of his study is *how* we read the subject matter of the painting. Should we read it as a narrative, or, as Brinkmann argues, a set of associations created to engage in further discourse?[26]

A number of studies in recent years have attempted to create a historical framework within which to analyse and understand a broad range of witchcraft images from different regions of Europe. In a lengthy essay of 1998, Wolfgang Schild, a German legal historian from the University of Bielefeld, developed a functional taxonomy of witch-craft images according to their broader and narrower functions.[27] Schild argued that some images were created to establish credibility for witchcraft theory, while others were created as propaganda in campaigns to eradicate witchcraft, and yet others to elaborate a visual aesthetic of witchcraft. Although Schild's concentration on the textual, social, legal, political, and cultural functions of witchcraft has been extremely valuable, the multivalent and multifunctional character of most of these images, as well as their chronological and geographical specificity, become lost in the face of functional categorization.

The 2005 book by Linda Hults, the broadest and most significant account of witchcraft imagery since the study of Sigrid Schade two decades earlier, takes a not uncommon art historical approach that focuses on the role of the witch in the imagination of leading artists, from Baldung to Goya.[28] Yet despite this range, Hults takes seriously the different political, social, and cultural environments, as well as the intellectual, religious, and artistic discourses, in response to which most of these images were produced. Artistic self-fashioning—the role that the witch plays in the self-identity of individual artists—drives this study. But it is not simply their artistic self-identity, argues Hults; it is also their gendered male self-identity. Through witch-craft, artists align themselves with the rhetorical and political strategies of the powerful, display their creative prowess, win intellectual respect and social status, and carve out a space for the articulation of fantasy.

My own 2007 study, limited to the later fifteenth and sixteenth centuries and therefore not nearly as expansive as Hults' work, has looked at the creation and dissemination of witchcraft images from the perspective of cultural communication and meaning.[29] I have been interested to explore how and why witchcraft began to take on a particular visual shape over its first one hundred years, and how it became a

[26] Bodo Brinkmann, ed. (2007). *Hexenlust und Sündenfall: die seltsamen Phantasien des Hans Baldung Grien. Witches' Lust and the Fall of Man: The Strange Fantasies of Hans Baldung Grien*, exhibition catalogue, Städel Museum, Frankfurt.

[27] Wolfgang Schild, 'Hexen-Bilder', in Gunther Franz and Franz Irsigler, eds, *Methoden und Konzepte der historischen Hexenforschung* (Trier, 1998), 329–413. See also Schild 'Hexenglaube, Hexenbegriff und Hexenphantasie' above. For the other important contributions of this historian, see Zika, 'Images and Witchcraft Studies'.

[28] Linda Hults, *The Witch as Muse: Art, Gender and Power in Early Modern Europe* (Philadelphia, PA, 2005).

[29] Charles Zika, *The Appearance of Witchcraft: Print and Visual Culture in Sixteenth-century Europe* (London, 2007). Also see Zika, *Exorcising our Demons: Magic, Witchcraft and Visual Culture in Early Modern Europe* (Leiden, 2003).

subject for artists, many of them unknown, to consider and depict. I have been especially interested in how the links to particular visual motifs and themes, such as sexuality, disorder, death, and apocalypse, shaped the social meanings of these images and gave them particular social traction, wider currency, greater credibility and power. And I have endeavoured to show how printing played a crucial role in disseminating and recycling these images, creating certain stereotypes of the witch but also making her figure and her practices far more visible, concrete, and real. Together with the recent work of Linda Hults and Wolfgang Schild, we now have different models for constructing a historical understanding of witchcraft imagery that incorporates chronological and geographical development and variation, artistic intention, and audience readership, as well as a sensitivity to the particular environments in which these images were produced and read, and the many and varied social and cultural functions they were meant to serve. But as Rita Voltmer has reminded us in a recent article on the multimedia production of witchcraft images in broadsheets, and in particular the fascinating 1593 broadsheet depicting a witches' sabbath in Trier— attached to a pamphlet by Thomas Sigfrid—we are still at a very early stage in understanding the relationship of image and text in many such broadsheets, and how such combinations serve to create the image of a dangerous enemy that needs to be defeated.[30]

So what conclusions can we draw from this historiography of witchcraft images, which is less than four decades old, and has only recently begun to provide a more systematic and historically based account of the field? The most obvious, yet fundamentally important contribution of the historiography is that witchcraft imagery is not universal and unchanging but has undergone significant change across time and space. It is only slowly that the field is beginning to define and refine such change. We know, for instance, that the images produced by Hans Baldung and his fellow artists in the early sixteenth century have quite different iconographical emphases from those of artists like Frans Francken the Younger and David Teniers the Younger a century and more later. Whereas the witchcraft images of the early sixteenth century are saturated with anxiety about female power and sexuality, those of the later sixteenth and early seventeenth centuries are characterized more by violence and death. Whereas the early sixteenth-century images represent witches meeting and acting in small groups in undefined or uninhabited spaces, and with hardly a devil or sabbath in sight, images from the last decade of the sixteenth and through the seventeenth century depict witches in almost massed formation, meeting more often in enclosed domestic spaces, engaged more obviously in pseudo-religious rituals with the paraphernalia of necromantic and invocatory magic, and sometimes performing the diabolical sabbath rituals elaborated by authors such as Jean Bodin and Pierre de Lancre. There are recognizable

[30] Rita Voltmer, '"Hört an neu schrecklich abentheuer/von den unholden ungeheuer"—Zur multimedialen Vermittlung des Fahndungsbildes "Hexerei" im Kontext konfessioneller Polemik', in Karl Härter, Gerhard Sälter and Eva Wiebel, eds, *Repräsentationen von Kriminalität und öffentlicher Sicherheit: Bilder, Vorstellungen und Diskurse vom 16. bis zum 20. Jahrhundert* (Frankfurt, 2010), 89–163.

themes in the work of south German and Swiss artists of the early sixteenth century, but we have not yet clearly identified those associated with an artistic shift of interest to artists in Flanders and the Netherlands in the early seventeenth century. Yet we can identify some iconographical shifts quite precisely—such as the role of Pieter Bruegel's *c.*1565 drawing of the chamber of the Hermogenes in introducing into German iconography the besoms or brooms on which witches are depicted riding in Francophone culture, and which gradually displace the forked cooking sticks typical of German images prior to this time.[31]

The changing emphases of witchcraft images in the seventeenth and eighteenth centuries, then, still remain to be explored.[32] We need to study far more systematically the nature of the witches' assemblies and sabbaths that appear at this time with respect to their lines of iconographic development; their relationship to witchcraft treatises, legal change, and prosecution; their links to visual discourses concerned with the performance of magic and the activity of the devil; their representation of witchcraft as imaginative fantasy and delusion; the points at which they introduce irony, parody, or scepticism. The fact that visual representations of sabbath do not appear until late in the sixteenth century, and only become more frequent from the second decade of the seventeenth century demands greater attention. Why do we find this cultural lag in comparison to literary description? What implications does it have for our understanding of a 'witchcraft stereotype' in Europe more generally? And why is it that during the decades around the turn of the seventeenth century such representation becomes more common? It would certainly seem to be related to a second wave of witchcraft treatises in the later sixteenth century and also a growing sense of witchcraft as a (Western) Europe-wide phenomenon. But can we trace these visual developments in more detail, with respect to particular works, regional trials, and persecutions, particular artists and patrons, and a geographical shift of this artistic activity from southern Germany in the early sixteenth century to Flemish and Dutch localities in the early seventeenth?[33]

Lyndal Roper has rightly argued that many witchcraft images and texts of the seventeenth century—such as the woodcut frontispiece to Johannes Praetorius' 1668 work, *Performance at the Blocksberg* (*Blockes-Berges Verrichtung*)—need to be understood as forms of entertainment.[34] This is undoubtedly correct, but also needs much closer exploration. For we have few guidelines to distinguish between entertainment and the theatricality of baroque culture, and we have little idea whether this development is geographically limited or whether it is the trademark of particular artists and

[31] Zika, *Appearance of Witchcraft*, 120–1, 162–3.

[32] I have endeavoured to elucidate some basic themes in Zika, 'Art and Visual Images', in Richard M. Golden, ed., *Encyclopedia of Witchcraft: The Western Tradition* (Santa Barbara, CA, 2006), i, 59–63.

[33] On these points see Zika, *Appearance of Witchcraft*, 209; Zika, *Exorcising our Demons*, 376–7. For the significance of the 1593 etching of *The Witches' Dance in Trier* for this development, see Voltmer, 'Hört an neu schrecklich abentheuer', 108ff.

[34] Lyndal Roper, 'Witchcraft and the Western Imagination', *Transactions of the Royal Historical Society*, 16 (2006), 117–41; Roper, *The Witch in the Western Imagination* (Charlottesville, VA, 2012).

printers. Similarly, there have been no studies exploring whether and when changes in legal ordinances in different territories impacted on depictions of witchcraft, nor of the different ways confessional allegiance or propaganda might have promoted one particular form of visual imagery rather than another.[35]

One of the underlying limitations for such studies is that our knowledge of the artists who created images of witchcraft remains very patchy. For while Linda Hults and other art historians have invested considerable energy on the work of major artists from Dürer and Baldung through to Salvator Rosa and Goya, we know little of the work of less important artists such as Cornelis Saftleven, Adrian Huberti, or Claude Gillot, let alone of the creators of the many 'anonymous' depictions of witches that illustrate witchcraft treatises and related works. It is telling that only very recently have we had detailed studies of the very influential illustrations to the twenty-one editions of Ulrich Molitor's treatise on witchcraft, which have been reproduced over and over in modern studies of the European witch-hunt.[36] But we still do not have a detailed study of the large print series that illustrated the two editions of Francesco Maria Guazzo's work of more than a century later.[37]

The gaps in our knowledge of witchcraft images are not limited to particular artists or illustrations of certain works; they span whole geographical regions and major time periods as well as artistic subjects. From the ongoing survey it is clear that the German-speaking territories of the Holy Roman Empire are best covered by the historiography, with reasonable attention also given to France, Switzerland, and the Netherlands. Visual materials from Britain have not been examined in any systematic fashion, even if the number of visual images created in England is not great, and that in Scotland even less. Representations of witchcraft and various forms of magic from the states of the Italian peninsula, on the other hand, are likely to be significantly more numerous, but the focus remains limited, concentrating on Salvator Rosa, and on individual paintings or prints.[38] Attention to illustrations in the witchcraft treatises themselves is very selective rather than systematic; while examination of the supposedly large number of images of

[35] Voltmer, 'Hört an neu schrecklich abentheuer', 163, suggests that the iconography in some witchcraft images might act as a 'cover' for confessional positions.

[36] Anita Komary (2000). 'Text und Illustration. Ulricus Molitoris "De lamiis et phitonicis mulieribus". Die Verfestigung und Verbreitung der Vorstellungen vom Hexereidelikt in Bildern um 1500', Diplomarbeit, University of Vienna; Natalie Kwan, 'Woodcuts and Witches: Ulrich Molitor's *De lamiis et pythonicis mulieribus*, 1489–1669', *German History*, 30/4 (2012), 493–527.

[37] Francesco Maria Guazzo, *Compendium Maleficarum* (Milan, 1608); Guazzo, *Compendium Maleficarum* (Milan, 1626); Guazzo, *Compendium maleficarum: The Montague Summers Edition* (New York, 1988).

[38] However, see (1994). *Bibliotheca Lamiarum: Documenti e immagini della stregoneria dal Medioevo all'Età Moderna*, exhibition catalogue, Biblioteca Universitaria, Pisa and Ospedaletto; Eugenio Battisti, *L'antirinascimento* (Milan, 1962), 138–57. For Salvator Rosa and witchcraft, see Charles Zika, 'The Corsini *Witchcraft Scene* of Salvator Rosa: Magic, Violence and Death', in David R. Marshall, ed., *The Italians in Australia: Studies in Renaissance and Baroque Art* (Florence, 2004), 179–90; Helen Langdon, 'Salvator Rosa in Florence 1640–49', *Apollo*, 100 (1974), 190–7; Luigi Salerno, 'Four Witchcraft Scenes by Salvator Rosa', *Bulletin of the Cleveland Museum of Art*, 65 (1978), 223–31. See also the articles on Agostino Veneziano's *Lo Stregozzo* at note 21, and the articles concerning Circe and Medea at note 40.

classical witches in single-leaf prints and in illustrations to classical texts has also been limited. The situation is the same for illustrated Bibles published in Italy, some of which surely contain images of the biblical witch of Endor, which might help us contextualize the very influential painting of the subject by Salvator Rosa. I am likewise unaware of any studies of witchcraft imagery in the Iberian peninsula, or in the various Slavic societies of Eastern Europe. Some attention has been paid to the witches, for the most part witches engaging in milk magic, found among the rich iconography of the wall paintings of village churches in Denmark and southern Sweden,[39] but it is unclear whether any of these images find their way into panel painting or print in the seventeenth and eighteenth centuries.

As this historiographical survey has shown, an important aspect of the study of witchcraft images is the manner in which they relate to, and draw upon, allied visual imagery and discourses. One very important yet largely unexplored related field is the depiction of classical literature and the role of sorcerers and witches in that literature. Circe and Medea, for instance, are constantly referred to in witchcraft treatises as examples of the reality of witchcraft; and they appear in numerous prints and paintings from the fifteenth to eighteenth centuries, and in manuscript illuminations before that. But how they were precisely depicted, what influence their depiction had on the visual representation, and possibly even the general understanding, of early modern European witchcraft, let alone whether their depiction in early modern Europe was influenced in turn by the new iconography of witchcraft, are questions to which we only have very limited answers.[40] This is even more the case for lesser-known figures such as Palaestra, Pamphile, Meroe, Canidia, Erictho, and the Furies.[41] The visual representation of each of these classical witches has its own history, of course, as do the different texts they illustrate. But until we explore the nature of their relationship or non-relationship to the images of early modern witches, our understanding of witchcraft

---

[39] Jens Christian Johansen, 'Hexen auf mittelalterlichen Wandmalereien: Zur Genese der Hexenprozesse in Dänemark', in Andreas Blauert, ed., *Ketzer, Zauberer, Hexen: Die Anfänge der europäischen Hexenverfolgungen* (Frankfurt, 1990), 217–40; Ebbe Nyborg, *Fanden på væggen* (Århus, 1978); Jan Wall, *Tjuvmjölkande väsen*, i: *Äldre nordisk tradition* (Uppsala, 1977).

[40] However, see the following contributions: Guy Tal, 'Disbelieving in Witchcraft: Allori's Melancholic Circe in the Palazzo Salviati', *Athanor*, 22 (2004), 57–66; Charles Zika, 'Images of Circe and Discourses of Witchcraft, 1480–1580', *Zeitenblicke: Online-Journal für die Geschichtswissenschaften*, 1 (2002), <www.zeitenblicke.historicum.net/2002/01/zika/zika.html> (accessed 22 August 2012); Astrid Wooton, 'On Circe's Island: Subversive Power Relationships in a Painting by Sinibaldo Scorza', *Melbourne Art Journal*, 1 (1997), 17–24; Bertina Suida Manning, 'The Transformation of Circe: The Significance of the Sorceress Subject in Seventeenth-century Genoese Painting', in Federico Zeri, *Scritti di storia dell'arte in onore di Federico Zeri* (Los Angeles, CA, 1984), ii, 689–708; Andrea Emiliani, ed., *Bologna 1584: Gli esordi dei Carracci e gli affreschi di Palazzo Fava* (Bologna, 1984); Norberto Gramaccini, 'La Médée d'Annibale Carracci au Palais Fava', in *Les Carraches et les décors profanes: Actes du colloque organisé par l'École Française de Rome, 2–4 Octobre 1986* (Rome, 1988), 491–519; Lieselotte E. Saurma-Jeltsch, 'Die Zähmung der Maßlosigkeit: Die Darstellung Medeas in der deutschen Buchmalerei', in Annette Kämmer, Margret Schuchard, and Agnes Speck, eds, *Medeas Wandlungen: Studien zu einem Mythos in Kunst und Wissenschaft* (Heidelberg, 1998), 96–128.

[41] For attention to some of these figures, see Zika, *The Appearance of Witchcraft*, 129–33, 141–52.

images will necessarily remain partial. And only after this process will we be able to answer the important question posed by Margaret Sullivan concerning the role of classical witches in the artistic 'discovery' of witchcraft.[42]

An even stronger case can be made for a concerted study of the most frequently represented witch in European culture, the biblical witch of Endor, who appears in the story of King Saul in 1 Samuel 28. My own research on this figure demonstrates how the passive role of this woman in depictions of the story in the late Middle Ages begins to change in the later fifteenth century, and is radically transformed by the seventeenth century.[43] From the mid-seventeenth century, most depictions of this biblical necromancer are clearly recognizable as a witch, but they also include the quite distinctive attributes of a male ritual magician—a book, a wand, or a magical circle. Whereas some visual clues from the early sixteenth century survive, such as the witch's wild flying hair, the absorption of the attributes of the male ritual magician are striking and wholly novel. And in the later seventeenth century these male attributes are employed as a visual code for witchcraft itself. Although the reasons for the new-found interest in this biblical necromancer turned witch are far from simple, it would seem that growing scepticism about the reality of witchcraft and doubts about the role of the devil in the world—views that were tarred with the accusation of 'atheism' in the later seventeenth century—promoted interest in the only witch authorized by biblical tradition.[44] While such an argument must depend on an analysis of texts as well as images, it demonstrates the value of the visual in opening up quite new lines of interpretation and enquiry.

The imagery of male ritual magic also requires systematic examination and analysis, in order to understand its relationship to the visual discourse of witchcraft. As with the cases of Circe, Medea, and the witch of Endor, we need sustained analysis of the visual representations of those male magicians who have played an important role in Christian discourse concerning the distinctions between demonic magic and divine miracle.

---

[42] Sullivan, 'Witches of Dürer and Hans Baldung Grien'.

[43] See Charles Zika, 'The Witch of Endor before the Witch Trials', in Louise Kallestrup, ed., *Heresy, Magic and Witchcraft: Contesting Orthodoxy in Medieval and Early Modern Europe* (forthcoming); Zika, 'The Baillieu Library's Etching of André Laurent, *Saul and the Witch of Endor*, after Salvator Rosa', in Stephanie Jaehrling and Kerrianne Stone, eds, *Print Matters at the Baillieu* (Melbourne, 2011); Zika, 'Images in Service of the Word: The Witch of Endor in the Bibles of Early Modern Europe', in *Anzeiger des Germanischen Nationalmuseums* (2009), 151–65; Zika, 'The Witch of Endor: Transformations of a Biblical Necromancer in Early Modern Europe', in C. Zika and F. W. Kent, eds, *Rituals, Images and Words: The Varieties of Cultural Expression in Late Medieval and Early Modern Europe* (Turnhout, 2005), 235–59; Zika, 'Reformation, Scriptural Precedent and Witchcraft: Johann Teufel's Woodcut of *The Witch of Endor*', in I. Breward, ed., *Reforming the Reformation: Essays in Honour of Peter Matheson* (Melbourne, 2004), 148–66. See also Paolo Lombardi, 'La strega come necromante: Il caso della pittonessa di Endor', in Giovanni Bosco and Patrizia Castelli, eds, *Stregoneria e Streghe nell'Europa Moderna* (Rome, 1996), 181–206; Jean-Claude Schmitt, 'Le spectre de Samuel et la sorcière d'En Dor: Avatars historiques d'un récit biblique: I Rois 28', *Études Rurales*, 105–6 (1987), 37–54 ; François Lecercle, *Le retour du mort. Débats sur la sorcière d'Endor et l'apparition de Samuel (XVIᵉ–XVIIIᵉ)* (Geneva, 2011).

[44] I touch on this argument in 'Images in Service of the Word', 156–62.

These are, firstly, Hermogenes and Simon Magus, two ancient magician figures who represent the long struggle of Christian forces—in this case, the Apostles St James and St Peter—against the magical powers of the devil.[45] Linked to Simon Magus in the visual tradition, moreover, is that consummate magician and trickster at the end of time, the Antichrist, who is also frequently associated with Jewish magic. And another story of biblical magic that often appears in demonological treatises in the early modern period is the contest at the court of the Egyptian Pharaoh between Aaron and the pagan magicians, in which the serpents created from Aaron's rod swallow the serpents created by the pagan magicians. If such stories were so frequently drawn upon in demonological treatises to support the reality of witchcraft, it is possible that they may well have influenced the ways artists imagined and depicted various scenes of witchcraft. Moreover, studies of such visual stories and their iconography would help us contextualize witchcraft imagery within a broader visual culture of which it was inevitably a part, rather than limit its meanings to some kind of self-enclosed pictorial system to be explained and understood only by reference to literary accounts of witchcraft in demonological treatises or in reports of evidence actually or supposedly derived from witch trials.

While witches are depicted as actors who do harm to individuals and bring disasters to bear on whole communities through their spells, potions, rituals, and the alliances or pacts they create with demonic powers, they are also identified as members of that broad underworld community of chthonic powers. Another desideratum in the study of witchcraft imagery is to explore the broad range of scenes and scenarios in which witches are known to appear—usually in the company of demons, spirits, and all manner of monsters and hybrids. They are prominently featured, for instance, in Pieter Bruegel's depiction of Hermogenes' chamber. But they also appear in many images of the temptations of St Anthony, in scenes of the pagan Tartarus or Underworld, in representations of a Christian Hell and Satan's court.[46] Evaluation of the frequency and nature of such appearances would help assess the extent to which witches ever became, for some artists at least, an established element within Christian cosmology. An appearance of witches in representations of the religious and magical practices and rituals of non-Christian peoples in the Americas, Asia, or Africa would likewise suggest a firming up of this new category of threat within Christian communities at home.

Since the emergence of modern witchcraft studies in the 1970s, trial evidence and the judicial process has rightly been the driver of understanding witchcraft as a new phenomenon in the cultural landscape of early modern Europe, and evaluating its social and cultural impact. But for that trial evidence to have been expressed by the

---

[45] For a brief treatment of the two figures in the sixteenth century, see Zika, *The Appearance of Witchcraft*, 162–78.

[46] For some examples of witches in the underworld, see Zika, *The Appearance of Witchcraft*, 129–32; and for the temptations of St Anthony see Ortrud Westheider and Michael Philipp, eds (2008). *Schrecken und Lust: Die Versuchung des heiligen Antonius von Hieronymus Bosch bis Max Ernst*, exhibition catalogue, Bucerius Kunst Forums, Hamburg and Munich.

accused, for it to have been understood and considered credible by the members of the court, and for the judicial process that produced the evidence to have been socially or political meaningful in the broader community, witchcraft also needs to be perceived as a cultural phenomenon rooted in intellectual beliefs, cultural discourses, and emotional engagements well outside the realm of the law.[47] One of the primary challenges for a history of witchcraft images is to show how this visual imagery is crucial to the elaboration of witchcraft as a social and cultural reality. For despite the growing number of studies devoted to the subject, visual images remain rather marginal to the field of witchcraft as a whole. Historians still tend to see images as illustrations of the harder documentary or even literary materials that speak of witchcraft belief or practice. Images are a third-level reality at best, frequently used to illustrate or enliven the text, or to operate as 'scriptures of the unlettered', as Gregory the Great dubbed them, both for viewers then and for readers now. I also think that a recent tendency to group images under the heading of 'fantasies',[48] as though in contrast to the reality of witchcraft elaborated in literature, legal handbooks, and courts, simply compounds the problem. Images are certainly constructed from imaginative phantasies, as are treatises, interrogations, and even trial evidence.[49] But we need to employ images to help identify the emotional pressures and cultural beliefs that have nurtured those 'fantasies', rather than relegating them to personal individual experience and thereby removing the need for further analysis.

Witchcraft images, whether appearing in panel paintings, single-leaf prints or print series, in drawings, book illustrations or broadsheets, are notoriously difficult to analyse with respect to their intended audience. They are for the most part multifocal with respect to their messages, uses, meanings, values, and audiences. But their fascination for us and their power for contemporaries frequently lie in the manner in which they draw on and combine a variety of literary and also visual discourses, whether from learned theological and literary references, more widely recognized visual traditions of fresco painting, oral descriptions in church sermons, or the rituals and displays of social celebration performed during pre-Lenten carnival. Although it is doubtless the case that most witchcraft representation was primarily intended for an audience that would be interested in examining or even purchasing these images, and/or reading the accompanying texts, the lines between learned and popular traditions as expressed through these artefacts are seriously blurred and often quite irrelevant. But by uncovering the different strains and traditions from which these images and their meanings were constructed, historians can gain a much richer and complex understanding of how witchcraft could appeal to a broad and socially differentiated community, and how

[47] See especially Stuart Clark, *Thinking with Demons: The Idea of Witchcraft in Early Modern Europe* (Oxford, 1997); Stuart Clark, ed., *Languages of Witchcraft: Narrative, Ideology and Meaning in Early Modern Culture* (London, 2001).

[48] See Beier-de Haan, Voltmer, and Irsigler, *Hexenwahn*, 248ff; Schild, 'Hexen-Bilder'.

[49] As well as the elaboration of 'fantasy' in works cited above by Swan and Hults, the work of Lyndal Roper is fundamental: Lyndal Roper, *Witch Craze: Terror and Fantasy in Baroque Germany* (New Haven, CT, 2004); Roper, *The Witch in the Western Imagination*.

through that process it might gain added weight, currency, credibility, and legitimacy. This, I believe, constitutes one of the most important reasons for continuing, deepening, and expanding our study of witchcraft images—a field of scholarship that is still very much in its infancy.

FURTHER READING

Beier-de Haan, Rosemarie, Voltmer, Rita, and Irsigler, Franz, eds (2002). *Hexenwahn: Ängste der Neuzeit*, exhibition catalogue, Deutsches Historisches Museum, Berlin.

Hults, Linda, *The Witch as Muse: Art, Gender and Power in Early Modern Europe* (Philadelphia, PA, 2005).

Marrow, James H. and Shestack, Alan, eds (1981). *Hans Baldung Grien, Prints and Drawings*, exhibition catalogue, National Gallery of Art, Washington, DC, and Yale University Gallery, New Haven, CT.

Préaud, Maxime, *Les Sorcières* (Paris, 1973).

Roper, Lyndal, *The Witch in the Western Imagination* (Charlottesville, VA, 2012).

Schade, Sigrid, *Schadenzauber und die Magie des Körpers: Hexenbilder der frühen Neuzeit* (Worms, 1983).

Schade, Sigrid, 'Kunsthexen—Hexenkünste', in Richard van Dülmen, ed., *Hexenwelten: Magie und Imagination, vom 16.-20. Jahrhundert* (Frankfurt, 1987), 170–218.

Schild, Wolfgang, 'Hexen-Bilder', in Gunther Franz and Franz Irsigler, eds, *Methoden und Konzepte der historischen Hexenforschung* (Trier, 1998), 329–413.

Sullivan, Margaret, 'The Witches of Dürer and Hans Baldung Grien', *Renaissance Quarterly*, 53 (2000), 332–401.

Swan, Claudia, *Art, Science and Witchcraft in Early Modern Holland: Jacques de Gheyn II (1565-1629)* (Cambridge, 2005).

Voltmer, Rita, '"Hört an neu schrecklich abentheuer/von den unholden ungeheuer"—Zur multimedialen Vermittlung des Fahndungsbildes "Hexerei" im Kontext konfessioneller Polemik', in Karl Härter, Gerhard Sälter, and Eva Wiebel, eds, *Repräsentationen von Kriminalität und öffentlicher Sicherheit: Bilder, Vorstellungen und Diskurse vom 16. bis zum 20. Jahrhundert* (Frankfurt, 2010), 89–163.

Zika, Charles, *Exorcising our Demons: Magic, Witchcraft and Visual Culture in Early Modern Europe* (Leiden, 2003).

Zika, Charles, *The Appearance of Witchcraft: Print and Visual Culture in Sixteenth-century Europe* (London, 2007).

Zika, Charles, 'Images and Witchcraft Studies: A Short History', in Marko Nenonen and Raisa Maria Toivo, eds, *Writing Witch-Hunt Histories: Challenging the Paradigm* (forthcoming).

PART II

WITCHCRAFT PROSECUTIONS

CHAPTER 9

....

THE FIRST WAVE OF TRIALS FOR DIABOLICAL WITCHCRAFT

....

RICHARD KIECKHEFER

WHILE the witch trials of the fifteenth century were fewer, and on the whole more sporadic, than those of the sixteenth and seventeenth centuries, it was during the fifteenth century that notions of diabolical witchcraft were first developed. If we want to understand how these ideas emerged, what alternative notions coexisted with them, and most basically how the European witch trials began, it is to late medieval texts and trials that we must turn.

Writing at the turn of the twentieth century, Joseph Hansen referred to a 'cumulative concept' of witchcraft that he saw as having developed in later medieval Europe, a composite to which elements were added one by one: the sabbath, flight to the sabbath, a pact with the devil, sex with *incubi* and *succubi*, and bewitchments (*maleficia*) carried out at the behest of the devil and with his aid.[1] In Hansen's evolutionary account of how witch beliefs emerged, each innovation remained as an accomplished fact. While much has changed in the historiography of witchcraft since Hansen's day, historians writing on this subject still tend to speak of a conception of witchcraft in later medieval Europe as evolving along a one-way path. We speak of 'the sabbath' as a more or less fixed notion that took hold in the early fifteenth century and admitted only incidental variation. We think of other elements in the mythology as building on the basic theme of the sabbath. We distinguish the point in the 1320s when demonic magic was defined

---

[1] Joseph Hansen, *Zauberwahn, Inquisition und Hexenprozeß im Mittelalter, und die Entstehung der großen Hexenverfolgung* (Munich, 1900; repr. Aalen, 1964).

as heresy, and we take that too as an accomplished fact that could be transferred unproblematically to later notions of witchcraft.[2]

We would do more justice to the evidence, however, by speaking instead about a more complex process of coalescence, diffusion, fusion, and attenuation. When we examine the trials in a particular region—and when we read late medieval writings about witchcraft—we find ideas brought together in discernible but fragile coalescence, which then sometimes became diffused over broader areas, and in the process were fused with ideas taken from different sources. Therefore, when we look back at the cluster that was once formed we may find that in its diffusion it has become attenuated, with key notions abridged or omitted. This survey will suggest some of the ways this more complex pattern of coalescence and attenuation, diffusion, and fusion is reflected in sources from the late medieval West.

9.1 THE LAUSANNE PARADIGM OF DIABOLICAL WITCHCRAFT IN TEXTS AND TRIALS

Two blocks of sources give at an early date a fully articulated conception of witchcraft: first, a set of writings produced around the 1430s, describing the activities of witches in parts of western Switzerland and nearby territories;[3] secondly, a manuscript from Lausanne with inquisitorial protocols beginning in the 1430s and extending into the early sixteenth century.[4] The themes that emerge from these sources might easily be taken as simply *the* late medieval conception of witchcraft, but it is important first to recognize them for what they are—the products of specific circumstances in particular locations—and only then to inquire what happens in their diffusion. The mythology of witchcraft articulated in these sources will be called the 'Lausanne paradigm', because it is in the Lausanne manuscript that it receives its fullest and most enduring articulation.

The writings in the first block all claim to be reporting on forms of witchcraft that are supposed to have come to light in earlier prosecution, although we cannot assume that they give faithful record of the charges raised in that prosecution. The chronicle of Hans Fründ, written in German at Lucerne between 1428 and 1430, refers to witches (*hexsen*) in the French-speaking part of the Valais who are guilty of evil, heresy, and

---

[2] Richard Kieckhefer, 'Witchcraft, Necromancy and Sorcery as Heresy', in Martine Ostorero, Georg Modestin, and Kathrin Utz Tremp, eds, *Chasses aux sorcières et démonologie: entre discours et pratiques (XIVᵉ–XVIIᵉ siècles)* (Florence, 2010), 133–53.

[3] The best repository of all these writings is Martine Ostorero, Agostino Paravicini Bagliani, and Kathrin Utz Tremp, eds, in collaboration with Catherine Chène, *L'imaginaire du sabbat: Edition critique des textes les plus anciens (1430 c.–1440 c.)* (Lausanne, 1999).

[4] Martine Ostorero, Kathrin Utz Tremp, and Georg Modestin, *Inquisition et sorcellerie en Suisse romande: Le registre Ac 29 des Archives cantonales vaudoises (1438–1528)* (Lausanne, 2007), reprints the records published earlier in the same series, with documents from five further trials not previously edited.

sorcery (*boßheit und ketzerÿe und zöberÿe*). However, we have independent documentation for witchcraft in this region, and the charges there bear little resemblance to those in Fründ's chronicle. The *Formicarius* (Ant-Hill) of Johannes Nider, written in Latin in the 1430s, tells about activities in the Bernese Alps and other territories, based mainly on testimony Nider had obtained from a secular judge from Bern and from an inquisitor. Much of what Nider reports is said to have occurred in the Simme Valley at the turn of the fifteenth century, decades before Nider wrote.[5] Again, the *Errores Gazariorum* (The Errors of the Gazarii), first written in Latin before 1437, probably in the Aosta Valley, was probably brought to Lausanne soon thereafter. Presumably written by an inquisitor, it gives little indication precisely when and where he carried out witch trials,[6] but it tells of 'heretics' who go to a 'synagogue' where they perpetrate their misdeeds. *Ut magorum et maleficiorum errores* (That the Errors of Magicians and Witches . . .) is a treatise written in Latin by the French judge Claude Tholosan around 1437, based on his prosecution of witches in the Dauphiné. Once again it appears to give a more extravagant depiction of witches' activities than that emerging from trial records in this region: in the judicial records, reference to the witches' assemblies is less developed than in Tholosan's imagination.[7] A fifth work, Martin Le Franc's *Champion des Dames* (Defender of Women), written in the early 1440s, again citing activity in the Dauphiné, is a debate between a misogynist who accuses women of being inclined to witchcraft and a defender who admits that they are gullible and duped by the devil but insists that their worst offences are imaginary.[8]

Setting Le Franc's ambiguous testimony aside, we find several beliefs coalescing in these writings, most importantly these:

1. witches attend an assembly presided over by Satan or a demon;
2. they renounce the faith, desecrate holy things, and make sacrifices to the devil;
3. they learn bewitchment—which includes the use of harmful potions and the hindering of human fertility—from the devil or a demon;
4. they kill children, bring their bodies to the assembly to be eaten, and make maleficent powders from their remains.

[5] Michael D. Bailey, *Battling Demons: Witchcraft, Heresy, and Reform in the Late Middle Ages* (University Park, PA, 2002); Werner Tschacher, *Der Formicarius des Johannes Nider von 1437/38: Studien zu den Anfängen der europäischen Hexenverfolgungen im Spätmittelalter* (Aachen, 2000).

[6] There is reference in sect. 17 to a place called Chambanaz, on which see Martine Ostorero's comments in Ostorero, et al., *L'imaginaire du sabbat*, 331.

[7] Pierrette Paravy, *De la chrétienté romaine à la Réforme en Dauphiné: évêques, fidèles et déviants (vers 1340–vers 1530)* (Rome, 1993); see the earlier publications by Paravy, 'A propos de la genèse médiévale des chasses aux sorcières: le traité de Claude Tholosan, juge dauphinois (vers 1436)', *Mélanges de l'Ecole Française de Rome: Moyen Age—Temps modernes*, 9l (1979), 333–79, and 'Faire croire: quelques hypothèses de recherche basées sur l'étude des procès de sorcellerie du Dauphiné au XVe siècle', in *Faire croire: modalités de la diffusion et de la réception des messages religieux du XIIe au XVe siècle: Table ronde, Rome, 22–23 juin 1979* (Rome, 1981), 119–30.

[8] Apart from the edition cited above, see Steven M. Taylor, 'Le procès de la sorcellerie chez Martin Le Franc: *Le Champion des dames*, livre IV', in Danielle Buschinger and Wolfgang Spiewok, eds, *Zauberer und Hexen in der Kultur des Mittelalters* (Greifswald, 1994), 203–12.

To be sure, there are also differences among these works. The *Errores Gazariorum* tells of indiscriminate sex among the witches at their assembly, and Tholosan speaks of sexual orgies involving both witches and demons, while neither Fründ nor Nider includes this among the witches' activities. Fründ and the *Errores Gazariorum* accept the witches' flight as real, but Nider and Tholosan dismiss it as illusion. Nider alone says women are more prone to witchcraft than men. Tholosan and the *Errores Gazariorum* emphasize that the devil punishes those who betray the sect's secrets. The *Errores Gazariorum* is exceptional in saying that the devil keeps possession of a charter written in the blood of each person inducted into the sect, in effect a pact. On the whole, however, these works are consistent in portraying a new type of sect or heresy that is expressly allied with the devil and threatens to undermine Christian society.[9]

The significance of these texts becomes clearer in the light of a fundamental change occurring in the first half of the fifteenth century. Daniel Hobbins has depicted Jean Gerson as a pioneer in the development of a kind of public intellectual, a university-trained scholar who turned away from traditional genres of academic writing to produce tracts: relatively short works on specific questions of public interest.[10] A tract might deal with a moral or political question of the day, might seek to promote reform or to counter some error, might provide special professional expertise of relevance and use to laypeople. Tracts were meant to have wide circulation, and frequently they achieved this goal. They were a means by which scholars could have broad impact on public affairs. But tracts were not the only means by which intellectuals sought and gained a public audience: dialogues and other genres could also serve this purpose, although tracts were perhaps important in leading the way and advertising the availability of scholars as commentators on questions of public interest.

Of the four major works on witchcraft from around the 1430s, only the *Errores Gazariorum* and the work of Tholosan strictly speaking qualify as tracts; Nider's *Formicarius* was a much longer work in the form of a dialogue dealing with witchcraft among a wide range of issues, while Fründ's chronicle touched on witchcraft as an event in Swiss history. It was Nider's work, however, that gained a wide public audience and qualified its author as the kind of public intellectual now coming into prominence. The other works, important no doubt to a local or regional audience, are of interest to us mainly as witnesses to the effort at publicity so many were seeking, and to the variety of ways witchcraft could be represented in contemporary literature that intended to have influence on public affairs.

It is tempting to speculate that the intense preoccupation with witchcraft in the 1430s was exacerbated by the widespread famine of that decade, brought on by exceptionally

---

[9] Michael Bailey, 'The Medieval Concept of the Witches' Sabbath', *Exemplaria*, 8 (1996), 419–39, especially the chart on 438–9.

[10] Daniel Hobbins, 'The Schoolman as Public Intellectual: Jean Gerson and the Late Medieval Tract', *American Historical Review*, 108 (2003), 1308–37; Daniel Hobbins, *Authorship and Publicity before Print: Jean Gerson and the Transformation of Late Medieval Learning* (Philadelphia, PA, 2009).

cold winters and wet summers and reaching a climax in 1437–8, precisely the time when at least two of the key writings on witchcraft were produced. The witch trials more generally have been associated with the Little Ice Age that began at this time; the link is perhaps most convincing for these early years, when the onset of unfavourable climate correlates so closely with these expressions of anxiety.[11] Given the concern with witches' manipulation of the weather and their destruction of crops, the link seems particularly plausible—if, in the end, unprovable. Less specifically relevant, but still no doubt to be reckoned a significant background factor, is the susceptibility to disease largely traceable to rapidly growing and overcrowded cities. One historian has commented that the later medieval centuries saw 'the most unhealthy epoch in the history of Central Europe'.[12] A society afflicted with famine and epidemics will not necessarily turn to witchcraft as an explanation, but if that cause is proposed it may seem more plausible in the context of widespread sudden death and an unfavourable climate, which seem unprecedented and without another plausible explanation.

The image of witchcraft articulated in these texts is echoed in a series of trial records from 1438 to 1528, involving sixteen men and eleven women, contained in an exceptionally full and important manuscript in the Archives Cantonales Vaudoises at Lausanne, Ac 29. The trials occurred on the southern edge of the Pays de Vaud, in the diocese of Lausanne, on the north shore of Lake Geneva (Lac Léman). Typically, the trials were conducted by vice-inquisitors or inquisitorial vicars from the Dominican convent of Lausanne, acting on papal authority, while the local bishop (who also held the title of count) was represented by a vicar or official. No one inquisitor was active in more than three of the trials; prosecution was the work of the Dominican community, represented by whichever members happened to be serving at the time as inquisitor. Throughout the period covered in this manuscript, the accusations and confessions follow a script that suggests the inquisitors were using a more or less fixed interrogatory, asking the same leading questions of the accused, in much the same order each time, and with expectation of very similar, although not necessarily identical, responses. The records are full enough to allow a great deal of individual detail, alongside confessions conforming to the preordained script. Typically these confessions included the following elements:

1. The relationship between the witch and the devil:
   (a) the appearance of the devil or demon to the witch, in human or bestial form;
   (b) homage paid by the witch to the devil, which included the obscene kiss *sub cauda* (under the tail) and the giving of a bodily part and other offerings;
   (c) denial of God, the Virgin, the sacrament of baptism, and sometimes other holy persons and objects;

---

[11] Wolfgang Behringer, 'Weather, Hunger and Fear: Origins of the European Witch-hunts in Climate, Society and Mentality', tr. David Lederer, *German History*, 13 (1995), 1–27.

[12] Ernst Schubert, *Einführung in die Grundprobleme der deutschen Geschichte im Spätmittelalter* (Darmstadt, 1992), 10.

   (d) desecration of the sacred, often involving the trampling on a cross;
   (e) payment to the witches of a specified sum of money, which was generally not
        paid, or when paid turned out illusory.
  2. Participation in activities along with other witches:
   (a) attendance at the assemblies, called either sects or synagogues (not sabbaths);
   (b) transport to those assemblies, usually on an anointed stick, and usually
        instantaneous;
   (c) eating the flesh of infants whom the witches had previously killed and
        exhumed;
   (d) anal sex with other witches;
   (e) illumination of the assemblies by candles and by a fire that emitted a
        mysterious blue light.
  3. Misdeeds carried out in the broader society at the command of demons:
   (a) violation of religious duties and profanation of the Eucharist;
   (b) bewitchments (*maleficia*), chiefly the killing of persons and animals by use of
        powders given by the demon.

Even the sequence of interrogation tended to be formulaic in these trials, again
suggesting use of a standard interrogatory. The accused were asked at the outset if
they knew the reason for their arrest, if they had previously been defamed for
witchcraft, or if they knew what it was witches were said to do. In effect, their recitation
of what witches did was a rehearsal for confession later in the trial of what they
themselves had done. When they broke down and began confessing their deeds as
witches, they often told how they had been seduced into the sect: in a moment of
despondency, perhaps in poverty, they had been approached by a stranger who offered
them aid if they went with him to an assembly and did as they were told. This emphasis
on the circumstances of seduction follows the precedent of the *Errores Gazariorum*,
which takes special interest in the motives and means for induction into the sect. Apart
from these points of confession, the witches were expected to give the names of as
many accomplices as possible in all these deeds. If at any point they did not give the
expected testimony, or make sufficiently full confession, if they could not name
accomplices, or if they wavered and retracted parts of what they confessed, they were
tortured; the trial record does not hesitate to record the use of torture.

   The paradigm of diabolical witchcraft found in these trial records was not limited to
the diocese of Lausanne; there were other places, especially in the vicinity of that
region, where the paradigm articulated in the writings of the 1430s and found in the
Lausanne protocols was found intact. Across Lake Geneva in Savoy, at the castle of
Villard-Chabod, a woman named Antonia Rose was interrogated and made confession
in a manner so closely resembling that of the trials in the diocese of Lausanne that one
can only assume the judges were following the same interrogatory, or a similar one. Not
surprisingly, the inquisitor at Villard-Chabod had presided over a witch trial in the

diocese of Lausanne three years previously.[13] Again, in 1462, when four women and four men were tried by an inquisitor at Chamonix (also in Savoy), and in 1493 at Vacheresse in the region of Gruyère when a woman named Jehanneta Lasne was prosecuted by a secular court, the confessions closely resemble those of the witches in the diocese of Lausanne, although in these cases we have only the final confessions, not records of the interrogation.[14] These places were close enough to Lausanne that we may safely suppose the judges were familiar with trials there and may again have used the same interrogatory. The coalescence of themes in these trials no doubt owes a great deal to the lingering influence of the literature from the 1430s, but, more directly, it can be accounted for as the result of inquisitors' fidelity to a more or less fixed list of leading questions.

9.2 FACTORS CONTRIBUTING TO DEVELOPMENT OF THE CLASSIC PARADIGM

The Lausanne trial records, along with the literature of the 1430s, shed light on issues that have long been discussed by historians of witchcraft. One that admits no simple answer is the relationship between trials and texts. Was it typically the noteworthy trials that inspired textual commentary, or was it more often texts that gave rise to trials? This may seem an instance of a chicken-and-egg question, to which the inevitable answer is that neither came first, they were interdependent. Several other important texts on witchcraft written over the fifteenth century were inspired largely by the authors' experience of witch trials: the writings of the 1430s, Jean Tinctor's *Contre le Vauderie* (inspired by a high-profile trial at Arras), the *Malleus maleficarum* (largely provoked by Heinrich Kramer's trials at Ravensburg and Innsbruck), Ulrich Molitoris' *De lamiis et phitonicis mulieribus* (also a response to the trial at Innsbruck), and others. Still, a good argument can be made that it was the writings of the 1430s that made it possible for inquisitors and other judges to prosecute people for diabolical witchcraft: it was texts that suggested the idea of such activity, texts that persuaded people such witchcraft was possible and indeed real, texts that countered possible objections. In the early sixteenth people were still reading Nider and being influenced by him: a cleric at Eberhardsklausen had been a sceptic, but after reading Nider wrote, 'I confess that I was ignorant. One who wishes to read and know ample material on how much the witches are able to do, whom they can harm [and] how . . . should read [the work] of

---

[13] Jh. M. Lavanchy, *Sabbats ou synagogues sur les bords du lac d'Annecy: procès inquisitorial à St. Jorioz en 1477* (2nd edn, Annecy, 1896); Joseph Hansen, ed., *Quellen und Untersuchungen zur Geschichte des Hexenwahns und der Hexenverfolgung im Mittelalter* (Bonn, 1901; repr. Hildesheim, 1963), 467–99.
[14] Hansen, *Quellen*, 590–2.

Johannes Nider . . . I had not read it when I began to write about these things.'[15] The cleric now began to promote the prosecution of witches. In this case it was chiefly texts that influenced the course of prosecution. Yet it is worth remembering that Nider's work is based largely on the testimony of judges, both secular and ecclesiastical, who told him of their experience in the prosecution of witches.

It would probably be most accurate to speak of an interplay of texts, trials, and local incidents. The third of these factors, the incidents that get reported in both texts and trials—the quarrels among villagers that gave rise to suspicion of witchcraft, the threats and counterthreats that were hoarded in the bank of communal memory until some crisis of incivility precipitated legal action—were a constant element in people's experience, waning and waxing in frequency and intensity but never rare. The alleged witches had reputations among their neighbours for malfeasance, often built up over a period of several years. A long history of marginalization was almost always grounded in suspicions of bewitching cattle, sometimes causing physical harm to the neighbours themselves, or, more rarely, use of erotic magic. Both texts and trials emerged out of this background of endemic tensions and provocations. The effect of texts was to compile both incidents and trials in the context of an inflammatory commentary, which in turn could heighten the severity of prosecution. The impact of texts was all the greater in an era when intellectuals were coming into their own as authorities on questions of public interest. Texts and trials both gave form and opportunity for the expression of anxieties that had built up over time, and they reinforced each in the process.

Another perennial issue in the historical literature is the relationship between diabolical witchcraft and heresy. In one way or other, the prosecution of witches has been represented as an outgrowth of inquisitorial heresy-hunting. One interpretation, now discredited, is that the inquisitors had extirpated most of the heretics and now turned their attention to witches.[16] Jeffrey Russell saw the accused as, in fact, heretics, who had been so disaffected with orthodox religion that they had begun a devil-worshipping sect, while Kathrin Utz Tremp has traced the complex history of negative stereotyping by which heretics (especially the so-called Luciferians) were falsely deemed to be devil worshippers.[17] What is clear is that many of the elements found in the literature of the 1430s and in the Lausanne trials were recycled from long-

---

[15] Walter Rummel, 'Gutenberg, der Teufel und die Muttergottes von Eberhardsklausen: Erst Hexenverfolgung im Trierer Land', in Andreas Blauert, ed., *Ketzer, Zauberer, Hexen: Die Anfänge der europäischen Hexenverfolgungen* (Frankfurt, 1990), 91–117.

[16] This construction of developments was more plausible before Norman Cohn and I demonstrated independently that an entire set of trial records, suggesting that the mythology of diabolical witchcraft extended back well into the fourteenth century, was forged in the early nineteenth century. See Norman Cohn, *Europe's Inner Demons: The Demonization of Christians in Medieval Christendom* (London, 1975), 128–38, and Richard Kieckhefer, *European Witch Trials: Their Foundations in Popular and Learned Culture, 1300–1500* (London, 1976), 16–18.

[17] Jeffrey Burton Russell, *Witchcraft in the Middle Ages* (Ithaca, NY, 1972); Kathrin Utz Tremp, *Von der Häresie zur Hexerei: 'Wirkliche' und imaginäre Sekten im Spätmittelalter* (Hanover, 2008).

standing allegations that heretics held nocturnal assemblies, engaged in sexual orgies, and were devoted to the devil.[18]

The link between witches and heretics is not simply a discovery or invention of historians: contemporaries in the fifteenth century also perceived some kind of connection. The dossier from Lausanne and some of the writings of the 1430s refer to the witches as heretics (*heretici*), and when the term *Vauderie* came to be used for diabolical witchcraft, even if some people may have taken it to have a connection with the Pays de Vaud as a kind of heartland of witchcraft, the more usual construction made this a synonym for Waldensianism, one of the most widespread heresies of later medieval Europe.[19] Wolfgang Behringer has argued that certain features of Waldensianism, such as the itinerant heretical masters' claims to supernatural power, gave plausibility to the connection between this heresy and witchcraft.[20]

Still, the questions posed to alleged witches make it clear that they were not thought of as heretics in any usual sense. The inquisitors in the diocese of Lausanne asked the accused whether they believed in God and in the devil, and they were interested in evidence of conventional piety: they wanted to know whether the accused knew the basic prayers laypeople were expected to know, and whether they had received communion at Easter time. But they did not ask about visits of itinerant masters, or refusal to take oaths, or any of the other beliefs and practices specific to Waldensians, nor did they ask questions that would have served as litmus tests for Catharism or any other recognized heresy. If witchcraft was a 'sect' or 'heresy'—and the inquisitors surely believed it was—it was a different kind of heresy, not an outgrowth of some previously existing heresy. Calling it a heresy would have been important to justify the intervention of inquisitors, who, after all, were delegated specifically as 'inquisitors of heretical depravity',[21] but perhaps even more importantly it was a way of emphasizing that the witches were a cohesive and powerful threat to Christendom, a conspiracy organized under the leadership of the devil, a collectivity dedicated to mocking and desecrating the Eucharist and the cross, and requiring of its members a total denial of God and the faith. It was set forth as the *ultimate* heresy. It did not pretend to restore Christianity to its original purity; it expressly devoted itself to the enemy of the Church and of everything holy. When we know about the circumstances that led to prosecution, they almost always involve bewitchment, not heresy. The testimony of neighbours shows that before the trials the accused were thought of as sorcerers, or maleficent magicians, and the charge of heresy was introduced only in the course of prosecution. To be sure, the Latin court records say that neighbours accused people of being 'heretics' (*heretici*), but what this meant in context clearly has nothing to do with

[18] On this see Cohn, *Europe's Inner Demons*.

[19] Richard Kieckhefer, 'Mythologies of Witchcraft in the Fifteenth Century', *Magic, Ritual, and Witchcraft*, 1 (2006), 100.

[20] Wolfgang Behringer, 'How Waldensians Became Witches: Heretics and their Journey to the Other World', in Gábor Klaniczay and Éva Pócs, eds, *Communicating with the Spirits* (Budapest, 2005), 155–92.

[21] The bull of Alexander IV, *Quod super nonnullis*, issued in 1258, had restricted inquisitors of heresy to action against magic only if it entailed heresy. See Hansen, *Quellen und Untersuchungen*, 1.

ordinary heresy, and we can only speculate what French term was used to translate and transcribe this Latin word.

A third question that recurs in the literature is the relevance of geography. Fernand Braudel and H. R. Trevor-Roper called attention to the importance of Alpine regions as centres of the early witch trials.[22] This suggestion is problematic, however. It is true that the literature of the 1430s suggests that Alpine valleys—the Simme Valley in the Bernese Alps, the Valais, the mountains of Dauphiné—were the breeding grounds for the paradigm of diabolical witchcraft we have sketched, but when we are able to compare this propaganda with court records we find little reason to accept that claim.[23] Nider's *Formicarius* refers to testimony from several locations, and it is not clear how far he means to ascribe this diabolical witchcraft specifically to Alpine territory;[24] furthermore, in general these writings seem to reflect outsiders' fantasies about mountain culture rather than what was happening in that culture itself. In any case, the mythology of diabolical witchcraft appears earliest and most fully in sub-Alpine territories in and around western Switzerland, in the *shadow* of the Alps.

The importance of sub-Alpine regions is twofold. We might speak here of a double borderland. First, the heartland of witchcraft was a region where languages and cultures abutted each other: Italian, French, and German. It is perhaps no coincidence that in the 1430s the classic paradigm was articulated in or near this region in a series of writings representative of these different cultures, which now were sharing their belief in a newly begotten sect of witches. As the Alps represented the product of tectonic activity, so too was this a region of cultural tectonics, where the interaction of cultures was reflected in this remarkable conjunction of writings, which came out of different linguistic communities, with ideas about witchcraft that had erupted into prominence across linguistic boundaries. Secondly, this was a borderland between rural communities that, until recently, would have been relatively remote, and urban complexes that were very much linked with broader cultural trends. To say that witchcraft emerged in the shadow of the Alps is not to say that either the practice or the accusation of witchcraft was specific to remote Alpine valleys. Rather, the trials tended to occur in or near urban areas, or in territories subject to urban authority: along the urbanized north banks of Lake Geneva, in parts of the Bernese Alps under the jurisdiction of Bern, along parts of the Upper Rhône by the town of Sion, and in other places where urban culture

---

[22] Oscar di Simplicio, 'Mountains and the Origins of Witchcraft', in Richard M. Golden, ed., *Encyclopedia of Witchcraft: The Western Tradition*, 4 vols (Santa Barbara, CA, 2006), iii, 790–1; H. R. Trevor-Roper, 'The European Witch-craze of the Sixteenth and Seventeenth Centuries', in *The European Witch-Craze of the Sixteenth and Seventeenth Centuries and Other Essays* (New York, 1969), 90–192; Pierrette Paravy, 'La sorcellerie, une spécialité montagnard? Le cas du monde alpin occidental', *Heresis*, 39 (2003), 19–33.

[23] Arno Borst, 'The Origins of the Witch-craze in the Alps', in *Medieval Worlds: Barbarians, Heretics, and Artists in the Middle Ages*, tr. Eric Hansen (Chicago, 1992), 101–22; Kieckhefer, *European Witch Trials*, 20; Paravy, *De la chrétienté romaine à la Réforme en Dauphiné*, 849.

[24] See here especially Catharine Chène's detailed analysis of Nider's sources of testimony in Ostorero, et al., *L'imaginaire du sabbat*, 233–44.

was encroaching on Alpine or sub-Alpine terrain. The accused typically came from the more traditional rural society of the valleys, or from the elevated hinterland above Lake Geneva. while the judges came from the more cosmopolitan elite of the towns. Confrontation between rural and urban culture would have been commonplace throughout the late medieval West, but there were few places where the contrast would have been so sharp as between the entrenched Alpine or sub-Alpine culture now exposed to the glare of sophisticated urban judges. The clash would have been all the greater when the authorities had themselves migrated across linguistic frontiers, as when Bishop George de Saluces moved from Aosta to Lausanne with his clerical retinue and soon began presiding over the Lausanne witch trials.[25] It was hard enough for a native of Lausanne to understand the rural culture of the hinterland, but all the harder for a bishop or priest recently arrived from Italy.

9.3 DIFFUSION OF THE LAUSANNE PARADIGM IN ATTENUATED FORM: FRENCH-SPEAKING TERRITORIES

Throughout the century there were people who suggested that diabolical witchcraft had originated in or around western Switzerland, Savoy, and the Dauphiné. For contemporaries, this was the heartland of diabolical witchcraft.[26] But other heresies had spread beyond their regions of origin—Waldensianism, Hussitism, and so on—and now this new conspiracy against Christendom seemed also to be marching beyond its original breeding grounds. However, when the mythology appeared in judicial records of other territories it rarely remained altogether intact. Perhaps the greatest problem with the 'cumulative concept' of witchcraft is that this way of formulating the history of witchcraft does not take into account one of the most important factors in the early trials: the spread of the classic paradigm in partial or attenuated form. What we see here is not accumulation but the opposite, a paring down of the pre-existing paradigm.

For example, Andrée Garaude was executed at Bressuire in the region of Poitou in 1475. In the opening stages of her confession she admitted performing image magic, but then she confessed to having been inducted into an assembly of witches and having attended the sabbath (now called by that term), carried by the devil or riding on a broom. At the sabbath she had sex with the devil and received a mark on her body. The devil was intent on her hating God and the Virgin Mary, and on her committing sacrilege with the consecrated host; she also urinated in the holy water stoup and defecated in the church nave at the devil's command. But in comparison with the protocols from Lausanne the recitation is relatively brief, and key features of the classic

---

[25] On George de Saluce, see Martine Ostorero, in Ostorero, et al., *L'imaginaire du sabbat*, 333–4.

[26] Ostorero et al., *L'imaginaire du sabbat*, 511–13.

paradigm of diabolical witchcraft are missing, such as the eating of human flesh.[27] At Boucoiran in 1491 Martiale Espaze confessed to attending the sabbath (again using that term), paying homage to the devil in the form of a goat, kissing him on the posterior, having sex with a demon, renouncing God and the Virgin and the faith, and trampling and spitting on a cross traced on the ground. But again the account is less developed than in the Lausanne documents, and much of what is done there at the witches' assembly is here transferred to a different context. Her relations with a demon are mostly outside the setting of the sabbath, sometimes en route to or from it, and it was evidently outside the sabbath that he made her renounce the faith.[28] Throughout the French territories there were trials in the second half of the fifteenth century that follow this pattern: they repeat some but not all of the charges in the Lausanne trials, and the accounts of diabolical witchcraft tend to be less extended and developed.[29]

The themes of diabolical witchcraft had been articulated in detail by writers of the 1430s referring to western Switzerland, Savoy, and the Dauphiné, and the trials in the diocese of Lausanne were faithful to this paradigm—in case after case they seemed to confirm its reality. Once it coalesced, the mythology then became known in other French-speaking regions, but without the aid of the inquisitors' interrogatory. Under these circumstances, judges might expect the accused to make confessions resembling those they had heard reported from afar, but the recitals were abridged, fragmentary, undeveloped.

9.4 Regional Alternatives to the Classic Paradigm: Italian-speaking Territories

A further difficulty with the notion of a 'cumulative concept' of witchcraft is that it tends to neglect alternative mythic complexes that coexisted with what we are here calling the Lausanne paradigm of diabolical witchcraft. Probably the most important alternative was the Italian concept of the *strega*, the night-flying witch who broke into people's homes, often accompanied by one or perhaps two other *streghe*, and killed infants by sucking their blood. Ugolino Nicolini has brought to light a set of trial records from Perugia in which the charge of *stregoneria* is made from 1445 into the

---

[27] René Filhol, 'Procès de sorcellerie à Bressuire (Août–Septembre 1475)', *Revue historique de droit française et étrange*, 4th ser., 42 (1964), 77–83.

[28] Édouard Bligny-Bondurand, 'Procédure contre une sorcière de Boucoiran (Gard), 1491', *Bulletin philologique et historique* (1907), 380–405.

[29] Kieckhefer, 'Mythologies of Witchcraft', 100–2.

early sixteenth century; this is perhaps the closest Italian equivalent to the Lausanne manuscript with its charges of *Vauderie*, and in Perugia as in the Lausanne collection the charges remained quite stable throughout a period of over half a century.[30] The *strega* was not regularly thought of as attending a nocturnal assembly, and the infants were killed but not taken to be eaten by *streghe*. If there was a conspiracy among them, it was a small-scale one. Whereas the witches in the diocese of Lausanne presented an affront to the Church and its sacraments, the *streghe* of Italy were disruptive more to the sanctity of the home and the family. If we try to represent the *streghe* as a regional variation on what is found in and around the Pays de Vaud, we will not get very far. The phenomena are in fact quite distinct. The trial records from Perugia suggest coalescence of a paradigm different from that in Lausanne, more deeply grounded in local mythology that had been known for centuries (ultimately traceable to Roman notions of the night-flying owl or *strix*).[31] If the trials in the diocese of Lausanne coalesced largely around an inquisitorial interrogatory, those in central Italy coalesced around long-standing traditions of folklore.

Still, once this mythic complex became known outside its native region it too could become fused with other, previously distinct, concepts. Perhaps the best instance of this is the case of Martiale Espaze, previously mentioned, who was tried at Boucoiran in 1491. The trial record begins with charges of bewitchment, but these are followed by fundamentally different accusations, first by an attenuated version of the Lausanne paradigm, but then also by accusations reminiscent of the Italian *strega*. Like the *strega*, Espaze attacked infants in their beds, in this case by pressing down on them, and at least once also putting powder into a child's mouth, causing lingering illness and death. As in the case of the *strega*, Espaze's activities remained almost wholly unassimilated into the context of the sabbath, although there is one reference to a child-killing that took place *after* a sabbath. Thus, while there were distinct regional mythologies, over time they did become fused, albeit partially and sporadically.

A further pattern is found in northern Italy and in Italian-speaking Switzerland. As early as 1384 and 1390 there were women at Milan who confessed they had participated in a gathering known as the 'play' (*ludus*) of Diana.[32] The purposes seem to have been fundamentally benign: they were instructed in the art of healing. Elsewhere in this region the devil brought bread and cheese to an assembly. The activities were not always benign: one woman did say she had devoted herself to Lucifer, who took

---

[30] Ugolino Nicolini, 'La stregoneria a Perugia e in Umbria nel Medioevo: con i testi di sette processi a Perugia e uno a Bologna', *Bollettino della Deputazione di storia patria per l'Umbria*, 84 (1987), 5–87; Kieckhefer, 'Mythologies of Witchcraft', 88–91.

[31] Paul Murgatroyd, *Mythological and Legendary Narrative in Ovid's* Fasti (Leiden, 2005), 4–6; and Samuel Grant Oliphant, 'The Story of the Strix: Ancient', *Transactions and Proceedings of the American Philological Association*, 44 (1913), 133–49.

[32] Ettore Vergo, 'Intorno a due inediti documenti di stregheria Milanese del secolo XIV', *Rendiconti del Reale Instituto Lombardo si Scienze e Lettere*, 2nd ser., 32 (1899), 166–8; Kieckhefer, 'Mythologies of Witchcraft', 96–8.

her to this gathering; in one case Lady Abunda presided over a large group that ate human flesh; elsewhere the participants were offered the blood of children (*puerorum striatorum*) or animals.[33] In short, we have suggestions of the mythology that came to be associated with those of both Lausanne and central Italy, yet these elements are probably overlays on a distinct mythic complex, native to this region, and marked chiefly by the presence of a female presider and by a spirit of bounty and fellowship. This is also the setting in which the postulate of realism becomes most plausible: the assumption that there really were folkloric customs, actual celebratory gatherings, interpreted *in sensu malo* by inquisitors and other uncomprehending outsiders. It is in this context that the views of Carlo Ginzburg become most plausible: that the mythology of witchcraft can be represented as resting on a misconstruction of actual folk beliefs and customs.[34]

The image that emerges from this survey is one of persistent regionalism, and in the judicial sources more or less distinct regional traditions that were fairly tenacious through the fifteenth century, if not beyond. There was more conflation of these traditions in contemporary treatises on witchcraft, which were more likely than the court records to reflect the viewpoints of individual writers, often reflecting the eclecticism that came from their reading of works from various parts of Europe. The Dominican Girolamo Visconti wrote a treatise whose title *Lamiarum sive striarum opusculum* (A Short Work on Witches or Streghe) already suggests a conflation of traditions: alongside the northern Italian notion of the assembly as a 'game' presided over by a woman, Visconti speaks of the offenders as members of a sect that assemble to perform sacrilegious acts such as host desecration.[35] Here and elsewhere in the literature on witchcraft we find that the fusion of traditions is relatively easy when nothing has to be proven: the spilling of ink is more painless than the spilling of blood, and mingling of ink from various sources presents no difficulty.

9.5 REGIONAL ALTERNATIVES TO THE CLASSIC PARADIGM: GERMAN-SPEAKING TERRITORIES

The impression of persistent regionalism is only reinforced when we bear in mind that in much of Europe there was no strong leaning towards any of these mythic patterns:

---

[33] Carl Binz, 'Zur Charakteristik des Cusanus', *Archiv für Kultur-Geschichte*, 7 (1909), 145–53; Binz, 'Le streghe nella Leventine nel secolo XV', *Bollettino Storico della Svizzera Italiana*, 6 (1884), 144–5; Paolo Guerrini, ed., *Chronache bresciane inedite dei sec. XV–XIX* (Brescia, 1922), i, 185–6; and Pierangelo Frigerio and Carlo Allessandro Pisoni, 'Un brogliaccio dell'Inquisizione milanese (1418–1422)', *Libri & Documenti: Rivista quadrimestrale (Archivio Storico Civico e Biblioteca Trivulziana)*, 21 (1995), 46–65.

[34] Carlo Ginzburg, *Ecstasies: Deciphering the Witches' Sabbath*, tr. Raymond Rosenthal (repr. Chicago, 2004).

[35] Hansen, *Quellen*, 200–7.

no pattern of explicit pact with the devil, or nocturnal assemblies, or of sucking the blood of infants. Germany seems on the whole to have been remarkably resistant to these notions. Trials there were conducted by secular, usually municipal, judges, both in the free imperial cities and elsewhere.

In Nuremberg, and to some extent elsewhere, the records are often vague, focusing more clearly on the materials used in sorcery than on the effects desired: the accused are said to have used sorcerous plants, or materials taken at the gallows from the bodies of executed criminals, but what they meant to achieve with these materials is not always specified.[36] Still, when all the evidence is taken together, four types of sorcery constitute the known majority: weather magic, bodily harm to fellow humans, harm to animals (especially theft of cows' milk), and love magic. Overwhelmingly, the most important accusation, occurring in well over half the documented cases, especially in Switzerland but further north as well, was weather magic, usually meant to cause storms that would destroy crops. That this accusation arises so commonly in municipal courts may seem surprising; storms that ruined the crops might destroy buildings as well, but the prevalence of this accusation points mainly to the interdependency of towns and the surrounding countryside, and to the tendency for cases in the territory of a town to be brought into the town proper for adjudication. The second most frequent accusation was the use of sorcery to cause bodily harm and death to fellow humans.

Municipal judges appear at times to have been uncertain how to proceed in these trials. On occasion they consulted the clergy, or even called in an inquisitor known as a 'witch-master',[37] but they were just as likely to consult with magistrates in other cities where witches had been prosecuted. When two women were tried at Cologne in 1456, one of them had come from Metz, where she had once destroyed all the crops within a circuit of two miles with her arts. The burgomaster and council of Cologne wrote requesting information about proceedings in Metz that might help with current proceedings. Later in the fifteenth century it was the turn of the town fathers at Cologne to give counsel to those elsewhere. The secular authorities at Zutphen wrote in 1491 to those of Cologne about three women who had been imprisoned for stirring up destructive storms and causing harm to livestock. Because the government at Cologne had experience in such matters, those at Zutphen hoped they could provide some useful counsel.[38]

---

[36] Hartmut Kunstmann, *Zauberwahn und Hexenprozess in der Reichsstadt Nürnberg* (Nuremberg, 1970); Richard Kieckhefer, 'The Role of Secular Authorities in the Early Witch-trials', in Johannes Dillinger, Jürgen Michael Schmidt, and Dieter R. Bauer, eds, *Hexenprozess und Staatsbildung/Witch-Trials and State-Building* (Bielefeld, 2008), 25–39.

[37] Andreas Schmauder, 'Frühe Hexenverfolgung in Ravensburg: Rahmenbedingungen, Chronologie und das Netzwerk der Personen', in Andreas Schmauder, ed., *Frühe Hexenverfolgung in Ravensburg und am Bodensee* (Konstanz, 2001), 39–44.

[38] Hansen, *Quellen*, 565–70. On Metz see also William Monter, *A Bewitched Duchy: Lorraine and its Dukes, 1477–1736* (Geneva, 2007), 30–3.

During this era town governments often exercised their judicial authority not only over witchcraft but over blasphemy, sodomy, even conspicuous religious idiosyncrasies, as well as sorcery.[39] Still, they showed relatively little interest in the mythic paradigms of diabolical witchcraft. The possibility of demonic involvement in magic is at times acknowledged. Witches were sometimes said to work under diabolical instigation, and even to have dedicated themselves to the devil as a precondition for being able to work their sorcery. A woman burned at Constance in 1493 confessed to sexual relations with a devil. Three women at Wolfsberg, Carinthia, had devoted themselves to particular devils and had repudiated God, the Virgin Mary, and the Christian faith, which sounds like a faint echo of the classic paradigm; nevertheless, they were not said to have attended a sabbath, and there is no suggestion that they belonged to a vast conspiracy of witches.[40] Even when a chronicler told of witches in the Upper Palatinate who rode at night on cats and brooms, rode out on Ember days to arouse storms, and made people lame (although they could also cure), there is no suggestion of the witches' assembly or sabbath, with all the practices associated with it.[41]

There were other nations and territories, such as England, that remained even less affected by these mythic patterns than Germany, but the focus on sorcery without any fully developed diabolical paradigm is remarkable in German lands because one might have thought conditions there were ripe for the spread of such a paradigm. Johannes Nider was German-speaking and probably wrote his *Formicarius* in Vienna. Later in the fifteenth century, the German inquisitor Heinrich Kramer (Institoris), main author of the *Malleus maleficarum*, borrowed heavily from the *Formicarius* and thus clearly knew its version of what became the Lausanne paradigm, but so far as we know it made little impact even in his own trials. When he prosecuted witches in Ravensburg and in Innsbruck, the charges were fundamentally indistinguishable from those brought forward in German secular courts.[42]

The *Malleus maleficarum* does contain strangely distorted echoes of the mythic paradigm. Kramer tells of an assembly in which the devil appears, demands that the witches abjure the faith and the Virgin Mary, requires that they give themselves to him soul and body, and leaves them with maleficent unguents made from the bodies of children, all of which derives from the mythology acted out in the Lausanne trials. But when he grasps for a German example from his own inquisitorial experience, he finds a story that does not really match his imported mythology. He tells an odd tale of a

[39] Laura Patricia Stokes develops this point in important ways in her *Demons of Urban Reform: Early European Witch Trials and Criminal Justice, 1430–1530* (New York, 2011).
[40] Hansen, *Quellen*, 592 (Constance); Fritz Byloff, ed., *Volkskundliches aus Strafprozessen der osterreichischen Alpenländer, mit besonderer Berücksichtigung der Zauberei- und Hexenprozesse 1455 bis 1850*, Quellen zur deutschen Volkskunde, 3 (Berlin and Leipzig, 1929), 12f., no. 14 (Wolfsberg).
[41] Hansen, *Quellen*, 235.
[42] Richard Kieckhefer, 'Magic at Innsbruck: The Case of 1485 Reexamined', in Thomas Wünsch, ed., *Religion und Magie in Ostmitteleuropa: Spielräume theologischer Normierungsprozesse in Spätmittelalter und Früher Neuzeit* (Münster, 2007), 11–29.

young woman whose aunt ordered her to go upstairs, where fifteen young men dressed in green presented themselves as her suitors. She did not want any of them, but after a beating she agreed to take one, and then (Kramer tells us peremptorily) she was solemnly initiated into witchcraft.[43] Kramer was one person we might have expected to serve as the ideal source for introducing paradigms of diabolical witchcraft into German lands, but instead he remained rooted in the traditions of his homeland. His mind was schooled in the international currents of demonology, but his eyes and his ears remained German. Here, as elsewhere, regionalism remained in force throughout the last decades of medieval Europe.

9.6 CRITICISM AND SCEPTICISM

There is poignant irony in the coexistence of two currents in fifteenth-century religious literature: alongside writings arguing the reality of witchcraft and the urgency of its suppression, there was a rich body of literature critical of superstitions.[44] These writings against superstitions could be directed first against *practice* of superstition, secondly against belief in its *efficacy*, thirdly against belief in its *reality*, meaning belief that there really were people who practised it. These three foci of critique were not always sharply distinct, but when the practices in question were the sort that arose in witch trials, it was the same critical impulse, which could be directed sometimes against the accused and at other times against the accusers. For example, it was superstitious to practise weather magic believing it effective, but it could also be superstitious to believe that *other people* practise weather magic and should be prosecuted for doing so. Hans von Vintler's didactic poem *Die Pluemen der Tugent* (1411) castigates superstitious practices such as the use of a consecrated host against a fever. Elsewhere, however, he criticizes belief in weather magic, in sorcery to affect cows' production of milk or to steal butter, and bewitchment to effect impotence.[45] Would a man such as Hans von Vintler oppose the prosecution of alleged witches, or would he support it? Faced with a set of concrete cases, he would have to decide whether it was the accused or the accusers who were being superstitious. Even if both were superstitious in their assumptions about the efficacy of bewitchment, the accused might still be guilty of vincible error in allowing herself to be duped by the devil.

One specific issue that was intensely controversial in late medieval sources was the possibility of witches' flight. The early medieval canon *Episcopi*, which had been taken up in authoritative collections of canon law, forbade belief in the possibility of night

---

[43] Henricus Institoris and Jacobus Sprenger, *Malleus maleficarum*, pt. 2, qu. 1, ch. 2, ed. and tr. Christopher S. Mackay (Cambridge, 2006), i, 396.

[44] Michael D. Bailey, 'A Late-medieval Crisis of Superstition?' *Speculum*, 84 (2009), 633–61.

[45] Wolfgang Ziegeler, *Möglichkeiten der Kritik am Hexen- und Zauberwesen im ausgehenden Mittelalter: Zeitsgnössische Stimmen und ihre soziale Zugehörigkeit* (Cologne, 1973; 2nd edn, 1983), 34–60.

flight. But did the canon *Episcopi* truly apply to the kind of witchcraft seen as prolifer-
ating in the fifteenth century? Those who feared the contagion of a new type of threat
argued that this canon—valid as it might be in a different context—did not apply here,
and thus it was not superstitious to try witches for offences that included flying to the
sabbath. The *Malleus maleficarum* came down on the side of credulity on this point. In
opposition, others argued that not only the witches' flight but the sabbath itself was an
illusion and should not be grounds for criminal conviction.[46]

Scepticism might, however, be partial and thus of limited relevance to the course
of prosecution. The lawyer Ulrich Molitoris, counsellor to Archduke Sigismund of
Austria, concluded in his *De lamiis et phitonicis mulieribus* (On Witches and Fortune-
Telling Women) that many of the activities ascribed to witches are impossible: their
flight to the sabbath, their transformation into the forms of animals, their weather
magic, even their divination and their harm to human bodies. Still, he recognized that
they might indeed form a pact with the devil, renouncing God, and for this idolatry and
apostasy they deserved execution.[47] Martin Plantsch, theologian at the University of
Tübingen, argued in his *Opusculum de sagis maleficis* (1507) that witches' flight was
impossible, but he did believe in weather magic and other bewitchments.[48]

It is striking, then, to find an instance of vigorous scepticism in the Valais, not far
from the heartland of the Lausanne paradigm, in 1467. Three witches about to be
executed had alleged that a widow from Chermignon d'en Haut named Françoise
Bonvin was among their accomplices. Bonvin herself was thus arrested and brought to
trial for witchcraft. She was fortunate, however, in having influential protectors who
came forward with a vigorous and successful defence.[49]

The first argument for Bonvin's defence had to do with how the devil tempts people.
Her accusers had told hair-raising tales of their encounter with the devil, who appeared
in hideously misshapen form with fire coming from his mouth. The defence insisted
that when the devil seeks to deceive people he begins not by terrifying them but by
blandishments to allure them. Secondly, the confessions of Bonvin's accusers had
centred largely on witches' manipulation of the weather, but weather is under the
control not of the devil or of humans but of God. To believe otherwise is heresy,
ascribing to a creature the power belonging to God alone. The accusers told of killing a
child and taking its body to their synagogue, where they ate it. But the cemetery where
the child was buried was surrounded by many houses, and the witches could hardly
have exhumed the body without being seen and heard. Further, it was not clear how
many days had passed between the killing and the eating of the child, or whether the

---

[46] See Edward Peters, 'Canon Episcopi', in Golden, ed., *Encyclopedia of Witchcraft*, 164–5. The title of
this article makes the common mistake of referring to the 'canon *Episcopi*' as the '*Canon Episcopi*'.

[47] Ulrich Molitor, *Schriften* (Constance, 1997).

[48] Martin Plantsch, *Opusculum de sagis maleficis* (Pforzheim, 1507); Gunther Franz, 'Martin Plantsch
(ca. 1460–1533/1535)', in Golden, ed., *Encyclopedia of Witchcraft*, iii, 904–5.

[49] Sandrine Strobino, *Françoise sauvée des flammes? une Valaisanne accusée de sorcellerie au XVe
siècle*, Cahiers Lausannois d'Histoire Médiévale, 18 (Lausanne, 1996).

body had been preserved with salt or had decomposed, or how they could have eaten it once decomposition set in.

Sixty-seven witnesses from the vicinity were then interrogated, including the clergy at Bonvin's parish church. They testified that she was of a good family, had lived an upright life, and had had a favourable reputation until recently defamed. She adhered to the Catholic faith, performed good works, attended church regularly, heard mass devoutly (although not always arriving on time), made the sign of the cross, confessed her sins and received communion at Easter time, and gave alms. She knew the Catholic faith 'in the manner of peasants', and had taught it to a young girl competently if simply. She had been charged with arousing a destructive storm, a flood, and a snowfall in July, but at the times each of these events occurred she had a convincing alibi. Witnesses also told of enmity between Bonvin and one of the accusers, with whom she had quarrelled over rights of pasturage. Bonvin evidently had a quick tongue and was eager to spread her own suspicions about her neighbours' misconduct. Still, the evidence in her favour was overwhelming, and the bishop issued a formal statement of her innocence, restoring her to freedom and possession of her property. Alas, another witch then accused her; she was again arrested, interrogated, and tortured, but seems a second time to have been also released as innocent.

Was scepticism more likely or less so when the allegations were of more ordinary bewitchment, without the mythic overlay? It is difficult to generalize, but Heinrich Kramer complained about resistance he had encountered to his prosecution at Innsbruck, and the documents from that case make clear that the local opposition to his trial—which centred on magic of various sorts, especially love magic—was considerable. The *Malleus maleficarum* was written largely to overcome such resistance, as was the bull *Summis desiderantes affectibus*, produced by Pope Innocent VIII at Kramer's behest. Both forms of accusation—ordinary bewitchment and diabolical witchcraft—could be scrutinized and challenged in a particular case, but the former was more widely and deeply established and was therefore harder to deny in principle.

9.7 CONCLUSION

The first wave of trials for diabolical witchcraft turns out to be more complex than has usually been suggested in the historical literature. The notion of an accumulation, in which one concept after another was added to the brew and remained there as an accomplished fact, is simply untenable. Regionalism remained persistent throughout late medieval Europe. There were voices of caution, although rarely of total denial. And yet the story is not one of endlessly splintering perspectives. Within broad territories there were paradigms that remained fairly stable: the recently invented paradigm that emerged in and around western Switzerland, the indigenous and traditional Italian notion of the *strega*, German concepts of bewitchment. Even when ideas about witchcraft were transported across regional lines, they did so in ways that allow some generalization. French echoes of the classic paradigm may rarely have captured the full force of that conceptual complex, but the fear of a conspiracy making its way across from Alpine or sub-Alpine regions and infecting more and more of Christian society was itself a strong trend. What late medieval witch-hunters and demonologists bequeathed to early modern Europe was thus not a fixed set of convictions and anxieties, but a more complex network of issues that called to be resolved and eventually were, at great cost.

Further Reading

Bailey, Michael D., 'From Sorcery to Witchcraft: Clerical Conceptions of Magic in the Late Middle Ages', *Speculum*, 76 (2001), 960–90.

Cohn, Norman, *Europe's Inner Demons: An Enquiry Inspired by the Great Witch-Hunt* (London, 1975).

Decker, Rainer, *Witchcraft and the Papacy: An Account Drawing on the Formerly Secret Records of the Roman Inquisition*, tr. H. C. Erik Midelfort (Charlottesville, VA, 2008).

Kieckhefer, Richard, *European Witch Trials: Their Foundations in Popular and Learned Culture, 1300–1500* (London, 1976).

Kieckhefer, Richard, 'Mythologies of Witchcraft in the Fifteenth Century', *Magic, Ritual, and Witchcraft*, 1 (2006), 79–107.

Levack, Brian P., ed., *Witchcraft, Magic and Demonology*, ii: *Witchcraft in the Ancient World and the Middle Ages* (Hamden, CT, 1992).

Mackay, Christopher S., *The Hammer of Witches: A Complete Translation of the 'Malleus maleficarum'* (Cambridge, 2009).

Stephens, Walter, *Demon Lovers: Witchcraft, Sex, and the Crisis of Belief* (Chicago, 2001).

Williams, Gerhild Scholz, *Defining Dominion: The Discourses of Magic and Witchcraft in Early Modern France and Germany* (Ann Arbor, MI, 1995).

CHAPTER 10

···

THE GERMAN WITCH TRIALS

···

THOMAS ROBISHEAUX

THE German lands have long been known as the 'heartland of the witch craze'. Of the estimated 90,000 individuals prosecuted for witchcraft in Europe, at least 30,000 and possibly as many as 45,000 came from the Germanies, roughly encompassed at the time by the Holy Roman Empire and nearby territories. Approximately 25,000 of an estimated 50,000 legal executions for witchcraft took place within the lands of modern-day Germany. The German lands also developed several large chain-reaction witch-hunts: terrifying panics that could claim hundreds of lives within a year or so. Understanding the German trials, therefore, takes one deeper into witchcraft, the trials, their dynamics, and the reasons for them. The large body of scholarship that treats German witchcraft since the 1970s—scholarship that rests on exceptionally rich archival records of trials—therefore lies at the centre of witchcraft studies in general. This body of scholarship has shaped views of witchcraft and the witch trials in decisive ways. German witchcraft studies have established the regional and comparative study as the dominant approach to trials, revealed the long-term temporal rhythms of witch-hunting, shown the necessity of multi-causal explanations for trials, revealed the popular village-level impulses that often drove the dynamics of fear of witchcraft, recognized the role of fragmented local state structures and legal practices in making trials more likely, and unearthed rich new insights into the varied kinds of beliefs about witches.[1]

---

[1] Still the best overview of the historiography of the German trials remains Wolfgang Behringer, 'Witchcraft Studies in Austria, Germany and Switzerland', in Jonathan Barry, Marianne Hester, and Gareth Roberts, eds, *Witchcraft in Early Modern Europe: Studies in Culture and Belief* (Cambridge, 1996), 64–95. For a more complete overview see Wolfgang Behringer, 'Geschichte der Hexenforschung', in Sönke Lorenz and Jürgen Michael Schmidt, eds, *Wider alle Hexerei und Teufelswerk: Die europäische Hexenverfolgung und ihre Auswirkungen auf Südwestdeutschland* (Ostfildern, 2004), 485–668.

10.1 THE GERMAN LANDS

Most of the Germanies came under the often fragile and fragmented structures of authority of the Holy Roman Empire. This decentralization of authority in the empire's roughly two thousand semi-independent territories shaped the overall patterns of witch trials. The weak institutions of the empire shared authority and power with seven prince-electorates, forty-three secular principalities, thirty-two ecclesiastical principalities, 140 independent lordships, seventy imperial abbacies, four cantons of the Teutonic Order, seventy-five imperial cities, and scores of imperial knights (670 in Swabia, 700 in Franconia, 360 along the Rhineland). In the old settled lands of the western and southern parts of the empire—characterized by small, fragmented lord-ships, weak territorial and ecclesiastical states, and small towns—elites, courts, and the local administrative institutions of government were often drawn into the community dynamics of witchcraft accusations, making the region's densely populated regions particularly receptive to witch trials. The few more centralized territorial states—Bavaria, Austria, the duchy of Württemberg, the electorate of the Palatinate, electoral Saxony and Brandenburg—tended to rein in the activities of local courts. As a result, these states tended to approach witchcraft with caution and even scepticism.

In northern and north-western Germany the duchies of Westphalia and Mecklen-burg, the county of Lippe, together with the ecclesiastical states of Osnabrück, Münster, and Paderborn, often exercised only nominal central control over lords and other splintered jurisdictions with their own law courts and legal traditions. Along the Rhine an even more extreme dispersal of authority characterized principalities like those of Jülich, Cleves, and Berg, the prince-bishopric of Cologne, and the counties of Nassau and dozens of small and weak secular lordships. At the heart of the empire, the prince-bishopric of Mainz, one of the most influential principalities of the empire, exercised only nominal control over a sprawling, complex, and contested set of lands and jurisdictions at the intersection of the Rhine and Main rivers. The central German lands of Thuringia, the long-settled regions along the Upper Rhine, the Odenwald and most of south-west Germany, were also classic lands of decentralized and shared authority. They included ecclesiastical states, such as the prince-bishoprics of Cologne, Mainz, Würzburg, and Bamberg; abbey lands like those of Fulda; ecclesiastical preb-ends such as Ellwangen; the great monastic states of Upper Swabia; free and imperial cities like Frankfurt, Nuremberg, Strasbourg, Augsburg, Ulm, and many smaller ones; and a host of small princely states, counties, and free and imperial knights. German witch trials tended to take place in the most splintered lands of Europe, the regions where early modern states were late to develop.[2]

---

[2] See Jörn Sieglerschmidt, 'Social and Economic Landscapes', in Sheilagh Ogilvie, ed., *Germany: A New Social and Economic History*, ii: *1630–1800* (London, 1996), 1–38.

The Reformation brought additional divisions to these territories. No firm correlation exists between religious confession and a propensity to hunt witches. But swings from Protestantism to Catholicism and back again, intense campaigns to renew Catholicism around 1600, or conditions where elites and populations felt vulnerable or threatened by zealous religious reformers could add urgency and intensity to local fears of witchcraft.

The vagaries of subsistence agriculture created an immediate backdrop of uncertainty to many of the witchcraft accusations in these territories. While the trials were by no means determined by economic uncertainties—many vulnerable regions that experienced harvest failures and famines did not hunt witches—a rough correlation exists between the worsening conditions for agriculture and witch trials after 1560. Most regions depended upon cereal production for food and even in the best of years productivity remained low and variable. Seed yield ratios averaged 1:3 or 1:4, adequate to feed a peasant family, but when crops failed, shortages, malnourishment, and famine threatened.[3] In areas of viticulture—along the Upper and Middle Rhine, the Main River and parts of Franconia and Swabia—winegrowers might enjoy decent incomes in good years, but downturns or early frosts quickly threatened livelihoods. Animal husbandry provided additional support for many families, but illnesses and murrains made cows vulnerable. In these often precarious conditions the loss of a single harvest or cow could tip a family into desperation.

More than one scholar has noted the association of the Little Ice Age with heightened tensions within agricultural communities and witchcraft accusations. Between roughly 1560 and 1720 the Little Ice Age reduced average annual temperatures, bringing on harsh winters, late springs, early autumns, and the increased likelihood of heavy rainfalls and storms in summer. The growing season contracted. Marginal agricultural lands became more vulnerable to harvest failures, famines, and disease. The village population then contracted. Following a decade of harvest failures and hunger in the 1570s the number of witch trials surged in the 1580s and 1590s. The years around 1600 were marked by extremely cold and prolonged winters, lingering frost in the spring, and short growing seasons. In the winter of 1600/1 temperatures averaged 5.5 degrees cooler than normal in Central Europe. In 1601 harvest yields fell off sharply. When a period of late frosts, unusually heavy rains, and summer storms and late frosts followed these setbacks in 1602, famine and the fear of more losses and hardship increased. The same cycle repeated itself in the late 1620s. A hailstorm around Stuttgart in 1626 damaged crops. Throughout south-west Germany hard and late frosts sharply reduced harvests. By late spring harvest failures and food shortages had spread. Lean and hungry years, inflation, and food shortages preceded the surge in witch trials between 1626 and 1630 across south-west Germany and Franconia. The wine-growing areas of Styria, Franconia, Swabia, and the Rhineland were even more vulnerable to uncertainty in the 1620s and 1630s. At the height of the trials between the 1580s and

---

[3] Thomas Robisheaux, *Rural Society and the Search for Order in Early Modern Germany* (Cambridge, 1989).

1630s witches were often accused of weather magic, spreading toxic powders on fields, and poisoning domestic animals and people. Such accusations were likely to be made in densely populated rural areas where agonistic village social relationships fuelled fears of loss, illness, and hardship.

10.2 CHRONOLOGY OF TRIALS

The years around 1560 mark a temporal turning point in German witch trials. The extent and distribution of trials in the early sixteenth century has not yet been systematically investigated, but research suggests a pattern of isolated and individual prosecutions centred around accusations of harmful magic. There were some note-worthy cases, such as the burning of a maid for witchcraft in the Black Forest for burning down the town of Schiltach, or the trials in the city of Nuremberg. Customar-ily, historians note the trials and executions of sixty-three people for witchcraft in the imperial lordship of Wiesenstieg in 1562 as inaugurating a new era of more trials. In addition, in these and many subsequent trials accusations of harmful magic (*malefi-cium*) came increasingly to be linked with diabolism, an elaborated concept of witch-craft first laid out in the *Malleus maleficarum*. Developments in Austrian lands in Swabia, especially the county of Hohenberg, illustrate this wider trend. Isolated indi-vidual trials took place in 1521, 1528, 1530, 1531, and again in 1554. Then, starting in 1558, the number of prosecutions increased.[4] In Austrian Vorarlberg trials increased notice-ably around 1550.[5] Along the Lower Rhine in the duchy of Jülich fifty-three executions are documented between 1490 and 1540, fewer in neighbouring Berg and Cleves. In the county of Lippe and its provincial capital, Lemgo, investigations into allegations of witchcraft increased markedly in the 1560s.[6] At the same time many territories issued new ordinances dealing explicitly with the crimes of sorcery and witchcraft: the law codes of the duchy of Württemberg (1567) and electoral Saxony (1572) having particular influence.

Around 1580 the reporting of witch trials shifted from accounts of sensational individual cases to more alarming reports about the widespread threat from witches and witchcraft, the harm witches occasioned, and the intensified efforts of the author-ities to root out the sect. The reports about the shockingly large number of trials in and

---

[4] Johannes Dillinger, 'Hexenverfolgungen in der Grafschaft Hohenberg', in Johannes Dillinger, Thomas Fritz, and Wolfgang Mährle, *Zum Feuer verdammt: Die Hexenverfolgungen in der Grafschaft Hohenberg, der Reichstadt Reutlingen und der Fürstpropstei Ellwangen* (Stuttgart, 1998), 1–162.

[5] Manfred Tschaikner, *Magie und Hexerei im südlichen Voralberg zu Beginn der Neuzeit* (Constance, 1997).

[6] For the best study of the Lippe trials see Rainer Walz, *Hexenglaube und magische Kommunikation im Dorf der Frühen Neuzeit: die Verfolgungen in der Grafschaft Lippe* (Paderborn, 1993). See also Gisela Wilbertz, Gerd Schwerhoff, and Jürgen Scheffler, *Hexenverfolgung und Regionalgeschichte: die Grafschaft Lippe in Vergleich* (Bielefeld, 1994).

around the Catholic archbishopric of Trier in the 1580s and 1590s played a pivotal role in ratcheting up the fears of witches throughout the empire. In north-western Germany and along the Middle Rhine the number of trials surged, especially in lands with dispersed and contested local jurisdictions, and small principalities and lordships. Prosecutions became almost continuous in the bishopric of Paderborn after 1572. In 1584 a major set of trials took place in the nearby prince-bishopric of Osnabrück. Around this time the Lutheran duchy of Mecklenburg and its fragmented jurisdictions, owned by feudal lords, became the centre of a long and virtually continuous set of trials, approximately 4,000 overall between 1560 and 1700. Peaks in the Mecklenburg trials occurred in 1600 and again around 1630.[7] A similar pattern developed in Pomerania where the duchy of Pomerania-Wolgast carried out about 1,000 trials with at least 600 victims. The fragmented and confusing jurisdictions of the duchies of Schleswig and Holstein also had sizable numbers of trials. Some of the most intense witch-hunts took place in the small counties of Isenburg-Büdingen, Schaumburg, and Lippe in the late 1580s and 1590s. Farther to the east the fewer trials in the electorates of Brandenburg and Saxony suggest a pattern of restraint and caution typical of the larger, more consolidated states of the empire. But just to the south, in Thuringia, where the authority of lordship and courts was split up among dozens of small Saxon dynastic lines, imperial cities, and lordships, sizable numbers of prosecutions took place: between 1,000 to 1,500 trials, with 500 executions.[8] Along the Middle Rhine a similar pattern emerged, as the fragmented counties of Nassau executed up to 400 witches, and the politically divided landgraviate of Hessen-Kassel another 250.

Farther to the south the number of trials surged around 1590 in Franconia, the Franconian-Swabian borderlands, and across the politically fragmented landscape of south-west Germany. Major Catholic ecclesiastical territories, such as the prince-bishoprics of Bamberg and Würzburg and the bishopric of Eichstätt recorded large numbers of witch trials. A wave of trials swept across some of the region's smallest territories in the Franconian-Swabian borderlands, such as the counties of Hohenlohe and the margraviate of Ansbach.[9] Even free and imperial cities like Augsburg, Nuremberg, Ulm, Rothenburg ob der Tauber, Reutlingen, and Nördlingen had their share of trials. In the compact territory at the centre of the south-western corner of the empire—the duchy of Württemberg—heavy hailstorms in 1562 contributed to the first surge in trials. A peak was reached between 1590 and 1630, but individual trials remained the norm in the duchy. Stuttgart's firm central control over local courts and the duchy's cautious jurists contributed to fewer trials than in the neighbouring territories. In Bavaria, following an increase in trials around 1590, authorities in Munich and in local courts tightened up legal procedures, changed the laws, and

---

[7] Katrin Moeller, *Dass Willkür über Recht ginge: Hexenverfolgung in Mecklenburg im 16. und 17. Jahrhundert* (Bielefeld, 2007).

[8] Ronald Füssel, *Die Hexenverfolgungen in Thüringener Raum* (Hamburg, 2003).

[9] Susanne Kleinöder-Strobel, *Die Verfolgung von Zauberei und Hexerei in den fränkischen Markgräftümern in 16. Jahrhundert* (Tübingen, 2002).

actively discouraged prosecutions.[10] The changes made it difficult for local prosecutions to gather support and momentum.

A second peak in German witchcraft prosecutions came in the 1620s. In southern Germany the differing attitudes of elites towards witchcraft and trials began to make a noticeable difference in local and regional patterns of trials. Bavaria and Austria, especially the government in Innsbruck, urged caution and judicial restraint on lower courts, thus moderating local tendencies to hunt witches. A handful of Catholic ecclesiastical territories, however, engaged in fierce chain-reaction witch trials between 1600 and 1610. Massive witch panics rippled across the princely prebend of Ellwangen, the bishoprics of Eichstätt, Mainz, and Würzburg, and the abbey of Fulda. But Catholic ecclesiastical territories were by no means alone in experiencing large witch-hunts. In northern Germany in the duchy of Mecklenburg a new peak in trials came between 1604 and 1615. None of these, however, compared in intensity to the terrifying witch panics of the late 1620s and early 1630s in the Franconian bishoprics of Würzburg and Bamberg between 1626 and 1630. The Cologne trials (1624–34) became the largest and most frightening of all the German witch-hunts.[11] The trials peaked in small secular lordships and principalities as well. Between 1633 and 1635, and again between 1651 and 1654, 283 executions took place in the small territory of Isenburg-Büdingen. In Berg, the town of Siegburg executed twenty-one people for the crime of witchcraft between 1636 and 1638. Similarly, a peak of intensity in the trials came to Paderborn and the duchy of Westphalia between 1628 and 1631. While towns rarely prosecuted large number of people for witchcraft, Lemgo, in the principality of Lippe, carried out a terrible series of trials between 1628 and 1637, resulting in 110 accusations and eighty-four executions. These hunts coincided with a period of deep agrarian distress due to crop failures, cold winters, inflation, and the heightened tensions and violence associated with the Thirty Years' War.

After 1630 German witch trials became more infrequent. In some areas decisive interventions on the part of governments brought an end to trials. Austria was a case in point. When Innsbruck finally intervened in the Swabian county of Hohenberg in 1630, replacing the land's key administrative personnel and changing the laws, witch trials abruptly ended. When the Tyrolean valley of Prättigau broke free of their Austrian overlords in Innsbruck between 1652 and 1660 a wave of witch trials, resulting in 100 executions, followed, but these ceased when Innsbruck regained control over the small region. In other cases lands deeply affected by the Thirty Years' War often lost the administrative and social cohesion necessary to carry out trials. In still other cases, rising revulsion against religious zeal and fanaticism deterred elites from indulging popular accusations of witchcraft. Still, some of the most intense witch-hunts took place after 1650. If one considers the number of trials per capita, the prosecutions that

---

[10] See the fine study by Wolfgang Behringer, *Witchcraft Persecutions in Bavaria: Popular Magic, Religious Zealotry and Reason of State in Early Modern Europe* (Cambridge, 1997).

[11] For a slightly out-of-date view of the Cologne trials as 'state terror' see Gerhard Schormann, *Der Krieg gegen die Hexen: das Ausrottungsprogramm des Kürfürsten von Köln* (Göttingen, 1991).

took place in tiny Liechtenstein between 1648 and 1651, again in the 1660s, and yet again in 1679–80 were arguably the most intense witch panics in the German territories. In the free and imperial city of Esslingen alarming accusations and terrifying trials disrupted the community; under the leadership of a zealous chief inquisitor, Daniel Hauff, seventy-five trials with thirty-seven executions took place between 1662 and 1665.[12] As other trials took place in nearby Reutlingen and northern Württemberg, rumours and fear spread across the Odenwald and the Swabian-Franconian borderlands. The alarming deaths of cattle and children led to fears that a nest of witches, secretly organized by the fierce Turk Anna, were poisoning food and fields around the Hohenlohe town of Langenburg. The witch trials held there between 1668 and 1672 claimed ten victims. They came to an end in the notorious case of a miller's wife, Anna Schmieg of Hürden, thought to have learned the black arts from Turk Anna.[13] By the end of the 1670s, however, the old patterns were changing noticeably. Not only were panics rare and individual trials far fewer in number, but the dynamics of the trials changed completely. The famous 'Sorcerer Jack' trials in Salzburg (1678–80) revolved around accusations against adolescent and young men, not peasant women, with Jacob Koller, a vagabond, their suspected witch leader. One hundred and forty of his alleged followers were tried and executed.

By the 1680s witch trials were rare events. In Calw a panic involving the town's children was averted in 1683–4.[14] In north-western Germany a final wave of trials took place in the duchy of Westphalia in the 1650s, the town of Lemgo in Lippe in the 1650s and 1660s, and the duchy of Mecklenburg in the 1660s and 1670s. The severe orthodox Lutheran ruler of Mecklenburg, Duke Gustav Adolf, launched a campaign to eradicate witchcraft and superstition from his duchy altogether, and a final wave of witch trials associated with his stern crusade rippled across the territory in the 1660s and 1670s. By the 1680s trials were rare in Holstein, Mecklenburg, and along the Rhineland. In the 1690s and well into the eighteenth century trials were mostly isolated occurrences. Among theologians and jurists, however, witchcraft remained a topic of controversy throughout the eighteenth century. The last trial took place against Anna Schwägelin of Kempten in 1775.

10.3 CHAIN-REACTION HUNTS

During the most zealous period of witchcraft prosecutions, between 1590 and 1630, an extraordinary and terrifying type of witch-hunt developed in a few German lands: the

---

[12] Günter Jerouschek, *Die Hexen und ihr Prozeß: die Hexenverfolgung in der Reichstadt Esslingen* (Esslingen, 1992).

[13] Thomas Robisheaux, *The Last Witch of Langenburg: Murder in a German Village* (New York, 2009).

[14] H. C. E. Midelfort, *Witch Hunting in Southwestern Germany, 1562–1684: The Social and Intellectual Foundations* (Stanford, CA, 1972), 158–63.

large chain-reaction hunt. Often occurring in territories, especially ecclesiastical principalities, where poorly developed local court systems operated with little effective central oversight, restraint, and review, the new model hunt claimed hundreds, and in a few cases a thousand or more victims, within a short period of time (one to four years). In these territories magistrates and local elites were easily drawn into witchcraft accusations. In some cases they actively organized and directed witch-hunts through extraordinary legal innovations. Catholic ecclesiastical territories were more vulnerable to such a development, in part because they exercised authority over dispersed, fragmented, and even contested local jurisdictions, where they often shared jurisdictions with local nobles and communities. These terrifying campaigns were distinctive not only for their numbers but for the powerful effects they exercised on surrounding areas. The Trier hunts around 1590 were the first widely known such events of this kind. But already in south-west Germany, Rottenburg and Obermarchtal had experienced large chain-reaction hunts in the mid- and late 1580s.

Perhaps the most noteworthy and significant witch-hunt of this type occurred in the electorate of Mainz between 1602 and 1604. The archbishop of Mainz, who also served as the chancellor of the Holy Roman Empire, exercised considerable influence by virtue of his office. The archdiocese of Mainz spanned much of the empire itself, from Hamburg down the Rhine to Strasbourg, Augsburg, and Constance. In addition, Mainz's lands sprawled across the Rhineland, Franconia, and Thuringia. Witchcraft accusations in Mainz therefore easily spilled over into hundreds of nearby small lordships, ecclesiastical lands, and small and fragmented principalities. The trials in Mainz quickly escalated out of control, in large part because power and authority was widely dispersed, shared, and contested between local elites, noblemen, and communities. In a short time Mainz's witch trials had claimed the lives of 650 people.[15]

It was not by accident that terrifying witch-hunts quickly developed in nearby Catholic ecclesiastical lands. In 1602 the abbey of Fulda also experienced a terrifying hunt for witches. Fulda's prosecutions, however, were organized 'from above' by Prince-abbot Balthasar, who orchestrated a relentless campaign of revenge against witches, personal enemies, and noblemen. When the trials ended in 1606, his campaign had claimed the lives of 276 victims. At the same time, the Teutonic Knights at Mergentheim, their cantons lying adjacent to Mainz, began their first massive witchcraft prosecutions.

Around 1600 a new dynamic emerged within these large chain-reaction witch-hunts. Instead of accusations building up slowly over several years, trials were started deliberately, gained momentum quickly, and resulted in large numbers of victims. While authorities did not usually instigate these hunts, they often took advantage of popular fears of witchcraft so that they might expand their authority. Armed with extraordinary legal powers, an awe-inspiring kind of prosecutor emerged: the witch commission or witch commissioner (*Hexenkommisar*). In 1611 the number of accusations of witchcraft

---

[15] Herbert Pohl, *Hexenglaube und Hexenverfolgung im Kürfürstentum Mainz: ein Beitrag zur Hexenfrage im 16. und beginninenden 17. Jahrhundert* (Stuttgart, 1988).

in the ecclesiastical territory of Ellwangen exploded when the princely prebend appointed a witch commission. The judges quickly introduced shortened criminal procedures and relaxed the restrictions on the use of torture. In 1611–12 Ellwangen's witch commission executed 300 witches. Before the panic ran its course in 1618, a total of 430 witches were executed.[16] In some cases zealous Catholic rulers and magistrates who displayed an almost fanatical devotion to the cause of Church reform played a decisive role in these chain-reaction hunts.

The most frightening of these large-scale witchcraft prosecutions did not take place until around 1630. In a contiguous string of Catholic ecclesiastical states and some small secular states stretching across Franconia from Mainz eastwards across the bishoprics of Würzburg and Bamberg, massive hunts swiftly and unexpectedly gained momentum, starting in 1626. Initial waves of trials had earlier swept through Mainz in 1616–18 (361 executions), Würzburg in 1616–18 (300 executions), and Bamberg in 1616–19. Then, between 1626 and 1630, a further wave of trials swept across the region: Mainz (768 executions), Würzburg (900 executions), and Bamberg (600 executions).[17] These prosecutions not only tore the social fabric but created political chaos, as they claimed the lives of mayors, town councillors, canons of the cathedral, and even members of the princely governments. These panics helped spark nearby witch-hunts in the small counties of Wertheim (1629–44), and in the canton of the Teutonic Knights at Mergentheim (1627–31).

The largest example of this new and terrifying kind of panic took place in the electorate of Cologne. Between 1626 and 1634 the trials there claimed 2,000 victims. Scholars once thought that the Cologne trials had been orchestrated from above. New research, however, shows that these trials, like those in the electorates of Trier and Mainz, developed in large part from local accusations, which quickly overwhelmed a sprawling system of local courts lacking central control and oversight. Courts and district officers introduced summary justice in witchcraft cases, and individual trials turned into panics as local elites were swept up in their neighbours' fears.

One of most distinctive feature of these panics—aside from the scale and scope of the prosecutions—was that the familiar stereotype of the witch broke down. In individual and medium-sized trials (five to ten executions) women—usually older women— accounted for 70 to 80 per cent of the victims. In the larger panics, however, this pattern was shattered as the pattern of accusations and prosecutions reached into the ranks of governing elites. The Bamberg trials were symptomatic of this breakdown: mayors, councillors, even high government officials were accused. More men were prosecuted as the large trials gathered momentum. Elites were implicated when confessions extracted by torture and permitted by relaxed standards of evidence yielded long lists of alleged accomplices. In addition, the normal machinery of the

---

[16] Wolfgang Mährle, '"O wehe der armen seelen": Hexenverfolgungenen in der Fürstpropstei Ellwangen (1588–1694)', in Dillinger, et al., *Zum Feuer verdammt*, 325–491.

[17] A little dated but still comprehensive is Friedrich Merzbacher, *Die Hexenprozesse in Franken* (Munich, 1970).

law tended to break down. A number of these large panics ended in part because the collapse in recognizable patterns among witches drained the confidence out of witch finding altogether.[18] Adam Tanner, a prominent Catholic theologian from Ingolstadt and Vienna, denounced these trials not because he doubted the existence of witches but because, he argued, the law simply could not identify them with confidence. In the wake of the Cologne trials Friedrich von Spee famously took up a similar argument in his *Cautio criminalis* (1631).

10.4 CLIMATE OF FEAR

One additional feature of the period between 1590 and 1630 was a darkening of the intellectual, cultural, and religious climate. The heightened tensions and unsettled cultural and ideological climate did not cause the witch trials, of course, but developed in complicated ways independently of and in close association with them. The roots of this change lay not only in the fears of witches but developed out of a hardening of the political and religious camps into ideological blocks of Protestants and Catholics in the Holy Roman Empire, growing worries about the fragility of the empire's institutions, popular fears of rootless vagabonds and criminals, widespread harvest failures and famines, economic difficulties, population crises, and the beginnings of war.

One contribution of the trials to this unsettled cultural climate came from the acrimonious debates over witchcraft. These contentious disputes increasingly divided dogmatic hardliners and sensationalists from moderates and sceptics. The debates revolved around a number of issues: the reality of witchcraft, the degree to which God and the devil actively caused misfortune, the pact with the devil, the material dangers posed by witches, the evidence for witchcraft, and the role of princes, magistrates, and the law in fighting witchcraft. When Johann Weyer wrote his famous sceptical treatise on witchcraft, *De praestigiis daemonum* (On the Conjuring of Demons, 1562), arguing that witches were not able to make weather magic, that they were just delusional old women, polemical preachers from south-west Germany countered his arguments in sermons and in print, arguing that witches were specifically adept in the dark arts of weather magic. In other places Protestant polemicists might cede the point that witches could not actually perform harmful magic, but they then pressed the point that witches should be persecuted all the more fiercely because they were guilty of the more dangerous spiritual crimes of apostasy and diabolism. The new and more rigorous demonological works supporting the prosecution of witches, especially Johann Fischart's translation of Jean Bodin's *De la demonomanie des sorciers* (*On the Demon-Mania of Witches*, 1580) into German in 1582, and Peter Binsfeld's treatise based on the Trier trials, *Tractatus de confessionibus maleficorum et sagarum* (Treatise

---

[18] Midelfort, *Witch Hunting in Southwestern Germany*, 121–63.

on the Confessions of Malefactors and Sorcerers, 1589), provided fresh and powerful arguments for treating witchcraft as a crime of *lèse-majesté* against the ruler and God himself. So alarmed was Binsfeld by the danger of witchcraft that he also argued for treating witchcraft as an 'exceptional crime' (*crimen exceptum*). Less rigorous, but widely circulated, was the Protestant Abraham Sawr's vernacular reader on witchcraft, *Theatrum de veneficiis* (The Theatre of Poisoners, 1586). Broadsides and anonymously written news-sheets circulated widely at the big book fair in Frankfurt. New works by Nicolas Remy, and especially Martin Del Rio's *Disquisitionum magicarum libri sex* (Disquisition on Magic in Six Books, 1599–1600), summed up a vast knowledge about demons and witches. These works rested on the fresh and compelling evidence of the recent trials, and helped explain precisely why and how demons and witches plagued Christians and Christian authorities.

These debates often divided highly placed government advisors, jurists, and university professors into political factions or loosely organized parties. The case of Bavaria and the Catholic political networks shaped by Bavarian influences offer the best case of this polarization. After the shocking rise of trials in the 1580s a group of moderate counsellors in Munich around Duke William V (1579–1597) and Maximilian I (1597–1623) gained the upper hand over the hardliners at the court and established a state policy of treating witchcraft accusations with caution and judicial restraint. Nobles and townspeople provided a wider base of support for a cautious approach to witchcraft. Countering them, however, and pressing for more prosecutions, was a faction of hardliners centred at the university in Ingolstadt. Their debates were taken up among theologians and government officials within the sphere of Bavaria's influence across southern Germany, shaping the regional politics of witchcraft through the era of the big trials in the 1620s and into the eighteenth century.[19] Similar positions characterized the Austrian governments in Innsbruck and Vienna. The Habsburg imperial court in Prague and Vienna became well known for discouraging trials, and even provided safe haven for victims of the witch-hunts in the Franconian Catholic prince-bishoprics.

A culture of judicial scepticism also developed in almost all of the large centralized Protestant states of the Holy Roman Empire. Even though Protestant Württemberg issued the first witchcraft ordinance that criminalized witchcraft as a spiritual crime in 1567, the duchy became known for its restraint in prosecuting witches. This came in part through the strong influence of the faculty of law at the University of Tübingen, which consistently argued in favour of caution in witch trials. Despite the fact that one of its most illustrious theologians, Thomas Erastus, strongly supported witch trials, the Rhineland Palatinate's Calvinist rulers and high-level counsellors remained staunchly sceptical towards witchcraft. The law faculty at Heidelberg was also a bulwark of support for the sceptics. Even when neighbouring territories engaged in fierce witch-hunts, the Palatinate kept a firm grip on its local courts and consistently discouraged

[19] See Behringer, *Witchcraft Persecutions in Bavaria*.

witch trials.[20] Government and judicial elites in electoral Saxony also approached witchcraft with comparative restraint and caution. If one were to judge by its harsh laws, such as the Saxon law code of 1572, which prescribed harsh penalties for witchcraft as a spiritual crime, and the published work of some its prominent jurists, such as Benedict Carpzov, one would expect this bulwark of Protestantism to be dominated by hardliners regarding witchcraft. But this was far from the case. The moderate number of trials in electoral Saxony indicates that pragmatic judicial sceptics dominated the courts.

By the 1640s and 1650s the cultural and political climate had shifted. Even though polemicists quickly and repeatedly denounced Friedrich von Spee's *Cautio criminalis*, the work clearly resonated among government elites in many quarters of the empire in the 1630s. To the old core arguments advanced by judicial sceptics came new and more relevant arguments against religious zeal and zealotry in any form. Religious fanaticism—frequently understood as an inclination to hunt witches—was met in many quarters with distaste. Towards the end of the Thirty Years' War, especially among the young graduates from law schools, one notices a generational change in which jurists and even some theologians tended to view the state and the law as a bulwark against partisanship, zeal, and chaos. Elites who leaned towards the new arguments about 'reason of state' also tended to distance themselves from beliefs in witchcraft. New approaches in medicine and the growing use of forensic medical investigations in controversial legal cases also led elites to play down mystical or diabolical explanations of poisons and look instead towards chemical explanations. Still, in some cases, elites, under certain conditions, could generate a climate of fear and support for witch trials, as happened in Hohenlohe-Langenburg, Mecklenburg, and Salzburg for short periods of time. The welcome reception of Christian Thomasius's famous sceptical work, *Kurze Lehrsätze von dem Laster der Zauberei mit dem Hexenprozess* (Short Propositions on the Vile Belief in Sorcery in the Witch Trial, 1704) was long prepared by a generation of jurists and civil servants more attentive to legal process, order, and restraint, and more sceptical about 'religious fanaticism', 'superstition', and popular passion in any form.

10.4.1 Community Dynamics

The impulse for most witch trials came from within small village communities. In contrast to the Rhine-Moselle borderlands, where semi-autonomous village witch committees often levelled the initial accusations, few such popular institutions are documented in other parts of the Holy Roman Empire. In these areas the accusations tended to work through local systems of village, district, and seigneurial courts. Given that villagers so often shared in many of the institutional aspects of local government, the dependence of many lords on the goodwill and material support of their peasants,

---

[20] Jürgen Michael Schmidt, *Glaube und Skepsis: die Kurpfalz und die abendländische Hexenverfolgung 1446–1685* (Bielefeld, 2000).

and the authorities' need to offer 'protection' to their subjects, it is no surprise that villagers turned to local courts to press their cases. Many witchcraft accusations drew on a host of agonistically structured conflicts among and between family members, neighbours, and other close and well-established relationships.[21] Accused witches were almost always familiar figures in the community. Given that fears of witchcraft could be insinuated into many different kinds of village conflicts—over honour, misfortunes, illness and unexpected deaths, property losses, pregnancy and childbirth, the illness of domestic animals, or even slander and communal norms governing neighbourly conduct, among others—the potential for witchcraft allegations and prosecutions was immense. Scholars still do not fully understand why suspicions aroused fears of witchcraft in one circumstance, while the very same behaviour in another time and place was perceived in strikingly different ways.

At the height of the trials approximately 80 per cent of all of those prosecuted for witchcraft were women, mostly women over forty. The pattern for late medieval and early sixteenth-century trials, where half of the accused were men, changed dramatically. This shift in the 1560s is still not fully understood. One reason for this change was that so much of the material harm and misfortune tended to be closely associated with the work of women. So many of the activities for which village women were responsible were prone to uncertainty and, especially after 1560, misfortune. When harvests failed and malnourishment, illness, and mortality rates spiked during famines, blame might easily fall on those women responsible for the care of pregnant women and children, preparing food, and nursing the ill. All of the activities around motherhood could become both more important and, at the same time, tinged with more anxiety and even suspicion. During the trial of Magdalena Dürr for murder and witchcraft in Rothenburg, the town magistrates focused on her 'unmotherly' behaviour towards children.[22] In Augsburg lying-in maids sometimes found themselves accused of harming pregnant women, new mothers, and infants. Anger and envy, it was commonly understood, consumed witches and drove them to *maleficium*.[23] Pamphleteers accused female witches of blighting the natural fertility of the fields through weather magic and poison. In the witch trials in the bishopric of Augsburg between 1586 and 1588 the authorities executed 150 witches, 9 per cent of whom were women usually accused of poisoning the fields and livestock. In other cases everyday disputes over reputation and honour escalated, an accusation of witchcraft becoming the final attack in long and bitter disputes among neighbours. The cases involving women from Lippe point also to disputes over property as triggers for witchcraft accusations.[24] In addition, community

[21] See especially Walz, *Hexenglaube und magische Kommunikation*.

[22] Alison Rowlands, *Witchcraft Narratives in Germany: Rothenburg, 1561–1652* (Manchester, 2003), 136–43.

[23] Lyndal Roper, *Witch Craze: Terror and Fantasy in Baroque Germany* (New Haven, CT, 2004), 127–59.

[24] Ingrid Ahrendt-Schulte, 'Schadenzauber und Konflikte: Sozialgeschichte von Frauen im Spiegel der Hexenprozesse des 16. Jahrhunderts in der Grafschaft Lippe', in Heide Wunder and Christina Vanja, eds, *Wander der Geschlechterbezieungen zu Beginn der Neuzeit* (Frankfurt, 1991), 198–228.

and religious norms governing marital and communal behaviour—with their emphasis on obedience, deference, harmony, piety, restraint in speech, dress, and decorum— could make women who seemed repeatedly to violate such norms vulnerable to accusations of witchcraft.

During witch panics the hunt for accomplices broke down communal and public order in shocking and unpredictable ways. Where authority was fragmented and localized this often meant that local elites themselves were drawn into the dynamics of witchcraft accusations and trials. In Austrian Swabia, for example, local town magistrates and district officers became intimately involved in the witch-hunts between 1583 and 1605. While magistrates may themselves have levelled accusations against poor or weak women, a fair number of these public officials were accused of witchcraft themselves.[25] In the abbey of Fulda, one of the most notoriously politicized witch-hunts, the prince-abbot and his judges directed accusations against local noblemen and elites. Prosecutions for witchcraft reached high into the political establishments of both Bamberg and Mergentheim in the early seventeenth century.

Yet witchcraft insinuated itself into so many different kinds of community relation-ships that the dynamics of accusations and trials and even panics could develop along surprising new lines. Johann Weyer never mentioned child witches in his treatise from 1562, for example. Just twenty years later, in some of the massive trials of the 1580s and 1590s, children began to step forward as witnesses. In the early seventeenth-century trials in Würzburg children even appeared as witches, curious and eager to learn the dark arts. By the 1670s and 1680s the dynamics of many trials came to revolve, in shocking and new ways, around children and adolescent boys.[26] These changes are not fully understood. In the Salzburg 'Zauberer Jackl' trials of 1678–81 the authorities directed their prosecutions against the adolescent boys and young men who formed roving gangs of vagrants, beggars, and thieves. In Calw in 1683–4 fears centring around children and child witches nearly brought on an avalanche of witchcraft accusations. In the Augsburg trials of the 1720s children were accused of forming secret cults, engaging in indecent sex, and attacking their parents, sometimes with violence and at other times with the aid of poisoned powders spread under their beds. So malleable and so deeply woven into the fabric of everyday life was witchcraft that it was feared it lurked invisibly within almost any troubling or troubled social relationship.

10.5 LEGAL PROCEDURES

Secular laws against *maleficium* or 'harmful magic' were well established long before jurists and theologians associated diabolism with witchcraft. Roman law provided a compelling precedent for punishing sorcery and harmful magic. Most courts of the

---

[25] Dillinger, 'Grafschaft Hohenberg', 75–81.
[26] Roper, *Witch Craze*, 204–21.

Holy Roman Empire also drew upon medieval customary law and law codes to punish harmful magic. In this regard many of the new territorial law codes of the middle of the sixteenth century, such as in the duchy of Jülich (1537) and Württemberg (1552), continued medieval precedents. While laws clearly treated harmful magic as a material crime—injury to life, health, and property—most did not clearly distinguish it from poisoning. For this reason many suspected witches were accused of mixing poison into food, spreading noxious powders over fields and pastures, or murdering victims in some other mysterious way. Moreover, in territories that lacked strong states and a rigorous and centralized judicial apparatus, the decentralization and splintering of legal jurisdictions often meant that no checks or rigorous appellate reviews curbed witch trials once they got under way.[27]

The Imperial Criminal Law Code or *Carolina* (1532) set a common legal standard for witchcraft prosecutions throughout the Holy Roman Empire. Like many medieval laws, nowhere did it mention diabolical witchcraft. Instead the code identified 'harmful magic' (Article 52) as a material crime that damaged persons or property by means of 'words or other instruments'. The *Carolina* also established standards of evidence for proving witchcraft, criteria that included evidence about where or how someone learned sorcery, associations with known sorcerers, a reputation for using spells or possessing poisons or other paraphernalia used in the working of sorcery.[28] Magistrates were to treat cases of suspected harmful magic through applying the standard rules of inquisitorial procedure, documenting the entire procedure, applying the ordinary rules of the law (*processus ordinarius*) and rigorously following well-defined rules of testimony and evidence. The code allowed torture, but magistrates could prescribe it only when a certain weight of evidence pointed to the guilt of the accused. Given that sorcery and witchcraft were secret crimes this meant, in practice, that the confession of the accused was vital for a conviction. Moreover, in controversial cases the *Carolina* required magistrates to seek legal review and advice from appellate courts, university faculties of law, or other higher legal instances. Finally, while by the early seventeenth century most courts widely cited the *Carolina* in their proceedings, the imperial law remained subordinate to territorial and local laws. In practice, many lower courts operated virtually independent of central review and oversight.[29]

[27] For a general introduction see Sönke Lorenz, 'Der Hexenprozeß', in Sönke Lorenz, ed., *Hexen und Hexenverfolgung im deutschen Südwesten* (Karlsruhe, 1994), ii, 67–84.

[28] Gustav Radbruch, ed., *Die Peinliche Gerichtsordnung Kaiser Karls V. von 1532 (Carolina)* (Stuttgart, 1962), 53–4.

[29] See Michael Ströhmer, 'Carolina (*Constitutio Criminalis Carolina CCC*): Die Peinliche Gerichtsordnung Kaiser Karls V. im Kontext der frühneuzeitlichen Hexenprozesse', in Gudrun Gersmann, Katrin Moeller, and Jürgen Michael Schmidt, eds, *Lexikon zur Geschichte der Hexenverfolgung*, <http://www.historicum.net/themen/hexenforschung/lexikon/alphabethisch/a-g/art/Carolina_Const/html/artikel/1586/ca/9334b35039adb8e85e2b4b73d747b6a4/> (accessed 20 September 2011). In English still the most accessible study is John H. Langbein, *Prosecuting Crime in the Renaissance: England, Germany, France* (Cambridge, MA, 1974), 167–209.

In the first wave of witch trials in the late sixteenth century courts therefore applied a wide variety of legal standards and procedures. In many cases magistrates even violated their own procedures and standards of evidence in proving witchcraft and using torture to extract confessions. Many public critics denounced these trials as illegal. Others called for immediate reforms. In the 1580s and 1590s, for example, magistrates and other elites often added to the evidence of *maleficium* accusations of diabolism, even when local laws made no such provisions for it. The new law codes of the duchy of Württemberg (1567) and the electorate of Saxony (1572) were the first to make the spiritual crime of apostasy and pact with the devil into a criminal offence. Later, through the work of Saxon jurists and legal reformers, and especially through the influence of Benedict Carpzov and his *Practica nova Imperialias Saxonica rerum criminalis* (New Practices of Imperial Saxony in Matters of Criminal Law, 1635), the more rigorous Saxon legal standards gained widespread influence. Drawing on the precedent in Roman law, these jurists treated witchcraft as treason against the sovereignty of God and the ruler (*crimen laesae majestatis*). Invoking this dire threat to public order then allowed lower courts to introduce abbreviated judicial procedures, adhere to lower standards of evidence, rely more on oral testimony, and relax the rules governing torture. In a 'secret crime' like witchcraft, where finding material evidence of diabolism and poisoning was virtually impossible, magistrates relied heavily on confessions. A new type of legal institution also began to appear in some areas around 1600: a witch commission that adopted the summary process. Such a commission was introduced in Ellwangen and subsequently adopted by Eichstätt in 1613.[30] In 1616 similar commissions were established in Würzburg and Bamberg. Locally appointed witch commissioners played a prominent role in driving the massive prosecutions around Cologne in the 1620s and 1630s. These extraordinary legal institutions aroused fierce legal controversy. Catholic Bavaria openly refused to adopt the new model. In northern Germany the influential Protestant jurist Johann Georg Godelman insisted that witchcraft be treated like any other crime, that is, according to ordinary legal procedures.[31]

The *Carolina* also prescribed that courts have their procedures reviewed by appellate courts or other higher legal bodies, such as the law faculties of universities. In the sixteenth century such reviews took place in a very uneven fashion.[32] But by the middle of the seventeenth century they were much more common, even routine. The influence of these legal consultations depended on time and place. In the electorate of the Palatinate the central government kept strict control over lower courts and had their cases sent to the University of Heidelberg for careful and sceptical review. Even

---

[30] Mährle, '"O wehe der armen seele"', 383–92.

[31] See especially Winfried Trusen, 'Rechtliche Grundlagen der Hexenprozesse und ihrer Beendigung', in Sönke Lorenz and Dieter R. Bauer, eds, *Das Ende der Hexenverfolgung* (Stuttgart, 1995), 203–26.

[32] For one of the best studies of the reception of the *Carolina* see Michael Ströhmer, *Von Hexen, Ratsherren und Juristen: Die Rezeption der Peinlichen Halsgerichtsordnung Kaiser Karls V. in den frühen Hexenprozessen der Hansestadt Lemgo 1583–1621* (Paderborn, 2002).

torture was forbidden to local magistrates. Witch trials were therefore infrequent. The relatively modest number of witch trials in the duchy of Württemberg—only 450 trials with 205 executions took place over two centuries—can be traced, in part, to the influence of the cautious law professors at the University of Tübingen. They consistently insisted on restraint and moderation, requiring that lower courts follow the *Carolina* and not use severe forms of torture. Similarly, the influence of the law faculty at the University of Rostock almost certainly moderated the trials in the duchy of Mecklenburg.[33] The Imperial Chamber Court (*Reichskammergericht*), which heard several hundred cases on appeal, also treated witch trials with scepticism. At the end of the 1620s the court harshly denounced the Franconian witch-hunts. This supreme court of the Holy Roman Empire may have had more influence in turning the sentiments of jurists and magistrates against witch trials than previously thought.[34]

By the middle of the seventeenth century legal reforms and the strong tendency to treat witchcraft in accordance with the requirements of the *processus ordinarius* made witch trials less common. When prosecutions did occur convictions were difficult to secure. Therefore, when Christian Thomasius published his stinging denunciation of witch beliefs and the witch trial in 1704 a new generation of rulers, magistrates, and jurists were receptive to his arguments.

10.6 QUESTIONS AND RESEARCH DIRECTIONS

While the scholarship on the German witch trials has contributed decisively to our understanding of early modern European witchcraft a number of unanswered questions remain. Most of the studies of the last forty years have concentrated on the peak period of the witch trials between 1560 and 1660. Within that period attention has been drawn to the massive waves of prosecutions and the sensational chain-reaction witch-hunts around 1590, 1600, and 1630. The large numbers of trials and the rich documentary record on them has made this a quite natural focus of investigation for this generation of scholarship. Yet this knowledge has come at a price. Scholars still remain puzzled by a relative 'lack' of witch trials in the early sixteenth century, that is, right after the appearance of the learned theory of diabolism. If the learned theory of witchcraft was as important as is commonly argued in the construction of witchcraft, why the long hiatus until the large trials begin around 1560? What patterns are discernible in the early sixteenth-century trials? The fewer and more isolated trials

---

[33] The work of Sönke Lorenz on legal reviews and consultations has been pioneering. See Sönke Lorenz, *Aktenversendung und Hexenprozeß: Dargestellt am Beispiel der Juristenfakultät Rostock und Greifswald (1570/82–1630)*, 3 vols (Frankfurt, 1982–3).

[34] Peter Oestmann, *Hexenprozesse am Reichskammergericht* (Cologne, 1997).

between 1660 and 1780 pose just as many questions about the 'decline' of the witch trial and doubts about witchcraft. For both of these periods, but also for the peak period of the trials, more understanding of the common everyday experience—harmful magic and the individual trial—still needs careful study.

Such new studies will need to treat witchcraft not as 'irrational' but as a 'rational' belief that expressed itself in a multitude of complicated ways. Terms such as 'craze' and 'panic' or 'fantasy' or 'imaginary belief' should be retired in favour of more precise concepts that allow for a more unprejudiced understanding of the early modern experiences of witchcraft.[35] Certainly there is now a sophisticated understanding of learned diabolism—one such historically specific concept—but its importance has likely been overstated, and its central focus in so many studies has not only obscured the many competing concepts of witchcraft but made it difficult to understand the complicated process by which people perceived some events as 'witchcraft' in one circumstance but not another. Even at the height of a so-called 'panic' witchcraft took on many different meanings to different people: harmful magic; poisoning; mysterious illness and death; superstition; slanderous insult; unneighbourly, impious, or wanton behaviour; an unproven belief; diabolism; and more.

This malleable, changeable quality of witchcraft and its intimate connections to a host of other experiences is precisely what has led scholars to abandon simple causal models of the witch trials. While some scholars are critical of the 'failure' to identify the exact 'causes' of such a major set of events in European history as the German witch trials, this finding actually points to the need for new historical methods in the investigation of witchcraft. It is doubtful that more systematic regional and comparative studies of German witch trials and witchcraft will yield important new insights into this problem. Microhistories, however, have shown one possible solution to this impasse in research. Microhistorical investigations that examine trials closely associated with crop failures, for example, show how misleading it can be to try to identify a single or even dominant 'trigger' for an accusation of witchcraft.[36] Other approaches will be needed as well.

A number of lacunae related to witchcraft also need further investigation. The figure of the old woman as witch is a familiar one in witchcraft, and yet this stereotype dominates the trials during only one period (1560–1660). Male witches have received more recent attention, but very little is understood about the key witch figure from the late trials: the 'child witch'. Children began to figure as witnesses in trials from the 1580s, then began to appear as prominent suspects in trials from the early seventeenth century. How and why did the 'child witch' come to dominate trials of the late seventeenth and eighteenth centuries? Studies of witchcraft and medicine have also been too limited by modern questions that look for the association of witchcraft with

---

[35] H. C. Erik Midelfort, 'Witch Craze? Beyond the Legends of Panic', *Magic, Ritual and Witchcraft*, 6 (2011), 11–33.

[36] Two such microhistories are Robisheaux, *The Last Witch of Langenburg* and Wolfgang Behringer, *Shaman of Oberstdorf: Chonrad Stoeckhlin and the Phantoms of the Night* (Charlottesville, VA, 1998).

'irrational' and 'delusional' mental disorders, such as melancholy or even 'madness'. Of much greater significance over the long term was the close association of witchcraft with poisoning—hence our need for new investigations of other branches of medicine, including folk medicine, toxicology, physiology, chemical medicine, and especially forensic medicine. And while attention has been lavished on the mental states presumably associated with witchcraft, too many studies pass over the much more readily available evidence about witchcraft and the emotions. Trial records are full of reports about the feelings of accusers and the accused. How are we to understand the emotions generated by witchcraft within the broader registers of early modern emotional states?

Long ago, in writing about 'the decline of magic', the historian Keith Thomas carefully placed English witchcraft and witch trials within the context of broad and complex cultures of magic and religion. Since that time the scholarship has focused intensively on just one aspect of this issue, the witch trial, making it sometimes difficult to understand the ways witch beliefs and practices were actually embedded in much larger sets of cultural, intellectual, and social systems of belief and practice. Given that old concepts of 'elite' and 'popular culture' no longer explain very much and the new semiotic approaches to culture beg the questions about social and institutional contexts for witchcraft, new concepts, methods, and approaches will need to be found. The unusually rich sources that have made studies of the German witch trial so productive may yet enable new studies, showing just how the experience of witchcraft related to the wider cultures of everyday life and magic.

FURTHER READING

Behringer, Wolfgang, *Witchcraft Persecutions in Bavaria: Popular Magic, Religious Zealotry and Reason of State in Early Modern Europe* (Cambridge, 1997).

Behringer, Wolfgang, *Shaman of Oberstdorf: Chonrad Stoeckhlin and the Phantoms of the Night* (Charlottesville, VA, 1998).

Decker, Rainer, *Die Hexen und ihre Henker: Ein Fallbericht* (Freiburg, 1994).

Dillinger, Johannes, *'Evil People': A Comparative Study of Witch Hunts in Swabian Austria and the Electorate of Trier* (Charlottesville, VA, 2009).

Jerouschek, Günter, *Die Hexen und ihr Prozeß: Die Hexenverfolgungen in der Reichsstadt Esslingen* (Esslingen, 1992).

Lorenz, Sönke, ed., *Hexen und Hexenverfolgungen im deutschen Südwesten*, 2 vols (Ostfildern, 1994).

Midelfort, H. C. E., *Witch Hunting in Southwestern Germany, 1562-1684: The Social and Intellectual Foundations* (Stanford, CA, 1972).

Pohl, Herbert, *Hexenglaube und Hexenverfolgung im Kurfürstentum Mainz: ein Beitrag zur Hexenfrage im 16. und beginnenden 17. Jahrhundert* (Stuttgart, 1998).

Robisheaux, Thomas, *The Last Witch of Langenburg: Murder in a German Village* (New York, 2009).

Rolands, Alison, *Witchcraft Narratives in Germany: Rothenburg, 1561-1652* (Manchester, 2003).

Roper, Lyndal, *Witch Craze: Terror and Fantasy in Baroque Germany* (New Haven, CT, 2004).

Schmidt, Jürgen Michael, *Glaube und Skepsis: die Kurpfalz und die abendländische Hexenverfolgung 1446–1685* (Bielefeld, 2000).

Scholz Williams, Gerhild, *Defining Dominion: The Discourses of Magic and Witchcraft in Early Modern France and Germany* (Ann Arbor, MI, 1995).

Tschalkner, Manfred, *Magie und Hexerei im südlichen Voralberg zu Beginn der Neuzeit* (Constance, 1997).

Walz, Rainer, *Hexenglaube und magische Kommunikation im Dorf der frühen Neuzeit: Die Verfolgungen in der Grafschaft Lippe* (Paderborn, 1993).

CHAPTER 11

....

WITCHCRAFT AND THE LOCAL COMMUNITIES: THE RHINE-MOSELLE REGION

....

ROBIN BRIGGS

THE territories on either side of the Moselle valley, and between that river and the west bank of the Rhine, lie near the heart of Western Europe. This was once the eastern extremity of the Roman Empire, with Trier as the capital, and a line of fortress towns along the Rhine that have become modern cities. In medieval and early modern times, by contrast, almost infinite political division characterized these classic borderlands. The nominal sovereignty of the Holy Roman Empire over virtually the whole region had negligible effects on the patchwork of middling-sized and puny states that held varying degrees of power over their nominal subjects. Even the Duchy of Luxembourg and the province of Franche-Comté, when they became part of the Spanish Habsburg Empire, were normally ruled with a light touch. The more significant local rulers, such as the Duke of Lorraine and the Prince-Archbishop-Electors of Trier and Mainz, often had to share authority with others, in territories full of enclaves and exemptions. Much of Alsace, the richest agricultural region, was divided between several powerful towns. Elsewhere, local loyalties naturally tended to overshadow those to distant and largely uninvolved rulers, while in the Saarland it was not uncommon for villages to be ruled by *condominia*, with agents acting for two or three rather nominal overlords. There was also a linguistic division; most of Lorraine, Franche-Comté, and the western part of Luxembourg were French-speaking, while elsewhere German dialects prevailed. Although the Reformation was not very successful in most of this area, by the later sixteenth century there were various scattered Protestant centres, with a much more substantial presence in Alsace, where Strasburg was a major Reformed city.

The physical geography, and in consequence the economy, also exhibited great variety. The alluvial plains along the Rhine, most notably in Alsace, were fertile arable zones, as were some parts of Lorraine. Elsewhere, uplands prevailed, encouraging a mixed agriculture that could be quite productive, and exceptionally so with regard to the vineyards of Alsace and the lower Moselle valley, whose wines had an international reputation. At the other extreme the Vosges and the Ardennes were largely barren massifs, which formed important natural barriers. There was, however, significant east–west trade through the passes across the Vosges, accompanied by important seasonal migrations of working people, while the rivers linked the region both to the Netherlands and to some flourishing parts of western Germany on the other side of the Rhine. There was salt mining in Lorraine, a range of ores were mined in the hills, and numerous local industries existed, with an inevitable predominance of textiles. From the late fifteenth century to the Thirty Years' War there was remarkably little military activity to disrupt ordinary life or trading patterns. The German Peasants' War of 1525 was one exception, as was the Schmalkaldic War of 1547 and its aftermath to 1552. Later, the frequent passage of Spanish troops en route for the Netherlands, and more sporadic movements of Protestant forces to intervene in the French Wars of Religion, were reminders of the vulnerability of this disunited region—although they represented only local or occasional problems. This all changed dramatically after 1620, as the Thirty Years' War brought armies, epidemics, and devastation to much of the region. A whole series of military operations affected the Rhineland, while the French moved into Lorraine and then Alsace and Franche-Comté, which became major campaigning areas. In many cases it would take decades after the Peace of Westphalia in 1648 for population levels to recover, despite extensive immigration.

The relatively peaceful times of the sixteenth century had nevertheless seen a typical European pattern of rising population and prices, with important effects on local society. Harvest crises became more frequent, as the most traumatic evidence of the pressures that forced small peasant landowners to sell their property, so that most of the population became wage labourers, competing for scarce work and declining real wages. Towns had to find ways of coping with the long-term poor and with migrants, who were increasingly viewed as a threat to law and order. Wherever court records survive there is evidence for more repressive attitudes and practices, with a striking rise in both prosecutions and harsh sentences, whether for theft or for acts of violence. The later sixteenth century was a hard time for ordinary people, exacerbated by bad weather conditions sometimes described as the Little Ice Age, with harvest failures becoming more frequent and building to a major crisis in the early 1590s. The vineyards that played an important role in many areas were also highly vulnerable to frost and hail; these disasters, along with animal epidemics, seem to have had a long association with witchcraft in the popular mind, probably dating back before the time of formal prosecution.

11.1 THE CHRONOLOGY AND SCALE OF WITCHCRAFT PROSECUTIONS[1]

The chronology of witchcraft trials was broadly similar across the whole region, particularly in the earlier phases. From around the middle of the fifteenth century there is evidence for scattered trials, often with links to specific episodes of bad weather, especially in Lorraine and Luxembourg. Their frequency declined, if anything, until the final decades of the sixteenth century, then between roughly 1570 and 1590 much more intensive persecution began virtually everywhere. Although the patchiness of record survival renders precise calculations impossible, there do seem to be variant local patterns. In Lorraine, Luxembourg, and the Saarland the persecution was more endemic than epidemic, with few marked peaks or troughs. Overall figures for Alsace (still lacking a full modern investigation) would probably look quite similar, but particular jurisdictions in this fragmented region saw significant local panics. Trials in the Trier region were concentrated in two major outbreaks: the larger centred on the years 1587–94, with a smaller but significant episode around 1630. Franche-Comté and Mainz each had several waves of persecution, affecting different parts of their territory. In Lorraine, Trier, and Mainz trial numbers fell to insignificant levels from the 1630s, with wartime devastation and changing attitudes among rulers or judges as the likely reasons. Elsewhere they took longer to disappear, but with the exception of a final moderately large outbreak between 1657 and 1660 in Franche-Comté (which led to relatively few executions) numbers had declined markedly. Estimates for the total numbers of executions would suggest around two thousand each for the Duchies of Luxembourg and Lorraine, and for the Electorate of Mainz, with 1,000 for the Electorate of Trier and 450 for Franche-Comté. The Mainz figure should, however, be heavily discounted, because the majority of executions took place in the upper Electorate around Erfurt, far into central Germany, not in the lower Electorate on the Rhine. Alsace presents special difficulties for the historian, so a wide bracket allowing for between one thousand and two thousand executions has to be used. If various smaller territories are included the whole region may have seen 10–12,000 executions, which probably represented 75 per cent or more of those put on trial. Known rates for

[1] I am particularly grateful to Dr Rita Voltmer for her expert advice on witchcraft in the Luxembourg and Trier regions, both in conversations over the past decade and more specifically through her comments on drafts of this chapter. For her own overview of the region see Rita Voltmer, 'Hexenverfolgungen im Maas-Rhein-Mosel-Raum—Ergebnisse und Perspektiven', in F. Irsigler, ed., *Zwischen Maas und Rhein? Beziehungen, Begegnungen und Konflikte in einem europäischen Kernraum von der Spätantike bis zum 19. Jahrhundert. Versuch einer Bilanz*, Trierer Historische Forschungen, 61 (Trier 2006), 153–87, and Voltmer, 'Die politischen Funktionen der frühneuzeitlichen Hexenverfolgungen: Machtdemonstration, Kontrolle und Herrschaftsverdichtung im Rhein-Maas-Raum', in M. Ostorero, G. Modestin, and K. Utz Tremp, eds, *Chasses aux sorcières et démonologie: Entre discours et pratiques (XIVᵉ–XVIIᵉ siècles)* (Florence, 2010), 89–115.

convictions range from 60 per cent in Franche-Comté to about 80 per cent in Lorraine and Luxembourg, and 85 per cent for Trier. The proportion of male witches varied considerably, from only 11 per cent in Trier to between 25 and 30 per cent in most other places.[2]

These statistics emphasize the fact that the region was one of the major centres of persecution in Western Europe, accounting for perhaps 20 to 25 per cent of all known trials and executions. Since the total population is unlikely to have been much in excess of two million at its peak in the early seventeenth century, this would suggest a ratio of about five executions for every thousand persons, according to the accepted mode of calculation, which is exceptionally high—perhaps five or six times the average for Europe west of the Elbe. It should, of course, be understood that the normal risk to any individual was significantly less than this ratio might suggest, because far more than two million persons lived and died in the region over the whole period of persecution. In addition there were some notable 'hot spots', whose intense persecutions contributed much more than their share to the total. The contiguous villages of Longuich and Kirsch, on the Moselle just north of Trier, had 73 trials, and sixty-seven of perhaps 250 inhabitants were executed between 1587 and 1596. These were among a group of villages subject to the abbey of St Maximin, which, with a total population of around 2,200, generated no less than five hundred executions, four hundred of them in the decade 1586–96. Trials in the *prévôté* of Saint-Dié, in the extreme south-east of Lorraine, ran at around two and a half times the already high average for the duchy as a whole. Yet even in such active micro-regions there are inexplicable variations from one village to the next, and on the broader canvas it looks as if at least half of the rural communities had no recorded trials, with many others only having one or two over the whole period. In some cases we know that the majority of those identified as known suspects from a group of villages, or named as accomplices seen at the sabbath, were never formally accused. A handful of the most intense witch-hunting episodes may have swept up virtually all the plausible candidates, along with numerous more accidental victims. More generally, however, we must suppose that there were far more potential defendants than ever reached the courts, as the evidence from the trials strongly implies that witchcraft and counter-magic were routine aspects of life for ordinary people and even local elites across the whole region.

11.2 LEGAL PROCEDURES

When many nominal rulers were absentees, and even the more substantial, the Dukes of Lorraine and the episcopal Electors of Mainz and Trier, were decidedly

---

[2] Recent calculations for many regions can be found in the relevant entries in Richard M. Golden, ed., *Encyclopedia of Witchcraft: The Western Tradition*, 4 vols (Santa Barbara, CA, 2006). For comparative tables for Europe see Wolfgang Behringer, *Witches and Witch-Hunts: A Global History* (Cambridge, 2004), 130 and 150, and Robin Briggs, *The Witches of Lorraine* (Oxford, 2007), 52.

second-division figures in comparative European terms, most criminal jurisdiction predictably remained with distinctly amateurish local courts. Only Franche-Comté had a reasonably effective appeal system, operated by the Parlement of Dôle, whose effects were immediately visible in a lower conviction rate. Several other territories had central courts, like the Lorraine Change de Nancy or the Provincial Council of Luxembourg, but in general these merely sought to enforce certain modest legal standards, not to review convictions or modify verdicts. Nowhere can we find legislation from the persecution period that made a serious attempt to define witchcraft and related offences; this was evidently thought to be such a well-established crime, condemned by both divine and human law, that specific enactments were hardly necessary. On the other hand, there were a fair number of procedural ordinances and decisions, such as the German *Carolina* code of 1532, various pronouncements from the Brussels government applicable in Luxembourg, and some often ineffective declarations by the Elector of Trier. From an early stage in the sixteenth century the jurists who were so prominent in either advising rulers or exercising delegated authority seem to have recognized that witchcraft trials were problematic. Most of the ordinances veer uneasily between supporting the search for these ultimate deviants and trying to prevent the numerous abuses that disfigured the trials. It was not until the middle of the seventeenth century that these efforts to raise standards seem to have become fairly effective in some places, then, along much of the west bank of the Rhine, French occupation or annexation in the time of Louis XIV meant that the very sceptical royal ordinance of 1682 was applied.

The seemingly endless minor variations in practice from one court to another should not conceal the broad similarities in style, and, indeed, outcome. Witches were almost always tried in secular courts, which used more or less the same inquisitorial methods. A *prima facie* case was made out through the collection of witness statements and repeated interrogations of the suspects, to justify the application of torture, which normally produced a confession. The key players in this process were the local administrative or judicial officials, who gathered the evidence and questioned the suspect, and the executioners, who were specialists with the rack, thumbscrews, strappado, and their like. Gaolers might also play a significant part, exploiting isolation and the fear of torture to secure notionally 'free' confessions. The peculiar nature of witchcraft, as an occult crime that was virtually incapable of proof by established legal standards, rendered the confession, and therefore the torture, the crucial part of the procedure. As a result, the nominal judges, usually local men devoid of legal training who might be illiterate, were commonly spectators rather than actors, who simply put their name or their mark to the papers when required. Such supervision as there was tended to concentrate on the decision to proceed to torture; in areas subject to the *Carolina* this should have involved consultation with a university law faculty, although it is far from certain how effectively this operated. In Lorraine the Change de Nancy had to approve torture, which it rarely chose to prohibit, but after 1634 the imported

French judges of the Metz Parlement took a far more rigorous and sceptical line.[3] The high rate of convictions across the region reflected the relative ease with which permission to torture was granted, although it must be said that in many cases the prosecution evidence would have looked quite compelling, so the authorities had no obvious reason to refuse their approval. It is hard to judge just how much the ferocity of the torture varied in different jurisdictions. In Franche-Comté, Lorraine, and Luxembourg fairly strict rules should have restricted its duration and intensity; courts and executioners quite often went over the limits, but really grave breaches seem to have been rare. Further east, where very local rules tended to apply, there are more signs of savage and repeated torture sessions, especially during major bouts of persecution.

11.3 WITCHCRAFT COMMITTEES, LOCAL ACTION, AND PATTERNS OF ACCUSATION

The other major difference between the eastern German-speaking regions and the Francophone ones to the west was the extent of local participation in organizing the trials. This was relative rather than absolute, because everywhere the state of village opinion was crucial to a successful prosecution, and official power-holders were open to influence of various kinds. The decisive factor in several areas was the emergence of the witch-hunting committee or *Hexenausschüsse*, an ad hoc body at least nominally elected by the villagers to take action against witches. It was committees of this type that largely drove the Trier and St Maximin persecutions either side of 1590, while they became widespread in the German-language parts of Luxembourg, and later developed in the Rhineland and elsewhere.[4] There may be some connection with the routine existence of elected officials and jurors in the village societies concerned, which provided a model for these much more sinister bodies; perhaps they first took shape where some local people were unhappy that (as they saw it) efforts to prosecute witches were being deliberately frustrated. In some Trier villages there were other precedents for collective action through an institution of *Herschaw*, which allowed communities to resort to limited violence when immediate danger threatened. The subsistence crisis of the 1580s, and the abnormal frosts that devastated the vineyards, could easily have been construed in these terms as a time of immediate danger. Whatever the origins, once the

---

[3] C. Petry, 'Das *Parlement de Metz* und das Ende der lothringischen Hexenverfolgung', in Herbert Eiden and Rita Voltmer, eds, *Hexenprozesse und Gerichtspraxis* (Trier, 2002), 227–51.

[4] An outstanding study of these committees is that by Walter Rummel, *Bauern, Herren und Hexen: Studien zur Sozialgeschichte sponheimischer und kurtrierische Hexenprozesse 1574–1664* (Göttingen, 1991). See also Rita Voltmer, 'Konspiration gegen Herrschaft und Staat? Überlegungen zur Rolle gemeindlicher Klagekonsortien in den Hexenverfolgungen des Rhein-Maas-Mosel-Raumes', in Johannes Dillinger, Jürgen Michael Schmidt, and Dieter R. Bauer, eds, *Staatsbildung und Hexenprozess* (Bielefeld, 2008), 213–44.

model had been set imitation clearly played an important role in disseminating it. While villages were natural units, in a city like Trier guilds formed their separate committees, which then set up a kind of federated super-committee to press the elector for more action against witches. The alarming power of the committees became evident not just from the high rates of prosecution they inspired, but also from the inability of the authorities to establish control over them. The Elector of Trier, for example, had initially been an enthusiastic supporter of the witch-hunt, then became dismayed to see central authority undermined by such grass-roots organizations—and found his belated prohibitions largely ignored. In Luxembourg the officials also had great diffi- culties applying central decrees, while the existence of many small independent jurisdictions created additional problems.

Informal proceedings of the kind associated with the committees are hard to trace, because specific documentation is naturally rare. Where we do have glimpses of their activities these are as unattractive as one might expect. Committees tended to be created in an excited atmosphere, which made it dangerous for individuals to object, since any resistance might bring on suspicions of witchcraft. There are many indica- tions that they readily became agencies for the murderous extension of village feuds; in the affected areas unusual numbers of elite figures were accused, these often being the wives of village office-holders and wealthy peasants. In other words these were not democratic arrangements, being more in the nature of little coups in which a deter- mined group used terror to impose a false external unity. Oaths were required, sworn on such symbols of authority as a mace, or even on a knife driven into a table. A key objective was to make the whole community liable for the costs of starting a prosecu- tion, which might otherwise have fallen on an individual or a small group; this would inevitably create wider pressure for witnesses to give hostile testimony. It readily became the basis on which committees raised what amounted to witchcraft taxes, and borrowed considerable sums to finance themselves by exploiting the credit of the village. Trials were expensive for the villagers because a fair number of other people could batten on them and make significant profits. Lawyers and executioners naturally took fees for their work, then they and the officials would share a banquet on the day of the executions, while probably securing a rake-off from any confiscated goods and property. Some communities ran up heavy debts that burdened them for decades, another reason for the authorities to feel grave disquiet. Ultimately, then, the commit- tees were highly divisive, and the rulers were not deceived, quickly realizing the potential dangers of what they quite appropriately stigmatized as 'conspiracies' or 'monopolies'.

Unfortunately such developments tended to reveal the true weakness of many rulers in the Rhine-Moselle lands. Since even more powerful monarchs usually struggled to exert control at the village level, this was wholly predictable. The local officials, on whom everything really hinged, were most unreliable agents in matters of this kind. Often they found it far more convenient, and potentially lucrative, to go along with local feeling and condone blatant abuses. Until at least the middle decades of the seventeenth century their ideas and attitudes were probably closer to those of the ordinary people than to the more critical views found among some educated elites—to such an extent that there were enthusiasts for persecution among them. Some of the most dangerous were local lawyers and notaries who compiled lists of names, taken from the confessions of those who named accomplices allegedly seen at the sabbath; an extraordinary surviving example is the witch-register kept by the St Maximin *Amtmann* (chief magistrate) Claudius Musiel, which contains nearly 1,400 names. Even under the witch-hunting Abbot Reiner Biewer (finally removed in 1613) the great majority of these denunciations did not lead to an actual trial.[5] Nevertheless, there are signs that in places (not just St Maximin) some crude equivalent of the 'three strikes' rule was edging into existence, so those whose names appeared repeatedly were clearly at greater risk. This did not require the production of actual lists, because in small regions collective memory was good enough to do the job. On closer inspection the role of denunciations is more problematic than it might seem; had the authorities taken the notion of the diabolical conspiracy at face value then surely they ought to have followed up even a single identification with much greater zeal than even the most credulous actually did. In practice a kind of mitigated scepticism normally seems to have operated on this point, with an awareness that both malice and undue pressure by judges had to be allowed for. Even zealots for persecution must not be dismissed as fools—they would have seen that many of those convicted withdrew their charges against others at the stake. The more astute might also have noticed how suspects sometimes made threats to denounce their neighbours in order to discourage any move against themselves.

Committees were far from being found everywhere across the region—even the German-speaking zones and those with weak or divided lordship were often free from them. As with virtually every other aspect of witchcraft, no single pattern emerges from the evidence, nor are there wholly convincing reasons for the wide variations from one small area to the next, or between neighbouring villages. The potential for devastating slides into persecution and factional struggles must have been present almost any-where, yet apparently needed some particular combination of factors to kick-start this into action. Sometimes the attitude of the rulers seems to have been decisive. The Dukes of Lorraine, who had developed a respectably effective administrative and judicial system, plainly disliked any type of independent local action, reacting strongly in a few instances where something of the kind threatened to develop. Another factor in the duchy was that the costs of trials had been kept very low, perhaps only a third of that in some other territories, so there was less reason for individual accusers to fear potential costs. An additional suspicion is that local officials were responsive to popular feeling and showed little reluctance to take up cases themselves. In the Franche-Comté the Dôle Parlement also managed to exert a reasonable degree of control; here the appeal system gave the accused an important second chance, with the corollary that

---

[5] R. Voltmer and K. Weisenstein, *Das Hexenregister des Claudius Musiel* (Trier, 1996).

abuses in the first instance courts risked becoming known to the authorities.[6] The Provincial Council of Luxembourg was apparently unable to exert any reliable control in the eastern administrative districts, where the many autonomous lordships allowed local nobles to collaborate with the witchcraft committees that proliferated, yet succeeded rather better in the French-speaking west. The contrast was arguably less than it might seem, because in the west there were quite frequent opportunities to put forward charges through the *enquêtes générales* or general enquiries ordered by the Council, after which an official prosecution was likely to follow. So, as in Lorraine, this represented a safety valve for popular feelings against notorious suspects.[7]

The vast majority of those accused were humble people, members of the settled population. Although they tended to be female rather than male, and older rather than younger, there is little else to mark them out from the mass of peasants and artisans. Certain sub-groups can be identified, such as widows with no surviving children, regular beggars, and male herdsmen, yet none of these fairly obvious categories features in such numbers that much significance can be attached to them. Quite a few members of wealthier peasant families also fell victim to prosecution, probably not too far out of line with their relative numbers in the population as a whole. Where committees operated this group might actually have suffered disproportionately, because village factions naturally centred around the more powerful figures in village society. A genuine panic was also liable to drag in more members of the elites, as denunciations multiplied and spread out beyond the normal limits. An awareness that very few people could feel completely safe against a random accusation may well have operated to check enthusiasm for persecution among leaders at every level from the village upwards, except when matters got temporarily out of hand. Reactions of this kind provide one of the most plausible explanations of why bursts of intense prosecution, notably those in Trier and its hinterland around 1590, always seemed to peter out within a few years, or sometimes a few months. With the lower-level prosecutions, exemplified by those in Lorraine, a much steadier flow of trials generated a rather different pattern. Here most of the accused had established reputations as witches in their communities, to such an extent that it can be hard to understand how they survived so long. Paradoxical though it may seem, detailed study of the trial records suggests that everywhere in the Rhine-Moselle region there were always substantial numbers of suspected witches living among their neighbours, despite the terrifying figures for executions. Even where an intense bout of persecution eliminated all the principal suspects, it would have not taken long for new ones to emerge, quite possibly from among the children or relatives of those already executed.

---

[6] For this province see E. William Monter, *Witchcraft in France and Switzerland: The Borderlands during the Reformation* (Ithaca, NY, and London, 1976) and B. Rochelandet, *Sorcières, diables et bûchers en Franche-Comté aux 16e et 17e siècles* (Paris, 1997).

[7] For Luxembourg see Rita Voltmer, '. . . ce tant exécrable et détestable crime de sortilège'. "Der "Bürgerkrieg" gegen Hexen und Hexenmeister im Herzogtum Luxemburg (16. und 17. Jahrhundert)', *Hémecht: Revue d'Histoire Luxembourgeoise. Zeitschrift für Luxemburger Geschichte*, 56 (2004), 57–92.

11.4 HIGH-PLACED VICTIMS AND
THE LOCAL DEMONOLOGISTS

In exceptional circumstances witchcraft charges could extend up to the very top of the social ladder. One spectacular and much discussed case was that of Dietrich Flade, allegedly the wealthiest man in Trier apart from the elector himself, and holder of the important office of *Stadtschultheiss* or town bailiff. Flade seems to have been distinctly unpopular locally, perhaps because he had acted for the elector in a bitter lawsuit between the latter and the municipality of Trier, which ended in a financially and politically disastrous defeat for the city. He also had a reputation for sharp financial dealing, which turned into charges that he was the leader of the sect of witches who intended to benefit from harvest failures and high grain prices. There are grounds for believing that a powerful rival, the governor Johann Zandt von Merl, had manipulated witnesses to develop these accusations, which gradually built up over the years between 1587 and 1589 until the elector was persuaded to put Flade—once a trusted servant—on trial, and a confession was extracted under torture. Although Flade was certainly not a true sceptic about witchcraft, and had himself presided over trials that brought condemnations, it is quite likely that awareness of his own vulnerability encouraged him to drag his feet over the developing persecution, providing another reason for the governor, an enthusiast for large-scale burnings, to engineer his downfall. His condemnation opened the way for many other prominent men and women to be accused and condemned, notably those who were thought to have failed to defend the city against the elector. The Jesuits were also prominent in organizing the Trier prosecutions, not least by extracting damning evidence from children, as well as preaching in support of the witch-hunt; ultimately the General of the Society in Rome would reprimand them for this conduct. Meanwhile the Jesuit-trained suffragan bishop of Trier, Peter Binsfeld, published his *Tractatus de confessionibus maleficorum et sagarum* in 1589, a work that would go into several more editions and was quickly translated into German.[8]

Binsfeld took an expansive view of the powers and influence of the devil, developing the doctrine of the implicit pact to categorize all magic as diabolical, and granting him virtually unlimited powers of deception. He was particularly determined to confront a key issue from the Flade case, that of the reliability of denunciations. Flade himself had

---

[8] For the Trier prosecutions see the volumes in the series *Trierer Hexenprozesse: Quellen und Darstellungen* (Trier 1995–); Johannes Dillinger, *'Evil People': A Comparative Study of Witch-hunts in Swabian Austria and the Electorate of Trier* (Charlottesville, VA, 2009); Rita Voltmer, 'Zwischen Herrschaftskrise, Wirtschaftsdepression und Jesuitenpropaganda. Hexenverfolgungen in der Stadt Trier (15.–17. Jahrhundert)', *Jahrbuch für westdeutsche Landesgeschichte*, 27 (2001), 37–107, and Voltmer, 'Die Hexenverfolgungen im Raum des Erzbistums (15.–17. Jahrhundert)', in B. Schneider, ed., *Geschichte des Bistums Trier, iii: Kirchenreform und Konfessionsstaat 1500–1801* (Trier, 2010), 709–49.

originally claimed that those who claimed to have seen him at the sabbath could not be trusted, because devils could assume the shape of anyone they chose. The response from Binsfeld was that God would never allow the innocent to suffer the penalties imposed on witches, so devils could only do this with the permission of those whom they impersonated. In fairness it should be said that Binsfeld balanced his enthusiasm for confessions under torture and denunciations with concern over procedural abuses; he also rejected ordeals, including pricking for the diabolical mark, and denied the significance of the inability to shed tears. For all its harshness this was a logical and well-argued stance, which had considerable influence on such contemporary demon-ologists as Del Rio. It attracted a passionate refutation from the Dutch Catholic theologian Cornelius Loos, who was living in Trier at this time, in an unpublished work on true and false magic. From the surviving sections it is clear that the book drew on humanist techniques to deny that the devil could perform many of the acts attributed to him and his followers, then went on to attribute confessions to the effects of either inhuman torture or mental disturbance. Loos also emphasized how readily the trials could be manipulated to serve personal ends, and lead to the shedding of innocent blood. This controversy was important because Binsfeld reacted by contriving to have Loos arrested and forced into a humiliating recantation, while the authorities took steps to halt the printing of his book; together with a series of formal statements on behalf of the Church this widely publicized recantation ensured that denial of belief in witchcraft would in future be treated as heresy.

The region produced three other well-known demonologists, the first being none other than Heinrich Kramer (Henry Institoris) of the *Malleus maleficarum*, born in Sélestat in Alsace, who seems to have begun his persecuting activities in that region. Most of Kramer's more significant career was, however, in other parts of Germany, so it is not clear how much weight should be put on his local associations. The widespread involvement of the Dominicans with the Inquisition, and with early witchcraft trials, is probably the most relevant factor here. Nicolas Remy was a French-trained jurist who had a long and successful career in the service of the Duke of Lorraine, eventually rising to the position of *procureur général* of the duchy in 1591, after fifteen years as a member of its central tribunal, the Change de Nancy. His *Demonolatry* of 1595 was a self-consciously literary work in Latin, which was not translated at this time, but was much cited by other writers. This was because Remy supplied an abundance of detailed stories about Lorraine witches and their doings, based on the trial records to which he had privileged access. His discursive text, which took many key issues for granted rather than arguing them through, is a classic example of a growing tendency to treat witchcraft almost as *grand guignol*, writing to amuse and titillate the reader rather than to argue a case. Remy did not bother to argue for more persecution or to provide advice for judges, so his book had no perceptible influence on events in the region. It is, however, very interesting in one negative sense, because this panegyrist of the dukes never made the slightest claim that witchcraft persecution was a sign of their Christian virtues; instead he was distinctly critical of the inadequacies of the local clergy in Lorraine. This silence is very damaging to those historians who would argue that rulers of this type naturally linked state-building (especially in the form of the godly state) with a self-conscious campaign against witches. Indeed, nothing else in the extensive Lorraine records suggests that there is any force in such claims.[9] Here as elsewhere the authorities reacted to growing socio-economic tensions by much harsher treatment of all types of crime, without making any special statements at all about witchcraft.

Despite Remy's legal knowledge, his book offered little help to judges, and was never cited in the Lorraine trials. When the much less prominent Franche-Comtois lawyer Henri Boguet published his *Discours des Sorciers* in 1602, on the other hand, he gave extensive advice on legal procedure, and provided a special appendix to guide judges in dealing with witches. This book was based on his activities as the senior judge in the lands of the abbey of St Claude, where he would ultimately try around 35 individuals as witches and sentence 80 per cent of them to death.[10] On the strength of his writings Boguet developed something of a local reputation as a witchcraft expert, for example being called in to advise the fiercely independent imperial city of Besançon on a difficult case in 1604. The *Discours* is in truth a rather naïve work (Lucien Febvre dismissed its author as an imbecile), which displays an embarrassingly cavalier attitude to legal principles. Standard authorities are on numerous occasions misrepresented or taken out of context to justify abusive practices. Actions which in themselves are not criminal are interpreted as showing that something much worse must have followed out of sight, various kinds of deception are permitted to the judge, and dubious witnesses are to be taken on trust (all under the elastic concept of *crimen exceptum*, twisted and distorted from its original meaning). It is easy to believe in the suggestion that Boguet prevented further reprints of his book after 1611 because he feared it would damage his chances of promotion to a place in the Parlement, although this story cannot be proven. While he is the one of these three writers whose book can be shown to have had some direct effect on local practice, this influence does not seem to have extended beyond his own province and was relatively short-lived. Like the others, therefore, his work is most interesting for what it tells us about contemporary perceptions; it can be compared with the surviving records of some of the trials in which he was involved.

---

[9] Among the best-known advocates of this interpretation are R. Muchembled, *Le roi et la sorcière: l'Europe des bûchers XVᵉ–XVIIIᵉ siècle* (Paris, 1993) and other books by the same author and Christina Larner, *Witchcraft and Religion: The Politics of Popular Belief* (Oxford, 1984).

[10] Many of these trials were published in F. Bavoux, *Hantises et diableries dans la terre abbatiale de Luxueil (1529–1630)* (Monaco, 1956); Bavoux, *La sorcellerie au pays de Quingey* (Monaco, 1954); Bavoux, *Les procès inédits de Boguet en matière de sorcellerie dans le Grand Judicature de St.-Claude (XVIᵉ–XVIIᵉ siècles)* (Dijon, 1958).

11.5 SOME SPECIFIC CASES AND
THE END OF THE PROSECUTIONS

Despite Boguet's shabby attempts to load the dice against the suspects, the more sophisticated appeal system in Franche-Comté clearly reduced the number of prosecutions and resulted in a rather lower ratio of executions to trials than elsewhere in the region. There was also considerably less recourse to torture. The seventeenth century saw three middling-sized waves of prosecutions, each following a rather similar course. The first, between 1599 and 1612, centred around Boguet's prosecutions; the second, between 1627 and 1631, on those encouraged by the *bailli* of Luxueil, Jean Clerc. Since there was no automatic appeal to the Parlement, these local judges were able to proceed for some time without much interference. Indeed, at first the Parlement was inclined to confirm their sentences, until doubts surfaced and a series of acquittals or reduced sentences checked the whole process. A final belated outbreak in 1658–61 differed slightly, because the principal instigator is thought to have been the local inquisitor Pierre Symard, who used a dangerous technique by having *monitoires* read from the pulpits, calling on parishioners to denounce witchcraft suspects. Again the Parlement apparently had to learn from experience; this time, however, its move away from confirming death sentences was linked to a much more decisive policy. A French translation of Spee's *Cautio Criminalis*, with its forthright attack on abuses in the trials, was published by a Besançon doctor in 1660, and when the papacy was informed about Symard's activities he was removed from his position. In this province the French occupation of 1674 came more than a decade after the last execution for witchcraft.

Mass trials had evidently been a feature of the Trier persecutions, as they were in a more localized and therefore smaller and more spasmodic form for Alsace and Luxembourg. Elsewhere in the region a more persistent style of scattered yet quite frequent trials obtained; this could include very nasty little episodes in specific villages, either in short bursts or spread out over a decade or more. Lorraine and the Saarland were the most striking examples of this kind, but of course the areas that saw mass trials also had their trickle of isolated and small group trials. Lorraine did have one belated local outbreak in and around the large textile-producing village of Mattaincourt, where some fifty executions took place between 1627 and 1631; there was a certain likeness to the famous Salem trials, with a large group of possessed women and girls naming suspects. In this part of the duchy there was a prehistory of local *curés* using exorcisms to identify witchcraft suspects, which is likely to have created dangerous precedents and paved the way for this episode. As in other panics, the odd wealthy individual was dragged in and condemned, alongside the humble people who predominated among the victims.[11] In the higher levels of Lorraine society there had been two

---

[11] For this affair see E. W. Monter, *A Bewitched Duchy: Lorraine and its Dukes 1477–1736* (Geneva, 2007), 111–13, and Briggs, *The Witches of Lorraine*, 83–5.

striking affairs in the previous decade. One surrounded the possession of the devout noblewoman Elisabeth de Rainfaing from 1618, which saw her accuse a doctor who had tried to help her as well as leading members of the Minim order. The doctor was finally executed, while a rare critic from among the Minims, Claude Pithoys, had to write from the safety of French-controlled territory. He remarked on how anyone who questioned the claims made by Elisabeth was immediately said to have been invaded by a demon, adding 'I am certain that posterity will be astonished that there were people in the world so simple-minded as to believe such idiocies.'[12] The other episode arose from the succession struggle when Duke Henri II died in 1624, to be succeeded by his nephew Charles IV, who had been forced into a very unwilling marriage with Henri's daughter Nicole. Within months the old duke's favourite, André des Bordes, was executed on a trumped-up witchcraft charge, then in 1631 a prominent ecclesiastic, Melchior de la Vallée, met a similar fate.[13] The 1631 case was part of a bizarre (and futile) attempt to persuade the pope that the ducal marriage was invalid, so that Charles IV could dispose of his wife in order to marry his mistress. At this time the rulers of Lorraine evidently found no problem in exploiting witchcraft charges for political and personal ends.

As already noted, most of the trials in the territories of the Elector of Mainz did not belong to the Rhine-Moselle region at all. It is, however, interesting to note that in both the upper and lower Electorates this was yet another instance where the driving force behind the trials came from below, with the electors largely reduced to making some attempt to control the process. A regulation of 1612, apparently intended to bring greater fairness, proved very unsatisfactory in practice, serving to allow far too much licence to local courts and thereby actually encouraging witch-hunting. Only with Elector Johann Philipp von Schönborn (1642–73) did matters improve, because he was influenced by Spee's critical views on procedure and established much firmer personal supervision of a rapidly diminishing number of trials. At roughly the same time (1652) Elector Karl Kaspar von der Leyen of Trier outlawed witchcraft trials completely, to signal a remarkable turnaround in the attitude of these high-born prelates. It is less clear why official disapproval became so much more effective at this time; admittedly earlier electors had been much less decisive, but their genuine efforts to prevent serious abuses had been notably unsuccessful. The general decline in persecution at this time rather suggests that there was much less pressure from below, probably because in the aftermath of the Thirty Years' War the massive population losses in the region had completely altered the situation at village level. When previously sedentary village populations experienced disruption and dispersal on this scale, the social memory that underlay the identification of witches and witchcraft families was virtually erased, while the survivors and the waves of new immigrants enjoyed more favourable conditions for several decades. This pattern would have prevailed in

---

[12] P. J. S. Whitmore, *A Seventeenth-Century Exposure of Superstition: Select Texts of Claude Pithoys (1587–1676)* (The Hague, 1972), 47.

[13] Etienne Delcambre and J. Lhermitte, *Élisabeth de Rainfaing, l'énergumène de Nancy, fondatrice de l'Ordre du Refuge; un cas énigmatique de possession diabolique en Lorraine au XVIIᵉ siècle* (Nancy, 1956).

Alsace, Franche-Comté, Lorraine, and parts of Luxembourg, as well as in the smaller territories along the Rhine. Meanwhile attitudes were shifting among rulers and ruling elites, who, while they may not yet have abandoned belief in witchcraft as such, had learned from bitter experience that persecution too readily became a surrender to popular action at the grass-roots level.

11.6 MAGIC, WITCHCRAFT, AND HEALING IN THE COMMUNITY

The survival of large numbers of fully documented trials from the region has allowed historians to go beyond the history of persecution, with analyses of witchcraft beliefs and practices as they were experienced even in the absence of legal action.[14] These materials provide exceptional opportunities to reconstruct a worldview that revolved around a magical and animistic universe, contained rather than controlled within a broadly conceived Christian scheme of things. Peasants and artisans combined a pragmatic, hard-headed approach to everyday life with complex views about agency and causation when misfortune struck. Once this happened supernatural beings and invisible yet potent forces were readily invoked to explain it. Many human illnesses were attributed to saints, so pilgrimages and offerings to their shrines were often the first line of defence. The obvious alternative explanation, however, was a diabolical affliction brought about through the agency of a local witch, one of the internal traitors to the community through whom the devil worked. Judges, witnesses, and confessing witches all agreed that such action was not unmotivated, but usually resulted from either a quarrel or longer-term animosity. Another general belief was that since witchcraft afflictions were effectively spells they could only be cured by the witch in person, who must remove the spell. There was a strong preference for physical explanations here, so witches were supposed to use the powders supplied by the devil (often sprinkled on food) to make their enemies ill, then to give them food or nurse them as the means of a cure. In Lorraine, at least, a remarkable associated claim made by numerous witches when they confessed was that the devil gave them a white powder to cure their victims; this bizarre reversal of normal ideas about diabolical conduct emphasized that witchcraft was conceived as a form of power, with harming and healing firmly linked. As a result witchcraft belief merged into a therapeutic system, for once the human cause of a sickness had been discovered the witch could be pressurized into making some gesture towards reconciliation that was also expected to bring about a cure. This applied to sick animals as well, for this was the other principal type of suspicion found in the trial records. Although all these witchcraft illnesses were supposed to be unnatural, the

[14] Among these one should particularly note the works by Delcambre, Labouvie, Simon, and myself listed in Further Reading.

dismal state of medical knowledge (even among trained physicians) meant that these identifications were wholly subjective and unreliable. One must add that modern understandings of the relationship between mind and body make it plain that those who believed themselves bewitched would be likely to fall sick, and might even die, while healing gestures would be effective in many cases.

What the records also show is that most of those brought to trial had a prehistory stretching back for years, often well over a decade, made up of a series of episodes where suspicions had been created, often followed by what was interpreted as a healing gesture. In many cases quite significant numbers of people and animals had supposedly died after quarrels with the suspect, yet no action had followed, beyond threats or name-calling. Suspects could evidently live for many years among their supposed victims, while every village must be assumed to have contained several individuals with a more or less established reputation as witches. So even in the areas with high rates of persecution the vast majority of alleged witches clearly escaped any legal action and died in their beds. There is an extremely difficult problem here for any historical explanation, that of the persistent reluctance to bring formal charges. Possible answers include an awareness that such identifications were never reliable, fears that those on trial would denounce vulnerable members of other families, or that they would resist the torture and return in vengeful mood, and the difficulties of building a coalition of witnesses without opening oneself up to retaliation. No doubt many people were reluctant to initiate proceedings that openly sought the death of a neighbour, while local officials probably operated as a kind of filter. Since so many of the accused were poor it was rare for confiscated goods to cover trial costs, and busy officials had little incentive to initiate these time-wasting procedures; for individuals to bring a case themselves made them liable for the costs, as well as making their hostility to the suspect all too public. So the fit between the extensive witchcraft beliefs and the legal system was always imperfect; the belief system had existed for centuries before there was significant persecution, and would persist into very recent times at village level.

Most suspicions were therefore dealt with by informal means, which commonly involved some sort of confrontation and a demand for reparative action by the witch. This pattern was reinforced by the dense network of healers, many of whom shaded into the more specialized category of witch doctors, who identified illnesses, confirmed suspicions, and provided varieties of counter-magic. In four hundred or so complete trials from Lorraine these people are a widespread presence, yet there is not a single case in which they can be positively identified as having instigated legal action; the inference is clearly that they were very anxious to keep out of sight. That was understandable, because although they only made up a small proportion of the accused, they were probably at greater risk than anyone else of ending up at the stake. This was not just because of hostility from the officials and the clergy, for there is ample evidence that in the popular mind their status was deeply ambiguous, with their claim to healing powers carrying a strong implication that they were equally capable of harming. Indeed many of their counter-magical techniques involved turning the evil back onto the witch who had sent it, easily construed as a form of magical aggression. Dissatisfied clients might readily come to see them as more than just cheats and come to think their activities were diabolical. A fair number of clerics performed in similar fashion, conduct which occasionally led to their own downfall, but more generally seems to have been regarded as a natural extension of their role as the guardians and dispensers of protective power. Sacramentals such as holy water and blessed bread or palms played a major role in anti-witchcraft rituals, and these clerics frequently performed exorcisms as cures for a range of disorders, particularly mental illness. Sufferers under exorcism could easily use their devils to make accusations; Mattaincourt is far from the sole example of this practice in the region. On the whole, however, the local clergy seem to have fitted in with the informal ways of handling witchcraft, and there are several examples where they can be seen acting to damp down suspicions.

Popular belief in witchcraft was evidently deeply ingrained, supported by a rich folklore and by the endless swell of village gossip. Once the trials began it was augmented by the practice of reading out confessions at the executions. In conse-quence, those put to the torture knew all too well what was expected of them, and came out with predictable confessions, whose similarity was regarded as confirmation of the whole system. They had been seduced by the devil when angry or in despair, been forced to attend the sabbath, and then harmed neighbours after quarrels, with the devil whispering in their ear. This was all remarkably convincing in psychological terms; it seems likely that some at least of the accused came to believe in their own powers to harm. Even the more fantastic elements of their confessions, such as stories of the sabbath, may have reflected dream experiences based on the shared culture. The meetings of witches were portrayed as inverted versions of village festivals and cere-monies, and their most important feature was weather magic carried out under diabol-ical compulsion, usually to cause hailstorms. This was another inversion, for the symbolic and real attack on fertility (also expressed when witches attacked children or animals) was the counterpart of the protective rituals that were so central to communal religious practice. However, the stories of the sabbath did not invert the normal social order, with the rich witches allegedly combining with the devil to damage the crops and ensure the high grain prices from which only they would benefit. Confessions were not all identical, of course, and there are some striking variations between those in the French- and German-speaking areas, which demonstrate that language was a significant cultural barrier. Specific beliefs, such as those regarding the way in which witches carried out their nefarious plans, or their capacity for shape-shifting (as with werewolves) marked out particular localities within the region, although few of them were not found in some form almost anywhere. On the whole the beliefs were more consistent than the persecution into which they fed, and which probably made them more intense so long as it lasted.

The Rhine-Moselle region therefore provides a superb opportunity to analyse the phenomenon of European witchcraft in depth, rather than simply concentrating on the history of persecution. Even in this latter field the work of the Trier group on the complex witch-hunt in the Electorate; of Rita Voltmer on the intense activity in Luxembourg; and of Walter Rummel on the social dynamics linked to witchcraft committees in the villages near Koblenz, have all opened up pathways for some fresh thinking, which could profitably be extended to other parts of the region. Much of this research emphasizes the fact that there were crucial differences in the dynamics of persecution, from intense short-term witch-hunts, with St Maximin as the most extreme case, shading through the zones where committees flourished, down to the endemic village accusations of Lorraine. Further work may well clarify the interplay between local power structures, patterns of lordship, legal practices, and the 'hot spots' where abuses proliferated and might have terrifying consequences. Alsace remains the largest relatively blank area on the historiographical map, in urgent need of both local and overall studies. That crucial gap apart, the most exciting way forward probably lies in the close examination of trial records, wherever these survive in any number, to uncover the beliefs and practices of the ordinary people who ultimately shaped the whole phenomenon. In an area where no government had much grip at the local level it was peasants and artisans whose input was crucial. Although they often acted in concert with minor officials and the lesser clergy, it was they who identified suspects, dealt with them by informal means, and sometimes mobilized group action to seek their elimination. Across the Rhine-Moselle region, therefore, persecution cannot plausibly be seen as linked to processes of state formation; it was largely driven by older communal values, while the rulers had the greatest difficulty imposing any kind of procedural constraints.[15] There is still much to learn about the way these processes worked, as there is about witchcraft as part of a therapeutic system.

FURTHER READING

Briggs, Robin, *The Witches of Lorraine* (Oxford, 2007).

Delcambre, Etienne, *Le concept de la sorcellerie dans le duché de Lorraine au XVIe et au XVIIe siècle*, 3 vols (Nancy, 1948–51).

Dillinger, Johannes, *'Evil People': A Comparative Study of Witch-hunts in Swabian Austria and the Electorate of Trier* (Charlottesville, VA, 2009).

Golden, Richard M., ed., *Encyclopedia of Witchcraft: The Western Tradition*, 4 vols (Santa Barbara, CA, 2006). Much of the latest research is covered in the entries on specific regions such as Luxembourg in this crucial summation of current knowledge, which also has excellent bibliographies.

Labouvie, Eva, *Zauberei und Hexenwerk: ländlicher Hexenglaube in der frühen Neuzeit* (Frankfurt am Main, 1991).

Labouvie, Eva, *Verbotene Künste: Volksmagie und ländlicher Aberglaube in den Dorfgemeinden des Sarraumes (16.–19. Jahrhundert)* (St Ingbert, 1992).

Monter, E. William, *Witchcraft in France and Switzerland: The Borderlands during the Reformation* (Ithaca, NY, and London, 1976).

---

[15] This is particularly well explained in Dillinger, *'Evil People'*.

Monter, E. William, *A Bewitched Duchy: Lorraine and its Dukes 1477–1736* (Geneva, 2007).

Rochelandet, B., *Sorcières, diables et bûchers en Franche-Comté aux 16e et 17e siècles* (Besançon, 1997).

Rummel, Walter, *Bauern, Herren und Hexen: Studien zur Sozialgeschichte sponheimischer und kurtrierische Hexenprozesse 1574–1664* (Göttingen, 1991).

Simon, Maryse, *Les affaires de sorcellerie dans le Val de Lièpvre (XVIe et XVIIe siècles)* (Strasbourg, 2006).

Voltmer, Rita, '. . . ce tant exécrable et détestable crime de sortilège. Der "Bürgerkrieg" gegen Hexen und Hexenmeister im Herzogtum Luxemburg (16. und 17. Jahrhundert)', *Hémecht. Revue d'Histoire Luxembourgeoise. Zeitschrift für Luxemburger Geschichte*, 56 (2004), 57–92.

Voltmer, Rita, 'Hexenverfolgungen im Maas-Rhein-Mosel-Raum—Ergebnisse und Perspektiven', in F. Irsigler, ed., *Zwischen Maas und Rhein. Beziehungen, Begegnungen und Konflikte in einem europäischen Kernraum von der Spätantike bis zum 19. Jahrhundert. Versuch einer Bilanz*, Trierer Historische Forschungen, 61 (Trier, 2006), 153–87.

Votmer, Rita, 'Die politischen Funktionen der frühneuzeitlichen Hexenverfolgungen: Machtdemonstration, Kontrolle und Herrschaftsverdichtung im Rhein-Maas-Raum', in M. Ostorero, G. Modestin, and K. Utz Tremp, eds, *Chasses aux sorcières et démonologie: Entre discours et pratiques (XIVe–XVIIe siècles)* (Florence, 2010), 89–115.

CHAPTER 12

WITCHCRAFT TRIALS IN FRANCE

WILLIAM MONTER

THE most noteworthy feature of the history of witchcraft in France is that, from the fifteenth century until the end of the Old Regime, throughout Europe's most populous kingdom this crime was judged in secular rather than ecclesiastical courts. One court dominated all others: the Parlement of Paris, Europe's oldest and largest appellate court, whose *ressort* or judicial district covered about half of a kingdom boasting approximately twenty million subjects around 1600. Between seven and twelve smaller parlements—among which Toulouse in southern France was the second oldest and had the second largest district—divided appellate justice over the French king's remaining ten million subjects.[1]

While the centrality of the Paris Parlement in the history of French witchcraft has never been in doubt, the major scholarly controversy about this subject during the past generation erupted less than a decade after Robert Mandrou published his grand *thèse* on the decline of witch-hunting in seventeenth-century France in the tumultuous year of 1968. In 1977, Mandrou's assumption that until the mid-1600s the Parlement of Paris had followed a 'traditional' judicial approach, with about 90 per cent of all witches it judged being sentenced to death, was dramatically challenged through a careful investigation of the reputedly illegible sixteenth-century Parisian interrogation records by an expatriate American. Alfred Soman began publishing his findings about the persistent leniency of Parisian judges towards accused witches in French in 1977 and in English a year later. In 1979, Mandrou counter-attacked by editing a collection of

---

[1] The map of French parlements in 1610 by Alfred Soman, 'Le role des Ardennes dans la decriminalisation de la sorcellerie en France', in *Revue historique ardennaise*, 23 (1988), 32, also includes the parlements of Rouen, Rennes, Bordeaux, Aix, Grenoble, and Dijon; the French Crown subsequently created parlements for Navarre (1620), Metz (1633), Alsace (1658), Franche-Comté (1678), and Flanders (1682).

ten unpublished texts composed between 1603 and 1702, prefaced by a vitriolic but unconvincing assault on his rival.[2]

Arguably, this controversy produced some light as well as much heat; the current scholarly consensus is that Soman has established an early and consistent pattern of judicial scepticism by the Paris Parlement with respect to both the physical reality and legal provability of witchcraft. However, one unfortunate side effect has been to undermine the value of the remainder of Mandrou's original work. Because Mandrou, unlike Soman, explored this subject in other parts of France over a longer period, both the middle section of his work—dealing with the growth of sceptical attitudes and judicial leniency among French appellate judges by the second quarter of the seventeenth century—and its final sections about the spread of such attitudes throughout France around the mid-seventeenth century and about royal intervention in such matters after 1670, still retain much of their usefulness. Soman has relatively little to say once the Paris Parlement began enforcing the principle of automatic appeals of any witchcraft trial after 1625, and largely ignores the revival of trials, condemnations, and even a few executions for diabolical magic that followed the royal edict, although it had supposedly decriminalized witchcraft in 1682.

Now that the dust from this controversy has settled, we can see that the Paris Parlement consistently displayed three features that made its practice in witchcraft cases uniquely important. First, it ensured that even in the fifteenth century no ecclesiastical tribunals under French suzerainty were permitted to make final judgements in witchcraft cases. Second, it took a sceptical position about the reality of the cumulative concept of witchcraft (which had been developed mainly by late medieval clerics), especially the witches' sabbath. Finally, while the Paris Parlement permitted the use of torture in criminal cases, including witchcraft, it was far more sceptical about its value than were most lower-tier courts in France, or elsewhere in Europe. After 1500, torture could not be applied more than once and could not inflict permanent physical harm on a prisoner. Consequently, the Paris Parlement obtained few confessions through torture for *any* capital crimes: already less than 10 per cent by 1540, this ratio had fallen to barely 2 per cent by the early seventeenth century.[3]

This combination of anticlerical scepticism and limited reliance on judicial torture ensured that, once its surviving decisions in criminal cases become reasonably complete after 1564 (precisely when major outbreaks of witch-hunting began throughout Western Europe), the Paris Parlement condemned surprisingly few people to death for witchcraft. Soman tabulated only 104 death sentences upheld between 1550 and 1625

[2] Robert Mandrou, *Magistrats et sorciers en France au XVIIe siecle* (Paris, 1968); see also the introduction to Mandrou's documentary collection, *Possession et sorcellerie au XVIIe siècle* (Paris, 1979), 13–15. Fifteen of Soman's articles published between 1977 and 1990 were collected in *Sorcellerie et justice criminelle; le Parlement de Paris (16e–18e siècles)* (Brookfield, VT 1992).

[3] Alfred Soman, 'La justice criminelle aux XVIe–XVIIe siècles: le Parlement de Paris et les sièges subalternes', in *Actes du 107e Congrès national des Sociétés savantes*, 2 vols (Brest, 1982; repr. Paris, 1984), i, 38–49.

among 930 defendants appealing condemnations for witchcraft.[4] After 1625, the Paris Parlement not only enforced automatic appeals in any witchcraft trials held throughout its vast jurisdiction, but also consistently refused to condemn anyone to death for this crime. All other French parlements, led by Toulouse, were fully autonomous, but they generally followed the example set by Paris. Consequently, although every French appellate court upheld at least a few death sentences for witchcraft in the sixteenth and seventeenth centuries, only one—the Parlement of Rouen in Normandy—is known to have condemned as many as a hundred witches to death between 1564 and 1660.[5] In most other French parlements, recorded decisions in criminal cases are far less complete than those from Paris, and often preserve only a handful of death sentences for witchcraft. For example, only ten executions for *sortilège* survive from the Parlement of Aix-en-Provence during twenty-eight years between 1581 and 1625; even fewer are known from the Parlement of Bordeaux, whose trial records are less extensive.

The French legal system had other peculiarities. For example, its procedure for appealing condemnations for witchcraft to a parlement were relatively simple: a defendant condemned to any physical punishment (death, torture, a whipping) had only to say four words, 'I appeal to Parlement', when his sentence was pronounced, whereupon both he himself and his trial record had to be sent, at public expense, to the nearest appellate court. Moreover, appealing any condemnation for witchcraft by a local court became obligatory in the Paris *ressort* by the 1620s, and this policy was soon followed by other parlements throughout the kingdom.

12.1 LATE MEDIEVAL LEGAL ANTICLERICALISM

Although hundreds of local witchcraft trials were held during the 1420s and 1430s in the Alpine districts of Dauphiné, an eastern French province bordering western Switzerland (the birthplace of the witches' sabbath and the location of Europe's earliest large-scale prosecutions for witchcraft), higher-level French courts soon displayed sceptical attitudes towards the reality of this new crime. As early as 1445, France's second oldest parlement, sitting at Toulouse in Languedoc, released a plaintiff charged with witchcraft because the evidence against her was clearly perjured; but it intervened too late to save half a dozen others, who had died after trials that displayed various irregularities.[6] In 1450, the French monarchy ordered an inquiry into the trial and condemnation of Joan of Arc, a process leading to an enquiry by two high-level French ecclesiastics in

[4] Alfred Soman, 'Le sabbat des sorciers: preuve juridique', in N. Jacques-Chaquin and M. Préaud, eds, *Le sabbat des sorciers (XVe–XVIIIe siècles)* (Grenoble, 1993), 98.

[5] William Monter, 'Toads and Eucharists: The Male Witches of Normandy, 1564–1660', *French Historical Studies*, 20 (1997), 573.

[6] William Monter, 'Languedoc', in Richard M. Golden, ed., *Encyclopedia of Witchcraft: The Western Tradition*, 4 vols (Santa Barbara, CA, 2006), iii, 624–5.

1452, then to a papally sanctioned rehabilitation trial held at Paris in 1455, and ultimately to her full rehabilitation at Rouen a quarter-century after her execution. These procedures marked the final time that ecclesiastical justice decided any significant case involving charges of witchcraft in the kingdom of France.

Not long after Joan of Arc's rehabilitation, the most important intervention of French royal justice in fifteenth-century witchcraft trials followed appeals to the Parlement of Paris by some prominent victims of the so-called *Vauderie* of Arras (1459–61), when a special inquisitorial court held a cluster of trials that eventually produced twenty-nine arrests and twelve executions, plus a death in prison. Because these trials took place in Artois, a province governed by the Dukes of Burgundy, but which had traditionally belonged to the *ressort* of the Paris Parlement, some prisoners and their relatives appealed to their territorial lord in Brussels, while three men fled as far as Paris. French justice proved more willing than its Burgundian counterpart to intervene on their behalf. By autumn 1461, an ecclesiastical court at Paris, presided over by the chief inquisitor of France, strongly condemned the operations of the Arras tribunal.

However, because of justified doubts that a distant court would not be able to enforce its ruling against the opposition of the territorial overlords, it took the Parlement of Paris until 1468 to pronounce in favour of the appellants. Only in 1491, long after the military defeat of the Burgundian dukes in 1477 and an ensuing French occupation of Arras—a time when the Parlement's rulings could be enforced, but when only one of the original plaintiffs (who had escaped from prison more than thirty years before) was still alive—did the Paris Parlement finally issue a definitive verdict nullifying all punishments imposed on the city's convicted witches and ordering the ecclesiastical judges to make elaborate restitution. When it declared the Arras trials 'abusive, false, null and contrary to all form and order of justice', the Paris court was particularly vehement about the 'intolerable cruelties' resulting from the misuse of torture by the inquisitorial tribunal that had convicted these so-called *Vaudois*.[7] It may not have been coincidence that, eight years later, the French Crown forbade reapplications of torture. Witchcraft was certainly not the only area where the Parlement of Paris developed the *appel comme d'abus* ('appeal from abusive jurisdiction') in order to override decisions of ecclesiastical courts, but its actions on the appeals from Arras provided an extremely important early precedent.

12.2 WITCH TRIALS INCREASE (1560–1624)

In the first half of the sixteenth century, recorded witch trials remained extremely rare throughout the kingdom of France, as in much of Western Europe, and few reached its

---

[7] Franck Mercier, *La Vauderie d'Arras: Une chasse aux sorcières à l'Automne du Moyen Âge* (Rennes, 2006), 219 (quote), 287 (list of cases), 319–20, 325–50.

appellate courts. In the early 1540s, only one witchcraft case was appealed to the Paris Parlement during a two-year period; this number would later increase to sixteen such appeals during twelve months in 1572–3, and to thirty-four in another twelve-month period in 1609–10. The 1540 defendant, a young man whose parents made the appeal, was one of four people sentenced to death for witchcraft by a local court in Beaujolais. The Parlement released him and ordered royal officials to investigate both the local *seigneur* and his legal officers.[8] Around this time, the Parlement of Normandy at Rouen executed two shepherds who had been caught stealing Eucharists on behalf of a witch (*sorcier et enchanteur*) who was never found. In 1542, it reduced the punishment of a man convicted of witchcraft from hanging to banishment. Similar examples have yet to be found elsewhere in France, although traces exist of witches being lynched in the vicinity of Lyon in 1544 and 1552.[9]

Until its interrogation records became available after 1564, Soman detected only a handful of appeals in witchcraft cases to the Paris Parlement. But beyond this point they rose sharply, from an average of barely five appeals per year between 1565–74 to more than twenty per year in the early 1580s. No useable records of local witch trials survive anywhere in the French kingdom. While our information from other French parlements is much less complete, scattered indications suggest that they too began receiving more appeals in witchcraft cases in the 1560s. In the spring of 1555 France's second-largest and second-oldest appellate court flatly rejected an attempt by the Seneschal of Bigorre (near the Spanish border) to send some of its judges there 'to make and complete the trials of some prisoners charged with using enchantments, spells (sorceries), poisonings (venefices) and charms, in order to extirpate this sect of scandalous and pernicious people from the country'. Instead, the court at Toulouse court blamed these crimes on the failure of parish priests to instruct people correctly and proposed that such defendants be tried 'according to holy decrees and canonical constitutions'. But only seven years later, while the first French war of religion was raging in Languedoc, the Parlement of Toulouse heard appeals from several prisoners charged with witchcraft, and upheld at least three death sentences for this crime, all against women.[10]

In northern France, the Parlement of Rouen, whose records for these years are far less complete than those for Paris, heard a dozen appeals from death sentences for witchcraft between 1564 and 1579, but did not confirm any of them until 1574. After 1580, appeals in witchcraft trials mushroomed at both courts—except during the apogee of religious warfare in 1589–93, when almost every French parlement split into separate royalist and Catholic-extremist factions, and ordinary judicial business almost ceased. After 1594, Parisian cases quickly rebounded to their previous levels of twenty witchcraft defendants per year and continued to average twenty or more such

---

Alfred Soman, 'Aux origines de l'appel de droit dans l'ordonnance criminelle de 1670', *XVIIe siècle*, 32 (1980), 23 and n. 6.

[9]   Monter, 'Male Witches of Normandy', 565; Soman, 'La justice criminelle', VII, 27 n. 23.

[10]   Archives Départementales, Haute-Garonne (Toulouse), B 3408, 3440–4.

cases per year until 1620.[11] At Rouen, the Parlement of Normandy judged at least one appeal from a death sentence for witchcraft every year from 1582 until 1619 (except 1589–93); and it upheld at least one death sentence for this crime every year but one between 1585 and 1615.

Although their records are far less complete, other French parlements apparently behaved similarly at this time. Surviving records from the parlements of Burgundy and Provence show that both handled witchcraft cases in most years.[12] At Dijon, where criminal-case rulings are rarely available before 1612, the Parlement of Burgundy judged twenty-three witchcraft defendants during ten of the eleven years between 1582 and 1592, upholding five death sentences and reducing four others. At Aix, for the period before the all-too-famous Gaufridy case of 1611, usable records of the parlement's criminal decisions survive from 1581 until August 1585 and during twelve years between 1596 and 1610 (two years are missing). In the early 1580s, the Parlement of Provence judged twelve witchcraft cases, upholding two death sentences and reducing three others. In the latter period, it judged twenty-three witchcraft defendants, torturing a half-dozen of them but pronouncing only one death sentence.

Recorded witch-hunting peaked throughout the French kingdom early in the seventeenth century. At Paris and Rouen, the two parlements with the best available records, appeals in witchcraft cases reached their numerical peak around 1610. South-western France had been a bastion of parlementary scepticism about the reality of witches' *maleficia*; no documented death sentences for witchcraft are known from the Bordeaux court (whose judges included Montaigne) until 1594, later than any other provincial parlement. But in 1609, this region experienced a famous witch-hunt in the Basque-speaking lands along the Spanish border, directed by a royally commissioned judge, Pierre de Lancre.

This judicial operation had significant repercussions on both sides of the border with Spain. Accused witches fleeing south triggered the final witch-hunt undertaken by the Spanish Inquisition, ending in a major auto–da–fé in 1610. Meanwhile, after his commission had expired, de Lancre's colleagues at Bordeaux released many prisoners whom he had arrested. In Spain, the episode soon led the Inquisition to stop executing witches altogether. In France, similar scepticism provoked de Lancre to publish a defence of the reality of the sabbath in 1612.[13] De Lancre was not without emulators elsewhere in France. His commission coincided with the first public exorcisms of Ursuline nuns at Marseilles in south-eastern France. Their accusations began a famous trial that ended with the well-publicized execution of a prominent priest by order of a

---

[11] See graph in Soman, VII, 26.

[12] For the Parlement of Burgundy, see Archives Départementales de la Côte d'Or (Dijon), B 46 II/1–2; for the Parlement of Provence, see Archives Départementales des Bouches-du-Rhone (dépot d'Aix), B 5467–70, 5476–89.

[13] The best modern edition of de Lancre's *Tableau de l'Inconstance des mauvais anges et demons*, first published in 1612, is by Nicole Jacques-Chaquin (Paris, 1982); see also Jonathan Pearl, 'Lancre, Pierre de (1533–1630)', *Encyclopedia of Witchcraft*, iii, 622–3.

French parlement, on charges of sending demons into nuns by means of a diabolical pact. It began a trend.

12.3 PARLEMENTARY SCEPTICISM (1625–50)

If the first part of Robert Mandrou's now-classic account of 1968 has been overturned by Soman's meticulous investigations of the actual workings of the Paris Parlement, its second part—about the seventeenth-century 'crisis of Satanism' and the emergence of an increasingly sceptical orientation towards the reality of witchcraft among the magistrates of Paris—retains much of its validity. Mandrou's account, which pivots around French public debate over some extremely famous early seventeenth-century cases involving priestly sorcerers in various parts of France, received valuable reinforcement from Michel de Certeau's 1970 account of the most notorious case in France, involving the demonic possession of many Ursuline nuns of Loudun by a local Jesuit named Urbain Grandier.[14]

The 'print trail' left by these famous cases of diabolical possession by priests is revealing. After the first case in Provence in 1609–11, only two noteworthy treatises were printed. One, by a professor of medicine, defended the method and value of searching suspected witches for diabolical marks; the other, by a veteran inquisitor, defended the value of testimony taken during exorcisms. However, the Loudun case of 1632–4 sparked a virtual explosion of publications. Certeau identified three pamphlets about Grandier's death, followed by fifty editions of thirty-five different works before 1638. Several accounts came from Protestants, and those from physicians were extremely critical of the proceedings. The next such case, in Normandy, eventually provoked more than a hundred public exorcisms and inspired almost three dozen editions from 1643–54.[15] Critical voices were again heard, this time from Catholics; as at Loudun, the most important came from the medical profession, including a court physician. A more original contribution was the autobiography of one of the principal nuns involved, Madeleine Bavent, who had confessed to causing the possession of her sisters; it was purportedly dictated to a priest a decade after the scandal began. Instead of being tried and sentenced for witchcraft, Bavent had been locked up in an asylum, where she would die a year later.

However, Mandrou's framework presents a chronological problem. He emphasized the vitally important procedural ruling of the Paris Parlement in 1624, requiring all

---

[14] Michel de Certeau, *La Possession at Loudun* (Paris, 1970) is available in English: *The Possession at Loudun*, tr. Michael B. Smith (Chicago, 1996). Previously, this episode was memorably treated by Aldous Huxley in *The Devils of Loudun* (London, 1952) and has been revisited more recently in English by Robert Rapley, *A Case of Witchcraft: The Trial of Urbain Grandier* (Montreal, 1998) and Sarah Ferber, *Demonic Possession and Exorcism in Early Modern France* (London, 2004). See also Robert Rapley, 'Loudun Nuns', in *Encyclopedia of Witchcraft*, iii, 669–72.

[15] Certeau, *Possession de Loudun*, 268–75; compare Rapley, 'Louviers Nuns', 672.

subordinate courts to send all witchcraft cases to it, and noted that afterwards 'one cannot find a single example [in a witch trial] where the parlement purely and simply upheld any decision of a subaltern court'.[16] But this ruling and the Parlement's subsequent systematic reduction of penalties for witchcraft fits poorly with his causes célèbres. It precedes Grandier's trial—the first of these three to generate sceptical discussions in print—by almost a decade. More than twenty years later, the royal parlement closest to Paris still ordered a priest burned for causing demonic possession in nuns, while ignoring the witchcraft confession of Sister Bavent.

In 1634, Cardinal Richelieu carefully ensured that Grandier (a personal enemy) would be unable to appeal his death sentence for witchcraft to the Paris Parlement. But to what extent were this parlement's two key decisions—to impose automatic appeals in witchcraft cases and to eliminate capital punishment for this crime—followed in the half of the French kingdom that lay outside its jurisdiction? Trying to extend his investigation beyond the Parisian district, Mandrou saw clearly that the Parlement of Normandy continued to follow a very different drummer from Paris, at least until Colbert and Louis XIV forcibly overturned some of its death sentences on witchcraft cases in 1670. He also saw that the other parlement closest to Paris, at Dijon, was clearly following Parisian guidelines by ordering automatic appeals in witchcraft cases in 1635 and drastically reducing its punishments for witchcraft during a panic nine years later, although it still upheld three death sentences for this crime.[17]

In fact, the first French parlement outside Paris to apply these new guidelines consistently was not even created until 1633, and its early record on judging witchcraft was not published until 2006.[18] The Parlement of Metz was located in a city that had been a republic rather than a provincial capital, and had experienced severe witch-hunts as recently as 1588. Established at a time when French armies were invading and occupying the united Duchy of Lorraine and Bar, this new court was designed to bring modern French jurisprudence into the kingdom's expanding eastern edge, and more specifically into one of the most intensive zones of witch-hunting in Western Europe. Under such circumstances, this new appellate tribunal drew its judges not from local notables but from younger men with elite Parisian backgrounds; several of them went on to distinguished careers, and young Nicolas Fouquet later played a major role at the French court.

France occupied Lorraine and Bar from 1634 until 1660, and again from 1670 until 1697. The first witchcraft case judged by the Metz Parlement involved two local sisters; it sentenced them to banishment, but both were stoned to death at the city limits. Although unable to enforce automatic appeals in witchcraft cases under wartime

[16] Mandrou, *Magistrats et sorciers*, 341–63 (quote at 349). Soman found one death sentence for witchcraft, from Orléans, upheld in 1625.

[17] Mandrou, *Magistrats et sorciers*, 385–90.

[18] André Brulé, *Sorcellerie et emprise démoniaque à Metz et au Pays messin (XII–XVIII⁰ siècles)* (Paris, 2006), 335–434; William Monter, *A Bewitched Duchy: Lorraine and its Dukes, 1477–1736* (Geneva, 2007), 128–9.

conditions in hostile territory, it reduced such sentences as relentlessly as their Parisian elders. The twenty cases of witchcraft heard by the Parlement of Metz from 1644 to 1660, when its effective control over this district gradually improved, included nine appeals from death sentences; it freed five defendants and imposed lesser sentences on the others.[19]

Perhaps the most serious test for French parlements confronting accusations for witchcraft occurred during three almost-simultaneous major outbreaks in the mid-1640s. They affected the appellate districts of Toulouse, Dijon, and Paris—all places which now enforced automatic appeals. The panic began, and was most severe, in Languedoc, where the Parlement of Toulouse judged at least 641 accused witches between spring 1643 and spring 1645. It initially upheld many local decisions, until parlementary judges learned in December 1643 about the activities of professional witchfinders in various parts of their district. They shifted their targets, and by summer 1644 they had hanged at least three witchfinders (some of whom had forged commissions from the parlement) and sent several others to the galleys. At the same time, they confirmed extremely few sentences of local tribunals and released almost two-thirds of the final six hundred suspected witches, mostly because of insufficient evidence.[20]

During a nearly simultaneous outbreak in Burgundy in 1644, the Parlement of Dijon reacted similarly to their colleagues at Toulouse: they confirmed the first two death sentences for witchcraft, but only one of the next thirteen. Then they captured a local witchfinder and sent him to the galleys, while releasing many of the next hundred prisoners charged with witchcraft. During the next few years, they uncovered nine episodes where suspected witches had been lynched with the complicity of local officials; however, nearly all of the ringleaders escaped their grasp.[21] However, the ripple effect seems extremely minor in the Ardennes of north-eastern France, where previous scandals (in 1587, 1601, and 1623) had played major roles in Parisian parlementary jurisprudence about witchcraft. In 1644 there were only half a dozen instances of judicial abuses in the Ardennes, primarily ducking suspected witches in water; unlike previous outbreaks in this region, neither professional witch-hunters nor lynchings are recorded here in 1644.[22]

12.4 'DECRIMINALIZATION' AND ITS DISCONTENTS

The final part of Mandrou's classic 1968 thesis recounts the direct interventions by Louis XIV's government, beginning with overturning death sentences for witchcraft

---

[19] Brulé, *Sorcellerie et emprise demoniaque à Metz*, Table XIV, 428–9.
[20] Monter, 'Languedoc', 625.
[21] William Monter, 'Burgundy, Duchy of', in *Encyclopedia of Witchcraft*, i, 152–3.
[22] Alfred Soman, 'Le role des Ardennes dans la décriminalisation de la sorcellerie en France', in *Revue historique ardennaise*, 23 (1988), 30–1, 36.

pronounced by the Parlement of Rouen in 1670, and culminating a dozen years later with a major royal edict that has often been assumed to mark the official 'decriminalization' of witchcraft in France. However, this account seems a bit too rose-tinted, for several reasons. First, French appellate justice does not seem particularly 'enlightened' when judging witchcraft cases on the kingdom's outer margins during this period. In Béarn, the local parlement apparently sponsored the activities of a young witchfinder in 1670. In the recently conquered parts of the Low Countries where Louis XIV created a sovereign council in 1668 (it became the Parlement of Flanders in 1686), jurists at Douai exhibited very traditional attitudes during a witch-hunt at a nearby village in 1679. In July 1683, a year after the new royal edict, the French appellate court for Alsace (created in 1658) upheld a death sentence for witchcraft.[23]

Second, Louis XIV's 1682 edict seems a bureaucratic response designed to cover up the greatest scandal of his reign. From 1679 until 1681, the events now conventionally and somewhat euphemistically known in France as the 'Affair of the Poisons' had provided endless gossip in Paris. Its official name imperfectly conceals something better described as sophisticated Europe's first encounter with the sulfurous phenomenon better known as the 'black mass'. One prominent prisoner, Abbé Guibourg, had served in several Parisian churches for half a century until Louis XIV's police chief arrested him in 1680 for performing various black masses, including some for the king's mistress Madame de Montespan. Like Grandier's scandalous execution almost fifty years earlier, 'reason of state' removed these culprits from the jurisdiction of the Paris Parlement. Instead, the 'Sun King' and his new Parisian police chief assigned the affair to a top-secret Chambre de l'Arsenal, which arranged several public executions but kept the most embarrassing prisoners, like Guibourg, chained up in faraway secret locations.

The famous 1682 edict followed the final dissolution of this special court. Its preamble, complaining that 'the execution of our predecessor kings' in this area 'having been neglected for a long time, and this relaxation having attracted from foreign countries many of these impostors', combines two significant falsehoods. No edict of Louis XIV's predecessors had ever defined the crime of witchcraft, let alone black masses; and the 'impostors' whom he now targeted were not foreigners but native Frenchmen living in Paris. The text of the edict avoided using the word 'witchcraft' (sorcellerie) and essentially redefined the crime by reducing maleficium to poisoning, and the diabolical pact to either fraud or sacrilege.

As Mandrou's final chapter noted, the 1682 edict apparently stimulated legal prosecutions and even capital punishments for felonies that had previously formed part of the cumulative witchcraft concept. As late as 1691, so-called sorciers were even executed by the Parlement of Paris (which had stopped executing witches long ago) for crimes traditionally identified closely with witchcraft. Even later, the Parlement of Normandy behaved similarly by condemning three men to death in 1703 for sacrileges directly

---

[23] Robert Muchembled, *Les derniers bûchers: Un village de Falndre et ses sorcières sous Louis XIV* (Paris, 1981), 40–2; Mandrou, *Magistrates et sorciers*, 491.

related to magical healing. In Franche-Comté, an eastern province conquered by Louis XIV in 1678 (and whose appellate court was dismissing condemnations for witchcraft fourteen years earlier), a witch confessing to 'unheard-of maléfices' against livestock was reportedly executed two years after Louis XIV's death.[24]

Throughout the Enlightenment, the pursuit of auxiliaries to witch trials, especially overzealous exorcists and professional witchfinders, continued on France's southern border. Between 1734 and 1787, the Parlement of Navarre published no fewer than six edicts condemning popular superstitions. The most general of these, in 1763, constituted 'a genuine admission of powerlessness [to combat such beliefs] at the same time that it proved the existence of an important co-existence of popular and elite beliefs'. It followed their investigation of a witch-finding exorcist and a folk healer, both of whom escaped their clutches; the exorcist returned six years later and settled quietly in Navarre's capital. In 1779—more than a century after Colbert's intervention in Navarre against the activities of a youthful witchfinder—a complex local trial ended with the condemnation of yet another youthful witchfinder, who was ultimately sent to the galleys. Technically, the crime of witchcraft would not be finally abolished in revolutionary France, along with other judicial debris of the Old Regime, until 1791.[25]

12.5 PROBLEMS FOR FUTURE RESEARCH

A major French peculiarity—one which has yet to be widely acknowledged, let alone satisfactorily explained—runs counter to one of the most fundamental assumptions about witchcraft throughout Europe, namely that it was essentially a female crime. This error was propagated by the first great French historian of witchcraft, Jules Michelet, who entitled his famous and often-reprinted work of 1862 *La sorcière*. As you will find elsewhere in this work, modern research about gender distribution among accused witches in French-speaking areas outside the borders of the early modern French kingdom—from Francophone Belgium or Luxembourg to eastern regions like Lorraine, Franche-Comté, or Francophone western Switzerland—conform to more general Continental patterns, although with significant percentages of male witches (often slightly above one-fourth). But these ratios do not necessarily hold across much of the kingdom of France, especially its northern and central parts; both saw a remarkably high percentage of men among defendants known to have been tried and executed for witchcraft. The pattern began early. Men comprised two-thirds of the defendants in the *Vauderie* of Arras; three of the four people condemned to death for witchcraft in Beaujolais in 1539 were male. Although local witchcraft trials from the peak era of witch-hunting in France have almost never been preserved, one of the very

---

[24] Muchembled, *Les derniers bûchers*, 40–2; Mandrou, *Magistrates et sorciers*, 491.
[25] Christian Desplat, *Sorcières et diables en Béarn (fin XIVe–début XIXe siècle)* (Pau, 1988), 118–19 (quote), 185–206.

rare exceptions (held near Sancerre in 1582–3) counted five men among six defend-ants.[26] One striking similarity among France's three most famous seventeenth-century cases of demonic possession was that every time, a priest was burned to death by order of a parlement or a specially appointed royal court, while no women—even one who confessed—were ever prosecuted. Throughout the 'Affair of the Poisons', clerical sorcerers remained prominent among the defendants and men received most of the harshest punishments. In the heart of the kingdom, men comprised a slight majority of the thousand-plus witchcraft defendants tried before the Parlement of Paris between 1550 and 1670, and they formed approximately two-thirds of the several hundred people tried for witchcraft at Rouen. Further east, men comprised about 40 per cent of witchcraft defendants tried by the Parlement of Dijon in the 1580s and fully half of the larger number tried in Burgundy between 1628 and 1646.

However, as one moves further away from Paris and north-central France, this phenomenon diminishes. At the edges of the French kingdom—in Alsace or the Pays de Labourd— the usual suspects were women. In the Ardennes and Burgundy, most people lynched as witches were women. Those identified by professional witchfinders (who in France were invariably male) were overwhelmingly women, particularly in southern France, a region dominated more than northern France by Roman law. In the kingdom's south-eastern corner, Provence, women comprised three-fourths of the three dozen witchcraft defendants tried by its parlement until 1610, but this ratio changed abruptly after the Gaufridy case; during the next fifteen years, men comprised over two-thirds of its sixty-seven witchcraft defendants.

One could also argue that men also formed the most spectacular practitioners of witchcraft in French causes célèbres. The most important Frenchwoman ever tinged with this crime was Joan of Arc, who was ultimately (although posthumously) cleared of such charges after a rehabilitation trial by French royal justice. On the other hand, famous French male witches were seen as dangerous scoundrels, and some of them were burned. The list begins in the 1570s with the exploits of the magician Trois-Echelles at the French court, as told by Jean Bodin in his widely read and translated *Démonomanie des sorciers* (1580). Trois-Echelles was a layman, but his most prominent seventeenth-century successors, Louis Gaufridy and Urbain Grandier, were secular clerics. The last male celebrity, a century after Trois-Echelles, was Abbé Guibourg, whose black masses reputedly included child sacrifice. Behind them was a male supporting cast; forty-six other priests besides Guibourg were eventually implicated in the 'Affair of the Poisons', and two of them were executed.[27]

---

[26] N. Jacques-Chaquin and M. Préaud, eds, *Les sorciers du carroi de Marlou: Un procès de sorcellerie en Berry (1582–1583)* (Grenoble, 1996).

[27] Lynn Mollenauer, *Strange Revelations: Magic, Poison and Sacrilege in Louis XIV's France* (University Park, PA, 2007), 109–10.

Although Stuart Clark, the leading expert on witchcraft treatises, has noted that most French demonologies were not strongly gendered,[28] a second major problem awaiting further investigation is the relationship—if any—between treatises of demonology and the actual conduct of witch trials. This problem is particularly acute in the kingdom of France, because it produced Europe's most widely read demonologist of the early modern era, Jean Bodin, while, at the same time, its leading court utterly rejected Bodin's judicial recommendations regarding witchcraft. Bodin was a great political theorist but a political nonentity at the French Estates-General of 1576, and he never practised law before the Paris Parlement. In the light of Soman's research, it is impossible to believe (as Mandrou, among others, apparently did) that Bodin's arguments about the legal treatment of accused witches had even the slightest effect on French jurisprudence.

At the same time, demonologists writing in French abounded around the borders of the kingdom (Damhouder in the Low Countries, Remy in Lorraine, Boguet in Franche-Comté, and Daneau in Savoy); some of them were judges and all were intimately familiar with current legal practice. In south-western France, the other well-known French demonologist, Pierre de Lancre, had been a judge at the Parlement of Bordeaux, and had arrested many witches in 1609 while a special royal commissioner in a Basque-speaking region. But his evident failure to convince his parlementary colleagues about the reality of the sabbath explains his continuing obsession with the subject in a second witchcraft treatise that he published a decade later. On the other side, with the significant exception of Michel de Montaigne, who had spent many years as a parlementary judge in Bordeaux before publishing his *Essays* in 1580, one finds little scepticism about the reality of witchcraft printed in French until the 1630s. It seems beyond doubt that Montaigne rather than de Lancre spoke for most *parlementaires* at Bordeaux—a tribunal not known to have approved a death sentence for witchcraft until 1594, almost a generation after most other French appellate courts. A few years before de Lancre's mission, it sent a confessed teenage werewolf to serve in a local monastery for the rest of his life.[29]

Another subject deserving further examination is how seriously the French legal system took the issue of the witches' sabbath, which we know was developed during the fifteenth century primarily in Francophone areas, including the French province of Dauphiné. In his most recent essay on witchcraft in France, Soman examined its role in witchcraft cases judged by the Paris Parlement, and found an increasing importance given to the sabbath in the early seventeenth century, especially with respect to capital punishment. Among the vast group of accused witches—over a thousand—whom this court did not sentence to death, sabbaths figured in only 20 per cent of cases before 1588, but in over half of those after 1609. Among the hundred witches whom it sentenced to death, barely half admitted to attending sabbaths until 1588, while 82 per

---

[28] Stuart Clark, 'The "Gendering" of Witchcraft in French Demonology: Misogyny or Polarity?' *French History*, 5 (1991), 429–31.

[29] Mandrou, *Possession et sorcellerie*, 33–109.

cent had inflicted physical harm on people or animals. These ratios were reversed after 1610, when over 90 per cent of those executed had attended sabbaths, while only 69 per cent had inflicted physical harm on people or animals.[30] Can these results be confirmed elsewhere in France or in nearby Francophone areas? Yet another possible task of future research is to investigate the long-term continuity of sceptical legal approaches to the 'cumulative concept' of witchcraft in France, not just from the fifteenth to the eighteenth century but also well beyond. In other words, did the consistently anticlerical prejudice of lay judges in Old Regime France (which can be seen in many areas other than witchcraft) prefigure or even condition post-revolutionary official attitudes in a land whose de facto modern national religion is *laïcité*.

FURTHER READING

Bostridge, Ian, 'The Case of France', in *Witchcraft and its Transformations, c. 1650–c. 1750* (Oxford, 1997), 205–31.

Certeau, Michel de, *The Possession at Loudun*, tr. Michael B. Smith (Chicago, 2000).

Desplat, Christian, *Sorcières et diables en Béarn (fin XIVᵉ–début XIXᵉ siècle)* (Pau, 1988).

Mandrou, Robert, *Magistrats et sorciers en France au XVIIᵉ siècle* (Paris, 1968).

Mandrou, Robert, ed., *Possession et sorcellerie au XVIIᵉ siècle* (Paris, 1979).

Mercier, Franck, *La Vauderie d'Arras: Une chasse aux sorcières à l'Automne du Moyen Âge* (Rennes, 2006).

Mollenauer, Lynn, *Strange Revelations: Magic, Poison and Sacrilege in Louis XIV's France* (University Park, PA, 2007).

Monter, William, 'Toads and the Eucharist: The Male Witches of Normandy, 1564–1660', *French Historical Studies*, 20 (1997), 563–95.

Pearl, Jonathan L., *The Crime of Crimes: Demonology and Politics in France, 1560–1620* (Waterloo, ON, 1999).

Scholz Williams, Gerhild, ed., *On the Inconstancy of Witches: Pierre de Lancre's* Tableau de l'inconstance des mauvais anges et demons *(1612)* (Tempe, AZ, 2006).

Soman, Alfred, *Sorcellerie et justice criminelle (16e–18e siècles)* (Farnham, 1992).

Soman, Alfred, 'Le sabbat des sorciers: preuve juridique', in N. Jacques-Chaquin and M. Préaud, eds, *Le sabbat des sorciers (XVᵉ–XVIIIᵉ siècles)* (Grenoble, 1993).

[30] Soman, 'Sabbat des sorciers', 98.

CHAPTER 13

WITCHCRAFT AND WEALTH: THE CASE OF THE NETHERLANDS

HANS DE WAARDT

THE late medieval and early modern Low Countries were anything but united. At first glance it might seem as if there was at least some sort of political cohesion, at least up till 1581, as, until that time, these domains shared one overlord. In 1581, however, most of the northern provinces and parts of the southern provinces abjured King Philip II of Spain. But even the previous political bond had been only superficial at best.

In the course of the preceding two centuries these provinces had been annexed one after the other by the Dukes of Burgundy or their Habsburg successors, with the notable exception of the domains of the bishop of Liege. In most of the Burgundo-Habsburg provinces three central institutions were introduced: provincial states to discuss taxes and other political matters, provincial courts of appeal, and audit offices to control financial matters. But in each province these institutions were composed, and functioned, in different ways. The bottom line for each province was the wish to preserve its privileges and to ward off all attempts for further centralization.

The coastal area was highly developed, and until 1585 Antwerp was the centre of international trade. Other towns in the coastal area had specific roles in a grid of economic interdependencies. Amsterdam, for instance, focused on the massive transport of grain from the Baltic. After 1585 an unprecedented economic boom began in the western parts of the new Dutch Republic, with Holland and, more specifically, Amsterdam as the centre of world trade. The Republic's inland provinces, however, benefited far less from this economic expansion.

13.1 Prosecuting Heresy and Witchcraft

The Habsburgs wished to suppress all religious dissent in the Netherlands. In the 1520s Charles V introduced an ecclesiastical court modelled on the Spanish Inquisition. Provincial and municipal administrators identified this new institution as just another instrument of centralization. Even the provincial courts of law did what they could to obstruct the activities of the inquisitive friars. As early as 1527 the Court of Holland and Zeeland received complete jurisdiction in heresy cases, and the inquisitors in these provinces were degraded to the status of assistants.[1] In Friesland, where the adminis tration of justice was more centralized than in any other province, the provincial court effectively sabotaged the work of the inquisitor Wilhelmus Lindanus, even though King Philip II had made him an extraordinary member of this institution.[2] In 1544, just one year after he had conquered the duchy of Gelderland, Charles V ordered local author ities to expel all Jews on the pretext that they were responsible for the rise of the new Protestant sects. Nothing happened, however, not even when the emperor renewed his order two years later.[3] In 1560 the Inquisition in the Low Countries was abolished.

The opposition of local authorities to the Inquisition did not imply that they were crypto-Protestants. To be sure, they usually did not pursue Protestant heretics with great determination, but in specific instances they could be very effective in this regard, such as when the Anabaptists attempted to found a New Jerusalem in the German town of Münster in 1534. This religiously inspired attack on the social order led to a massive concerted hunt for these radical Protestants. But local administrators again lost much of their prosecutorial zeal when finding some years later that the militancy of the Anabaptists had given way to the pacifism of the Mennonites. This occurred even in Amsterdam, where the Anabaptists had attacked the town hall in April 1535. This assault enabled a minority faction to gain control of the city council with the support of the central government in Brussels. The new rulers styled themselves the *sincere Catholique factie*, but nevertheless tended to neglect their duty when it came to persecuting religious dissenters.[4] It will be discussed below how other factions tried to erode their opponents' power by concocting accusations of witchcraft against female relatives of the sincere Catholics.

[1] Serge ter Braake, *Met recht en rekenschap: de ambtenaren bij het Hof van Holland en de Haagse Rekenkamer in de Habsburgse tijd (1483–1558)* (Hilversum, 2007), 225, 234.

[2] Oebele Vries, *De Heeren van den Raede: biografieën en groepsportret van de raadsheren van het Hof van Friesland, 1499–1811* (Hilversum, 1999), 61; S. Zijlstra, *Om de ware gemeente en de oude gronden: geschiedenis van de dopersen in de Nederlanden 1531–1675* (Hilversum, 2000), 234–5.

[3] J. H. J. Geurts and J. A. E. Kuys, 'Kerkelijke en godsdienstige verhoudingen in Gelre vóór en ná 1543', in F. Keverling Buisman, ed., *Verdrag en Tractaat van Venlo: herdenkingsbundel, 1543–1993* (Hilversum, 1993), 192–4.

[4] J. J. Woltjer, 'Het conflict tussen Willem Bardes en Hendrick Dirckszoon', *Bijdragen en mededelingen betreffende de geschiedenis der Nederlanden*, 86 (1971), 178–99.

The particularism of local authorities in combination with the wish to avoid civic unrest led to a situation in which no central authority, either temporal or ecclesiastical, was strong enough to launch, let alone coordinate, a campaign to wipe out witchcraft. Just as in heresy cases, only local benches of aldermen and provincial courts were competent in this matter. In theory other ecclesiastical courts besides the unsuccessful Inquisition were also qualified to hear such cases. In reality, however, these other institutions were just as ineffective.[5] The centralist pretensions of these authorities were perhaps gargantuan, but their real power was much smaller.

Until the final decades of the fifteenth century witchcraft was not really a concern of the secular authorities. Local bailiffs and sheriffs tended to interpret complaints against supposed witches as reparation claims.[6] People who were believed to have suffered some sort of damage by the magical activities of another individual could ask the judicial authorities to impose a financial compensation. The local officer then allowed the defendant to buy off further judicial proceedings. Dozens of such fines or 'compositions', as they were called, have been discovered in the accounts of local officers. But these entries are usually very short and more often than not it is impossible to establish what the accused were exactly supposed to have done.

This shortage of information is aggravated by the fact that in the sources the terms used to identify either the crime or the perpetrator had very broad and therefore vague meanings. The usual term for witchcraft was *toverij* and that for a witch *toveres*, male *tovenaar*. The overwhelming majority of the people accused in the Low Countries were female, while the first of these terms could literally refer to any kind of magical activity. In *De praestigiis daemonum*, the first edition of which appeared in 1563, Johan Wier, often identified as Johann Weyer, the German spelling of his name, discussed this linguistic problem. From 1545 till 1550 Weyer had been municipal physician of the capital of the province of Gelderland, Arnhem, and had then been appointed chief physician to the Duke of Cleves and Jülich. In these functions he had had ample opportunity to witness several witchcraft trials. One of the many things he discussed in

---

[5] The statist view of the French historian Robert Muchembled—according to whom it was the central authorities in Brussels who instigated witchcraft prosecutions in the context of a large-scale cultural offensive, which was meant to strengthen their absolutist pretensions—should be rejected. See, e.g. his *La sorcière au village, XVIe–XVIIIe siècle* (Paris, 1979). A year earlier he postulated that for 'the social elites and certainly for the authorities the stake was a procedure to extirpate a very powerful diabolic sect and at the same time a method to subdue in body and mind all who were watching this drama'. Robert Muchembled, 'Avant-propos. Satan ou les hommes? La chasse au sorcières et ses causes', in Marie-Sylvie Dupont-Bouchat, Willem Frijhoff, and Robert Muchembled, eds, *Prophètes et sorciers dans les Pays-Bas XVIe–XVIIIe siècles* (Paris, 1978), 13–32, here 30.

[6] There were two types of local officers in the Low Countries. The one who represented the prince in a country district was often referred to as the *baljuw*, although there were quite a few local variations, whereas an officer in a town was ordinarily designated as *schout*. The first term is here translated as bailiff and the second as sheriff.

his book was the ambiguous meaning of the German word for sorcerer, *Zauberer*, a term closely linked to the Dutch, or really Low German, *toverij*.[7]

Maleficent witchcraft, the counter-magic of cunning folk, fortune-telling, even the learned natural magic of people like Wier's mentor Agrippa of Nettesheim, were all different forms of *toverij*. This often makes it difficult to understand what offence people were accused of. In 1371, for instance, the sheriff of Heusden, a small town in the province of Holland, reported to have received from two individual women, respectively three and nine pounds, without giving any further specification than that they had been accused of witchcraft.

This vagueness is indeed frustrating, but should be perceived as the reflection of a constitutive element of the magical worldview of this period in this part of Europe. The boundaries between activities conceived as magical were often unclear and could easily be blurred. An effect of an action that one person saw as highly negative could have much more positive qualities in the eyes of another. Searches for treasure by magical means, rites meant to stop husbands from battering their wives, attempts to recover stolen property, or the expulsion of demons and spectres—all had this two-edged character.

Even though bailiffs and sheriffs preferred to interpret accusations of witchcraft as demands for compensation until the final decades of the fifteenth century, they could, and sometimes did, institute legal proceedings of a more serious nature. In these cases a formal indictment could eventually lead to a death sentence. In 1472 a parish priest's housekeeper in a village in Gelderland was executed, and in 1469 or 1470 a man was burnt for sorcery in Nijmegen. Sometimes witchcraft was linked with poisoning, as for instance in 1462, when a woman was burnt in the town of Utrecht on the charge of having caused another person to become insane. Her use of poison was interpreted as sorcery. But it could also happen that in this period crimes that in later centuries merited the harshest possible penalties were punished with less severity. In 1380 for example, a woman in Maastricht who was supposed to have commended herself to the devil 'for profit', was banished.[8] Banishment was certainly not inconsequential, but of course was not as severe as the death penalty.

All in all, there was little consistency in the way that authorities proceeded in witchcraft cases. For such uniformity to become possible, a number of changes were necessary. First of all, witchcraft had to be identified as a crime so heinous that only execution by burning could rectify it. Dutch theologians never incorporated the new demonology of the fifteenth century in their writings. They were more concerned with the counter-magic of laypeople and the distinction between superstition and acknowledged religious practices. As to the demonic pact, they held on to the traditional

---

[7] Johan Wier, *Opera omnia* (Amsterdam, 1660), 94–5; cf. *Witches, Devils, and Doctors in the Renaissance. Johann Weyer. De praestigiis daemonum*, ed. George Mora (Binghamton, NY, 1991), 97–8. The German term for sorcery is *Zauberei*.

[8] Regionaal Historisch Centrum Limburg, Archief van de Indivieze Raad Maastricht, Raadsverdragen nr. 1, fo. 5[r.]

teachings of Augustine and Aquinas. While admitting that superstitious activities could only have effect with demonic assistance, they argued that this resulted in an implicit pact, the implications of which did not need to be known to the humans who performed them. These people should therefore not be prosecuted as if they had willingly concluded a demonic pact, but should instead receive religious instruction and renounce their sinful behaviour. The *Malleus maleficarum*, Heinrich Kramer's manual for witchcraft inquisitors, was almost never quoted in the Netherlands, and when the Brabant Jesuit Martín Del Rio, probably the most influential demonologist of the seventeenth century, published his disquisitions on magic in 1599, the northern provinces had already established themselves as an independent and, at least nominally, Protestant state.

Nevertheless, the interpretation of the demonic pact as the *sine qua non* of all magical activity, notions of the absolute antisocial character of the witch, and execution as the only possible punishment for witchcraft found their way into the minds of secular authorities. In the middle of the fifteenth century a version of the German law book *Sachsenspiegel*, which was heavily influenced by Roman law, was introduced in the Netherlands. This code prescribed death by fire as the penalty for those found guilty of witchcraft.

Another major innovation was the introduction of a new role for the bailiffs and sheriffs. In medieval law it was left to the victim of a crime to lodge a complaint with the legal authorities, who would then treat the matter in a way very similar to modern civil cases. In this accusatory procedure it was the complainant who collected the necessary evidence. In the fifteenth century the Burgundian rulers presented themselves as modern monarchs whose primary goal was to maintain domestic peace and administer justice. This implied that they and their representatives were now expected to take the initiative in the prosecution of criminals. Thus an inquisitorial procedure was introduced, in which the sheriffs and bailiffs had the explicit obligation to initiate criminal trials and to supervise the execution of sentences. Under the old accusatory procedure, complainants who had failed to produce enough evidence could be sentenced to receive the punishment that would otherwise have been meted out to the defendant. As long as this so-called *talio* was in force, legal accusations of witchcraft remained a rare phenomenon, because it was very difficult for individuals to furnish a court with sufficient proof. Together with the inquisitorial procedure, torture was introduced to extract confessions, which in the eyes of jurists was the most reliable form of proof.

However, it took inquisitorial procedure a while to supplant the accusatorial approach, and for several decades both forms of judicial procedure more or less existed side by side. In 1515, for instance, a woman in the eastern town of Kampen, who had lodged a complaint against another woman but had been unable to provide enough evidence, was beheaded after the defendant had managed to resist serious torture. In 1502 the sheriff of Haarlem arrested a woman after a married couple had complained that she had regularly entered their house in the form of a cat and had caused a variety of problems there. The woman was severely tortured but did not confess. Several of the suspect's bones had been crushed on the rack, and the sheriff was now forced to pay the hospital costs himself. He tried to recover the costs from the two people who had made the initial charges, arguing that it was their case and that they were therefore responsible for the financial consequences. But both the Court of Holland and the Great Council of Mechelen, the supreme judicial institution of the Low Countries, ruled against him. As men well trained in Roman law, the justices evidently saw no room for such an appeal to an outdated legal principle.

In another case, which occurred between 1497 and 1503, the bailiff of a country district south-east of Amsterdam arrested two women who, according to their neighbours, were responsible for defaults in the production of butter and paint. Notwithstanding repeated torture—the second time by the executioner of Haarlem, who was also responsible for the serious injuries in the case discussed in the previous paragraph—they persisted in denying their guilt. They therefore had to be released. One of them, who had admitted some petty theft, received for that crime the relatively huge fine of £45 4s.

13.2 New Torture Techniques, Roman Law, and the Responsibilities of the State

The traditional rack was clearly not very effective in this sort of trial. Other, more sophisticated techniques were evidently needed. These were introduced from neighbouring territories at the close of the fifteenth and the beginning of the sixteenth century. In 1491 the council and the bailiff of the town of Zutphen in the eastern part of Gelderland sent a letter to the burgomasters and council of Cologne in which they asked for advice on how to extract confessions from witches. They had submitted three women to fierce torture, and with the help of holy water and other sacred tools they had also attempted to break the power they believed the devil was wielding over these defendants, but all to no avail. The answer of the rulers of Cologne has not been preserved, but it may be assumed that it was quite satisfying. From then on, administrators in Zutphen were themselves often asked by colleagues from other places for advice on such matters. In 1514 Duke Charles of Gelderland hired the executioner of Zutphen to examine witches. The duke explicitly stated that it was his intention to suppress all 'devil worship and witchcraft' in his domains. The sources are very incomplete for this period, but it may be assumed that at that time Gelderland was involved in a large witch-hunt. A year later, in 1515, this executioner was called to Kampen to probe a woman there, but, as already mentioned, he failed to get the desired confession. In 1537 the administrators of the small town of Harderwijk, also in Gelderland, asked Zutphen 'how one should examine' a witch, and Zutphen responded by lending them their executioner. In this case the outcome of the proceedings against the witch is unknown.

The new expertise in prosecuting witches also spread throughout the northern Low Countries via other routes. When three women were arrested in Nijmegen in 1513, the town government invited the executioner of the Duke of Cleves to assist them in the prosecution. It took the executioner only a few days to wring a confession from one of the accused, who was then promptly burnt. The daughter of this accused witch was also tortured but apparently not executed, while the third defendant was released. In 1519 another trial began in Nijmegen. The aldermen first tried to break the arrested woman's will by having her exorcised by a mendicant friar. This clergyman asked the help of another specialist, a certain Doctor Wynant, a layman, who lived in Arnhem, but he too was unsuccessful. Then finally, Master Symon, the executioner of Cleves, was called in, and produced the desired effect. Within a few days the suspect confessed and was therefore sentenced to death. The town incurred additional costs to carry her to the stake, as she could no longer walk as a result of the executioner's handiwork.

By then Symon had built up a reputation as an expert in these matters. When another woman was arrested in Utrecht in 1519, Symon was called in again, and the whole process ended in just a few days with an execution. In the same town and in the same year another woman was put in gaol after she had failed to prove that a man had accused her of witchcraft. She was kept in prison for six years and then released on bail, but a year later she was again imprisoned, together with her daughter and two other women. In this case the town officials decided to hire the executioner from 's-Herto-genbosch, in Brabant, rather than the one from Cleves. The three older women confessed and were executed; the fate of the daughter is unclear. In 1528 the adminis-trators of Utrecht commissioned an envoy with explicit instructions to find out whatever he could about the most effective techniques to test witches. In the course of the 1530s 11 witches, all female, were executed in this town, thereby earning the municipal authorities a reputation for expertise as witch-hunters. When in the autumn of 1541 a woman was arrested in Amsterdam, the local bench first sent two of its members to The Hague to ask the Court of Holland for advice. But the justices answered that they should turn to Utrecht for assistance, which they did. The city secretary and a Franciscan friar then came to Amsterdam. The secretary supervised the interrogations, while the Minorite was entrusted with the necessary exorcism. In January 1542 the supposed witch was indeed executed. At the end of that same year the executioner of Utrecht was employed by the bailiff of another town in Holland; this time he managed to force the culprit to confess that she had concluded a pact with the devil and had committed a series of outrages. Again, seven years later, in 1549, the administrators of Haarlem invited the secretary of Utrecht to assist them in their dealings with three defendants. This time, however, his activities produced no convic-tions. As Haarlem is located very close to the North Sea, the spread of this new practical experience along this specific route had come to an end. In the south-eastern part of Gelderland it had been diffused from nearby Jülich, and in a succession of trials that slowly worked itself through the north-west of the Holy Roman Empire it also reached the northern province of Groningen in the 1540s.

Essentially, this new technique was a mix of physical and psychological torture. In his advice to the authorities of Kampen, in 1515 Duke Charles of Gelderland told them that they should first investigate the reputation of the accused and also that of her parents and children. Then, on a Saturday evening, during a divine service, they should force her to drink holy water mixed with incense, a piece of the priest's stole, and shavings of the Easter candle. During this procedure she should wear a stole and a necklace of 13 balls made of the wax of the Easter candle. If she still refused to confess she should be sprinkled with holy water and only then submitted to torture. As late as 1586 a clerk in the small town of Goedereede in the south-western part of the province of Holland, noted during a trial on the backside of the file: 'Shave all the hair. Put on new clothes sprinkled with holy water. Prepare and force her to consume beer and bread mixed with a lot of sugar, a bit of a consecrated wax candle, a piece of a priest's stole, some consecrated salt.' According to the local bailiff's account the accused were indeed forced to put on long vests and slippers sprinkled with holy water. It is remarkable that these ceremonial, very Catholic ingredients were still in use at a time when Goedereede was already—at least in name—a Protestant town.

About the middle of the sixteenth century a new, probably even more efficacious, technique was introduced. It now became common practice to keep a suspected witch awake for days, sometimes as long as a whole week or even longer. Together with the search for the devil's mark, which actually does not seem to have been performed very often, this combination of keeping the witch awake and forcing her to wear clothes loaded with sacral power, would cause the victims of this psychological torture to lose all sense of reality, as their physical limits were symbolically rescinded and their body invaded. The infliction of severe pain could then be expected to finish the job. It would effectively break the culprit's will, and she would be willing to confess to anything.

A final precondition of the increase in witchcraft prosecutions was a sense of impending danger, the fear that certain individuals were conspiring to destroy society. In the 1520s the Low Countries were hit by a severe outbreak of plague. In 1521 the sheriff of 's-Hertogenbosch in the north of Brabant arrested two men and one woman on the charge that they had been spreading the epidemic by infecting doorposts, thresholds, and wells They were followed two years later by another two women. Three of these five culprits were sentenced to the stake and the other two were released after they had managed to endure torture. These people were all so-called scrubbers, which meant that they nursed sufferers of the plague. The bailiff of a country district in Holland that bordered on Brabant also arrested a scrubber woman, who was then sentenced to be strangled and subsequently burnt. Between 1530 and 1533 this bailiff took yet another woman into custody who, according to her husband, had 'brought death into houses by way of witchcraft'. Plague never became a major issue in trials for witchcraft in the sense that supposed witches were charged with the crime of spreading this disease. But these trials show that in this period the belief was spreading that certain categories of individuals could be blamed collectively for sudden outbreaks of massive disaster. The last case suggests that witchcraft was put on a par with other heinous crimes.

This suggestion finds corroboration in a case that was brought before the aldermen of Dordrecht in 1545. A married couple, Jacob Loenis Smidt and Neelken Aerts, were accused of having eaten meat on Ash Wednesday. Jacob had also manipulated clover leaves for magical purposes, and under torture had confessed that he 'had known his wife in a way that was very abominable and counter nature'. Neelken then also confessed that she had concluded a pact with the devil and had bewitched several people. Consequently, the two were sentenced to be strangled to death and then burnt. The investigation started with what, a few decades earlier, would have been interpreted as minor offences. It would have been left to an ecclesiastical court to deal with the violation of the fast. Magical acts such as Jacob's juggling witch clover would then have been settled with a composition, in other words, with a fine. But such a confined arrangement was now no longer possible. After the couple had been submitted to torture it was discovered that they were also guilty of activities that transgressed the laws of nature. The woman was then forced to admit that she was a witch and had concluded a demonic pact. The confession to having made a pact with the devil also appears to have aggravated the severity of the other crimes. It is remarkable that the man, who had admitted to having performed magic, was not accused of witchcraft but his wife was, even though she had not been involved in her husband's botanic conjuring. This conforms to the pattern in the western provinces in which only women were accused of witchcraft. In eastern regions men could also be accused of such crimes. In the majority of these cases, most of them trials for slander, men were blamed by other men of having wrought havoc, in the shape of wolves, among their cattle and other possessions. In the course of the second quarter of the sixteenth century all the preconditions for an increase of witchcraft trials were thus fulfilled.

From about 1500 until 1608 several hundreds of trials were indeed conducted in the northern Netherlands, but their geographical and chronological distribution was uneven. In the northern province of Groningen the majority of the trials occurred in the 1540s and around 1590. Utrecht saw an upsurge in the 1520s and 1530s, and then again around 1590; Gelderland in the 1540s and 1550s; and Holland in the mid-1560s, in 1585, and in 1591. The real peak occurred in the middle of that century. There was a further upsurge in the 1590s, but on a much smaller scale than in the Holy Roman Empire, France, or the Southern (now Spanish) Netherlands. By that time the intensity of the fear for witches and witchcraft was already decreasing in the Dutch Republic. A real witch-hunt never took place in the territory of the Republic. Table 13.1 shows the numbers of people accused of witchcraft who died in the course of the trials, either because they were sentenced to death, or as a result of heavy torture, or while in prison.

The first thing that catches the eye in Table 13.1 is the differences between the provinces. It should be noted that about a third of the population of the Republic lived in Holland, the most densely populated province of the Union. Around 1500 the northern Low Countries as a whole had a population of somewhat less than one

Table 13.1 Casualties in Witchcraft Trials in the Northern Low Countries

Province	Women	Men	Total
Holland	39	0	39
Zeeland	4	0	4
Utrecht	21	2	23
Friesland	0	0	0
Groningen	46	4	50
Drenthe	1	0	1
Overijssel	1	0	1
Gelderland	43	3	46
Total*	155	9	164

* These are minimum figures. An estimation of a total of about 200 victims within the boundaries of the Dutch Republic seems to be acceptable. If casualties are included from regions that were under Spanish domination at the time of the trials but were later conquered by the Republic (North-Brabant, the northern part of Flanders, the Meuse towns Maastricht, Roermond, and Venlo), an estimated total of 250, perhaps even 300, seems to be acceptable.

million, a number that doubled by the year 1650.[9] This, of course, puts the total of 39 victims in Holland in a different perspective. In comparison to provinces like Utrecht, which had a much smaller population, or Groningen or Gelderland, which were even more sparsely populated, the number of victims in Holland was proportionally quite small. It is also very likely that in Gelderland the total number of executions was considerably higher, since there is evidence that the province experienced a large number of unrecorded trials in the second decade of the sixteenth century. The source material for later decades is also incomplete. Several sources from that period refer to trials that have left no other traces in the records, as, for instance, when it was noted that a trial began because a culprit in another jurisdiction had named the defendant as an accomplice. Many lords in Gelderland enjoyed a considerable degree of autonomy but kept rather untidy archives. Because of these gaps it will probably never be possible to establish a more precise figure. The very high number of casualties in Groningen, the province that, relatively, witnessed the largest number of trials, can also be explained as the result of local jurisdictional autonomy. In this province the town of Groningen held sway over a large part of the countryside, and in these areas trials were a very rare phenomenon. In other districts, however, where this town had little or no direct influence, local officers had much greater judicial latitude.

It is possible that there was more than one casualty in Overijssel, but the total number was probably not much higher. The same holds true for Zeeland where only four witches died. One of these victims, a cunning woman who was burnt in 1541, had been banished a few years earlier from nearby Flanders but had resumed her practice in

[9] Jan de Vries and A. M. van der Woude, *The First Modern Economy: Success, Failure, and Perseverance of the Dutch Economy* (Cambridge, 1997), 50–2.

Flushing.[10] The reason for the total absence of death sentences in Friesland was the strong position of the provincial court there, which was considerably more robust than that of the courts of other provinces. All these courts were staffed with academically trained jurists and, like their Frisian counterparts, these professionals disliked the violation of due process in witchcraft trials. Officially, torture could not be applied at random but only if the indicia, or pieces of circumstantial evidence, amounted to a half-proof, the equivalent of one eyewitness. In witchcraft cases it was usually not possible to produce any other initial evidence besides hearsay, and a bad reputation was in itself insufficient to sentence a defendant to be tortured. The Court of Friesland adhered to these procedural rules closely, not because the justices did not believe that witchcraft was possible, but because they realized that it was impossible to produce acceptable evidence of guilt.

Most authorities displayed little enthusiasm for these trials. It was difficult to produce sufficient evidence, which presented a serious problem in the eyes of professional lawyers, and the trials almost always proved to be very costly. Executioners had to be hired, expert exorcists were engaged before the Reformation, and people had to be employed to keep the defendants awake. Bailiffs and sheriffs leased their offices, and expensive procedures made it difficult for them to pay the expenses of the trials. As most defendants were rather poor, there was little chance that the officers would be able to recover their costs from their confiscated properties.

Defendants whose financial situation was stronger had several possibilities to throw a spanner in the works. They could hire professional lawyers, but that would only be of use in provinces where the administration of justice was well organized. At several locations in Groningen or Gelderland local judges would not feel particularly impressed by such legal assistants. In several provinces it was also possible to address the court and ask for a 'purge', that is, for an official declaration that this person was 'pure, clean and innocent'. The court then summoned its attorney general, the bailiff or the sheriff of the place where the initiator was residing, and the individuals who had tarnished the reputation of that person. By taking such an initiative a woman, when noticing that the local sheriff or bailiff was taking testimony against her, could hope to force the officer to disclose his findings before he was ready to bring them before a judge. If the court then stated that the accused was indeed innocent, she could hope that this would prevent any further criminal procedure. But this strategy did not always work. In a trial in Schiedam in 1585, one of the five witches who were sentenced to the stake had actually been purged three years earlier by the Court of Holland.

In 1591 two women from that same town asked this court to purge them from all suspicion of witchcraft. In their hometown the local bailiff had recently instigated several trials, and they feared that they too would be indicted. It took the court a whole

---

[10] The other three occurred in 1564 and 1565. In Middelburg a woman named Catherine van Wommele, who had been imprisoned, committed suicide in 1564, and a year later two women were burnt in a town nearby called Veere. On Middelburg see W. S. Unger, ed., *Bronnen tot de geschiedenis van Middelburg in den landsheerlijken tijd* (The Hague, 1923), i, 356–7.

year to come to a preliminary decision, and in February 1592 it sentenced the two women to be tortured. From this verdict they appealed to the High Council, and after more than another year of deliberations, the supreme court acquitted them completely in July 1593. The bailiff had produced a large number of incriminating testimonies, but the two women had responded by bringing forward a series of certificates from high-ranking citizens, who all declared that the conduct of the two suspects was beyond reproach. The Council thus created new jurisprudence that made it impossible to use torture in future witchcraft trials.

Only a few weeks after the High Council had delivered this verdict, the aldermen of a tiny town in the north of Holland decided to submit a female suspect to the water test. When she appealed to the Court of Holland against this interlocutory sentence, the justices decided to ask the professors of the faculties of medicine and philosophy of the recently founded University of Leiden for their opinion on the admissibility of evidence produced in this way. The professors answered that the water test was invalid. One of their arguments was strictly medical: women who were suspected of witchcraft, they wrote, were often melancholic. This implied that they tended to be rather fat and consequently would float more easily than other women. Of a more theological nature was their argument that the devil was the great deceiver and could therefore be expected to hide in the water under the suspected woman and then lift her up so that she would not sink. The court found these arguments convincing enough to forbid the administration of this test.

This decision made it virtually impossible to prove that somebody was a witch. A suspect could not be tortured, nor could she be submitted to the water test. Theoretically this jurisprudence was only valid in the provinces of Holland and Zeeland, but the other provinces soon adopted it as well. Hence it was only possible to convict a person for witchcraft if the culprit confessed of her own free will. This actually happened in 1608, when in the small town of Gorcum, located in the south-east of Holland, a woman named Anna Mugge handed herself over to the local magistrates, telling them that she had concluded a pact with the devil and, with his help, had bewitched a number of people. On this evidence she was sentenced to death, which made her the last person in the Dutch Republic to be executed for witchcraft. The Republic thus became the first country in Europe where witchcraft trials came to an end.

13.3 AFTER THE TRIALS

This did not mean, however, that the belief in witchcraft had disappeared. Slander trials in which people who had been accused of witchcraft or of being werewolves sued, to force their slanderers to retract their defamation, took place till the nineteenth century and beyond. But in Holland, the most affluent and powerful province, the nature of these accusations changed after 1600. Whereas witches were previously believed to have operated in all social environments, they now came to be feared almost exclusively in the female domain. They still attacked pregnant women, women in labour, and infants, but withdrew from economic activities that were part of the male domain. In other words, accusations that a woman had stirred up a storm and had caused shipwrecks, or had prevented milk from turning into butter, or had made cattle and other animals sick, became a rare phenomenon.

This limitation of the activities of witches to the female space resulted from the economic boom that was transforming the culture and society of Holland. Men did not stop believing that witchcraft was possible, but came to see it as a minor threat. Unprecedented economic growth created numerous new jobs, so anybody who failed in one type of occupation had ample opportunity to try his luck elsewhere. This development had already begun in the sixteenth century in the coastal provinces, where the soil mainly consisted of peat. Towards the end of the medieval period the ground here had begun sinking below sea level and was becoming ever more watery. Peasants had responded to this by shifting from agriculture to cattle-raising. They now turned into proto-capitalistic entrepreneurs, who produced cheese, butter, and meat for an anonymous market, and purchased things they could not, or were now unwilling, to make themselves from craftsmen who specialized in the production of such commodities.[11]

The sixteenth and seventeenth centuries were a period of high inflation, and everywhere else in Europe real income lagged behind rapidly rising prices. But this was not so in Holland, where wages were actually rising faster than prices. This meant that for considerable sections of the population the quality of life was improving. In other parts of Europe, for instance in nearby Westphalia, famines were often followed by large-scale witch-hunts. But in the Dutch Republic there was always enough food, thanks to the steady importation of Baltic grain. Under such circumstances witchcraft lost much of the menacing force it had formerly possessed. It thus withdrew, so to say, from the male, that is, the public, domain, but was still very present in the female domestic area.

Professional jurists could now reject any formal accusations more easily than in the preceding period. In the mid-sixteenth century it had been a concern in both the higher and the lower levels of society. In 1547, for instance, the itinerant Flemish cunning man Jacob Judoci de Rosa was hired in Amsterdam, first by a man who earned his daily bread by transporting small cargoes in his barge, and then by a brewer; both asked him to help them to get rid of the effects of witchcraft. This brewer was a member of the faction that had lost its power after 1534, and he was convinced that the danger was coming from his wife's godmother. This woman, however, was the mother and mother-in-law of members of the sincere Catholic faction that was now in command. The accusation against this woman therefore had strong political implications and,

---

[11] On this development see Jan de Vries, *The Dutch Rural Economy in the Golden Age* (London, 1974).

in the event, she was, as could be expected, completely exonerated. The cunning man managed to escape but was caught a year later in Gelderland. There he was tried and convicted, with Johan Wier as one of the many people who took an interest in this case.[12] Almost twenty years later, in 1566, at a time when political and religious tensions were rapidly building everywhere in the Low Countries, a daughter of this woman was, in turn, accused of being a witch. This time the orphans of the municipal orphanage, who were believed to be demonically possessed and were roaming the streets, blamed her for causing their afflictions. They climbed the tower of one of the main churches of Amsterdam while shouting that it was this woman, Jacoba Bam, who was responsible for their distress. Jacoba was also fully acquitted. The possessed boys seem to have been manipulated by political opponents of the ruling coterie.

These two incidents show that, at that time, witchcraft was still an issue in the eyes of the elites. But after 1594 leading circles preferred to prevent such accusations from developing into real problems. In this sense there was a fundamental difference between their approach and the attitude of their colleagues in the Spanish Netherlands. After Antwerp had been captured by the Spanish in 1585, the economic system, of which this city had been the centre, collapsed. Soon after, the number of trials and executions began to rise in Brabant and even more so in Flanders. Invariably such proceedings were called to a halt when a town or rural district was conquered by the army of the Republic. In December 1589 five woman and four girls were brought before the aldermen of the town of Breda in Brabant. The trial had not yet been fully concluded when the town was captured by the army of the Republic. The new administrators immediately put an end to these proceedings.

In the autumn of 1595 Brabant was swept by a veritable wave of trials that took the lives of more than twenty alleged witches. It started in the north-eastern corner of this province and reached Brussels a few weeks later. In 1645 a bailiff in that area, which in 1629 had been conquered by the Republic, again tried to instigate a new trial, but his superiors in The Hague decidedly put an end to this endeavour. In the most eastern part of Gelderland, which was under Spanish control until 1635, several women were executed in 1623 and 1626. In towns along the Meuse the fear of witchcraft was so intense that in 1613 a massive panic in the town of Roermond led to the execution of more than forty people. In 1632 this town was seized by the army of the Republic and the trials stopped, but flared up again as soon as it had been recaptured by the Spanish in 1638. These incidents show that the political allegiance of the local authorities was not without importance. But this element certainly was not the decisive factor. It should be emphasized that it was not the Spanish but local rulers who instigated these trials.

---

[12] Wier, *Opera omnia*, 465; *Witches, Devils, and Doctors*, 484.

13.4 THE DECLINE OF DEMONIC POWER

The mental outlook of these local administrators was at least as important as their political and religious sympathies. In the north the elites no longer believed in the reality of diabolical conspiracies. In the south Del Rio was now one of the chief advocates of the trials. In the Republic no such figure came forward. Indeed, it was quite the opposite—authors of almost all religious denominations agreed that witchcraft was a matter of little importance or even that it did not exist at all. In 1592 the Catholic priest Cornelius Loos (1545–1595), who had been forced to flee his hometown in Holland, wrote a treatise in which he argued that the idea that witches should be prosecuted was nothing but a chimera which had been planted by the devil in order to distract attention from his real helpers, the heretical Protestants.[13] In 1659, at a time when the numbers of slander trials again reached a peak in Holland, the Haarlem Mennonite Abraham Palingh published a book attempting to dissuade the authorities from taking witchcraft accusations seriously once again. In his eyes, just as in those of other Mennonites, the devil was incapable of assuming an anthropomorphic appearance, let alone concluding pacts with humans or having sex with them. Spiritualism, the conviction that man could only find God deep within himself and that it was pointless to prosecute people for religious reasons because everybody had the right to develop his contact with God individually, was close to the concepts of the Mennonites. For spiritualists the devil was more an abstract principle of evil than an independent force. Johan Wier had been deeply inspired by the thought of spiritualist prophets like David Joris, Hendrik Niclaes, and his own brother, Matthias.[14] He argued that the devil was unable to change the course of nature, but was such a clever deceiver that many people believed that, with his help, they were able to perform witchcraft. Such people were not to be prosecuted but be treated by good physicians, for in reality they were melancholics whose minds had been clouded by a surplus of black bile. His arguments were adopted by the Leiden professors when they were consulted by the Court of Holland. The rector at that time was Johannes Heurnius, who was also one of the professors of medicine, and there are some indications that he was in close contact with spiritualists. It is more than probable that the president of the High Council, the

---

[13] In 1593 the printing of his *De vera et falsa magia* (On True and False Magic) was suppressed on the orders of papal nuncio Frangipani, and Loos was forced to sign a recantation. In 1886 a manuscript of the first part of his treatise was retrieved by George Lincoln Burr in Trier, and two years later a printed version of the same chapters was discovered in Cologne. See, for a close analysis of Loos' argument, P. C. van der Eerden, 'Cornelius Loos und *magia falsa*', in Hartmut Lehmann and Otto Ulbricht, eds, *Vom Unfug des Hexen-Process: Gegner der Hexenverfolgungen von Johann Weyer bis Friedrich Spee* (Wiesbaden, 1992), 139–60.

[14] On this see Hans de Waardt, 'Witchcraft, Spiritualism, and Medicine: The Religious Convictions of Johan Wier', *Sixteenth Century Journal*, 42 (2011), 369–91. See also Hans de Waardt, '"Lightning strikes, wherever ire dwells with power": Johan Wier on Anger as an Illness', in Yasmin Haskell, ed., *Diseases of the Imagination and Imaginary Disease in the Early Modern Period* (Turnhout, 2011), 261–74.

court that suppressed the use of torture in witchcraft trials, actively participated in the activities of Hendrik Niclaes' Family of Love.

The last person to be mentioned in this context is Balthasar Bekker (1634–1698). In 1692 the Reformed Synod of the northern half of the province of Holland banned Bekker from his pastoral duties after he had published his *De betooverde wereld* (*The Bewitched World*). However, the burgomasters of Amsterdam, the city where he was then employed, continued to pay his wages until he died, six years later. It was not so much his argument that witchcraft was impossible or that the demonic pact could not have any real effect that brought him the ultimate wrath of his fellow ministers. It was his attempt to found his arguments on a Cartesian line of reasoning. Traditional, that is, Aristotelian, Reformed theologians were perceiving the new philosophy of Descartes, who had composed and published all his major works in the Republic, as a menace. In the 1670s the pantheism of Spinoza only added to their certainty that true religion was now under serious threat. For many of them Bekker, this avowed Cartesian, was the embodiment of this danger, but what made matters worse, he was one of them. Thus the search for the human assistants of the devil now turned into a perhaps more modern pursuit of unwelcome innovators.

13.5 Possibilities for Further Research

Much research has already been done on the history of witchcraft in the Netherlands. But the archives of some provinces have not been explored in depth (Utrecht, Overijssel, North-Brabant, Limburg). Thematic approaches could also prove to be rewarding. Witchcraft was only at specific times a major issue in the Netherlands, yet the production of paintings and other images in which witchcraft was portrayed was indeed massive. A balanced analysis of this dichotomy could throw new light on the ways in which the Dutch coped with witchcraft and magic. A similar observation can be made regarding the religious aspects. Reformed ministers repeatedly discussed the nature and range of demonic power. The commotion that Bekker caused with his book is only one example, albeit the most conspicuous, of this divergence. A large part of the population of Amsterdam was Jewish, both Sephardic and Ashkenazic, but very little is known of their ideas and concerns regarding witchcraft.

Further Reading

Blécourt, Willem de, *Termen van toverij: De veranderende betekenis van toverij in Noordoost-Nederland tussen de zestiende en de twintigste eeuw* (Nijmegen, 1990).

Blécourt, Willem de, 'Mangels Beweisen: Über das Ende der Verfolgung von Zauberinnen in Niederländisch und Spanisch Geldern 1590–1640', in Sönke Lorenz and Dieter R. Bauer, eds, *Das Ende der Hexenverfolgung* (Stuttgart, 1995), 77–95.

Blécourt, Willem de and Waardt, Hans de, 'De regels van het recht. Aantekeningen over de rol van het Gelderse Hof bij de procesvorming inzake toverij, 1543–1620', *Bijdragen en mededeelingen Gelre*, 80 (1989), 24–51.

Blécourt, Willem de and Waardt, Hans de, 'Das Vordringen der Zaubereiverfolgungen in die Niederlande: Rhein, Maas und Schelde entlang', in Andreas Blauert, ed., *Ketzer, Zauberer, Hexen: die Anfänge der europäischen Hexenverfolgungen* (Frankfurt, 1990), 182–216.

Fix, Andrew C., *Fallen Angels: Balthasar Bekker, Spirit Belief, and Confessionalism in the Seventeenth Century Dutch Republic* (Dordrecht, 1999).

Gijswijt-Hofstra, Marijke and Frijhoff, Willem, eds, *Witchcraft in the Netherlands: From the Fourteenth to the Twentieth Century* (Rotterdam, 1991).

Waardt, Hans de, *Toverij en samenleving: Holland 1500–1800* (The Hague, 1991).

Waardt, Hans de, 'Verlöschen und Entfachen der Scheiterhaufen: Holland und Brabant in den 1590er Jahren', in Herbert Eiden and Rita Voltmer, eds, *Hexenprozesee und Gerichtspraxis* (Trier, 2002), 315–29.

Waite, Gary K., '"Man is a Devil to Himself": David Joris and the Rise of a Sceptical Tradition Towards the Devil in the Early Modern Netherlands, 1540–1600', *Nederlands Archief voor Kerkgeschiedenis*, 75 (1995), 1–30.

CHAPTER 14

....

WITCHCRAFT
PROSECUTIONS IN
ITALY

....

TAMAR HERZIG

ITALY only became a nation-state in the nineteenth century, and although parts of the peninsula were subject to different political powers in the pre-modern era, this chapter deals with the prosecution of witchcraft in the regions that form part of present-day Italy, excluding Sicily. In Italy, the terminology used when referring to individuals suspected of sorcery varied according to gender, with the term 'witch' (*strega*) denoting women guilty of magical crimes, and 'magician' (*mago*), 'enchanter', or 'necromancer' designating their male counterparts. As Anne Jacobson Schutte has shown, although Italian (female) 'witches' and (male) 'magicians' usually belonged to distinct social groups, they pursued similar ends: causing or solving health problems, obtaining riches or sexual favours, and gaining knowledge of secret or future events. Since the late sixteenth century, the prosecution of diabolic witch-craft and *maleficium* (harmful magic) in Italy formed part of a broader attack on 'superstitious' practices, which targeted female as well as male practitioners of the magical arts.[1] Hence, this chapter conceives of witchcraft in a broad sense, and the term 'witch' is used to denote both women and men prosecuted for meddling in illicit magic.

---

[1] Anne Jacobson Schutte, 'I processi dell'Inquisizione veneziana nel Seicento: La femminilizzazione dell'eresia', in Andrea Del Col and Giovanna Paolin, eds, *L'inquisizione Romana in Italia nell'Età moderna: Archivi, problemi di metodo e nuove ricerche* (Rome, 1991), 162; Peter Burke, 'Witchcraft and Magic in Renaissance Italy: Gianfrancesco Pico and his *Strix*', in Sydney Anglo, ed., *The Damned Art: Essays in the Literature of Witchcraft* (London, 1977), 32–4.

14.1 WITCH-HUNTING IN
RENAISSANCE ITALY

Perhaps the most striking aspect of Italian witchcraft trials is that their bloodiest phase occurred in the period generally associated with the Italian Renaissance. As Gene Brucker has demonstrated, while humanist values triumphed in the urban centres of early Renaissance culture, their courts began prosecuting witches. The preaching of Observant Franciscan friars such as Bernardino of Siena (d.1444) often provoked prosecutions. Even though these preachers did not fully adhere to the notion of diabolic witchcraft as elaborated north of the Alps, they vehemently opposed 'superstitious' practices and advocated the harsh punishment of sorcerers. From the late fourteenth until the mid-fifteenth century, witchcraft scares ending with capital punishment broke out in Milan (in 1385 and 1390), Venice (1422), Rome (c.1420 and 1426), Florence (1427), Todi (1428), Perugia (in 1433, 1437, and 1446), and in Alpine regions such as Val d'Aosta (in 1419, 1428–30, 1434–7, 1445–9), Val d'Adige (1433), and Morbegno (1438).[2]

The repression of witchcraft intensified during the second half of the fifteenth century. Witches were burned in Perugia (in 1455 and 1456), Ferrara (1454), Tortona (1456), Val d'Aosta (in 1460–2, 1466, 1484, 1493), Salussola (1479), Mantua (1493–4), and Milan (in 1457 and 1472), as well as in the region of Como (in 1456, 1460–82, 1487), in Tollegno (1470), and in Canavese (in 1472 and 1474–5). Mass trials ended with multiple capital punishments in Cuneo (1477), in the region of Pavia (1479), in the Valtellina (in 1460, 1483, and 1485), in Peveragno (in 1485 and 1489), in Carignano (1493–4), and in Valcamonica in 1455 (Venetian officials probably prevented the execution of convicted witches in Valcamonica in 1485–7).

Witch prosecutions reached their climax during the Italian Wars (1494–1530). In these years Italian witch-hunters, including the philosopher Giovanni Francesco Pico (1469–1533), count of Mirandola, published books justifying the harsh punishment of witches, while a few sceptics began criticizing the witch-hunts. In northern Italy, witches were burned in Rifreddo and Gambasca (1494–5), Bologna (in 1498, 1508, and 1509), Brescia (in 1499 and 1518), Val di Fiemme (1501), Piacenza (1502–3), Mantua (in 1505 and 1507), Parma (1510), Milan (in 1515 and 1519), Peveragno (1512–13), Monza

---

[2] Gene A. Brucker, 'Sorcery in Early Renaissance Florence', *Studies in the Renaissance*, 10 (1963), 7–24; Franco Cardini, 'La predicazione popolare alle origini della caccia alle streghe', in M. Cucco and P. A. Rossi, eds, *La strega, il teologo, lo scienziato* (Genoa, 1986), 277–93; Franco Mormando, *The Preacher's Demons: Bernardino of Siena and the Social Underworld of Early Renaissance Italy* (Chicago, 1999), 52–108; Marina Montesano, *'Supra acqua et supra ad vento': 'Superstizioni', maleficia e incantamenta nei predicatori francescani osservanti (Italia, sec. XV)* (Rome, 1999), 97–152; Montesano, 'Milan', in Richard M. Golden, ed., *Encyclopedia of Witchcraft: The Western Tradition* [hereafter *EW*], 4 vols (Santa Barbara, CA, 2006), iii, 764; Silvia Bertolin and Ezio Emerico Gerbore, eds, *La stregoneria nella Valle d'Aosta medievale* (Quart, 2003), 36–60; Andrea Del Col, *L'Inquisizione in Italia: Dal XII al XXI secolo* (Milan, 2006), 195–7.

(1520), and Venegono Superiore (1520). Documented witch panics, ending with at least ten deaths, occurred in Val di Fiemme (1504–5), in the region of Como (in 1512–17 and 1519–22), in the Valcamonica (in 1510–12, 1516–17, and 1518–21), in Suno (1519), in the region of Valtellina (1523), and in Mirandola (1522–5). Isolated executions also took place in central Italy: in Perugia (1501), Siena (1507–8), and Rome, where at least three witches were executed between 1505 and 1524. In Fiano Romano in 1528, the female healer Bellezza Orsini evaded execution only by committing suicide. Small panics also broke out in southern Italy, with three witches executed in the kingdom of Naples in 1506.[3]

Before 1542, only about ten Italian witchcraft trials were prosecuted by episcopal tribunals, and about thirty took place in secular courts; all others were conducted by papal inquisitors. If, in the early fifteenth century, Franciscan preachers contributed to spreading the fear of witchcraft, from the second half of this century Dominican inquisitors, notably members of the Observant Congregation of Lombardy, were largely responsible for major witchcraft prosecutions. Scholars have recently focused their attention on these inquisitors, trying to marry their witch-hunting with their other religious concerns.[4]

Much of the documentation concerning witchcraft trials conducted before 1542 was destroyed in the eighteenth and nineteenth centuries, but some of the trials are referred to in other sources: chronicles, letters, sermons, and demonological treatises. The problems inherent in relying on such sources become clear when considering what was probably the largest witch-hunt conducted by papal inquisitors in Italian lands, which broke out in the bishopric of Como in the early sixteenth century. Witch-hunting in Como had begun in the 1480s, with the burning of perhaps as many as forty-one witches. Prosecutions were renewed three decades later, peaking in 1512–17. The records of their proceedings were burned in 1782, when Emperor Joseph II suspended the inquisitorial tribunal in Como.

One sixteenth-century chronicler describes the burning of three hundred women in Como in 1514. The jurist Andrea Alciati (1492–1550), who reportedly consulted the trial records, asserted in 1516 that the inquisitor in Como had already sent more than one hundred women to the stake and continued to pursue witches. However, in 1517 the Dominican Isidoro Isolani (c.1475–1528) proudly reported that more than sixty witches

    [3] Alessandro Luzio and Rodolfo Renier, 'La coltura e le relazioni letterarie d'Isabella d'Este ed Elisabetta Gonzaga', *Giornale storico della letteratura italiana*, 38 (1901), 53; Del Col, *L'Inquisizione in Italia*, 197–211; Albano Biondi, 'Gianfrancesco Pico e la repressione della stregoneria: Qualche novità sui processi Mirandolesi del 1522–1523', in Giordano Bertuzzi, ed., *Mirandola e le terre del basso corso del Secchia dal Medioevo all'età contemporanea* (Modena, 1984), i, 331–49; Paolo Potrone, 'Naples', in *EW*, iii, 801; Michael Tavuzzi, *Renaissance Inquisitors: Dominican Inquisitors and Inquisitorial Districts in Northern Italy, 1474–1527* (Leiden, 2007), 253–8; Del Col, 'L'attività dell'Inquisizione nell'Italia moderna: Un bilancio complessivo', in *Caccia alle streghe in Italia tra XIV e XVII secolo: Atti del Convegno nazionale di Studi storico-antropologici, Triora, 22–24 Ottobre 2004* (Bolzano, 2007), 392–3.

    [4] Tavuzzi, *Renaissance Inquisitors*, 149–208; Tamar Herzig, 'Heinrich Kramer e la caccia alle streghe in Italia', in Dinora Corsi and Matteo Duni, eds, *'Non lasciar vivere la malefica': Le streghe nei trattati e nei processi (secoli XIV–XVII)* [hereafter *NLV*] (Florence, 2008), 167–96.

convicted by the inquisitor in the bishopric of Como had been burned around 1514. The Dominican historian Leandro Alberti (c.1479–1552) affirmed in 1517 that the inquisitor of Como and his vicars had just more than thirty culprits burned. Six years later, Alberti's confrere Bartolomeo Spina (c.1475–1546) asserted that the inquisitor and his vicars had proceeded against one thousand witches, sending over a hundred witches to the stake each year. The discrepancies among the sources are too great to arrive at any consensus, and estimates of the number of executions in Como in 1512–17 range from about thirty to several hundreds.

In the absence of the actual records of trials in pre-Tridentine Italy, then, our knowledge is only fragmentary, but obviously more trials took place, and more witches were burned, than the numbers attested by extant documentation. Relying on the conservative approximation of sixty burnings for the Como trials, Andrea Del Col proposes the figure of between 251 and 269 executions for the era preceding 1542, estimating the number of all witchcraft trials conducted in this period as between 639 and 693. Michael Tavuzzi, however, argues that the number of executions in witchcraft trials conducted only by Dominican inquisitors in northern Italy alone between 1450 and 1525 must have totalled several hundreds. To these should be added the death sentences in trials conducted by inquisitors in northern Italy before 1450 and from 1525 to 1541; in those held elsewhere in the peninsula throughout the fifteenth and early sixteenth centuries; and in the trials conducted by secular magistrates and episcopal courts in the north between 1450 and 1525. All these probably add up to a number of executions significantly higher than 269, in keeping with Wolfgang Behringer's view of the scope of witch-hunting in Renaissance Italy, which Behringer equates with the intensity of prosecutions in Switzerland and France during that period.[5]

The cessation of devastating warfare in Italian lands around 1530 was followed by a decline in burnings, but did not bring witchcraft trials to an end. Proceedings leading to death sentences continued to occur until mid-century, not only in the Alpine regions of Val d'Aosta (in 1532 and 1537) and Trentino (1540), but also in Pienza (1540) and San Miniato (1540) in central Italy. Even in the city of Bologna—whose university boasted a distinguished faculty of law in which Alciati, an early critic of witch-hunting, was teaching during the 1530s—Marta of Budrio was burned for witchcraft in 1531, and subsequent executions occurred in 1543, 1545, and 1549. Torture was employed during trials in Modena (1539) and Rome (1540), and there and elsewhere convicted witches occasionally received harsh punishments such as exile or prolonged imprisonment.[6]

---

[5] Adriano Prosperi, *Tribunali della coscienza: Inquisitori, confessori, missionari* (rev. edn, Turin, 2009), 388; Rainer Decker, *Witchcraft and the Papacy: An Account Drawing on the Formerly Secret Records of the Roman Inquisition*, tr. H. C. Erik Midelfort (Charlottesville, VA, 2008), 75–6, 212, 223 n. 3; Del Col, 'L'attività', 392–4. Cf. Tavuzzi, *Renaissance Inquisitors*, 197–8, 253–8; Wolfgang Behringer, *Witches and Witch-Hunts: A Global History* (Cambridge, 2004), 78–9, 150.

[6] Guido Dall'Olio, 'Tribunali vescovili, inquisizione romana e stregoneria: I processi bolognesi del 1559', in Adriano Prosperi, ed., *Il piacere del testo: Saggi e studi per Albano Biondi*, 2 vols (Rome, 2001), i, 66–67 nn. 7–9; Dall'Olio, 'Leandro Alberti, inquisitore e mediatore', in Massimo Donattini, ed., *L'Italia dell'inquisitore: Storia e geografia dell'Italia del Cinquecento nella 'Descrittione' di Leandro Alberti*

14.2 THE ROMAN INQUISITION AND WITCHCRAFT

With the bull *Licet ab initio* (It is Allowed from the Beginning) promulgated in 1542, Pope Paul III (r. 1534–1549) instituted the Congregation of the Holy Office of the Inquisition, known as the Roman Inquisition. Unlike its medieval predecessors, the Roman Inquisition was an organ of the Curia, and was presided over by the pope. A strong, centralized institution, it reached beyond the Papal States and assumed responsibility for the prosecution of all types of heresy. These included witchcraft, which theologians since the late Middle Ages had defined as a heresy involving apostasy from the faith and devil worship.

From the mid-sixteenth century, the Roman Inquisition was active throughout the central and northern Italian states, with the exception of the republic of Lucca, which established its own inquisitorial office to curb the spread of heresy. In the Spanish-ruled duchy of Milan and in the republic of Venice, representatives of the state became part of the Inquisition's tribunals. In the kingdom of Naples, which belonged to the Spanish Crown, two inquisitorial tribunals were operating by the late sixteenth century: one presided over by the Neapolitan bishop, and the other headed by a delegate of the Holy Office in Rome.[7]

Only five complete archives (Venice, Modena, Siena, Naples, and Aquileia) of the original forty-five provincial tribunals in Italy proper have survived intact. Moreover, much of the material originally preserved in the central archive of the Holy Office was lost or destroyed.[8] This archive, whose name was changed to *Archivio della Congregazione per la Dottrina della Fede* (hereafter ACDF) after the Second Vatican Council, was opened to scholars in 1998; their findings now enable us to make the following observations.

During the first years following its establishment, the Roman Inquisition was mainly concerned with curtailing Protestantism and did not invest significant efforts in devising a defined policy towards witchcraft. However, as Guido Dall'Olio observes, even in this early phase the Congregation of the Holy Office occasionally intervened in cases of magic involving the invocation of demons, abuse of sacraments, or apostasy. In 1559 Pope Paul IV (r. 1555–1559), who headed the Congregation, authorized the execution of four women condemned as witches in Bologna, even though they were

(Bologna, 2007), 30–31 n. 21; Giacomo Moro, 'Menzogna o sortilegio? Giovan Battista Pallavicino, Lope Hurtado de Mendoza e un'accusa di stregoneria nella Roma Farnesiana (1540)', *Rivista di storia e letteratura religiosa* [hereafter *RSLR*], 28 (1992), 215–75; Matteo Duni, *Under the Devil's Spell: Witches, Sorcerers, and the Inquisition in Renaissance Italy* (Florence, 2007), 31–2, 118–23.

[7] Giovanni Romeo, 'Una città, due inquisizioni: l'anomalia del Sant'Ufficio a Napoli nel tardo '500', *RSLR*, 24 (1988), 42–67; Prosperi, *L'inquisizione Romana: Letture e ricerche* (Rome, 2003), 60–3.

[8] John Tedeschi, *The Prosecution of Heresy: Collected Studies on the Inquisition in Early Modern Italy* (Binghamton, NY, 1991), 23–45.

first-time, penitent heretics. This decision broke with established inquisitorial tradition, and was opposed by some members of the Congregation, who favoured less
severe punishments for witchcraft.[9]

In 1569, the more moderate cardinal-inquisitors had the upper hand, when the
Congregation refused to confirm the death sentences of seven women from Lecco
who had confessed to participating in the witches' sabbath and causing the death of
children. One of the accused died as a result of her incarceration, but the Congregation
prevented the execution of six others, notwithstanding pressure from Carlo Borromeo
(1538–1584), archbishop of Milan, who wished to secure their death. In subsequent
years, an ever growing number of cardinal-inquisitors came to regard the pursuit of
witchcraft accusations as a potential source of trouble, which could arouse opposition
to the Holy Office. Nonetheless, scattered witchcraft cases tried by inquisitorial,
episcopal, and secular courts led to capital punishments in Rome (1559 and 1572),
Siena (1569), Lucca (1571), and Bologna (1577 and 1579).[10]

After the defeat of evangelical currents in the first four decades of the Inquisition's
activity 'superstition', namely unorthodox rituals of healing or predicting the future,
became the Holy Office's main concern. In 1586 Sixtus V (r. 1585–90), a former
Franciscan inquisitor, issued a bull condemning a long list of popular practices,
including astrology and unauthorized invocations of saints (previously deemed harmless), as superstitious. In another bull of 1587, Sixtus charged inquisitors with punishing
'simple' spells, formerly prosecuted in episcopal courts. The bulls signalled a hardening
of papal policy against unorthodox practices. They also expanded the jurisdiction of the
Roman Inquisition—hitherto limited to cases of diabolic witchcraft and magical
practices involving the invocation of demons—over all forms of magic, which were
now regarded as 'savouring of heresy'.

Sixtus V's bulls led to a remarkable rise in the number of trials that inquisitorial
tribunals conducted against practitioners of magic. Thus, whereas cases of magic
constituted a small part of the proceedings that the Venetian tribunal had conducted
before the mid-1580s, around 1586 such trials amounted to one-third of all its prosecutions. From the end of the sixteenth century until 1631, sorcery cases comprised one half
of inquisitorial trials in Venice, and in the early eighteenth century illicit magic made
up almost 70 per cent of inquisitorial trials. The Inquisition's tribunal in Modena
conforms to a similar pattern, with a marked increase in the number of magic cases
tried after the 1580s, and a continual rise after 1600. In Naples, magic constituted over
40 per cent of all trial procedures by the Inquisition's court in the seventeenth century,
and about 60 per cent of all cases in the early eighteenth century.[11] The overall number

---

[9] Dall'Olio, 'Tribunali', 63–82.

[10] Vincenzo Lavenia, '"Anticamente di misto foro": Inquisizione, stati e delitti di stregoneria nella
prima età moderna', in Giovanna Paolin, ed., *Inquisizioni: Percorsi di ricerca* (Trieste, 2001), 41–53;
Decker, *Witchcraft*, 96–8.

[11] William Monter and John Tedeschi, 'Toward a Statistical Profile of the Italian Inquisitions,
Sixteenth to Eighteenth Centuries', in Tedeschi, *Prosecution*, 94–6; Ruth Martin, *Witchcraft and the
Inquisition in Venice, 1550–1650* (Oxford, 1989), 215–18; Duni, *Under the Devil's Spell*, 34.

of trials for magic and witchcraft prosecuted by tribunals of the Roman Inquisition before the end of the eighteenth century is estimated as between 22,000 and 33,000, with the total number of denunciations that did not lead to full-blown trials rising to 66,000, and possibly even 100,000.[12]

As William Monter and John Tedeschi have shown, since the late sixteenth century the Roman Inquisition became much more concerned with magic and witchcraft than its Spanish and Portuguese counterparts ever were. However, the Roman Inquisition's systematic prosecution of divination, love magic, magical healing, magical treasure hunting, and, more rarely, *maleficium*, often ended with 'light' punishments. These included whipping through the streets or other forms of public humiliation, house arrest, or confinement to a geographical area such as one's village or even an entire city. In grave cases and those of repeated offenders, the condemned were exiled, imprisoned, or, in severe cases, sent to the galleys. Death penalties were usually reserved for cases of explicit demonic magic, often performed by clerical necromancers, and to magical practitioners convicted of misusing the sacraments.[13] Rainer Decker proposes that the overall number of witch executions ordered by the Holy Office from 1542 through the eighteenth century was below three hundred, and Del Col estimates that trials for magic conducted by inquisitorial tribunals resulted with at least 240, but perhaps as many as 350, executions.[14]

Paradoxically, about the time Sixtus V's bulls called for eradicating all magical practices, the Holy Office was adopting an increasingly careful attitude towards diabolic witchcraft. Already, in 1582, the Congregation had punished a judge responsible for the abuse of alleged witches in Parano (near Orvieto), following the death of two accused women and the rape of a third. The protests of Cardinal Giulio Antonio Santori (1532–1602), a leading figure in the Congregation, against the violation of judicial norms in the proceedings against witches from the Ligurian village of Triora did not prevent the death of at least eight women in 1588, due to torture and to the harsh conditions of their incarceration. Nonetheless, following the death of another suspect in the Inquisition's jail in Naples in 1588, Santori's intervention led to the freeing of two other women accused of participating in the witches' sabbath.

Santori instructed the representative of the Holy Office in Naples to dismiss the accusations of suspects who provided names of accomplices reportedly seen at the sabbath. His insistence that proceedings against witches be based on sufficient judicial grounds, proving the connection between cases of sickness or death and malevolent spells, signals what Giovanni Romeo has called the Roman Inquisition's 'turn to moderation'.[15] Although, like all other European court systems, inquisitorial tribunals

---

[12] Del Col, 'L'attività', 392.

[13] Monter and Tedeschi, 'Toward a Statistical Profile', 102; Tedeschi, 'Inquisitorial Law and the Witch', in Bengt Ankarloo and Gustav Henningsen, eds, *Early Modern European Witchcraft: Centres and Peripheries* (Oxford, 1990), 104–15; Dall'Olio, 'Tribunali', 67 n. 9.

[14] Del Col, 'L'attività', 392; Decker, *Witchcraft*, 212–13.

[15] Claudio Copo and Gian Maria Panizza, 'La pace impossibile: Indagini ed ipotesi per una ricerca sulle accuse di stregoneria a Triora (1587–1590)', *RSLR*, 26 (1990), 34–74; Giovanni Romeo, *Inquisitori, esorcisti e streghe nell'Italia della Controriforma* (Florence, 1990), 3–29.

continued to rely on the use of torture well into the seventeenth century, after 1588 the Holy Office instructed its tribunals to disregard confessions concerning fellow participants in diabolical gatherings. In 1589 the Holy Office reprimanded the vicar of the inquisitor of Florence for subjecting three suspected witches from Pistoia to undue torture. In 1594, its intervention facilitated the liberation of an accused witch from San Miniato, who had confessed under torture to participating in the sabbath and copulating with the devil.[16]

In 1593, a witchcraft panic broke out in the town of Bitonto. Two possessed women claimed to have participated in the witches' sabbath, and their admissions led to the arrest of supposed accomplices. Their trials were conducted by the local bishop and archdeacon, who turned to the Congregation of the Holy Office for advice. By the time the Congregation intervened, one accused witch had died due to severe torture; another was killed in jail in unclear circumstances; a third had a miscarriage during her interrogation; and one man suffered fatal injuries while running away after being denounced as a witch. Only when the demoniacs were finally summoned to Rome did Clement VIII (r. 1592–1605) order the release of all remaining suspects. The Congregation had the bishop and archdeacon who had conducted the trials banished from Bitonto, yet in spite of the severity of their transgressions they were allowed to return by 1601, and took up their offices again.[17]

During the 1620s, the Congregation began sending inquisitorial tribunals the *Instructio pro formandis processibus in causis strigum, sortilegiorum et maleficiorum* (Instruction for Proceeding with Cases of Witchcraft, Sorcery, and Harmful Magic). This manual summarized the Congregation's attitude, as manifested in its dealing with cases of witchcraft in the preceding half century. In 1625 parts of the *Instruction* appeared in Italian translation in Eliseo Masini's *Sacro Arsenale* (Sacred Arsenal). The full text of the *Instructio* was first published as an official curial statement only in 1657, perhaps because the Congregation feared exacerbating its conflicts with secular authorities, which accused its tribunals of treating witches too leniently.

The *Instructio* stressed the need to refrain from prosecuting individuals denounced by others, who claimed to have seen them at the sabbath. It prohibited suggestive questioning and excessive torture, and forbade inquisitors to regard defendants' failure to cry as a proof of their culpability, or to shave their bodies in search of witches' marks. The *Instructio* insisted on the need to consult physicians and establish material evidence for the perpetration of crimes involving *maleficium*. It also prohibited the pursuit of witchcraft accusations made by exorcists, because of their notoriety for assuming ubiquitous demonic activity.

The *Instructio* circulated on both sides of the Alps, but it is difficult to detect its impact on actual prosecutions. Italian secular judges who were familiar with the *Instructio* or with Masini's manual did not necessarily adhere to the judicial caution

---

[16] Franco Cardini, ed., *Gostanza, la strega di San Miniato: Processo a una guaritrice nella Toscana medicea* (Rome-Bari, 1989); Tedeschi, 'Inquisitorial Law', 99.

[17] Romeo, *Inquisitori*, 155–9; Decker, *Witchcraft*, 96–111.

that they called for.[18] Indeed, in 1647 judges in Friuli, who had borrowed a copy of Masini's book from a local inquisitorial vicar, nonetheless relied on the admissions of an accused witch to arrest accomplices that she claimed to have seen at the sabbath.[19]

Strikingly, at about the same time that the Congregation began dispatching manuscripts of the *Instructio* to its tribunals, the pope who headed it, Gregory XV (r. 1621–23), expressed a much harsher view of witchcraft. In his 1623 bull *Omnipotentis Dei* (Of Omnipotent God), Gregory argued that witches convicted at inquisitorial tribunals of causing death by means of *maleficium* should be turned over to the secular arm for execution, even if they were first-time, repentant heretics. If their spells led solely to illness or damaged crops or domestic animals, witches should be punished by life imprisonment.

Gregory's motives for issuing a bull that violated inquisitorial tradition concerning first-time offenders remain unclear. Historians also disagree on whether the cardinal-inquisitors of the Holy Office supported the promulgation of the bull, and on whether the propagation of the *Instructio* was meant to mitigate its severity.[20] In any case, the apparent ambiguity in Church policy concerning witchcraft may help to explain why the Congregation refrained from taking action against judges outside its jurisdiction who did not comply with the guidelines of the *Instructio*.

This brings us to the issue of trials conducted by secular or episcopal courts, which continued to operate in the Italian peninsula after the establishment of the Roman Inquisition. Since 1587, the authority of the tribunals of the Holy Office had gained precedence over all other courts in the prosecution of magic. Nonetheless, civil magistrates continued to claim jurisdiction over cases involving *maleficia*, which had traditionally been considered *mixti fori* (i.e. crimes within the jurisdiction of either lay or ecclesiastical authorities), long after the promulgation of Gregory XV's bull.

Recent studies indicate that secular tribunals continued to sentence witches to death well into the eighteenth century.[21] Thirty-two documented witchcraft cases tried by civil magistrates in post-Tridentine Italy ended with executions. Dozens of other known trials, mainly in the Alpine valleys, probably resulted in numerous executions. Until the records of trials by civil courts are studied systematically, estimates of the scope of Italian witch prosecutions remain largely hypothetical.

Taking into account the known trials conducted by *all* types of courts in the late sixteenth and seventeenth centuries, it becomes clear that witchcraft panics broke out in Alpine regions such as Val di Fassa (in 1573, 1627–31, and 1643–4), Nogaredo (1646–7), Val di Non (1611–15), and the Valtellina (in the 1670s), as well as in Turin (1619), leading to multiple deaths. Trials ending with individual executions occurred in

[18] Tedeschi, *Prosecution*, 212–13; Lavenia, '"Anticamente"', 70–80.

[19] Luigi De Biasio, 'Esecuzioni capitali contro streghe nel Friuli orientale alla metà del secolo XVII', *Memorie storiche forogiuliesi*, 58 (1978), 147–58.

[20] Tedeschi, *Prosecution*, 216 n. 6, 225 n. 57; Prosperi, *Tribunali*, 400–11; Del Col, *L'Inquisizione in Italia*, 589–90; Giovanni Romeo, 'Inquisizione, Chiesa e stregoneria nell'Italia della Controriforma: Nuove ipotesi', in *NLV*, 57–62.

[21] Lavenia, '"Anticamente"', 35–80; Romeo, 'Inquisizione', 53–64.

Rome (in 1587, 1630, 1635), Velletri (1587), Perugia (1590), Mantua (in 1595 and 1600), Florence (1612), Venice (1617), Padua (1629), in the region of Friuli (1647), and on repeated occasions in Milan (in 1590–1610, 1619–20, 1641, and 1643). The last Italian witchcraft trials to end with capital punishments took place in the eighteenth century in Venice (in 1705 and 1724) and in the region of Piedmont (in 1709, 1717, and 1723).

Adding the estimated number of executions in post-Tridentine witchcraft scares to the figures for fifteenth- and sixteenth-century trials mentioned earlier, Del Col assesses the total number of individuals executed for witchcraft in Italy as between 418 and 546. Behringer, who relies on the highest figures for the victims of the early Como witch-hunts, proposes an estimate of 2,500 victims.[22] Neither historian takes into account the many suspects who died as a result of interrogations. Twenty-nine accused witches are known to have perished before the end of their trials in post-Tridentine Italy. In 1611, twelve women died in the course of witchcraft trials conducted by the episcopal tribunal in Novara; another died during her investigation in the witchcraft scare in Soraggio (1607); and brutal torture killed one witchcraft suspect in Lucca in 1589 and another from Monte San Savino in 1616. Fourteen others died before the end of their investigation during the above-mentioned trials in Milan, Parano, Triora, Naples, and Bitonto.[23] Abuse of alleged witches in the course of their trial or incarceration sometimes involved rape, as in Parano in 1582, and even as late as 1724, when a nun prosecuted for witchcraft was raped in the jail of the Inquisition in Faenza.[24]

14.3 THE HISTORIOGRAPHY OF ITALIAN WITCHCRAFT

Witchcraft posed a problem for the pioneer of Italian Renaissance studies, Jacob Burckhardt. As the Swiss historian knew, Italian philosophers and artists often shared the fear of witchcraft prevalent in other segments of the population. However, Burck-hardt suggested that Italy would have overcome the fear of witches had it not been invaded by foreign powers during the Italian Wars. The early historians of witchcraft, Joseph Hansen and Henry Charles Lea, followed Burckhardt in contrasting the atroci-ties that took place north of the Alps with the enlightened attitude towards witches that supposedly prevailed in Renaissance Italy. Only after the mid-twentieth century

[22] Del Col, 'L'attività', 382, 394; cf. Behringer, Witches, 150, 154–5.
[23] Thomas Deutscher, 'The Role of the Episcopal Tribunal of Novara in the Suppression of Heresy and Witchcraft, 1563–1615', Catholic Historical Review, 77 (1991), 403–21; Christopher F. Black, The Italian Inquisition (New Haven, CT, 2009), 41, 88.
[24] Decker, Witchcraft, 99; Anne Jacobson Schutte, 'Asmodea, A Nun-Witch in Eighteenth-Century Tuscany', in Kathryn Edwards, ed., Werewolves, Witches, and Wandering Spirits: Traditional Beliefs and Folklore in Early Modern Europe (Kirksville, MO, 2001), 132.

did historians begin to question such assumptions by seriously investigating Italian witchcraft.

Gene Brucker, Giuseppe Bonomo, and Albano Biondi have studied the witch prosecutions in major cultural centres of Renaissance Italy.[25] Domenico Mammoli called attention to the trial of Matteuccia of Todi, who in 1428 confessed to shape-shifting, flying to the witches' assembly, and sucking children's blood. Matteuccia's trial is one of the earliest known descriptions of witches' crimes to include key elements of the so-called cumulative concept of witchcraft, and is the fullest early account of the witches' sabbath. Luisa Muraro has analysed an even earlier allusion to the peculiarly Italian version of the sabbath in the confessions of Sibilla Zanni and Pierina Bugatis, who were executed in Milan in 1390 after describing their participation in assemblies presided over by a female figure, whom their judges took to be the devil in disguise. These studies have revealed that the Italian peninsula played an important role in the development of the belief in diabolic witchcraft, as well as in the early phase of European witch-hunting.[26]

Peter Burke has suggested that the revival of interest in ancient magic during the High Renaissance corresponded to the rise of witch-hunting. As many intellectuals got interested in Hermeticism, Neoplatonism, and other occult traditions, Italian rulers and churchmen became alert to the presence of magical activities, and began suspecting demonic conspiracies.[27] Another scholar now argues, *pace* Burckhardt: 'whatever might have been the defining traits of the *Civilization of the Renaissance in Italy*, witch-hunting was an integral part of it'.[28]

The historian who revolutionized the study of Italian witchcraft was Carlo Ginzburg; his research into the archives of inquisitorial tribunals in northern Italy led to the publication of *I benandanti* (The Night Battles) in 1966. The *benandanti* (do-gooders) were members of an agrarian cult that had probably existed since pagan times. They believed that because they had been born 'with the caul' (amniotic sac), they were predestined to practise ecstatic rites, in which their souls would leave their bodies and battle witches to ensure the fertility of their fields. According to Ginzburg, once they came to the attention of the Inquisition in Venice, inquisitors interpreted their nocturnal experiences as the witches' sabbath. In a process of acculturation that lasted

[25] Jacob Burckhardt, *The Civilization of the Renaissance in Italy*, tr. S. G. C. Middlemore (4th rev. edn, London, 1951), 303–41; cf. Brucker, 'Sorcery', 7–24; Giuseppe Bonomo, *Caccia alle streghe: La credenza nelle streghe dal sec. XIII al XIX con particolare riferimento all'Italia* (Palermo, 1959); Albano Biondi, 'Streghe ed eretici nei domini estensi all'epoca dell'Ariosto', in Paolo Rossi, ed., *Il rinascimento nelle corti padane: Società e cultura* (Bari, 1977), 165–99.

[26] Domenico Mammoli, ed., *The Record of the Trial and Condemnation of a Witch, Matteuccia di Francesco, at Todi, 20 March 1428* (Rome, 1972); Luisa Muraro, *La Signora del gioco: Episodi della caccia alle streghe* (Milan, 1976), 147–55. See also Richard Kieckhefer, *European Witch Trials: Their Foundations in Popular and Learned Culture, 1300–1500* (London, 1976), 21–38, 106–47; Sergio Abbiati, Attilio Agnoletto, and Maria Rosario Lazzati, eds, *La stregoneria: Diavoli, streghe, inquisitori dal Trecento al Settecento* (Milan, 1984).

[27] Burke, 'Witchcraft', 32–53.

[28] Tavuzzi, *Renaissance Inquisitors*, 198.

for almost a century, the learned, urban inquisitors convinced the illiterate, rural *benandanti* to think of themselves as devil-worshipping witches.[29]

Ginzburg's microhistorical studies have exemplified how rewarding a close reading of trial records could be. The publication of *I benandanti* inspired in-depth investigations of local witchcraft scares and the discovery of records from previously unknown trials.[30] Important studies have focused on specific trials, such as that of the midwife Gostanza da Libbiano and the Modenese 'witch-priest' Guglielmo Campana. More recently, historians began turning their attention to episodes of demonic possession involving suspicions of witchcraft.[31]

Although Ginzburg acknowledged the suggestive questioning employed in inquisitorial interrogations, he argued that the confessions of accused witches and the depositions of witnesses could reveal much about the lives of people from the lower classes.[32] Following his lead, historians have analysed trial records from Venice, Modena, Naples, and Siena. Their findings indicate that resorting to 'superstitious' magic could enable poor villagers, urban labourers and streetwalkers, as well as members of the lower clergy, to earn a modest income. However, after 1587 magical practitioners risked denunciation to the Holy Office, often by disappointed clients.[33]

Ginzburg's anthropological approach also paved the way for the study of witch beliefs by historians and cultural anthropologists, who pondered aspects peculiar to the Italian version of the sabbath, known as the game (*gioco*), that surface in demonological literature and trial records. As their studies demonstrate, pre-modern Italians believed that witches met regularly in designated places such as the walnut tree of Benevento, and that a female figure known as the Lady of the Game (*Domina Ludi* or *Signora del Gioco*) presided over their gatherings. The belief in a benevolent 'Lady' may have grown out of a female deity's cult in an archaic agricultural civilization, a remnant of pagan beliefs that were only completely eradicated in the post-Tridentine era. However, the

---

[29] Carlo Ginzburg, *The Night Battles: Witchcraft and Agrarian Cults in the Sixteenth and Seventeenth Centuries*, tr. John and Anne Tedeschi (Baltimore, MD, 1983).

[30] Grado Giovanni Merlo, *Streghe* (Bologna, 2006); Anna Marcaccioli Castiglioni, *Streghe e roghi nel ducato di Milano: Processi per stregoneria a Venegono Superiore nel 1520* (Milan, 1999); Giovanna Bosco and Patrizia Castelli, eds, *Stregoneria e streghe nell'Europa moderna* (Rome, 1996).

[31] Cardini, *Gostanza*; Matteo Duni, *Tra religione e magia: Storia del prete modenese Guglielmo Campana (1460?–1541)* (Florence, 1999); Vincenzo Lavenia, 'I diavoli di Carpi e il Sant'Uffizio (1636–1639)', in Mario Rosa, ed., *Eretici, esuli e indemoniati nell'età moderna* (Florence, 1998), 77–139; Jeffrey R. Watt, *The Scourge of Demons: Possession, Lust, and Witchcraft in a Seventeenth-Century Italian Convent* (Rochester, 2009).

[32] Carlo Ginzburg, *Clues, Myths, and the Historical Method*, tr. John and Anne Tedeschi (Baltimore, MD, 1989), 156–64.

[33] Jean-Michel Sallmann, *Chercheurs de trésors et jeteuses de sorts: La quête du surnaturel à Naples au XVIᵉ siècle* (Paris, 1986); Mary Rose O'Neil, '*Sacerdote ovvero strione*: Ecclesiastical and Superstitious Remedies in Sixteenth-Century Italy', in Steven L. Kaplan, ed., *Understanding Popular Culture: Europe from the Middle Ages to the Nineteenth Century* (Berlin, 1984), 53–83; David Gentilcore, *From Bishop to Witch: The System of the Sacred in Early Modern Terra d'Otranto* (Manchester, 1992); Guido Ruggiero, *Binding Passions: Tales of Magic, Marriage, and Power at the End of the Renaissance* (Oxford, 1993); Oscar Di Simplicio, *Inquisizione, stregoneria e medicina: Siena e il suo Stato, 1580–1721* (Siena, 2000).

'Lady' was also believed to have the power to resuscitate oxen eaten by witches during their gatherings, a motif typical of myths originating in hunters' societies.[34] Ginzburg himself dedicated a controversial monograph (discussed in other chapters of this volume) to exploring the origins of the early modern belief in the witches' sabbath in shamanistic myths and popular rituals.

Ginzburg's study of the *benandanti* eventually came under scrutiny, when anthropological research in Friuli revealed the survival of beliefs in the *benandanti*'s therapeutic powers and contacts with the dead until the twentieth century, calling into question the thesis concerning the Inquisition's repression of popular culture. Re-examining records from the *benandanti*'s trials, Franco Nardon argues that they saw themselves primarily as magical healers, downplaying the shamanistic elements that Ginzburg emphasizes. Rather than portraying a linear process of acculturation, Nardon suggests that the inquisitors, not the individuals they were interrogating, were the ones whose interests changed over time. The first inquisitor to encounter the *benandanti*, in 1574, was concerned with heresy and was therefore obsessed with their nocturnal battles, which he interpreted as the witches' sabbath. Seventeenth-century inquisitors, on the other hand, were preoccupied with their 'superstitious' healings and possible abuse of the sacraments.[35]

Ginzburg's study of the *benandanti* called attention to the possibility of hearing the voices—even weak, mediated ones—of the accused through the records of inquisitorial investigations. Nardon's critique suggests that records from the *benandanti*'s trials mainly reveal the concerns of their interrogators. It thus reinforces the historiographical tendency to focus on the mechanisms of power and modes of operation of the Roman Inquisition and other judicial systems, rather than on the beliefs and practices of those brought before their tribunals.[36]

The study of the Roman Inquisition and its dealing with witchcraft has actually been one of the most fruitful fields of research in Italian religious history in the last few decades. During the 1970s and 1980s, Tedeschi's path-breaking studies have demonstrated how, by upholding high standards of judicial procedure, the Holy Office avoided large-scale witch-hunts of the type that became common north of the Alps. A few years before the opening of the ACDF, Romeo attempted to explain the 'turn to moderation' of the Holy Office. Decker, who consulted ACDF materials in subsequent years, underscored the importance of this 'turn' in his exploration of the papacy's attitude towards witchcraft.[37]

[34] Maurizio Bertolotti, 'The Ox's Bones and the Ox's Hide: A Popular Myth, Part Hagiography and Part Witchcraft', in Edward Muir and Guido Ruggiero, eds, *Microhistory and the Lost Peoples of Europe: Selections from 'Quaderni Storici'* (Baltimore, MD, 1991), 42–70; Albano Biondi, 'La signora delle erbe e la magia della vegetazione', in *Cultura popolare nell'Emilia Romagna: Medicina, erbe e magia* (Milan, 1981), 185–203; Pinuccia di Gesaro, 'La "Società del Gioco" in Tirolo ovvero la "compagnia delle streghe" tra tolleranza e repressione', in *Caccia alle streghe in Italia*, 129–49.

[35] Franco Nardon, *Benandanti e inquisitori nel Friuli del Seicento* (Trieste, 1999).

[36] Moshe Sluhovsky, 'Authority and Power in Early Modern Italy: Recent Italian Historiography', *The Historical Journal*, 47 (2004), 508–10.

[37] Tedeschi, *Prosecution*; Tedeschi, 'Inquisitorial Law'; Romeo, *Inquisitori*; Decker, *Witchcraft*.

Adriano Prosperi placed the Roman Inquisition's treatment of witchcraft within the broader context of the Church's efforts to refashion Catholicism. According to Prosperi, after the Council of Trent, inquisitors, confessors, and missionary preachers collaborated in uprooting popular 'superstitions' by employing various means of persuasion, indoctrination, and repression. Preachers taught the faithful how to tell licit from 'superstitious' practices, and confessors denied absolution to anyone who confessed to holding heretical beliefs or engaging in unorthodox behaviour. Such confessants were instructed to turn to the local inquisitor, confess their heresies, provide names of accomplices, and return to their confessor with the inquisitor's permission to receive penance and absolution. Inquisitors usually treated first-time penitent offenders, who presented themselves spontaneously, rather mildly.

The joint efforts of preachers, confessors, and inquisitors, which ensured an effective control of the populace, transformed the nature of the Inquisition. The Holy Office preferred a close, intense monitoring of the masses, inflicting only light penances when necessary, in contrast to the severe punishments that inquisitors before 1542 had often favoured. At the same time, the reinvigorated efforts to ensure better training of the lower clergy were complimented by the fairly harsh punishment of priests or friars who meddled in magic.[38]

14.4 CURRENT TRENDS AND DIRECTIONS FOR FUTURE RESEARCH

Some revisionist historians interpret the relatively low number of witches executed at the end of trials conducted by the Roman Inquisition as the outcome of its 'progressive' attitude towards witchcraft. That Italian witches continued to be burned until the eighteenth century was, they propose, mainly because of the uncouth masses. Although the Church did its best to educate the faithful, and the jurists of the Holy Office did all they could to prevent executions, persisting pressure 'from below' led to the deaths of many suspected witches. Decker further argues that most witches that the Holy Office sentenced to death were *magicians*, who were *really* guilty of attempting to cause harm by invoking demons. Others condemned by the Inquisition had misused Eucharistic hosts, a *real* crime that the Tridentine Church could not tolerate. That the Holy Office condemned such *magicians* to death should not blemish its reputation as a sceptical body that, unlike secular courts elsewhere in Europe, cannot be blamed for executing imaginary *witches* charged with illusory crimes such as copulating with the devil.[39]

---

[38] Prosperi, *Tribunali*, 219–43, 368–99, 418–30.
[39] Annibale Cogliano, *La svolta illuminata del Santo Officio a fine Cinquecento* (Naples, 2006); Decker, *Witchcraft*.

Matteo Duni recently criticized such attempts to shift the blame away from the Inquisition to the lay populace.[40] Vincenzo Lavenia has noted that although the Holy Office insisted on its theoretical prerogative in trying cases of witchcraft, in practice it often put up with civil magistrates' prosecution of cases involving malevolent magic. Unlike the Iberian Inquisitions, which were responsible to rulers of politically unified states, the Roman Inquisition's tribunals outside the Papal States operated in a politically fragmented peninsula and relied on the support of local authorities to carry out their task of eradicating heresy. At a time when the Church depended on the cooperation of lay magistrates to ensure the implementation of the Tridentine reforms, inquisitors sometimes authorized, or simply overlooked, the prosecution of *maleficia* and the execution of their alleged perpetrators by secular courts.

Romeo goes even further, in a study that reconsiders his earlier thesis of the Roman Inquisition's 'turn to moderation'. Rather than bringing witch prosecutions to an end, Romeo proposes that this 'turn' paved the way for bloodier witch-hunting, mostly carried out by secular courts. The Holy Office, Romeo asserts, never repudiated the theological presumptions that justified the repression of witchcraft, and maintained an ambivalent stand towards the crime. Romeo does not question the fact that most cardinal-inquisitors came to doubt the reality of the sabbath by the late sixteenth century. Nonetheless, he proposes that the Holy Office tolerated the persistence of witch executions, and that it did not have a moderating effect on the prosecution of witchcraft comparable to that which the Spanish or Portuguese Inquisitions had. Further studies of hitherto unexplored trials by civil magistrates are required before this re-revisionist thesis can be proven valid.

As Romeo remarks, the Holy Office frequently tarried in curtailing the excesses of its own inquisitors or inquisitorial vicars, and punished overzealous judges rather lightly, as in the Bitonto affair. Moreover, the lynching of presumed witches, sometimes following their release by the Inquisition, became all the more common in the seventeenth century and usually went unpunished.[41] We currently know little about what happened to accused witches who were not executed, unless their names resurface in later court records. More work needs to be done on the long-term effects of witchcraft prosecutions on suspects who had been exonerated, or had received relatively light punishments.

The fate of one recent study, based on records of the diocesan archive in Sarno (in southern Italy), attests to the risks that still await scholars who uncover unpleasant evidence about the early modern Church. The ecclesiastical censure and eventual destruction in 2008 of a book by Gaetana Mazza, which dealt, inter alia, with the prosecution of witchcraft, serves as a reminder that clergymen still have control over archives holding records from trials conducted by Church representatives in previous centuries. Clerical archivists occasionally prohibit the consultation of documents

---

[40] Matteo Duni, 'Le streghe e gli storici, 1986–2006: Bilancio e prospettive', in *NLV*, 10–15 and n. 25.
[41] Lavenia, '"Anticamente"', 35–80; Romeo, 'Inquisizione', 53–64.

pertaining to accused witches tried by ecclesiastical authorities in the past.[42] It is hoped that in the future historians gain access to such records, whose exclusion from consultation impedes a comprehensive assessment of Italian witchcraft trials.

Even at the present state of research, though, it is clear that we have come a long way since the days of Burckhardt and Hansen. We now know that the Renaissance was also the heyday of Italian witch-hunting, and that even during the so-called Counter-Reformation considerably more witches were tried in Italy than in Spain or Portugal. Once hailed by historians as an enlightened body that had a moderating influence on prosecutions, the Roman Inquisition now appears to have had a more ambiguous effect on the repression of witchcraft.

Scholars of the Roman Inquisition have made the most significant contribution to the study of Italian witchcraft, while the trials of the fifteenth and early sixteenth centuries remain relatively understudied. These early panics, as well as the trials conducted by non-inquisitorial courts after 1542, should be explored more thoroughly, and more attention should also be given to the social history of witchcraft. Christopher Black has lately called attention to the invaluable information on family relations, neighbourhood tensions, and contacts among members of different ethnic affiliations, social class, or religious status, which can be gleaned from extant trial records.[43]

Additional work also needs to be done in elucidating the significance of gender in witchcraft accusations, prosecutions, and beliefs. Ginzburg, whose publications have considerably influenced Italian witchcraft studies, largely ignored questions of gender.[44] Popular myths such as that of the Lady of the Game—who, it was commonly believed, taught witches to employ herbs for healing various maladies—have mainly been explored by feminist scholars from non-historical disciplines; such studies have had minimal impact on mainstream Italian historiography.[45]

Historians of Italian medicine point to the efforts of university-educated physicians to monopolize the healing arts. Together with the Church's concurrent campaign to eradicate 'superstition' by ensuring its exclusive control of supernatural forces, such efforts were aimed at eliminating competition from the uneducated laity. This dual process, which led to the criminalization of practitioners of the magical arts, had a strong gender dimension, because while all authorized exorcists were male and most licensed doctors were men, most folk healers accused of witchcraft were women.[46]

---

[42] Adriano Prosperi, 'Presentazione', in Gaetana Mazza, *Streghe, guaritori, istigatori: Casi di inquisizione diocesana in Età moderna* (Rome, 2009), 9–14; Schutte, 'Asmodea', 127 n. 25.

[43] Black, *Italian Inquisition*, 236–54, 259. See also Oscar Di Simplicio, *Autunno della stregoneria: Maleficio e magia nell'Italia moderna* (Bologna, 2005).

[44] Oscar Di Simplicio, 'Ginzburg, Carlo', in *EW*, ii, 444; William Monter, 'Gendering the Extended Family of Ginzburg's Benandanti', *Magic, Ritual, and Witchcraft*, 1 (2006), 226.

[45] E.g. Muraro, *La Signora del Gioco*. Notable exceptions are Biondi, 'La signora', 185–203; Luisa Accati, 'The Spirit of Fornication: Virtue of the Soul and Virtue of the Body in Friuli, 1600–1800', in Edward Muir and Guido Ruggiero, eds, *Sex and Gender in Historical Perspective: Selections from 'Quaderni Storici'* (Baltimore, MD, 1990), 110–40.

[46] Jole Agrimi and Chiara Crisciani, 'Savoir médical et anthropologie religieuse: Les représentations et les fonctions de la vetula (13ᵉ–15ᵉ siècle)', *Annales ESC*, 48 (1993), 1282–308; Katharine Park, 'Medicine

Female healers and diviners, however, were not the only ones who risked prosecu-tion; so did practitioners of learned magic, who were usually male. As noted at the beginning of this chapter, the distinction between 'magician' and 'witch' in Italy was often blurred. In 1521, the Dominican witch-hunter Silvestro Prierias (1456–1527) even coined the term *strigimaga* (witch-magician) and used it in the title of his influential demonological work.[47] This term also proves helpful for designating the practitioners of magic that the Roman Inquisition targeted. Since the late sixteenth century, men were frequently charged with meddling in illicit magic: in Friuli, 45 per cent of the *benandanti* denounced to the Inquisition were men, though the harshest punishment ever given to a *benandante* went to a woman. In Venice and Modena, witchcraft accusations were sex-related and women comprised the majority of the accused, and in Siena all those tried for witchcraft were women. Some studies suggest that clerical necromancers were in greater danger than poor female healers of being sent to the stake,[48] but the correlation between the accused's gender and the severity of punish-ment in witchcraft trials conducted by secular, episcopal, and inquisitorial tribunals still awaits a thorough investigation.

Although Italian witchcraft theorists were influenced by the *Malleus maleficarum* (*c.*1486/7), they were more hesitant than their northern European counterparts in associating witchcraft with women. Writing to justify the early sixteenth-century panics, Prierias and other demonologists felt the need to account for the high propor-tion of men among those convicted as *strigimagi*. Giovanni Francesco Pico even resorted to Italians' notoriety for sodomy and devised an original explanation for the predominance of male witches in Italy, arguing that some of them were lured to entering a pact with the devil after committing same-sex relations with demons in the shape of young boys.[49]

The gendered construction of witchcraft in the works of early sixteenth-century witch-hunters needs to be examined in the context of their fascination with female spirituality. In her seminal studies, Gabriella Zarri has noted that some of the most vigorous Italian witch-hunters were devoted to women mystics, whom they revered as counter-witches. My work on Heinrich Kramer's admiration for Italian holy women, and his collaboration with the inquisitors who backed them, has called into question assumptions concerning the notorious demonologist's notion of the female sex. Studies of the Roman Inquisition suggest that its concern over feigned female sanctity went hand in hand with its lenient prosecution of witchcraft. Prosperi proposes that the

and Magic: The Healing Arts', in Judith Brown and Robert Davis, eds, *Gender and Society in Renaissance Italy* (London, 1998), 133–49.

[47] Burke, 'Witchcraft', 32–4; Giorgio Galli, 'Cultura delle streghe e cultura dei maghi', in *Oltre Triora: Nuove ipotesi di indagine sulla stregoneria e la caccia alle streghe. Atti del convegno Triora-Toirano, 29–30 ottobre 1994* (Milan, 1997), 43–52.

[48] Monter, 'Gendering', 223; Martin, *Witchcraft*, 226–30; Schutte, 'I processi', 159–73; Oscar Di Simplicio, 'Italy', in *EW*, ii, 578; Duni, *Under the Devil's Spell*, 71–3.

[49] Tamar Herzig, 'The Demons' Reaction to Sodomy: Witchcraft and Homosexuality in Gianfrancesco Pico della Mirandola's *Strix*', *Sixteenth Century Journal*, 34/1 (April 2003), 53–72.

cardinal-inquisitors who rejected admissions of participation in the sabbath concurrently repudiated claims of female mystics who believed they enjoyed unmediated contacts with the divine.[50] A *longue durée* examination of the gendered construction of witchcraft and sanctity (and also of heresy) in Italy, how they affected one another, and how and why they were modified over time, is still needed.

Finally, although the historiography of Italian witchcraft has been extremely rich and stimulating, it comprises mainly microhistorical or local studies. Aware of the political and cultural diversity of pre-modern Italy, scholars often prefer focusing on a geographically confined area, and are wary of proposing grand narratives. Excellent surveys of the prosecution of witchcraft by inquisitorial tribunals are included in recent studies of the Roman Inquisition. However, it is high time for broad syntheses that explore common themes and variations in Italian witchcraft trials from the late fourteenth through the eighteenth centuries.

FURTHER READING

Black, Christopher F., *The Italian Inquisition* (New Haven, CT, 2009).
Bonomo, Giuseppe, *Caccia alle streghe: La credenza nelle streghe dal sec. XIII al XIX con particolare riferimento all'Italia* (Palermo, 1959).
Bosco, Giovanna and Castelli, Patrizia, eds, *Stregoneria e streghe nell'Europa moderna* (Rome, 1996).
Caccia alle streghe in Italia tra XIV e XVII secolo: Atti del Convegno nazionale di Studi storico-antropologici, Triora, 22–24 Ottobre 2004 (Bolzano, 2007).
Corsi, Dinora and Duni, Matteo, ed., '*Non lasciar vivere la malefica': Le streghe nei trattati e nei processi (secoli XIV–XVII)* (Florence, 2008).
Decker, Rainer, *Witchcraft and the Papacy: An Account Drawing on the Formerly Secret Records of the Roman Inquisition*, tr. H. C. Erik Midelfort (Charlottesville, VA, 2008).
Del Col, Andrea, *L'Inquisizione in Italia: Dal XII al XXI secolo* (Milan, 2006).
Di Simplicio, Oscar, *Autunno della stregoneria: Maleficio e magia nell'Italia moderna* (Bologna, 2005).
Duni, Matteo, *Under the Devil's Spell: Witches, Sorcerers, and the Inquisition in Renaissance Italy* (Florence, 2007).
Ginzburg, Carlo, *The Night Battles: Witchcraft and Agrarian Cults in the Sixteenth and Seventeenth Centuries*, tr. John and Anne Tedeschi (Baltimore, MD, 1983).
Nardon, Franco, *Benandanti e inquisitori nel Friuli del Seicento* (Trieste, 1999).

---

[50] Gabriella Zarri, 'Living Saints: A Typology of Female Sanctity in the Early Sixteenth Century', in Daniel Bornstein and Roberto Rusconi, eds, *Women and Religion in Medieval and Renaissance Italy* (Chicago, 1996), esp. 244–8; Peter Dinzelbacher, 'Sante o streghe? Alcuni casi del tardo medioevo', in Gabriella Zarri, ed., *Finzione e santità tra medioevo ed età moderna* (Turin, 1991), 52–87; Dinora Corsi, 'Mulieres religiosae e mulieres maleficae nell'ultimo Medioevo', in *NLV*, 19–42; Prosperi, *Tribunali*, 431–64; Schutte, '"Saints" and "Witches" in Early Modern Italy: Stepsisters or Strangers?', in Anne Jacobson Schutte, Thomas Kuehn, and Silvana Seidel Menchi, eds, *Time, Space, and Women's Lives in Early Modern Europe* (Kirksville, MO, 2001), 153–64; Tamar Herzig, 'Witches, Saints, and Heretics: Heinrich Kramer's Ties with Italian Women Mystics', *Magic, Ritual, and Witchcraft*, 1 (2006), 24–55.

Paolin, Giovanna, ed., *Inquisizioni: Percorsi di ricerca* (Trieste, 2001).

Prosperi, Adriano, *Tribunali della coscienza: Inquisitori, confessori, missionari* (rev. edn, Turin, 2009).

Romeo, Giovanni, *Inquisitori, esorcisti e streghe nell'Italia della Controriforma* (Florence, 1990).

Tedeschi, John, *The Prosecution of Heresy: Collected Studies on the Inquisition in Early Modern Italy* (Binghamton, NY, 1991).

CHAPTER 15

....

WITCHCRAFT IN IBERIA

....

WILLIAM MONTER

THROUGHOUT the early modern Iberian peninsula, the history of witch-hunting was dominated to a remarkable extent by the scepticism of both the Spanish and Portuguese Inquisitions about the cumulative concept of witchcraft. Reversing the policy of France, their nearest European neighbour, both Spain and Portugal tried to prevent secular courts from punishing a crime that Continental jurists agreed was of 'mixed' jurisdiction; and thanks to royal support, they succeeded in doing so much of the time in most of Iberia. After 1550 neither Holy Office (whose records are much more complete than those from most other early modern institutions) permitted no more than a handful of executions for witchcraft, largely because of their persistent doubts about the reality of witches' assemblies, and even more about the reality of physical harm attributed to witches. For such reasons, torture played a relatively minor role in witch trials held under inquisitorial jurisdiction, although both Iberian Holy Offices often employed it against suspected Jews, Muslims, or Protestants.

The Spanish Inquisition had much less jurisdictional control over the crime of witchcraft than its Portuguese counterpart, particularly in the north-eastern lands that belonged to the Crown of Aragon rather than the Crown of Castile. In Portugal, very little evidence survives of secular tribunals judging witchcraft cases, and we know of fewer than a dozen public executions for witchcraft and related crimes (secular courts executed over half of these in 1559). In the Spanish dependency of Sicily, where our knowledge of witchcraft trials is limited to inquisitorial sources, there were no recorded executions for this offence. Most of our recorded evidence comes from Spain's northernmost provinces, where inquisitorial courts executed about two dozen witches between 1498 and 1610, secular courts put several hundred witches to death, mainly between 1520 and 1625.

Both cultural and political geography help explain this unusual record. Spain's Pyrenean regions held the peninsula's deepest and most tenacious beliefs about malevolent witchcraft, and tales about *maleficia* and sabbaths informed village quarrels here every bit as thoroughly as they did in so many other parts of Continental Europe.

However, as we shall see, such 'classical' witches seem unknown among villagers, either in other parts of Iberia or in Sicily. At the same time, the witches of northern Spain inhabited a region boasting considerable local autonomy and individual legal rights, where central control (including the Inquisition) was generally weak. Across Pyrenean Spain, the legal history of the repression of witchcraft shifts as one moves from west to east. Among the Basques in the small kingdom of Navarre (which was administratively attached to Castile rather than Aragon after its conquest in 1513), special commissioners, armed with extensive but temporary powers, occasionally wreaked havoc among suspected witches in its northern mountains, before the Inquisition gradually wrested effective control over the crime of witchcraft from them during the second half of the sixteenth century. Further east, in the mountains of the kingdom of Aragon, such commissioners were unknown, and fellow villagers had to strip suspected witches of their civic privileges before they could be legally arrested and punished. Outlawing a suspected witch, even an old woman from an undistinguished clan, was a cumbersome process that was seldom properly recorded. Further east in Catalonia, witch-hunting was conducted primarily by professional witchfinders, who had been invited by village notables in cooperation with local seigneurs holding the rights of high justice. Vigilante justice seldom preserves usable paper trails for historians to follow, and this problem bedevils any attempt to provide satisfactory statistics on witchcraft prosecutions in the parts of Spain that witnessed most of them.

The history of witchcraft in Europe's south-western corner has other peculiarities. The single most influential modern study of the subject, Julio Caro Baroja's *Las brujas y su mondo*, is now fifty years old, but still defines the basic paradigm within which research continues in Spain. This magisterial overview of witchcraft, from the perspective of Western cultural history—which devoted much of its second half to contemporaneous witchcraft trials in neighbouring Basque regions of Spain and France in the early seventeenth century—was largely overlooked abroad.[1] Various reasons help explain this undeserved neglect: the perceived parochialism and backwardness of Franco's Spain contributed as much as the unconventional academic background of a fiercely independent author whose anthropological guidelines derived as much from Greco-Roman classicism as from 'fieldwork' in the Basque country, where he spent part of every year. Caro Baroja's most authentic and most prominent disciple in the history of Basque witchcraft has been a Danish ethnographer, Gustav Henningsen, who has greatly enriched our knowledge of the key events affecting the Spanish Inquisition's approach to witchcraft during the decisive outbreak of witchcraft accusations and confessions in Spain's Basque regions between 1609 and 1614. Meanwhile, no significant modern publication on this subject appeared in Spain's smaller and more remote

---

[1] Julio Caro Baroja, *Las brujas y su mondo* (Madrid, 1961). An English translation, *The World of the Witches*, appeared as early as 1965 (University of Chicago Press) partly through the efforts of an anthropologist, Julian Pitt-Rivers, but it received few reviews from historians. Its greatest success abroad was a German translation in 1968 that added both a foreword and an additional chapter on German aspects by a professor of folklore, Will-Erich Peuckert. Its first French edition came in 1972.

neighbour, Portugal, until after it entered the European Community in 1986. Although neither of the basic studies on the history of Portugal's efforts to control and punish harmful illicit magic is yet available in English, this subject is now better known on a national level than are parallel events in its larger Iberian neighbour.

It was a Portuguese rather than Spanish expert who first attempted, in 1994, to place this subject not in an Iberian but in a more general Mediterranean context. In a synthetic essay, still unavailable in English, entitled '*Un univers saturé de magie*' (A Universe Saturated with Magic), Francisco Bethencourt emphasized the central importance of the diabolical pact in linking the theoretically opposed notions of beneficial and harmful witchcraft throughout Mediterranean Europe. He also noted that reports of witches' sabbaths seem much less common in southern than in northern Europe. Instead, throughout Mediterranean Europe, 'the great majority of accusations of illicit magic concern love potions or minor spells attributed to minor witches in urban settings', while 'the witch linked to the myth of the sabbat (a *bruja* in Spain, *bruxa* in Portugal, or *strega* in Italy) plays a threatening but less visible role'. In Iberia, 'contradicting one of the most widespread presuppositions of the bibliography of witchcraft', synodal constitutions and handbooks for confessors paid great interest to diabolical pacts while almost completely ignoring witches' sabbaths. On balance, therefore, the Spanish Inquisition normally considered diabolical witchcraft a relatively minor problem in regions full of poorly converted Jews and Muslims. At least, by the 1520s it began following a 'coherent and systematic' policy of caution about the physical reality of this crime, while simultaneously doing its best to maintain jurisdiction over it.[2]

An excellent test for Bethencourt's 'Mediterranean' perspective on witchcraft comes from the history of its prosecution in Sicily, a part of today's Italy where the Spanish rather than the Roman Inquisition held jurisdiction over this crime (another large Italian island, Sardinia, also fell under the jurisdiction of the Spanish Inquisition, but its history of witchcraft has been less well studied). We shall therefore look first at the treatment of witchcraft in mainland Spain, then at Sicily, its semi-colonial Italian dependency, before examining Portugal (which was also united with the Spanish Crown from 1580 to 1640—the period when witch-hunts were most severe everywhere else in Western Europe). As in Bethencourt's larger comparative history of the three major Mediterranean inquisitions, the institutional and cultural similarities between Spain and Portugal seem greater than those between either Iberian kingdom and continental Italy, where the Roman Inquisition held jurisdiction over witchcraft. What has been missing so far is any systematic approach to those Iberian similarities before, during, and after the personal union of the Spanish and Portuguese Crowns.

---

[2] Francisco Bethencourt, 'Un univers saturé de magie: l'Europe méridionale', in Robert Muchembled, ed., *Magie et sorcellerie en Europe du Moyen Âge à nos jours* (Paris, 1994), 159–94 (quotes at 178 and 180).

15.1 SPAIN

Our knowledge of the general outlines of the Spanish Inquisition's involvement with witchcraft changes very slowly. More than a century ago, the first scholar to investigate the problem, the great American historian Henry Charles Lea, emphasized this Inquisition's persistent scepticism about the cumulative concept of witchcraft. Lea, who was certainly no apologist for traditional Catholicism or for clerical bureaucracy, asserted that 'no land was more exposed to the contagion of this insanity [which he called the "witch-madness"] than Spain', but 'that it was repressed and rendered comparatively harmless was due to the wisdom and firmness of the Inquisition'. Lea's paradox remains a central aspect—perhaps *the* central aspect—of the subject. Over fifty years later, it reappeared in Caro Baroja's discussion of the differences between early seventeenth-century French and Spanish approaches to Basque witchcraft. Even my sketch of this subject, now over twenty years old, which contrasted an early period of vigorous inquisitorial intervention in northern Spain with a half-century after 1550, when this offence was all but ignored by the Holy Office, still remains generally valid. So does my observation that Spain's largest outbreak of witch-hunting occurred after, rather than before, the Inquisition's *crise de conscience* of 1609–14, and that it affected northern regions that the Holy Office was sometimes unable to control satifactorily.[3]

The early seventeenth-century witch craze in Navarre's Basque country—now relatively well known, thanks mainly to Henningsen—became pivotal for two reasons. First, it marked the final (and by far the best-publicized) occasion when the Spanish Inquisition executed several witches and punished dozens more at an *auto de fe* held at Logroño in 1610. Second, during its follow-up activities, the tribunal's junior inquisitor, Alonso Salazar y Frías, investigated almost two thousand confessed witches, most of them children and adolescents. After conducting various controlled experiments, both to corroborate versions of the same witches' gathering and to test various substances confiscated from these confessed witches, he concluded that the offence was purely imaginary: nothing that was either heretical or physically harmful had actually occurred. His activities can now be studied through Henningsen's detailed account of 1980, complemented by his bilingual collection of pertinent documents a quarter-century later. Henningsen's first work enriches Caro Baroja's account in various ways, including by providing direct early links between events and people across the French–Spanish border. At the outset of this panic, the first confessing Spanish witch had just returned home from France. At its apex, an unnamed Bordeaux *parlementaire* (probably not Pierre de Lancre) attended the famous 1610 *auto de fe* in disguise;

---

[3] H. C. Lea, *A History of the Inquisition of Spain*, 4 vols (New York, 1906–8), iv, 206 (quote); William Monter, *Frontiers of Heresy: The Spanish Inquisition from the Basque Lands to Sicily* (Cambridge, 1990), 255–75.

afterwards, he praised the clemency of the inquisitors and requested a copy of their sentences.[4]

Henningsen's second work publishes some early clerical criticisms of the inquisitorial tribunal's actions, which preceded the careful on-site investigations of Logroño's junior inquisitor. The first written doubts about the confessions of the Basque witches came from a young Basque-speaking Jesuit and, even more significantly, from Bishop Antonio Venegas of Pamplona, himself a former inquisitor; he both requested that the Inquisition's central governing board curb these excesses and converted Salazar y Frías to his views before the decisive local visitation to the thousand-plus confessed witches. Meanwhile, Logroño's senior inquisitors defended their actions in a thoughtful 134-page counter-memorandum refuting Salazar y Frías, which was discovered in Navarre's state archives. Buttressed with more than two thousand references to current cases, its 'evidence' literally far outweighs their junior colleague's forty-five page summary of his criticisms of their assumptions, which had previously been sent to Madrid. Ultimately, after five further reports by their doggedly critical colleague, the inquisition's governing council adopted policies that prevented further capital punishment for accused witches.[5]

Four years after Logroño's famous *auto de fe*, exactly when the Inquisition's Supreme Council was deciding that witches' sabbaths in the Basque country were imaginary, what became by far the worst witch-hunt in early modern Spain broke out at the opposite end of the Pyrenees, in Catalonia. Here, the Barcelona tribunal of the Spanish Inquisition did absolutely nothing to control it for several years, and played at most a marginal role when secular authorities finally halted it in 1622. Augustí Alcoberro has recently established the parameters of this panic. It began north of the Pyrenees in 1614, in the north-eastern district of Rosselló (now part of France); it was exacerbated by unusually wet weather in 1617; and it spread throughout much of Catalonia between 1618 and 1622. In many places, professional witchfinders identified suspects who were rapidly convicted and hanged by seigneurial courts with rights of high justice. Although the total number of victims remains unknown, scattered local sources provide information about 150 known deaths in almost fifty different locations, mostly in central Catalonia. After prolonged consultation with Catalonia's seven bishops (two seats being vacant) and high-level negotiations at court, the royal administration finally halted the hunt in 1622 by ordering that all accused witches be transferred to Catalonia's appellate tribunal, the Audiencia Real, which apparently released them. This centralization measure occurred two years before the French Parlement of Paris

---

[4] Gustav Henningsen followed *The Witches' Advocate: Basque Witchcraft and the Spanish Inquisition* (Reno, NV, 1980) with an edited volume, *The Salazar Documents: Inquisitor Alonso de Salazar Frías and Others on the Basque Witch Persecution* (Leiden, 2004). On cross-border connections see Henningsen, *Witches' Advocate*, 30–1, 120–3, 130–1, 194–5.

[5] The first half of Henningsen's *Salazar Documents* is largely devoted to letters from the Jesuit Solarte and from Bishop Venegas; see also Henningsen, *Witches' Advocate*, 127–8, 230–1, 236, 314–17, 336–45. Their counter-memorandum was published by Florencio Idoate, *Un documento sobre brujería en Navarra* (Pamplona, 1972); see also Henningsen, *Salazar Documents*, 351–491.

claimed jurisdiction over all witch trials in its vast district, but it has left no paper trail: the records of Catalonia's Audiencia have vanished, and Alcoberro believes that no single order of this type was ever issued. In any event, Spain's greatest witch-hunt hunt finally ended in spring 1622 with minimal participation by Barcelona's Inquisition, which later that year investigated a woman who reputedly said that 'there were no witches and Hell did not exist'.[6]

A few more witches were executed in Catalonia in the late 1620s, but none afterwards. In the central Pyrenees between Navarre and Catalonia, however, local witch-hunts continued sporadically for much longer. Saragossa's inquisitors arrested professional witchfinders in 1636 and 1657, and they judged accused witches as late as 1658. Aragonese secular justice pursued witches longer than anywhere else in Spain; *desaforamientos* were still proclaimed in Pyrenean districts as late as 1680 and 1691.

One of Henningsen's most intriguing suggestions emerged from his unmatched familiarity with the *relaciones de causas* or annual reports of inquisitorial tribunals throughout Spain. He noticed that while a wide range of illicit magical spells or *hechicería* were found throughout Spain, fully developed European witchcraft or *brujería* was never mentioned in inquisitorial records from such southern Spanish regions as Estremadura, Andalucia, Granada, Murcia, or Valencia, and very rarely in New Castile, the centre of Spain. Jean-Pierre Dedieu first tested Henningsen's idea in the inquisitorial district of Toledo, and found only twenty mentions of *brujas* among hundreds of trials for 'superstition' between 1530 and 1650. All but one of these came from the north-western edge of this district, on the southern slopes of Spain's central mountain range; none came from the southern or eastern plains of La Mancha. A subsequent exploration of this subject in the other Castilian inquisitorial tribunal at Cuenca revealed only a handful of charges of *brujas* murdering babies.[7]

Henningsen's idea of a geographical limit to 'classical' witchcraft in Spain has been expanded by a young Norwegian scholar, Gunnar Knutsen, whose recent book explores its unusually sharp boundary in eastern Spain between Catalonia and Valencia. Both regions saw numerous inquisitorial trials for 'superstition', but *brujas*, although abundant throughout Catalonia, seem unknown in Valencia except in one far northern corner. Valencia held no trials for demonological witchcraft while its northern neighbour (in an area where the Barcelona Inquisition was often unable to

[6] Augustí Alcoberro, 'Cacera de bruixes, justicia local i Inquisició a Catalunya, 1487–1643: alguns criteris metodològics', *Pedralbes: Revista d'Historia Moderna*, 28 (2008), 485–504, with a map of all known Catalan trials and executions for witchcraft on 501.

[7] Henningsen originally drew this line in 'The Database of the Spanish Inquisition', in H. Mollenhaupt and D. Simon, eds, *Vorträge zur Justizforschung, Geschichte und Theorie* (Frankfurt, 1993), ii, 72. It is now more accessible in Gunnar W. Knutsen, *Servants of Satan and Masters of Demons: The Spanish Inquisition's Trials for Superstition, Valencia and Barcelona, 1478–1700* (Turnhout, 2009), 50. On *brujería* in Castile, see Jean-Pierre Dedieu, *L'administration de la foi: L'Inquisition de Tolède (XVᵉ–XVIIIᵉ siècle)* (Madrid, 1989), 320–8, esp. 322 n. 33; Ana Conde, 'Sorcellerie et Inquisition au XVIᵉ siècle en Espagne: l'exemple du diocèse de Cuenca', in A. Molinié-Bertrand and J.-P. Duviols, eds, *Inquisition d'Espagne* (Paris, 2003), 95–107.

enforce its jurisdiction over this crime) had several hundred of them, mainly in secular courts. Knutsen explains this contrast through cultural, social, and religious differences. Because most of Valencia's rural population, where most witchcraft trials occurred throughout Europe, were Moriscos rather than traditional Christians, Valencian magical culture usually saw people as able to control and force demons rather then being manipulated by them,[8]

In Castile, only four *brujas* mentioned sabbaths at Toledo, always after spending much time in prison, and there were no convictions for *brujería* at Cuenca after 1527. But even northern Spanish regions, where *brujería* seems more extensive, provide few details about sabbaths except in its Basque-speaking districts. It is no accident that the usual Spanish word for such gatherings, *aquellares*, comes from Basque, or that its original meaning has been misunderstood. In the kingdom of Aragon, the Holy Office occasionally executed witches until 1537, and in Catalonia until 1549, when a local inquisitor defied orders from headquarters. A full-fledged sabbath appears in Aragon's first preserved inquisitorial witch-trial at the very end of the fifteenth century; afterwards, Gari Lacruz found barely three dozen, mostly vague, references here among several hundred cases of what the Holy Office labelled 'superstition.' The next two recorded sabbaths (1534 and 1579) were held in the *aire de Touiouse*—that is, north of the border with France—a site still widespread in modern Aragonese folklore.[9]

Far south of the 'Henningsen-Knutsen line', traces of harmful *brujería* have also been found in sixteenth-century records from an unlikely location: the Canary Islands, so close to northern Africa that the devil occasionally appeared here in the form of a camel. Here, as at Cuenca, *brujas* specialized in sucking the blood of babies. In 1529, before the Holy Office gained control of their cases, the deputy governor arrested several women charged with killing infants by this method. Such accusations peaked in the late sixteenth century but continued sporadically until 1766, with forty cases in all. Meanwhile, inquisitorial efforts to punish other forms of illicit magic in public had unfortunate consequences. In 1691, a woman was stoned to death after an auto; public riots forced them to suspend another such punishment in 1718. In 1740, hundreds of masked vigilantes attacked suspected witches. By mid-century, Canariot inquisitors admitted that if they punished *hechiceras* in public, they not only risked disorderly scenes but also raised the professional reputations of their prisoners. Instead, secular authorities meted out popular justice. In 1763, the civil magistrates of Gran Canaria sentenced a male *brujo* to two hundred lashes and eight years of service in an African fortress, and also imposed public whippings on three women who were 'notorious witches'.[10]

---

[8] Knutsen, *Servants of Satan*, esp. 85–115 (Barcelona), 119–54 (Valencia).

[9] Angel Gari Lacruz, 'Les sabbats en Aragon d'après les documents et la tradition orale', in N. Jacques-Chaquin and M. Préaud, eds, *Le sabbat des sorciers, XVᵉ–XVIIIᵉ siècles* (Grenoble, 1993), 281–98, esp. 289–91. See also Gustav Henningsen, 'El invento de la palabra "aquelarre"', in *Historia y Humanismo: Estudios en honor del profesor, Dr. D. Valentín Vázquez de Prada*, ed. Jesús María Usunáriz Garoya, 2 vols (Pamplona, 2000), i, 351–9.

[10] Francisco Fajardo Spinola, *Hechicería y brujeria en Canarias en la Edad Moderna* (Las Palmpas, 1991), 226–32, 451, 470–2, 482–3.

In 1754, Canariot inquisitors had suggested to their Spanish headquarters that their local witches be deported to mainland Spain, 'where people are less credulous'. By this time, 'Enlightened' Spain had begun to publish suitably cautious and discreet attacks on an important part of the witchcraft complex—demonic possession. A tireless Benedictine monk, Benito Feijoo, expressed puzzlement that men formed a majority among the 'genuinely' possessed persons described in the New Testament, 'but now-adays there are a hundred possessed women for every man'. He also estimated that there were only twenty or thirty 'genuine' possessions among five hundred cases, and revived the argument made a century earlier in Navarre by Venegas and Salazar that clerical publicity inevitably multiplied witchcraft accusations.[11]

By 1800, the whole conceptual baggage of witchcraft had fallen into official disfavour in Spain. Several commentators, including Caro Baroja, have noted the bitingly satirical form of Francisco Goya's numerous depictions of the fantastic irrationality of witch-craft, particularly in his *Caprichos* and *Dark Paintings*. However, they could not match this famous pictorial evidence with written confirmation from 'Enlightened' Spanish authorities—at least not until María Tausiet discovered an early nineteenth-century trial record in the diocesan archive of Saragossa. Entitled 'Los energúmenos de Tosos' (*energumeni* being Latin for possessed persons), it turned the traditional picture upside down. In this instance, the supposed *bruja* denounced her supposedly demonically possessed accusers before her local episcopal court, which defended her. By 1812, much of Spain's upper clergy apparently shared Goya's scepticism about the reality of witchcraft; the bishop himself saw possession as a fraud. Thirty-two people main-tained that Joaquina Martinez had sent demons into them and had driven her from her village, Villanueva de Huerva; whenever she tried to return, they threw stones at her or attacked her with knives. Aragon's episcopal authorities attempted unsucess-fully to punish the ringleaders and advised the plaintiff to move to a less hostile environment.[12]

15.2 SICILY

The record of the Sicilian tribunal of the Spanish Inquisition in judging cases of illicit magic and witchcraft has obvious similarities both to its record in mainland Spain and to that of the Roman Inquisition in mainland Italy. At the same time, Sicily offers a distinctive feature of local folklore related to witchcraft that separates it from either of

---

[11] María Tausiet, 'From Illusion to Disenchantment: Feijoo versus the "Falsely" Possessed in Eighteenth-century Spain', in Willem de Blécourt and Owen Davies, eds, *Beyond the Witch Trials: Witchcraft and Magic in Enlightenment Europe* (Manchester, 2004), 45–60 (quote at 54).

[12] For an English condensation of Tausiet's *Los posesos de Tosas (1812–14): Brujería y justicia popular en tiempos de revolución* (Saragossa, 2002) see 'The Possessed of Tosos (1812–1814): Witchcraft and Popular Justice during the Spanish Revolution', in Hans de Waardt, Jürgen Michael Schmidt, and Dieter Bauer, eds, *Dämonische Bessessenheit* (Bielefeld, 2005), 263–80.

them. Like Spain south of the Henningsen–Knutsen line and much of Italy, Sicily had
no local 'witches' in the northern European sense. As Bethencourt noted, both the
Italian and Iberian peninsula shared a colourful 'Mediterranean' underworld of illicit
magicians selling love potions, defences against the evil eye, and high-end ventures to
find buried treasures. Moreover, inquisitors in Sicily, like their colleagues throughout
Iberia, prosecuted roughly equal numbers of men and women for illicit magic.
Although Sicily's trial records were publicly burned when its inquisitorial tribunal
was abolished in 1782, two sources provide considerable evidence about the Spanish
Inquisition's activities here. Many annual reports of its activities between 1540 and 1700
are preserved in Madrid, and about four hundred volumes of its fiscal records survive
in Palermo. The latter have enabled a local researcher, Maria Sofia Messana, both to
identify no fewer than 195 *autos de fe* held between 1501 and 1744 and to underline the
close involvement of the Spanish inquisition with colonial rule on the island, for
example by holding an unprecedented four public *autos* and discovering at least two
further Sicilian conspiracies in the immediate aftermath of a failed revolt in 1647.[13]

Sicily held two dubious distinctions within the Spanish inquisitorial system. Its
blasphemers received exceptionally stiff galley sentences from shocked Spanish-born
inquisitors because of the extravagant inventiveness of their oaths, and its magical
treasure-seekers far exceeded their Iberian counterparts by creating what is probably
Europe's earliest testimony about 'black masses' in 1586, including both animal sacrifice
and ritual homosexuality.[14] Jurisdictionally, the Spanish Inquisition worked in
extremely close cooperation with Sicilian episcopal authorities, who participated in
all its activities from denunciations to torture, and voted on punishment in every case.
Together, they maintained almost complete control of prosecutions for illicit magic.
Although Sicily's parliament discussed making diabolical witchcraft a capital crime in
1630, the island's secular courts rarely investigated it; barely 1 per cent of the inquisition's magical cases had been transferred from secular courts. As elsewhere, lay justice
seems harsher. In 1789, with the Sicilian Inquisition legally abolished, Palermo's Gran
Corte condemned an old crone, known as the 'vinegar woman', for poisoning.

In addition to his work on Basque witchcraft, Gustav Henningsen has also studied
Sicily's most distinctive contribution to Mediterranean (and European) witchcraft.
This involved the activities of nocturnal groups known to the inquisitors as 'ladies
from outside' (*donni* [*sic*] *di fuora*). These women mediated between humans and
fairies, who were also known in Sicily as *donne di fori*. Like witches, they could
transform themselves into animals, fly around at night in groups, and heal supernatur-
ally inflicted illnesses. Unlike a classical witches' sabbath, no devils attended their

---

[13] Maria Sofia Messana, *Inquisitori, negromanti e streghe nella Sicilia moderna 1500–1782* (Palermo,
2007), 137–9, 415–16, 593–607 (list of autos).

[14] Monter, *Frontiers of Heresy*, 164–85; William Monter, 'Black Mass', in Richard M. Golden, ed.,
Encyclopedia of Witchcraft: The Western Tradition, 4 vols (Santa Barbara, CA, 2006), i, 125 (The
ringleader was sent to serve in the galleys, where he continued his activities and was rearrested).

nocturnal meetings; instead, everything was delightful—music, dancing, fine clothes, good food—and as they left, they said 'stop the dance and may prosperity increase'.

But Sicilian clerics had mistrusted the activities of good fairies since the mid-fifteenth century, and Spanish inquisitors, who began interrogating them in 1579, immediately concluded that these people were witches (*brujas*). Because the 'ladies from outside' had male as well as female ringleaders, ten of these ninety suspects were men (two of them were sent to the galleys). At the opposite end of modern Italy, the Roman Inquisition had diabolized the mostly male nocturnal (and also originally benevolent) *benandanti* of north-eastern Friuli by the mid-seventeenth century. In Sicily, although Messana considers that the long-serving inquisitor Trasmiera (1634–1665) gradually 'succeeded in turning fantastic tales into diabolical realities', Henningsen insists that, despite numerous shared features of the *donne di fuora* and the witches' sabbath, not even the Spanish Inquisition could give 'cumulative' witchcraft a firm foothold in a Sicilian folk culture that—unlike the folklore of a region on the Austrian border—lacked a harmful parallel group of diabolical *stregoni* (witches).[15]

15.3 Portugal

Francisco Bethencourt noted in 1994 that 'in Portugal, [witchcraft] was an even more residual phenomenon for the Inquisition than in Spain, not only with respect to the volume of cases, but also the quality of punishments'. Over its whole history, he observed, such cases comprised roughly half of their level in Castile: barely 3 per cent of all trials at Coimbra, even less at Évora, and only slightly more at Lisbon. And being much smaller than Spain, with only three inquisitorial tribunals, all possessing well-preserved records, Portugal's history of witchcraft and superstitious magic seems in some ways more easily accessible than that of its larger neighbour. Consequently, a combination of two recent investigations, Bethencourt's 1987 exploration of sixteenth-century evidence and José Paiva's larger survey in 1997 covering the next two centuries, provides a satisfactory overview.[16]

Three other aspects of this subject also deserve attention. First, Portugal lacks preserved records of criminal trials from its secular courts, so that apart from a handful of cases punished at Lisbon in 1559 and 1560 we know virtually nothing about non-ecclesiastical involvement with maleficent magic anywhere in this kingdom. Second,

---

[15] Gustav Henningsen, '"The Ladies from Outside": An Archaic Pattern of the Witches' Sabbath', in B. Ankarloo and G. Henningsen, eds, *Early Modern European Witchcraft: Centres and Peripheries* (Oxford, 1990), 191–215; Henningsen, 'Sicily', in *Encyclopedia of Witchcraft*, iv, 1032–4; cf. Messana, *Inquisitori, negromanti e streghe*, 550–69 (quote at 554).

[16] Bethencourt, 'Univers saturé de magie', 186–7, 188–9 (quote at 188). Neither Francisco Bethencourt's *O Imiaginario da magia: feiticerias, saludadores e nigromantes no séc. XVI* (Lisbon, 1987), nor José Pedro Paiva's *Bruxaria e superstição num país sem 'caça às bruxas' (1600-1774)* (Lisbon, 1997) has been translated into English.

Portuguese inquisitorial interest in illicit magic did not reach its peak until the eighteenth century, with the largest number of cases occurring between 1715 and 1755—a chronology matched on Spanish soil only in the Canary Islands. Such trials accelerated after 1690, with new edicts against magical healers, *curanderos* and *saludadores*. Timothy Walker links the accelerated Holy Office persecution of folk healers in 'Enlightenment' Portugal to its increasing use of university-trained physicians as inquisitorial familiars and expert witnesses in such cases.[17]

A third Portuguese peculiarity, largely a consequence of the first two, is that public executions for anything that we might want to label as 'witchcraft' seem extraordinarily rare here. Among 818 formal trials for superstitious magic, Portugal's Holy Office recorded only four death sentences between 1626 and 1744—fewer than the five witches executed at Lisbon in 1559 by secular justice. However, several inquisitorial prisoners charged with illicit magic, twenty-seven in all, died in prison. Other Portuguese peculiarities include the complete absence of weather magic or printed manuals for exorcists. Few clergymen or highly educated laypeople were tried for illicit magic; Paiva found only ten clerics among 818 defendants, including an Italian alchemist arrested in 1619.[18]

Like other Europeans, the Portuguese never doubted that people could inflict physical harm through magical means, and Portugal's churchmen were as obsessed as their counterparts elsewhere in Christendom by the possibility of making direct or indirect pacts with demons for a variety of purposes. Even though they employed torture increasingly over time, Portugal's Holy Office managed to wring confessions of diabolical pacts from only 12 per cent of its 654 prisoners who made confessions; half of these confessed only after torture. But Portugal's inquisitors paid so little attention to reports of physical harm inflicted by witches that when they captured a suspect who had been accused of murdering fifty people, they questioned her *only* about her dealings with the devil. In fact, in a complete reversal of the priorities of Europe's secular courts, none of the four people whom Portugal's Holy Office executed for diabolical magic had been charged with inflicting any physical harm on either people or property. What they *had* done was confess on two separate occasions to making pacts renouncing Christianity, thus making them eligible for capital punishment as relapsed apostates.[19]

Portuguese inquisitors believed that people who had made such pacts met at collective nocturnal assemblies, but they had considerable trouble imposing this idea on Portugal's largely rural population. Only forty-two confessions made by defendants accused of illicit magic (about half of those who admitted some form of diabolical pact)

---

[17] Timothy Walker, *Doctors, Folk Medicine and the Inquisition: The Repression of Magical Healing in Portugal during the Enlightenment* (Leiden, 2005).

[18] Paiva, *Bruxaria*, 64, 125, 163–4; Paiva, 'Portugal', in *Encyclopedia of Witchcraft*, iii, 920; Francisco Bethencourt, 'Portugal: A Scrupulous Inquisition', in Ankarloo and Henningsen, eds, *Early Modern European Witchcraft*, 405.

[19] Paiva, *Bruxaria*, 144–8, 151, 355.

mentioned such gatherings. The word *sabbat* never appears in Portuguese trial records (although, in a land full of 'New Christians' of Jewish ancestry, *sinagogas* does). One prisoner, after admitting attending several festivals (*festas*) in honour of the 'prince of demons', told the surprised inquisitors that at these events he had joined the brotherhood of Our Lady of the Rosary and received a rosary to help him pray. The fullest description of such an assembly came very late, in 1735, and one of its most curious details was the prisoner's assertion that she summoned the devil by naming John Calvin![20]

15.4 FUTURE RESEARCH

Spain and Portugal, two nations with a long and sometimes painful history of coexistence on the Iberian peninsula, joined the European Community simultaneously over a quarter-century ago, but they still rarely cooperate with each other. The history of witchcraft typifies this situation and obscures some important similarities between these neighbours. For example, publications about witchcraft seem extremely rare throughout the Iberian peninsula during the major phase of witch-hunting in Western Europe, and it is only a slight exaggeration to claim that 'Iberian demonology' is an oxymoron. With few exceptions, Spanish and Portuguese titles discussing such subjects are 'anti-superstitious', composed by theologians and dedicated primarily to attacking incorrect religious practices. Only the most obscure Spanish title, published at Huesca in northern Aragon in 1632, directly encouraged witch-hunting. The only Portuguese author with experience as an inquisitor discussed magical healing but ignored *maleficium*; Portugal's only other 'demonologist', a physician, confined himself to Italian evidence when doubting the possibility of spreading plague through diabolical means.[21]

As this last detail illustrates, the interrelationship between early modern Iberia—where the Spanish and Portuguese Crowns were united on a personal (but not institutional) level from 1580 to 1640—and Italy (much of it dominated politically by the Spanish Habsburgs during most of the era of witch trials) raises various problems for historians of witchcraft. For example, the author of the most widely read handbook for confessors in Catholic Europe during the apogee of witch-hunting was a Basque, Martin de Azpilcueta, known as 'Navarro' from his northern Spanish birthplace, who taught canon law at Portugal's only university when he first published his *Enchiridion* in Portuguese in 1549. In it, Azpilcueta grouped all forms of illicit magic as sins against

---

[20] Paiva, *Bruxaria*, 137, 149, 154–5. Paiva noted that this ratio of sabbaths resembled what Gari Lacruz [*supra*, n. 9] found in Spanish Aragon, although Portuguese chronology is different, with the fullest descriptions coming at the end rather than the beginning of the series.

[21] María Tausiet, 'Le sabbat dans les traités espagnols sur la superstition et la sorcellerie aux XVIe et XVIIe siècle', in Jacques-Chaquin and Préaud, *Le sabbat des sorciers*, 259–80; Paiva, *Bruxaria*, 19–36; José Pedro Paiva, 'Moura, Manuel Vale de (d. 1560)', in Golden, ed., *Encyclopedia of Witchcraft*, iii, 792–93.

the first commandment, and laid special emphasis on possible misuses of sacred objects (e.g. Eucharistic hosts, holy water, altar stones) for such purposes. He next taught at Salamanca and his *Enchiridion* appeared in Spanish by 1556. Azpilcueta ended his career as a judicial consultant to the standing committee that governed the Roman Inquisition. Ninety-one editions of Azpilcueta's handbook had appeared by 1625. Fifty-seven were in Latin, nineteen in Spanish, eight in Italian, four in French, and three in Portuguese. Although dismissed as unimaginative Thomism by the leading intellectual historian of demonology, Azpilcueta's enormously popular guide fits almost perfectly with the intellectual framework shared by all three great Mediterranean inquisitions.[22]

Other problems are more strictly Iberian. For example, Portugal occasionally borrowed bits of popular folklore from Spain (e.g. invoking 'Maria Padilla', later identified as the 'wife of the lame devil', in conjurations), but was this process ever reversed? More importantly, does the east–west 'Henningsen-Knutsen line' separating fully conceptualized witchcraft from less malevolent forms of superstitious magic extend into Portugal? There is reason to suspect that the cumulative concept of witchcraft, especially sabbaths, weakened both west and south of the Basque country. In Spain's north-western corner, Jaime Contreras found an 'almost absolute absence of witchcraft in the strict sense' among the thousands of inquisitorial cases from the Galician tribunal of Santiago de Compostela. When Galician secular courts began trials of witches (here called *meigas*) in 1611 and 1626, complete with torture, multiple arrests, and accusations against 200 people, the Holy Office intervened and stopped them. Portugal's richest evidence about assemblies of witches comes from the Douro valley, south of Galicia.[23]

A more ambitious research programme might explore the relationship between Iberian inquisitorial repression of illicit magic and Africans who were nominally Christians but often slaves. James H. Sweet has recently explored this problem with brio, following the career of an African-born magical healer from Brazil back to Portugal.[24] Such men and women appear more often in inquisitorial records from the Canary Islands (where 20 per cent of all such defendants were full-blooded Africans and another 25 per cent were mulattos) and from Lisbon (which also handled serious cases from Brazil) than anywhere else in Europe. Both tribunals share an overlapping chronology, with interest in such issues peaking from the late seventeenth through the mid-eighteenth century, and each provides some tantalizing pieces of information. In the Canaries, 'witches' seem obviously responsible for the occasional appearance of the devil in the form of a camel; at Lisbon, one finds African women using original invocations and several African men selling special forms of magical charms to protect

[22] María Tausiet, 'Le sabbat dans les traités espagnols sur la superstition et la sorcellerie aux XVIe et XVIIe siècle', in Jacques-Chaquin and Préaud, *Le sabbat des sorciers*, 259–80; Paiva, *Bruxaria*, 19–36.
[23] Paiva, *Bruxaria*, 101–2, 141, 155; Jaime Contreras, *El Santo Oficio de la Inquisición de Galicia* (Madrid, 1982), 687–91 (quote at 687).
[24] James H. Sweet, *Domingos Álvares, African Healing, and the Intellectual History of the Atlantic World* (Chapel Hill, NC, 2011).

the wearer against physical harm in quarrels. The most noteworthy peculiarity, which bothered Lisbon's inquisitors in 1731, was an African's confession that he and his companions had been sodomized by the devil at a nocturnal assembly; the inquisitors finally concluded—on the basis of Italian evidence!—that such behaviour was theologically possible.[25]

Another problem that deserves investigation across national borders is the role of professional witchfinders throughout the Pyrenees. Although they seem absent during the decisive events on both sides of the French–Spanish border from 1609–14, witchfinders appear in most other outbreaks of intensive witch-hunting on both sides of the mountains. One finds them as early as the two young girls hired by the Navarrese witch-hunter Balanza in 1525, and as late as the teenage boy taken to many villages of Béarn by judges from its parlement in 1670. This phenomenon extended all the way across the Pyrenees, on both sides, and proved extremely difficult for high-level sceptical officials to control in either Spain or France. Pyrenean witchcraft apparently flowed from north to south. The most dangerous witchfinders, often men born in France, drove Spain's deadliest witch-hunt, in Catalonia between 1618 and 1621. Later, we find them at work on the French side of the border in 1643 and 1644, during the largest recorded outbreak of witch trials in Languedoc, where they preoccupied the Parlement of Toulouse, who caught and punished some of them. At the same time, a mock-heroic Catalan chapbook celebrated a mythical Frenchman who had identified over three thousand witches.[26]

Interesting gender differences appear to exist within the groups of 'real' witches in northern Spain. It seems highly pertinent that although *desaforamientos* mentioned both male and female witches in their preambles, secular justice in early modern Aragon and Catalonia almost never arrested a man for witchcraft. In Aragon, Tausiet identifies seventy women (and no men) named in surviving secular and inquisitorial sources.[27] Catalonia seems similarly gender-specific during its great hunt of 1614–22, although the evidence has yet to be sifted. However, the Basque country looks very different. Here one can find several men among Navarre's witches in both the early and late waves of prosecution. It also seems pertinent that Navarre's very first recorded publicly paid witchfinders, back in the 1520s, should have been two little girls, whereas twenty years later Catalonia's first recorded witchfinder was a Morisco – and only men did this job afterwards in the central and eastern Pyrenees.

FURTHER READING

Alcoberro, Agustí, 'Cacera de bruixes, justícia local i Inquisicío a Catalunya, 1487–1643: alguns criteris metodològics', *Pedralbes: Revista d'Història Moderna*, 28 (2008), 485–504.

---

[25] Fajardo Spinola, *Hechicería y brujeria en Canarias*, 324–6; Paiva, *Bruxaria*, 37, 114, 129, 156.
[26] Monter, *Frontiers of Heresy*, 120–2, 274–5.
[27] Tausiet, *Pozoña*, 548–51.

Bethencourt, Francisco, *O Imiaginario da magia: feiticerias, saludadores e nigromantes no séc. XVI* (Lisbon, 1987).

Bethencourt, Francisco, 'Portugal: A Scrupulous Inquisition', in Bengt Ankarloo and Gustav Henningsen, eds, *Early Modern European Witchcraft: Centres and Peripheries* (Oxford, 1990), 403–22.

Caro Baroja, Julio, *The World of the Witches*, tr. O. N. V. Glendinning (Chicago, 1964).

Fajardo Spinola, Francisco, *Hechicería y brujería en Canarias en la Edad Moderna* (Las Palmas, 1992).

Gari Lacruz, Ángel, *Brujería e Inquisición en Aragón* (2nd edn, Saragossa, 2007).

Henningsen, Gustav, *The Witches' Advocate: Basque Witchcraft and the Spanish Inquisition* (Reno, NV, 1980).

Henningsen, Gustav, '"The Ladies from Outside": An Archaic Pattern of the Witches' Sabbath', in Bengt Ankarloo and Gustav Henningsen, eds, *Early Modern European Witchcraft: Centres and Peripheries* (Oxford, 1990), 191–215.

Henningsen, Gustav, ed., *The Salazar Documents: Inquisitor Alonso de Salazar Frías and Others on the Basque Witch Persecution* (Leiden, 2004).

Knutsen, Gunnar W., *Servants of Satan and Masters of Demons: The Spanish Inquisition's Trials for Superstition in Valencia and Barcelona, 1478–1700* (Turnhout, 2009).

Messana, Maria, Sofia, *Inquisitori, negromanti e streghe nella Sicilia moderna 1500–1782* (Palermo, 2007).

Monter, William, *Frontiers of Heresy: The Spanish Inquisition from the Basque Lands to Sicily* (Cambridge, 1990).

Paiva, José Pedro, *Bruxaria e superstiçao num país sem 'caça às bruxas'* (Lisbon, 1997).

Sweet, James H., *Domingos Álvares, African Healing, and the Intellectual History of the Atlantic World* (Chapel Hill, NC, 2011).

Tausiet, María, *Ponzoña en los ojos: Brujería y superstición en Aragon en el siglo XVI* (2nd edn, Madrid, 2004).

Tausiet, María, 'The Possessed of Tosos (1812–1814): Witchcraft and Popular Justice during the Spanish Revolution', in Hans de Waardt, Jürgen Michael Schmidt, and Dieter Bauer, eds, *Dämonische Bessenheit* (Bielefeld, 2005), 263–80.

Walker, Timothy D., *Doctors, Folk Medicine and the Inquisition: The Repression of Magical Healing in Portugal during the Enlightenment* (Leiden, 2005).

CHAPTER 16

....

WITCHCRAFT TRIALS
IN ENGLAND

....

MALCOLM GASKILL

HISTORICAL enquiry into English witch trials began with two books in the second decade of the eighteenth century. The best known was by Francis Hutchinson, a Suffolk clergyman who had finished writing some years earlier, but delayed publication until 1718 due to the political sensitivity of his subject. No witch had been executed in England since the 1680s, but trials continued into the eighteenth century, most famously that of Jane Wenham, whose conviction in 1712 sparked off a pamphlet war between sceptical Whigs and traditionalist Tories. Hutchinson was a Whig but an ambitious one, and had no desire to offend the conservative archbishop of Canterbury. However, after the publication in 1715 of a credulous book by a writer named Richard Boulton the time felt right. Hutchinson's work, then, was not merely a contribution to knowledge but a calculated assault on the defenders of superstition and persecution. His strategy paid off and by 1720 he was the bishop of Down and Connor. Of Boulton we hear little more.[1]

It is easy to portray Hutchinson as a harbinger of the Enlightenment and Boulton as a benighted reactionary. In truth, their opposing claims shared common ground. Most of Hutchinson's ideas were asserted rather than reasoned, involving mockery of witch beliefs in general and Boulton in particular. Nor did he surrender his belief in the agency of evil spirits; men who did risked being accused of atheism. Boulton, by contrast, used a method that had served thinkers well for generations: he accumulated ancient precept and telling example to establish witchcraft's reality. He was Oxford-educated, steeped in the latest natural philosophy, and his opinions, though not consensual, were far from eccentric. Attitudes to witchcraft were shaped not just by

---

[1] Francis Hutchinson, *An Historical Essay Concerning Witchcraft* (London, 1718); Richard Boulton, *A Compleat History of Magick, Sorcery, and Witchcraft*, 2 vols (London, 1715); Andrew Sneddon, *Witchcraft and the Whigs: The Life of Bishop Francis Hutchinson, 1660–1739* (Manchester, 2008).

academic disciplines but by natural inclination and the voice of conscience. Fashion played a part, too, with an educated middle class self-consciously distancing itself from the 'foolish' beliefs of the lower orders. Hutchinson and Boulton were not modern empiricists as neither properly tested a hypothesis. Instead, both belonged to an age of divine providence and revelation, and differed only in the extent to which they managed to suspend disbelief.[2]

The shape of this debate owes less to the eighteenth century per se and more to the history of witchcraft as a whole. From the Tudors to the Hanoverians, there was no simple trajectory between credulity and scepticism: these positions coexisted through-out the early modern period.[3] Key aspects of the Hutchinson–Boulton disagreement appeared earlier: Glanvill versus Webster in the 1670s; controversy surrounding the witch trials of the 1640s; disputed possession cases around 1600; and Reginald Scot's critique and its backlash in the 1580s. The Continental writers Jean Bodin and Johann Weyer also locked horns, and in England were read by Scot and his successors.[4] Intellectually, these commentators resembled each other more than the 'sceptics' resemble us. This blurring of the battle lines demonstrates how witchcraft was forever poised between probability and improbability, certainty and impossibility. Had equivo-cation been confined to university disputations it would hardly have mattered. But judges and juries *also* had to decide the truth of witchcraft: the guilt or innocence of individuals on trial for their lives.[5]

The courts' fear of hanging blameless women is reflected in the low conviction rate: 22 per cent in south-eastern England.[6] Reliable runs of indictments do not survive for the most part, but it is unlikely that even during bursts of paranoia more than half of prosecutions—the European average—were successful.[7] This wariness may also explain why, given the omnipresence of causal factors—religious polarization, godly demonization, endemic witch beliefs, legislation against witchcraft, an expanding legal culture, and neighbourly tensions—trials were comparatively rare.[8] There was no mass scapegoating by peasants unwilling to accept misfortunes as divine punishments. Communities lived with their witches for years, deterred by the expense of prosecution, and fear of revenge and counter-suit, and preferring informal methods of protection

---

[2] James Sharpe, ed., *The Final Debate*, in James Sharpe and Richard Golden, eds, *English Witchcraft, 1560–1736*, 6 vols (London, 2003), vi, pp. vii–xv.

[3] William Monter, 'Re-contextualizing British Witchcraft', *Journal of Interdisciplinary History*, 35 (2004), 105–11, esp. 107.

[4] Stuart Clark, *Thinking with Demons: The Idea of Witchcraft in Early Modern Europe* (Oxford, 1997), 195–213.

[5] Malcolm Gaskill, 'Witchcraft and Evidence in Early Modern England', *Past & Present*, 198 (2008), 33–70. See also Brian P. Levack, *The Witch-Hunt in Early Modern Europe* (3rd edn, Harlow, 2006), 78–108, 213–34; James Sharpe, *Instruments of Darkness: Witchcraft in England, 1550–1750* (London, 1996), 80–102, 231–4.

[6] Sharpe, *Instruments of Darkness*, 105–27, esp. 111.

[7] Levack, *Witch-Hunt*, 22–3.

[8] See Wolfgang Behringer's comparison of European executions and populations: *Witches and Witch-Hunts* (Cambridge, 2004), 150.

and retaliation, including counter-magic.[9] Potential accusers must have known their chance of success at law was poor. Most people accepted witches' existence, but proving their crimes was supremely difficult. We might wonder why there were any convictions at all.[10]

An understanding of how private suspicions became public accusations is a comparatively recent achievement. It was not something Hutchinson or Boulton would have been concerned with or able to explain. An interpretative thread runs through histories of witchcraft from the eighteenth to the twentieth centuries, namely that witch-hunts were the product of ignorance from below and religious zeal from above. Hutchinson rooted persecution in popish intolerance, but Puritans were also fair game, most notoriously the witchfinder Matthew Hopkins.[11] Witch beliefs were a vivid symbol of pre-Enlightenment unreason, a key to everything that progressive thinkers had overturned. For decades, rationalist writers could not explain the 'witch craze' any other way.[12]

Things did not change until the historical profession adopted the empirical habit of scientists, whose mechanical universe had helped banish witches. By 1650, when the legal basis of witchcraft was crumbling, natural philosophers were already favouring inductive over deductive reasoning. The path to truth was cleared of old assumptions and paved with evidence from which new ideas might be formed—established paradigms began to shift.[13] Something similar dawned on historians of witchcraft in the twentieth century. Rationalist triumphalism was set aside, and primary sources examined. The first milestone was a book by Wallace Notestein in 1911. Notestein praised Hutchinson for his 'epoch-making history', but began by observing that 'few subjects have gathered about themselves so large concretions of misinformation as English witchcraft'. Implicit here was the suggestion that, for all his wry detachment, Hutchinson's legacy had been negligible.[14] In 1929 George Lyman Kittredge also completed a vast amount of research to form some penetrating insights into the world of witch beliefs. He emphasized both popular and elite obsessions and explored their interactions.[15]

Notestein and Kittredge were Americans: what had England to offer? Two figures stand out: Margaret Murray, an ethnologist who claimed that witches had belonged to

[9] Described in Robin Briggs, *Witches and Neighbours: The Social and Cultural Context of European Witchcraft* (London, 1996), 135–68.

[10] Some tribunals suspended evidential rules: Christina Larner, 'Crimen Exceptum? The Crime of Witchcraft in Europe', in V. A. C. Gatrell, Bruce Lenman, and Geoffrey Parker, eds, *Crime and the Law: The Social History of Crime in Western Europe since 1500* (London, 1980), 49–75.

[11] Hutchinson, *Historical Essay*, esp. 59–72.

[12] See, for example, W. E. H. Lecky, *A History of the Rise and Influence of the Spirit of Rationalism in Europe*, 2 vols (London, 1865), i, 27–154.

[13] Barbara J. Shapiro, *Probability and Certainty in Seventeenth-Century England* (Princeton, 1983), 163–226.

[14] Wallace Notestein, *A History of Witchcraft in England from 1558 to 1718* (Washington, DC, 1911), pp. v–xi, quotations at pp. v, ix.

[15] George Lyman Kittredge, *Witchcraft in Old and New England* (New York, 1929).

a proscribed cult, and Montague Summers, a fanatical Catholic obsessed with Satanism.[16] In 1929, however, a remarkable publication abstracted 790 witchcraft indictments from the Home Circuit assize records, 1560–1701. The author, C. L'Estrange Ewen, was rigorous and dispassionate, and, bypassing 'the disgusting habits and filthy orgies commonly ascribed to devil-worshippers' (Summers' territory), delivered 'an account of the official machinery of conviction and punishment and statistics of its functioning'. Four years later he assembled another body of evidence from nationwide sources.[17] Ewen's work went beyond Notestein and Kittredge, who had relied mainly on print, and established for the history of English witchcraft what the archivist Joseph Hansen had in Germany: the need to learn what had happened in the courts.[18]

In the mid-1940s two new books appeared. The folklorist Christina Hole's account was aimed at general readers, yet by noticing the sources and eschewing myth she gave a sober 'impression of witchcraft in England as it appeared when all believed in it'.[19] In its wake came a monograph by historian R. Trevor Davies, which delved deep into English sources, displaying an obvious debt to Kittredge, Notestein, and Ewen. Davies' interest in the Civil Wars led him to exaggerate the role of witch-hunting in great events, but he still demonstrated the potential for a tighter chronology, a socio-political focus, and an empirically based methodology.[20] Twenty years passed before the next important contribution, an extended essay by Hugh Trevor-Roper, which took witchcraft seriously as a philosophical and political idea. For his analysis of English witch trials, Trevor-Roper drew appreciatively upon Ewen—the subject's 'closest student'—but expressed indifference to underlying beliefs and social conditions.[21]

The year 1967 saw not only Trevor-Roper's publication but the completion of a doctoral thesis by Alan Macfarlane, an analysis of witchcraft accusations in Essex supervised by Keith Thomas, who himself was writing a book on popular beliefs. Their work, which appeared in the early 1970s, made Trevor-Roper's high-mindedness seem old-fashioned.[22] This was scholarly history from the bottom up, setting a new

[16] Margaret Murray, *The Witch Cult in Western Europe* (Oxford, 1921); Montague Summers, *The History of Witchcraft and Demonology* (London, 1926). See also Juliette Wood, 'The Reality of Witch-cults Reasserted: Fertility and Satanism', in Jonathan Barry and Owen Davies, eds, *Witchcraft Historiography* (Basingstoke, 2007), 69–89.

[17] C. L'Estrange Ewen, *Witch Hunting and Witch Trials* (London, 1929), quotation at p. xii; C. L'Estrange Ewen, *Witchcraft and Demonianism* (London, 1933). See also Ewen's *Witchcraft in Star Chamber* (n.p., 1938).

[18] Joseph Hansen, *Zauberwahn, Inquisition, und Hexenprozessen im Mittelalter und die Entstehung der Grossen Hexenverfolgung* (Munich, 1900).

[19] Christina Hole, *Witchcraft in England* (London, 1945), 8.

[20] R. Trevor Davies, *Four Centuries of Witch-Beliefs with Special Reference to the Great Rebellion* (London, 1947).

[21] H. R. Trevor-Roper, *The European Witch-Craze of the Sixteenth and Seventeenth Centuries* (London, 1969), 89–91, quotation at 89. Reprinted from *Religion, the Reformation and Social Change* (London, 1967).

[22] Alan Macfarlane, *Witchcraft in Tudor and Stuart England: A Regional and Comparative Study* (London, 1970); Keith Thomas, *Religion and the Decline of Magic: Studies in Popular Beliefs in Sixteenth- and Seventeenth-Century England* (London, 1971).

agenda for English witchcraft studies. Both Thomas and Macfarlane were indebted to Ewen, and, like him, sedulous combers of archives.[23] But they also employed socio-logical and anthropological models, which aligned them with a generation of 'new social historians', who used myriad sources and put the politics back in. Thomas and Macfarlane linked the rise of witch trials to wider changes, specifically post-Reforma-tion orthodoxies, population increase, inflation, and the growth of poverty. According to the 'charity-refused' model, suspicions followed refusal to give alms, creating resentment on one side and guilt on the other; misfortune was then interpreted as magical revenge. The typical witchcraft accusation was not random, but arose from a relationship between a modestly prosperous householder and someone without a defined role in the community, usually an elderly woman.[24]

Criticisms and developments followed.[25] For one thing, some evidence from else-where in the country did not fit the 'charity-refused' model. Furthermore, counties on the Home Circuit that were very like Essex in society, economy, and religion produced considerably fewer witch trials. Abroad, the model had limited applicability. Some critics objected to overly prescriptive distinctions between religion and magic, and the crude determinism sociology and anthropology imposed on witchcraft accusations; twentieth-century Africa and seventeenth-century England were too dissimilar for parallels to be meaningful. Finally, sweeping inferences about long-term cultural change seemed too neat, plus Thomas' conclusions differed from Macfarlane's. The former saw, in the prosecution of witches' communities, bonding in an age of social crisis; the latter believed that crisis encouraged individualism.[26]

Neither historian was interested in pursuing the matter further; others were. Micro-studies demonstrated the importance of local politics, involving complicated commu-nity tensions and factions.[27] The communication of ideas received attention, as did the confluence of attitudes that created the witch image and affected the outcome of

---

[23] Thomas, *Religion and the Decline of Magic*, n. 517.

[24] Macfarlane and Thomas were influenced by E. E. Evans-Pritchard, *Witchcraft, Oracles and Magic among the Azande* (Oxford, 1937). See also Keith Thomas, 'The Relevance of Social Anthropology to the Historical Study of English Witchcraft', in Mary Douglas, ed., *Witchcraft Confessions and Accusations* (London, 1970), 47–81.

[25] E. P. Thompson, 'Anthropology and the Discipline of Historical Context', *Midland History*, 1 (1972), 43–8; David D. Hall, 'Witchcraft and the Limits of Interpretation', *New England Quarterly*, 58 (1985), 254–61; Jonathan Barry, 'Introduction: Keith Thomas and the Problem of Witchcraft', in Jonathan Barry, Marianne Hester, and Gareth Roberts, eds, *Witchcraft in Early Modern Europe: Studies in Culture and Belief* (Cambridge, 1996), 1–45; James Sharpe, 'Introduction', in Macfarlane's *Witchcraft* (2nd edn, London, 1999), xi–xxvi.

[26] Macfarlane changed his mind: *The Origins of English Individualism* (Oxford, 1978), 1–2, 59–61; *The Culture of Capitalism* (Oxford, 1987), 98–176.

[27] Annabel Gregory, 'Witchcraft, Politics and "Good Neighbourhood" in Early Seventeenth-century Rye', *Past & Present*, 133 (1991), 31–66; Peter Elmer, 'Towards a Politics of Witchcraft in Early Modern England', in Stuart Clark, ed., *Languages of Witchcraft: Narrative, Ideology and Meaning in Early Modern Culture* (Basingstoke, 2001) 101–18; Malcolm Gaskill, 'The Devil in the Shape of a Man: Witchcraft, Conflict and Belief in Jacobean England', *Historical Research*, 71 (1998), 142–71.

trials.[28] Law, evidence, and legal process were scrutinized.[29] We learned more about the adjuncts to witchcraft: cunning folk, animal familiars, demonic possession.[30] The question of gender, neglected by Macfarlane and Thomas, was addressed, involving not just male–female antagonisms but subtle identities within households and neighbourhoods.[31] Female subjectivities were teased from the evidence, especially confessions.[32] Work on Scotland, Europe, and America provided valuable comparisons and contexts, casting England's experience in a different light. The underlying assumption that continental cases focused more on diabolism and English cases on *maleficium* was revised.[33] The larger picture of English witch trials became deeper and richer, less static and predictable; its meanings were complex, nuanced, and ambiguous. The social reality of witchcraft existed in intricate details, in discretion and decision-making, in fear and fantasy, anger and loss of restraint.

Historians might be running out of things to say. Some excellent book-length case studies have added detail to the spatial and chronological picture without adding much

---

[28] Stuart Clark, 'Protestant Demonology: Sin, Superstition and Society (*c.* 1520–*c.* 1640)', in Bengt Ankarloo and Gustav Henningsen, eds, *Early Modern European Witchcraft: Centres and Peripheries* (Oxford, 1990), 45–81; Clive Holmes, 'Popular Culture? Witches, Magistrates and Divines in Early Modern England', in Steven L. Kaplan, ed., *Understanding Popular Culture* (Berlin, 1984), 85–111; Marion Gibson, *Reading Witchcraft: Stories of Early English Witches* (London, 1999).

[29] Gregory Durston, *Witchcraft and Witch Trials: A History of English Witchcraft and its Legal Perspectives, 1542 to 1736* (Chichester, 2000); J. A. Sharpe, 'Women, Witchcraft and the Legal Process', in Jenny Kermode and Garthine Walker, eds, *Women, Crime and the Courts in Early Modern England* (London, 1994), 106–24; Brian P. Levack, 'Possession, Witchcraft and the Law in Jacobean England', *Washington and Lee Law Review*, 52 (1996), 1613–40.

[30] Owen Davies, *Cunning Folk: Popular Magic in English History* (London, 2003); James Sharpe, 'The Witch's Familiar in Elizabethan England', in George W. Bernard and Steven J. Gunn, eds, *Authority and Consent in Tudor England: Essays Presented to C. S. L. Davies* (Aldershot, 2002), 219–32; J. A. Sharpe, 'Disruption in the Well-ordered Household: Age, Authority and Possessed Young People', in Paul Griffiths, Adam Fox, and Steve Hindle, eds, *The Experience of Authority in Early Modern England* (London, 1996), 187–212.

[31] Clive Holmes, 'Women: Witnesses and Witches', *Past & Present*, 140 (1993), 45–78; J. A. Sharpe, 'Witchcraft and Women in Seventeenth-century England: Some Northern Evidence', *Continuity and Change*, 6 (1991), 179–99; Deborah Willis, *Malevolent Nurture: Witch-Hunting and Maternal Power in Early Modern England* (London, 1995).

[32] Diane Purkiss, *The Witch in History: Early Modern and Twentieth-Century Representations* (London, 1996), 91–176; Malcolm Gaskill, 'Witchcraft and Power in Early Modern England: The Case of Margaret Moore', in Kermode and Walker, eds, *Women, Crime and the Courts*, 125–45; Louise Jackson, 'Witches, Wives and Mothers: Witchcraft Persecution and Women's Confessions in Seventeenth-century England', *Women's History Review*, 4 (1995), 63–83. Cf. Malcolm Gaskill, 'Masculinity and Witchcraft in Seventeenth-century England', in Alison Rowlands, ed., *Witchcraft and Masculinities in Early Modern Europe* (Basingstoke, 2009), 171–90.

[33] William P. Monter, *Witchcraft in France and Switzerland: The Borderlands during the Reformation* (London, 1976); H. C. Erik Midelfort, *Witch Hunting in Southwestern Germany, 1562–1684* (Stanford, CA, 1972); Christina Larner, *Enemies of God: The Witch-Hunt in Scotland* (London, 1981); Brian P. Levack, *Witch-Hunting in Scotland: Law, Politics and Religion* (London, 2008); Richard Godbeer, *The Devil's Dominion: Magic and Religion in Early New England* (Cambridge, 1992); Richard Weisman, *Witchcraft, Magic and Religion in Seventeenth-Century Massachusetts* (Amherst, MA, 1984).

to wider understanding.[34] Explaining long-term change remains one of the most challenging tasks. The future of witchcraft studies in England may lie in several directions: case studies that dig beneath the surface, demonstrating the intellectual and political linkages that made witch trials happen in some places and not in others; work that cross-fertilizes the history of witchcraft with expert legal or medical history, or perhaps theology or literary criticism; and genuinely comparative studies, using samples of different English regions, or England and other early modern states.[35]

16.1 ELIZABETHAN WITCHCRAFT PROSECUTIONS

In the Middle Ages, maleficent witchcraft featured in political conspiracies—including some at court—and the Church was hostile to magic and occasionally censured practitioners. Theologians were de facto demonologists, and the devil featured in the legends and superstitions of the multitude. But until the mid-sixteenth century, concern never erupted as official policy or popular protest.[36] In 1542 Henry VIII introduced the first Witchcraft Act, part of a legislative programme to establish the Tudor state. Death was prescribed for conjuring spirits, attempting to hurt or kill, finding treasure, and provoking love. The law did not attract much attention, and was repealed in 1547 and not replaced by Edward or Mary.[37] Witchcraft was, however, included by Cranmer in his canon law reforms of the 1550s, and also appeared as a new interrogatory in ecclesiastical visitation articles.[38] Although the history of English witch trials was guided by secular legal initiatives, it may have been the Church that got things started. After Elizabeth's accession in 1558, returning Marian exiles warned her of sorcery by Catholic enemies. A bill was read in parliament in 1559, and, though not fully ratified until 1563, was in force by 1560.[39]

Indictments from this time involved neither treason nor apostasy but social conflict: neighbourly disputes in obscure Essex villages. In one case, strange deaths were blamed

[34] For example: Philip C. Almond, *The Witches of Warboys* (London, 2008); Michael Honeybone, *'Wicked Practise & Sorcerye': The Belvoir Witchcraft Case of 1619* (Buckingham, 2008).

[35] On trajectories, see Ronald Hutton, 'Anthropological and Historical Approaches to Witchcraft: Potential for a New Collaboration?' *The Historical Journal*, 47 (2004), 413–34; Brian P. Levack, 'Themes of Recent Witchcraft Research', *ARV: Nordic Yearbook of Folklore*, 62 (2006), 7–31; Malcolm Gaskill, 'The Pursuit of Reality: Recent Research into the History of Witchcraft', *The Historical Journal*, 51 (2008), 1069–88.

[36] Notestein, *History of Witchcraft*, ch. 1; Kittredge, *Witchcraft*, ch. 2.

[37] Ewen, *Witch Hunting*, 13–15.

[38] I owe this observation to Michael Zell.

[39] Norman Jones, 'Defining Superstitions: Treasonous Catholics and the Act against Witchcraft of 1563', in Charles Carlton, Robert L. Woods, Mary L. Robertson, and Joseph S. Block, eds, *States, Sovereigns and Society in Early Modern England: Essays in Honour of A. J. Slavin* (Stroud, 1998), 187–203; Ewen, *Witch Hunting*, n. 15; Sharpe, *Instruments of Darkness*, 88–94.

on a brewer, in the other a woman was accused of harming neighbours and extorting money.[40] Earlier *maleficium* cases appear in the records of the church courts—which usually only dealt with trivial folk magic—perhaps indicating growth in popular anxiety about witches as economic conditions deteriorated.[41] Neither Church nor state had any special interest or capability in conducting witch-hunts: bishops and archdeacons relied on information from churchwardens, and secular justice followed accusatory principles where the onus lay with ordinary accusers. Cases could be shaped by clergymen, magistrates, and judges, but prosecutorial momentum came from below. The enforcement of Protestantism may have heightened sensitivity to the diabolic, and it is possible, as Keith Thomas suggested, that the proscription of medieval rituals left many feeling vulnerable to malign forces.[42] In these years, shortages of work and resources also bred competition and animosity between neighbours—prime conditions for the incubation of witchcraft suspicions.

What actually happened in these accusations? In his trawl through the Home Circuit assize records, Ewen uncovered the case of four women from Hatfield Peverel in Essex, tried in 1566. In their particulars, the indictments were much like the others: between them the suspects were said to have bewitched a man (who died), a woman (left disabled), an infant child, and various livestock. Two of the suspects, Laura Winchester and Joan Waterhouse, were acquitted, but Elizabeth Francis confessed to bewitching the child and was imprisoned according to statute. Agnes Waterhouse, Joan's mother, also confessed and was hanged; her crime murder.[43]

Given the brevity of indictments, in most instances this is all we could know. But the Hatfield Peverel witches are unusual in that within a month of their trial, a pamphlet was published—the earliest of its type—which adds detail to the story.[44] Elizabeth Francis was taught witchcraft by her grandmother, who also induced her to surrender her soul to a cat-like creature called 'Satan'. She used her power for personal gain, including avenging herself upon a wealthy man who had spurned her, and initiating Agnes Waterhouse, a poor widow, into her craft. Waterhouse quarrelled with neighbours and attacked their interests in farmyard, brewery, and dairy. She killed one man with a bloody flux, then tiring of her husband had Satan despatch him too. Her 18-year-old daughter Joan admitted asking Satan to frighten a girl who had refused her bread and cheese; this he did 'in the lyknes of an evyll favoured dogge with hornes on his head'.[45] In court, the victim confirmed this, saying the beast had appeared with the key to the dairy in its mouth.

On 29 July 1566, Mother Waterhouse was brought to the gallows, where she confessed, begging God's mercy. A spectator asked if she had bewitched a local tailor,

[40] Ewen, *Witch Hunting*, 117.
[41] For example, Canterbury Cathedral, City, and Diocesan Record Office, DCb/X.1.2, f. 1/50; X.1.3, ff. 156–8; X.1.5, ff.162$^\mathrm{v}$–163.
[42] Thomas, *Religion and the Decline of Magic*, 315–16, 588–93.
[43] Ewen, *Witch Hunting*, 120.
[44] *The examination and confession of certaine Wytches at Chensforde* (London, 1566).
[45] *The examination and confession*, sig. B4.

to which she replied that he 'was so strong in fayth that he [Satan] hadde no power to hurt hym'. Others quizzed her about religion, revealing that she was stuck in her old Catholic ways. Whether or not these conversations really happened, it is significant that the pamphleteer made them his finale. Popery and witchcraft were fused, and Protestant godliness endorsed. Waterhouse's wickedness was mitigated by her pious end, demonstrating the redeeming power of grace. As the rope tightened, 'she yelded up her sowle, trusting to be in joye with Christe her saviour, whiche dearely had bought her with his most precious bloudde'.[46] Elizabeth Francis served her sentence and returned to Hatfield Peverel, where she resumed her malevolent campaign. In 1572 and again in 1579 she confessed and was tried; first she was gaoled, then hanged. Again, her story made it into print. We read that Alice Poole had denied her some yeast so she 'badde a mischief to light uppon her', invoking the devil in the shape of a dog; she identified other witches and described their crimes. The author urged anyone with information about witchcraft to 'prevente or stop the mischief by all possible meanes'.[47]

Increased incidence of trials, and their reporting, contributed to a feeling that witches abounded but could be resisted in the courts. 'All possible means' did not include counter-magic: it meant orthodox religion and the law. Disincentives to prosecuting meant that a moment of confidence—or reckless desperation—had to intervene. The mood in Hatfield Peverel comprised heightened awareness of diabolism and a hardened resolve to act. The same was true of many other Essex parishes; but not all England was this resolute. Ewen's data indicate that in the fifty years between 1558 and 1607, 187 people were indicted in Essex, an average of around thirty-seven per decade (although in the median decade the number was nearly twice that). Sussex, by comparison, indicted just thirteen people in this period; in Kent it was twenty-five, in Hertford twenty-nine, and in Surrey thirty-five. Outside Essex, then, the decadal average was about five—one person in each county, every two years.[48] Rapid economic transformation, intense puritanism, advanced literacy, and the nucleation of communities may have raised prosecution levels in Essex. But why these should have been seven times higher than any neighbouring county is unknown.[49]

Educated men were influenced by the books available in later sixteenth-century England, but arguments for and against witch-hunting were equally compelling. In 1584, Reginald Scot, a Kentish gentleman, wrote a sceptical treatise after attending a witch trial in Rochester. The key witness was a vicar whom Scot thought misguided and malicious, hinting at his puritanism, which Scot saw as as socially divisive as Catholicism was spiritually corrupting.[50] Scot's defence of the equilibrium of the Elizabethan

---

[46] *The examination and confession*, 'The ende and last confession of mother Waterhouse at her death'.

[47] Ewen, *Witch Hunting*, 125, 138; *A Detection of damnable driftes, practized by three Witches arraigned at Chelmisforde* (London, 1579), sigs. A3ᵛ, A4.

[48] Decadal statistics are taken from Ewen, *Witch Hunting*, 99.

[49] Macfarlane, *Witchcraft*, 147–207, does not reach firm conclusions.

[50] Reginald Scot, *The Discoverie of Witchcraft* (London, 1584), 5–6; Ewen, *Witch Hunting*, 143. I am indebted to Peter Elmer for information about Scot.

state, a reformed land purged of witches and superstitions, had parallels elsewhere, even in the work of his critics. Henry Holland, a Cambridgeshire minister whose treatise was published in 1590, was implacably opposed to witchcraft, but worried more about his parishioners' inability to accept God's providence. Not only were misfortunes caused by sin blamed on witches, but ubiquitous cunning folk seduced 'victims' with their charms.[51] Other clerical authors, including George Gifford and William Perkins, said the same. White witches were, if anything, worse than maleficent ones, but the law did not concur.[52]

16.2 THE EARLY STUARTS AND THE INTERREGNUM

The most infamous Elizabethan witch trials, including that of the witches of Warboys in Huntingdonshire, were as likely to divide opinion as to unite it. In the Warboys' case, the daughters of Robert Throckmorton accused Alice Samuel of afflicting them with spirits, a charge given force by tensions between established farmers and rising Puritan gentry. The accused witch, her husband and daughter were all executed in 1593, not because the evidence against them was unimpeachable, but because political conditions for a conviction were ideal: the Throckmortons were well-connected, and the Cromwells, lords of the manor of Warboys, also accused Samuel.[53] It is hard to know who read pamphlets and what they thought about them, but we can identify two readers of the Warboys' account: William Sommers and Anne Gunter. Both copied the Throckmorton girls' ordeal to fake their own demonic possessions.[54]

The seventeenth century began with controversy over the exorcist John Darrell. For fifteen years previously, the Church had watched with alarm as Catholics and Protestants competed to cast out demons. Darrell's denunciation as a fraud—he may have coached William Sommers—discouraged trust in religious extremists and reasserted ecclesiastical authority.[55] But it had another effect. Given the conflation of

---

[51] Henry Holland, *A Treatise against Witchcraft* (Cambridge, 1590).

[52] George Gifford, *A Dialogue Concerning Witches and Witchcraftes* (London, 1593); William Perkins, *A Discourse of the Damned Art of Witchcraft* (Cambridge, 1608).

[53] *The most strange and admirable discoverie of the three Witches of Warboys* (London, 1593); Anne Reiber DeWindt, 'Witchcraft and Conflicting Visions of the Ideal Village Community', *Journal of British Studies*, 34 (1995), 427–63.

[54] James Sharpe, 'Witches of Warboys', in Richard M. Golden, ed., *Encyclopedia of Witchcraft: The Western Tradition*, 4 vols (Santa Barbara, CA, 2004), iv, 1180.

[55] Michael MacDonald, *Witchcraft and Hysteria in Elizabeth London* (London, 1991); Thomas Freeman, 'Demons, Deviance and Defiance: John Darrell and the Politics of Exorcism in Late Elizabethan England', in Peter Lake and Michael Questier, eds, *Conformity and Orthodoxy in the English Church, c. 1560–1660* (Woodbridge, 2000), 34–63; Marion Gibson, *Possession, Puritanism and Print: Darrell, Harsnett, Shakespeare and the Elizabethan Exorcism Controversy* (London, 2006).

bewitchment and possession by the 1590s, this reaction also promoted scepticism about the accusation of witches. The anti-Puritan archbishop of Canterbury passed the Darrell case to Richard Bancroft, bishop of London, who tasked his chaplain, Samuel Harsnett, to rebuke exorcists in print. This Harsnett did in 1603, displaying his admiration for Scot.[56] In the same year, James VI of Scotland became king of England, where, a reputation for witch-hunting notwithstanding, he took a sceptical line about witches and demoniacs. In 1605 he met the allegedly possessed Anne Gunter, but was unimpressed, and again the matter passed to Bancroft and Harsnett, who had the Gunters tried in Star Chamber for their imposture. The Church that had encouraged Elizabeth I to punish witches now encouraged her successor to investigate their accusers.[57]

From this point, it became difficult to say anything about witchcraft in public that was uncontroversial. Cases had been exposed to the royal gaze and found wanting. The issue was not whether witchcraft existed. Clerics were as wary of undermining the world of spirits, and so being accused of atheism, as they would be in Francis Hutchinson's day. Privately some may have considered witch trials a tragedy, or at least an embarrassment, but the Witchcraft Act stood and prosecutions continued. Indeed, James I introduced a new statute in 1604, not, as is sometimes supposed, to express his hatred of witches, but to suppress attempted invocation of spirits; in parallel with this, the Church's canons tightened injunctions about exorcism.

Ewen shows that in the thirty years between 1598 and 1627—James was succeeded by Charles I in 1625—ninety-one people were indicted on the Home Circuit, a fall of over 60 per cent from the three preceding decades. Almost half the accused came from Essex; the other four counties saw very few prosecutions, with none recorded for Surrey. Between the two periods, 1558–97 and 1598–1627, the conviction rate remained roughly constant at between 23 and 28 per cent, suggesting that the magistrates who forwarded accusations to the assizes, and possibly the grand jurors who screened cases, had advanced further in their scepticism than trial juries. When a case came to court in James I's reign, the defendant's chances were the same as in Elizabeth's; but now far fewer cases made it that far. Under Charles, the trickle of witch trials almost dried up. In the decade 1628–37, there were just eleven Home Circuit prosecutions—five in Essex, four in Kent, and two in Surrey—none of which resulted in a hanging.[58]

The religious politics that had influenced James' attitude became, under Charles, even more polarized—part of the cause and context of the war that began in 1642. Charles declined to support puritanical preoccupations like sorcery, possession, and idolatry, and his justices and judges knew it. In 1634 when a witch panic broke out in Pendle, Lancashire, not only were the accusers (including an eleven-year-old boy) sent to London to be questioned, but the king ordered his physician, William Harvey, to

---

[56] Samuel Harsnett, *A Declaration of egregious popish Impostures* (London, 1603); Clive Holmes, 'Witchcraft and Possession at the Accession of James I', in John Newton and Jo Bath, eds, *Witchcraft and the Act of 1604* (Leiden, 2007), 69–90.

[57] James Sharpe, *The Bewitching of Anne Gunter* (London, 1999).

[58] Ewen, *Witch Hunting*, 99.

examine the suspects' bodies. The accused were cleared, the accusers censured.[59] A more famous Pendle episode in 1612 had ended differently. Ten of the sixteen witches tried had been executed—a conviction rate of over 60 per cent—contrasting sharply with the Home Circuit experience, and providing an indication of what could happen when social, political, religious, and legal opinions were fatally aligned. The assize judges, so often impartial purveyors of law, in this instance probably obliged the Lancashire authorities, who were at war with ungodliness (of which popery and witchcraft were its most heinous manifestations). The proactive conduct of the magistrate Roger Nowell was critical in determining the scale of the trials, the force of the evidence, and the number of convictions.[60]

The lengthy pamphlet published by a court official at Lancaster might suggest that the judges anticipated criticism.[61] There is no evidence of their censure, but the writing was on the wall. At Leicester in 1616, nine women were hanged and another six saved by the intervention of James I, who saw through the pretended bewitchment. The judges were disgraced, and their peers took careful notice, as did magistrates in the shires.[62] The effect at the Home Circuit assizes was dramatic. We find seven indictments for 1618, none for 1619, and one for 1620; in 1621 two women were tried on five indictments, then nothing is recorded until 1626. All the trials between 1618 and 1621 ended in acquittal, except that of a widow reprieved after judgement.[63] This decline can also be seen in the literature. The flurry of print in the 1590s dwindled quickly after 1600. Between 1606 and 1625, we know of only five full-length pamphlets, including the one about the Lancashire witches. A tract from 1619 described, seriously, bewitchment in the earl of Rutland's household, but aimed 'not to make any contentious Arguments about the discourses, distinction or definition of Witchcraft'. In 1621 an account of the trial of Elizabeth Sawyer included a similar disclaimer, and after that no English witchcraft stories appeared in print for over twenty years.[64]

The pamphlet which, in 1643, broke the silence, told of the witch of Newbury, a woman who may have been a royalist spy, but whose story suited the witch stereotype: she was secretive, cold-blooded, and rebellious.[65] The extent to which this publication turned back the clock should be assessed alongside the political inversions of the Civil Wars, and the collapse of the royal policy and higher courts that had restrained

[59] National Archives, London, SP 16/271/15; Ewen, *Witchcraft and Demonianism*, 244–51.
[60] Jonathan Lumby, *The Lancashire Witch-Craze: Jennet Preston and the Lancashire Witches, 1612* (2nd edn, Lancaster, 1995); Robert Poole, ed., *The Lancashire Witches: Histories and Stories* (Manchester, 2002).
[61] Thomas Potts, *The Wonderfull Discoverie of Witches in the Countie of Lancaster* (London, 1613).
[62] *Calendar of State Papers, Domestic, 1611–18*, 398; Notestein, *History of Witchcraft*, 140–1.
[63] Ewen, *Witch Hunting*, 210–12.
[64] Marion Gibson, ed., *Early English Trial Pamphlets*, in Sharpe and Golden, eds, *English Witchcraft*, ii, xv–xvii; *The Wonderfull Discoverie of the Witchcrafts of Margaret and Phillip Flower* (London, 1619), sig. B1; Henry Goodcole, *The wonderfull Discoverie of Elizabeth Sawyer a Witch* (London, 1621), sigs. A3–A3ᵛ.
[65] *A Most Certain, Strange, and True Discovery of a Witch* (London, 1643); *Mercurius Civicus* (21–8 September 1643), 140.

witch-hunting. Around the country, pent-up anti-witch feeling was released. Where puritanism flourished trials increased, not least in Essex, where 45 people were tried between 1638 and 1647, compared to five in the preceding decade.[66] The witch-hunt of 1645, which accounted for most of these prosecutions, was part of a wider eastern outbreak, in which as many as 300 people were interrogated, and a third hanged. Just as previous witch-hunts had been started by an enthusiastic magistrate, now a campaign launched by two witchfinders, Matthew Hopkins and John Stearne, made the difference. Between 1645 and 1647 English courts heard an unprecedented number of confessions to diabolic allegiance—involving pacts with Satan in return for revenge and material possessions—harking back to the Hatfield Peverel trials, except now with a stronger sexual element. In the 1640s the conviction rate rose to between 42 and 46 per cent.[67]

The East Anglian witch-hunt, and the tracts it inspired, did not alter things permanently. Although there were more prosecutions on the Home Circuit in the late 1640s and 1650s, the conviction rate plummeted. Had it not been for a mass trial at Maidstone in 1652 the change would have been even more striking.[68] In contrast to Jacobean circumstances, by mid-century magistrates and grand jurors were relatively willing to allow witchcraft cases to go to trial, expecting that most juries, probably under judicial direction, would acquit those charged. The mood of the people, encouraged by apocalyptic images in Puritan preaching and widespread experience of wartime disorder, supported the idea that the devil stalked the land.[69] But the kind of confessions procured by Hopkins and Stearne, and their illegal means of extracting them, further undermined the crime for which, controversially, hard evidence was generally absent. Local borough courts could still follow their own rules. In 1650 authorities in Newcastle hired a witch-pricker who identified thirty suspects, fifteen of whom were executed.[70] But by 1660 this sort of irregularity was frowned upon, and had become unthinkable on the assize circuits.

16.3 Prosecutions and Attitudes after 1660

The fact that witchcraft trials disappeared from English life with a whimper not a bang is unsurprising given the intellectual and legal limbo they occupied for most of the

---

[66] Ewen, *Witch Hunting*, 99.

[67] Malcolm Gaskill, *Witchfinders: A Seventeenth-Century English Tragedy* (London, 2005); Ewen, *Witch Hunting*, 99.

[68] H. F., *A Prodigious & Tragicall History of the Arraignment, Tryall, Confession, and Condemnation of six Witches at Maidstone, in Kent* (London, 1652).

[69] Nathan Johnstone, *The Devil and Demonism in Early Modern England* (Cambridge, 2006), 213–86; Frederick Valletta, *Witchcraft, Magic and Superstition in England, 1640–70* (Aldershot, 2000), esp. 27–61.

[70] Roger Howell, *Newcastle upon Tyne and the Puritan Revolution* (Oxford, 1967), 232–3.

period. Trials fluctuated, varied from place to place, and, outside particular witch panics (always the exception to the rule), conviction rates were low. As Restoration assize records show, for as long as there was a statute, and officers willing to use it, trials were possible, even if numbers declined and the chance of securing a conviction fell almost to zero. Indeed, on the Home Circuit there was just one execution in the decade 1658–67, the last recorded for the south-east. Yet trials kept on happening: twenty-three in that period alone, followed by twelve in the next decade, and nine after that; between 1688 and 1697 there were four; and two between 1698 and 1707. And the qualitative evidence is extraordinary. In 1664, fifteen people in Putney, including a doctor, were willing to endorse an indictment against a gentlewoman and her daughter; and in 1671 a grand jury deemed plausible the charges against Widow Barren of Woolwich, namely that she had covenanted with, employed, and rewarded an evil spirit in the likeness of a rat. These cases ended in failure for the plaintiffs, but that could not have been a foregone conclusion or it would be puzzling why anyone, including the court officials, would have wasted their time.[71]

Even panics were still possible, given favourable conditions on the ground. In 1664–5 Robert Hunt, a Somerset justice of the peace, gathered evidence against twenty-five witches, some of whom made elaborate confessions. The devil appeared to Alice Duke and told her she should want for nothing, empowering her to curse anything by saying 'A Pox take it'; she signed his paper with her blood and he gave her sixpence. Despite the sheer weight of such evidence, or perhaps because of it, it appears that the Privy Council intervened in Somerset to prevent a major witch-hunt.[72] Reprieves for three women had been sent from Westminster after the Maidstone trials of 1652, although by the time news arrived they had been hanged.[73] In other cases, magistrates regulated each other. When, in 1672, fourteen witches were apprehended in Wiltshire, a JP advised his peers that in this 'age of scepticism' they would be foolish to proceed.[74] We can see this caution even during the Essex witch trials of 1645, when JPs and clergy persuaded the judge—the inexperienced earl of Warwick—to reprieve nine of the twenty-nine convicted women.[75] Judges could be caught between competing local interests. In 1682, Sir Francis North sentenced three women to death at Exeter merely, by his own admission, to prevent an angry mob stirring up an extra-legal witch craze.[76]

Whereas Puritan witchfinders had been exercised by popery in their midst, men like Robert Hunt were at least as concerned with Protestant nonconformity, a source of disobedience and dissension considered to be diabolical in instigation. Hunt was a

---

[71] Ewen, *Witch Hunting*, 99, 254, 258.
[72] Joseph Glanvill, *Saducismus Triumphatus* (London, 1681), 126–65, quotation at 148; Notestein, *History of Witchcraft*, 273.
[73] *Journals of the House of Commons, 1651–9*, 60, 173.
[74] *Gentleman's Magazine* (June 1832), 489–91.
[75] Gaskill, *Witchfinders*, 128–9.
[76] Roger North, *The Lives of the Norths*, ed. Augustus Jessopp, 3 vols (London, 1890), i, 166.

moderate Protestant hostile to Quakers, a sect periodically associated with witchcraft.[77] Yet again the kaleidoscope had turned so as to present witches as enemies of the status quo. Moreover, public controversy about witches raged on, providing an intellectual and cultural context, reported in books and pamphlets, for their continued prosecution. By the 1680s, the 'rage of party' was under way, ensuring that both pro- and anti-witch-trial positions, corresponding to Tories and Whigs respectively, were both robustly asserted and socially acceptable. If a gentleman declared that witches existed and should be punished, it was not ridiculous that witches should be arraigned at the assizes. This remained true when Hutchinson and Boulton were writing thirty years later. Intense political antagonism kept the issue of witchcraft alive in the public sphere.[78]

The convenient historical shorthand here is the quarrel between Joseph Glanvill, clerical defender of the spirit world, and John Webster, a materialist physician. They had fundamentally different views of evidence, and so reached contrasting conclusions about the world. Webster's ideas were close to Reginald Scot's, but what stands out is his insistence that legal testimonies were inherently flawed. If one charge of witchcraft was false, they all could be. Glanvill focused on the vast quantity of evidence generated by witch trials, including the book of examinations lent to him by Robert Hunt, many of which he reproduced in *Saducismus Triumphatus* (1681).[79] Neither Glanvill nor Webster was much concerned with specific demonic threats or party politics. Rather, they were pursuing basic philosophical truths about the universe, the essence of God's creation. They simply adopted different methods and neither thesis predominated for another fifty years. Polite discussion at the Royal Society, and political furore in parliament, permitted a wavering, open-ended debate because no one's life was in the balance. In the courts it was a different matter, and by 1680 controls had to be imposed upon the admissibility of evidence. The last death sentence in England was handed down in 1685, hastening the end of the history of witchcraft as an indictable felony, and curtailing the kind of proof on which Glanvill and his disciples depended to sustain their arguments.[80]

The office of the Lord Chief Justice points to changing legal attitudes. In 1662 Sir Matthew Hale, a gifted lawyer tolerant of nonconformists, condemned two old women from Lowestoft in Suffolk. To do this, it was necessary to give witnesses the benefit of

---

[77] Jonathan Barry, 'Somerset Witches', in Golden, ed., *Encyclopedia of Witchcraft*, iv, 1061. See also Peter Elmer, '"Saints or Sorcerers": Quakerism, Demonology and the Decline of Witchcraft in Seventeenth-century England', in Barry, Hester, and Roberts, eds, *Witchcraft in Early Modern Europe*, 145–79.

[78] Ian Bostridge, *Witchcraft and its Transformations, c. 1650–c. 1750* (Oxford, 1997), 108–54; Malcolm Gaskill, *Crime and Mentalities in Early Modern England* (Cambridge, 2000), 79–119; Sharpe, *Instruments of Darkness*, 213–75.

[79] Thomas H. Jobe, 'The Devil in Restoration Science: The Glanvill–Webster Witchcraft Debate', *Isis*, 72 (1981), 343–56.

[80] Alice Molland was condemned at Exeter in 1685, but there is no evidence that sentence was carried out; the last confirmed executions were in 1682, also at Exeter.

the doubt, and excuse flaws in their evidence, using the argument that Satan was cunning. Hale believed that the truth of a witchcraft accusation could be determined at law, although by the end of his life in 1676 he was unsure.[81] As ever, achieving absolute certainty about specific cases required an effort of will and concentration of mind. Other senior officials, like Chief Justice North in 1682, put pragmatism before conscience. But within a few years this was no longer necessary. In 1689 Sir John Holt, a sceptical Whig, became Lord Chief Justice and began directing jurors to acquit witches. Holt's successors followed suit.[82] In 1712 a jury at Hertford found Jane Wenham guilty, contrary to the wishes of the judge, Sir John Powell, who treated the evidence with disdain and arranged a reprieve. The ensuing controversy followed party lines, and had little to do with philosophy or theology. Francis Hutchinson made much of the case in his book, condemning the absurdity of the testimony and the superstition of the clergy. He met Wenham, who lived out her days protected by a local Whig landowner, and found her to be 'a pious sober Woman'.[83]

Jane Wenham was the last person known to have been convicted for witchcraft in England. Her case demonstrates not just the collapse of the legal principles behind witch trials, and the vitality of witchcraft as a topic for debate, but the unabated credulity and fury of the common people. In 1736 a row broke out in the Yorkshire parish of Baildon, in which Mary Hartley accused Bridget Goldsbrough of transmuting into cats and riding her son like a horse to Pendle Hill.[84] Fifty years earlier, the case might have developed into a trial, but now this was impossible. Not only had over two decades passed without a single conviction (and hardly any cases at all), but a few months earlier parliament had repealed the Witchcraft Act. This was not a progressive measure befitting the age of enlightenment, but the Whig government thumbing its nose at the Tories.[85] High Church traditionalists and Low Church firebrands alike continued to lament the passing of the statute, as if English Christianity were now defenceless against the onslaught of Satan. But by 1750 it was more usual for educated men to treat witch beliefs as the unique property of the illiterate lower orders—a useful boundary by which to delineate class.[86]

---

[81] Gilbert Geis and Ivan Bunn, *A Trial of Witches: A Seventeenth-Century Witchcraft Prosecution* (London, 1997); Alan Cromartie, *Sir Matthew Hale 1609–1676: Law, Religion and Natural Philosophy* (Cambridge, 1995), 237–9.

[82] Thomas, *Religion and the Decline of Magic*, 547.

[83] Phyllis J. Guskin, 'The Context of Witchcraft: The Case of Jane Wenham (1712)', *Eighteenth Century Studies*, 15 (1981), 48–71; Hutchinson, *Historical Essay*, 130.

[84] J. A. Sharpe, *Witchcraft in Seventeenth-Century Yorkshire: Accusations and Counter Accusations*, Borthwick Papers, 81 (York, 1992), 200.

[85] Bostridge, *Witchcraft and its Transformations*, 180–202.

[86] Owen Davies, *Witchcraft, Magic and Culture, 1736–1951* (Manchester, 1991), 1–78.

FURTHER READING

Bostridge, Ian, *Witchcraft and its Transformations, c. 1650–c. 1750* (Oxford, 1997).

Clark, Stuart, 'Protestant Demonology: Sin, Superstition and Society (*c. 1520–c. 1640*)', in Bengt Ankarloo and Gustav Henningsen, eds, *Early Modern European Witchcraft: Centres and Peripheries* (Oxford, 1990), 45–81.

DeWindt, Anne Reiber, 'Witchcraft and Conflicting Visions of the Ideal Village Community', *Journal of British Studies*, 34 (1995), 427–63.

Elmer, Peter, 'Towards a Politics of Witchcraft in Early Modern England', in Stuart Clark, ed., *Languages of Witchcraft: Narrative, Ideology and Meaning in Early Modern Culture* (Basingstoke, 2001), 101–18.

Gaskill, Malcolm, *Witchfinders: A Seventeenth-Century English Tragedy* (London, 2005).

Gibson, Marion, *Reading Witchcraft: Stories of Early English Witches* (London, 1999).

Gregory, Annabel, 'Witchcraft, Politics and "Good Neighbourhood" in Early Seventeenth-century Rye', *Past & Present*, 133 (1991), 31–66.

Holmes, Clive, 'Women: Witnesses and Witches', *Past & Present*, 140 (1993), 45–78.

Jackson, Louise, 'Witches, Wives and Mothers: Witchcraft Persecution and Women's Confessions in Seventeenth-century England', *Women's History Review*, 4 (1995), 63–83.

Macfarlane, Alan, *Witchcraft in Tudor and Stuart England: A Regional and Comparative Study* (2nd edn, London, 1999).

Poole, Robert, ed., *The Lancashire Witches: Histories and Stories* (Manchester, 2002).

Sharpe, James, *Instruments of Darkness: Witchcraft in England, 1550–1750* (London, 1996).

Thomas, Keith, *Religion and the Decline of Magic: Studies in Popular Beliefs in Sixteenth- and Seventeenth-Century England* (London, 1971).

Valletta, Frederick, *Witchcraft, Magic and Superstition in England, 1640–70* (Aldershot, 2000).

Willis, Deborah, *Malevolent Nurture: Witch-Hunting and Maternal Power in Early Modern England* (London, 1995).

CHAPTER 17

....

WITCHCRAFT IN
SCOTLAND

....

JULIAN GOODARE

SCOTLAND's witches have always attracted attention. One reason for this is the modern romantic image of Scotland as a land of mists, ghosts, and Celtic twilight; we expect weird and uncanny things to happen in Scotland. Even the actual words 'weird' and 'uncanny' have entered standard English from Scots. This image need not be taken too seriously, but we shall see that romantic ideas have contributed constructively to the scholarly study of Scottish witchcraft. Scotland also attracts attention because of James VI—the intellectual king who took part in witchcraft panics, who published a book on witchcraft, and for whom Shakespeare wrote his witch play *Macbeth*. Finally, one reason to pay attention to Scottish witchcraft is simply that it has been well served by scholars. Scotland, a medium-sized country on the northern margins of Europe, has become an influential case study of witch-hunting and witch belief.

17.1 HISTORIOGRAPHICAL DEVELOPMENT
....

The idea that Scotland was an important place for witchcraft may have begun with Sir Walter Scott in the early nineteenth century. Scott's romantic novels were popular all over Europe, and he also encouraged the study of Scottish history. The antiquarian writings on witchcraft by Scott and his contemporaries, Charles Kirkpatrick Sharpe and Sir John Graham Dalyell, are still worth reading.[1] Scott and Sharpe were keen to condemn the witch-hunters, freely using terms like 'superstition', 'delusion',

---

[1] Sir Walter Scott, *Letters on Demonology and Witchcraft* (London, [1830] 1884); Charles K. Sharpe, *A Historical Account of the Belief in Witchcraft in Scotland* (London, [1818] 1884); J. G. Dalyell, *The Darker Superstitions of Scotland* (Edinburgh, 1834).

'persecution', and 'villainy', which today seem less like explanations for witch-hunting than substitutes for explanations. Yet they and Dalyell were fascinated by the exotic popular beliefs and practices that surfaced in the trials. These too were 'superstitions', as Dalyell made clear in the title of his work, but they represented a rich seam of romantic folklore that could be mined to benefit Scottish culture.

In the early twentieth century, the mainstream of writing on Scottish witchcraft remained romantic, with Scotland a key location for Margaret Murray's theory of a surviving pagan witch cult. One of Murray's most important witches, Isobel Gowdie, in Auldearn in 1662, confessed to being a member of a coven of thirteen, and Murray claimed that the whole European cult was organized in this way. However, Murray's well-known misuse of evidence destroyed the credibility of her theory. Norman Cohn, who in the 1970s played a key role in discrediting Murray, also encouraged Christina Larner to return to witchcraft research. Larner was to become the most important scholar that Scottish witchcraft had ever had, setting the subject on a firm foundation and inspiring lines of research that have continued to bear fruit up to the present.

Larner completed a Ph.D. thesis in 1962 on Scottish demonology, and went on to a career as a sociologist. In the 1970s she headed a research team that established the first realistic figures for the scale of the Scottish witch-hunt. Her team found around 3,000 'cases', of which, she reckoned, 1,500 or fewer had led to executions. Previous figures for executions alone had ranged from 3,000 to 30,000. Larner's own figures have since been revised upwards, but the old era of exaggerated speculation was gone.

Larner also conducted a careful reading of individual witchcraft trials; her best work, indeed, may have been qualitative rather than quantitative. Previous scholars had ascribed all witch-hunting to the Church and its allegedly dour Calvinism, but Larner showed that this was only part of the story. Ordinary folk cooperated in the prosecution of witches who angered their neighbours, while witch-hunters at a higher level were lairds, secular judges, and privy councillors, as well as ministers. The book in which Larner brought her findings together, *Enemies of God: The Witch-Hunt in Scotland*, appeared in 1981 to much acclaim, and has influenced subsequent research, not just in Scotland, but in Europe as a whole. She herself died in 1983, but her reputation has remained high.

In the 1990s, research on Scottish witchcraft resumed, and has taken a number of directions. Several of these have continued Larner's own work: reassessing numbers and social profiles of witches, refining the chronology and geography of prosecutions, and developing more sophisticated understandings of witch-hunting. A new statistical resource, the online Survey of Scottish Witchcraft, appeared in 2003 and superseded Larner's statistics. The Survey found many fresh cases, especially in local church records, and increased the overall size of the Scottish witch-hunt by about a third. It also gathered far more information on each case, enabling researchers to search for individual cases displaying particular motifs, and to make connections between cases.

17.2 OUTLINE OF THE SCOTTISH WITCH-HUNT

What, then, has research to date told us? In answering this question, it must constantly be borne in mind that the records of Scottish witchcraft are good in some respects, disappointing in others. Many questions can be answered, but some issues remain intractable. Witchcraft was a secular crime between 1563 and 1736, and almost all trials occurred in this period. However, it was mainly after 1589 that large numbers of cases began. There was a pronounced tendency for cases to cluster in short bursts, as we shall see. After 1662, a protracted decline set in, with the last execution in 1727. Most trials were authorized centrally, and a record of this authorization usually survives, at least after 1608, so we can get a good statistical sense of the pattern of accusations. The trial record itself is much less likely to have survived, unless the trial was held in the central justiciary court, as it was in about one-tenth of cases. The other nine-tenths of trials were mostly held in temporary local courts, which rarely preserved archives. The survival of detailed trial records has been patchy; there is enough for most qualitative purposes, but some statistics are hard to come by.

Statistics do show that the Scottish witch-hunt was one of the most severe in Protestant Europe. Out of a population of about a million, about 4,000 witches were formally accused and perhaps around 2,500 were executed. Scotland, with about 2.5 executions per thousand of population, thus had about five times the European average of 0.5 executions per thousand.[2] Of course the European average conceals wide variations, but Scotland's witch-hunt was not just more severe than that of its neighbour England—it was severe in absolute terms.

Some more statistics may help here.[3] Scottish witches were 85 per cent female, probably a larger proportion than for Europe as a whole. They tended to be in later middle age. Statistics on age are difficult, but, from a small sample, 22 per cent were in their thirties, 41 per cent in their forties, and 13 per cent in their fifties. A woman aged over forty was probably already seen as old, with fertility ceasing and visible changes of ageing beginning. It sometimes took a while to bring a witch to trial, so those witches with reputations in the community may have acquired them when they were younger. However, witches named by their neighbours were probably a minority of the total; more were accused after being named as an accomplice in the confession of another witch. Few were midwives, but a number had been involved in magical healing—a figure of 40 per cent can be extracted from a subset of the data, although this probably

---

[2] For the European average see Richard M. Golden, 'Satan in Europe: The Geography of Witch Hunts', in Michael Wolfe, ed., *Changing Identities in Early Modern France* (Durham, NC, 1997), 216–47. The Survey of Scottish Witchcraft found 3,837 witchcraft suspects, a minimum figure because of missing records. The figure of 2,500 executions will be discussed further below.

[3] These mostly come from Lauren Martin and Joyce Miller, 'Some Findings from the Survey of Scottish Witchcraft', in Julian Goodare, Lauren Martin, and Joyce Miller, eds, *Witchcraft and Belief in Early Modern Scotland* (Basingstoke, 2008), 51–70.

represents a maximum, with the real proportion being lower. Data on marital status and on socio-economic status are fragmentary, but the general impression is that most Scottish witches were typical members of their communities rather than marginal vagrants.

A typical witchcraft accusation passed through several stages. Things began in the local community, with neighbours deciding that a person was a witch. Whether the neighbours then complained to the authorities, or whether the authorities initiated action on hearing of community discussion, is not entirely clear, but the records then show us the suspect under investigation. The pre-trial investigation was usually organized by a local church court, either the kirk session, the parish committee of post-Reformation Scotland, or its superior court, the presbytery. These courts were powerful bodies, keen to enforce godly discipline. They could not execute anyone, but they could summon suspects and witnesses, interrogate them, and compile dossiers of evidence. In cooperation with local lairds or urban magistrates, they could also imprison suspects and torture them; torture is a disputed topic, as we shall see.

The next stage was to seek authority to hold a criminal trial. Here, the kirk session would have to involve local lairds or urban magistrates. Usually, they would assemble a small group of influential, propertied laymen, who would submit the dossier of evidence to the Privy Council in Edinburgh—the central coordinating body for the government. If the council thought the evidence sufficient, they would usually grant a 'commission of justiciary' authorizing the group of laymen to constitute themselves as criminal judges to convene a court to try the named suspect or suspects. Such ad hoc local courts tried about nine-tenths of the witches, with most of the remainder being sent to the central justiciary court in Edinburgh. Local courts usually convicted; the justiciary court had a higher acquittal rate, either because it was more professional, or because the Privy Council sent trickier cases to it, or both. In either court, an assize (jury) of local propertied men would deliver a verdict. If they convicted, the witch was usually sentenced to be strangled at a stake and have her or his body burned.

17.2 RECENT DEBATES (1): WITCH-HUNTING

These, then, are some broad outlines of the subject as it is generally understood at present. Research has also probed into many details, and these have led to debate. What follows will indicate the main lines of some debates. Recent research has revised some of Christina Larner's assumptions, though it has also confirmed the soundness of her general approach. Here I will begin with debates on the process of witch-hunting, and then outline some of the work that has been done on witch belief. It is, perhaps, on this latter topic that recent work has taken directions that Larner did not anticipate.

The North Berwick panic of 1590–1, and especially the role of King James VI, have attracted debate. This was a dramatic episode, taking its name from the alleged meeting of two hundred witches in the church of North Berwick, near Edinburgh, on the night of Hallowe'en 1590. The witches, who had all sailed there in sieves, met the devil, who preached to them and encouraged them to plot the destruction of the king. One of Larner's earliest publications concerned James's role.[4] She pointed out that the North Berwick panic, involving treason, resembled the kind of political sorcery that was feared in the late Middle Ages. James had recently returned from Denmark to fetch his bride, with Scottish and Danish witches allegedly conspiring to raise storms against their North Sea voyages. Larner argued that the king had learned about Continental demonology in Denmark, and brought its ideas back to a Scotland that had not previously heard of them. In particular, she argued, James imported the demonic pact. As king of England after 1603, James later became sceptical of the witchcraft threat, but in Scotland he had launched a series of prosecutions—and justified them in his book, *Daemonologie* (1597). In *Enemies of God*, Larner expanded on this idea, writing that a 'general commission for trying witches' was established in the closing stages of the North Berwick panic.[5] She thought that the commission continued until 1597, when miscarriages of justice caused it to be revoked.

Although influential in their time, these ideas have since been subjected to severe criticism. Thomas Riis objected that Denmark was an unlikely source for the demonic pact, since witchcraft accusations there were largely based on village malefice.[6] P. G. Maxwell-Stuart added that Niels Hemmingsen, the famed Danish theologian with whom James had held discussions, had not in fact foregrounded the demonic pact in his writings on witchcraft.[7] Finally, Jenny Wormald showed that the outlines at least of the demonic pact had been known in Scotland earlier.[8]

The North Berwick panic became more accessible in 2000, when Lawrence Normand and Gareth Roberts produced a detailed edition of the key documents.[9] They and Wormald independently attempted to revise Larner's 'general commission for trying witches', in a technical discussion that became even more technical when I entered it.[10] Normand and Roberts and Wormald assumed that Larner's 'general commission' existed, but moved its origin from 1591 to 1592. My critique was more radical and

---

[4] Christina Larner, 'James VI and I and Witchcraft', in Alan G. R. Smith, ed., *The Reign of James VI and I* (London, 1973), 74–90; reprinted in Christina Larner, *Witchcraft and Religion: The Politics of Popular Belief* (Oxford, 1984), 3–22.

[5] Christina Larner, *Enemies of God: The Witch-Hunt in Scotland* (London, 1981), 35.

[6] Thomas Riis, *Should Auld Acquaintance Be Forgot: Scottish–Danish Relations, c.1450–1707*, 2 vols (Odense, 1988), i, 266–9.

[7] P. G. Maxwell-Stuart, 'The Fear of the King is Death: James VI and the Witches of East Lothian', in W. G. Naphy and Penny Roberts, eds, *Fear in Early Modern Society* (Manchester, 1997), 212–13.

[8] Jenny Wormald, 'The Witches, the Devil and the King', in Terry Brotherstone and David Ditchburn, eds, *Freedom and Authority: Scotland, c.1050–c.1650* (East Linton, 2000), 165–80, at 170–2. It has been argued that John Knox was aware of the demonic pact as early as 1556: Julian Goodare, 'John Knox on Demonology and Witchcraft', *Archiv für Reformationsgeschichte*, 96 (2005), 224–9.

[9] Lawrence Normand and Gareth Roberts, eds, *Witchcraft in Early Modern Scotland: James VI's Demonology and the North Berwick Witches* (Exeter, 2000).

[10] Julian Goodare, 'The Framework for Scottish Witch-Hunting in the 1590s', *Scottish Historical Review*, 81 (2002), 240–50, and references there cited.

ultimately simpler: the 'general commission' was illusory, no such thing being established either in 1591 or in 1592, or being revoked in 1597. Procedures for trying witches remained fairly constant, if flexible, throughout the 1590s, and indeed throughout the whole Scottish witch-hunt. Witchcraft trials could be held either in the justiciary court in Edinburgh, or in the locality by the authority of a commission of justiciary—a document usually issued by the Privy Council, empowering one or more local lairds or officials to hold a court.

King James's responsibility for the prosecutions of the 1590s has also been debated. Traditional accounts attributed most responsibility to him, but we are now seeing more different strands of activity in both the 1590-1 and 1597 panics. Wormald gave James a more nuanced role in the former of these. More controversially, she argued that James became a 'sceptic' before or during the 1597 panic, and that his 'doubts' about witch-hunting were evident in his book *Daemonologie*, published shortly afterwards.[11] I argued against this, saying that the order of 12 August 1597 revoking recent witchcraft trial commissions was not simply a 'sceptical' measure but could also be supported by witch-hunting enthusiasts, and that there was evidence in September of the king's keenness to prosecute witches—for which others, the genuine 'sceptics', were criticizing him. As for *Daemonologie*, it was not credible to suggest that this was a 'sceptical' work.[12] Since then, Clive Holmes has indicated his continued support for Wormald's position;[13] Brian Levack, by contrast, has taken a view close to mine, and indeed shown how it fits his own broader interpretation of James. To Levack, the most important aspect of James's involvement was that it politicized Scottish witchcraft, both in 1590-1 and in 1597.[14]

Another debate has concerned responsibility for witch-hunting and indeed the nature of the Scottish state. Again it was Larner whose ideas launched the controversy. The general thrust of her argument emphasized local elites—especially lairds—in contrast to previous scholars who had emphasized ministers. But she was also struck by what she (erroneously, it seems) took to be central government's initiatives in first promoting and then curtailing witch-hunting in the 1590s, and throughout her text she scattered remarks like 'the rise and fall of witch-hunting has to be related in the first place to the concerns of central government'.[15]

---

[11] Jenny Wormald, 'The Witches, the Devil and the King', 177–80.

[12] Julian Goodare, 'The Scottish Witchcraft Panic of 1597', in Goodare, ed., *The Scottish Witch-Hunt in Context* (Manchester, 2002), 60–6.

[13] Clive Holmes, 'Witchcraft and Possession at the Accession of James I: The Publication of Samuel Harsnett's *A Declaration of Egregious Popish Impostures*', in John Newton and Jo Bath, eds, *Witchcraft and the Act of 1604* (Leiden, 2008), 86–8. Holmes's main point is not controversial: James was more 'sceptical' after 1603 when he was also James I of England. On this see also P. G. Maxwell-Stuart, 'King James's Experience of Witches, and the 1604 English Witchcraft Act', 31–46 in the same volume.

[14] Brian P. Levack, 'King James VI and Witchcraft', in *Witch-Hunting in Scotland: Law, Politics and Religion* (London, 2008), 41–2.

[15] Larner, *Enemies of God*, 87. She continued: 'and in the second place to the interest of the local landowners and church authorities', going on to point out that peasant accusations also played a role.

These remarks led to trouble when Brian Levack, one of the leading scholars of the European witch-hunt, became involved. In 1995, in the second edition of his famous textbook, Levack stressed his view that 'the original impetus for prosecution came mainly from the localities rather than from the centre and that the central authorities of the state had more to do with the restriction of witch-hunting than with its spread'.[16] He then extended this argument in a paper, using Scotland as a test case and criticizing Larner in the process. Most Scottish trials, he argued, were held by local lairds using commissions of justiciary, and they were not accountable centrally for their decisions— unlike in England, where centrally appointed judges visited the localities. Levack also deployed his unrivalled expertise in the decline of witch-hunting to argue that in Scotland, as in Europe generally, the central authorities' role was to intervene to prevent injustice and ultimately to bring witch-hunting to a halt.[17]

The next stage in the debate came from me. Although I too had criticized Larner, I argued for a higher degree of central control overall than Levack had indicated. Commissions of justiciary were implemented locally, but granted centrally—usually by the Privy Council. I showed that the council expected prospective commissioners to produce a detailed written case against the suspect, and refused to grant a commission if this was inadequate. It was not surprising that most local trials ended in convictions, because local trials only occurred once a central body had decided to authorize them.[18] In his reply, Levack accepted much of this but continued to emphasize that authorizing local elites to hold trials represented a lower degree of central control than holding trials in courts directly organized from the centre—a point that I would, in turn, accept.[19]

The issue of the state is related to that of legal procedure. Debate here has focused on torture. Stuart Macdonald has provided a clear summary of the difficult issues, though his distinction between 'judicial torture', which he says was rare, and 'sleep deprivation', which he says was common, is not particularly clear.[20] If judicial torture consisted of ill-treatment designed to get the suspect to confess, then surely sleep deprivation *was* judicial torture? Brian Levack, in a broader survey of torture, shows that it was. His penetrating comparison with England places Scotland's legal system, in this respect, closer to English practice than to the Romano-canonical system used on much of the Continent. He points out that cases of torture of Scottish witches were

[16] Brian P. Levack, *The Witch-Hunt in Early Modern Europe* (2nd edn, Harlow, 1995), x. A third edition has since appeared (Harlow, 2006).

[17] Brian P. Levack, 'State-building and Witch Hunting in Early Modern Europe', in Jonathan Barry, Marianne Hester, and Gareth Roberts, eds, *Witchcraft in Early Modern Europe: Studies in Culture and Belief* (Cambridge, 1996), 96–115.

[18] Julian Goodare, 'Witch-Hunting and the Scottish State', in Goodare, ed., *The Scottish Witch-Hunt in Context*, 122–45.

[19] Brian P. Levack, 'Absolutism, State-building and Witchcraft', in *Witch-Hunting in Scotland*, 98–114.

[20] Stuart Macdonald, 'Torture and the Scottish Witch-Hunt: A Re-Examination', *Scottish Tradition*, 27 (2002), 95–114.

hardly ever authorized by Privy Council warrant, and on that basis calls them 'illegal' (or, on one occasion, 'technically illegal').[21] This raises the question of why so little effort was made to stop it. Levack's own answer is that the local elites who were administering the torture were largely autonomous, and this is certainly part of the story. However, the Privy Council did intervene in some blatantly irregular cases that came to its attention, such as a trial in Brechin in 1608 where no commission had been sought and where the convicted witches were burned alive.[22] If it was accepted that sleep deprivation was 'illegal', did anybody say so, and if not, why not? Answers to these questions await further research. In the meantime, Liv Helene Willumsen has surveyed the cases of reported torture in more detail than before, arguing that it may have been more prevalent for women. She also suggests that cases of confession 'without torture' may be deliberate denials that torture had occurred.[23] Again, more research is needed.

Torture was employed to extract confessions, and there have been some remarkable studies of witches' confessions. Louise Yeoman has shown that the Calvinist conversion process could be traumatic for some people, heightening perception of the devil's assaults.[24] Diane Purkiss has discussed the 'stories' told by confessing witches, showing how some reshaped traumatic events from their own past or wove folkloric material into their narratives.[25] Liv Helene Willumsen's use of 'narratology', a technique of literary scholarship, has enabled the different 'voices' in witchcraft texts to speak more clearly. These include the 'voice of the scribe', the 'voice of the law', the 'voices of the witnesses', and—particularly valuably—the 'voice of the accused person'.[26] Emma Wilby has read the confessions of Isobel Gowdie with an eye to reconstructing the interrogation process, showing that different types of questioning can be read back from the recorded answers.[27]

Most witches were women—probably a higher proportion in Scotland than in Europe as a whole. I have surveyed the issue in a paper on women, followed by another on men.[28] These papers set witch-hunting in a broader context of criminalization of

[21] Brian P. Levack, 'Judicial Torture in Scotland during the Age of Mackenzie', *Stair Society Miscellany*, iv (2002), 185–98; Brian P. Levack, 'Witchcraft and the Law in Early Modern Scotland', in *Witch-Hunting in Scotland*, 21–4; quotation at 22.

[22] *Register of the Privy Council of Scotland*, xiv, 605.

[23] Liv Helene Willumsen, 'Seventeenth Century Witchcraft Trials in Scotland and Northern Norway', Ph.D. thesis, University of Edinburgh, 2008, 78–84, 104, 204.

[24] Louise A. Yeoman, 'The Devil as Doctor: Witchcraft, Wodrow, and the Wider World', *Scottish Archives*, 1 (1995), 93–105.

[25] Diane Purkiss, 'Sounds of Silence: Fairies and Incest in Scottish Witchcraft Stories', in Stuart Clark, ed., *Languages of Witchcraft: Narrative, Ideology and Meaning in Early Modern Culture* (London, 2001), 81–98.

[26] Willumsen, 'Seventeenth Century Witchcraft Trials', 28–33 and *passim*.

[27] Emma Wilby, *The Visions of Isobel Gowdie: Magic, Witchcraft and Dark Shamanism in Seventeenth-Century Scotland* (Brighton, 2010), 53–80.

[28] Julian Goodare, 'Women and the Witch-Hunt in Scotland', *Social History*, 23 (1998), 288–308; Goodare, 'Men and the Witch-Hunt in Scotland', in Alison Rowlands, ed., *Witchcraft and Masculinities in Early Modern Europe* (Basingstoke, 2009), 148–70.

women's offences and assault on women's ungodliness. The Scottish emphasis on sex with the devil was related to the intense attack on extramarital sex mounted by the Scottish Reformation. Witchcraft accusations against men usually omitted the sexual element, tending to make male witchcraft a paler and milder variant of its female counterpart. Exceptions came with those witches who were thought to bear authority in the witch organization; these were almost all men. Witchcraft was ultimately a patriarchal matter.

This general pattern has not been challenged, but there have been debates on related issues. Lauren Martin has found a notably broad range of women's quarrelling that is of comparative interest. Studies from some other countries had tended to characterize witch-related quarrels as being about 'motherhood' or 'fertility', but Martin showed that many Scottish quarrels were about the household as an economic unit—businesses like dairying, brewing, or cloth production.[29]

The drive for godly discipline was particularly relevant to women, since by far the largest item of business in most church courts was the punishment of extramarital sex—usually revealed by a woman's pregnancy. Women thus found themselves in the front line of discipline, with men being drawn in, if at all, as accomplices. The early Reformers had little understanding of popular magical practices, assuming in the 1563 witchcraft act that 'witches' were public practitioners with clients.[30] However, this soon changed once kirk sessions were established more widely. The impact of the Reformation has been seen in notably positive terms by Margo Todd, and—in its effects on women at least—in notably negative terms by Gordon DesBrisay.[31] The outcome of this debate is likely to affect our understanding of the place of witch-hunting in the prosecution of crime and moral regulation of women. It may also enable us to return to the question of the responsibility of the Church for witch-hunting, especially once we recognize that 'the Church' was not a self-contained entity but a collection of local courts with considerable lay involvement.[32]

One debate, prompted by the works of P. G. Maxwell-Stuart, has concerned the reality of witches' activities.[33] Maxwell-Stuart views Scottish witchcraft as something practised by an organized cult of self-identified 'witches', who danced together, cast evil

---

[29] Lauren Martin, 'The Devil and the Domestic: Witchcraft, Quarrels and Women's Work in Scotland', in Goodare, ed., *The Scottish Witch-Hunt in Context*, 73–89.

[30] Julian Goodare, 'The Scottish Witchcraft Act', *Church History*, 74 (2005), 39–67.

[31] Margo Todd, *The Culture of Protestantism in Early Modern Scotland* (New Haven, CT, 2002); Gordon DesBrisay, 'Twisted by Definition? Women under Godly Discipline in Seventeenth-century Scottish Towns', in Yvonne G. Brown and Rona Ferguson, eds, *Twisted Sisters: Women, Crime and Deviance in Scotland since 1400* (East Linton, 2002), 137–55.

[32] For a good survey of the Church's role see Stuart Macdonald, *The Witches of Fife: Witch-Hunting in a Scottish Shire, 1560–1710* (East Linton, 2001), 169–94. For an effort to integrate witchcraft into the outlines of a broader picture see Julian Goodare, *The Government of Scotland, 1560–1625* (Oxford, 2004), 260–3.

[33] Especially P. G. Maxwell-Stuart, *Satan's Conspiracy: Magic and Witchcraft in Sixteenth-century Scotland* (East Linton, 2001) and P. G. Maxwell-Stuart, *An Abundance of Witches: The Great Scottish Witch-Hunt* (Stroud, 2005).

spells, and quite possibly worshipped the devil.[34] This perhaps echoes Larner's work in demystifying Scottish witchcraft and in portraying witches as real people active in their communities. However, the idea of an organized cult is not supported by any other scholarly account of European witchcraft. Maxwell-Stuart regrettably ignores the way in which reputations were built up by quarrels followed by misfortune. His detailed reconstructions of some individual cases—at least those demonstrably involving magical practitioners—have been welcomed. But he has been criticized by reviewers for taking witches' confessions as transparent accounts of real events, for collapsing the categories of witches and magical practitioners, and for treating almost all witchcraft prosecutors as fair-minded men whose only motive was the justified suppression of real crime.[35]

The idea of fair-minded witchcraft prosecutors is not, of course, far-fetched, but it is hardly the whole story—especially during the witchcraft panics. This has led to further debate. Larner produced a chronology of the periods of intense witchcraft prosecution, and the Survey of Scottish Witchcraft confirmed its reliability. She saw five 'peaks of intensive prosecution': 1590–1, 1597, 1629–30, 1649, and 1661–2.[36] The Survey's additional cases, plus more careful examination of the evidence, have revised these dates slightly, with recent studies dating the largest panics as 1590–1, 1597, 1628–31, 1649–50, and 1661–2.[37] There is also a study of a period of judicial caution *between* panics.[38]

Lauren Martin has recently built on this work to produce a remarkable statistical analysis of the panics, paying detailed attention to geography as well as chronology, and incorporating a provocative attack on the very concept of 'panic'.[39] She points out that the term 'panic' has been used both to describe the groups of prosecutions themselves and to characterize the state of mind in which prosecutors may have approached them,

---

[34] His view of witchcraft as an organized activity is most clearly articulated in P. G. Maxwell-Stuart, 'Witchcraft and the Kirk in Aberdeenshire, 1596–97', *Northern Scotland*, 18 (1998), 1–14. For a detailed critique see Julian Goodare, 'The Aberdeenshire Witchcraft Panic of 1597', *Northern Scotland*, 21 (2001), 26–32. Maxwell-Stuart also presents witches' magical spells as taking genuine effect (*Satan's Conspiracy*, 3–4), and says that accounts of the demonic pact may represent 'a genuine impulse reported by the witch' (*Abundance of Witches*, 227).

[35] E.g. Louise Yeoman in *Scottish Archives*, 8 (2002), 134–5; Brian P. Levack in *English Historical Review*, 122 (2007), 191–2.

[36] Larner, *Enemies of God*, 60.

[37] There are now individual studies of each of these five panics, notably: Normand and Roberts, eds, *Witchcraft in Early Modern Scotland*; Wormald, 'The Witches, the Devil and the King'; Julian Goodare, 'The Scottish Witchcraft Panic of 1597'; Goodare, 'The Aberdeenshire Witchcraft Panic of 1597'; Elizabeth Robertson, 'Panic and Persecution: Witch-Hunting in East Lothian, 1628–1631', MSc by Research thesis, University of Edinburgh, 2009; Paula Hughes, 'The 1649–50 Scottish Witch-Hunt, with Particular Reference to the Synod of Lothian and Tweeddale', Ph.D. thesis, University of Strathclyde, 2008; Brian P. Levack, 'The Great Scottish Witch-Hunt of 1661–2', in *Witch-Hunting in Scotland*, 81–97. Two panics, 1649–50 and 1661–2, are compared by Anna L. Cordey, 'Witch-Hunting in the Presbytery of Dalkeith, 1649 to 1662', MSc by Research thesis, University of Edinburgh, 2003.

[38] Michael Wasser, 'The Privy Council and the Witches: The Curtailment of Witchcraft Prosecutions in Scotland, 1597–1628', *Scottish Historical Review*, 82 (2003), 20–46.

[39] Lauren Martin, 'Scottish Witchcraft Panics Re-examined', in Goodare, Martin, and Miller, eds, *Witchcraft and Belief*, 119–43.

arguing that this makes it a 'slippery' term that should be abandoned. She claims that the terms 'investigation' and 'prosecution', plus 'witch-hunt' when extraordinary measures were used, are adequate to describe the ways in which the authorities dealt with witches.

Martin's attack involves more than terminology. She argues that historians studying panics in the Larner tradition have primarily engaged in what she calls 'suspect-counting', using the dramatic leaps in the graph of suspects to show that something extraordinary was happening. However, this may fail to bring out the importance of witchcraft prosecution for the community as a whole. She proposes replacing the 'suspect-counting' model for most purposes with a 'community-focused' model, treating the key event as being a community's experience of, and involvement in, a decision to prosecute local witches. Using parishes as 'communities', she produces alternative graphs and tables that count, not numbers of witchcraft suspects, but numbers of parishes in which prosecutions occurred. She shows that even during intense periods of prosecution, most parishes did not prosecute any witches, and most of those that did so prosecuted only one or two. How, she asks, can that be a 'national panic', or even a 'panic' at all?

The most obvious problem with this is that the 'community-focused' model produces a graph with dramatic peaks that are virtually indistinguishable from those provided by the 'suspect-counting' model.[40] Moreover, although most prosecutions during peak periods were still of one or two witches at a time, the proportion of multiple cases rose sharply. Martin provides no explanation for the dramatic clustering of these cases within peak periods, nor for their wide scattering across Scotland. Evidently a process was at work that widely and suddenly transmitted encouragements to witchcraft prosecution across the country. Local initiation of prosecutions meant that such encouragements would be taken up only patchily, but the process was still a 'national' one.[41]

Clearly, more assessment of this is required. One major work that has appeared since Martin's, the Ph.D. thesis by Liv Helene Willumsen, uses statistics extensively but retains the term 'panic' on the grounds that 'within scholarly witchcraft research to date, the word has been used of intensive witch-hunting in defined periods'.[42] Willumsen has also analysed the fragmentary data on executions in more detail than before, breaking them down into categories and producing a significantly larger estimate for executions: 2,500.[43] As for Martin's work, my own view at present is that she has

---

[40] Martin, 'Scottish Witchcraft Panics Re-examined', 137.

[41] For some suggestions on the processes at work see Goodare, 'Witch-Hunting and the Scottish State', 136–9. This discussion of 'national' panics also makes their 'patchwork' nature clear.

[42] Willumsen, 'Seventeenth Century Witchcraft Trials', 38. See also her analysis of 'panic versus non-panic periods', 40–4.

[43] Liv Helene Willumsen, 'Rates of Execution in Scottish Witchcraft Trials', paper (forthcoming). This is what we might expect from knowing that the largest group of trials, those held under local commission, proceeded in ways that were likely to produce very high conviction rates; however, this paper is the first to apply statistical analysis to the issue.

successfully ended an era in which it could be assumed that 'suspect-counting' was a simple matter. In some ways this needs to be extended, for instance by looking in more detail at the 'community experience' of witch-hunting. Did people in the 'community' welcome the serial prosecution of witches with no prior reputation, whose arrest arose solely from their being named in a previous witch's confession? However, I feel that the concept of 'panic' is still valid, and indeed that the concept of 'national panic' should be retained. The fact that the term 'panic' embraces both a set of events and a state of mind is hardly unusual; other terms used by historians, such as 'Reformation' and indeed 'witch-hunt', also do so.

Study of the chronology of witch-hunting would not be complete without paying attention to its decline. Here the major work is that of Brian Levack. He has shown that the broad picture was one of procedural reform, with judges insisting on following due process and avoiding the excesses that occurred during panics. Torture was curtailed, witch-pricking was curtailed, central supervision was stepped up, and an increased proportion of acquittals made it harder for multiple cases to begin. He distances the topic from the decline of witch beliefs, pointing out that the 'sceptical' judges who did most to rein in prosecutions were careful to indicate their assent to the principles of demonology.[44] Levack has also investigated demonic possession; the headline cases of this occurred late in Scotland, concentrated in three outbreaks of 1697, 1699, and 1704. These initially fuelled some prosecutions, but also stirred up debate and opposition.[45] Michael Wasser has argued that the possession debates are a small part of a broader picture, in which new intellectual ideas can indeed be seen as undermining the credibility of witch belief in the later stages of the hunt.[46]

17.3 RECENT DEBATES (II): WITCH BELIEF

Scotland is a diverse place, and this has provided opportunities for fruitful cross-cultural comparison. In early modern times, a cultural barrier separated the Gaelic-speaking Highlands and the Scots-speaking Lowlands, with the former constituting one-third of the population. Larner wrote that 'In the Highlands, especially those parts outside the Kirk sessions system and within the dominion of the clans there was no witch-hunting, or none that reached the records.'[47] This statement was perhaps

---

[44] Brian P. Levack, 'The Decline and End of Scottish Witch-Hunting', *Witch-Hunting in Scotland*, 131–44.

[45] Brian P. Levack, 'Demonic Possession in Early Modern Scotland', in Goodare, Martin, and Miller, eds, *Witchcraft and Belief*, 166–84; revised as 'Demonic Possession and Witch-Hunting in Scotland', in Levack, *Witch-Hunting in Scotland*, 115–30.

[46] Michael Wasser, 'The Mechanical World-View and the Decline of Witch-Beliefs in Scotland', in Goodare, Martin, and Miller, eds, *Witchcraft and Belief*, 206–26.

[47] Larner, *Enemies of God*, 80. The text reads 'Kirk sessions, system', but this appears to be a typographical error.

extreme, and she herself cited Highland cases that might seem to qualify it, but it was left to Lizanne Henderson to reveal the extent of Highland witch-hunting.[48] Meanwhile, Martin's geographical analysis showed that the 'Highland' region came only eighth out of ten in 'intensity of prosecution', with her 'Grampian' and 'Tayside' regions having even fewer cases per head of population.[49] In favour of Larner it might be noted that most 'Highland' cases came from areas on the edges of the Highlands like Bute and Tain, where Gaelic-speakers could be caught up in witch-hunts driven by recognizably Lowland elites.

Does this show that indigenous Gaelic culture was free of witch-hunting impulses? This is not yet proven, but it seems possible—and may have far-reaching implications. Ronald Hutton sees the division between the Gaelic-speaking and Scots-speaking zones as an example of a fault line, traceable in principle among traditional societies all over the globe, between those that ascribed misfortune to witches and those that ascribed misfortune to other causes. The 'other causes' were typically angry or evil spirits (either ghosts or nature spirits), who had to be defeated or propitiated by specialist magical practitioners. Hutton argues that Siberia, with its tribal shamans, is a vast and paradigmatic witch-free region, and that the Gaelic world may have been similar to the extent that it blamed misfortune on its own nature spirits: fairies.[50] Henderson has raised the obvious objection that lowlanders believed in fairies too, but Hutton's latest work shows in more detail that the issue is not simply fairy belief but the propensity to ascribe misfortune to fairies.[51] There is clearly more to be learned from the study of cultural regions.

A related strand of research has focused on folk belief and ritual practice. Rather than demystifying witches as Larner did, some scholars have emphasized the weird and exotic material that appears in witches' confessions—and have begun to develop explanations for it. Lizanne Henderson and Edward J. Cowan opened up new avenues by showing that fairies were taken seriously by the common folk. In their work, *Scottish Fairy Belief*, they devoted a chapter to the demonization of fairies during the witch-hunt. Suspects, interrogated about the devil, sometimes volunteered information about fairies. Unfortunately, interrogators readily construed fairies as demons.[52] Emma Wilby has taken this further, focusing on lived experience. She has analysed a pattern of encounters between humans and other beings—principally fairies in Scotland and animal familiars in England—as deriving from visions and trances. Some magical practitioners worked with spirit guides, often fairies but sometimes other beings

[48] Lizanne Henderson, 'Witch Hunting and Witch Belief in the *Gàidhealtachd*', in Goodare, Martin, and Miller, eds, *Witchcraft and Belief*, 95–118.

[49] Martin, 'Scottish Witchcraft Panics Re-examined', 125.

[50] Ronald Hutton, 'The Global Context of the Scottish Witch-Hunt', in Goodare, ed., *The Scottish Witch-Hunt in Context*, 16–32.

[51] Henderson, 'Witch Hunting and Witch Belief in the *Gàidhealtachd*', 101–2; Ronald Hutton, 'Witch-Hunting in Celtic Societies', *Past & Present*, 212 (August 2011), 43–71.

[52] Lizanne Henderson and Edward J. Cowan, *Scottish Fairy Belief: A History* (East Linton, 2001), 106–41.

(angels, ghosts, or indeterminate beings), who gave them special knowledge and powers. Anthropological studies of trances and shamanistic practices can shed light on the lived nature of such experiences.[53]

Visions and trances, though knowledge of them may have shaped many people's attitude to witchcraft, were probably rare and exotic. There were also everyday magical practices occurring in all communities. Joyce Miller's pioneering work on 'charmers' has revealed the types of rituals involved.[54] Edward J. Cowan has pointed out more links with witchcraft belief, and has set charming in a broader context—that of the Reformation's attack on popular culture—while Owen Davies has focused on 'charmers' themselves, arguing that a division between amateur healers (the category for which the term 'charmer' was used in England) and professional 'cunning folk' (as they were termed in England) can be perceived in Scotland.[55] 'Nicneven', apparently a name or soubriquet used by more than one witch or magical practitioner as early as the 1560s, presents a continuing puzzle that may be solved by further study of magical practices.[56]

The issue of popular belief in the devil has been debated. Stuart Macdonald, using mainly pre-trial material from local church courts in Fife, has pointed to the rarity of mentions of the devil; sometimes the investigators failed to follow up obvious allusions to demonic involvement.[57] Yet the importance of the demonic pact in most Scottish trial documents, first remarked by Larner, seems unshakeable.[58] What we need now is more study of folk belief, including the folkloric devil—a topic recently opened up by Joyce Miller.[59]

Larner's original topic, Scottish demonology, has been less well served by research, though there have been studies of John Knox and, of course, of James VI.[60] Even work on James is often subsumed in broader studies of witch-hunting (cited earlier) rather

[53] Emma Wilby, *Cunning Folk and Familiar Spirits: Shamanistic Visionary Traditions in Early Modern British Witchcraft and Magic* (Brighton, 2005); Wilby, *The Visions of Isobel Gowdie*.

[54] Joyce Miller, 'Devices and Directions: Folk Healing Aspects of Witchcraft Practice in Seventeenth-century Scotland', in Goodare, ed., *The Scottish Witch-Hunt in Context*, 90–105.

[55] Edward J. Cowan, 'Witch Persecution and Popular Belief in Lowland Scotland: The Devil's Decade', and Owen Davies, 'A Comparative Perspective on Scottish Cunning-folk and Charmers', in Goodare, Martin, and Miller, eds, *Witchcraft and Belief*, 71–94, 185–205.

[56] Alison Hanham, '"The Scottish Hecate": A Wild Witch Chase', *Scottish Studies*, 13 (1969), 59–65; Julian Goodare, 'Nicneven (fl. 1560s)', in Elizabeth Ewan, Sue Innes, and Siân Reynolds, eds, *The Biographical Dictionary of Scottish Women* (Edinburgh, 2006), 284.

[57] Stuart Macdonald, 'In Search of the Devil in Fife Witchcraft Cases, 1560–1705', in Goodare, ed., *The Scottish Witch-Hunt in Context*, 33–50.

[58] Larner, *Enemies of God*, 134–74.

[59] Joyce Miller, 'Men in Black: Appearances of the Devil in Early Modern Scottish Witchcraft Discourse', in Goodare, Martin, and Miller, eds, *Witchcraft and Belief*, 144–65.

[60] Goodare, 'John Knox'; Stuart Clark, 'King James' *Daemonologie*: Witchcraft and Kingship', in Sydney Anglo, ed., *The Damned Art: Essays in the Literature of Witchcraft* (London, 1977), 156–81; Daniel Fischlin, '"Counterfeiting God": James VI (I) and the Politics of *Daemonologie* (1597)', *Journal of Narrative Technique*, 26 (1996), 1–27; Normand and Roberts, eds, *Witchcraft in Early Modern Scotland*, 327–52.

than focusing on the details of his beliefs. For the later period there is Larner's study of two tracts, and a good deal of Scottish material in Ian Bostridge's survey of the political aspects of witchcraft debates.[61]

17.4 FUTURE RESEARCH DIRECTIONS

This survey of recent work on Scottish witchcraft can only be a snapshot of a moving target. Many of the debates discussed above are still continuing, and work is in progress in various areas. What I would like to do now is to stand back from these debates and sketch some broader issues that seem ripe for further development.

There has been much work on witch-hunting, but more research is certainly needed on witch-hunters. Various scholars have pointed out that there is a distinction to be drawn between the witchcraft prosecutor who carries out his assigned duties diligently and the witchcraft prosecutor who takes the initiative to search out fresh witches—to *hunt* them, in fact. There is qualitative evidence that both types of people operated in Scotland, but the details are unclear. The Witchcraft Survey has now done the basic work of identifying 'people involved' in witchcraft cases, and provides links between cases that enable the identification of likely serial witch-hunters; this lead should now be followed up.

The law on witchcraft needs more work. Levack has opened up the subject, with an excellent study focusing on legal procedure;[62] what we now need is a study of the substantive law as it was articulated in court. Why did courts find one suspect guilty, and another innocent? Why did judges order some charges to be dropped, while finding others competent? What value was placed on different types of evidence— neighbours' statements, the suspect's confession, the issue of 'habit and repute' (reputation), pricking for the devil's mark, and so on?

There is more work needed on popular belief and practice. Shape-shifting is a common motif in confessions, and also occurs in neighbours' accusations; its role in the witch-hunt overall is a project waiting to be done. A full study of magical practitioners is needed in its own right, and it would also clarify the role of magical practice in witchcraft trials.

Neighbourhood relationships may not seem like a neglected topic, but the details of quarrels and curses could be further investigated, especially from the perspective of gender. Larner herself pointed out the fact that witchcraft trials were not 'natural' methods of 'witchcraft control', with peasants normally preferring to seek

<hr/>

[61] Christina Larner, 'Two Late Scottish Witchcraft Tracts: *Witch-Craft Proven* and *The Tryal of Witchcraft*', in Anglo, ed., *The Damned Art*, 227–45; Ian Bostridge, *Witchcraft and its Transformations, c.1650–c.1750* (Oxford, 1997), 139–54 and *passim*.
[62] Brian P. Levack, 'Witchcraft and the Law in Early Modern Scotland', in *Witch-Hunting in Scotland*, 15–33.

reconciliation with someone who had cursed them after a quarrel; this should be followed up.[63] Research could also broaden out to use witchcraft documents to investigate matters other than witchcraft; after all, in them we often see intimate details of people's everyday lives, details that may not be recoverable from any other source.[64]

Returning to the beliefs of the elite, we need to set Scottish demonology in a broader context of intellectual life. Michael Hunter has begun this, with an edition of the works of Robert Kirk and related correspondence on fairy belief and second sight.[65] These works have sometimes been seen as 'folklore', but Hunter shows that they represent scientific enquiry—an enterprise in which such luminaries as Robert Boyle participated. Further work on scientific understanding of ghosts, 'apparitions', and 'providences' will no doubt shed light on the complex relationship between the decline of witchcraft belief and the rise of modern science.

As well as science, we need to look at literature. Several literary scholars have discussed the sixteenth-century Scottish genre of 'eldritch' (spooky) writing; much of this involves demons, fairies, monsters, and even witches.[66] Following a suggestion of Lyndal Roper, we should integrate this 'imaginative' material into historical study of witchcraft prosecution.[67] A study by Jacqueline Simpson of a famous 'eldritch' poem, Alexander Montgomerie's 'Flyting with Polwart', shows that Montgomerie drew extensively on folklore as well as classical literature.[68] Such works surely influenced the way in which prosecutors approached witches, but how?

Finally, we need more comparative studies. Was the North Berwick panic of 1590–1 influenced by the recent panic of 1587–9 in the German electorate of Trier? This, after all, was a highly political panic, involving the spectacular execution of the capital's prominent bailiff, Dietrich Flade, in September 1589, and the publication of a book

[63] Christina Larner, 'Natural and Unnatural Methods of Witchcraft Control', in *Witchcraft and Religion*, 127–39.

[64] Lauren Martin, 'Witchcraft and Family: What can Witchcraft Documents Tell Us about Early Modern Scottish Family Life?' *Scottish Tradition*, 27 (2002), 7–22; Scott Moir, 'The Crucible: Witchcraft and the Experience of Family in Early Modern Scotland', in Elizabeth Ewan and Janay Nugent, eds, *Finding the Family in Medieval and Early Modern Scotland* (Aldershot, 2008), 49–59.

[65] Michael Hunter, ed., *The Occult Laboratory: Magic, Science and Second Sight in Late Seventeenth-Century Scotland* (Woodbridge, 2001).

[66] Priscilla Bawcutt, 'Elrich Fantasyis in Dunbar and Other Poets', in J. D. McClure and M. R. G. Spiller, eds, *Bryght Lanternis: Essays on the Language and Literature of Medieval and Renaissance Scotland* (Aberdeen, 1989), 162–78; Keely Fisher, 'Eldritch Comic Verse in Older Scots', in Sally Mapstone, ed., *Older Scots Literature* (Edinburgh, 2005), 292–313; Alaric Hall, 'The Etymology and Meanings of *eldritch*', *Scottish Language*, 26 (2007), 16–22.

[67] Lyndal Roper, 'Witchcraft and the Western Imagination', *Transactions of the Royal Historical Society*, 6th ser., 16 (2006), 117–42. For recent studies linking *Macbeth* with Scottish witchcraft see Laura Kolb, 'Playing with Demons: Interrogating the Supernatural in Jacobean Drama', *Forum for Modern Language Studies*, 43 (2007), 337–50, and Roy Booth, 'Standing within the Prospect of Belief: *Macbeth*, King James, and Witchcraft', in Newton and Bath, eds, *Witchcraft and the Act of 1604*, 47–67.

[68] Jacqueline Simpson, '"The Weird Sisters Wandering": Burlesque Witchery in Montgomerie's *Flyting*', *Folklore*, 106 (1995), 9–20.

against witches in that year by Peter Binsfeld.[69] Or was the 1628–31 panic connected with the enormous surge of German witch-hunting at that time?[70] It has been argued that writings about demonic possession in the celebrated Bargarran panic of 1697 were influenced by writings about the recent panic of 1692 at Salem, Massachusetts.[71] As well as importing witchcraft, Scotland may have exported it. The 1649–50 'Scottish' panic spilled over into northern England.[72] A Scottish cunning man in the Netherlands, James Cunningham, was pilloried and banished for practising counter-magic against witches in 1608.[73] The first witchcraft panics in Finnmark, northern Norway, seem to have been inspired by its new Scottish governor, John Cunningham, in 1620.[74]

Comparative study can thus take many forms. James Sharpe and Brian Levack have made a start by comparing Scotland and England, bringing out many points of similarity despite the radically different intensity of witch-hunting in each country.[75] I have carried out a study placing Scottish witchcraft beliefs in their European context; again Scotland emerges as a fairly typical European state, though it naturally had some locally distinctive traits.[76] These are merely preliminary surveys, however, and we need more detailed work. This Handbook may itself assist international comparisons. As well as detailed work, we need to develop the big picture. The Survey of Scottish Witchcraft has proven to be useful, and this surely indicates that a Survey of European Witchcraft would also be helpful.

FURTHER READING

Goodare, Julian, ed., *The Scottish Witch-Hunt in Context* (Manchester, 2002).
Goodare, Julian, ed., *Scottish Witches and Witch-Hunters* (Basingstoke, 2013).
Goodare, Julian, Martin, Lauren, and Miller, Joyce, eds, *Witchcraft and Belief in Early Modern Scotland* (Basingstoke, 2008).
Goodare, Julian, Martin, Lauren, Miller, Joyce, and Yeoman, Louise (2003). 'The Survey of Scottish Witchcraft, 1563–1736', ⟨http://www.shc.ed.ac.uk/witches/⟩ (accessed 13 October 2010).

[69] George L. Burr, 'The Fate of Dietrich Flade', *Papers of the American Historical Association*, 5 (1891), 189–243. James's *Daemonologie* has been compared with Binsfeld's work: Levack, 'King James VI', 44.
[70] H. C. E. Midelfort, *Witch-Hunting in Southwestern Germany, 1562–1684: The Social and Intellectual Foundations* (Stanford, CA, 1972), 121–63.
[71] Hugh McLachlan and Kim Swales, 'The Bewitchment of Christian Shaw: A Reassessment of the Famous Paisley Witchcraft Case of 1697', in Brown and Ferguson, eds, *Twisted Sisters*, 54–83.
[72] Brian P. Levack, 'Witch-Hunting in Revolutionary Britain', in *Witch-Hunting in Scotland*, 69–70.
[73] Hans de Waardt, 'Prosecution or Defense: Procedural Possibilities Following a Witchcraft Accusation in the Province of Holland before 1800', in Marijke Gijswijt-Hofstra and Willem Frijhoff, eds, *Witchcraft in the Netherlands*, tr. Rachel M. J. van der Fall (Rotterdam, 1991), 84.
[74] Willumsen, 'Seventeenth Century Witchcraft Trials', 24–5.
[75] James Sharpe, 'Witch-Hunting and Witch Historiography: Some Anglo-Scottish Comparisons', in Goodare, ed., *The Scottish Witch-Hunt in Context*, 182–97; Brian P. Levack, 'Witch-Hunting in Scotland and England', in *Witch-Hunting in Scotland*, 1–14.
[76] Julian Goodare, 'Scottish Witchcraft in its European Context', in Goodare, Martin, and Miller, eds, *Witchcraft and Belief*, 26–50.

Henderson, Lizanne, ed., *Fantastical Imaginations: The Supernatural in Scottish History and Culture* (East Linton, 2009).

Henderson, Lizanne and Cowan, Edward J., *Scottish Fairy Belief: A History* (East Linton, 2001).

Hunter, Michael, ed., *The Occult Laboratory: Magic, Science and Second Sight in Late Seventeenth-Century Scotland* (Woodbridge, 2001).

Hutton, Ronald, 'Witch-Hunting in Celtic Societies', *Past & Present*, 212 (August 2011), 43–71.

Larner, Christina, *Enemies of God: The Witch-Hunt in Scotland* (London, 1981; repr. Edinburgh, 2000).

Larner, Christina, *Witchcraft and Religion: The Politics of Popular Belief* (Oxford, 1984).

Levack, Brian P., *Witch-Hunting in Scotland: Law, Politics and Religion* (London, 2008).

Macdonald, Stuart, *The Witches of Fife: Witch-Hunting in a Scottish Shire, 1560–1710* (East Linton, 2001).

Normand, Lawrence and Roberts, Gareth, eds, *Witchcraft in Early Modern Scotland: James VI's* Demonology *and the North Berwick Witches* (Exeter, 2000).

Wilby, Emma, *Cunning Folk and Familiar Spirits: Shamanistic Visionary Traditions in Early Modern British Witchcraft and Magic* (Brighton, 2005).

Wilby, Emma, *The Visions of Isobel Gowdie: Magic, Witchcraft and Dark Shamanism in Seventeenth-Century Scotland* (Brighton, 2010).

Willumsen, Liv Helene, *Witches of the North: Scotland and Finnmark* (Leiden, 2013).

CHAPTER 18

WITCHCRAFT IN POLAND: MILK AND MALEFICE

MICHAEL OSTLING

In the summer of 1674 the court of Słomniki, a small town north of Kraków in southern Poland, heard accusations of 'witchcraft and dew-gathering' against the peasant woman Krystyna Gajowa Danielecka. Tied hand and foot and dunked in the river, Krystyna 'could not sink, but floated to the other side', failing the water ordeal. Interrogated under torture (suspension from the strappado three times, twice with the application of hot irons), she confessed to nothing, but blamed one Dorota Pilecka for her misfortunes. Sometime previously, Dorota had come to her house asking for butter; Krystyna gave it and received some peas and turnips in return, from which moment 'everything spoiled': her butter stank and there were worms in her cheese and milk.

As a result of Krystyna's denunciation, the village court of Kalina Wielka brought Dorota Pilecka to trial. Before the assembled commune of land-holding peasant men and the lord of the manor, a series of witnesses brought forth their suspicions: Dorota washed cattle in herbal decoctions; she collected manure, grass, and soil from the hoofprints of other people's cattle as they went out to pasture; she always showed up when cows were calving, ostensibly to borrow a bit of flour or lard but really to steal the afterbirth; she had been seen collecting herbs in the cemetery, mixing these cemetery-herbs into her posy to be blessed at the feast of 'Our Lady of the Herbs' (15 August, the Assumption of the Virgin Mary); she owned a dried bat. In general, 'people say that she must know how to do something'. Under such a weight of evidence, Dorota was turned over to the Słomniki town court for interrogation under torture. Pulled three times and burned with hot irons, she never confessed but was nevertheless pronounced guilty: she had 'practised all sorts of witchcraft and enchantment with herbs', and had offended against the First Commandment: 'Thou shalt not have other gods before me.' Krystyna

Danielecka was beheaded. To punish Dorota's more serious crimes, the Słomniki court sent to Kraków for an executioner to burn her properly at the stake.[1]

The executions of Krystyna and Dorota constitute just two of many hundreds of such executions for witchcraft in the Commonwealth of the Two Nations of Poland and Lithuania—a vast and diverse state in the early modern era, stretching from the Baltic to the trans-Dnieper steppes, and comprising most of the territory of present-day Poland, Lithuania, Belarus, and Ukraine. We know of at least 867 witch trials and at least 558 accused witches under the Polish Crown between 1511 until the abolition of witchcraft as a capital crime in 1776, and a much smaller number—ninety-seven trials, of which twenty-seven included death sentences—in the Grand Duchy of Lithuania. Given the preliminary state of scholarship on Polish witch trials, and the poor state of the Polish archives—nearly 80 per cent of the records of the Central Archives of Old Records was deliberately burnt by the Nazis in the dying days of the Second World War—these numbers must be treated as minimum figures only. A total of perhaps two thousand witches burnt, while undemonstrable, seems likely.[2]

No single set of small-town trials can hope to embody all the themes and issues of hundreds of trials over three centuries, and indeed the two Słomniki trials of 1674 lack many central motifs encountered elsewhere in Poland. We hear of no verbal curse against neighbours—'eat a devil!' or 'you won't live to enjoy the profit from this field'. We find no burial of 'disgusting things'—ashes and bones and toads, or the whole rotting head of a mare—under a threshold or in a child's bedchamber, bringing sickness and death. Neither Krystyna nor Dorota travelled to the witches' feast at Łysa Góra (Bald Mountain), to dance with demon consorts while the rare male witch provided music played on a hoe, a needle, or a foxes' tail; by contrast, in northern and western Poland in the late seventeenth century, the Bald Mountain motif had become so common that many witchcraft confessions devolve into long lists of denunciations, naming the other witches seen at the feast. At Słomniki, neither Krystyna nor Dorota enjoyed the services of the demon-familiars found in witch trials throughout central Poland and eastwards into Ruthenia. Hybrid creatures, part Christian devil, part Slavic house spirit, part ghost of an unbaptized baby, such *diabły* or *latawcy* or *złe duchy* (devils, flying ones, evil spirits) could be sent to strangle a cow or push a neighbour into the lake to drown; they also flew in and out of the witches' hovel, their tails sparking fire, bearing stolen grain or milk or treasure.

In many respects, however, the Słomniki trials are typical. Like at least 90 per cent of the accused Polish witches, both Krystyna and Dorota were women—an identity so

[1] Władysław Siarkowski, *Materiały do etnografii ludu polskiego z okolic Kielc* (Kielce, [1878–9] 2000), 84–7.

[2] I take the numbers for the Polish Crown (roughly ethnic Poland plus Ruthenia, Wołyn, Podole, and Ukraine) from Małgorzata Pilaszek, *Procesy o czary w Polsce w wiekach XV–XVIIII* (Kraków, 2008), 266, 292; and those for the Grand Duchy (roughly Lithuania and Belarus) from the same author's 'Litewskie procesy czarownic w XVI–XVIII w.', *Odrodzenie i Reformacja w Polsce*, 46 (2002), 7–35. On the destruction of the Polish archives see Adam Stebelski, *The Fate of Polish Archives during World War II* (Warsaw, 1964).

close that the Polish word *baba*, like its Russian cognate, can connote 'old village woman', 'cunning woman', and 'witch'. Like most, they were village serfs or commoner inhabitants of the small agrarian towns sprinkled throughout the Polish countryside (the large cities of the Commonwealth—Kraków, Gdańsk, Warsaw, Poznań, Lublin, Lwów—all recorded witch trials, but in disproportionately small numbers). Krystyna seems to have been a widow while Dorota was the wife of the village cobbler; both were caught up in the relationships of petty borrowing and lending, the reciprocal food and labour exchanges, which could so easily lead to the conflict and envy expressed in witchcraft accusations. Krystyna allegedly received her own power to bewitch through accursed food, a common motif blurring the distinction between perpetrator and victim, witch and bewitched. Like many suspected witches, Krystyna was dunked in the river—an ancient Slavic practice still resorted to, albeit illicitly, right into the mid-nineteenth century, despite repeated ecclesiastical condemnation of the practice from the early seventeenth century onwards.[3]

Like many accused witches in early modern Poland, Krystyna and Dorota only came to trial after many years of gradually consolidated reputations for sinister, suspicious behaviour. Krystyna had gathered dew—that is, she had taken the life-giving moisture from fields of grain or (more likely), from pastureland on the village common, metonymically transferring the dew's fecundity to her own fields and milch cows. Dorota stood accused of a series of rituals, all also tending to increase the milk production of her own cattle at the expense of others. So central was milk-theft to Polish conceptions of witchcraft that a woman could come under suspicion simply because 'she has plenty of butter from just one cow'; conversely, the husband of another accused witch attempted to prove his wife's innocence by declaring 'I have nine cows, but I don't have even a drop of milk, and my wife always used to say, "they call me a witch, even though I have to buy cheese".' It would be misleading to treat this dairy obsession in purely nutritional terms, or to derive it from a superstitious ignorance of Pasteur. In the early modern Polish popular cosmology, a cow's yield of milk represented a central moment in what Lyndal Roper has called 'the economy of bodily fluids': it provided both an 'objective' index of a household's prosperity and a symbolic index of its health and well-being. The witch was, above all, an over-consumer of these limited goods: she stole milk and the health it symbolized while her neighbours, their cattle, their fields, and their fat juicy babies, dried up and shrivelled away.[4] Hence the stereotypical rhyming spell of Polish witches, attested to in dozens of trials: 'Biorę pożytek, ale nie wszytek'—'I take the profit, though not the whole thing.'

[3] Russell Zguta, 'The Ordeal by Water (Swimming of Witches) in the East Slavic World', *Slavic Review*, 36 (1977), 220–30; Jósef Rosenblatt, *Czarownica powołana: Przyczynek do historii spraw przeciw czarownicom w Polsce* (Warsaw, 1883), 63–4.

[4] Lyndal Roper, *Oedipus and the Devil: Witchcraft, Sexuality and Religion in Early Modern Europe* (London, 1994), 207–9; George M. Foster, 'Peasant Society and the Image of the Limited Good', *American Anthropologist*, 67 (1965), 293–315.

Moreover, most of the Słomniki witches' suspicious activities constitute excesses or inversions of the ordinary counter-magic practised by any conscientious housewife. Krystyna gathered dew from communal fields—others protected their cattle, or restored stolen milk, with holy water or with water gathered from a running river before sunrise. Dorota washed her cows with herbs blessed at the feast of Our Lady of the Herbs—so did everyone else. The only difference is that Dorota, allegedly, gathered some of her herbs in the cemetery. Witches differed from their neighbours not through special knowledge or ability, but through *little* illicit departures from common folk practices. And yet one woman's 'recovery' of her cow's lost milk must have looked, to an outsider, very like another woman's 'theft'—one might say that the best defence is a good offence. It follows that, while milk magic was widely practised, few practitioners thought of themselves as milk-thieves—as witches. The imagined activity of thieves generated the real activities of protectors and recoverers, and the imagined rituals and spells of thieves generated, through inversion, the real rituals and spells of their adversaries. Thus one finds a characteristic paradox of the Polish witch trials: despite the lack of self-identified witches, there was always plenty of quite real evidence for the practice of witchcraft.

Finally, the outcome of the Słomniki trials is typical. Like perhaps two-thirds of accused witches before town courts in Poland, Krystyna and Dorota were sentenced to death—nearly always, as with Dorota, by burning alive at the stake.

18.1 LAW AND PRACTICE

Criminal justice in the early modern Polish–Lithuanian Commonwealth presented a mosaic of overlapping courts and jurisdictions, each with its own legal traditions and norms. Only in the Grand Duchy, where the Third Lithuanian Statute of 1588 assigned jurisdiction over witch trials to the noble palatinate courts, do we find clear, though ill-enforced, norms for the prosecution of witches. In the Polish Crown, witches could be tried before manorial courts, village courts, ecclesiastical courts, even the special Cossack tribunals of eastern Ukraine or the guild courts of large cities: in 1670, the baker's guild of Bydgoszcz heard accusations that a member had mixed ground bones from a hanged thief into his flour, seeking thereby to increase sales.[5] Witchcraft cases involving the desecration of the Eucharistic host could be referred to regional noble courts or to the Crown Tribunal at Lublin; however, the statutory law guiding such noble courts took so little notice of witchcraft that the word appears not at all in the first five volumes of the *Volumina Legum*, the great compendium of Polish law. Not

---

[5] Z. Malewski, 'Procesy o czarnoksięstwo i zabobony w Bydgoszczy: Przyczynek do dziejów czarownictwa w Polsce', *Przegląd Bydgoski*, 4 (1936), 80–1.

until the state sought belatedly to regulate witch trials in the 1670s did Polish statutory law become relevant to witch trials in the country.[6]

Ecclesiastical courts tried women variously described as *incantatrices, sortilegae,* or *mulieres antiquas* throughout the fifteenth century and well into the sixteenth. Such women allegedly made amulets from roots, divined with wax and lead, or (an especial concern of the ecclesiastical courts, in Poland as in the West), made use of holy water, chrism, and blessed candles for this-worldly ends. However, cases involving magic constituted less than 1 per cent of church-court trials in this period; Joanna Adamczyk, who has recently provided a thorough study of these trials, finds them to exhibit a 'relatively minimal interest in the problem of magical practices'.[7] Only in the seventeenth century, when de facto jurisdiction over criminal witchcraft had decisively shifted to the secular courts, did the Catholic Church hierarchy take a strong interest in witchcraft. In a concerted campaign beginning in the 1630s and intensifying through decades of polemical publications, the Church denounced the excesses of secular courts and the bloody-mindedness of secular judges, described disparagingly as 'analphabetic hillbillies' and as 'legal ignoramuses who can hardly recite the Lord's Prayer'.[8] Drawing on the text of a parliamentary *constitutio* of 1543 (an act which, however, had never been ratified or enacted into law), the bishops of northern and western Poland issued a series of pastoral letters and synodal decrees in the first four decades of the eighteenth century, insisting that witch trials be returned to church-court jurisdiction, and threatening secular magistrates with ecclesiastical censure.[9] With the partial exception of the diocese of Włocławek, where Bishop Krzysztof Antoni Szembek intervened personally in several town-court witch trials in the early eighteenth century, this ecclesiastical campaign seems to have had little effect on the behaviour of secular town courts—the courts before which some 80 per cent of accused Polish witches were tried.

Although ecclesiastical court records mention a trial before the secular town court of Poznań as early as 1434, the earliest clear cases come from Gdańsk in 1501 and Waliszew, a suburb of Poznań, in 1511, where a *vetula* accused of magically spoiling the brewing of beer was burnt at the stake.[10] The code of Saxon law employed by Polish

---

[6] Stanisław Salmonowicz, 'Procesy o czary w Polsce: Próba rozważań modelowych', in G. Bałtruszajtis, ed., *Prawo wczoraj i dziś* (Warsaw, 2000), 310; Michael Ostling, 'Konstytucja 1543 r. i początki procesów o czary w Polsce', *Odrodzenie i Reformacja w Polsce*, 49 (2005), 93–103.

[7] Joanna Adamczyk, 'Czary i magia w praktyce sądów kościelnych na ziemiach polskich w późnym średniowieczu (XV-połowa XVI wieku)', in Maria Koczerska, ed., *Karolińscy pokutnicy i polskie średniowieczne czarownice* (Warsaw, 2007), 249; Pilaszek, *Procesy*, 144–53.

[8] Serafin Gamalski, *Przestrogi Duchowne, Sędziom, Inwestygatorom, y Instygatorom Czarownic* (Poznań, 1742), 7; Anon., *Czarownica powolana, abo krotka nauka y prestroga z strony czarownic* (Gdańsk, [1639] 1714), 52.

[9] Ostling, 'Konstytucja 1543'; Henryk Karbownik, 'Management of Witchcraft Trials in the Light of Synod Resolutions and Bishops' Regulations in Pre-partition Poland', *Review of Comparative Law*, 2 (1988).

[10] Krzysztof P. Szkurlatowski, 'Gdańskie procesy czarownic w XV–XVII w. na tle ówczesnych przemian religijnych', in Jan Iluk and Danuta Mariańska, eds, *Protestantyzm i protestanci na Pomorzu*

town courts called for death at the stake for *maleficium*, a position strengthened in the mid-sixteenth century when the Kraków jurist Bartłomiej Groicki translated selections from the *Carolina* into Polish, including its provision of capital punishment for any magic resulting in harm to persons or property.[11] Nevertheless, throughout the sixteenth century secular witch trials remained rare and rarely resulted in execution. The accused, often semi-professional cunning women, confessed to milk-theft and love magic but also to healing with herbs and prayers, finding lost or stolen items, and laying protective blessings on cattle and on brewing beer. They were punished with fines, oaths of apology, or banishment: where they received a capital sentence, this was often for a combination of crimes. A witch sentenced to decapitation in Poznań seems to have worked as a procuress, while two women eventually burnt in Kalisz for demon-assisted milk-theft first came to the court's attention for vagrancy, robbery, and prostitution.

By the early seventeenth century, noble and burgher attitudes towards witchcraft had shifted decisively. A notation in the village-court records of Klimkówka traces this shift in attitude: in 1611 the village's noble owner reminded the court that 'concerning witch-craft . . . the law commands that if [a witch] should threaten, she must be punished with death'.[12] Three years later, the little-known petty nobleman Stanisław Ząbkowic published his translation of Kramer's *Malleus maleficarum*—the earliest vernacular translation of this seminal work of demonology.[13] Meanwhile, notions of witchcraft as a species of blasphemous treason entered Polish jurisprudence through the influence of Continental legal scholars such as Joos de Damhouder and Benedict Carpzov, whose writings nudged the local Polish version of Saxon law in the direction of Western inquisitorial norms.[14] A rare crime in the sixteenth and early seventeenth century, confined largely to the northern and western palatinates of Wielkopolska and Royal Prussia, witchcraft was becoming a topic on everybody's mind; according to the polemical pamphlet *The Witch Denounced*, 'one hears about witch-trials more than

---

(Gdańsk, 1997), 218–19; Bolesław Ulanowski, ed., *Acta iudiciorum ecclesiasticorum diocesum gneznensis et poznaniensis (1403–1530)* (Kraków,1902), item 1660.

[11] Bartłomiej Groicki, *Ten postępek wybran jest z praw cesarskich* (Kraków, 1559), art. 24.

[12] Ludwik Łysiak, ed., *Księga sądowa kresu klimkowskiego, 1600–1762* (Wrocław, 1965), item 72.

[13] Stanisław Ząbkowic, *Młot na czarownice: Postępek zwierzchowny w czarach, także sposob uchronienia sie ich, y lekarstwo na nie w dwoch częściach zamykaiący* (Kraków, 1614); on translations of the *Malleus*, see H. C. Erik Midelfort's review of Christopher Mackay, *The Hammer of Witches: A Complete Translation of the* Malleus Maleficarum, *Catholic Historical Review*, 97 (2011), 99. Although the influence of such texts on practice is notoriously difficult to establish, it is worth noting that copies of the *Malleus*, in Latin or in Ząbkowic's Polish translation, have been found in the personal libraries of a Poznań magistrate and a juryman of Lublin.

[14] Karol Koranyi, 'Wpływ prawa flandryjskiego na polskie w XVI wieku (Damhouder-Groicki)', *Pamiętnik historyczno-prawny*, 4 (1927), 165–218; Witold Maisel, *Poznańskie prawo karne do końca XVI wieku* (Poznań, 1963), 211; Wacław Uruszczak, 'Proces czarownicy w Nowym Sączu w 1670 roku: Z badań nad miejskim procesem karnym czasów nowożytnych', in E. Borkowska-Bagieńska and H. Olszewski, eds, *Historia Prawa. Historia Kultury: Liber Memorialis Vitoldo Maisel* (Poznań, 1994), 193.

Table 18.1 Intensive Witch-Hunts in Poland

Town	Region	Number of Trials	Number Executed	Dates
Fordon	Wielkopolska	60	?	1675–1711
Grodzisk	Wielkopolska	5	20+	1700–1720
Kleczew	Wielkopolska	21	41	1682–1700
Łobżenica	Wielkopolska	?	c. 30	1675–1700
Nieszawa	Wielkopolska	12+	?	1698–1722
Nowe	Royal Prussia	18	?	1701–1719
Płońsk	Mazowsze	16	26+	1699–1713

about any other subject'.[15] Over half the Polish witch trials (and over half the executions) occurred in the seventeenth century; after 1650, such trials became nearly as common in southern Poland (Małopolska) as in the north and west. Between 1648 and 1660 the country was devastated by a series of disasters: Cossack uprising, Russian invasion, peasant *jacquerie*, and, above all, the catastrophic Swedish war known to Polish historiography as the Deluge. The last quarter of the seventeenth century, when the countryside had begun to recover demographically but not economically, saw the peak of the witch trials and executions: perhaps a quarter of the total. Moreover, though most trials continued to be initiated through accusation and to feature just one or a few suspects, the half-century 1675–1725 saw an increase in intensive witch-hunts and chain-reaction trials.

By far the bloodiest outbreak of witch panic occurred in the small town of Kleczew in central Wielkopolska. As Tomasz Wiślicz has ably shown, the Kleczew court became a magnet for witchcraft cases, drawing in suspects from villages and small towns within a 15 kilometre radius.[16] To understand the mechanisms underlying the Kleczew witch-hunt we must briefly consider its opposite: the everyday, ordinary trials before Polish village courts.

Village-court witch trials differed radically from the trials before town courts. Testimony before a village court could function as a sort of pre-trial hearing, as with the proceedings against Dorota Pilecka before her trial in Słomniki. In general, however, village courts functioned on a model of restorative justice, the court focusing not on who was wrong but on how to set things right. Wiślicz has shown that of fifty-three village-court witch trials from 1529 to 1766, the great majority ended with sentences of a small fine, an oath of expurgation, or a court-enforced apology and reconciliation between accuser and accused. Village courts could level corporal punishments such as flogging, and (with the manor's permission), might order the banishment of a troublesome witch—as when the court of Iwkowa ordered a *succubita*

---

[15] *Czarownica powołana*, f.3.
[16] Tomasz Wiślicz, 'The Township of Kleczew and its Neighborhood Fighting the Devil (1624–1700)', *Acta Poloniae Historica*, 89 (2004), 65–95.

to depart the village territory 'before sundown'.[17] But village magistrates could not legally adjudicate capital crimes. To permanently eradicate a dangerous witch from their midst, a village community had to send the accused to the Saxon law court of a nearby town.

This consideration helps to account for several features of that large proportion (about two-thirds) of town-court witch trials originating in villages. Because the nobility maintained almost proprietary rights over their peasant subjects, a serf could not stand accused before a town court without at least the tacit permission of the lord of the manor—Dorota Pilecka was sent to the Słomniki town court only after her master, *Pan* Michał Oraczewski, had heard the village-court testimony against her and chose to proceed. The appearance of class warfare discernible in some Polish witch trials derives in part from this juridical situation: a peasant witch simply could not come to trial unless her manor-lord himself had reason to take village suspicions seriously—often because he or his family had themselves become victims of the witch. However, once the lord of the manor had become convinced of a suspected witch's guilt, his active cooperation often assured her conviction. He covered the costs of magistrate, scribe, and executioner, sending his serf to the town for trial or even inviting the court to the manor, putting them up as his guests while they tried the case *in situ*. A nobleman who paid for a local town court to come to his property expected, and often got, the verdicts and sentences he was looking for; the popularity of the Kleczew court among the petty nobility of central Wielkopolska, even where the courts of other small towns were sometimes nearer at hand, correlates with that court's willingness to accede to such noble desires for conviction. On the other hand, the need for manorial cooperation tended to inhibit witch panics or chain-reaction trials: when an accused witch denounced collaborators from another village, the serfs belonging to another manor, it could often prove impossible to bring these newly suspected witches to justice.[18]

To thoughtful observers the local, small-town witch trials of the late seventeenth century could appear as thinly legitimated lynchings; but without a strong central government little could be done to stop them. Over a third of the Polish witch trials, and two-fifths of the executions, occurred in the eighteenth century, primarily in its first quarter. The Catholic Church hierarchy had been campaigning against the trials for decades; now the state also tried, albeit ineffectually, to intervene. The Assessory Court, an organ of the Royal Chancellery exercising limited appellate oversight over the Saxon-law judiciaries of royal towns, attempted to regulate witch trials in 1673, forbidding small-town magistrates from hearing cases for 'sacrilege, sorcery, or malefice'. However, royal rescripts in 1703, 1727, and 1740, and repeated decrees of the Assessory

---

[17] Tomasz Wiślicz, 'Czary przed sądami wiejskimi w Polsce XVI–XVIII wieku', *Czasopismo Prawno-Historyczne*, 49 (1997), 47–63; Stanisław Płaza, ed., *Księga sądowa wsi Iwkowej, 1581–1809* (Wrocław, 1969), item 284.

[18] Michael Ostling, *Between the Devil and the Host: Imagining Witchcraft in Early Modern Poland* (Oxford, 2011), 94–9. On witchcraft as class war, see Genowefa Adamczewska, 'Magiczna broń i jej rola w walce między wsią a dworem w Sieradzkiem w XVI–XVIII w.', *Łódzkie Studia Etnograficzne*, 5 (1963), 5–16.

Court in 1749, 1750, and 1768 had almost no effect. Despite draconian penalties, on paper, against offending magistrates, such directives of the weak central government remained unenforceable so long as local nobility supported the witch trials.[19] Such support began to erode by the second half of the eighteenth century, by which time educated Poles were increasingly embarrassed by the Western perception of their Commonwealth as backward and superstitious. Rampant witch-burnings formed part of this unsatisfactory image: in a mid-century polyglot dictionary, the Professor of Polish at Leipzig could complain that 'en Pologne on brûle les sorciers souvent sans aucune inquisition'.[20] The noble leaders of Poland's late-blooming Enlightenment could not abide continued witch trials in the country. At the reforming parliamentary session of 1776, King Stanisław August proposed a *constitutio* abolishing judicial torture; it passed unanimously, together with an amendment 'forever abolishing the penalty of death in cases of witchcraft'.[21] The crime of witchcraft had been legislated out of existence, although scattered reports of dunkings, assaults, or even lynching of suspected witches continued through the nineteenth and twentieth centuries. The milk-theft motif remains current even today: in 2004, the Kraków regional court ordered a woman to apologize after publicly accusing her neighbour of spoiling the milk in the udders of her cows.[22]

18.2 PROGRESS AND PROSPECTS

Nineteenth and early twentieth-century Polish folklorists, like their compeers elsewhere in Europe, looked to witch trials in search of the timeless, essential genesis of their nation as preserved in the practices of the common folk. In witch-trial testimony they found both remnants of pre-Christian Slavic religion and antecedents for present-day superstition, evidence either way for just such a substratum of ahistorical national culture. Early on, the brilliant Ryszard Berwiński critiqued this folkloric approach, insisting instead on the derivative, foreign provenance of most Polish witchcraft beliefs. Berwiński portrayed the Polish witch as a 'cosmopolitan, not born or raised in this or that country, but conceived at the cross-roads between this temporal and the everlasting world': an image that fits well with recent models placing witch trials at the conjuncture of transnational and local, literary and oral, elite and popular

---

[19] Malgorzata Pilaszek, 'Apelacje w polskich procesach czarownic (XVII–XVIII w.)', *Odrodzenie i Reformacja w Polsce*, 49 (2005), 113–36; Ostling, *Devil and the Host*, 53–9.

[20] M. A. Trotz, *Nouveau Dictionnaire François, Allemand et Polonais* (1749); quoted after Pilaszek, *Procesy*, 68.

[21] Jerzy Michalski, 'Jeszcze o konstytucji sejmu 1776 roku "Konwikcje w sprawach kryminalnych"', *Kwartalnik Historyczny*, 103 (1996), 89–101.

[22] Aldona Christina Schiffmann, 'The Witch and Crime: The Persecution of Witches in 20th-century Poland', *ARV: Scandinavian Yearbook of Folklore*, 43 (1987), 147–65; Anon., 'Pierwszy od 300 lat w Polsce proces o czary', *Gazeta Wyborcza*, 10 March 2004.

worldviews.[23] Nevertheless, it was the ahistorical, essentializing folklorists who hunted down and published a great many trial records, preserving these from the catastrophes of the twentieth century. Oskar Kolberg's vast but disorganized survey of Polish folklore, together with pre-war articles from the folklore journals *Wisła* and *Lud*, remain valuable resources for the historian of Polish witch trials.[24]

In contrast, nineteenth-century Polish historians paid witchcraft little mind. A few deployed witch trials to illustrate the deficiencies that had led to the partition of the Commonwealth by its imperial neighbours at the end of the eighteenth century: thus Józef Łukaszewicz could inveigh against 'the obscurantism of the Jesuit schools' filling up the nobility with superstitious nonsense, thanks to which one finds witch trials on 'nearly every page' of the early modern Polish court records. But the same author used witch trials to impugn the partitioning powers: the prosecutions were 'bred in Germany and were brought to our country along with the barbaric Magdeburg Law'.[25] In contrast, the legal scholar Jósef Rosenblatt examined the Polish witch trials as evidence for a judicial system in disarray, but he also found, in texts like the *Witch Denounced*, proof that *some* early modern Poles stood up for tolerance against the superstitious fanaticism of the times.[26] Although witch trials remained marginal to Polish historiography of this period, the parameters for twentieth-century discussion of the subject were thus set: witch trials represented the worst, most backward aspects of the pre-Partition era; witch beliefs derived from external sources and were thus not essentially Polish; though Polish witch trials were comparatively mild, they inspired great works of sceptical toleration representing the best, most progressive characteristics of the nation. This tendency to invidious comparison proved remarkably stable right into the twenty-first century, informing brief but influential essays by such well-known historians as Janusz Tazbir and Maria Bogucka. Even Małgorzata Pilaszek, despite having analysed more Polish trials and chronicled more Polish executions than any previous researcher, insists that the Polish witch prosecutions were 'among the least intensive of the entire continent', constituting 'only a pale reflection of events in the West'.[27]

Bohdan Baranowski's *Witch-Trials in Poland in the 17th and 18th Centuries*, the first and until very recently the only monograph on the Polish witch trials, shared this tendency to compare Polish mildness to the 'millions' of witches burnt in Germany. But it added a second contrast: between the progressive, socialist, atheist present and the superstitious, feudal, fanatical past. Published in 1952 at the height of Poland's brief

[23] R. Berwiński, *Studia o gusłach, czarach, zabobonach i przesądach ludowych* (2nd edn, Warsaw, [1862] 1984), ii, 181.

[24] Oskar Kolberg, *Dzieła wszystkie Oskara Kolberga*, ed. Julian Krzyżanowski *et al.*, 84 vols (Wrocław and Poznań, [1857–1907] 1961–2011).

[25] Józef Łukaszewicz, *Krótki historyczno-statystyczny opis miast i wsi w dzisiejszym powiecie krotoszyńskim od najdawniejszych czasów aż po rok 1794* (Poznań, 1869–75), i, 74–6.

[26] Rosenblatt, *Czarownica powołana*.

[27] Janusz Tazbir, 'Procesy o czary', *Odrodzenie i Reformacja w Polsce*, 23 (1978), 157–77; Tazbir, 'Liczenie wiedźm', *Polityka*, 37 (2001), 74–5; Maria Bogucka, 'Law and Crime in Poland in Early Modern Times', *Acta Poloniae Historica*, 71 (1995), 191; Pilaszek, *Procesy*, 128.

Stalinist phase, and written by an author committed to legitimating the new regime by creating a black legend of the system it replaced (between 1950 and 1953 Baranowski collaborated on a series of publications exposing the intolerance, fanaticism, and brutal despotism of the Catholic Church and the Polish nobility), *Witch-Trials* depicted the Polish prosecutions as a product of 'Popish politics and the Inquisition' wedded to class warfare: the nobility used witchcraft accusation to eliminate uppity serfs, 'the bold fighters, male and female, for the rights of the peasant masses'.[28] For Baranowski, the 'gloomy superstition' of witchcraft stood for all that was cruel, ignorant, and savage in the Polish past, and he systematically exaggerated the scope of the persecutions to bolster his dark vision of that past. His assertion that 10,000 witches were burnt in Poland, and a further 5,000 lynched (an assertion widely cited in Western scholarship until very recently, after the French resumé to *Witch-Trials*) derives entirely from this dark vision: Baranowski simply multiplied the number of towns in early modern Poland by an arbitrary four trials per town, then doubled the resulting product.[29] Although he edited a valuable collection of the early witch trials in Kalisz,[30] and later wrote useful histories of everyday life in early modern Poland, Baranowski's legacy will remain his systematic, long-influential misrepresentation of the Polish witch trials.

At the turn of the twenty-first century, Stanisław Salmonowicz surveyed the scholarship on Polish witchcraft and found little to like—Baranowski's dubious synthesis; Janusz Tazbir's brief programmatic corrective to that synthesis; a few scattered archival studies of limited ambition.[31] Much has changed in the intervening years. Although the scholarship on Polish witchcraft remains young, recent work has broadened its scope enormously and provided a firm footing for future research. Tomasz Wiślicz's research on village courts and on the great Kleczew witch-hunt has already been noted; he has also begun an investigation into popular demonology as expressed in exorcism narratives.[32] The tireless Jacek Wijaczka has produced a stream of regional and thematic studies, and his monograph on Ducal Prussia demonstrates the similar trajectory of witchcraft prosecution in this erstwhile fiefdom of the Polish Crown: a late peak of trials in the last three decades of the seventeenth century; women constituting about 85 per cent of the accused.[33] Kateryna Dysa's important study, 'Witchcraft Trials and Beyond', focuses on the understudied Ruthenian regions of the Crown. Despite a persistent early modern stereotype of Ruthenia as a nest of witches (such that a seventeenth-century

---

[28] Bohdan Baranowski, *Procesy Czarownic w Polsce w XVII i XVIII wieku* (Łódź, 1952), 10–11, 39.

[29] Baranowski, *Procesy Czarownic*, 30, 178.

[30] *Najdawniejsze procesy o czary w Kaliszu* (Lublin, 1951).

[31] Salmonowicz, 'Procesy o czary w Polsce'; Tazbir, 'Procesy o czary'.

[32] Tomasz Wiślicz, 'Talking to the Devil in the Early Modern Popular Imagination', in O. Z. Pugliese and E. M. Kavaler, eds, *Faith and Fantasy in the Renaissance: Texts, Images, Religious Practices* (Toronto, 2009), 135–46.

[33] See especially Jacek Wijaczka, 'Procesy o czary w regionie świętokrzyskiego w XVII XVIII wieku', in Wijaczka, ed., *Z przeszłości regionu świętokrzyskiego od XVI do XX wieku* (Kielce, 2003); Wijaczka, 'Procesy o czary w Polsce w dobie Oświecenia: Zarys problematyki', *Klio*, 17 (2005), 17–62; Wijaczka, *Procesy o czary w Prusach Książęcych/Brandenburskich w XVI–XVIII wieku* (Toruń, 2007).

Polish–Latin dictionary glossed *saga* as both *czarownica* and *Rusiianka*, 'witch' and 'Ruthenian woman'), Dysa's study confirms that the magistrates in this region showed little interest in eradicating witches. Acquittals were common, sentences mild: of 189 witch trials in the period 1600–1800, Dysa finds just thirteen executions.[34] Finally, two book-length monographs on Polish witch trials have recently appeared. Brief consideration of these books will demonstrate that the scholarship on Polish witchcraft has come of age, while also suggesting directions for future research.[35]

More than half a century after Baranowski's *Witch-Trials*, Małgorzata Pilaszek's massive *Trials for Witchcraft in Poland* has brought the study of witchcraft in Poland into the twenty-first century. Strongly grounded in the broadest survey of Polish archives so far undertaken—Pilaszek perused or sampled the criminal records of twenty-nine towns scattered throughout Poland, and made use of the published records for several dozen more—Pilaszek's book marks a new era in Polish historiography.[36] Her cautious analyses of this large database and her appreciation for the social and legal forces driving the witch trials present a decisive departure from Baranowski's inflationary speculations: after Pilaszek, it should no longer be possible to dismiss witch trials as the tragic result of 'feudal fanaticism'. Importantly, Pilaszek has introduced recent Anglo-American social history to a Polish scholarly audience—and she has theoretical contributions to export in return. As has been standard since historians discovered the anthropology of E. E. Evans-Pritchard, Pilaszek reads the witch-trial records as evidence of interpersonal conflicts, but she goes further. Bringing this conflict model into conversation with the cognitive linguistics of George Lakoff and Mark Johnson, Pilaszek finds parallels between the spells and curses of a quarrelsome woman, generating suspicions; the malicious gossip and slander of neighbours, generating accusations; and the formal witch trials that generate convictions. All are *verbal* attacks with real-world consequences, all are permutations of the master metaphor of 'argument as war'. As Katarzyna Mączarka, an accused witch before the Poznań court, declared: 'nie byłyby czary bez gwary'—'there would be no witchcraft without squabbling'.[37]

With its historiographically sophisticated presentation of a rich and variegated body of archival source material, Pilaszek's work will remain the point of departure for research into Polish witch trials into the foreseeable future. However, as Pilaszek acknowleges, her study takes little interest in the subjective experience of witchcraft or its basis in folk cosmology and popular Christianity. My own *Between the Devil and the Host*, which reflects a background in religious studies and the anthropology of

---

[34] Kateryna Dysa, 'Witchcraft Trials and Beyond: Right-Bank Side Ukrainian Trials of the Seventeenth and Eighteenth Centuries', Ph.D. dissertation, Central European University, Budapest, 2004.

[35] A third has appeared very recently: Wanda Wyporska, *Witchcraft in Early Modern Poland, 1500–1800* (Basingstoke, 2013).

[36] Pilaszek, *Procesy*, 266–7.

[37] Pilaszek, *Procesy*, 57–61.

religion, attempts to fill some of the gaps left by Pilaszek's work. On the basis of a survey of 254 trials from over eighty towns and villages, I cover much the same ground as Pilaszek's study: surveying the social dynamics that motivated accusations of witchcraft, the legal basis for prosecution, and the judicial procedures that transformed village suspicions of magical milk-theft into abominable crimes. However, I also read the trial records as documents illuminating the history of Christianity in early modern Poland. On the one hand, witches and victims described the activities of *szatany* and *diabły*—'satans' and 'devils'—which in their appearance and behaviour resemble the house spirits, riverside demons, and treasure-hauling imps of Slavic folklore. While such folk-demons represent a partial 'indigenization' of the Christian devil, the reverse is also true: their frequently attested origin as the ghosts of unbaptized babies points to a thorough if unorthodox integration of Catholic sacramentalism into popular demonology. Meanwhile, widespread allegations that witches desecrated the Most Holy Sacrament of the Eucharistic host—tossing it into pigsties, stabbing it until it transformed into a bloody, crying baby (or hiding it in beehives to help the honey thrive)—express both elite Counter-Reformation anxieties and, through the inversionary prism of witchcraft confession, the piety of ordinary women. When under torture the accused witch Anna Ratajka cried out 'Most Holy Virgin Mary—Most Holy Sacrament—Image of Studzianna!' she sought succour through the intercession of the Virgin, through a wonder-working image of the Holy Family, and through the Body of Christ—itself tormented and broken just as she was being tortured and broken. During and by means of the interrogation, in which the secular court reconfigured Anna as a Eucharist-desecrating, child-killing witch who 'cared nothing but nothing for God or for Salvation, forsaking Heaven', she testified unwittingly to her Catholic orthodoxy.[38] Recent Polish historiography has tended too easily to agree with contemporary reformers that early modern popular Christianity was young, superstitious, half-pagan, and worldly.[39] Yet when an accused witch acquiesced to the sexual demands of her diabolical lover with the words 'if God so wills it', this should complicate our understanding of popular piety in early modern Poland.[40]

18.3 CONCLUSIONS

A century and a half of sporadic, largely programmatic research into Polish witchcraft produced little beyond invidious comparison—of the fanatical feudal past against the

[38] L. Tassilion Tripplin, ed., *Tajemnice społeczeństwa wykryte ze spraw kryminalnych krajowych* (Wrocław, 1852), iii, 267–74.

[39] Stanisław Brzeżański, *Owczarnia w Dzikim Polu* (Lwów, 1717), fols 5–6v; Jan Kracik, 'Katolicka indoktrynacja doby saskiej w parafiach zachodniej Małopolski', *Roczniki Teologiczno-Kanoniczne*, 20 (1973), 13–27; Tomasz Wiślicz, 'Jak gdyby wśród pogan lub heretyków: Polityka potrydenckiego Kościoła wobec religii ludowej i jej osobliwości w Rzeczypospolitej', in Robert Kołodziej and Filip Wolański, eds, *Staropolska ogląd świata* (Toruń, 2009) ii, 37.

[40] Quotation after Pilaszek, *Procesy*, 423.

progressive present, or of foreign barbarism against Polish mildness and toleration. Only in the last few years has this scholarship undertaken serious archival research, eschewing polemic in favour of a commitment to understanding the past. Grounded in the foundational work of the early twenty-first century, future research can take up the many questions remaining ripe for exploration. By way of conclusion, I outline three such questions below.

First, there remains a great need for further archival research. The records of Polish witch trials, many still scattered throughout poorly catalogued regional archives, have left nothing like the centralized paper trails characteristic of the Roman Inquisition or the Muscovite petition records. Intensive witch-hunts such as those at Kleczew or Płońsk, the records for which were fortuitously preserved or rediscovered in the twentieth century, *might* be the rarities they currently appear to be.[41] Or, they could represent the tip of an iceberg. The challenge of archival research in Poland is also an opportunity—such research has only begun, and nobody can say what further investigations might bring to light.

Secondly, the connections between witch trials and trials for alleged ritual murder deserves careful attention. In the seventeenth and eighteenth centuries, the Commonwealth included the largest Jewish community in Europe. A series of host-desecration and ritual murder trials beginning in the late sixteenth century closely mirrored the accusations against witches, and Catholic polemicists did not hesitate to equate witchcraft and Judaism—as when Sebastian Klonowic bemoaned 'godless ones' who, 'seized by a Satanic greed... sell the holy Sacrament to Jews and witches' for their anti-Christian purposes.[42] In an important essay entitled 'The Wholly Other? Jews as Witches and Witches as Jews', the anthropologist Joanna Tokarska-Bakir has enlisted the early modern Polish witch trials to understand the demonization of Jews in twentieth-century pogroms—especially the Jedwabne massacre of 1941, around which re-examinations of Polish/Jewish relations have recently crystalized.[43] Although Tokarska-Bakir deploys the historical materials rather crudely, the polemical question of her title deserves exploration: its answer will further complicate Poland's self-understanding as 'the state without stakes'.

Finally, the witch trials provide an unrivalled source for gender studies and the history of early modern Polish women. The extremely high proportion of women executed for witchcraft—at over 90 per cent, one of the starkest gender disproportions anywhere in Europe—demands closer analysis. Demonological misogynist stereotypes account incompletely for this gender disparity. One finds the same high proportion of

[41] Zygmunt Lasocki, 'Szlachta płońska w walce z czartem', *Miesięcznik Heraldyczny*, 12 (1933), 1–8, 18–22, 37–42; Wiślicz, 'Township of Kleczew'.

[42] Zenon Guldon and Jacek Wijaczka, 'The Accusation of Ritual Murder in Poland, 1500–1800', *Polin*, 10 (1997), 99–140; Sebastian Fabian Klonowic, *Worek Ivdaszow: to iest Złe nabyćie Máiętności*, ed. Kazimierz Budzyk (Wrocław, [1600] 1960), 139.

[43] Joanna Tokarska-Bakir, '*Ganz Andere?* Żyd jako czarownica i czarownica jako Żyd w Polskich i obcych źródłach etnograficznych, czyli jak czytać protokoły przesłuchań', *Res Publica Nowa*, 8 (2001), 3–32.

female witches in Orthodox and Greek Catholic Ruthenia (88 per cent), with a much lower prevalence of women accused in Lithuania (c.60 per cent) or in Orthodox Muscovy (c.25 per cent)—and yet gender stereotypes are almost invariant across the whole region.[44] Future work should also go beyond questions of causation, examining the testimony of accused witches for what it might tell us of women's ordinary, non-diabolical lives. Attending to the voices of accused witches, one learns not only about hatred and fear, but also about neighbourhood solidarity, family relations, even love. Dysa has initiated such an approach, finding, in the Ruthenian witch trials, narratives of neighbours who came to the defence of neighbours; or husbands who testified movingly about the kindness and decency of their wives.[45] In the interrogation record of Zofia Baranowa, prosecuted in Lublin for selling amulets of dried snakeskins and the herb belladonna, we learn that her demon lover 'appeared to me in the shape of my [deceased] husband, because I loved that husband of mine'.[46] Examining confessions of this kind, with due caution as to their context of production, we learn something about Polish witchcraft of course, but we also catch a glimpse into a world otherwise lost to historical scrutiny—the private lives and loves of early modern Polish women.

FURTHER READING

Adamczyk, Joanna, 'Czary i magia w praktyce sądów kościelnych na ziemiach polskich w późnym średniowieczu (XV-połowa XVI wieku)' [Witchcraft and Magic in the Practice of Church Courts in the Polish Lands in the Late Middle Ages (from the Fifteenth to the Mid-Sixteenth Century)], in Maria Koczerska, ed., Karolińscy pokutnicy i polskie średniowieczne czarownice (Warsaw, 2007).

Baranowski, Bohdan, Procesy Czarownic w Polsce w XVII i XVIII wieku [Witch-Trials in Poland in the Seventeenth and Eighteenth Centuries] (Łódź, 1952).

Dysa, Kateryna. 'Witchcraft Trials and Beyond: Right Bank Side Ukrainian Trials of the Seventeenth and Eighteenth Centuries', Ph.D. dissertation, Central European University, Budapest, 2004.

Ostling, Michael, Between the Devil and the Host: Imagining Witchcraft in Early Modern Poland (Oxford, 2011).

Pilaszek, Malgorzata, 'Litewskie procesy czarownic w XVI–XVIII w.' [Lithuanian Witch-Trials in the Sixteenth-Eighteenth Centuries], Odrodzenie i Reformacja w Polsce, 46 (2002), 7–35.

Pilaszek, Małgorzata, Procesy o czary w Polsce w wiekach XV–XVIIII [Trials for Witchcraft in Poland, 15th–18th Centuries] (Kraków, 2008).

Schiffmann, Aldona Christina, 'The Witch and Crime: The Persecution of Witches in 20th-century Poland', ARV: Scandinavian Yearbook of Folklore, 43 (1987), 147–65.

---

[44] Dysa, 'Witchcraft Trials', 41–7; Pilaszek, 'Litewskie procesy czarownic'. Jacek Wijaczka's 'Men Standing Trial for Witchcraft at the Łobżenica Court in the Second Half of the Seventeenth Century', Acta Poloniae Historica, 93 (2006), 69–85, suffers somewhat for lack of material.

[45] Dysa, 'Witchcraft Trials', 89–102.

[46] Archiwum Państwowe w Lublinie, Akta Miasta Lublina sig. 140 (Criminalia), fols 50–1, 60–64v.

Tazbir, Janusz, 'Hexenprozesse in Polen' [Witch-Trials in Poland], *Archiv für Reformation-geschichte*, 71 (1980), 280–307.

Tokarska-Bakir, Joanna, '*Ganz Andere*? Żyd jako czarownica i czarownica jako Żyd w Polskich i obcych źródłach etnograficznych, czyli jak czytać protokoły przesłuchań' [Wholly Other? The Jew as a Witch and the Witch as a Jew in Polish and Foreign Ethnographic Sources, or How to Read Interrogation Records], *Res Publica Nova*, 8 (2001), 3–32.

Wijaczka, Jacek, 'Procesy o czary w Polsce w dobie Oświecenia: Zarys problematyki' [Trials for Witchcraft in Poland in the Enlightenment Period: A Sketch of the Problem], *Klio*, 17 (2005), 17–62.

Wijaczka, Jacek, 'Men Standing Trial for Witchcraft at the Łobżenica Court in the Second Half of the Seventeenth Century', *Acta Poloniae Historica*, 93 (2006), 69–85.

Wiślicz, Tomasz, 'Czary przed sądami wiejskimi w Polsce XVI–XVIII wieku' [Witchcraft before Village Courts in Poland, 16th–18th Centuries], *Czasopismo Prawno-Historyczne*, 49 (1997), 47–63.

Wiślicz, Tomasz, 'The Township of Kleczew and its Neighborhood Fighting the Devil (1624–1700)', *Acta Poloniae Historica*, 89 (2004), 65–95.

Wyporska, Wanda, *Witchcraft in Early Modern Poland, 1500–1800* (Basingstoke, 2013).

....

CHAPTER 19

WITCH-HUNTING IN EARLY MODERN HUNGARY

....

ILDIKÓ SZ. KRISTÓF

THE establishment in 1983 of an interdisciplinary research group for the study of witch-hunting in Hungary coincided with the last years of communism in the country. The group was based in the Department of Folk Beliefs and Customs of the Institute of Ethnology of the Hungarian Academy of Sciences in Budapest. It was headed by the renowned folklorist Éva Pócs, and had as one of its founding members the historian Gábor Klaniczay. The group consisted of a handful of folklorists, historians, and archivists, working together in an increasingly open academic atmosphere with the aim of renewing local religious studies, as well as the discipline of history, by studying and appropriating methods of Western historical research. The fall of the communist regime, with its promotion of Marxist ideology, in 1989–90 made the introduction of a number of modern approaches to the writing of history possible. Social and intellectual history, quantitative studies, the *histoire de la mentalité*, the history of popular culture, historical anthropology, microhistory, the *new cultural history* as well as postmodern criticism all penetrated the academic world of Hungary during the 1990s. It was mainly at this time that witchcraft research became, as it remains to a large extent today, attractive and fashionable in the eyes of Hungarian scholars, although it was not altogether new in local historical and ethnographical studies. Within the research group, however, the individual choices of research topics depended largely upon methodological preferences, linguistic knowledge, and the disciplinary and institutional affiliation of the scholars involved. The mosaic-like, fluctuating, and rather diffuse nature that characterizes witchcraft studies nowadays in Hungary is rooted to some extent in these early, formative years.

One of the initial projects of the witchcraft research group was to create a database of early modern Hungarian witch trials. To facilitate this undertaking the group used

KLEIO, a computer programme developed originally for the quantitative analysis of inventories in the Max Planck Institut für Geschichte in Göttingen, Germany. Almost two thousand witchcraft trials and approximately twenty thousand so-called *maleficium* or *bewitchment narratives*, which were found mostly in the testimony of witnesses in witch trials, were encoded at that time, according to a set of questions that the members of the research group developed. In this way the group gathered basic information about the individual trials: the accused witch's name, sex, age, family and social status, and religion. The same data was acquired for all the accusers, together with their relation to the accused. Another questionnaire was designed to codify information in the narratives of bewitchment. Inspired by historical anthropology and social studies of witch-hunting in Western Europe, these questions were intended to emphasize the *social* and *narrative* features as well as the *constructed* nature of witchcraft accusations. The testimonies of the individual witnesses were to be coded according to the morphological sequence of a model or 'ideal' bewitchment narrative. They were intended to reveal how the act of *maleficium* was imagined in the minds of the witnesses, and how the accused person became a 'witch' in the eyes of others.[1]

The discovery of new archival material since the formation of the research group has led to a steady expansion of the database. By the year 2000 the number of known witchcraft accusations had almost doubled, and archival research on the subject, inside as well as outside modern-day Hungary, is still ongoing. Local historians and archivists, who were not necessarily members of the research group, also contributed to this enterprise. These historians have come not only from Hungary, but from Austria, Croatia, Romania, and Slovakia.

Despite the limitations of *KLEIO*, its use has provided a deeper understanding of the importance of *locality* in early modern witchcraft prosecutions, and has led to the publication of a number of local and regional studies of witch-hunting. The most notable of these studies includes an in-depth, historical–anthropological study of witch-hunting in a Calvinist region of Hungary (the town of Debrecen and the neighbouring county of Bihar);[2] a narrative–morphological analysis of bewitchment stories from the mostly Catholic county of Sopron; social–legal studies of the earliest, sixteenth-century, witch trials of the towns of Kolozsvár (Cluj in present-day Romania) and Sopron; wider regional statistical–legal studies of witchcraft inside and outside modern-day Hungary; and numerous studies of local witch-hunts in various urban and village communities, based on a close reading of trial documents and other local historical sources.

In addition to these local and regional studies, important statistical, bibliographical, social, and folkloristic summaries of the overall history of witch-hunting in early

---

[1] For a detailed description of the programme *KLEIO* and its uses for studying witchcraft trials see Gábor Klaniczay, Éva Pócs, Péter Tóth G. and Robert Wolosz, 'A Kleio boszorkányper-adatbázis' [The Kleio Witchcraft-trial Database], in Pócs, ed., *Demonológia és boszorkányság Európában* [*Demonology and Witchcraft in Europe*] (Budapest, 2001), 293–335, summary in English, 372–95.

[2] See Ildikó Kristóf, *Ördögi mesterséget nem cselekedtem* (Debrecen, 1998). For an earlier version see Kristóf, '"Wise Women", Sinners and the Poor: The Social Background of Witch Hunting in a 16/18th-Century Calvinist City of Eastern Hungary', *Acta Ethnographica*, 37 (1990), 93–119.

modern Hungary have resulted from the work of the research group.[3] Individual researchers have also investigated specific aspects of Hungarian witchcraft, including demonology, folk beliefs, methods of elite and popular healing, midwifery, criminal law, and the micro-sociology of local witch-hunts. In addition, some scholars working mostly in the earlier research tradition, and outside the witchcraft research group, have used witchcraft trial documents to illuminate various aspects of early modern material culture, such as furniture, building materials, and minerals.

19.1 THE HISTORY OF WITCH-HUNTING IN THE KINGDOM OF HUNGARY

One of the most important features of witch-hunting in the ancient kingdom in Hungary is that it seems to have remained relatively moderate in intensity. There is documentary evidence of 848 executions for witchcraft before 1800 in a population that

---

[3] General statistical/legal/social summaries include Gábor Klaniczay, 'Witch Hunting in Hungary: Social or Cultural Tensions?', Acta Ethnographica, 37 (1990), 67–91; Gábor Klaniczay, 'Hungary: The Accusations and the Universe of Popular Magic', in Bengt Ankarloo and Gustav Henningsen, eds, Early Modern European Witchcraft: Centres and Peripheries (Oxford, 1990), 219–25. Historiographical summaries and bibliographies are to be found in Klaniczay, 'A Cultural History of Witchcraft', Magic, Ritual, and Witchcraft, 5 (2010), 188–212; Éva Pócs, 'Bevezetö: Egy munkacsoport tizenöt éve' [Preface: Fifteen Years of a Research Team] in Pócs, ed., Demonológia és boszorkányság, 9–19, summary in English, 337–46; Péter Tóth G., 'Boszorkányos hagyaték: A magyarországi boszorkányperek feltárásának kutatástörténete a kezdetektöl napjainkig' [A History of the Exploration of Witchcraft Trials in Hungary from the Beginning to These Days], in Gábor Vargyas, ed., Párbeszéd a hagyománnyal: A néprajzi kutatás múltja és jelene [In Dialogue with Tradition: The Past and Present of Ethnographical Research] (Budapest, 2011), 637–94. An index of witchcraft trials known until 2000 is to be found in Péter Tóth G., A magyarországi boszorkányság forrásainak katasztere (1408–1848) [A Catalogue of the Sources of Hungarian Witchcraft, 1408–1848] (Budapest, 2000), with an introduction in English. For thorough analyses of folkloristic beliefs (e.g. fairies, táltos, etc.) providing, in many respects, the foundation of diabolic witchcraft, see the many works of Éva Pócs, including 'The Popular Foundations of the Witches' Sabbath and the Devil's Pact in Central and Southeastern Europe', Acta Ethnographica, 37 (1991/2), 305–70; 'Le sabbat et les mythologies indo-européennes', in Nicole Jacques-Chaquin and Maxime Préaud, eds, Le sabbat des sorciers XVᵉ–XVIIIᵉ siècles (Grenoble, 1993), 23–31; 'Feenflug und Hexenflug in Mittel-Südosteuropa. Ritus und Mythos, Erlebnis und Bericht', in Dieter R. Bauer and Wolfgang Behringer, eds, Fliegen und Schweben: Annäherung an eine menschliche Sensation (Munich, 1997), 146–67; 'Shamanism, Witchcraft and Christianity in Early Modern Europe', in Ülo Valk, ed., Studies in Folklore and Popular Religion (Tartu, 1999), iii, 111–35; and, Between the Living and the Dead: A Perspective on Witches and Seers in the Early Modern Age (Budapest, 1999). For a survey of the activity of the witchcraft research group until 2001, see Pócs, ed., Demonológia és boszorkányság Európában, 9–19. For a relatively recent summary on witch-hunting in early modern Hungary see Sz. Kristóf, 'Hungary', 515–20. And for a summary of the beliefs and practice of treasure hunting, not infrequently related to witchcraft beliefs in Hungary, see Benedek Láng and Péter Tóth G., eds, A kincskeresés 400 éve Magyarországon: Kézikönyvek és olvasóik [Four Hundred Years of Treasure Hunting in Hungary: Handbooks and their Readers] (Budapest, 2009), which has a summary in English.

ranged between 3.5 million and 5.3 million people.[4] This number should, however, be considered a minimum, since the records of some executions have probably been lost. Moreover, the boundaries of Hungary changed from time to time during this period, and included, at one time or another, parts of modern Austria, Croatia, Romania, Serbia, Slovakia, and Ukraine. As a consequence, plenty of the historical documents relating to witchcraft and witch-hunting in such areas are now to be found in archives outside the current boundaries of Hungary—and have not yet been explored as fully as possible.

19.1.1 Early Modern Witch-Hunts

Witch-hunting in early modern Hungary coincided with an unstable period in the country's political history. The Ottoman Turks defeated the Hungarian armies at Mohács in 1526 and occupied Buda, the capital, in 1541. For the next 150 years the country was divided into three parts, and this division, together with the accompanying politico-socio-cultural developments that it engendered, provided the geopolitical setting for early modern witchcraft accusations. During this period the kingdom of Hungary was limited to the north-western part known as Upper Hungary, which was ruled by the Habsburg monarchy. The central and southern parts (approximately the area of the Great Hungarian Plain), was occupied by the Turks, and belonged to the Ottoman Empire, while the eastern part, Transylvania (today in Romania), became a more or less independent principality, ruled mostly by Hungarian noble dynasties. In the 1680s and 1690s the Turks were driven out of Hungary with the help of the Habsburg army, bringing the whole country, including Transylvania, under the rule of the Habsburg monarchy.

19.2 THE LEGAL FOUNDATION OF WITCH-HUNTING

During the early modern period the prosecution of magic and witchcraft in the kingdom of Hungary acquired a new legal foundation. King Ferdinand I (r. 1526–1564)

---

[4] Hereafter, the statistical figures for early modern witch-hunting in Hungary are provided according to the unpublished register of the accused witches, created by Péter Tóth G., indicated as UROW in the following. The last survey of national relevance accessible in English before that is to be found in Klaniczay, 'Witch-Hunting in Hungary'; Klaniczay, 'Hungary'; and Sz. Kristóf, 'Hungary'. The discrepancy in the statistical data given in these essays, as well as in the present survey, is due to the gradual increase in the archival findings on the one hand, and the constant refinement of the methods of interpreting historical data on the other. This is especially true for the possible number of capital sentences.

issued a decree against *incantatrices* (enchantresses or witches) in 1527, and the *Constitutio Criminalis Carolina*, the criminal codex promulgated by Emperor Charles V in 1532, facilitated the prosecution of these offenders. In 1614 the Transylvanian Diet also issued a decree in order to punish 'sorcerers' and 'witches' to be found in that region. Witchcraft, however, has never been considered a *crimen exceptum*, that is, an excepted crime, in the kingdom of Hungary, and it was prosecuted together with other crimes in municipal, county, and landlords' courts. The most frequently used legal text was *Forma processus judicii criminalis seu praxis criminalis* (Form of the procedure of jurisdiction or the practice of criminal investigation), based on the teachings of the Leipzig Lutheran lawyer Benedict Carpzov, and codified for Austria by Emperor Ferdinand III in 1656. It was published in Latin in 1687 by the Catholic university of Nagyszombat, and appended to the *Corpus iuris* of Hungary in 1696. *Praxis criminalis* constituted the most important channel through which Western demonological ideas, including those of the sabbath and the demonic pact, entered Hungary. Although its publication history is not well researched, it went into a minimum of six editions (all in Latin and without any textual change) between 1687 and 1748. The late publication of this legal manual in Hungary may help to explain why Hungarian witch-hunting reached its peak only during the second half of the seventeenth and the first half of the eighteenth centuries. Only then did witch trials become widespread in the country.

Municipal customs also provided a legal foundation for some local trials. For example, a clause in the customs of the seven free royal cities published in 1701 ordered that anyone abusing the sacraments and the pictures of saints, that is, using them for magical purposes, should be put to death. Where municipal law made no reference to witchcraft, as in the Transylvanian Saxon cities, local courts relied on to the *Constitutio Criminalis Carolina*. In early modern period most Hungarian witchcraft trials were held in the secular courts, but these tribunals often cited Exod. 22:18 to claim divine as well as temporal authority for proceeding against witches.

The long life and relatively frequent use of the water ordeal and other features of medieval criminal procedure testify to the survival of the accusatorial system of criminal justice well into the first half of the eighteenth century. But the increased reliance upon the production of material proof (such as 'magical' objects or instruments found with the accused person), the use of torture to extract confessions, and the taking of written depositions from witnesses, show that Hungarian courts in the sixteenth and seventeenth centuries were gradually adopting some of the features of inquisitorial procedure, which was well established in most parts of Western Europe.[5]

---

[5] On the use of the water ordeal in early modern Hungary and elsewhere see Péter Tóth G., 'River Ordeal–Trial by Water–Swimming of Witches: Procedures of Ordeal in Witch Trials', in Gábor Klaniczay and Éva Pócs, in collaboration with Eszter Csonka-Takács, eds, *Witchcraft Mythologies and Persecutions* (Budapest, 2008), 129–63. For the city of Debrecen see Kristóf, *Ördögi mesterséget nem cselekedtem*, 49–50.

19.3 OVERALL CHRONOLOGY AND STATISTICS

As shown by a recent statistical assessment, it was the sixteenth century that saw the beginnings of a (more or less) regular witch-hunt in the kingdom of Hungary. It seems to have intensified during the 1580s and 1590s, reached one of its peaks towards the end of the seventeenth century, but only become truly massive during the first half of the eighteenth century.

The numbers of currently known accused witches in seven chronological periods are as follows:

1526–52	74
1553–1600	262
1601–50	544
1651–1700	781
1701–50	2,297
1751–1800	592
1801–48	32

The kingdom of Hungary has always been a multi-ethnic country. Upper Hungary had a fairly large population of Germans, Slovaks, and Czechs, while Germans and Romanians populated Transylvania, and, in the south, Croatians, Serbians, and—towards the end of this period—Slovaks, lived on the Great Plain. In addition to these minorities, Jews and Roma lived in various places throughout the country. Despite this wide ethnic diversity, the great majority (approximately 75 per cent) of those accused of witchcraft or instrumental in bringing the accusations were Hungarians. One explanation for this ethnic concentration is that witchcraft charges developed mainly among people who interacted with one another on a daily basis, unimpeded by linguistic or cultural barriers, and Hungarians formed the largest ethnic bloc in the kingdom.[6]

19.4 LEARNED DEMONOLOGY

Historians know much more about Protestant than Catholic demonology, the latter representing the ideas of educated people regarding witchcraft and the powers of the devil. Protestant theologians wrote more extensively than Catholics about the subject, and Protestant synods issued orders to punish 'sorcerers' and 'witches'. For example,

[6] UROW. The estimated per cents for other nationalities are very small: 9 per cent German, 7.5 per cent Croatian, 4 per cent Roumanian, 2 per cent Slovakian, 1 per cent Roma, 1 per cent Polish–Ruthenian, and 0.5 per cent Serbian.

the early Transylvanian Lutheran synod of 1577 threatened any person involved in magical acts with death. The first religious treatises that discussed witchcraft as such came from Protestant authors. The Lutheran preacher Péter Bornemisza published *Ördögi kísírtetekröl a vagy röttenetes utálatosságáról ez megfertéztett világnak* (About the Temptations of the Devil, or the Loathsomeness of this Infected World) in 1578. The book dealt with witch beliefs, related stories of witchcraft, and described various magical practices among peasants in north-west Hungary.[7] The presence of the devil in the world and the danger he represented to Christians were also emphasized in the early Lutheran liturgies, such as the *Agenda* of István Melotai Nyilas, which was published in Várad (Oradea, in present-day Romania) in 1563. The liturgical work included a number of formulas for performing exorcisms.

The first Hungarian Calvinist demonology was included in *Confessio Ecclesiae Debrecinensis* (Confession of Faith for the Church of Debrecen), which appeared in 1562. The work was compiled under the direction of Péter Méliusz Juhász, who became the first bishop of the Calvinist Church in Hungary. Méliusz, who was a follower of the teachings of the German Lutheran theologian Johann Brenz, manifested a high degree of scepticism regarding the reality of diabolical witchcraft. His demonological ideas laid the foundation for a vigorous and long-lasting sceptical tradition among Hungarian Calvinists.[8] Although Calvinist liturgical manuals also testified to the everyday works of the devil, and even contained a ritual of exorcism,[9] scholarly scepticism pervaded contemporary Calvinist theology. It characterized, for example, the two comprehensive treatises on demonology, both titled *Disputatio theologica de lamiis veneficis*, which were compiled by two students of Calvinist theology, Joannes C. Mediomontanus and Andreas P. Csehi, and were published in Várad in 1656. Both of them relied on the work of the sixteenth-century sceptic Johann Weyer, and almost entirely rejected the diabolical ideas that characterized the *Malleus maleficarum* as well as the credulous tract on witchcraft by the English Protestant demonologist, William Perkins. One point, however, on which Mediomontanus and Csehi agreed with Perkins, was that they both condemned *any* kind of 'witch', even one who was a victim of diabolic illusions or a humble practitioner of popular 'white' magic, such as love magic, healing, or divination. For them it was the *intention* of those witches and sorcerers to use diabolic power that made them guilty of a spiritual crime.[10]

Seventeenth-century Hungarian Calvinist views on witchcraft were not altogether sceptical or homogeneous. A Calvinist synod held in the town of Margita in Bihar

---

[7] Gábor Klaniczay, 'Die "Teuflischen Gespenster" (*Ördögi kisirtetek*) des Pfarrers Péter Bornemisza (1578) und die Debatte über Erscheinungen und Gespenster', in Claire Gantet-Fabrice Almeida, ed., *Gespenster und Politik 16. bis 21. Jahrhundert* (Munich, 2007), 51–65.

[8] Ildikó Kristóf, *Ördögi mesterséget nem cselekedtem*, 55–61 and Ildikó Kristóf, 'Elements of Demonology in Hungarian Calvinist Literature Printed in Debrecen in the Sixteenth and Seventeenth Centuries', *Cauda Pavonis: Studies in Hermeticism*, 16 (1997), 10–11.

[9] Éva Szacsvay, 'Az ördögüzés református szabályozása 1636-ban (I.)' [The Calvinist Regulation of Exorcism in 1636], in Gábor Barna and Erzsébet Kótyuk, eds, *Test, lélek, természet: Tanulmányok a népi orvoslás emlékeiböl* (Budapest, 2002), 79–92, with a summary in English.

[10] On Calvinist demonology see Kristóf, *Ördögi mesterséget nem cselekedtem*, 54–76; Kristóf, 'Elements of Demonology', 9–17; Kristóf, '"Wise Women", Sinners and the Poor', 93–119.

county in 1681, for example, threatened all sorcerers and those who consulted them with excommunication. This injunction appears to have functioned as a catalyst to witch-hunting in the region. The synod was chaired by Bishop Mátyás Nógrádi, a Calvinist preacher in Debrecen, who published his *Lelki próbakö* (Spiritual Touchstone) in 1651. This book included a short treatise, '*Az ördögi practicáról mint kellyen ítélni embernek*' (How to Judge Devilish Practices). Although Bishop Nógrádi argued for a rather prudent and careful handling and investigation of village witchcraft accusations, he analysed certain forms of the witches' pact with the devil, and even categorized them into types, and he gave greater credence to them than did his colleagues. It may be relevant to note that Bishop Nógrádi had travelled to England in the mid-1640s, when Matthew Hopkins, the notorious witchfinder, was conducting the largest witch-hunt in English history. Nógrádi may have also been influenced by the demonological treatise of William Perkins, *The Damned Art of Witchcraft* (1608), which he cited in his own work.[11]

Although the majority of Hungarian Calvinists rejected the idea of the witches' pact and the sabbath, considering them nothing but illusions or the product of melancholy, they condemned all forms of everyday popular magic, especially those of popular healers and cunning people. The Debrecen Calvinists also published *Lex politica Dei* (The Public Law of God) in 1610, which was a collection of the laws in the Hebrew Bible condemning sorcery and divination. The Calvinists made their strongest case against the practice of popular magic of this sort when discussing the origin and curing of illnesses, especially the plague. Seventeenth-century Calvinist preachers in Debrecen all insisted that popular healers and midwives who employed magical practices deserved severe punishment.[12]

Despite the harshness of these condemnations, Hungarian Protestant demonology manifested a rather 'gentle', sceptical attitude towards witchcraft. There is still research to be done on this question, but we already know that, for example, a group of seventeenth-century Protestant students studying in Wittenberg and Jena imported an explicitly anti-diabolical, anti-demonological concept of magic. Georgius Fridericus Magnus, a so-called 'Hungarus' (Latin for Hungarian but also for the greater kingdom of Hungary at the time) from the city of Pozsony (Bratislava in present-day Slovakia) defended the propositions of Johann Weyer and Kaspar Peucer in his *Disputatio physica de magia* (Physical Dispute about Magic), held in Wittenberg in 1665, and denied the possibility of the witches' pact with the devil. Later in the century Johannes Surmann, who came from Beszterce (Bistriţa in present-day Romania), supported the arguments of the late seventeenth-century Dutch sceptic Balthasar Bekker in his *De*

---

[11] On Bishop Nógrádi and Perkins see Kristóf, *Ördögi mesterséget nem cselekedtem*, 65–8 and Kristóf, 'Elements of Demonology', 12.

[12] For Protestant notions on the plague epidemic see Kristóf, *Ördögi mesterséget nem cselekedtem*, 70–2; Kristóf, 'Plague of the Plagues': Epidemic and Riot in Debrecen in 1739/42', *Ethnos*, 8 (1991), 64–77.

daemonologia recentiorum auctorum falsa (About the False Demonology of Recent Authors) of 1692. Gottofried Roesch, another 'Hungarus' from Körmöcbánya (Kremnica in present-day Slovakia), also rejected a diabolical interpretation of magic in his *Exercitatio historico philologica de cultu Simonis Magi* (Historical-philological Exercises on the Art of Simon Magus), published at Jena in 1683. Eighteenth-century scholarly writings, including *Keskeny ut* (The Narrow Road, 1719) by Imre Pápai Páriz contributed to this sceptical trend in the Hungarian Protestant tradition. These works also recommended the punishment of any form of popular or white magic.[13]

The demonology of the Hungarian Catholics in the early modern period has not received much scholarly attention. To be sure, the *Malleus maleficarum* was known in early modern Hungary. The libraries of the various Jesuit colleges in Upper Hungary had copies of this notorious witchcraft manual, as did Miklós Zrínyi, one of the greatest poets and writers of the seventeenth century. The trials that took place in Somorja (Šamorin in present-day Slovakia) in 1691 made an explicit reference to the *Malleus*, but the book apparently did not exert a significant influence on witch-hunting in subsequent years. During the same century, copies of Martin Del Rio's *Disquisitionum magicarum libri sex* (1599) could be found in some of the libraries of the Jesuit colleges in Upper Hungary, as could copies of Jean Bodin's *Daemonomania* (1580). Otherwise, the criminal courts in Catholic regions relied mainly on *Praxis criminalis* in prosecuting cases of witchcraft during the seventeenth and eighteenth centuries. Towards the end of the prosecutions, courts relied on other legal guides, such as István Huszty's *Jurisprudentia practica* (The Practice of Jurisprudence), published in 1758, which included chapters on the practice of magic, and recommended the use of torture when prosecuting witches.

Rituals of exorcism were routinely included in Catholic liturgical manuals. Franciscan and Jesuit missionaries (often Italians or southern Slavs) performed these rites on both noble and peasant demoniacs during the seventeenth century. Catholic rites of exorcism differed significantly from those of Calvinists, which relied exclusively on the methods of prayer and fasting. But Protestants and Catholics agreed in their condemnation of both witchcraft and popular magic, in eighteenth-century printed collections of sermons, such as Zsigmond Csúzy's *Evangéliomi trombita* (The Evangelical

---

[13] The majority of the authors and treatises mentioned here come from the research of Sz. Kristóf. The so-called learned magic (*magia naturalis*) and the occult sciences are not discussed in this chapter. Those interested in them should consult Benedek Láng, 'Research Problems of Magical Texts in Central Europe', in Blanka Szeghyová, ed., *The Role of Magic in the Past: Learned and Popular Magic, Popular Beliefs and Diversity of Attitudes* (Bratislava, 2005), 11–17, and Láng's *Unlocked Books: Manuscripts of Learned Magic in the Medieval Libraries of Central Europe* (University Park, PA, 2008); György Endre Szönyi, 'The Occult Sciences in Early Modern Hungary in a Central European Context', in Szeghyová, ed., *The Role of Magic in the Past*, 29–44, and Szönyi, *John Dee's Occultism: Magical Exaltation Through Powerful Signs* (New York, 2004), esp. 241–70. See also Márton Szentpéteri, 'Magic and Demonology in Albert Szenci Molnár's Personal Commonplace Book', in Szeghyová, ed., *The Role of Magic in the Past*, 64–72.

Trumpet), which appeared in print in 1724, and József Telek's *Tizen-két tsillagú korona* (Crown of Twelve Stars), published at Buda in 1769.

German demonology played an important role in Hungarian witch-hunting, both in its learned and popular forms. The first campaign against witches in the second half of the sixteenth century took place in the Upper Hungarian and the Transylvanian towns that had a predominantly German population, and was apparently inspired by the demonological teachings of the Lutheran Church. The first learned description of the witches' sabbath came from the area of Upper Hungary around the city of Pozsony, near the Austrian border, in 1578. The Lutheran preacher Péter Bornemisza's treatise on demonic temptation claimed that the local witches had a queen, that they could transform themselves into animals like cats, and that they made a great frenzy dancing and fornicating at their meetings.[14] A much later, Calvinist description of the sabbath by Mediomontanus also suggests a German influence. According to Mediomontanus, the witches usually gathered in the wine cellars on Mount St Gellért in Buda, a mountain that probably acquired its reputation as the location of witches' assemblies because the local German inhabitants called it *Blocksberg*, the highest peak in northern Germany where German witches were believed to have gathered.[15]

19.5 POPULAR DEMONOLOGY

Although it is difficult to trace the popular adoption of demonological ideas, they appeared for the first time in regions inhabited mostly by Germans and Slovaks within the ancient kingdom of Hungary. A witch's confession to having made a pact with the devil was recorded as early as 1581 in the Upper Hungarian mining town of Selmecbá-nya (Banská Štiavnica in present-day Slovakia). One of the first popular descriptions of the witches' sabbath, in which witches flew on broomsticks and copulated with the devil, was recorded in the city of Pozsony in 1602. In more or less the same region, in the communities of Sopron, Körmend, Lakompak, and Darázsfalva (Trausdorf in present-day Austria), numerous popular descriptions of the sabbath appeared during the 1650s and 1670s, which were periods of intense witch-hunting.[16] Other locations where popular diabolical beliefs flourished at an early date were the seven privileged Saxon cities (*Siebenbürgen*) in Transylvania. The cities of Segesvár (Sighişoara/Schäß-burg in present-day Romania), or Nagyszeben (Sibiu/Hermannstadt in present-day Romania) experienced a regular and intensive succession of witch-hunts from the

---

[14] Klaniczay, 'Die "Teuflischen Gespenster"', 51–65. Tünde Lengyel, 'Nyitra és Pozsony megye boszorkányperei a 16–18. században' [Witchcraft Trials in Nyitra and Pozsony County in the Sixteenth to Eighteenth Centuries], in *Archivum Sal'a—Levéltári Évkönyv* (2005), ii, 39–42.

[15] On Mediomontanus and Mount St Gellért see Klaniczay, 'Hungary', 232–4, 249.

[16] On the influence of German demonology upon Hungarian witch beliefs see Klaniczay, 'Hungary', 249–51, and Endre Hagenthurn, ed., *Segesvári boszorkányperek—Schäßburger Hexenprozesse* (Budapest, 2010).

1660s until the middle of the eighteenth century. Austrian German soldiers, lodged in Hungarian villages as part of the military occupation of the country during and after the Turkish wars, also seem to have introduced German ideas of witchcraft into Hungary. In a number of instances German soldiers, acting sometimes as witchfinders, accused their hosts of witchcraft.[17]

Early modern witch-hunting in Hungary was primarily an urban phenomenon. In addition to the Saxon towns of Upper Hungary, the city of Sopron in north-western Hungary, which was also exposed to German influences, held some of the earliest witch trials in 1528–9. Early trials also took place in the towns of Kolozsvár in Transylvania and Debrecen on the Great Plain, which were mostly inhabited by Hungarians. Kolozsvár, which had a religiously mixed population, held at least nineteen witch trials between 1565 and 1593, with thirteen of them resulting in burnings. Wandering preachers from Kolozsvár also helped to inspire the witch-hunts of the 1570s in Debrecen, whose confessional allegiance shifted from Lutheranism to Calvinism in the late sixteenth century. The towns and villages of the Great Plain, a frontier territory occupied by the Ottoman Turks from the middle of the sixteenth century until the end of the seventeenth century, did not experience intensive witch-hunting until the early years of the eighteenth century.[18] Although the Turks did not prevent local courts from functioning in this region, it was not until 1728 that one of the largest witch panics in Hungary developed—in the Catholic city of Szeged—when twenty-one persons were tried for witchcraft. Of these, thirteen were convicted and burned, three were drowned during the water ordeal, and three died in prison. Between 1728 and 1744 a total of forty-one persons were accused of witchcraft in Szeged. In the religiously divided town of Hódmezővásárhely another forty-one persons were brought to trial between 1724 and 1763, although only seven of these were executed. No fewer than twenty people were accused of being witches in Ottomány in 1724. One possible explanation for the late date of these witch-hunts is that the belated urbanization of the Great Plain and the

[17] Klaniczay, 'Hungary', 227, 229, 252–3, and Klaniczay, 'Witch-Hunting in Hungary', 80; Hagenthurn, ed., Segesvári boszorkányperek.

[18] For Debrecen see Kristóf, Ördögi mesterséget nem cselekedtem, 45–8 and '"Wise Women", Sinners and the Poor', 96–103. For Kolozsvár see Klaniczay, 'Hungary', 229–30; Klaniczay, 'Witch-Hunting in Hungary', 73–5; Klaniczay, 'A boszorkányvád mozgatórugói. Gondolatok az első kolozsvári boszorkányperek kapcsán' (The Triggers of Witchcraft Accusation. Thoughts in Connection with the First Witch Trials in Kolozsvár), Korunk, 16/5 (2005), 27–38; Klaniczay, 'Mely ördögtöl volt nyavalyája, azon ördög volna gyógyítója."A gyógyítók elleni boszorkányvád problémája a magyar boszorkányperekben' ('That Devilish Person who Caused the Harm, Would Also Take It Away.' The Problem of Witchcraft Charges against Healers in Hungarian Witch Trials), in Gábor Vargyas ed., Párbeszéd a hagyománnyal. A néprajzi kutatás múltja és jelene (Budapest-Pécs, 2011), 695–712; and Tünde Komáromi, 'Hat boszorkány rontásai. Kolozsvár, 1584' [The Harms Done by Six Witches Kolozsvár, 1584], in Árpád Töhötöm Szabó, ed., Életutak és életmódok (Kolozsvár, 2002), 5–41. As for the towns of Upper Hungary (today's Slovakia), archival research for witchcraft trials is still ongoing, but some local/regional analyses have been published, especially for the seventeenth and eighteenth centuries, such as Lengyel, 'Nyitra és Pozsony megye boszorkányperei' and Majtán, 'Servants of the Devil in Krupina', in Szeghyová, ed., The Role of Magic in the Past, 101–7.

resettlement of this area after the end of Ottoman rule caused considerable social and cultural turmoil in these communities.[19]

The popular image of the Hungarian sabbath was based not so much on foreign demonological concepts as local, originally non-diabolical, beliefs. Beliefs in the Hungarian *táltos*—who was a sort of shamanistic sorcerer—and south-eastern Slavic and Romanian fairies and sorcerers such as *kresnik* and *zduhać*, influenced these popular notions of witchcraft. Either learned demonologists diabolized these supernatural beings, or local accusers and judges referred to them in the trials in order to prove the suspicious supernatural connections and malevolence of accused witches.[20] The witches' sabbath, as represented in confessions and legal depositions made by town and village dwellers in early modern Hungary, tended to be more like a community feast, with excessive eating and drinking, playing music, and dancing in houses, churchyards, or the local tavern. In the majority of cases the sabbath resembled a rather profane feast in which the devil was not present. When, however, the devil was in attendance, he was imagined either as a he-goat (as in the trials at Szeged in 1728) or as having horse legs (as in the Pozsony area). Sometimes he took the shape of a human being, either a tall black man, a priest, or a handsome peasant lad. According to the testimony of some witnesses, he wore Hungarian dress in regions inhabited by Germans and German dress in predominantly Hungarian areas. He could also be represented as an ordinary animal, such as a dog or cat.[21]

[19] For Sopron see Ildikó Németh, 'Az 1528–1529. évi soproni boszorkányperek' [The Witchcraft Trials Held in 1528–29 in Sopron], in Éva Pócs, ed., *Közösség és identitás* (Budapest, 2002), 163–70, summary in English: 288–9 and Németh, 'Boszorkányperek a 16. századi Sopronban' [Witchcraft Trials in Sixteenth-century Sopron], *Soproni Szemle*, 2 (2006), 166–74. For Kolozsvár see Klaniczay, 'Hungary', 229–30; Klaniczay, 'Witch Hunting', 73–5, and Komáromi, 'Hat boszorkány rontásai', 5–41. For Debrecen and Ottomány see Kristóf, *Ördögi mesterséget nem cselekedtem*, 45–8, and Klaniczay, '"Wise Women", Sinners and the Poor', 93–119. For Szeged see István Petrovics, 'Witch-Hunt in Szeged in the Early Eighteenth Century', in Szeghyová, ed., *The Role of Magic in the Past*, 108–16. For Hódmezővásárhely see Barbara Benkéné Sándor, 'Hódmezővásárhely egészségügyi kultúrája a 18. századi boszorkányperek alapján' [The Medical Culture of Hódmezővásárhely, based on Eighteenth-century Witchcraft Trials], in *Néprajzi Tanulmányok*, Studia Ethnographica, 4 (Szeged, 2003), 69–74.

[20] For a survey of the popular beliefs on which the image of the witches' gathering could be founded see Pócs, 'The Popular Foundations of the Witches' Sabbath'; Klaniczay, 'Hungary', 243–55. For further analysis of certain beliefs see Éva Pócs, *Fairies and Witches at the Boundary of South-Eastern and Central Europe* (Helsinki, 1989); Klaniczay, 'Benandante-kresnik-zduhać-táltos. Samanizmus és boszorkányhit érintkezési pontjai Közép-Európában' [Benandante-kresnik-zduhać-táltos: Some Points of Contact between Shamanism and Witch-belief in Central Europe], *Ethnographia*, 94 (1983), 116–34, with a summary in English; Klaniczay, 'Shamanistic Elements in Central European Witchcraft', in Mihály Hoppál, ed., *Shamanism in Eurasia* (Göttingen, 1984), 131–69; Éva Pócs, '*Tündéres* and the Order of St Ilona', or, Did the Hungarians Have Fairy Magicians?', *Acta Ethnographica Hungarica*, 54 (2009), 379–96; Pócs, 'Hungarian *Táltos* and his European Parallels', in Mihály Hoppál and Juha Pentikäinen, eds, *Uralic Mythology and Folklore* (Budapest, 1989), 251–76.

[21] For examples see Klaniczay, 'Hungary', 250–3, and Gábor Klaniczay, 'Le sabbat raconté par les témoins des procès de sorcellerie en Hongrie', in Nicole Jacques-Chaquin and Maxime Préaud, eds, *Le sabbat des sorciers XV ͤ-XVIII ͤ siècles* (Grenoble, 1993), 227–46.

19.6 A STATISTICAL PROFILE OF
HUNGARIAN WITCHES

According to our present knowledge, a total of 4,592 accused witches were brought to trial between 1213 and 1800 in the kingdom of Hungary. The total number of trials was 2,291. These figures should be considered minimum totals, since the exploration of witchcraft trials in different archival collections is still ongoing. For the entire period, the great majority of the accused witches were women (3,962 or 86 per cent). Local studies provide similar gender distributions: only eleven men (roughly 9 per cent) were brought to trial in the city of Debrecen between 1575 and 1759, and eight (roughly 5 per cent) in the villages and towns of Bihar county between 1591 and 1766.

About two thirds or 3,444 of the accused witches were Hungarian, while most of the rest were German (428), Croatian (340), and Romanian (183). There were small numbers of Slovaks (92), Roma (47), Poles–Ruthens (41), and Serbs (18) as well.[22]

The exact number of executions cannot be determined. According to the most recent research, only 848 witches or roughly 51 per cent of those whose final sentences were known were given capital sentences. One should, however, take into consideration the fact that the final sentences are *not* known for roughly 64 per cent of the total number of accused witches. The majority of those not sentenced to death received corporal punishment or were banished from their communities either temporarily or permanently. The remainder were acquitted. Local rates of capital punishments varied. In the Calvinist city of Debrecen only 27 per cent of those whose sentences are known were executed, mainly by burning, while in the predominantly Calvinist county of Bihar the comparable figure was 38 per cent.

19.7 CHRONOLOGICAL PATTERNS OF
WITCHCRAFT PROSECUTIONS

Early modern Hungarian witch-hunting tended to increase in intensity during periods of peace that set in after or between wars and internal rebellions. These periods also coincided with periods of devastating plague epidemics and their immediate aftermath. Witch-hunting reached its first peak in the 1580s, a peaceful period that coincided with a plague epidemic. The intensity of prosecutions decreased during the Fifteen Years' War with the Turks (1591–1606) and also during the anti-Habsburg uprising of István Bocskai (1604–6).

[22] UROW.

The 1620s saw a new spike in the number of prosecutions. Although this was a time of rebellion, when Gábor Bethlen, Prince of Transylvania, led three campaigns against the Habsburgs, many individual trials were held in years of peace and in regions unaffected by military conflict. A decree issued by the Transylvanian Diet in 1614 to punish sorcerers, coupled with the outbreak of the plague, most likely contributed to the intensification of witch-hunting during these years.

Another increase in witch-hunting occurred after 1690, when the Ottomans were finally driven out of the country. Witch-hunting reached its highest peak in the first half of the eighteenth century, after the end of the War of Independence against the Habsburgs (1703–11). The two greatest plague epidemics of the eighteenth century, which took place between 1709 and 1711 and between 1738 and 1745, also seem to have contributed to this intense period of witch-hunting.

19.8 Decriminalization and Late Witch Trials

Although witch-hunting declined somewhat in the middle of the eighteenth century, it did not register a significant reduction in intensity until the Habsburg empress Maria Theresa took steps to stop the prosecutions after 1758, and until Hungarian witch beliefs underwent a profound transformation.

The person who was primarily responsible for the change in official policy was Gerard van Swieten, Maria Theresa's enlightened court physician. After having examined personally a Slovenian woman (a certain Heruczina) accused of witchcraft, van Swieten submitted a mémoire to the empress in 1758, arguing that the charges against this woman were based on false beliefs. In order to avoid future miscarriages of justice of this sort he suggested that the government end all such prosecutions. In keeping with his recommendation, the royal court reversed a number of local, municipal sentences passed against accused witches, and in 1768 a royal decree prohibited the execution of witches.[23] This decree did not, however, bring an immediate end to all witchcraft prosecutions in Hungary. County magistrates, who presided over their own criminal courts and resisted the centralizing efforts of the Habsburg rulers, continued to hold witchcraft trials during the last three decades of the eighteenth century, and in some regions even into the early years of the nineteenth century.

In addition to this change in royal policy, local magistrates began to interpret witchcraft as an imposture or the product of illness rather than a supernatural, diabolical act. This is what happened in the city of Debrecen, where prosecutions for

---

[23] Klaniczay, 'Hungary', 235; Lilla Krász and Péter Tóth G., 'Die Dekriminalisierung der Magie und der Kampf gegen Aberglauben in Ungarn und in Siebenbürgen 1740–1848', unpublished manuscript; UROW.

witchcraft ended well before the decrees of Empress Maria Theresa. A large volume of educational literature, including popular scientific texts, schoolbooks, and chapbooks, ridiculed witch beliefs as superstitious, and attributed its effects to natural causes. Lawyers used these attacks on traditional witch beliefs to defend witches at their trials, and they were successful in winning a number of acquittals in the mid-eighteenth century.

19.9 ACCUSERS AND ACCUSED: A MICRO-SOCIOLOGY

Accusations of witchcraft in early modern Hungary must be studied in their proper local, social, and cultural context. In many cases witchcraft charges involved other offences or crimes, such as adultery, fornication, arson, or malevolent curing, and they often reflected 'dangerous' social relations between the accused witches and their accusers.

Early modern Hungarian witchcraft accusations reveal three main patterns. The first is what may be called 'accusations from above', which occurred when a wealthier person or one of higher social or political status accused a person of lower status. This pattern was evident in politically initiated witch trials within the Transylvanian high nobility. Among the princes who accused family members of their political enemies of witchcraft were Sigismund Báthory, who blamed the mother of Boldizsár Báthory, whom he had murdered, for causing his impotence; Gábor Bethlen, who, after having taken power from the murdered Gábor Báthory in 1612, accused the sister of the latter as well as two other noblewomen of his entourage; and Mihály Apafy, who initiated a very large witch-hunt between 1679 and 1686. Apafy's main target was the wife of his exiled rival, Pál Béldi, whom he accused of inflicting a serious illness on the prince's wife, Anna Bornemisza, in revenge for her husband's defeat.[24]

This pattern was also apparent in early modern urban and village witchcraft. For example, in the city of Debrecen, well-to-do burghers (artisans and merchants) accused their lodgers, their house servants, or even city beggars of witchcraft in dozens of cases. These accusations seem to have formed part of an explicit local socio-political campaign against the poor. A variant of this pattern was evident when so-called 'honest' Calvinist citizens in Debrecen accused adulteresses, drunkards, thieves, and 'blasphemous' women of witchcraft. The latter group comprised fifty-three people, roughly 36 per cent of the total number of Debrecen witches. Another variant of this pattern, in which

---

[24] Klaniczay, 'Hungary', 238. János Herner, ed., *Bornemisza Anna megbüvöltetése* [*The Bewitchment of Anna Bornemisza*] (Budapest, 1988). Lengyel, 'Nyitra és Pozsony megye boszorkányperei', 36–7. For the witchcraft charges against Erzsébet Báthory see Tünde Lengyel and Gábor Várkonyi, *Báthory Erzsébet: Egy asszony élete* [*Erzsébet Báthory: The Life of a Woman*] (Budapest, 2011), 285–91.

a person of 'superior' social or moral status accused a subordinate of witchcraft, occurred when young female servants were accused of witchcraft (mostly love magic) and fornication by their landlords, hosts, or their mostly male acquaintances or clients.

Another manifestation of this pattern can be seen in two other forms of social conflict in the eighteenth-century frontier world of the Great Plain that were closely connected to its resettlement and the restructure of its social world. The first was evident when local village or town dwellers accused strangers or newcomers of witchcraft, a very common phenomenon in the period. The second was apparent when formerly privileged social groups, such as the *hajdú* (Haiduk) nobles who had lost their administrative, economic, and military liberties after the end of the Turkish occupation, accused their peasant neighbours of witchcraft. Suffering the loss of their ancient privileges, the nobles apparently used witchcraft accusations to retaliate against people of lower social status who had recently settled in their communities.[25]

The second main pattern of witchcraft accusations might be labelled 'accusations from below'. It was evident when a socially disadvantaged party accused a person of higher social or economic status. This pattern was most common in witch panics. We find it, for example, in the city of Szeged in 1728, when a poor wise woman and beggar accused a highly esteemed former judge, Dániel Rósa, of witchcraft. Town and village magistrates and judges were also accused during the witch panic in the villages of Ottomány and Nagykereki in 1724, and in the Kiskunhalas panic of 1734.[26]

Another manifestation of this pattern was evident when fourteen- to sixteen-year-old house servants or kitchen maids, and even younger children accused their landlords, hosts, and even parents or grandparents of witchcraft. Some of these accusations from below also occurred during witch panics, as in Kolozsvár towards the end of the witch-hunt that lasted from 1615 to 1629. Others, however, occurred in trials when only one person was accused, such as in Debrecen and the county of Bihar during the first half of eighteenth century.[27]

Accusations from socially subordinate groups also occurred during periods of moderate witch-hunting. In some trials in eighteenth-century Debrecen lodgers accused their hosts of witchcraft. In an even larger number of cases, patients and clients accused wise women, midwives, and healers who had failed in their efforts to

---

[25] Kristóf, *Ördögi mesterséget nem cselekedtem*, 132–43, 162–70, 171–6. For the trial of a young servant from Nyírgyulaj in 1728–9, accused of fornication and witchcraft, tortured, and then banned from the county, see György Szoboszlay, 'Egy falusi boszorkány és a közösség: Fodor Mária története' [A Village Witch and the Community: The Story of Mária Fodor], in István Czövek, ed., *Tanulmányok az egyetemes és magyar történelem köréből VI* (Nyíregyháza, 2008), 41–54.

[26] For Szeged see Petrovics, 'Witch-Hunt in Szeged', 114–16 and Klaniczay, 'Hungary', 239. For Kiskunhalas see Klaniczay, 'A halasi boszorkányok és az új kultúrtörténet' (The Witches of Kiskunhalas and the New Cultural History) in Zsombor Bódy, Sándor Horváth and Tibor Valuch, eds, *Megtalálható-e a múlt? Tanulmányok Gyáni Gábor 60. születésnapjára*, (Budapest, 2010), 118–39. For Ottomány and Nagykereki see Kristóf, *Ördögi mesterséget nem cselekedtem*, 224–5. For a case of a Calvinist preacher accused informally of having associated himself with the devil in the 1630s see Szentpéteri, 'Magic and Demonology'.

[27] Klaniczay, 'Hungary', 239; Kristóf, *Ördögi mesterséget nem cselekedtem*.

cure them. Cunning folk, who were mostly women in early modern Hungary, were called either *tudós* (wise), *orvos* (doctor), *tudós asszony* (wise woman), *orvosasszony* (doctor/medicine woman) or, referring more to the practices of divination and fortune-telling, *néző* (seer). Witchcraft accusations against cunning people reflected a broader transformation of the healing and medical culture in Debrecen, in which popular healers and experts of magic gradually suffered a loss in prestige. Debrecen was not an isolated case. Witchcraft accusations against wise women and cunning people occurred in South Transdanubia, Nagybánya (Baia Mare in present-day Romania), Kolozsvár, and in many other local communities throughout the country. They show, among other things, that relationships between patients and healers or diviners were not always amicable during this period.

Occasionally accusation from below reached the highest levels of society. For example, Anna Benkö, a Transylvanian noblewoman, was accused of witchcraft in the middle of the eighteenth century. Her trial involved both accusations from below, since it was servants and housemaids who accused her of various magical practices, and those from people of equal social status, namely her noble relatives who wanted to get her fortune.[28]

The third main pattern of witchcraft accusations involved individuals who had the same social status or occupation or possessed magical power. Many of the accusations of this kind reflected competition among cunning folk; a large number of witchcraft accusations in Hungary originated in this kind of magical status rivalry. Almost all the victims of the first witchcraft trial in Kolozsvár in 1565 were cunning folk who accused one another of witchcraft. The same was true in the early modern Debrecen trials, in which roughly 31 per cent of all the accused witches were practitioners of popular or magical healing. During these trials local wise women brought charges against other wise women, midwives accused other midwives, and city barber surgeons and licensed midwives testified against their popular equivalents, stigmatizing them as 'diabolical' and therefore illegal. These kinds of witchcraft accusations, as mentioned above, reflected the reorganization and institutionalization of the local health care system in Debrecen during the eighteenth century. Rivalry among wise women and midwives was also apparent in the Hódmezövásárhely and Nagybánya witch trials.[29]

    28 Krász, 'Bábák és boszorkányok a kora újkori Magyarországon' [Midwives and Witches in Early Modern Hungary], *Rubicon*, 7 (2005), 37–40; Krász, 'Zwischen Verbanntsein und Akzeptiertsein', in Glatz Ferenc, ed., *An der Schwelle der Europäischen Union: Begegnungen, Schriftenreihen*, x (Budapest, 2000), 217–32. On Anna Benkö see Szoboszlay, 'Riválisok és jó rokonok: Egy háromszéki boszorkányhistória néhány tanulsága' [Rivals and Good Relatives: Lessons from a Story of Witchcraft in Háromszék], in István Czövek and Gábor Reszler, eds, *Múlttöredékek. Tanulmánygyüjtemény Hársfalvi Péter emlékére* (Nyíregyháza, 2008), 208–21, and Zsuzsa Bokor, 'Történelmek–levéltárak–boszorkányok: A boszorkányperek kutatásának problémáiról' [Histories–archives–witches: About the Problems of the Research of Witchcraft Trials], in Árpád Töhötöm Szabó, ed., *Lenyomatok. Fiatal kutatók a népi kultúráról* (Kolozsvár, 2002), 47–62.
    29 Kristóf, *Ördögi mesterséget nem cselekedtem*, 143–70 and Kristóf, '"Wise Women", Sinners and the Poor', 107–11; Klaniczay, 'Hungary', 239; Klaniczay, 'Mely ördögtöl volt nyavalyája'; Benkéné Sándor, 'Hódmezövásárhely egészségügyi kultúrája'; András Kiss, 'Ante Claram Bóci (Egy 1565-beli ismeretlen

Same-status accusations and magical status rivalry contributed to the development of witch-hunts in various ways. In some eighteenth-century hunts, the magistrates forced cunning folk to furnish 'proofs' of alleged agreements with the witches, according to which the latter had agreed to bewitch people so that the cunning folk would have more patients to cure. These charges were based on the well-known adage in Hungary that 'Who can lift the spell, can cast it as well.'

A specific group of Hungarian cunning men known as *tudós pásztorok* or wise shepherds also found themselves accused of witchcraft, either by their village clients or their shepherd colleagues, during the seventeenth and especially the eighteenth century. A peculiar charge brought against them testified to popular beliefs in so-called werewolves, humans who were believed to be able to transform themselves into wolves. Such charges were made throughout the early modern period.[30] Charges against shepherds for practising witchcraft and acting as werewolves may have reflected the decline of the ancient practice of cattle-herding in the eighteenth century. Another aspect of the economic and social transformation of Hungary that occurred after its Turkish occupation was the undermining of the traditionally high prestige of the shepherds, who had reputations as popular healers. The resettlement and the profound economic–political reorganization of the country under the returned Habsburg rulers and the newly established institutions of absolute monarchy were responsible for this development.[31]

In sum, charges of witchcraft were used by individuals belonging to many different social groups to advance their interests and resolve their social conflicts. These charges were not limited to one social group, nor did they reflect a particular type of social

kolozsvári boszorkányper)' [Ante Claram Bóci: An Unknown Witch Trial from Kolozsvár, 1565], in his *Más források—más értelmezések* (Marosvásárhely, 2003), 291–309, and Kiss, 'Kömíves Prisca boszorkánypere 1565-böl' [The Witchcraft Trial of Prisca Kömíves from 1565], *Korunk*, 16 (2005), 16–25; Judit Kis-Halas and Péter Tóth G., 'Hával és conditióval' [With 'If' and 'Conditio'], in Béla Balogh, ed., *Nagybányai boszorkányperek* [*Witchcraft Trials of Nagybánya*] (Budapest, 2003), 28–9; Kis-Halas, 'Trial of an Honest Citizen in Nagybánya 1704-1705: A Tentative Microanalysis of Witchcraft Accusations', in Gábor Klaniczay and Éva Pócs, in collaboration with Eszter Csonka-Takács, eds, *Demons, Spirits, Witches 3: Witchcraft Mythologies and Persecutions* (Budapest, 2008), 213–36.

[30] Klaniczay, 'Hungary', 254. One of the earliest witchcraft trials held in 1528–9 in Sopron concerned a shepherd and his son said to have specific knowledge, and be able to send wolves to kill their rival/enemy shepherd, using various kinds of magical instruments. See Németh, 'Az 1528–1529. évi soproni boszorkányperek' and Németh, 'Az 1528–1529. évi soproni boszorkányperek' (The Witchcraft Trials Held in 1528–9 in Sopron), in Pócs, ed., *Közösség és identitás* (Budapest, 2002), 163–70, and Németh, 'Boszorkányperek a 16. századi Sopronban' (Witchcraft Trials in 16th-Century Sopron), *Soproni Szemle*, 2 (2006), 166–74.

[31] Klaniczay, 'Hungary', 254; Kristóf, *Ördögi mesterséget nem cselekedtem*, 85–6. For an analysis of the witchcraft trial held in 1759 of a shepherd from the village of Vaszar, accused of magical (and unsuccessful) healing, and sending wolves to kill his enemies see József Hudi, 'Az újjáépítés korszaka (1697–1847)' [The Period of Rebuilding 1697–1847], in József Hudi and Zsolt Mezei, eds, *Vaszar története* (Vaszar, 2010), 232–4.

conflict. Charges of witchcraft penetrated early modern Hungarian society as a whole and reflected the transformation of that society during the early modern period.[32]

19.10 FUTURE RESEARCH

One large gap in our knowledge of witch-hunting in Hungary is the way in which the prosecutions in the ecclesiastical courts corresponded with, contributed to, or overlapped with those of the secular courts. Early modern ecclesiastical records often dealt with offences related to witchcraft, and these have not been adequately explored. Some work has been done on the records of Calvinist tribunals, but very little has been conducted in the ecclesiastical records of other religious denominations.

Another gap is the importance of gender in understanding witchcraft prosecutions. Some Hungarian studies have investigated the influence of Calvinist concepts of female weakness and fallibility with those of diabolic temptation, but the views of Lutherans and Catholics regarding the connection between witchcraft and women remain relatively unknown. The degree to which clerical stereotypes of women coincided with popular attitudes towards women accused of witchcraft remains largely unexplored.

There is also a need for a better understanding of the cultural language of witchcraft narratives and the particular social and cultural context in which they were produced. For example, the locations where witches were thought to assemble might refer to specific sites in the local landscape, or more generally to locations such as private vineyards, whose access was restricted by law.[33] Gestures and ceremonies mentioned in the trial documents might refer to forms of legal ritual, while the dramatic character of these narratives made them appear to constitute a 'theatre of blood and pain'.[34] Finally, more attention needs to be paid to the construction of witchcraft narratives. In this respect the methodologies of microhistory, critical discourse analysis, and linguistic

---

[32] A thorough analysis of local conflicts resulting in witchcraft accusations in Hungary would show a broader perspective than the one proposed by Robert J. W. Evans, *The Making of the Habsburg Monarchy 1550–1700* (Oxford, 1979), 411, according to which witchcraft charges went hand in hand with efforts at social control, and formed 'another aspect of the pursuit of settled hierarchy' in Hungary and in Central Europe. A considerable number of the above-mentioned 'dangerous relations' involved in such charges would also testify to the subversive function of witchcraft, itself very much present in early modern Hungary.

[33] Melinda Égetö, 'Boszorkányszombat a szölöhegyen: A szölöhegy elkülönítettségének tükrözödése a népi mentalitásban' [Witches' Sabbath on the Vineyard Hill: The Reflection of the Separate Legal and Economic Status of the Vineyard Hill in Folk Mentality], in Éva Pócs, ed., *Demonológia és boszorkányság Európában*, 227–47, summary in English, 365–7.

[34] Ildikó Sz. Kristóf, 'How to Make a (Legal) Pact with the Devil? Legal Customs and Literacy in Witch Confessions in Early Modern Hungary', in Klaniczay and Pócs, *Demons, Spirits, Witches 3*, 164–83, and Klaniczay and Kristóf, 'Écritures saintes et pactes diaboliques: Les usages religieux de l'écrit (Moyen Age et Temps modernes)', *Annales: Histoire, Sciences Sociales*, 4–5 (2001), 947–80 (esp. 973–5); Tóth G., '"The Bloody Theatre of Europe". The Culture of Pain, Cruelty and Martyrdom in Early Modern Hungary', *Acta Ethnographica*, 48 (2003), 385–96.

analysis will continue to contribute to a deeper understanding of the subject, and bring us to a deeper knowledge of the mental worlds of those who initiated witchcraft prosecutions and those who staged them.[35]

FURTHER READING

Klaniczay, Gábor, 'Hungary: The Accusations and the Universe of Popular Magic', in Bengt Ankarloo and Gustav Henningsen, eds, *Early Modern European Witchcraft: Centres and Peripheries* (Oxford, 1990), 219–25.

Klaniczay, Gábor, *The Uses of Supernatural Power: The Transformation of Popular Religion in Medieval and Early Modern Europe* (Cambridge, 1990).

Klaniczay, Gábor, 'Witch Hunting in Hungary: Social or Cultural Tensions?', *Acta Ethnographica*, 37 (1990), 67–91.

Klaniczay, Gábor, 'Le sabbat raconté par les témoins des procès de sorcellerie en Hongrie', in Nicole Jacques-Chaquin and Maxime Préaud, eds, *Le sabbat des sorciers XVᵉ-XVIIIᵉ siècles* (Grenoble, 1993), 227–46.

Klaniczay, Gábor, 'A boszorkányvád mozgatórugói. Gondolatok az elsö kolozsvári boszorkányperek kapcsán' [The Triggers of Witchcraft Accusation. Thoughts in Connection with the First Witch trials in Kolozsvár], *Korunk*, 16/5 (2005), 27–38.

Klaniczay, Gábor 'A halasi boszorkányok és az új kultúrtörténet' [The witches of Kiskunhalas and the new cultural history] in Zsombor Bódy, Sándor Horváth and Tibor Valuch, eds, *Megtalálható-e a múlt? Tanulmányok Gyáni Gábor 60. születésnapjára*, (Budapest, 2010), 118–39.

Klaniczay, Gábor, 'Mely ördögtöl volt nyavalyája, azon ördög volna gyógyítója."A gyógyítók elleni boszorkányvád problémája a magyar boszorkányperekben' ['That Devilish Person who Caused the Harm, Would Also Take it Away.' The Problem of Witchcraft Charges against Healers in Hungarian Witch Trials], in Gábor Vargyas ed., *Párbeszéd a hagyománnyal. A néprajzi kutatás múltja és jelene* (Budapest-Pécs, 2011), 695–712.

Klaniczay, Gábor and Pócs, Éva, eds, 'Witch-Beliefs and Witch-Hunting in Central and Eastern Europe', *Acta Ethnographica*, 37 (1991/2).

Kristóf, Ildikó, '"Wise Women", Sinners and the Poor: The Social Background of Witch Hunting in a 16/18th-Century Calvinist City of Eastern Hungary', *Acta Ethnographica*, 37 (1990), 93–119.

Kristóf, Ildikó, 'Elements of Demonology in Hungarian Calvinist Literature Printed in Debrecen in the Sixteenth and Seventeenth Centuries', *Cauda Pavonis: Studies in Hermeticism*, 16 (1997), 9–17.

---

[35] Bokor, 'Történelmek'; Zsófia Frazon, 'Az ördögszövetség mint büntetöügyi igazság és létrehozásának mechanizmusa' [The Devil Pact as Truth of the Criminal Procedure and the Mechanisms of its Construction], *Tabula*, 1(3) (2000), 28–47 (with an abstract in English); Emese Ilyefalvi, '. . . akar mi lellyen benneteket mingyart Emberre gyanakoztok'. Boszorkányfenyegetések pragmatikai elemzése ['Whatever occurs to you, you suspect a human being behind'. A Pragmatical Analysis of the Threatenings of the Accused Witches], in Tünde Székely, ed., *Rodosz konferenciakötet* (Cluj, 2010), 75–92.

Kristóf, Ildikó, 'Ördögi mesterséget nem cselekedtem': A boszorkányüldözés társadalmi és kulturális háttere a kora újkori Debrecenben és Bihar vármegyében ['I Have Not Done Any Diabolic Deed': The Social and Religious Background of Witch-hunting in Early Modern Debrecen and Bihar County] (Debrecen, 1998), with a summary in English.

Németh, Ildikó, 'Az 1528-1529. évi soproni boszorkányperek' [The witchcraft trials held in 1528-29 in Sopron], in Pócs, ed., Közösség és identitás (Budapest, 2002), 163-170, and Németh, Ildikó, 'Boszorkányperek a 16. századi Sopronban' [Witchcraft Trials in 16th-century Sopron], Soproni Szemle, 2 (2006), 166–74.

Sz. Kristóf, Ildikó, 'Hungary', in Richard M. Golden, ed., Encyclopedia of Witchcraft: The Western Tradition (Santa Barbara, CA, 2006), ii, 515–20.

Pócs, Éva, Fairies and Witches at the Boundary of South-Eastern and Central Europe (Helsinki, 1989).

Pócs, Éva, 'The Popular Foundations of the Witches' Sabbath and the Devil's Pact in Central and Southeastern Europe', Acta Ethnographica, 37 (1991/2), 305–70.

Pócs, Éva, Between the Living and the Dead: A Perspective on Witches and Seers in the Early Modern Age (Budapest, 1999).

Pócs, Éva, 'Tündéres and the Order of St Ilona, or, Did the Hungarians Have Fairy Magicians?' Acta Ethnographica Hungarica, 54 (2009), 379–96.

Szeghyová, Blanka, ed., The Role of Magic in the Past: Learned and Popular Magic, Popular Beliefs and Diversity of Attitudes (Bratislava, 2005).

Tóth G., Péter, 'River Ordeal–Trial by Water–Swimming of Witches: Procedures of Ordeal in Witch Trials', in Gábor Klaniczay and Éva Pócs, in collaboration with Eszter Csonka-Takács, eds, Witchcraft Mythologies and Persecutions (Budapest, 2008), 129–63.

Tóth G., Péter, 'Objects, Worms, Demons: The Natural and Magical Miracle as Material Proof in the Demonological Literature of Early Modern Hungary', Acta Ethnographica Hungarica, 54 (2009), 411–51.

CHAPTER 20

....

WITCHCRAFT TRIALS IN RUSSIA: HISTORY AND HISTORIOGRAPHY

....

VALERIE KIVELSON

IN 1648 Vasilii Pavlov, a military man in the service of Tsar Alexei Mikhailovich, came to the court of the governor-general of the frontier fortress town of Belev to denounce his bondsman for working magic against him. The accusation was framed as a humble petition—as convention dictated—addressed directly to the tsar from his suppliant 'slave':

> To Sovereign, Tsar, and Grand Prince Alexei Mikhailovich, your slave Vaska, son of Andrei Pavlov, petitions.
> In this year, 1648, my bondsman, Ivashka Ryzhei, threatened in the presence of my [other] bondsman, Gavrilko Filipev, saying 'if my master is ever mad at me for any reason, then I will stand in the threshold or wherever, and say [a spell], and he will be able to do nothing to me. And as to the female sex, whomever I want, even if it is a *boiarinia* (mistress/noblewoman), my spells will cause [her] to fall in love with me.'

The horrified master took what he saw as appropriate steps:

> So I beat him and ordered him to write what he had boasted of in front of my bondsmen. He wrote it out with his own hand in the presence of people, my peasants. Merciful sovereign, tsar and grand prince . . . have mercy on me, your slave. Order, sovereign, that my man Ivashka Ryzhei be questioned and his criminal letter taken as evidence.

In many ways, this case typifies the prosecution of witchcraft in Muscovite and early imperial Russian courts. Initiated by petition, denunciations very often grew out of domestic tensions or hostilities between masters and serfs, slaves, or other dependents. They were normally heard in secular courts, overseen by the tsar or the central chancelleries in Moscow or, later, Petersburg. The charges usually involved acts of material or physical harm (*maleficium*, or, in Russian, *porcha*, literally, 'spoiling') or the magical alteration of emotions. Nearly three-quarters of cases that reached the courts identified men rather than women as practitioners of harmful magic. The tsar's courts took such charges very seriously. The accused in this case, Ivan Ryzhei, was interrogated, undoubtedly with torture, and found guilty as charged. Because it was discovered that he possessed written texts of the spells his master had described, the verdict was clear-cut. The sentence, issued in the name of the tsar, demonstrates just how egregious an infraction he had committed. The orders from Moscow to the local governor read:

> When you get this, announce his criminality before many people and order him beaten with a knout and give him to Vasilii Pavlov [his master, who had brought the suit]. And here is Ivashko's criminal writing sent back to you with this order. Order his criminal writing burned on his back, so that henceforth no one would dare write such criminal spells.[1]

Witchcraft trials in Russia are not only intriguing in their own right but also invite comparisons with those that took place in Western and Central Europe. Russian witchcraft trials were characterized by a high percentage of men among the accused, relatively infrequent discussion of diabolism, and harsh, inquisitorial legal procedures. The distinctive political, religious, and social history of Russia in the early modern period, its relative cultural isolation, the teachings of Orthodox Christianity, the inescapable pressures of social hierarchy, bondage, and dependency, all left their imprint on the trials.

20.1 WITCHCRAFT IN LAW AND LEGAL PROCESS

The courts of the Muscovite tsars conducted trials of witches which, at the most general level, resembled those of many of their European counterparts, with cases initiated from below but prosecuted from above by administrative officials, for the most part in secular courts. Chronologically, formal trials started in the early seventeenth century. Prosecution continued apace through the 1740s, and trailed off only in the 1760s, during the reign of Catherine the Great.

The Russian Orthodox Church condemned sorcery and witchcraft, identified variously as *koldovstvo*, *vedovstvo*, *charovanie*, *vorozhba*, or *chernoknizhestvo*, as 'devilish' and hazardous to Orthodox Christian souls, but for the most part religious authorities left the task of prosecution to secular courts. Suspects were identified by denunciations submitted against them by members of the community, and then were harshly

---

[1] Rossiiskii gosudarstvennyi arkhiv drevnikh aktov (RGADA) [Russian State Archive of Ancient Documents], Moscow, fol. 210, stolbtsy razriadnykh stolov, Prikaznyi stol, st. 567, ll. 202–6.

investigated by provincial officials or by officers of the central administration in Moscow. Courts of law were of a piece with the administrative infrastructure; in the seventeenth century the town governor served as chief administrator, enforcer, investigator, interrogator, and presiding judge. Moscow kept close watch on the performance of governors, and witchcraft cases, like all other major investigations, required incessant reference to Moscow for instructions on how to proceed. These exchanges left a dense documentary record tracking the conduct of trials. Most witchcraft cases were eventually transferred to one of the central chancelleries. In the seventeenth century they were usually brought to the Chancellery of Military Affairs (*Razriadnyi Prikaz*). In the eighteenth century secular jurisdiction over witchcraft cases shifted primarily to the Preobrazhenskii Prikaz, the investigative bureau responsible for sniffing out all forms of sedition, while some cases made their way to ecclesiastical courts under the Holy Synod. These institutions too left extensive paper trails. None of these legal venues allowed for the presence of lawyers—who did not exist in Russia until much later—or any form of representation for the accused.

As in Continental Europe, interrogators routinely employed torture as a mean of eliciting testimony. Russian law was not hampered by the requirements of Roman law that deemed confession 'the queen of proofs' or stipulated the kinds and qualities of evidence necessary for conviction. Instead, torture was regarded as a practical way to uncover hidden information about undiscovered crimes or unnamed accomplices. Although lawmakers and judges voiced some concern that excessive torture might kill and thereby silence their witnesses, they expressed no moral qualms or real doubt about the validity of torture as a route to establishing the truth. Administered in special torture chambers (*zastenki*), interrogative torture consisting of beating, suspension from the strappado accompanied by more beating (with or without weights attached to the feet), burning with fire or with hot iron pincers, and, rarely, water being poured on the head. Not only those charged with witchcraft were subject to torture; anyone else implicated during the interrogation process would be arrested and could be brought to the torture chamber if the testimony warranted such a step.

Russian law regarding witchcraft developed in fits and starts, and no single position or definition emerged. The openness and multiplicity of the crime were matched by a chronic uncertainty in the law. Muscovite law operated in a grey area between the great efforts at legal codification, which produced the law codes of 1550, 1589, 1606, the imposing Ulozhenie Law Code of 1649, and the New Statute Code of 1669, and an endless series of ad hoc decrees, issued in response to particular problems, directed towards individual officials or regions, and only poorly integrated into general practice. These decrees might repeat what was in the codified law, add to it, or directly contradict it.

Until the enactment of the New Statutes of 1669, codified laws contained no explicit legislation concerning witchcraft, so presiding officials necessarily invoked various tangentially related regulations when prosecuting such cases. These prove revealing with regard to how officials categorized witchcraft or what they understood to constitute the essence of the crime. Trial records refer to articles on blasphemy, treason, banditry, patricide, and murder of a superior. The episodic decrees censured the practice of witchcraft on equally heterogeneous grounds, denouncing it sometimes as a manifestation of criminal banditry (in decrees of 1555 and 1671, and again in the New Statute Code of 1669) or, elsewhere, as a more spiritual offence, along with blasphemy, impiety, or revelry (in decrees of 1649, 1653, and 1677). The wide variety in approaches indicates that ideas about witchcraft remained amorphous, without a single unifying conceptual or definitional core. Only under the Westernizing, reforming ruler Peter the Great did Russia import passages from the *Carolina* and condemn witchcraft as potentially, but not necessarily, involving a pact with the devil. Peter's Military Articles (1715) and Naval Articles (1720) incorporated this possibility into a newly formalized definition of witchcraft. His codes were immediately published and disseminated, and were adopted in courts of all kinds, including ecclesiastical courts. Even after Peter's legal reforms, however, other approaches to witchcraft and other codes of law remained operative, thereby continuing a pattern of murky ambiguity in the condemnation and prosecution of magic. Secular and church courts vied for jurisdiction, and a new strain of scepticism regarding the powers of witches, and particularly regarding the authenticity of those claiming to be possessed, ran alongside the equally novel condemnation of witchcraft as Satanism. The sceptical position finally triumphed in a series of decrees issued under the Enlightenment ruler Catherine the Great. A synodal decree of 1772 prohibited further trials of witchcraft, opining that the whole business should be considered a matter of charlatanry rather than of magic. This put an end to the formal prosecution of witchcraft as a felony, but lesser courts continued to hear charges of witchcraft and to investigate possession cases right through to the early twentieth century, administering small fines or even short jail sentences. While educated elites, like their European counterparts, came to adopt an attitude of derisive or indulgent condescension towards the ignorant superstitions of the *narod*, the folk, popular belief remained animated and continues to provide fodder for ethnographers and folklorists to this day.

Medieval chronicles document sporadic episodes of violence against suspected witches as early as the eleventh century, and suspicions and accusations of witchcraft plagued the courts and persons of the rulers from the late fifteenth century onwards, but no trial records survive before the early 1600s. This absence may reflect the disappearance of sources, particularly those from before the devastating fire of 1626 that devoured most of the official archives, but more likely few actual trials had been conducted prior to the seventeenth century. With the consolidation of the tsarist state under the Romanov rulers after 1613, a confluence of factors—an expanding judicial–administrative presence, a growing state ambition to control society at its most minute levels, and a series of official decrees prohibiting witchcraft and prescribing legal processes and punishments—created a fertile environment for a real increase in witchcraft prosecution.

If the source record has survived in representative numbers, as seems likely, Russian courts tried relatively few cases, and the total number of executions fails to impress those familiar with European death tallies. Records survive for about 230 trials, involving some 490 individuals in the seventeenth century, and approximately the same for the following century. Of those tried in the seventeenth century, about 15 per cent met their deaths at the hands of the court, while only a handful of people were executed in the eighteenth century. Seventeenth-century executions took various forms: hanging, beheading, and, in a minority of cases, burning. Some laws specified that female felons were to be buried alive, with their heads exposed, and were to be left to die a slow death, but, in fact, several of the few women who were executed went to the flames instead. The majority of those convicted of witchcraft endured lesser punishments. After surviving the ordeal of investigative torture, almost all suffered punitive beatings, with either bastinadoes or the knout, the infamous Russian leather whip. If they were judged to have inflicted serious physical harm through their magic, they might suffer the severing of a hand or a foot, or, as in the case of Ivan Ryzhei, have the text of their spells set on fire on their flesh as a palpable lesson to the general public. Subsequently, many convicted witches were exiled to the remote frontiers, where the men were registered as soldiers or peasants and put to work to defend the borders of the tsardom or to feed the tsar's subjects. The wives or husbands of the convicts and any children who were still minors travelled at state expense to join the exiles in their new places of perpetual banishment. Others were released back to their former positions in life, but under the watchful eyes of their families, masters, or neighbours, who were obliged to sign sureties guaranteeing their good behaviour. Tsarist decrees enumerated ever harsher penalties for repeat offenders, and the deterrent appears to have been effective, at least to the point that few recidivists appear in the surviving records. One elderly fortune-teller mentioned that she had served two earlier stints of penance and reeducation in a convent, but otherwise few of the accused make repeat appearances in the archives.

20.2 CONCEPTIONS OF WITCHCRAFT: ABSENT DEMONOLOGY

Just as the law was inconsistent in its definitions of, and responses to, witchcraft, so the theology and general conceptualization of witchcraft were ambiguous and amorphous. Neither the treatises of ecclesiastical elites nor the accusations and confessions of ordinary people contained any consistent demonology. While unclean spirits, demons, and even Satan himself make appearances, there was no effort either from above or below to tie up the loose ends into a systematic theory of magic or to represent witches as enjoying any particular relationship with the devil. Internal evidence suggests that most magic was tacitly understood to work by analogy or homology. Spells normally invoked the power of likeness ('as a log withers in the fire, so may my master wither; as a corpse feels no pain, so may my tooth not ache'), or called on the personified avatars of emotional states to visit their power on their target ('Go, woe, and make that slave of God pine for me'). With the simple ingredients of an herbal pharmacopeia, practitioners invoked the immanent powers of plants' familiar names (heartwort for heart problems; Mary-Mother-of-God plant for childbirth-related issues) or of their appearance (a red root for blood flow; a heart-shaped flower for heart disease).[2] Supernatural beings also entered in the mix: incantations invoked the assistance of relevant saints and Christian intercessors, demons, spirits, and 'unclean' or 'unknowable forces', and even, rarely, of Satan, with these assorted supernatural agents promiscuously jumbled together, heedless of their widely varying origins, genres, registers, and valences. Spells addressed to devils and demons treated them as submissive agents, carrying out the bidding of the practitioner, not as dreaded embodiments of evil or as manifestations of the 'Enemy of Mankind'.

Russian theorists and theologians expressed little interest in formulating a coherent demonology, so the absence of such a programmatic understanding among the broader population is not at all surprising. Conclusions about popular magical practice derive largely from the accusations and confessions of the accused and from spell books and ingredients introduced as material evidence in court. Confessions are notoriously slippery forms of evidence, given the combination of torture and leading questions that could distort the testimony. Nonetheless, trial transcripts give reason to believe that suspects were given quite free rein in their testimony, so long as they answered the questions that the court considered most relevant. Judges questioned their suspects to determine: who taught them their witchcraft, whom had they taught, whom had they bewitched, and what kind of witchcraft they practised. Never in the seventeenth century and only occasionally in the eighteenth century, after the Petrine legislation, did judges ask leading questions in the demonological mode commonly endorsed by European judges, such as 'when did you make a pact with the devil?'

20.3 CHARACTERISTICS OF THE ACCUSED

What rendered an individual vulnerable to witchcraft charges? What traits or behaviours raised suspicions and impelled Muscovites to lodge accusations in court? People of absolutely every social standing participated in early modern Russia's lively world of witchcraft and magic, up to and including the tsar himself, the women of the royal court, and pre-eminent churchmen, boyars, princes, and princesses. Denunciations for witchcraft were most commonly exchanged among social equals or directed down the social scale, towards social inferiors. In the eighteenth century, the arrow of accusation tipped slightly, and A. S. Lavrov even argues that instances of upwards accusation came

---

[2] A. B. Ippolitova, *Russkie rukopisnye travniki XVII–XVIII vekov: issledovanie fol'klora i etnobotaniki* [*Russian Herbal Manuscripts of the Seventeenth–Eighteenth Centuries: Research in Folklore and Ethnobotany*] (Moscow, 2008).

to dominate.[3] While elites regularly consulted with magical practitioners and employed their services, more humble people were commonly identified as the purveyors of those services, and simple townspeople, serfs, and slaves were most harshly persecuted. Men were more likely than women to be brought to trial. Three quarters of those prosecuted for witchcraft or magic were male. Among those of lower standing, non-Russian and non-Orthodox subjects of the empire were at slightly higher risk. Tatars, Cheremis (a Finnic people, also called Mari), Latvians, or Lithuanians, and non-Christians (Muslims, or animists) found themselves susceptible to accusation, especially if they lived in close proximity to Russians. For the most part, however, the magic practised by non-Christians was understood as different from Russian magic. Non-Russian sorcerers were usually termed *volkhvy*, an ancient word employed to describe pagan seers or biblical magi.

Another group at high risk included individuals who seem to have merited the charges, that is, people who were reputed to dispense some form of magical assistance, as healers, prognosticators, or providers of spells, and those who threatened or boasted publicly about their powers. In a society with essentially no professional physicians trained in what passed for scientific, Western-style medicine, the bulk of the population had no choice but to rely on the power of the clergy and prayer or to turn to the services of healers.[4] Healers ranged from a friend, neighbour, or family member who happened to know of a soothing tea, a curative plant, or an incantation that had proved efficacious in the past, to specialists who accrued large stocks of roots and herbs, collected books of spells, and attracted clientele from a wide area. Desperate clients confessed to consulting such people in order to heal their children from disease, win the love of their husbands or masters, or restore family members from the torment of spirit possession. Healers might enjoy the confidence of their patients until a cure went awry, at which point the slur of witchcraft might arise, particularly if money had changed hands. A number of healers found themselves accused of causing illness by sprinkling salt at crossroads or casting spells on the wind, and then charging to cure the conditions they themselves had caused. Muscovites did not articulate or observe any clear-cut divisions between good and evil or white and black magic, but few cases of benign magic or successful healing were brought to court, and the death penalty was reserved for those charged with magical murder or treason.

[3] A. S. Lavrov, *Koldovstvo i religiia v Rossii: 1700–1740 gg* [*Witchcraft and Religion in Russia: 1700–1740*] (Moscow, 2000).

[4] Eve Levin, 'Healers and Witches in Early Modern Russia', in Yelena Mazour-Matusevich and Alexandra S. Korros, eds, *Saluting Aron Gurevich: Essays in History, Literature and Other Related Subjects* (Leiden, 2010), 105–33.

20.4 A MALE MAJORITY

It would be convenient to argue that more men than women practised magic or healing, and to explain the gender disparity among the accused in that way. Since just about everyone seems to have practised or employed magic in some form or other, however, it is hard to establish a gender breakdown of the general pool of practitioners and their clients. Only those who were identified in court documents are visible, which brings us to the puzzling male majority among the accused. Prescriptive sources might lead us to expect instead an association of witchcraft with women. For instance, clerical treatises dwelled disapprovingly on the tendency of women to invite witches into their homes to cure their children, suggesting that this was seen as a particularly female proclivity. Linguistically, it must be significant that the term *baba*, meaning elderly lower-class woman, also connoted 'witch'. Nonetheless, the evidence of the courts indicates that men were the ones more often charged, whether or not they were more actively engaged in casting spells or indulging in other forms of magic.

The frequency with which men or women practised or employed magic in the population as a whole remains impossible to quantify by gender, but other characteristics and behaviours help to explain the preponderance of men among the accused. First, charges frequently targeted individuals perceived as insubordinate or defiant of accepted hierarchies, uppity troublemakers like Ivashka Ryzhei, who had the temerity to try to win any woman he wanted, even his landlord's wife. While women certainly found ways to express defiance, their movement in the world was generally so constrained that they had fewer venues in which to do so.[5] Muscovy and early imperial Russia were profoundly hierarchical societies, in which everyone was subject to and bound to serve and obey others, whether within the family, the serf- or slave-owning household, the village or town collective, the regiment, the church or monastic order, or the tsarist administration. All of these levels of domination and subordination were clear and manifest to all, established by law and reinforced by practice. Those who did not fit in an obvious way disturbed the harmony of the communities they encountered. Wandering people, people without assigned masters, people with no identifiable place of residence drew the suspicion of both the authorities and the general public. Outsiders whose fit in the social hierarchy was uncertain were vulnerable to the suspicion of witchcraft or of other misdeeds, which helps to explain the non-negligible presence of non-Russians among the accused.

Strangers, however, were not the only ones at high risk. Another noteworthy subset of accusations reflected the same preoccupation with social stability, but targeted, by contrast, the most intimate of insiders: family members, in-laws, household servants, or domestic slaves. These cases record the anxieties of commanding officers, masters,

---

[5] W. F. Ryan, 'The Witchcraft Hysteria in Early Modern Europe: Was Russia an Exception?' *Slavonic and East European Review*, 76 (1998), 49–84.

husbands, or sons-in-law who feared and suspected the curses and spells of rebellious inferiors. Fathers accused their sons of betraying filial piety through egregious acts of witchcraft. Landlords and estate bailiffs feared the magical retribution of angry serfs and slaves. Tsars interpreted challenges to their rule as acts of sorcery.

Subaltern figures apparently shared their masters' and patrons' view of magic as a medium through which social order could be managed and enforced, but of course they addressed it from the other end of the stick (or knout). The masters were right to be suspicious: a significant number of surviving spells and courtroom confessions reveal that magic was directed upwards from below towards the powerful. Spells were imagined as a way of navigating and ameliorating the conditions of subordination. While those in charge feared that their servants and dependants might use spells to bewitch, harm, or kill them and their loved ones, the accused confessed more commonly to adopting magical means to alleviate the violence or mitigate the hardship of their subordination. Stratification and hierarchy were universally understood and accepted as natural, but the terms on which they were enacted were constantly disputed. Magic was deployed when fathers and masters exceeded the tolerable norms of patriarchal governance. By the same token, accusations of magic served to rein in the rebellion of noncompliant subordinates.

The fierce inequities of hierarchy played out in interestingly different ways for men and women. While all Muscovites were subordinate to someone—even the tsar was expected to serve God in humility and piety—women generally answered to fewer masters. Men enjoyed greater licence to move about the realm, whether trading goods or looking for employment, fulfilling the biddings of their masters, going on pilgrimage, or serving the tsar in various capacities. In these movements, they encountered more opportunities to clash with more layers of authorities, and risked more occasions to incur accusations of witchcraft. Women by and large stayed at home, serving husbands, fathers-in-law, or masters. They wandered into fewer settings where suspicions of witchcraft might arise. Their circle of contact was more constrained, and those cases against women that did come to court bear traces of the more intimate context that produced them. The charges of witchcraft levelled against women by their immediate superiors often carried more emotive charge and revealed more ferocious levels of domestic violence than the rather more impersonal charges brought against men by their superior officers or business rivals.

Literacy factored into witchcraft accusations as another element freighted with gender-specific implications. In a society distinguished by its extremely low literacy rates, the power of writing was closely controlled by Church and state. In the wrong hands, rampant literacy might threaten the ability of the established authorities to control the written word. Hence, numerous cases emerged from bureaucratic–administrative circles, from low-level functionaries, monks and village priests, government clerks, or bailiffs and managers on provincial estates who had mastered the dangerous skills of reading and writing and might produce and disseminate seditious literature, forged documents, blasphemous texts, or magical spells. A sizeable number of the accused drew suspicion because they were known to collect pieces of paper or little notebooks covered with 'unknown writing'. Literacy was nearly exclusively a male prerogative, and hence the correlation between literacy and magic placed far more men than women at risk of accusation.

Russian Orthodoxy also contributed to a less gendered and, in particular, less female, understanding of witchcraft. Orthodox teachings and assumptions about women, witchcraft, the body, and sex differed sufficiently from common wisdom throughout Protestant and Catholic Europe to render the Western Christian logic of witchcraft inapplicable, and to make the association of women with witchcraft unnecessary or even unlikely. For instance, affective, sensory connections with the divine were generally valued above learned, rational theology, levelling the spiritual playing field for men and women. Although Eve was the target of lavish condemnation in Russia as in the West, sexual desire was not associated particularly with Eve or her daughters; all humans were assumed to suffer from this lamentable weakness. Celibacy, though admirable, was not considered the only pious path, and the married clergy served as an acknowledgement that allowances must be made for flawed mortals. Orthodox readings of the Fall of Man reflected the general preoccupation with order and hierarchy by stressing the couple's shared defiance of God's commands over their sexual transgression. More to the point, sexuality was not woven into the mythology of witchcraft, so whether sexual desire was considered in gendered terms or not, it figured little in the image of a witch.[6]

20.5 WITCHCRAFT SCHOLARSHIP IN RUSSIA AND THE SOVIET UNION

The study of witchcraft in Russia reflects in microcosm the tumultuous and often painful cultural and political history of that country in the past several centuries.

Across the nineteenth and twentieth centuries, people who studied witchcraft often invested the topic with potent and dangerous significance. Nineteenth- and early twentieth-century nationalists, reformers, and radicals, like many of their counterparts throughout Europe, went out to 'the folk' to collect their beliefs, stories, and practices, and they drew highly political conclusions about the condition of the national soul from the material they collected. As a rule, ethnographers and folklorists working in the nineteenth and early twentieth centuries assumed that the peasants could be read as timeless repositories of an ancient and authentic heritage. They read magical practices as continuing an unbroken tradition of archaic Slavic paganism, which, they claimed,

---

[6] Valerie Kivelson, 'Sexuality and Gender in Early Modern Russian Orthodoxy: Sin and Virtue in Cultural Context', in John-Paul Himka and Andriy Zayarnyuk, ed., *Letters from Heaven: Popular Religion in Russia and Ukraine* (Toronto, 2006), 100–25.

ran unchecked alongside and beneath a thin veneer of Orthodox Christianity.[7] The militantly atheist and determinedly rationalist Soviet regime took a very different tack: research and publication on the topic ground to a halt after the Revolution of 1917 and began again, tentatively, only in the late 1970s. Since 1991 and the collapse of the Soviet Union, publication has picked up apace, but necessarily still bears the imprint of a seventy-plus-year hiatus.

Culturally, for Russians and those who study its history, Russia's relationship with the rest of Europe has long been an animating question, and it remains a problem of urgent concern as Russians define themselves in the wake of the fall of the Soviet Union. Russian thinkers have agonized over the question of whether they are part of Europe, or, if not, whether their unique socio-cultural formations were inferior to those of the West, or, perhaps, morally and ethically superior. From its very inception, the study of witchcraft and witchcraft trials was swept into the general urge to compare Russia with a mythologized and homogenized vision of an imaginary West. Comparison with European witchcraft and witch-hunts, often argued in strongly polemical tones, forms one major axis along which research on Russian magic and witchcraft has developed.

Historians, as opposed to ethnographers, began publishing on the topic of Russian witchcraft and magic only in the last quarter of the nineteenth century, and made their first major contributions in the early decades of the twentieth, just prior to the Revolution. Once they discovered that their ancestors too had tried and executed witches in the early modern era, the comparative significance of that discovery took on pressing importance and drove the historical study of Russian witchcraft in several unproductive directions. By the time Russian researchers took up the subject, burning witches was understood to be a cruel, misguided practice. Thus, various scholars tried to assess how Russian trials and punishments measured up to a Western template, in order to assess Russia's relative moral standing. Here the evidence posed a troubling dissonance between the story told by the numbers and that told by the records of the trials. The total numbers of recorded trials that survive is relatively small, surprisingly small given the size of the population. Records of a meagre five hundred trials survive from the century and a half between 1611 and the 1760s, while the population reached roughly ten million in 1700. The low numbers spawned three disparate and mutually contradictory conclusions: first, that Russia's persecution was milder than Europe's, indicating an admirable tolerance of folk practices and non-doctrinal beliefs; second, that Russia must necessarily have launched a full-blown witch-hunt (to keep up with its more civilized neighbours!), and therefore thousands of trial records must have been lost; or, third, given the weaknesses and institutional inadequacies of the Russian Church and state, that witches were dispatched unceremoniously by local, extra-legal

---

[7] S. Maksimov, *Nechistaia nevedomaia i krestnaia sila* [*Unclean, Unknown, and Christian Force*] (St Petersburg, 1903). See also A. N. Afanas'ev, *Poeticheskie vozzreniia slavian na prirodu: spravochno-bibliograficheskie materialy* [*The Slavic Poetic Visions of Nature: Material for a Bibliographic Guide*], ed. T. A. Agapkina, V. Ia. Petrukhin, and A. L. Toporkov (Moscow, 2000).

collectives, on manorial estates or by community lynch mobs, thus leaving no trace in the written record.

The imputed 'mildness' of Russian witch-hunting does seem to be borne out at least quantitatively: the arguments maintaining that vast numbers of records have vanished or that witches were treated to rough community justice do not hold up under scrutiny. If many trials had occurred but were not preserved in the central archives, provincial archives would contain records of at least some of the missing cases, but those provincial archives that survive hold few, if any, cases not preserved in Moscow. Thus the central archival holdings represent more or less complete material on all formal trials of witches. As for informal or local justice, the claim is, on the face of it, implausible: the Russian regime was notorious for its ambition to monopolize all judicial power and to control behaviour throughout its realm to an extraordinary degree. Although much of this ambition remained merely aspirational, lynch mobs and unauthorized killings would inevitably have provoked investigations and produced reams of paperwork to record their findings. Violent assaults on suspected witches were investigated and prosecuted in the nineteenth century, once witchcraft was no longer judged a felony in official courts, but no such investigations for unsanctioned killings survive from earlier eras, when accusers could still be certain of receiving a hearing in court. Extra-legal solutions were simply not necessary, given the courts' willingness to address witchcraft charges. As for manorial justice, the numerous cases brought by landlords against their own peasants and slaves demonstrate that judges and litigants alike acknowledged the jurisdiction of the tsar's courts over matters of witchcraft. The low numbers, though undoubtedly incomplete, seem likely to reflect a genuinely small number of trials.

On the other hand, the self-congratulatory claim to 'mildness' shatters when the particulars of Russian legal process come into focus. N. Ia. Novombergskii, the real founder of historical witchcraft studies in Russia, observes in the introduction to his publication of trial materials, 'This struggle [against witchcraft] was [carried out] with no less cruelty than in western Europe: in the struggle with witches, Muscovite Rus' suffered the same general terrorizing investigation, torture, and public burning of those convicted of witchcraft.'[8]

The Russian Revolution put a stop to all research on witchcraft and related subjects. The field was preserved in amber in its pre-1917 state through most of the Soviet era. The Bolshevik regime and its later Soviet incarnations frowned upon research into religion and other forms of 'superstition'. In 1929, for instance, a book on folk healing was condemned as a 'most pernicious book', 'in no way differentiating itself from prerevolutionary ethnographic literature created by agents of tsarism, lackeys of the

---

[8] N. Ia. Novombergskii, *Koldovstvo v Moskovskoi Rusi XVII veka* [*Witchcraft in Muscovite Rus of the XVIIth Century*] [Materialy po istorii meditsiny v Rossii (Material in the History of Medicine in Russia), v. 3, pt. 1] (St Petersburg, 1906), rpt. *Slovo i delo gosudarevy*, ii: *Materialy. Prilozhenie: Koldovstvo v Moskovskoi Rus XVII-go stoletiia* [*Material. Appendix: Witchcraft in Muscovite Russia of the XVIIth century*] (Moscow, 2004).

bourgeoisie and the nobility'.[9] The prohibition of such research amounted to more than a discouraging academic environment: in 1930–1, dozens of leading humanists engaged in the study of medieval Russian history and culture were arrested and sent to hard labour camps in connection with the so-called 'Academic Affair'. Among others, L. V. Cherepnin, a young specialist on medieval sources who had recently published a serious article on Muscovite witchcraft, was arrested and sent to the camps in the Russian north for several years. He was one of the lucky ones, in that he survived and returned to a long and distinguished life of scholarship in Moscow—but he never again returned to such risky topics.[10] Not surprisingly, research into such dangerous areas ceased for almost forty years.

Only in the 1960s and 70s did a handful of scholars take the first tentative steps back into the area of popular religion, mostly under the protective guise of something else. In 1965, for instance, A. I. Klibanov published a study of popular religious sectarianism, a slightly safer topic when cast as a branch of the history of radicalism and protest. His further studies of popular utopian movements appeared in series such as 'Scientific-atheistic literature' under the auspices of the Academy of Sciences.[11] Archeologists, perhaps granted somewhat greater licence because of the material base of their research, began to delve into the history of Slavic paganism in the early 1980s. Philologists entered the field a bit later, contributing valuable works on the border between linguistics and folklore. The ethnolinguist N. I. Tolstoi, for instance, published influential articles on Slavic and Baltic folklore, which included material on magic and witchcraft.[12]

    [9] *Sovetskaia etnografiia*, 1/2 (1931), 59–60; quoted in L. N. Vinogradova, 'Put'' v nauke ot 'serebrianogo veka' fol'kloristiki do epokhi 'velikikh preobrazovanii' [Path of Scholarship from the 'Silver Age' of Folklore Studies to the Epoch of 'The Great Transformation'], in E. N. Eleonskaia, *Skazka, zagovor i koldovstvo v Rossii: sb. Trudov [Folktales, Spells, and Witchcraft in Russia: Collected Works]*, ed. L. N. Vinogradova (Moscow, 1994), 17.

    [10] L. V. Cherepnin, 'Iz istorii drevnerusskogo koldovstva XVII v.' [From the History of Old Russian Witchcraft of the Seventeenth Century], *Etnografiia*, 2 (1929), 86–109. His biography is documented in V. D. Nazarov, 'Lev Vladimirovich Cherepnin', in G. N. Sevost'ianov and L. T. Mil'skaia, eds, *Portrety istorikov: Vremia i sud'by*, i: *Otechestvennaia istoriia* (Moscow, 2000), 285–303. For a brief biography of a contemporary of Cherepnin's, the ethno-folklorist E. N. Eleonskaia, see Vinogradova, 'Put'' v nauke'. On Cherepnin in the Academic Affair, see *Akademicheskoe delo, 1929–1931 gg.: dokumenty i materialy sledstvennogo dela, sfabrikovannogo OGPU [The Academic Affair, 1929–1931: Documents and Materials from the Investigation Fabricated by the OGPU]*, ed. Zh. I. Alferov and V.P. Leonov (St Petersburg, 1993–8), ii, pt. 1, pp. xxxi–xxxiii.

    [11] A. I. Klibanov, *Istoriia religioznogo sektantstva v Rossii, 60-e gody XIX v.–1917 g. [History of Religious Sectarianism in Russia from the 1860s to 1917]* (Moscow, 1965); Klibanov, *Religioznoe sektantstvo v proshlom i nastoiashchem [Religious Sectarianism in the Past and Present]* (Moscow, 1973). By the late 1980s and 1990s, the atmosphere had changed significantly, allowing Klibanov to publish an edited collection, *Russkoe pravoslavie: vekhi istorii [Russian Orthodoxy: Milestones of History]* (Moscow, 1989); and his single-authored *Dukhovnaia kul'tura srednevekovoi Rusi [Spiritual Culture of Medieval Rus']* (Moscow, 1996).

    [12] Archeologists: T. V. Nikolaeva and A. V. Chernetsov, *Drevnerusskie amulety-zmeeviki [Old Russian Snake Amulets]* (Moscow, 1991); B. A. Rybakov, *Iazychestvo drevnikh slavian [Paganism of the Ancient Slavs]* (Moscow, 1994); philologists: N. I. Tolstoi, *Ocherki slavianskogo iazychestva [Essays on*

For the most part, until the early 1990s, historical research within Russia moved in patterns quite distinct from those in the West. A small number of Western scholars were working on witchcraft-related topics right through the years of the Cold War, and some limited intellectual dialogue crossed the divide. Most significant of the works produced in the Anglo-American literature was Russell Zguta's article, 'Witchcraft Trials in Seventeenth-Century Russia', which appeared in the *American Historical Review* in 1977.[13] Zguta's analysis garnered much attention both from specialists studying witchcraft in other areas of the world—in whose bibliographies his article figures as the citation of choice on Russian witchcraft—and from colleagues gingerly touching on the subject in the Soviet Union. Zguta's examination of published court cases isolated two salient axes of difference between Muscovite trials and those prosecuted in the courts of Europe: the majority of accused witches were male, and the devil was imagined to play a very limited role in their work.

As perestroika began to take effect and the ideological holds of Marxism–Leninism and Scientific Atheism relaxed their grip, scholars from a variety of disciplines edged into the newly accessible field of study. For the most part, the terrain was occupied by ethnographers, along with 'archeographers', a hybrid specialty of ethnographer–philologist who hunted for rare books and manuscripts in remote villages, and catalogued and described them in their cultural context. These field-workers were gratified to find that the pre-revolutionary traditions of popular belief in spirits, magic, and witchcraft remained alive and well in the post-Soviet country-side.[14] In short, they took up their pre-revolutionary predecessors' work right where it had been cut short.

The resurgence of interest in folk practices, spirituality, and popular belief lends an aura of liberation and triumph to the work taking shape in the post-Soviet era. Field research has turned up evidence of remarkable survivals of beliefs and practices despite the repression and disruption of the twentieth century, and of newly minted occult practices that take advantage of the world of twenty-first century possibilities offered by globalization and the Internet.[15] Yet inevitably this post-Soviet boom bears the mark of

Slavic Paganism] (Moscow, 2003); interdisciplinary contributions: R. A. Simonov, A. A. Turilov, A. V. Chernetsov, *Drevnerusskaia knizhnost: estestvennonauchnye i sokrovennye znaniia v Rossii XVI v., sviazannye s Ivanom. Rykovym [Old Russian Literary Culture: Natural Scientific and Occult Knowledge in Russia in the 16th Century, associated with Ivan Rykov]* (Moscow, 1994).

   [13] Russell Zguta, 'Witchcraft Trials in Seventeenth-Century Russia', *American Historical Review*, 82 (1977), 1187–207; and his 'Was there a Witch Craze in Muscovite Russia?' *Southern Folklore Quarterly*, 41 (1977), 119–28.

   [14] Archeographers: I. V. Pozdeeva and E. B. Smilianskaia, eds, *Mir staroobriadchestva [The World of Old Belief]* (Moscow, 1992); E. B. Smilianskaia and N. G. Denisov, *Staroobriadchestvo Bessarabii: knizhnost i pevcheskaia kultura [Bessarabian Old Belief: Book Culture and Singing Culture]* (Moscow, 2007).

   [15] On the question of persistence and invention, see Faith Wigzell, 'The Dreambook in Russia: Persistence and Popularity', *History Workshop Journal*, 48 (1999), 114–32; Galina Lindquist, *Conjuring Hope: Magic and Healing in Contemporary Russia* (New York, 2005).

the seventy-year stasis. Deprived of ongoing cross-fertilization with the international scholarly community, the first efforts to renew the study of witchcraft and folk belief dove in where late nineteenth and early twentieth-century methods and findings had left off. Most significantly, as A. V. Chernetsov notes, recent Russian publications often lack the rigorous historicism that would allow them to differentiate beliefs and practices of one period from another.[16] With the techniques of late imperial ethnography in mind, Russian philologists and ethnographers are often highly attuned to regional, geographic variation, but tend to show little interest in exploring issues of change over time. The temptation to read evidence from the last century or last week into the distant past, to assume a timeless continuity in peasant belief, continues to win adherents.

In the very last years of the Soviet Union, a new generation of more historically minded scholars began to work in the history of Russian witchcraft. In Moscow, an active circle coalesced in the 1990s, although the first salvo may have come from Novosibirsk, where, in 1987, N. N. Pokrovskii found a notebook of magical spells from 1734 and published an analysis of it in a journal, tellingly titled 'Scientific Atheism, Religion, and Current Times'.[17] Since the late 1990s, Russian scholars have produced an explosion of articles, edited collections, source publications, and monographs too numerous to review here individually. One of the first of this new boom to appear was O. D. Zhuravel's study, *The Motif of the Pact with the Devil in Old Russian Literature*. The book concentrates on literary representations of the satanic pact, which the author traces back through early medieval Slavic translations to Byzantine sources. From those imported beginnings, the motif took root within Russian culture, as evident in a spate of indigenous reworkings of the idea as an important plot element in saints' lives, miracle tales, and in the popular fiction that began to develop in manuscript culture in the early modern period. Turning to trial evidence, Zhuravel' shows that the concept of the satanic pact had spread beyond a narrow circle of literate clerics and cultured elites, and had begun to make incremental inroads into popular imagination by the seventeenth and eighteenth centuries.[18]

The first decade of the twenty-first century has witnessed an energetic push to republish old classics on witchcraft and has also produced a crop of new studies of witchcraft and magic, both within Russia and its former subject states and outside of it.

---

[16] See A. V. Chernetsov's review of A. L. Toporkov's, 'Zagovory v russkoi rukopisnoi traditsii' [(Spells in the Russian Manuscript Tradition], *Drevniaia Rus. Voprosy medievistiki*, 3(41) (2010), 85–104. Toporkov, however, brings a clear awareness of historical specificity to his work, as do Chernetsov himself and most of the authors listed below.

[17] N. N. Pokrovskii, 'Tetrad' zagovorov 1734 goda' [A Notebook of Spells of 1734], in *Nauchnyi ateism, religiia i soveremennost* (Novosibirsk, 1987), 239–66.

[18] O. D. Zhuravel', *Siuzhet o dogovore chelovekom s d'iavolom v drevnerusskoi literature* [The Plot Motif of the Pact with the Devil in Old Russian Literature] (Novosibirsk, 1996). An analysis of a fully developed satanic case is presented in A. T. Shastov, 'Iakutskoe delo o koldune Ivane Zheglove' [The Iakustsk Trial of the Witch Ivan Zheglov], in *Obshchestvennoe soznanie, knizhnost', literatura perioda feodalizma* (Novosibirsk, 1990), 83–8.

A. V. Chernetsov and A. A. Turilov's examination of the mysterious 'Rafli', a prohibited prognosticatory text that evoked much concern and grave censure among
Muscovite churchmen, paints a rich picture of the intellectual and textual world of
early modern Russian writers. A. L. Toporkov extends this work on the literary traces
of early modern magic with his studies of the literary tropes, poetic forms, biblical and
more ancient pagan borrowings, and uses of spells. His publications present large
numbers of spells that survive in spell books, in trial records, or interleaved into other
kinds of texts such as herbals or books of healing. A. B. Ippolitova's 'ethnobotanical'
study of the various herbs and plants named in spells and herbal remedies identifies the
plants, catalogues their uses, and speculates on the nature of the cures and of the magic
powers invested in them.[19]

Two important monographs analyse eighteenth-century trial records, each from a
very different angle. A. S. Lavrov presents a deeply researched account of witchcraft in
the formal conventions of the law and in the actual process of prosecution. His
Witchcraft and Religion in Russia situates early eighteenth-century trials of witches
in a broader context of popular religiosity and attempts at its regulation. Capturing a
sense of popular belief and practice is always a challenge, all the more so given the
limitations of early modern Russian sources, but Lavrov succeeds admirably. By
situating witchcraft as one among many explicitly *religious* matters, however, Lavrov's
approach yields an unintended side effect: the religious framing pre-empts the still-
open question of whether or not witchcraft and magic fell into the realm of religion in
the eyes of contemporaries. E. B. Smilianskaia treats witches, blasphemers, and heretics
all together, but she considers the applicability or meaning of the category of 'spiritual
crime' in each context. Her analysis, built on an impressive archival base, emphasizes
the everyday worldly worries and tribulations that underlay the use of magic in its
social context. Her psychological acuity, along with her vivid writing, brings to life the
experiences of the men and women who populate her case studies.[20]

During the late Soviet years and into the post-Soviet period, Anglo-American
authors working in the area of Russian magic for the most part adhered to the
ethnographic–folkloric approach established before the Revolution. Noteworthy
among these works are Linda Ivanits' compendium and efficient discussion of Russian
folk beliefs, and Andreas Johns' psychologically informed analysis of Baba Yaga, the

---

[19] On Rafli and The Gates of Aristotle, see A. L. Toporkov and A. A. Turilov, eds, *Otrechennoe chtenie
v Rossii XVII–XVIII vekov* [*Forbidden Reading in Russia, XVII–XVIII centuries*], (Moscow, 2002);
A. A. Turilov and A. V. Chernetsov, 'Otrechennaia kniga Rafli' [The Forbidden Book Rafli], *Trudy
Otdela drevnerusskoi literatury*, 40 (1985), 260–344; A. L. Toporkov, *Zagovory v russkoi rukopisnoi
traditsii XV–XIX vv.: istoriia, simvolika, poetika* [*Spells in Russian Manuscript Tradition of the Fifteenth-
Nineteenth Centuries: History, Symbolism, Poetics*] (Moscow, 2005). A useful guide to the subjects of
spells is: V. L. Kliaus, *Ukazatel' siuzhetov i siuzhetnykh situatsii zagovornykh tekstov vostochnykh i
iuzhnykh slavian* (Moscow, 1997). Ippolitova, *Russkie rukopisnye travniki XVII–XVIII vekov*, op. cit.

[20] Lavrov, *Koldovstvo i religiia v Rossii*; E. B. Smilianskaia, *Volshebniki, bogokhul'niki, eretiki:
narodnaia religioznost' i 'dukhovnye prestupleniia' v Rossii XVIII v.* [*Witches, Blasphemers, Heretics:
Popular Religiosity and 'Spiritual Crimes' in Eighteenth-Century Russia*] (Moscow, 2003).

classic Russian fairytale witch. The most important recent publication in the field, Will Ryan's magisterial survey of magical beliefs and practices throughout Russian history, *The Bathhouse at Midnight*, draws on many disciplines, combining ethnography, philology, folklore, and history, and has had a major impact across international boundaries. The book appeared in English in 1999 and in Russian translation in 2006, making quite a splash in both incarnations.[21]

Other Western works in related areas include Faith Wigzell's book on fortune-telling since the eighteenth century, and Eve Levin's elucidation of the porous line separating religion from magic, prayer from incantation, and Christianity from its various opposites. Claudio Sergio Ingerflom elucidates the importance of magic in fueling popular rebellion. My own work on seventeenth-century trials also explores the centrality of magic in Muscovite political thought, using witchcraft as a lens for better understanding the assumptions, values, and practices of Muscovite culture, society, politics, and law. Building on Zguta's observations about the inverted gender profile of Russia's accused and the absence of systematic demonology, my research explores the implications of these findings.[22]

A particular branch of witchcraft literature concerns the phenomenon of spirit possession, which shared many common characteristics with manifestations found throughout the world, but which took on particular Russian colouring. Christine Worobec's 2001 monograph, *Possessed: Women, Witches, and Demons*, traces changing understandings of the phenomenon of 'shrieking' or demon possession (*klikushestvo* or *besoderzhimost'*) across four centuries. Possession figures in few early modern trials, but appears prominently in saints' lives, miracle tales, and iconography. It remained a noteworthy phenomenon in Russia through the early twentieth century, and seems to be enjoying a renaissance in post-Soviet Russia. Worobec's book still holds pride of place as the definitive work on possession in Russia, but recently other scholars have been venturing into the field.[23]

At present, the old political divides are no longer operative, and the circulation of scholarly works, speeded along by the marvels of Internet technology, is producing far

[21] Linda J.Ivanits, *Russian Folk Belief* (Armonk, NY, 1989); Andreas Rainer Bormann Johns, *Baba Iaga, the Ambiguous Mother of the Russian Folktale* (New York, 2004); W. F. Ryan, *The Bathhouse at Midnight: Magic in Russia* (University Park, PA, 1999); Ryan, *Bania v polnoch': istoricheskiĭ obzor magii i gadanii v Rossii* (Moscow, 2006); Ryan, 'The Witchcraft Hysteria in Early Modern Europe: Was Russia an Exception?' *Slavonic and East European Review*, 76 (1998), 49–84.

[22] Faith Wigzell, *Reading Russian Fortunes: Print Culture, Gender, and Divination in Russia from 1765* (Cambridge, 1998); Eve Levin, '*Dvoeverie* and Popular Religion', in Stephen K Batalden, ed., *Seeking God: The Recovery of Religious Identity in Orthodox Russia, Ukraine and Georgia* (Dekalb, IL, 1993), 31–52; and Levin, 'Supplicatory Prayers as a Source for Popular Religious Culture in Muscovite Russia', in Samuel H. Baron and Nancy Shields Kollmann, eds, *Religion and Culture in Early Modern Russia and Ukraine* (DeKalb, IL, 1997), 96–114; Valerie Kivelson, *Desperate Magic: The Moral Economy of Witchcraft in Seventeenth-Century Russia* (Ithaca, NY, forthcoming).

[23] Christine D. Worobec, *Possessed: Women, Witches, and Demons in Imperial Russia* (DeKalb, IL, 2001); Ekaterina Mel'nikova, 'Otchityvanie besnovatykh: praktiki i diskursy' [Exorcizing the Demon-possessed: Practices and Discourses], *Antropolicheskii Forum*, 4 (2006), 220–63.

more fruitful intellectual exchange. Happily, it no longer makes sense to separate two streams of 'Russian' and 'Western' scholarship, and the kinds of questions addressed in the literature are broadening, departing from the constraining tracks of earlier historiography. In a 2010 article on 'Law and Religion in Muscovite Russia', for instance, Boris Uspenskii makes witchcraft the revealing focus of his exploration of the essence of Muscovite law, and argues, in conversation with scholars from all over, that the crime of witchcraft was feared primarily as a form of physical or material harm, rather than as a threat to the immortal souls of Orthodox Christians.[24]

Emerging from the forced hibernation of the seventy years of Soviet rule, the study of witchcraft has awakened at an auspicious time, when scholars of European witchcraft are welcoming comparative studies of witchcraft in other parts of the globe. A new generation of post-Soviet scholars is bringing fresh questions to bear on familiar and on newly discovered sources. Trained in both Russian and European traditions, equally at home in the Russian archives and at international scholarly forums, fully conversant with Russian and Western languages and literatures, these historians, philologists, and ethnographers are producing work at a level that promises to bring Russian witchcraft into engaged and productive conversation with witchcraft research writ large.[25]

20.6 CONCLUSION

A finite number of comparative questions have preoccupied scholars of Russian witchcraft, which has produced some good work but overall has constrained the field of inquiry and shut off the possibility of exploring less conventional aspects of the problem. Both as a vehicle for understanding Russia itself and for illuminating the phenomenon of witchcraft comparatively, Russian witchcraft study is poised on the brink of tremendous breakthroughs. As the topic opens out more organically in the coming years, it promises fresh insights into the inner workings of Muscovite and imperial society. Among many possible directions, it offers access to the normally inaccessible realms of domestic life, affective experiences, somatic and physical states. Explorations of attitudes towards the body expressed by judges, torturers, and

[24] Boris Uspenskii, 'Pravo i religiia v Moskovskoi Rusi' [Law and Religion in Muscovite Russia], in E.I. Pivovar, ed., *Rossica/Rusistika/Rossievedenie* (Moscow, 2010), 194–286. Operating on a far more abstract and highly theoretical hermeneutic plane, A. L. Iurganov's recent book, *To Kill the Devil: The Path from the Middle Ages to Modern Times*, situates Muscovite demonology in a narrative of modernization; A. L. Iurganov, *Ubit' besa: put' ot Srednevekov'ia k Novomu vremeni* (Moscow, 2006).

[25] For example, working on Ukrainian witchcraft, Kateryna Dysa, 'Orthodox Demonology and the Perception of Witchcraft in Early Modern Ukraine', in Jaroslav Miller and László Kontler, eds, *Friars, Nobles and Burghers—Sermons, Images and Prints. Studies of Culture and Society in Early-Modern Europe. In Memoriam István György Tóth* (Budapest, 2010), 341–60; and her *Witchcraft Trials and Beyond: Trials for Witchcraft in the Volhynian, Podolian and Ruthenian Palatinates of the Polish–Lithuanian Commonwealth in the Seventeenth and Eighteenth Centuries* (Budapest, 2011).

executioners, and embedded in spells and magical rituals may allow Russianists to engage with themes in the history of the body, so fruitfully developed in other literatures. The intellectual and theological dimensions, the gendered context and assumptions, the changing role of social status in a time of rapid cultural transformation, all of these themes are ripe for analysis.

The Russian example provides an ideal control group to counterpose to more familiar European histories of witchcraft belief and persecution. Russia offers a case study of a European Christian society practicing a different variant of Christianity, an anomaly in the expected gender distribution, a culture fully immersed in witchcraft and magic but largely uninterested in witches' connection with Satan. As Russianists will benefit from a more nuanced and carefully differentiated sense of what witchcraft connoted in the 'West', the introduction of a fully fleshed out Russian literature into the general corpus of witchcraft scholarship will add depth and richness to our general understanding of the phenomenon of witchcraft.

FURTHER READING

Ivanits, Linda J., *Russian Folk Belief* (Armonk, NY, 1989).

Kivelson, Valerie, *Desperate Magic: The Moral Economy of Witchcraft in Seventeenth-Century Russia* (Ithaca, NY, forthcoming).

Lavrov, A. S., *Koldovstvo i religiia v Rossii: 1700–1740 gg.* [*Witchcraft and Religion in Russia: 1700–1740*] (Moscow, 2000).

Levin, Eve, 'Dvoeverie and Popular Religion', in *Seeking God: The Recovery of Religious Identity in Orthodox Russia, Ukraine and Georgia* (Dekalb, IL, 1993).

Levin, Eve, 'Supplicatory Prayers as a Source for Popular Religious Culture in Muscovite Russia', in Samuel H. Baron and Nancy Shields Kollmann, eds, *Religion and Culture in Early Modern Russia and Ukraine* (DeKalb, IL, 1997), 96–114.

Levin, Eve, 'Healers and Witches in Early Modern Russia', in Yelena Mazour-Matusevich and Alexandra S. Korros, eds, *Saluting Aron Gurevich: Essays in History, Literature and Other Related Subjects* (Leiden, 2010), 105–33.

Lindquist, Galina, *Conjuring Hope: Magic and Healing in Contemporary Russia* (New York, 2005).

Novombergskii, N. Ia., *Slovo i delo gosudarevy*, ii: *Materialy. Prilozhenie Koldovstvo v Moskovskoi rusi XVII-go stoletiia* [*Material. Appendix: Witchcraft in Moscovite Russia of the XVIIth century*] (Moscow, 2004).

Ryan, W. F. *The Bathhouse at Midnight: Magic in Russia* (University Park, PA, 1999).

Smilianskaia, E. B. *Volshebniki, bogokhul'niki, eretiki: narodnaia religioznost' i 'dukhovnye prestupleniia' v Rossii XVIII v.* [*Witches, Blasphemers, Heretics: Popular Religiosity and 'Spiritual Crimes' in Eighteenth-Century Russia*] (Moscow, 2003).

Toporkov, A. L. *Zagovory v russkoi rukopisnoi traditsii XV–XIX vv.: istoriia, simvolika, poetika* [*Spells in Russian Manuscript Tradition of the 15th–19th centuries: History, Symbolism, Poetics*] (Moscow, 2005).

Toporkov, A. L. and Turilov, A. A., eds, *Otrechennoe chtenie v Rossii XVII–XVIII vekov* [*Forbidden Reading in Russia of the XVII–XVIII Centuries*] (Moscow, 2002).

Uspenskii, Boris, 'Pravo i religiia v Moskovskoi Rusi' [*Law and Religion in Moscovite Russia*], in E.I. Pivovar, ed., *Rossica/Rusistika/Rossievedenie* (Moscow, 2010), 194–286.

Worobec, Christine D. *Possessed: Women, Witches, and Demons in Imperial Russia* (DeKalb, IL, 2001).

Zguta, Russell, 'Witchcraft Trials in Seventeenth-Century Russia', *American Historical Review*, 82 (1977), 1187–207.

Zhuravel', O. D., *Siuzhet o dogovore chelovekom s d'iavolom v drevnerusskoi literature* [*The Plot Motif of the Pact with the Devil in Old Russian Literature*] (Novosibirsk, 1996).

CHAPTER 21

....

WITCHCRAFT CRIMINALITY AND WITCHCRAFT RESEARCH IN THE NORDIC COUNTRIES

....

RUNE BLIX HAGEN

THE five Nordic countries—Iceland, Norway, Denmark, Sweden, and Finland—were all involved in the European witch-hunts in the early modern period. Although the prosecutions in the entire region reached a peak between 1620 and 1660, trials took place both in earlier and later periods. Taking into account the total population of the Nordic countries at the beginning of the seventeenth century, which was estimated at about 2,200,000 inhabitants, the number of trials was considerable. There are no exact figures for the number of individuals formally charged with witchcraft in one form or another, but almost 1,200 death sentences have been recorded.

Although the Nordic countries constitute an integrated geographical area and have many similar institutions and cultures, the witch trials held in the individual countries varied in many respects. Some regions had a preponderance of men among those charged, while in others a number of indigenous people were indicted. The most intense prosecutions took place in Dalarna in Sweden in the period 1668–76—often referred to as the Blåkulla trials—and in four chain-reaction witch-hunts in a very sparsely populated coastal area in Øst-Finnmark in the most north-eastern part of Norway between 1621 and 1663.

The following table, *Executions of witches in the Nordic world*, provides estimates of the number of executions in the five Nordic counties in relationship to their populations. Although the figures are based on recorded cases, they must still be regarded as estimates.

Table 21.1 Executions of Witches in the Nordic world

Country	Execution	Population c.1600
NORWAY	310	400,000
DENMARK	400	570,000
ICELAND	22	50,000
SWEDEN	+ 300	800,000
FINLAND	120	350,000

A key development in the historiography of witchcraft in the Nordic countries was the publication of *Häxornas Europa*, edited by Bengt Ankarloo and Gustav Henningsen, in 1987. An English version was published in 1989 under the title *Early Modern European Witchcraft: Centres and Peripheries*. The book originated in a symposium held in Stockholm in 1984. The conference emphasized a comparative approach to the subject, and this resulted in the identification of many regional variations throughout Europe, especially those on the 'periphery' of Continental Europe. The book raises interesting challenges for the history of witchcraft, through explaining the cultural lag in the adoption of European demonology in the Nordic countries, and determining the degree of the state's involvement in the prosecutions, and it has become a foundational work for the study of witchcraft trials on the geographical fringes of Europe. In it, the American historian E. William Monter, one of the veterans in the field of witchcraft research, made some broad comparisons between witchcraft in Scandinavia and the British Isles. He described Norwegian witches in a few words as specialists in nautical witchcraft and uncritically repeated Trevor-Roper's long-standing claim that the Sami minority population was not affected by the violent trials in Finnmark.[1] Apart from a few general remarks about Sweden, Denmark, and Finland, Monter actually had little to say about the Nordic cases. This reflected the fact that, until the 1980s, Nordic historians had published very little in English. Only within the last few years have

---

[1] William E. Monter, 'Scandinavian Witchcraft in Anglo-American Perspective', in Bengt Ankarloo and Gustav Henningsen, eds, *Early Modern European Witchcraft: Centres and Peripheries* (Oxford, 1990), 430. All together the three counties that make up the northern region of Norway—Nordland, Troms, and Finnmark—prosecuted thirty-seven Sami individuals from 1593 to 1695. Of these, twenty men and eight women were burned at the stake for practising witchcraft. Between 1639 and 1749, in the regions of Swedish and Finnish Lapland, at least seventy-three Sami males but only three Sami females were prosecuted on charges of using drums and practising sacrificial rituals. Few of them received death penalties, however. For the cases of northern part of Finland and Sweden, see Karin Granqvist, '"Thou Shalt Have No other Gods before Me (Exodus 20:3)": Witchcraft and Superstition Trials in Seventeenth- and Eighteenth-century Swedish Lapland', in P. Sköld and K. Kram, eds, *Kulturkonfrontation i Lappmarken* (Umeå, 1998), 13–29. The different patterns of witch-hunting among the indigenous people of Norway, Finland, and Sweden highlight some very interesting issues. Prosecutions apparently became more severe in northern Norway because they took place at an earlier stage in the seventeenth century than in Finnish and Swedish Lapland. The differences in chronology should, moreover, be seen in context with the state power strategies of penetration and expansion in the areas up north.

English-language contributions come from Nordic historians, as they are gradually beginning to relate research in the field to international trends.

The legal dimension of witchcraft in the Nordic countries was one of the main subjects of the meeting of Nordic historians in Oslo in 1994. The papers at this conference focused on the courts' interaction with local communities. The Danish historian Jens Chr. V. Johansen gave an account of key findings in Nordic witchcraft research, identifying differences among the trials in the Nordic countries with regard to context, chronology, structure, and legal foundation. Johansen emphasized the fact that Nordic witchcraft cases originated in the local community and that most of the cases were tried in the ordinary secular courts. The Blåkulla trials in Sweden were the exception, since many of the cases there were judged by special witchcraft courts established by royal commissions. Chronologically, Denmark tried the largest number of Nordic witches in the first part of the seventeenth century, while the other countries adjudicated most of their cases in the second half of that century. One of Johansen's themes is the role of the clergy, and he makes the interesting observation that Norwegian, Swedish, and Icelandic local priests played a far more direct and active role in the course of the trials than did Danish priests.[2]

After several decades of local studies of witchcraft prosecutions, the pattern of Nordic witchcraft research appears to be moving towards that of comparative regional studies. Several such works have been carried out by Norwegian researchers in recent years, such as Liv Helene Willumsen's English-language dissertation of 2008, in which she compares the pattern of trials in the Danish–Norwegian county of Finnmark with similar witch-hunts in Scotland.[3] A postgraduate thesis by Ellen Janette Alm compared the role of the state in the witchcraft trials in Denmark and Norway.[4] In a similar vein, a thesis by Birger Andreas Marthinsen investigated accusations of sorcery against men in Iceland and Norway.[5] The Danish historian Louise Nyholm Kallestrup has published a comparative study of witch-hunts in Italy and Denmark, establishing the differences and similarities between the inquisitorial procedures used by the ecclesiastical courts in Italy and those followed by the secular courts in a Protestant country.[6] The Swedish historian Per Sörlin should also be mentioned in this context for

---

[2] Jens Christian V. Johansen, 'Trolddom', in Sølvi Søgner, ed., Rapport II, *Normer og sosial kontroll i Norden ca. 1550–1850* (Oslo, 1994), 98; Johansen, *Da Djævelen var ude ... trolddom i det 17. århundredes Danmark* [*When the Devil was Loose ... Witchcraft in Seventeenth Century Denmark*] (Odense, 1991).

[3] Liv Helene Willumsen, 'Seventeenth-Century Witchcraft Trials in Scotland and Northern Norway', Ph.D. thesis, University of Edinburgh, 2008.

[4] Ellen Janette Alm, 'Statens rolle i trolldomsprosessene i Danmark og Norge på 1500- og 1600-tallet' [The Role of the State during the Witch Trials in Denmark and Norway in the Sixteenth and Seventeenth Centuries: A Comparative Study], unpublished dissertation, University of Tromsø, 2000.

[5] Birger Andreas Marthinsen, *Trollmenn and Galdramenn: En undersøkelse av trolldom blant anklagede menn i 1600-tallets Norge og Island* [*Sorcerers: An Investigation of Sorcery among Men in Seventeenth-Century Norway and Iceland*] (Trondheim, 2010).

[6] Louise Nyholm Kallestrup, *I pagt med Djævelen: Trolddomsforestillinger og trolddomsforfølgelser i Italien og Danmark efter Reformationen* (Copenhagen, 2009). See also Further Reading for her article in English on the same topic.

his comparison of the involvement of children in the prosecutions of witches in Dalarna, Sweden, and in the Basque country.[7]

The crime that witches in Nordic countries had allegedly committed was usually identified as *trolldom* (sorcery). The correct legal term for the perpetrator was therefore *trollkvinne* (sorceress) and *trollmann* (sorcerer) respectively, with *trollfolk* (sorcerers) being used for the plural. The modern umbrella term *heks* (witch) was first introduced in Denmark, Norway, Iceland, and Sweden towards the end of the seventeenth century, and was thus not used in any of the laws against sorcery, and appeared very seldom in trial records.

Old legal documents from the Nordic countries describe sorcerers—or *trolls* as they are popularly referred to—as beings that people should avoid. For example, the ancient Norwegian Christian statutes from the eleventh and twelfth centuries contain a clear ban on contacting such *trolls* or seeking knowledge from them. Moreover, in Norway's and Iceland's first land laws, passed in 1276 and 1281 respectively, such contact was perceived as a very serious breach of law that carried the strictest penalty. The law forbids anyone to, as they say, 'sit outside to wake trolls'.[8]

The American historian Stephen A. Mitchell is the only scholar who has systematically conducted research on sorcery and witch-hunts in the Nordic countries during the pre-Reformation period. He uses saga texts, ancient legislation, and diploma material from the Middle Ages. Mitchell argues that the persecution of sorcerers before the era of the witch-burnings occurred in all the Nordic countries without exception. The sentences were relatively mild, and women were, for the most part, treated more leniently than men. Magical activities during the late Middle Ages were clearly linked to gender: women were often accused of magic connected to love and of offences connected to sexuality, while typical accusations against men concerned heresy and acts that reflected a political agenda. Women did not form a clear majority among the few people who were punished for sorcery prior to the Reformation.[9]

21.1 SWEDEN

The violent Swedish witchcraft trials in the period 1668–76 reverberated throughout large parts of the Western world. At that time the events became known far beyond Sweden's borders through pamphlets translated into various languages, one result of

---

[7] Per Sörlin, 'Djävulens barn: de nordsvenska och baskiska häxprocesserna under 1600-talet' [The Devil's Children: Witch Trials in Northern Sweden and the Basque Country during the Seventeenth Century], in Andreas Östborn, ed., *Dalarnas Häxprocesser* (Uppsala, 2000), 43–65.

[8] Gunnar W. Knutsen and Anne Irene Riisøy, 'Trolls and Witches', *ARV: Nordic Yearbook of Folklore* Vol. 63 (2007), 64; Stephen A. Mitchell, *Witchcraft and Magic in the Nordic Middle Ages* (Philadelphia, PA, 2011), 21, 214.

[9] Stephen A. Mitchell, 'Gender and Nordic Witchcraft in the Later Middle Ages', *ARV: Nordic Yearbook of Folklore*, Vol. 56 (2000), 17–18.

which was that it had some significance for the outbreak of the witch-hunt at Salem in New England in 1692. More than a hundred women were executed in Sweden in the course of eight years, as well as several children and a few men, for having visited Blåkulla and carousing with Satan and his demons. The prosecutions are usually referred to in the historical literature as the Blåkulla trials.[10] What was shocking about these trials were the tales of witches who had induced several small children to take part in the witches' sabbath in Blåkulla, a somewhat vague geographical location in the far north. During the years the trials took place, several thousand Swedish children appeared in local courts and bore witness against close relatives and neighbours. The prosecutions originated in the eastern parts of Dalarna. At the time of the trials there were twice as many women as men in this region, partly because of conscription to the Swedish army. Records also show that there were strong, emancipated, and independent women residing in Dalarna. Many of the women who were accused of witchcraft came from middle-income to wealthy farming families. An uneven division of the sexes, with a large proportion of single women and widows, might have posed a threat to patriarchal norms and social order. A large number of unmarried women could also have contributed to social unrest and increased the number of accusations.[11]

Swedish scholars have done the most important recent work on witchcraft trials and magic in the Nordic countries. In *Varken Gud eller natur* (Neither God nor Nature), published in 1999, the historian Linda Oja explores Swedish popular beliefs regarding magic. She establishes that there were significant changes in thought on the question of magic within a period of two hundred years, from the beginning of the seventeenth century until the end of the eighteenth century. Her book provides the first substantial investigation of the mentality and culture of a Nordic country regarding magic. The book represents an innovative venture that greatly broadens the comparative rationale for similar investigations in other Nordic countries.

Per Sörlin's monograph *Trolldoms- och vidskepelseprocessena i Göta hovrätt 1635–1754* (Wicked Arts' Witchcraft and Magic Trials in Southern Sweden 1635–1754), published in 1993, is based on an empirical study of 353 trials for witchcraft, and the less serious crime of magic, in the period. Sörlin uses this empirical data to test three explanatory models that have been prominent in recent decades in the field of Western witchcraft research: 1) the acculturation model; 2) the conflict model; and 3) the system model. In the preface Sörlin explains that he wrote the book as a response to some of the witchcraft studies of the 1980s in which the acculturation thesis was a key

---

[10] Bengt Ankarloo, 'Witch Trials in Northern Europe 1450–1700', in Bengt Ankarloo, Stuart Clark, William Monter, eds, *The Period of the Witch Trials* (London, 2002), 85–90, and Per Sörlin, 'Mora Witches', in Richard M. Golden, ed., *Encyclopedia of Witchcraft: The Western Tradition*(Santa Barbara, CA, 2006), iii, 783–5.

[11] Bengt Ankarloo, 'Witch Trials in Northern Europe', 74, see also Per Anders Östling, *Blåkulla, magi och trolldomsprocesser. En folkloristisk studie av folkliga trosföreställningar och av trolldomsprocesserna inom Svea Hovrätts jurisdiktion 1597-1720* [*Blåkulla, Magic, and Witchcraft Trials: A Folkloristic Study of Popular Belief and the Witch Trials in the Jurisdiction of Svea Circuit Court 1597-1720*] (Uppsala, 2002), 322.

component. By studying less serious witchcraft criminality in areas where prosecutions did not develop into panics, Sörlin concludes that the trials cannot be explained by the imposition of elite ideas on those of the broader population. Elites may have been more influential in cases from south Sweden, but their objectives had more to do with imposing discipline and control than acculturating, civilizing, or assimilating the rural population. He also shows that such cases did not often originate in crisis and conflict. Sörlin is of the view that it is most advantageous to study these witch cases on their own merit, that is, as independent episodes that follow their own logic. Sörlin's work supports the argument that the trials in Dalarna have, for far too long, been central to witchcraft research. As the Norwegian historian Gunnar W. Knutsen argues, 'the "Blåkulla" trials in the seventeenth century have dominated awareness of witch trials in Sweden, thus displacing other issues'.[12]

In *Livet går vidare* (Life Goes On), published in 1996, the historians Marie Lennersand and Linda Oja offer yet another new departure in Nordic witchcraft studies by investigating how small local communities dealt with the consequences of the witchcraft trials. They show that in the aftermath of the witchcraft crisis in Dalarna, local communities entered what could be characterized as a state of emergency. In the two communities of Älvdalen and Rättvik the trials led to a long and impenetrable silence. Local authorities consciously adopted this strategy to bring the crisis to an end and prevent new outbreaks of witch-hunting. Lennersand and Oja point out, however, that silence is not synonymous with forgetting, atonement, or total obliviousness.[13] Behind the decision to change the perception of conflict lies an acknowledgement that the witchcraft trials caused greater social insecurity than the activities of the local witches.

21.2 FINLAND

In the early modern period Finland constituted the eastern part of the Swedish principality. Almost two thousand people were formally accused of sorcery in the period 1520–1750. Approximately 120 of these were sentenced to death, and most of the sentences were imposed in the period 1649–84.[14] Witchcraft prosecutions in Finland did not conform to a single national pattern. A wave of witch trials at the end of the 1670s and the early 1680s took place in the aftermath of the Swedish Blåkulla trials, and involved a large number of women. Other trials further east in the country prosecuted more traditional pre-Christian forms of magic. The material contains a considerable number of sorcerers and consists of individual cases rather than a chain of trials. The

---

[12] Gunnar W. Knutsen, 'The Decline and End of Witch Trials in Scandinavia', *ARV: Nordic Yearbook of Folklore*, 62 (2006), 158.

[13] Marie Lennersand and Linda Oja, *Livet går vidare: Älvdalen och Rättvik efter de stora häxprocesserna 1668–1671* (Hedemora, 2006), 186.

[14] Marko Nenonen, 'Finland', in *Encyclopedia of Witchcraft*, ii, 376.

total number of men prosecuted for these crimes was exceptionally high, giving Finland one of the highest percentages of male witches in all of Europe. However, it is important to emphasize that this proportion was still less than 50 per cent of the total. The legal historian Marko Nenonen has emphasized the regional difference between west and east Finland in this respect. Elements of diabolism were almost absent in the cases from the Karelen area in the east, where witches were usually tried for traditional sorcery, which was often practised by men. 'The further from the west coast a trial was held, the more often men were accused', writes Nenonen. Men, moreover, were accused of malevolent sorcery, whereas women were often charged with practising healing magic.[15]

The underlying context of *Witchcraft and Gender in Early Modern Society* (2008) by the Finnish historian Raisa Maria Toivo is the web of folklore, gossip, and rumours, and how folklore currents were connected to the practice of different kinds of magic. One of the main goals of the study is to reconstruct the agency of a woman accused of witchcraft. Using the narrative of a peasant woman named Agata Pekantytär, Toivo discusses issues relating to household, family relations, power, and early modern women's living conditions in small farming communities. The book studies witchcraft prosecutions that did not involve the use of torture or develop into large panics. The charges against Agata and her sisters in this south-western region of Finland do not include references to the witches' sabbath or pacts with the devil. In other words, the study is not about diabolical witchcraft, but about individual cases that originated in social quarrels and disagreements among neighbours. Diabolical elements figure in only a small minority of all witch trials in Finland, and have been blown out of proportion in the historiography of European witchcraft. Toivo criticizes historians of witchcraft for painting far too grim a picture of the trials because they take 'the most gruesomely exceptional circumstances as the basis of their studies, the German witch-crazes'.[16]

21.3 ICELAND

In parts of Finland, in Iceland, and among the Sami people in Fennoscandia, witchcraft trials were linked to traditional magic that was primarily, but not exclusively, associated

[15] Marko Nenonen, 'Witch Hunts in Europe: A New Geography', *ARV: Nordic Yearbook of Folklore*, 62 (2006), 165–86; Nenonen, 'Finland', in *Encyclopedia of Witchcraft*, ii, 373–7. On the basis of findings not only from Finland but from other East European countries, Marko Nenonen has criticized the idea of what he calls 'the western European paradigm of witch-hunt historiography', and his critical assessments of a narrow geographical perspective has provoked an ongoing and unfinished debate. For discussions see H. C. Erik Midelfort, 'Witch Craze? Beyond the Legends of Panic', *Magic, Ritual, and Witchcraft*, 6 (2011), 11–33; and Valerie A. Kivelson, 'Lethal Convictions: The Power of a Satanic Paradigm in Russian and European Witch Trials', in *Magic, Ritual, and Witchcraft*, 6 (2011), 34–61.

[16] Raisa Maria Toivo, *Witchcraft and Gender in Early Modern Society: Finland and the Wider European Experience* (Aldershot, 2008), 167.

with men. In spite of a knowledge of gender-linked demonological works, such as the *Malleus maleficarum*, and legislation that identified witchcraft as diabolism, more than 160 men and only fifteen women were involved in cases in Iceland, and the devil's pact was hardly mentioned at all. A total of twenty-one men and *one* woman were sentenced to death and burnt alive. Iceland is, however, the Nordic country where knowledge of witchcraft cases is poorest. This might be due to the fact that the research on the subject has been limited, but also because little has been translated into other languages.

Like Norway, Iceland belonged to the Danish-dominated kingdom of Oldenburg. The Danish sorcery legislation of 1617 was extended to Iceland after 1630, and most of the trials were there held after that time. The 1617 legislation amended archaic witchcraft perceptions, placing them in a learned demonological context, but had no proven effect on the specific Icelandic cases. There is probably a clear correlation between trials based on medieval legislation and the high number of men involved in the cases. A type of magic that is more closely described in older statutes than in the diabolically inspired texts from the 1600s was attributed to men. The use of torture, including the water ordeal, was not known in the Icelandic cases.

The first witch-burnings in Iceland occurred in 1625, while the last execution took place in 1683.[17] After this time all death sentences had to be re-examined by the Supreme Court in Copenhagen. The main accusations in the Icelandic trials concern sorcerers who had allegedly cast a spell to inflict unnatural illnesses on their neighbours. Witches were also charged with injury to domestic animals, exorcism, illegal healing, and shipwrecks resulting from bad weather. Magical symbols were referred to in several of the cases, as well as grimoires and remedies, such as runic letters and occult writings. In his work on magic books, Owen Davies observes that 'the one place in Europe where grimoires did feature in the witch trials was Iceland'.[18] The most distinctive feature of witchcraft prosecutions in Iceland was the belief that sorcery was a body of traditional knowledge that operated in the masculine sphere. Furthermore, there was little diabolism in these charges: Icelandic sorcerers did not allegedly fly around in the air or participate in witches' sabbaths. Most of the cases arose in the western fjords, and individuals such as the dean Páll Björnsson (1621–1706) took the initiative in most of the serious cases in the 1660s and 1670s. The dean also wrote a short text called *Character bestiæ*, in which he quoted from *Malleus maleficarum*.

21.4 DENMARK

Despite the inadequacy of the sources, it seems clear that most of the witchcraft trials in Denmark took place in the period 1617–25. The law against sorcery was promulgated in

---

[17] Magnùs Rafnsson, *Angurgapi: The Witch-hunts in Iceland* (Hólmavík, 2003), 25–6.

[18] Owen Davies, *Grimoires: A History of Magic Books* (Oxford, 2009), 31, 71; see also Mitchell, *Witchcraft and Magic*, 47–8.

1617, and the increase in persecution was a direct consequence of the legislation.[19] Even though nearly four hundred people were sentenced to death, huge chain-reaction witch-hunts occurred rarely in Denmark. Denmark had prominent theologians who wrote about sorcery, but the more elaborate forms of witchcraft never gained a firm footing among the secular persecutors. As in Norway, there were no reports of sexual promiscuity or cannibalism, but other manifestations of diabolism, such as finding the devil's marks on the accused, appear in several cases. The prosecutions originated in everyday conflicts with neighbours, and the women had often had the reputation of being witches for a long time, indicating that the majority of those prosecuted were somewhat older, infertile, and married women.

Relatively little work has been done on Danish witch-hunting in the past two decades, but two works by Danish scholars have made important contributions to the field. The first is Louise Nyholm Kallestrup's comparison of witchcraft trials in a Catholic and a Protestant region of Europe during the early modern period. *I pagt med Djævelen* (In Pact with the Devil) suggests that there were relatively few similarities. Sorcery was regarded as a very serious crime in the sixteenth and seventeenth centuries in both Denmark and Italy, and the theological concept of magic held a central position among the authorities in both countries. All types of magic—white as well as black— were believed to be the work of the devil. Another common feature of witchcraft prosecutions in the two countries was that charges of sorcery originated in the general population.

The Italian cases mainly concentrate on magic related to love, which is almost absent in the Danish cases where bewitchment, that is, malevolent sorcery, is the essence. This disparity in the type of magic that was handled by the courts could also been seen in the great differences in sentences imposed. The strictest and most severe penalty for sorcery in Orbetello, Italy, was whipping in the streets followed by banishment, while several cases in north Jutland, Denmark, resulted in the imposition of the death sentence. The section of the book that concerns the general public's perception of witchcraft gives a good portrayal of the fact that ordinary people viewed magic as an inherent quality of human beings, believing magical powers could be intensified by invoking supernatural spirits of some kind of demonic or divine aspect.

Kallestrup finds that the main difference lies in the two fundamentally dissimilar systems of law, a difference that plays a major role in bringing people to trial and in sentencing them. The Inquisition perceived witchcraft as a religious offence that involved heresy and apostasy. For the inquisitors the trials were, therefore, about atonement, and the goal was to lead the sinner back on the right track through re-Catholicization. In Denmark there was also a religious dimension to witch-hunting, but the crime was viewed as a secular offence. It was not only prosecuted in the secular courts, but the use of accusatorial procedure ensured that the charges originated in the social and economic relationships among villagers rather than in the spiritual concerns

---

[19] Jens Christian V. Johansen, 'Denmark', in *Encyclopedia of Witchcraft*, i, 266.

of inquisitors. Witchcraft gained a clearer mundane and physical quality in Denmark than it did in Italy while malevolent sorcery motivated by revenge made witchcraft a more serious crime in the former in the seventeenth century. Finally, Kallestrup emphasizes the important Catholic difference between implicit and explicit pacts with the devil as an explanation of the Inquisition's mildness compared with the numerous sentences of burning to death in Denmark. Diabolism, however, was not a prominent feature in either Danish or Italian witchcraft trials, so the differences between the nature of the charges brought against Danish and Italian witches were arguably not as striking as the book claims.

A major work published in 2000 by the archivist and historian Tyge Krogh illustrates the ruling elite's gradual acknowledgement of the ideology that lay behind the public authorities' understanding of law and punishment.[20] In the context of witchcraft, Krogh writes about the final phase of witchcraft trials in Denmark and Norway. The demonstration of power and religious understanding manifested through painful and spectacular punishments is a key theme. Krogh's concept of magic is related to the perception of the anger the criminal aroused in 'our Lord' and thus the fight against everything that could invoke the wrath of God in the form of war, suffering, and pestilence. Krogh derives his broad and rather ahistorical concept of magic from anthropology, more precisely from Mary Douglas, who includes the practice of religion in the definition of magic.

The work's most comprehensive part, on the actual conclusions of judgement, focuses on the theological dimension that provides the framework for the interweaving of worship, absolute power, natural philosophy, and the penal system. Krogh discusses the importance of Lutheran orthodoxy, Pietism, and other religious movements for the understanding of criminal law. Although the development of law making and handling cases moved towards jurisprudence, forcing religion aside in the deliberations of justice, it was not until 1754 that the king stopped consulting the Faculty of Theology in serious cases. A separate chapter on crimes against religion discusses the extent to which the king was bound by the penal provisions of the Pentateuch in cases concerning heresy, pacts with the devil, sorcery, and blasphemy. The debate on the applicability of the Law of Moses shows that new fields of thought were gradually infiltrating the minds of scholarly theologians and their counselling. The last death sentences in Danish and Norwegian witchcraft trials were imposed during the 1690s, and towards the middle of the eighteenth century theologians and jurists gradually rejected so-called crimes against religion.

---

[20] Tyge Krogh, *Oplysningstiden og det magiske: henrettelser og korporlige straffe i1700-tallets første halvdel* [*The Enlightenment and the Magical: Executions and Corporal Punishments in Denmark in the First Half of the Eighteenth Century*] (Copenhagen, 2000).

21.5 NORWAY

In proportion to its population of approximately 440,000 in 1665, a relatively large number of Norwegians were prosecuted for witchcraft. From the 1560s until the beginning of the eighteenth century more than 750 named men and women were formally accused of breaches of the Danish–Norwegian laws against sorcery. About 310 of these were sentenced to death, 80 per cent of whom were women. Stricter penalties were usually imposed on women than men. It is worth noting that these statistics are based on cases for which we have documentary evidence; the legal archives of the seventeenth century are inadequate for several Norwegian areas.

Norwegian witchcraft cases have been the subject of commentary since the beginning of the seventeenth century, but historical research based mainly on archival records began only the 1980s. Since then scholars have transcribed and published a considerable amount of source material and have also produced numerous local studies and some general historical studies.[21] So far legal history has dominated research in the field, but cultural history is gradually beginning to gain ground.

Norwegian witchcraft trials began around 1560, with the most intense period of prosecution lasting from about 1620 to 1665. The frequency of cases gradually decreased towards the end of the seventeenth century. The last death sentence was imposed in Kvæfjord in the county of Troms in 1695. A woman by the name of Johanne Nielsdatter had renounced God, her holy baptism, and Christianity and had surrendered herself to the devil. She was receiving diabolical assistance and strength from a demon called Knut, who acted as a personal servant. Johanne confessed to having caused the death of four persons and injured the health and limbs of a number of others by means of witchcraft. In addition she was said to have perpetrated many evil deeds by various means. The judgement of 14 November 1695 decreed that Johanne was to be thrown alive into the flames and burnt to death. The court based its legal authority for the prosecution on Article 9 of the first chapter of Christian V's Norwegian law of 1687. Johanne is thus among the very few sorcerers in Norway who were sentenced on the basis of that judicial code.[22]

Although several people were sentenced on the basis of strict sorcery laws in the late sixteenth and the early seventeenth centuries, most of those in Norway were tried under the main Danish–Norwegian laws against sorcery that came into force in the

---

[21] Among source publications, Liv Helene Willumsen's monumental transcription of court records from Finnmark deserves special mention. The English version, *Witchcraft Trials in Finnmark, Northern Norway*, tr. Katjana Edwardsen (Bergen, 2010) is particularly valuable for comparative European research. Other publications include Hilde Sandvik and Harald Winge, eds, *Tingbok for Finnmark 1620–1633* [*Court Book of Finnmark 1620–1633*] (Oslo, 1987); Hans H. Lilienskiold, *Trolldom og ugudelighet i 1600-tallets Finnmark* [*Sorcery and Ungodliness in Seventeenth-Century Finnmark*], ed. Rune Blix Hagen and Per Einar Sparboe (Tromsø, 1998). For further references, see note 28.

[22] Rune Blix Hagen, *Dei europeiske trolldomsprosessane* [*The European Witch Trials*] (Oslo, 2007), 89.

autumn of 1617. The regulations were put into effect by King Christian IV, partly to mark the Protestant state Church's celebration of the one hundred-year anniversary of Martin Luther's publication of his ninety-five theses against contemporary Catholic ideas and practices. As was the case throughout Denmark, the number of witchcraft trials increased in parts of Norway, particularly in the Østland area in the east, during the period 1619–25.[23] The regulations differentiated between various types of witchcraft criminality. Making a pact with the devil was the worst offence and was to be punished by death. Those who practised white magic, so-called *signere* (healers and 'white' witches), were punished with fines and banishment. The clients of these sorcerers, defined as *medvitere* (accomplices), were also punished under the law with milder penalties. Almost one third of Norwegian sorcerers were convicted on the basis of accusations that identified them as either *signere* or *medvitere*.[24]

The Norwegian witch trials were unevenly distributed geographically. As in other places in Europe, one region might experience extensive prosecution while the neighbouring region had almost no experience at all of witch-hunts. The number of trials in the towns was proportionately higher than the size of the urban population throughout the kingdom,[25] and was particularly high in Stavanger and Bergen. Persecution in Bergen, the country's largest town at the time, began very early: there were at least sixteen cases in the town even before the beginning of the seventeenth century.[26] In addition, the confessions in the Bergen cases reflected elements of learned witchcraft beliefs, such as pacts with the devil, witches' sabbaths, and shape-shifting. Finnmark stands out among the counties, both for the scope of its prosecutions and their brutality. With a population of 3,200 Norwegians and Sami people at the end of the seventeenth century, more than ninety people were executed for witchcraft over the course of about sixty years. The entire territory of sparsely populated northern Norway had a total of more than 40 per cent of the recorded death sentences for the entire country. In male-dominated coastal communities such as Vadsø and Vardø, the prosecutions developed into panics and matched some the most terrible witch-hunts on the Continent in intensity. In the worst cases the trials exterminated almost the entire female population in some of the fishing villages. One special feature of the prosecutions in the northern part of Norway was the presence of indigenous people— Sami shamans—among those tried. Moreover, notions of diabolism appeared in many of the confessions. The water ordeal was used in approximately thirty of these cases, whereas this dubious legal procedure is known to have occurred in only a few

[23] Gunnar W. Knutsen, 'Norwegian Witchcraft Trials: A Reassessment', *Continuity and Change*, 18 (2003), 195.

[24] Hans Eyvind Næss, *Trolldomsprosessene i Norge på 1500–1600 tallet* [*The Witch Persecution in Norway during the Sixteenth and Seventeenth Centuries*] (Oslo, 1982), 135.

[25] Næss, *Trolldomsprosessene*, 33.

[26] Ragnhild Botheim, *Trolldomsprosessane i Bergenhus len 1566–1700* (Bergen, 1999), 49.

Norwegian cases outside Finnmark.[27] The strong trading link between coastal Finn-mark and Bergen in the early modern period greatly facilitated the transmission of witch beliefs and there is a clear correlation between cases involving diabolism in Bergen at the end of the sixteenth century and the first large, chain-reaction witch-hunts in Finnmark around 1621.

The first Norwegian scholars to exploit this rich source material were not historians but folklorists, and the folklore emphasis in studying Norwegian witchcraft dominated research in the field until the 1980s. The folklorists did not use legal sources to shed light on the witch trials as such, but rather as evidence of popular prayers of blessing, rituals, and formulas that illuminated witch *beliefs* and concepts of magic among the broader population. The abundant publications from the Institute for Comparative Research in Human Culture, an independent research institution established in 1922, contain much of this type of material. The institute also took the initiative to systemat-ically transcribe and duplicate the Norwegian witchcraft trials from county records, local registers, and other legal records. Today the material forms part of *Norsk Folke-minnesamling*—the national archive for folklorist and cultural history material—at the Department of Cultural Studies and Oriental Languages at the University of Oslo. The entire collection was digitalized and posted on the Internet early in 2010.[28] This database, together with copies of Norwegian witchcraft trial materials, constitutes the most important source of knowledge about Norwegian witchcraft.

The first large-scale publication on witchcraft cases in Norway, *Heksetro og trold-dom: Et studie i norsk heksevæsen* (Witch Belief and Sorcery: A Study of the Norwegian Witchcraft), which appeared in 1971, was written by the Danish folklore researcher Bente Gullveig Alver. The book, which was written in the older folkloric tradition, succeeded in making the subject of Norwegian witchcraft known to the broader Norwegian public.

Alver emphasized the low social status of Norwegian sorcerers. Those who were accused were generally old, single women who were often poor, and frequently earned their living as vagrants. Indeed, as Alver puts it, they were poverty-stricken and at times owned only the tattered clothes on their backs.[29] This description of the poverty of those accused of witchcraft in Norway was accepted and perpetuated until recent times, when the picture has gradually begun to change.

---

[27] Hagen, *Dei europeiske trolldomsprosessane*, 91–2. For an identifier list of all the people involved in the north Norwegian witch trials, see my website <http://ansatte.uit.no/rha003/nnhekser.htm> (accessed 29 October 2012).

[28] <http://www.edd.uio.no/ikos/trolldom.html> (accessed 29 October 2012). See also Henning Laugerud, 'The Collection of Norwegian Witchcraft-trials in the Norwegian Folklore Archives (*Norsk folkeminnesamling*) at the University of Oslo', *ARV: Nordic Yearbook of Folklore*, 65 (2009), 131–41. Most of the old court books are scanned and can be found at the Norwegian digital archives: <http://www.arkivverket.no/arkivverket/Digitalarkivet> (accessed 29 October 2012).

[29] Bente Gullveig Alver, *Heksetro og trolldom: en studie i norsk heksevæsen* (Oslo, 1971), 63; see also the discussion in her book *Mellem mennesker og magter: Magi i hekseforfølgelsernes tid* [*Between Humans and Magical Powers: Magic in the Time of the Witch Persecutions*] (Oslo, 2008), 20–2.

A great advance in Norwegian witchcraft research came with the publication of *Trolldomsprosessene i Norge på 1500–1600 tallet* (Witchcraft Trials in Norway in the Sixteenth and Seventeenth Centuries) by Hans Eyvind Næss in 1982. This book, based on Næss' doctoral thesis, is an empirical study based on archival materials that has a clear quantitative dimension, and has become a foundational work for the study of crime in early modern Norway. By comparing the prosecution of witchcraft with that of other crimes Næss presented an overview of the development of criminality in early modern Norway.

Næss applied the explanatory model of 'social strain' from Macfarlane, as did Alver and a number of other Nordic witchcraft researchers. Deterioration in living conditions and overpopulation led to social tensions and strained limited resources. As Næss portrays it, the turning point came in the 1620s, when the social cohesion and solidarity of many Norwegian local communities began to erode. The pressure to prosecute undesired individuals came from below as the deterioration of relationships among neighbours engendered fear and violence, and provided the social context of the prosecutions. Those who were labelled sorcerers were recruited from poverty-stricken groups. The most common Norwegian witch figure, as Næss describes her, is an elderly, poor, and often married woman. Næss' horrifying portrayal of social and neighbourhood relationships in Norway in the seventeenth century has since been criticized for being oversimplified, too general, and too imprecise.[30] His critics also place greater emphasis on the role of ruling elites in causing witch-hunts.

The historian Sølvi Sogner, who served as Næss' opponent when he defended his dissertation, criticized the work on several grounds. Objecting to his inclusion of slander cases in calculating the total number of witches, Sogner criticized him for overestimating the size of Norwegian witch-hunts. Arguing that he did not pay sufficient attention to the role of the elite, she contended that authorities were primarily responsible for instigating prosecutions at the local level. In this way witchcraft trials became the product of rational Danish–Norwegian state policy.[31] Sogner also emphasized the gender dimension of witchcraft studies, and has been eager to promote the importance of cultural history in studying Norwegian witchcraft.

Næss' article, 'Norway: The Criminological Context', remains the most widely cited source of information about Norwegian witchcraft by non-Nordic scholars. The article appears as an ultra-short version of his doctoral dissertation, but Næss accepted Sogner's criticism of some points, and scaled down his estimate of the number of Norwegian witchcraft trials from 870 to 789.[32]

---

[30] Sølvi Sogner, 'Trolldomsprosessene i Norge på 1500–1600-tallet', *Norveg—Tidsskrift for folkelivsgranskning*, 25 (1982), 155–82.

[31] Sølvi Sogner, 'Trolldomsprosessene', 168–73.

[32] Hans Eyvind Næss, 'Norway: The Criminological Context', in Bengt Ankarloo and Gustav Henningsen, eds, *Early Modern European Witchcraft: Centres and Peripheries* (Oxford, 1990), 373. The figures have been adjusted again in Naess, 'Norway', in *Encyclopedia of Witchcraft*, iii, 836–9.

In the early 1980s Næss maintained that Norway had displayed less scholarly interest in witchcraft prosecutions than any other European country.[33] The claim appeared to hold water—at least up until the later 1990s. Currently it appears that Norwegian witchcraft research is more than equal to that produced in other Nordic countries. In the period from 1984 to 2011 one substantial doctoral thesis and six master's dissertations have focused on the Norwegian witch trials.

All in-depth research in witchcraft trials after 1982 has taken Næss' arguments into account. Regional studies from the eastern, western, and northern parts of Norway have related their findings and explanations to his seminal work. The result has been revision, further elaboration, and a certain change of orientation. An examination of the sources from Finnmark shows that Næss had omitted almost twenty-five cases and recorded others twice.[34] In her study of the county of Bergenhus, Ragnhild Botheim replaced more than 30 per cent of Næss' quantitative material from that part of the country. She writes that the witches of western Norway were a relatively complex group; in particular many women from higher social levels in Bergen were exposed to accusations of malevolent magic.[35] This dissertation thus casts new light on the perception of Norwegian sorceresses as a poverty-stricken group, as well as on the extent of diabolism in Bergen prior to the witch laws of 1617.

Gunnar Knutsen revised 20 per cent of Næss' figures relating to the eastern part of Norway and found that the majority of the death sentences were imposed in the period 1619–25 as a direct consequence of the Danish–Norwegian 1617 regulations. This is a somewhat different pattern from the rest of the country, where the number of trials peaked around 1660. Knutsen finds stronger similarities between the development of trials in Jutland in Denmark and those in the eastern part of Norway, than between the latter and other Norwegian areas. In a related article he concludes: 'Indeed if one looks at witchcraft trials in Norway by county, very few counties actually conform to the pattern for the country as a whole.'[36]

Liv Helene Willumsen's thesis on Finnmark of 1984 (revised in 1994) was distinctive in several ways.[37] Rather than discussing Næss' material, she used it as a basis for taking several interesting approaches, including that of gender analysis. The witches from Finnmark, as revealed from entries in the court records, clearly make up a diverse social group: down-to-earth women among the ordinary people in the fishing villages, and more prosperous wives from the middle ranks of society. The historical witches in the true north were almost always accused of practising malevolent magic and only rarely of dabbling in white magic. Coastal women used magic to control winds and cause shipwrecks, bad weather, and death, or to frighten fish away from the coast. Several

[33] Næss, *Trolldomsprosessene*, 11.
[34] Alm, *Statens rolle*, Appendix., 205–38.
[35] Botheim, *Trolldomsprosessane*, 8–9, 78.
[36] Knutsen, 'Norwegian Witchcraft Trials', 193.
[37] Liv Helene Willumsen, *Trollkvinne i Nord i historiske kilder og skjønnlitteratur* [*Female Witches of the North, in Historical Sources and Fiction*] (Tromsø, 1994).

women used their malevolent powers against county authorities and merchants. They also made pacts with the devil and worshipped him in nocturnal assemblies. The women were accused of having 'bound' themselves to Satan. In other words, diabolism was a key feature of witchcraft trials in Finnmark. On the other hand, the devil that these witches in Finnmark allegedly worshipped did not resemble the devil described at sabbaths in other parts of Europe. For one thing he was rarely sexualized, and the witches did not participate in either sexual orgies or cannibalistic activities when they met at the witches' sabbath on the local Domen mountain pass or elsewhere. Their diabolical activities have a more innocent and festive character. The absence of 'sexual themes' in witchcraft confessions was also a feature in the Danish witchcraft trials.[38] In Swedish trials, however, during the late 1660s and 1670s, sexual motifs were common.[39]

In several contexts Willumsen established similarities between Norwegian and Scottish witchcraft. Her doctoral dissertation at the University of Edinburgh compared the narrative patterns of witchcraft confessions in Finnmark with those in Scotland.[40] Through a close reading of selected cases she identified essential common features in the narrative patterns with regard to folklore, mentality, and witch beliefs. Scottish women and those from northern Norway were both antagonistic towards powerful men. Learned witch beliefs were common in both regions, unlike most other parts of Norway and the British Isles. The issues Willumsen has raised provide an agenda for future research in the field.

Ellen Alm's comparative study of Danish and Norwegian witchcraft trials, *Statens rolle i trolldomsprosessene i Danmark og Norge på 1500- og 1600-tallet* (The State's Role in Witchcraft Trials in Denmark and Norway in the Sixteenth and Seventeenth Centuries) not only compiles a valuable list of the names of sorcerers accused in both countries, but challenges the thesis that witchcraft prosecutions originated in small communities. Alm argues that witchcraft trials in Denmark and Norway originated from above, that is, from the efforts of state authorities to pass witchcraft legislation and take the initiative in prosecutions.[41] She also reveals a number of differences between the two countries in their enforcement of witchcraft legislation. One of these differences is that those who practised white magic in Denmark were prosecuted more frequently and sentenced more harshly than those in Norway.

Nils Gilje's book *Heksen og humanisten: Anne Pedersdatter og Absalon Pederssøn Beyer: en historie om magi og trolldom i Bergen på 1500-tallet* (The Witch and the Humanist: Anne Pedersdatter and Absalon Pederssøn Beyer: A Story of Magic and Witchcraft in Bergen in the Sixteenth Century) uses a famous Norwegian witchcraft case in 1590 to provide a deeper understanding of the intellectual foundations of the trials. He emphasizes the importance of Protestant apocalyptical thought, with its belief that the world was in its Last Days, in giving urgency to the prosecution of witches. He also describes a semiotic cosmos in which magic belonged to a long series

---

[38] Johansen, 'Denmark', 267.   [39] Östling, *Blåkulla*, 318.
[40] Willumsen, 'Seventeenth-Century Witchcraft Trials'.
[41] Alm, *Statens rolle*, 170.

of communicative patterns. In his analysis of the case of Anne Pedersdatter, Gilje sees the witch figure as a social and cultural construct, one that was created by conflict in the neighbourhood and the cumulative notion of witchcraft that had currency among the intellectuals in Bergen towards the end of the sixteenth century.[42]

In my own research I have studied different aspects of the development of witchcraft trials throughout northern Norway, especially in Finnmark. By using a local centre-periphery model, with central political administrative functions in the east and west Finnmark on the periphery, I have studied key variables, such as gender and ethnicity, in the data. For example, west Finnmark appears as one of the few regions in Europe with a majority of men among those persecuted for sorcery, with the Sami people accounting for the large number of male witches. I have also directed attention to Sami witchcraft magic as a manifestation of shamanism, and especially for the impact on what is called Sami shamanism.[43] With regard to the preponderance of Norwegian coastal women in east Finnmark accused of witchcraft, I have interpreted the trials as an effort to demonize rebellious women and destroy potentially dangerous networks among women in the coastal villages.[44]

As discussed earlier in this chapter, one of the main trends in witchcraft research in the Nordic countries has been the publication of studies that compare witchcraft prosecutions within the Nordic countries, or between Nordic countries and other European states. Historians of witchcraft working in national fields outside Norway have also begun to adopt a comparative approach to the study of early modern witchcraft. It is hoped that the meeting of historians from the five Nordic countries in Tromsø in August 2011—to discuss the historiography of Nordic witchcraft studies—will lead to the creation of an active network of researchers, who will encourage work that taskes into account both the similarities and differences between witchcraft prosecutions in the five countries.

FURTHER READING

Ankarloo, Bengt, 'Witch Trials in Northern Europe 1450–1700', in Bengt Anarkloo and Stuart Clark, eds, *Witchcraft and Magic in Europe*, iv: *The Period of the Witch Trials* (London, 2002), 53–95.
Ankarloo, Bengt and Henningsen, Gustav, eds, *Early Modern European Witchcraft: Centres and Peripheries* (Oxford, 1990).

---

[42] Nils Gilje, *Heksen og humanisten: Anne Pedersdatter og Absalon Pederssøn Beyer: en historie om magi og trolldom i Bergen på 1500-tallet* (Bergen, 2003), 247.
[43] Rune Blix Hagen, 'Sami Shamanism: The Arctic Dimension', *Magic, Ritual, and Witchcraft*, 1 (2006), 227–33. See also Rune Blix Hagen, 'Traces of Shamanism in the Witch Trials of Norway: The 1692 Trial of the Sami Shaman Anders Poulsen', in Hans de Waardt, Jürgen Michael Schmidt, H.C. Erik Midelfort, Sönke Lorenz und Dieter R. Bauer, eds, *Dämonische Besessenheit: Zur Interpretation eines kulturhistorischen Phänomens* (Bielefeld, 2005), 306–25.
[44] Hagen, *Dei europeiske trolldomsprosessane*, 118.

ARV: Nordic Yearbook of Folklore, 62 (2006), special issue on witchcraft research in the Nordic Countries, with contributions from Brian P. Levack, Jari Eilola, Per Sörlin, Per Anders Östling, Rune Blix Hagen, Gunnar W. Knutsen, Marko Nenonen, and Raisa Maria Toivo.

Hagen, Rune Blix, 'Lapland', 'Olaus Magnus', 'Shamanism', 'Wind Knots', and 'Weather Magic', in Richard M. Golden, ed., *Encyclopedia of Witchcraft: The Western Tradition*, 4 vols (Santa Barbara, CA, 2006), iii, 625–7, 707–8; iv, 1029–31, 1185–8, 1199–200.

Hagen, Rune Blix, 'Seventeenth-Century Images of the True North, Lapland and the Sami', in Kajsa Anderson, ed., *L'Image du Sápmi* (Örebro, 2009), 138–68.

Kallestrup, Louise Nyholm, 'Lay and Inquisitorial Witchcraft Prosecutions in Early Modern Italy and Denmark', *Scandinavian Journal of History*, 36 (2011), 265–78.

Knutsen, Gunnar W. 'Norwegian Witchcraft Trials: A Reassessment', *Continuity and Change*, 18 (2003), 185–200.

Knutsen, Gunnar W., and Riisøy, Anne Irene, 'Trolls and Witches', *ARV: Nordic Yearbook of Folklore*, 63 (2007), 31–69.

Laugerud, Henning, 'The Collection of Norwegian Witchcraft-trials in the Norwegian Folklore Archives (*Norsk folkeminnesamling*) at the University of Oslo', *ARV: Nordic Yearbook of Folklore*, 65 (2009), 131–41.

Mitchell, Stephen A., *Witchcraft and Magic in the Nordic Middle Ages* (Philadelphia, PA, 2011).

Sörlin, Per, *'Wicked Arts': Witchcraft and Magic Trials in Southern Sweden, 1635–1754* (Leiden, 1999).

Rafnsson, Magnús, *Angurgapi: The Witch-hunts in Iceland* (Hólmavík, 2003).

Toivo, Raisa Maria, *Witchcraft and Gender in Early Modern Society: Finland and the Wider European Experience* (Aldershot, 2008).

Willumsen, Liv Helene, 'Witches in Scotland and Northern Norway: Two Case Studies', in Peter Graves and Arne Kruse, eds, *Images and Imaginations: Perspectives on Britain and Scandinavia* (Edinburgh, 2007), 35–66.

Willumsen, Liv Helene, *The Witchcraft Trials in Finnmark, Northern Norway*, tr. Katjana Edwardsen (Bergen, 2010).

....

CHAPTER 22

WITCHCRAFT IN
BRITISH AMERICA

....

RICHARD GODBEER

FEAR of witches was embedded within the culture that English migrants brought with them as they crossed the Atlantic to settle in North America, and so it is not surprising that witch-hunting became a part of the colonial experience. Over sixty trials for witchcraft took place in seventeenth-century New England, omitting the infamous Salem witch-hunt of 1692, which resulted in over one hundred and fifty formal charges. Accusations of witchcraft occurred throughout the British colonies. But there were far fewer prosecutions in the middle and southern colonies than in New England. There was one execution in Maryland and five in Bermuda, whereas in New England at least thirty-three (and perhaps as many as thirty-five) women and men were hanged as witches.[1] The disproportionate number of cases in the northern colonies was assuredly due to the powerful influence of religious culture in that region, as Puritan beliefs encouraged a preoccupation with evil forces that seemed to endanger individual souls and New England as a whole. This was also the case in Bermuda, where Puritan ministers who migrated to the island after being ousted from their parishes in England fought energetically against what they saw as the devil's intrusions into their new home. Given Bermuda's modest population, the twenty-one trials that took place there during the 1600s suggest an intensity of witch-hunting comparable to the northern mainland colonies. Yet most of the scholarship on witchcraft in British America has focused on New England, reflecting the richness of the evidence surviving from that region as well

[1] For a listing of witch trials in seventeenth-century New England, see Richard Godbeer, *The Devil's Dominion: Magic and Religion in Early New England* (New York, 1992), 235–42. For witchcraft cases elsewhere in British colonies on the mainland of North America, see John Demos, *The Enemy Within: 2,000 Years of Witch-Hunting in the Western World* (New York, 2008), 87–92; for witch trials in Bermuda, see Michael Jarvis, 'Bermuda', in Richard M. Golden, ed., *Encyclopedia of Witchcraft: The Western Tradition*, 4 vols (Santa Barbara, CA, 2006), i, 111–12, and Virginia Bernhard, 'Religion, Politics, and Witchcraft in Bermuda, 1651–55', *William and Mary Quarterly*, 67 (2010), 677–708.

as a disproportionate interest in the northern colonies both inside and outside academia.

22.1 A SUPERNATURAL WORLD

Seventeenth-century New Englanders believed that their world was filled with supernatural forces that could intrude upon their lives at any time. According to the worldview embraced by most New Englanders, God and the devil were constantly at work in their day-to-day lives, testing and tempting, rewarding and punishing as each individual deserved. God had ultimate authority over all that occurred in the universe, so that when the devil intervened in people's lives, he was able to do so because God allowed it to happen. Any extraordinary event that seemed to interrupt the natural order—comets and eclipses, dramatic fires and epidemics, deformed births and inexplicable crop failures, dreams and visions—carried supernatural significance.[2] Ministers argued that any unusual occurrence or misfortune carried a divine message. When misfortune struck, God was usually prompting sinners to self-examination, repentance, and a renewed commitment to obey His commandments. On some occasions God inflicted the warning himself; on others he allowed the devil or even a human witch to act on his behalf. In either case, the appropriate response was to repent and reform. Yet at the same time, godly New Englanders looked outward as well as inward for the source of their afflictions: they often suspected and sometimes accused particular neighbours of bewitching them. There was nothing unorthodox about such a strategy: as the Bible declared, 'Thou shalt not suffer a witch to live.'

Biblical mandate and religious ideology were not the only influences at work as New Englanders responded to adversities that might have been caused by witchcraft. Alongside Protestant Christianity there survived and flourished in New England less formal and yet influential folk beliefs that the settlers brought from England, including those which underlay the use of magic. Folk magic was based on the assumption that men and women could wield occult power for their own benefit. Many settlers believed that through the use of simple techniques, passed down from one generation to the next, they could predict the future, heal the sick, and protect themselves against witchcraft. Most divining, healing, and defensive techniques were quite straightforward, and so it was not unusual for colonists to experiment on their own. But in times of need New Englanders often turned to neighbours who had a reputation for occult expertise. These individuals, known as 'cunning folk', performed a valued social service, but they could also use their skills to harm or destroy those who crossed

---

[2] See David D. Hall, *Worlds of Wonder, Days of Judgment: Popular Religious Belief in Early New England* (New York, 1989), 71–116.

them. Neighbours who possessed occult powers were thus valuable allies, but also potentially deadly enemies.[3]

Many people did not see anything wrong with using magic for benevolent or defensive purposes; only those who deployed their skills for malign ends were a social menace. From this perspective, witchcraft was the misuse of otherwise benign supernatural skills. But ministers saw things differently. They insisted that scripture gave no sanction for such experiments and that human beings could not wield supernatural forces. The Puritan clergy did not doubt that magic worked, but according to them it did so because the devil intervened to assist whoever used it. Individuals might think that they were successfully harnessing occult powers, but in fact the devil was doing it for them and so luring them into his service.[4] Ministers were horrified by the popularity of magical techniques, especially among devout settlers. Some colonists may not have understood why magic was objectionable from a theological perspective; others may have understood quite well their ministers' objections, but quietly ignored official warnings or set aside their own misgivings—for the simple reason that magic answered a need for knowledge and control that Puritan theology reserved only for God. In general, colonists who turned to magic do not seem to have given much thought to where such powers came from. Their attitude was pragmatic: tradition taught that such forces existed and that they could be useful. When godly colonists turned to magic, they were not rejecting religious faith so much as turning to whatever supernatural resource seemed helpful at a given moment.[5]

The belief that magic could be used for both good and evil purposes placed people known for their magical cunning in an ambiguous and potentially perilous position. When New Englanders feared that they were bewitched, they often blamed men and women in their local communities who had a reputation for occult skill: such individuals might be using their skills to harm as well as to help their neighbours. Healers could easily become the target of suspicion if their patients grew sicker instead of

---

[3] Godbeer, *The Devil's Dominion*, esp. 24–54, and Jon Butler, *Awash in a Sea of Faith: Christianizing the American People* (Cambridge, MA, 1990), 67–97. Indian and African cultures also included belief in magic and witchcraft, yet it is difficult to tell from the surviving documentation whether cunning folk or other colonists of European descent incorporated occult techniques from these other cultures into their own magical repertoire. White colonists may well have been unwilling to adopt occult charms proffered by peoples whom they believed to be pagans and devil-worshippers. The records do contain occasional hints of supernatural exchange across racial lines, but they are little more than suggestive. See Charles J. Hoadly, ed., *Records of the Colony or Jurisdiction of New Haven*, 2 vols (New Haven, CT, 1857–8), ii, 80, 86; Butler, *Awash in a Sea of Faith*, 94; and Elaine G. Breslaw, *Tituba, Reluctant Witch of Salem: Devilish Indians and Puritan Fantasies* (New York, 1996).

[4] Godbeer, *The Devil's Dominion*, 55–84.

[5] Whereas Butler and I argue that many colonists combined magical and religious assumptions in a syncretic worldview, Richard Weisman depicts magical and religious beliefs in early New England as two 'competing cosmologies' and argues for a sharp conflict between 'proponents of magic' and the clergy; see Richard Weisman, *Witchcraft, Magic, and Religion in Seventeenth-Century Massachusetts* (Amherst, MA, 1984), 54, 66.

recovering. And anyone known for their magical expertise had reason to worry if they argued with a neighbour who then suffered a mysterious illness or mishap.

22.2 WOMEN AS WITCHES

Women known for their magical skills were much more likely than men to be accused of witchcraft. The power wielded by cunning folk was potentially dangerous whether in the hands of a man or a woman, but it seemed especially threatening if possessed by a woman because it contradicted gender norms that placed women in subordinate positions. Neither belief in folk magic nor its practice were gender-specific: men as well as women resorted to and functioned as cunning folk. Yet suspicions that magical skill had been used for malicious ends were much more likely to be directed against female practitioners.

Witchcraft was perceived on both sides of the Atlantic as a primarily female phenomenon. Around four fifths of those New Englanders tried for witchcraft were women. Puritan ministers did not teach that women were by nature more evil than men, but they did see them as weaker and thus more susceptible to sinful impulses. Elizabeth Reis has pointed out that 'colonists shared with their English brethren the belief that women's bodies were physically weaker than men's' and that therefore 'the Devil could more frequently and successfully gain access to and possess women's souls'. Ministers reminded New England congregations that it was Eve who first gave way to Satan and then seduced Adam, when she should have continued to serve his moral welfare in obedience to God; all women inherited that insidious blend of weakness and power from their mother Eve.[6]

Some women were much more likely to be accused of witchcraft than others. Throughout the seventeenth century, women became vulnerable to such allegations only if they were seen as having forsaken their prescribed place in a gendered hierarchy that Puritans held to be ordained by God. Puritan ministers insisted that women were not 'a necessary evil', as Catholic theologians had often claimed, but instead 'a necessary good', designed as a 'sweet and intimate companion' for men.[7] As Carol Karlsen has pointed out, Puritan thinkers needed to believe that women could play a constructive role within godly communities because men needed female companions and helpmeets to work with them in raising self-disciplined children, who would grow up to become committed Puritans. 'There was no place in this vision,' Karlsen writes,

---

[6] Elizabeth Reis, *Damned Women: Sinners and Witches in Puritan New England* (Ithaca, NY, 1997), 108, 110.

[7] John Cotton, *A Meet Help* (Boston, MA, 1699), 14, 21.

'for the belief that women were *incapable* of fulfilling such a role. Nor was in the ideal Puritan society for women who refused to fill it.'[8]

That caveat in Puritan gender ideology could prove fatal. Women whose c stances or behaviour seemed to disrupt social norms and hierarchies could easily their status as 'Handmaidens of the Lord' and become branded as the 'Servants o Satan'. Especially vulnerable were women who had passed menopause and thus no longer served the purpose of procreation, women who were widowed and so neither fulfilled the role of wife nor had a husband to protect them from malicious accusations, and women who had inherited or stood to inherit property in violation of expectations that wealth would be transmitted from man to man. Women who seemed unduly aggressive and contentious or who failed to display deference towards men in positions of authority were also more likely to be accused.[9]

New Englanders sought to ensure a positive and respected place for women in godly society, yet the lingering fear of 'women-as-witches' complicated and compromised their celebration of women as 'a necessary good'. Behaviour or circumstances that seemed disorderly could easily become identified as diabolical and associated with witchcraft: the devil had, after all, led a rebellion against God's rule in heaven. Eve's legacy as a female prototype was double-edged: on the one hand, a beloved and successful helpmeet in the Garden of Eden; on the other, Satan's first human ally. Women as well as men internalized the claim that women were more vulnerable to the devil's influence. As women accused other women, they participated in negative assumptions about their own sex.[10]

Prominent among these female accusers were girls and young women who claimed that they were not only bewitched but also possessed. During their fits, they engaged in disobedient and unruly behaviour: they questioned the authority of their parents, masters, and ministers; they refused to do housework, eat their meals, or to wash their hands; they shouted and screamed; they became violent, lewd, and blasphemous. And they accused older adults, mostly women, of tormenting them. Karlsen has argued that in order to understand their behaviour, we need to bear in mind that children and young women were expected to accept a subordinate position within their households and communities. Many of those who became possessed had personal histories that further weakened their position within colonial society. A significant number of the possessed accusers in 1692 had been orphaned in recent Indian attacks and were now living with relatives or family friends, often as servants; they had little or no dowry to offer and so their marital prospects were dismal. In a society that valued women largely in terms of their husbands' social and economic standing, they must have known that

[8] Carol Karlsen, *The Devil in the Shape of a Woman: Witchcraft in Colonial New England* (New York, 1987), 165.

[9] Karlsen discusses the demographic, economic, and temperamental characteristics of accused witches in *The Devil in the Shape of a Woman*, 46–152.

[10] Reis argues that women were more inclined than men to see themselves as wholly 'unfit and unworthy'. Whereas men differentiated between their sinful deeds and inner selves, women conflated the two. See *Damned Women*, 12–54 (quotation at 38).

omed to obscurity.[11] Having grown up in devout house-
: young women doubtless understood that any anger or
:ponse to their situation made them potential recruits for
istians, they would have feared rebellious emotions that
d evil, personified in the devil and his first recruit, Eve.
mediated between a young woman's rage at her place in
to acknowledge or validate that rage. By claiming and
; that they were possessed, they could express anger and
cknowledge full responsibility for such feelings: after all,
the devil and his followers were speaking through them. And by accusing others of
being witches, they shifted attention away from their own moral failings to those of the
women and men whom they now accused of allegiance to Satan. They may also have
relished the power that they exercised during the court's proceedings, a power that
children and young women would not otherwise have attained in seventeenth-century
New England. Yet this is not to suggest that the possessed girls and young women were
simply acting. They may have feared quite sincerely that the devil and his disciples were
after them: after all, their faith taught them that the resentment they felt made them
likely recruits.[12]

22.3 MALEVOLENT NEIGHBOURS

When seventeenth-century New Englanders suspected that they were bewitched,
whether by a woman or a man, the person they blamed was usually a close neighbour
with whom they had a history of personal tension or conflict. In most cases the
antagonism developed according to one of three scenarios. In the first of these,
neighbour A requested a favour, such as temporary shelter or the loan of a household
implement, from neighbour B, who refused and then felt guilty for having done so.
Neighbour A was disappointed and resentful, perhaps cursing neighbour B and vowing
to get even. Neighbour B now displaced his own sense of guilt onto neighbour A,
blaming her vengeful anger for subsequent misfortunes such as the unexplained death
of livestock or a mysterious illness within his family. According to neighbour B,

---

[11] Karlsen, *The Devil in the Shape of a Woman*, 226–30.

[12] Karlsen, *The Devil in the Shape of a Woman*, 222–51; Godbeer, *The Devil's Dominion*, 85–121, and
Godbeer, 'Chaste and Unchaste Covenants: Witchcraft and Sex in Early Modern Culture', in Peter
Benes, ed., *Wonders of the Invisible World, 1600–1900* (Boston, MA, 1995), 53–72. John Demos suggests
that adolescent girls may have accused older women who symbolized their mothers, against whom they
could not openly rebel (and some of whom were no longer present); see John Demos, *Entertaining
Satan: Witchcraft and the Culture of Early New England* (New York, 1982), 157–65. For a very different
perspective on the afflicted girls in 1692 see Peter Charles Hoffer, *The Devil's Disciples: Makers of the
Salem Witchcraft Trials* (Baltimore, MD, 1996). According to Hoffer, some of the afflicted showed
symptoms of child abuse. The psychological impact of that abuse would, he argues, help to explain at
least some of their behaviour.

witchcraft was at work and neighbour A was responsible. In the second scenario, an exchange of goods between neighbour A and neighbour B went awry; neighbour A considered herself the aggrieved party and was angry. In the weeks, months, or even years that followed, neighbour B's family suffered a series of misfortunes and became convinced that neighbour A was taking revenge by using occult forces against them. In the third scenario, neighbour A and neighbour B quarrelled because one of them had allegedly damaged property belonging to the other. Again neighbour A was enraged. Neighbour B was subsequently troubled by mysterious misfortunes and accused neighbour A of bewitching him. The assumption underlying accusations of witchcraft in each scenario was that an individual who felt mistreated (neighbour A) had turned to witchcraft as a form of revenge. The victim of witchcraft (neighbour B) had failed to be a good neighbour, whether through lack of generosity or by questioning a neighbour's honesty; they believed that the alleged witch (neighbour A) had retaliated by becoming the ultimately nightmarish neighbour, wreaking havoc and destruction among her enemies.[13]

If we are to understand why so many accusations of witchcraft originated in disputes between neighbours, we need to consider a crucial intersection between social values and supernatural beliefs in early New England. John Demos has pointed out that this social element was closely linked to the circumstances in which most pre-modern men and women lived. Most New Englanders lived in tiny communities where the quality of life was 'personal in the fullest sense'. Each resident not only knew everyone else in the town but also interacted with neighbours in many different roles and contexts. Personal interactions and influence were central to the experience of early New Englanders. It therefore made good sense to account for misfortune or suffering in personal terms. Witchcraft explained personal problems in terms of personal interactions. A particular neighbour had quarrelled with you and was now taking revenge for a perceived injury by bewitching you.[14]

The tiny communities in which New Englanders settled were clustered precariously on the margins of empire, separated from each other by roads that were sometimes impassable and by no means always safe. Neighbours knew that they depended upon each other for their survival. Townsfolk and villagers helped each other to put up new buildings or harvest crops; they exchanged food and simple products such as candles or soap in a local barter economy; and they gave each other emotional support as they navigated life's challenges and tragedies. The Puritan faith in which most of the colonists believed (albeit to varying degrees) taught that being a good neighbour had its spiritual as well as practical dimensions. Settlers must keep watch over each other, warn each other when they seemed to be in danger of giving way to sinful urges, and trust that others would keep an equally close eye on them.

---

[13] See Demos, *Entertaining Satan*, 275–312.
[14] Demos, *Entertaining Satan*, 311–12.

The Puritans' emphasis on community and mutual support meant that arguments between neighbours became not only irritating in their own right but also a betrayal of social and moral values on which their practical and spiritual welfare depended. It is, then, hardly surprising that such disputes gave rise to festering resentments. In many instances there was no institutional outlet for the tensions and hostilities that resulted. If someone trespassed upon a neighbour's property or assaulted another town resident, a law had been broken and the malefactor would be dealt with accordingly. But refusing to lend a neighbour food or a tool was not a crime and so the resulting animosity could not be expressed or mediated directly through civil or criminal proceedings. Witchcraft allegations provided an outlet for feelings of guilt or hostility rooted in confrontations between neighbours over issues of mutual support and responsibility.

Yet we should beware of concluding that New Englanders used such allegations simply as a ploy to get rid of their enemies. Most of those who accused their neighbours of witchcraft believed quite sincerely that they were guilty as charged. Allegations of witchcraft brought together three important components of pre-modern culture: the inability to explain or control illness and other forms of misfortune, a deeply embedded belief in supernatural forces that could be used to inflict harm, and the densely personal nature of human interactions. Given the density of interpersonal contact in these tiny communities, it is hardly surprising that one neighbour's suspicions about another often spread from household to household in a ripple effect that encouraged other townsfolk to interpret their own misfortunes as the result of witchcraft. The mysterious and the supernatural converged with what John Demos refers to as 'things most tangible and personal'. Along 'the seam of their convergence' emerged accusations of witchcraft.[15]

22.4 WITCH TRIALS IN SEVENTEENTH-CENTURY NEW ENGLAND

Once New Englanders became convinced that a particular individual had bewitched them, they had the right to lodge a formal complaint and so initiate a criminal prosecution. In England and its New England colonies, allegations of witchcraft were handled by secular courts, not ecclesiastical courts of inquisition such as conducted witch trials in some European countries. New England's legal system was rigorous and cautious in its handling of capital cases. Of the sixty-one known prosecutions for witchcraft in seventeenth-century New England, excluding the Salem witch-hunt, sixteen at most (perhaps only fourteen) resulted in conviction and execution, a rate of just over one quarter (26.2 per cent). Four of the accused individuals confessed,

---

[15] Demos, *Entertaining Satan*, 312.

which made the court's job much easier. If those cases are omitted, the conviction rate falls to just under one-fifth (19.7 per cent).[16]

New England's witchcraft laws were framed in theological terms, treating witches as heretical servants of the devil and demanding proof of diabolical allegiance. Yet ordinary men and women were interested less in where a witch's power came from than in the practical threat that she posed. Depositions in most witch cases prior to the Salem panic reflected that practical preoccupation and rarely made any mention of the devil. The evidence given against New England's accused witches generally fell into one of four categories. Most frequently, witnesses described quarrels followed by misfortune or illness, presumably brought on by witchcraft. Witnesses sometimes claimed that the accused was known as a fortune-teller or healer; this established that the accused had occult powers which, it was implied, had also been deployed for malign purposes. Witnesses also described having used defensive and retaliatory techniques such as burning the ear or tail of a bewitched cow so as to injure and thus identify the witch responsible; they reported the results of such experiments to the court as incriminating testimony. And, finally, neighbours of the accused would describe generally suspicious behaviour, such as extraordinary and perhaps superhuman strength.

Most testimony presented at witch trials in New England was circumstantial and unconvincing from the perspective of legal and religious experts. Magistrates were willing to convict and execute accused witches. But they generally refused to do so unless the evidence satisfied rigorous standards of proof: this meant either a voluntary confession, or at least two independent witnesses to an incident demonstrating the individual's guilt. Those giving testimony against the accused assumed that their personal experiences and impressions would be treated as hard evidence.[17] Yet judges were interested only in evidence that established the devil's involvement—and even then worried about its reliability. The only occasion on which New England courts gathered extensive evidence of diabolical allegiance was the Salem witch-hunt, which was also the one occasion on which the authorities made illegal use of physical torture and extreme psychological pressure to extract a large number of confessions. (English law forbade the use of torture during judicial interrogation, except in cases of sedition or treason, and the New England authorities operated under English jurisdiction.)

Accusers expected to be taken seriously and sometimes refused to accept an acquittal. They conferred with each other, gathered new evidence against the suspect, and then renewed legal charges. Three New Englanders were each prosecuted for witchcraft on three separate occasions; another five appeared in court twice on charges of

---

[16] Godbeer, *The Devil's Dominion*, 158; this section draws primarily on the argument developed in pp. 153–78 of that work.

[17] It is worth noting that New Englanders rarely accepted immediately or without question claims that a particular person was bewitched or that a specific individual was responsible. They were clearly committed to a process of empirical verification (even though the techniques they used might strike us as odd). See Richard Godbeer, *Escaping Salem: The Other Witch Hunt of 1692* (New York, 2005).

witchcraft. All of these cases resulted in acquittal.[18] As the difficulty of securing a legal conviction for witchcraft became increasingly apparent, so New Englanders became less inclined to initiate legal prosecutions against suspected witches. There were nineteen witch trials in New England during the 1660s, but only six during the 1670s and eight during the 1680s. Yet the dramatic fall in prosecutions for witchcraft during the 1670s and 1680s was not due to any decline in fear of witches, as became abundantly clear in 1692.

22.5 THE SALEM WITCH-HUNT

The Salem witch-hunt of 1692 was very different from other trials for witchcraft in seventeenth-century New England, both in its scale and in the intensity of the fears that gripped local residents that year. That crisis has become one of the most infamous events of early American history and has inspired a huge body of literature, including plays and novels as well as academic monographs and articles. Earlier scholars of the witch-hunt tended to focus on the issue of blame: some defended those involved as well-meaning if misguided; others condemned them as superstitious zealots or accused them of taking part in a murderous conspiracy.[19] Recent scholars have been more inclined to seek explanations for why a witch panic of this magnitude erupted at this particular time and in this specific locale. Some of these explanations have proven more convincing than others. A graduate student in biology at the University of California, Santa Barbara, proposed in 1976, for example, that the fits suffered by Salem villagers were symptoms of a disease, convulsive ergotism, which came from contaminated grain. Scholars have scrutinized this argument and exposed its fundamental flaws, yet it has proven resilient outside academic circles.[20]

Perhaps the most influential of recent attempts to explain what happened in 1692 focuses on the social and economic tensions within Salem Village, which contemporaries

[18] Godbeer, *The Devil's Dominion*, 172–3.

[19] For examples of works more sympathetic to those involved, see George L. Kittredge, 'Notes on Witchcraft', *Proceedings of the American Antiquarian Society*, 18 (1907), 148–212, and Samuel Eliot Morison, *The Puritan Pronaos: Studies in the Intellectual Life of New England in the Seventeenth Century* (New York, 1936); for more condemnatory works, see Charles W. Upham, *Salem Witchcraft*, 2 vols (Boston, MA, 1867) and James Truslow Adams, *The Founding of New England* (Boston, MA, 1921). Two recent books that do not flinch from placing blame for what happened at Salem are Enders A. Robinson, *The Devil Discovered: Salem Witchcraft 1692* (New York, 1991), which sees the witch-hunt as driven by conspiracy, and Bernard Rosenthal, *Salem Story: Reading the Witch Trials of 1692* (New York, 1993), which places much emphasis on the role played by 'simple fraud' in the trials (quotation at 185).

[20] Linnda R. Caporael, 'Ergotism: The Satan Loosed in Salem?', *Science* (2 April 1976), 21–6; for a critique of Caporael's thesis, see Nicholas P. Spanos and Jack Gottlieb, 'Ergotism and the Salem Village Witch Trials', *Science* (24 December 1976), 1390–94. For a more detailed account of how historians, scientists, and playwrights have sought to explain the witch-hunt over the past three hundred years, see Demos, *The Enemy Within*, 189–212.

understood in supernatural terms. Paul Boyer and Stephen Nissenbaum have shown in *Salem Possessed* that the village in which the panic began was a deeply divided and dysfunctional community.[21] Salem Village developed as an outgrowth of Salem Town, one of the region's largest seaports. The village was situated within the territorial bounds of Salem Town and had no civil government of its own; it was legally joined with and subordinate to the nearby seaport. Some villagers wanted independence from the town, in part because the latter had proven remarkably insensitive to their concerns. The church in Salem Town, for example, was reluctant to let the villagers form a congregation of their own, despite the inconvenience of having to travel so far to the town meeting house. Some villagers also wanted to separate themselves from the commercial spirit that increasingly characterized the town. According to Boyer and Nissenbaum, villagers who saw that way of life as spiritually suspect tended to perceive neighbours who lived nearer to the town or associated with its interests as morally deficient and untrustworthy.

Salem Village became increasingly conflict-ridden as those who associated with the town aligned against those who were eager to separate and form an autonomous community. Because the village had no formal institutions of its own, it proved extremely difficult to resolve the disputes that arose between these two groups (just as the individual quarrels described by John Demos focused on issues that were not amenable to resolution through regular institutional channels). As a result, animosities and mutual suspicions deepened with each passing year. Proponents of separation from the town eventually secured the establishment of an independent church in 1689 and the ordination of Samuel Parris as their pastor. Parris proved to be an unfortunate choice: a failed and bitter merchant who resented those who succeeded in the world of commerce, he fuelled local hostilities. Parris gave a series of inflammatory sermons that translated factional division into a cosmic struggle between the forces of good and evil. In the minds of his supporters, Salem Town became the symbol of an alien, corrupt, and even diabolical world that threatened the welfare of Salem Village.

Because supporters of Samuel Parris perceived their enemies as nothing less than evil, it was but a short step for them to become convinced that those aligned with the town and its interests were servants of Satan. Boyer and Nissenbaum argue that divisions within the village were reproduced in the pattern of accusations in 1692: a disproportionate number of accused witches and their defenders lived on the side of the village nearest to Salem Town, while most of the accusers lived on the western side.[22] Many of the accused had personal histories or interests that either associated them with Salem Town or otherwise marked them as threatening outsiders. But as Boyer and Nissenbaum emphasize, this was not just a cynical bid to dispose of enemies by labelling them as witches: villagers pointed the finger of accusation at particular individuals because they truly believed them to be morally deficient and thus likely

---

[21] Paul Boyer and Stephen Nissenbaum, *Salem Possessed: The Social Origins of Witchcraft* (Cambridge, MA, 1974).

[22] Boyer and Nissenbaum, *Salem Possessed*, 34.

members of a diabolical conspiracy. Those people who had become identified with forces of change, which their enemies construed as disorder and immorality, were now accused of having allied with radical evil, namely, the devil.

Critics of *Salem Possessed* have chipped away at various components of its argument, including the geographical divisions on which Boyer and Nissenbaum placed so much importance.[23] Yet the most serious problem with *Salem Possessed* is its focus on Salem Village, given that the witch-hunt of 1692 was, after all, a regional phenomenon involving two dozen towns and villages. Salem did not even produce the most accusations; that dubious distinction fell to Andover.[24] Other scholars have argued that a more comprehensive explanation for the witch panic must involve stepping away from Salem Village itself and examining the broader fears that ignited that year into witch panic.

A succession of attacks directed against the settlements of New England during the two decades prior to 1692 created intense anxiety among those who lived in the region. Perhaps the most terrifying of these attacks were Indian raids that came in two waves, the first in 1675–6 and the second beginning in 1689. Many colonists were convinced that Indians worshipped the devil and practised witchcraft. Given that association and the widespread fear generated by Indian attacks in the early 1690s, it is hardly surprising that anxiety about this apparently demonic threat surfaced repeatedly in the trial depositions at Salem. As recent scholars have restored Indians to visibility as central players in early American history, so a growing number of studies have examined the links between Indian attacks and the Salem witch-hunt.[25] The most recent of these is Mary Beth Norton's *In the Devil's Snare*. Norton demonstrates the impact of Indian raids on the witch panic in much greater detail than any previous study.[26] She notes the parallels between horrified responses to the Indians' mutilation of their enemies in contemporary accounts and the descriptions in 1692 of witches threatening to tear their victims to pieces. She shows that several male suspects who did not fit the usual witch stereotype became vulnerable to accusation in 1692 because of their association with the

---

[23] See especially the recent forum, 'Salem Repossessed', in *William and Mary Quarterly*, 65 (2008), 391–534.

[24] Elinor Abbot provides a thought-provoking analysis of divisions within seventeenth-century Andover in *Our Company Increases Apace: History, Language, and Social Identity in Early Colonial Andover, Massachusetts* (Dallas, TX, 2007), though she declines to suggest specific connections between those divisions and the accusations of 1692. See also Chadwick Hansen, 'Andover Witchcraft and the Causes of the Salem Witchcraft Trials', in Howard Kerr and Charles Crow, eds, *The Occult in America: New Historical Perspectives* (Urbana, IL, 1983), 38–57.

[25] These include Richard Slotkin, *Regeneration Through Violence: The Mythology of the American Frontier, 1600–1860* (Middletown, CT, 1973); David Konig, *Law and Society in Puritan Massachusetts: Essex County, 1629–1692* (Chapel Hill, NC, 1979); James E. Kences, 'Some Unexplored Relationships of Essex County Witchcraft to the Indian Wars of 1675 and 1689', *Essex Institute Historical Collections*, 120 (1984), 179–212; Carol Karlsen, *The Devil in the Shape of a Woman*, esp. ch. 7; Godbeer, *The Devil's Dominion*, ch. 6; John McWilliams, 'Indian John and the Northern Tawnies', *New England Quarterly*, 69 (1996), 580–604; and Breslaw, *Tituba, Reluctant Witch of Salem*.

[26] Mary Beth Norton, *In the Devil's Snare: The Salem Witchcraft Crisis of 1692* (New York, 2002).

frontier. And, perhaps most strikingly, she suggests that the support given by Massachusetts leaders to the Salem court may have been due in no small part to their own lack of success in repelling the Indian attacks: rooting out those responsible for invisible assaults on the colony could deflect attention from, and appease, their sense of guilt for failing to deal effectively with more visible assaults. Norton and her predecessors show convincingly that the witch-hunt of 1692 makes most sense if we step back from events in Salem itself and place them in a broader context of military and political crisis.

Yet Indians were by no means the only enemies to have launched assaults on New England during the years preceding 1692.[27] Political reforms imposed by the government in London had also threatened to undermine the colonists' way of life. In 1684 the Crown revoked the charter that had granted Massachusetts something akin to self-government. Two years later, the northern colonies were incorporated into a single entity, to be known as the Dominion of New England. There would henceforth be no representative assemblies and all power would be vested in the governor and his councillors. The new governor, Sir Edmund Andros, was a career soldier with an autocratic temperament. He was also an Anglican, much to the outrage of Puritans, who saw their new governor's religion as one short step away from Roman Catholicism, which they in turn associated with the Antichrist. Andros attempted unsuccessfully to negotiate a peace with the Indians, and then led an equally unsuccessful military expedition against them in Maine. Some suspected that he had travelled north to make a secret pact with the Indians and also French Catholics in Canada. It is, then, hardly surprising that when James II was deposed in 1688, the Bostonians carried out a coup of their own the following year, arresting Andros and reinstating their old charter of government until a new one could be negotiated.

But Andros was not the only purveyor of heresy into New England. In the summer of 1688, Quakers launched an evangelical campaign in the northern colonies. Quakers rejected many of the beliefs that other Protestants held dear and their egalitarian ideals horrified even those who did not care much about their religious views. Quakers claimed to receive revelation from God, but Puritans declared that these so-called revelations were really diabolical. The Quakers were so called because they tended to convulse when receiving revelation; the similarities between these convulsions and demonic possession did not go unnoticed by their enemies. And just as women who challenged social norms could end up being associated with Satan and his rebellion against rightful authority, so Quakers who refused to show respect for social hierarchy were seen as aligning themselves with the prince of disorder and sin. Though Quakers remained a tiny minority, the vehemence of anti-Quaker tracts that appeared in the early 1690s testifies to the danger that some Puritans saw them as posing.

What made matters worse was that the new charter of 1691 gave freedom of worship to all Protestants. Until 1684 only the male members of Puritan congregations had been allowed to vote in political elections, but now the right to vote would be based instead

---

[27] For a more detailed version of the argument put forward in the following paragraphs, see Godbeer, *The Devil's Dominion*, 182–203.

on land ownership (as in England and other North American colonies), which enfran-
chised property-owning dissenters such as Anglicans and Quakers. These two changes
struck a direct blow to Puritan dominance in New England. Puritans had felt for some
time that their godly society was under threat. During the second half of the seventeenth century the population became more diverse in its values and priorities: some
of those who migrated in these later decades were drawn more by economic opportunity than by religious ideals, and as the original settlers produced children, not all of
these native-born New Englanders grew up to share their parents' values. Those who
identified closely with the religious goals of the early settlers feared that they were
losing control of the region's culture and that New England was in a state of moral
decline. A more diverse population and a more worldly way of life struck them as the
devil's work.

That sense of decline and the siege mentality that it created among devout settlers
provided an important context for the ways in which colonists responded to crises that
struck New England during the years prior to the Salem panic. Indian raids, the
authoritarian Dominion, Quaker evangelism, and the dramatic implications of the
new charter left many colonists feeling imperilled. The colonists described these
various threats in much the same language used to characterize witches: as alien,
invasive, and malevolent. To be ruled by Andros and his cronies, to be attacked by
Indians, or to be evangelized by Quakers was equivalent to being assaulted by Satan.
From this perspective, the witch crisis of 1692 was not an isolated event but the climax
of a devilish assault upon the region.

The pattern of witch accusations that year suggests an intense preoccupation with
invasion: those who could be linked in some way to recent experiences of physical and
spiritual assault proved most vulnerable to accusations of witchcraft. A significant
number of the accused had close Quaker associations.[28] Fear of Indians resonated
through the testimony given at the trials. And many of the accused were clearly
perceived as outsiders, either literally or figuratively.[29] The tense situation within
Salem Village itself paralleled crises in the region at large, as those villagers who feared
and resented Salem Town came to see all those associated with it as the agents of a
corrupt and evil world that threatened to destroy their way of life. The afflictions in
Salem Village unleashed fears of alien, invasive, and diabolical forces that had accumulated throughout the region during the last two decades. As one commentator wrote
that year, '[t]he usual walls of defense about mankind have such a gap made in them
that the very devils are broken in upon us'.[30]

The magistrates charged with handling the panic of 1692 proved much more willing
to convict than those who had presided over previous witch trials. During the summer

[28] See Christine Leigh Heyrman, 'Specters of Subversion, Societies of Friends: Dissent and the Devil in
Provincial Essex County, Massachusetts', in David D. Hall, John M. Murrin, and Thad. W. Tate, eds,
Saints and Revolutionaries: Essays on Early American History (New York, 1984), 60.

[29] Godbeer, *The Devil's Dominion*, 201–2.

[30] Cotton Mather, *Wonders of the Invisible World* (Boston, MA, 1693), 80.

and early fall of that year, the special court tried twenty-seven individuals and found all of them guilty as charged. Yet with each passing month the court became more deeply mired in controversy over the evidence being used to justify convictions. In sharp contrast to earlier cases, the testimony accumulating at Salem contained plentiful evidence of the devil's involvement in the alleged bewitchments. Over fifty of those indicted in 1692 confessed that they were indeed witches who had covenanted with Satan. Yet by the end of the summer many of these confessing witches had recanted, claiming that their admissions of guilt had been forced from them through the use of psychological pressure and physical torture. Apart from confessions, almost all of the testimony that made reference to the devil came from the afflicted girls and young women. Most of their information apparently came from demonic spectres that appeared to them in the form of human witches. The magistrates took the position that devils could appear in the image of a particular individual only with that person's permission, so that the appearance of a spectre could be treated as proof that the individual represented was, in fact, a witch. Yet critics of the court argued that spectral evidence was unreliable as a basis for conviction. Because the devil was a notorious liar, any information subject to his influence might well be misleading and part of a scheme to incriminate the innocent. None of those attacking the court questioned the reality of witchcraft. What they did doubt was the possibility of proving who exactly was responsible for witchcraft, unless the witch freely confessed.

Once spectral testimony came under attack and once confessors began to recant, the court found itself in an extremely awkward position. An impressive number of townsfolk and villagers from communities across Essex County had come forward to testify against witch suspects; their depositions testified eloquently to a widespread and profound fear of witchcraft. But unlike the confessors and afflicted girls, these other witnesses rarely mentioned the devil's involvement as the law demanded. As the eagerness of the court to convict collided with a growing chorus of opposition to its proceedings, the governor felt that he had no choice but to suspend the trials and reassess the situation.[31]

Seventeenth-century critics of the court and most commentators since then have depicted the nineteen executions that occurred prior to the suspension of the trials as a tragic injustice. Yet from the perspective of people who wanted the courts to take decisive action against witches in their midst, the acquittal and release of so many suspects in the weeks and months following the suspension of the trials must have been both galling and frightening. That witch trials disappeared from the history of New England shortly thereafter was due as much to popular disillusionment with the legal process as to any reluctance on the part of officials to accommodate witch accusations. Yet belief in witchcraft and fear of witches would persist throughout the eighteenth

---

[31] That the accusers were now naming individuals from prominent families, including the governor's own wife, doubtless also figured in the decision to halt the trials. But that decision seems to have been driven primarily by controversy surrounding the magistrates' assessment of the evidence before them.

century, despite growing doubts about the reality of supernatural phenomena within educated circles. In the minds of many colonists witchcraft was still a very real threat.[32]

22.6 NEW DIRECTIONS

Recent scholarship on witchcraft in New England has taught us much about the cultural and social assumptions that shaped the northern colonies. Scholarly focus on that region is hardly surprising given that so much of the extant evidence is concentrated in New England. Yet a more determined investigation of surviving documentation from other parts of British America, including Bermuda, would broaden and enrich our understanding of witch-hunting as it operated within the British colonial context. In particular, it would enable scholars to ascertain which aspects of New England's supernatural lore and experience with witch-hunting were distinctive, and which were shared with other colonies. This is perhaps the most obvious and also elusive challenge awaiting scholars of early American witchcraft.

The case of Bermuda is particularly intriguing. In 1634 a ship returning to Boston from that island reported that clerical efforts to clean up the island had recently included the public exorcism of a man 'possessed with a devil'. Puritan ministers who settled there seem to have taken very seriously the Bermuda Company's call for 'all sorcerers, enchanters, charmers, witches, figure-casters or fortune-tellers, and conjurers' to be exposed and prosecuted. Between 1651 and 1696, twenty-one individuals (seventeen women and four men) were tried on charges of witchcraft; five of them were hanged. A cluster of trials in the early 1650s appears to have been caused in large part by political tensions: Bermudians on both sides of the political divide labelled their enemies as servants of the devil and sought to rid their island of evil influences through witch trials. In the eighteenth century a number of slaves were accused of having used supernatural means to poison or otherwise harm white islanders and other slaves.[33] Examining the process whereby witch-hunting became racialized in Bermuda, along with the impact of Caribbean and African culture on witch beliefs and the kinds of evidence presented at witch trials, the ways in which colonial officials, ministers, and other inhabitants of the island approached the challenges of dealing with alleged supernatural threats, and the degree to which Bermuda's witch-hunt in the 1650s

---

[32] For discussion of witch beliefs in the eighteenth century, see Herbert Leventhal, *In The Shadow of the Enlightenment: Occultism and Renaissance Science in Eighteenth-Century America* (New York, 1976), 66-125; Demos, *Entertaining Satan*, 387–400; Alan Taylor, 'The Early Republic's Supernatural Economy: Treasure Seeking in the American North-East, 1780–1830', *American Quarterly*, 38 (1986), 6–34; Butler, *Awash in a Sea of Faith*, 228–36; and Godbeer, *The Devil's Dominion*, 226–30.

[33] Richard S. Dunn and Laetitia Yeandle, eds, *The Journal of John Winthrop, 1630–1649* (Cambridge, MA, 1996), 119; J. H. Lefroy, ed., *Memorials of the Discovery and Early Settlement of the Bermudas or Somers Islands*, 2 vols (London, 1878–9; repr. Hamilton, Bermuda, 1981), i, 320; and in general, Michael Jarvis, 'Bermuda'.

resembled or differed from other early modern witch-hunts, would surely make a fascinating study.

There is also more to be done on New England witchcraft. Historians have paid close attention to contemporary witch beliefs, shaped as much by traditional folk culture as by Puritan theology. Yet in our eagerness to reconstruct popular attitudes and assumptions relating to witchcraft, we may have paid insufficient attention to the evolving perspectives of more educated colonial leaders and ministers. Attitudes towards the supernatural world, including witchcraft and demonology, were under constant debate in England and Europe during this period, and intellectuals in the colonies were very much engaged with those conversations.[34] Scholars have paid considerable attention over the years to Increase and Cotton Mather, but much less work has been done on the impact of new ideas about the supernatural world on other members of the colonial elite. It would be helpful to know whether and to what degree New England ministers and leading lay colonists drew on Scottish and continental as well as English demonological ideas. Walter Woodward's recent study of John Winthrop, Jr, reminds us that the attitudes of those in positions of authority could have a dramatic impact on judicial policy in general, and the handling of witch cases in particular.[35]

Elsewhere in the mainland colonies, leadership was doubtless important in shaping very different attitudes towards witch-hunting from those that predominated in New England. When a woman accused of witchcraft in Fairfield County, Connecticut, fled to New York in 1692, that colony's attorney general refused to cooperate with those who wanted the suspect returned to Connecticut for trial.[36] Whether sufficient evidence survives to enable a close study of official and clerical attitudes towards witchcraft and witch-hunting in other parts of British America remains to be seen. Yet fragmentary evidence suggests that popular belief in witchcraft and fear of the havoc that witches could wreak in their local communities were widespread throughout the mainland colonies. That evidence, including the records that survive from occasional witch trials, surely deserves more sustained analysis than has been attempted to date.[37]

Of those accused as witches in seventeenth-century New England, roughly four of every five were women, and recent scholars have paid close attention to the ways in which witch-hunting targeted women. But what of the remaining one in every five? Historians have pointed out that roughly half of the men charged with this crime were

[34] See, for example, Michael P. Winship, *Seers of God: Puritan Providentialism in the Restoration and Early Enlightenment* (Baltimore, MD, 1996).

[35] Walter W. Woodward, *Prospero's America: John Winthrop, Jr., Alchemy, and the Creation of New England Culture, 1606–76* (Chapel Hill, NC, 2010).

[36] See David D. Hall, ed., *Witch-Hunting in Seventeenth-Century New England: A Documentary History, 1638–1693* (2nd edn, Boston, 1999), 331–2; and Godbeer, *Escaping Salem*, 57–8.

[37] For some suggestive comments in this direction, see Demos, *The Enemy Within*, 87–92.

married or otherwise close to accused women: they were, in other words, guilty by association.[38] But at least some of these men were problematic in their own right and in ways that were clearly gendered. Take, for example, George Burroughs, one of the accused in 1692. Burroughs had links to the Indian wars and was implicated in Salem Village's internal conflict, both of which made him a likely target. But his own personality and behaviour may well have contributed to his vulnerability. It now seems clear that women who seemed to contravene gendered expectations were especially vulnerable to accusations of witchcraft. Yet the depositions against Burroughs suggest that this could also apply to men who violated masculine codes: in his case by failing in his duty to be a caring and protective husband. (John Willard, another male suspect in 1692, had also mistreated his wife.) Given the skewed gender ratio of witch accusations, it is difficult to imagine a satisfying examination of witch trials that does not take gender seriously. Yet, as a growing number of scholars now acknowledge, understanding gender is extremely difficult unless conceptions of manhood are thoroughly integrated into that emerging picture.[39]

FURTHER READING

Boyer, Paul and Nissenbaum, Stephen, *Salem Possessed: The Social Origins of Witchcraft* (Cambridge, MA, 1974).

Boyer, Paul and Nissenbaum, Stephen, eds, *Salem-Village Witchcraft: A Documentary Record of Local Conflict in Colonial New England* (1972; Boston, 1993).

Breslaw, Elaine G., *Tituba, Reluctant Witch of Salem: Devilish Indians and Puritan Fantasies* (New York, 1996).

Butler, Jon, *Awash in a Sea of Faith: Christianizing the American People* (Cambridge, MA, 1990).

Demos, John Putnam, *Entertaining Satan: Witchcraft and the Culture of Early New England* (New York, 1982).

Godbeer, Richard, *The Devil's Dominion: Magic and Religion in Early New England* (New York, 1992).

Godbeer, Richard, ed., *The Salem Witch Hunt: A Brief History with Documents* (Boston, MA, 2011).

Hall, David D., *Worlds of Wonder, Days of Judgment: Popular Religious Belief in Early New England* (New York, 1989).

Hall, David D., ed., *Witch-Hunting in Seventeenth-Century New England: A Documentary History, 1658–1693* (2nd edn, Boston, MA, 1999).

Hansen, Chadwick, *Witchcraft at Salem* (New York, 1969).

---

[38] Demos, *Entertaining Satan*, 60; Karlsen, *The Devil in the Shape of a Woman*, 47–8.

[39] For recent studies of male witches, see Lara Apps and Andrew Gow, *Male Witches in Early Modern Europe* (Manchester, 2003) and Elizabeth J. Kent, 'Masculinity and Male Witches in Old and New England, 1593–1680', *History Workshop Journal*, 60 (2005), 69–92.

Karlsen, Carol F., *The Devil in the Shape of a Woman: Witchcraft in Colonial New England* (New York, 1987).

Norton, Mary Beth, *In the Devil's Snare: The Salem Witchcraft Crisis of 1692* (New York, 2002).

Reis, Elizabeth, *Damned Women: Sinners and Witches in Puritan New England* (Ithaca, NY, 1997).

Rosenthal, Bernard, ed., *Records of the Salem Witch-Hunt* (Cambridge, 2009).

CHAPTER 23

MERGING MAGICAL TRADITIONS: SORCERY AND WITCHCRAFT IN SPANISH AND PORTUGUESE AMERICA

IRIS GAREIS

SPANISH colonization in the Americas began shortly after Columbus' first voyage in 1492, and Portugal took possession of Brazil in 1500. At the beginning of the sixteenth century, Spanish and Portuguese colonizers and missionaries poured into Central and South America, carrying with them their European ideas on witchcraft and, particularly in the urban centres of the colonies, interacting with the indigenous population. While Europeans introduced their notions of sorcery and witchcraft to the Amerindians, they also adopted some indigenous magical concepts and practices. In the second half of the sixteenth century, when numerous Africans were brought to Spanish and Portuguese America, another notion of witchcraft was added to those of Europeans and Native Americans, and eventually some features of their different concepts of witchcraft merged into new, hybrid notions.[1]

23.1 PARALLELS AND DIFFERENCES

In Spanish and Portuguese America different colonial cultures developed, due partly to different forms of colonialism and partly to the great variety of Amerindian social,

---

[1] Iris Gareis, 'Spanish America', in Richard M. Golden, ed., *Encyclopedia of Witchcraft: The Western Tradition*, 4 vols (Santa Barbara, CA, 2006), iv, 1070–4; William Monter, *Ritual, Myth and Magic in Early Modern Europe* (Brighton, 1983), 98–102.

political, and religious systems encountered by the colonizers. In the early sixteenth century, Spanish conquerors first subdued the Aztecs in Mexico (1519–21), then in 1532 set off for South America to conquer the Inca Empire in the central Andes. With regard to the realms of these two well-organized American empires, information on pre-Columbian religions is available in colonial historical sources. In spite of scanty information on pre-Columbian witchcraft, two different regional models emerge: one centred at the core of the pre-colonial Aztec state in Mexico, and another in highland Peru, the heart of the former Inca Empire. In colonial Mexico as well as in Peru, the great majority of the population was Amerindian, which accounts for the prominence of indigenous elements in the witch/sorcery beliefs of these regions. In Brazil, however, indigenous peoples were organized in smaller tribal societies, ruled by ethnic lords or war chiefs. No central institutions were responsible for the maintenance and transmission of their culture. Furthermore, until the end of the sixteenth century, the Portuguese did not control more than a relatively small strip of the coastal area, and therefore had contact only with the coastal tribes of Brazil. Consequently, little reliable information exists on pre-Columbian and early colonial Amerindian concepts of witchcraft.

The great bulk of information on colonial Spanish, Portuguese, and African witchcraft comes from inquisitorial records. In Spanish America, all inhabitants were subject to the Inquisition with the exception of Amerindians. Separate American tribunals were established at Lima in 1570, in 1571 at the city of Mexico, and in 1610 a third tribunal was founded at Cartagena on the Atlantic coast of modern Columbia. These tribunals in Spanish America regularly reported to the Supreme Council (*Suprema*) of the Inquisition in Madrid, sending them *relaciones de las causas* (reports of cases or trials) for review, and occasionally providing extracts of trial records.[2] Brazil had no tribunal of its own, but was subject to the Lisbon Inquisition. Commissioners of the Inquisition tried minor cases in Brazil and reported to the tribunal in Lisbon. Trial records of three visitations preserved in the archives of the Portuguese Inquisition yield information on witchcraft concepts among the colonial Brazilian population.[3]

Early modern Europeans believed that the deities venerated by the Amerindians were demons. The notion of the devil as personification of evil, so important to the early modern European concept of witchcraft, was, however, completely unknown to indigenous Americans. Amerindian societies regarded supernatural beings as neither good nor bad. Evil as conceived in Europe at the time, therefore, did not exist in pre-colonial indigenous cultures.[4] Consequently, the Amerindian concept of witchcraft was

---

[2] Gareis, 'Spanish America', 1071; Monter, *Ritual*, 102–3.

[3] Charles Amiel, 'The Archives of the Portuguese Inquisition: A Brief Survey', in Gustav Henningsen and John Tedeschi, in association with Charles Amiel, eds, *The Inquisition in Early Modern Europe: Studies in Sources and Methods* (Dekalb, IL, 1986), 79–99, 80–1; Iris Gareis, 'Brazil', in *Encyclopedia of Witchcraft*, i, 143–4; Laura de Mello e Souza, *The Devil and the Land of the Holy Cross: Witchcraft, Slavery, and Popular Religion in Colonial Brazil*, tr. Diane Grosklaus Whitty (Austin, TX, 2003), 184–186.

[4] Iris Gareis, 'Evil and Its Representations in Latin American Religions: Introduction', in Iris Gareis, ed., *Entidades maléficas y conceptos del mal en las religiones latinoamericanas/Evil Entities and Concepts of Evil in Latin American Religions* (Aachen, 2008), 12–23; Monter, *Ritual*, 101–2.

not classified as intrinsically evil, as in early modern Europe, but simply meant harmful magic. In this sense, however, witchcraft seems to have been a widespread and well-known concept in Amerindian cultures.[5]

In Spanish America Europeans and Africans were usually not allowed to settle among Amerindians. Although the Spanish segregation policy eventually failed to achieve its goal, in colonial towns Amerindians were usually outnumbered by Spanish, creoles, Africans, and their descendants. Thus, European concepts of sorcery and witchcraft flourished in the urban centres, while Amerindian ideas on harmful magic were more widespread in rural areas. In their attitudes towards African witchcraft, Spanish and Portuguese America shared some parallels, as both were slaveholding societies. In both cases it is extremely difficult to determine whether accusations of witchcraft against Africans were prompted by the fears that were typical of slaveholding societies or whether African slaves did actually use witchcraft to inflict harm on the slaveholders.[6]

Colonial Spaniards distinguished between sorcery (*hechicería*) and witchcraft (*brujería*). Several characteristic traits defined a magician as either a witch or sorcerer. In the Spanish learned tradition, witchcraft required an explicit pact with the devil, whereas sorcery involved an implicit pact. Another distinctive feature—the extraordinary powers attributed to witches—divided the learned community, for some sceptics did not believe witches were endowed with such powers. But at least until the end of the sixteenth century, the majority of learned people shared the popular belief that witches could fly through the air, transform themselves into animals, raise storms, and in general command the weather. Sorcerers, by contrast, were usually thought to lack such supernatural capacities but had to use spells, potions, plants, and other materials in their magical procedures. A third characteristic trait related witchcraft to harmful magic (*maleficium*), whereas sorcery, even though it occasionally inflicted harm on a victim, was usually not associated with *maleficium*. Inquisitorial records typically related *brujería* or witchcraft to harmful magic. Sorcery was merely regarded as superstition and therefore not punished with the death penalty. Witches, by contrast, if found guilty, were likely to be sent to the stake, at least until 1614 when the Supreme Council of the Spanish Inquisition demanded extreme caution in witchcraft cases and never again executed witches. In practice witchcraft and sorcery were subsumed under the category of superstition. Although the Spanish language no longer distinguishes between *brujería* (witchcraft) and *hechicería* (sorcery), early modern Spaniards and members of all layers of the colonial society evidently could tell the difference.[7] Similarly, the Portuguese language distinguishes between 'witchcraft' (*bruxaria*) and

[5] Wolfgang Behringer, *Witches and Witch-Hunts: A Global History* (Cambridge, 2004), 18–21; Souza, *The Devil*, 105–6, 172–3.

[6] James H. Sweet, *Recreating Africa: Culture, Kinship, and Religion in the African-Portuguese World*, 1441–1770 (Chapel Hill, NC, 2003), 161–4.

[7] Gareis, 'Spanish America', 1071–2; Hugo G. Nutini and John M. Roberts, *Bloodsucking Witchcraft: An Epistemological Study of Anthropomorphic Supernaturalism in Rural Tlaxcala* (Tucson, AZ, 1993), 90.

'sorcery' (*feitiçaria*), but unlike the Spanish emphasis on the different meanings of the notions, Portuguese trial records made no distinction between the two terms and used them interchangeably.[8]

In Portuguese as well as in Spanish America witchcraft was more often practised by individuals. Collective rituals to perform witchcraft and harmful magic of the kind attributed to the witches' gatherings in Europe were rarely mentioned in the historical sources. In general, many more sorcery cases involving charges of beneficent magic than witchcraft accusations involving charges of harmful magic were brought before the Spanish and Portuguese inquisitions. Another parallel can be drawn with regard to the similar social profile of the accused: in both regions the great majority of individuals practising magic came from the lower social strata of the colonial population. They made a living by performing rituals of love magic, healing, divination, or by selling potions, and the like. In sorcery trials female defendants by far outnumbered accused men.[9] Sorcery was clearly gendered in the early modern Hispanic world: learned magic using spell books, astrological tables, and other written devices usually fell into the domain of men. Occasionally women also used a written pact with the devil and employed other written texts, such as recipes for potions or prayers to conjure demons. But more often women's magical culture was transmitted by oral tradition.[10]

23.2 AMERINDIAN, EUROPEAN, AND AFRICAN MODELS

The demonization of the American religions and outward similarities of indigenous religious specialists to European witches account for an early assimilation of Amerindian beliefs into early modern European witchcraft. It is, therefore, difficult to identify pre-Columbian notions of witchcraft (i.e. harmful magic) in the colonial historical sources. Nevertheless colonial authors mention many different types of sorcerers and witches in pre-Conquest Mexico. Among these, three types of practitioners of harmful magic resembled European witches: the *nahualli*, the *teyolloquani*, and the *tlahuelpuchi*. In 1571 Fray Alonso de Molina's dictionary of Nahuatl and Spanish listed these terms under the Spanish word *bruxa* (*bruja*, female witch).[11] The *tlahuelpuchi* is still

---

[8] Laura de Mello e Souza, 'Witchcraft and Magic Practices in Colonial Brazil: 1580–1770', in Gábor Klaniczay and Éva Pócs, eds, 'Witch Beliefs and Witch-Hunting in Central and Eastern Europe', *Acta Ethnographica Hungarica*, 37 (1991/2), 243–56, 245.

[9] Gareis, 'Spanish America', 1072; Monter, *Ritual*, 103–4; Souza, *The Devil*, xvii, 253.

[10] Iris Gareis, 'Frauenkulturen im spanischen Kolonialreich: Transkulturalität, Geschlechterrollen und weibliche Identität in einer neuen Welt', in Martina Ineichen, Anna K. Liesch, Anja Rathmann-Lutz, and Simon Wenger, eds, *Gender in Trans-it: Transkulturelle und transnationale Perspektiven/ Transcultural and Transnational Perspectives* (Zürich, 2009), 183–90, at 186–8.

[11] Alonso de Molina, *Vocabulario en Lengua Castellana y Mexicana y Mexicana y Castellana* (Mexico City, [1571] 1977), fol. 21v.

much feared in the contemporary Mexican state of Tlaxcala as a bloodsucking witch, and might well have been considered as such in pre-colonial times, whereas the assimilation of *nahualli* into the Spanish concept of witch points to alterations in the meaning of the term. In pre-Conquest Mexico the term *nahual* was not restricted to practitioners of harmful magic but rather described individuals, usually religious or political leaders, with special capacities to transform themselves into animals—jaguars, birds, and the like. The power of shape-shifting was considered a divine gift and innate to the *nahual*. Only a few, powerful individuals could become *nahuales*. According to colonial sources the pre-colonial *nahual* was a healer and a diviner and made predictions, especially with regard to rainfall, which was of great importance in a region always threatened by drought. The pre-colonial *nahual* also exhibited the typical traits of a trickster, who was an ambivalent supernatural entity. Since trickster-like beings were believed to be both benevolent and malevolent, missionaries classified them as inherently evil during the process of evangelization. As missionaries redefined indigenous deities as evil entities, the *nahuales* were transformed into perpetrators of harmful magic. Gradually, the Spanish model of the witch overlapped and eventually penetrated the indigenous notion of the *nahual*. To early modern Spaniards the *nahual*'s capacity to transform into animals must have been the most striking parallel to the European witch. The ensuing process of assimilation of the *nahual* into the early modern Spanish model of the witch triggered the development of a hybrid notion that combined pre-Conquest and colonial elements. One such common belief was that if the animal form of the *nahual* was hurt in one of its nocturnal expeditions, the sores would appear in the human body of the witch. Comparison with contemporary notions of the *nahual* in modern Tlaxcala, particularly that of the *mujer-nahual* (woman-nahual) in Puebla, illustrates the transformation to a shape-shifting, bloodsucking witch, flying through the air and perpetrating her crimes in the dark of the night.[12]

Shamanic elements, such as ecstasy, the power of shape-shifting, flying, and commanding the forces of nature, were characteristic traits of early colonial indigenous priests and magicians in the realm of the former Aztec Empire. As early as 1536, the first apostolic inquisitor, Bishop Juan de Zumárraga, tried two priests of the Aztec rain god Tlaloc as idolaters. One of the two indigenous priests was said to be able to transform himself into a jaguar or a dog with the aid of a certain potion. The sacrifices performed by the priests were directed to Tlaloc in order to beg for rain and end a severe drought. Shortly thereafter, a nomadic sorcerer named Ocelotl (Jaguar) in Nahuatl (Martín Ucelo in Spanish) was denounced to the Inquisition by Amerindians in the modern states of Hidalgo and Tlaxcala. The indigenous witnesses testified that Ocelotl was a diviner and could transform himself at will into a jaguar, lion, or dog. He told the

---

[12] Gonzalo Aguirre Beltrán, *Medicina y magia: El proceso de aculturación en la estructura colonial* (Mexico City, 1992), 47, 97–105; Fernando Cervantes, *The Devil in the New World: The Impact of Diabolism in New Spain* (New Haven, CT, 1994), 61, 92–3; Antonella Fagetti, 'La mujer-*nahual*: Un personaje malévolo del imaginario colectivo', in Gareis, ed., *Entidades maléficas*, 138–49; Nutini and Roberts, *Bloodsucking Witchcraft*, 43–7, 85–6, 90–7, 102.

Amerindians that he was immortal, commanded the clouds to bring rain, and talked frequently to the 'devil' at night. The indigenous population worshipped Ocelotl as a great prophet and healer. There was even testimony that Ocelotl had predicted the downfall of the Aztec Empire to Motecuzoma, the last Aztec ruler, who imprisoned him for this prophecy. Andrés Mixcoatl (Cloud Serpent), also worshipped as a god, declared himself a brother of Ocelotl and of the rain god Tlaloc, who gave him the power to command the rain, cure illnesses, and make prophecies. Mixcoatl could punish communities with terrible floods or droughts. He used to ingest certain plants that produced visions and enabled him to communicate with the supernatural world.[13]

More explicitly, colonial authors attested that harmful magic was much feared in the realm of the pre-colonial Inca Empire. In less than a century the Inca had subdued the Andean peoples from south of modern Columbia to central Chile. Although the enormous extension of the empire brought hundreds of different ethnic groups under Inca rule, the Andean peoples shared a common fear of harmful magic. According to authors like Inca Garcilaso de la Vega (1609), a descendant from an Inca princess and a Spanish conquistador, or the Amerindian historian Felipe Guaman Poma de Ayala (c.1615), harmful magic was severely punished in the Inca state. If a person was found guilty of having practised harmful magic, Inca officials killed not only the witch but the whole family, with the exception of infants. The houses of the evildoers were destroyed and the soil was covered with lime. Special care was taken to protect the Inca ruler from harmful magic. All his belongings, clothes, nail parings, and hair were collected and kept in a safe place to prevent them from being used in magical procedures.

Public executions of witches occurred only on rare occasions. Historical sources mention only a single case in which the condemned were brought to the capital, Cusco, and publicly executed as witches. In the event, the ethnic lord of Quivi, a region conquered by the Inca in the late fifteenth century, was accused of conspiracy against Inca rule with the help of a local deity. The Inca judge charged with the investigation of the case eventually found the lord of Quivi guilty of having practised harmful magic, intending to kill the Inca ruler, and, consequently, of having committed high treason and rebellion against the Inca state. Evidently, the link between harmful magic and rebellion, as in the case against the people of Quivi, turned witchcraft accusations into powerful political weapons.[14]

In the Andes witchcraft was usually performed by individuals. Reports of witches' assemblies are only to be found in documents from the early seventeenth century referring to the north coast of Peru. In the course of a campaign against idolatry, the ecclesiastical judges discovered that the region was infested not only with 'idolatrous'

---

[13] Richard E. Greenleaf, *Zumárraga and the Mexican Inquisition, 1536–1543* (Washington, DC, 1961), 50–6; Serge Gruzinski, *Man-Gods in the Mexican Highlands: Indian Power and Colonial Society, 1520–1800*, tr. Eileen Corrigan (Stanford, CA, 1989), 36–59.

[14] Iris Gareis, 'Brujos y brujas en el antiguo Perú: apariencia y realidad en las fuentes históricas', *Revista de Indias*, 53 (1993), 583–613, at 605–11.

indigenous priests but also with witches (*brujos*). In four villages the judges charged with the visitation detected a total of sixty-three witches of this kind. Other settlements, however, seemed to be free of this infestation. Indigenous testimonies expressed the terrible fear instilled by these witches in the local population. They were called *cauchu* or *runamicuc*. The latter is a Quechua word with the meaning 'man-eater', thus alluding to the cannibalistic aspect of this kind of witch. The *runamicuc* were thought to enter the houses of their victims at night when everybody was fast asleep, suck some blood from the unfortunate sleepers, then fly through the air to their assemblies where they cooked the blood, transforming it into flesh for the witches' gruesome banquet. In order to understand the nature of the witches' flights, the Jesuit fathers did an experiment with a contrite *runamicuc* who, after having ingested a potion, fell to the floor as if dead. After having regained consciousness, he told the Jesuits that, while unconscious, he had attended a gathering of *runamicuc* in a distant place. Certainly, the ecstatic flight and several other elements characterizing these Andean witches, especially the descriptions of their nocturnal assemblies, were likely to be assimilated by early modern authors to the model of the European witch. The Augustinian chronicler Antonio de la Calancha (1638), well acquainted with European demonology, even called the attention of the readers to what he considered striking parallels between the Peruvian witches with their Basque counterparts, the famous witches of Zugarramurdi. Other beliefs regarding these Peruvian witches, however, corresponded to Andean notions of harmful magic, as, for example, the idea that by sucking the blood of the victim, the witch would abduct the victim's soul or a portion thereof. The loss of the soul would gradually weaken the person and inevitably bring about the death of the victim. A contrite *runamicuc* confessed that the witches of a village were organized in some sort of military way with their captains or masters, disciples or soldiers. It is little wonder that in the face of such a powerful organization their fellow villagers usually did not dare to testify against the witches.[15]

Trial records for magical healing dating from the eighteenth century show that northern Peru was still the scene of an ongoing struggle of magical healers against witches for the life of the patient. Healing sessions would start around midnight, usually in the wilderness. After ingesting a potion made of psychoactive plants, the shaman fell into trance and learned from his supernatural helpers who had inflicted harm on his patient. The healing session culminated in the shaman's dramatic fight to rescue the soul of the ill person. As a shamanic healer explained to the ecclesiastical judge, it was a fight to the death, reaching its climax when the 'adversary of the same kind' (the witch) would aim at the heart of the healer and try to kill him with his magical stones. If the shaman and his spirit helpers failed to ward off the attack, both the shaman and his patient would die.[16]

---

[15] Antonio de la Calancha, *Coronica Moralizada del orden de San Agvstin en el Perv, con svcesos egenplares vistos en esta monarqvia* (Barcelona, 1639), bk. III, ch. 18, 632–3; Gareis, 'Brujos y brujas', 598–605.

[16] 'Autos contra Marcos Marcelo por el delito de supersticiones y hechicerías', Pueblo Nuevo, 12 December 1768. Fs. 21, Archivo Arzobispal de Trujillo (Peru), Idolatrías, fol. 5^v; Iris Gareis, 'Una bucólica

The characteristics of the Peruvian *runamicuc* corresponded closely with those of early modern European witches. Like their European counterparts, the *runamicuc* could fly through the air, enter the houses of their victims, and cause them to fall asleep. Furthermore, they were bloodsucking witches who consumed the souls of the victims at a witches' gathering presided over by a supernatural being in the shape of a tiger or lion—soon identified by the ecclesiastical judges as the devil himself. In spite of some distortions in colonial descriptions of Peruvian witches, the concept of harmful magic was evidently well-known to Andean peoples.

Much less is known of Amerindian witchcraft models in Portuguese America. In the sixteenth and early seventeenth centuries, the majority of Amerindian peoples inhabiting the Brazilian coastal area belonged to the Tupi–Guarani language family and several of the numerous Amerindian nations were subsumed under the denomination of Tupinambá. Although, by the first decades of the seventeenth century, forced labour and European diseases had almost brought them to extinction, the Tupinamba are the most fully documented group of early modern Amerindians from the Brazilian coast. Colonial authors agreed that in Tupinamba society magicians called *pagé* played an important role. Every local group had several magicians acting as priests, diviners, and magical healers; they were also thought to command the weather, especially the rain. Some few *pagés*, however, became extremely powerful and rich. Since illnesses were usually attributed to harmful magic, only a *pagé* could heal the patient, usually by extracting the agents of the disease, such as stones, little sticks, or thorns. In healing sessions the *pagé* was assisted by his guardian spirit or several spirit helpers, which had bestowed the magical power on him. He also depended on them for his prophecies or divination. To communicate with the supernatural world, he would enter a trance by smoking tobacco and shaking a rattle that represented the spirit helper. In these sessions the spirits often appeared in the form of wild animals or birds of prey to answer the enquiries of the *pagé*. Tupinamba also believed that the most powerful magicians were able to transform at will into wild animals, such as jaguars.[17]

To early modern observers descriptions of these Brazilian shamans offered plenty of parallels to European notions of witches. On the other hand, the belief of the Tupinamba that disease and every other possible type of misfortune were caused by hostile magicians shows the important role harmful magic played in the everyday life of Amerindian societies. Obviously, colonial Brazilians shared these beliefs, because Amerindian *pagés* were much sought after as accomplished healers of illnesses inflicted by harmful magic.[18]

Spaniards and Portuguese brought their ideas on witchcraft to the colonies, and as early as the second half of the sixteenth century, European, Amerindian, and African

---

andina: curanderos y brujos en la costa norte del Perú (siglo XVIII)', in Luis Millones and Moises Lemlij, eds, *En el nombre del Señor: Shamanes, demonios, y curanderos del norte del Perú* (Lima, 1994), 211–30.

[17] Alfred Métraux, *La religion des Tupinamba et ses rapports avec celle des autres tribus Tupi–Guarani* (Paris, 1928), 79–95.

[18] Souza, *The Devil*, 100–6.

models of sorcery and witchcraft converged within the lower strata of colonial society. Since in Spanish America Europeans and Africans were excluded from Amerindian settlements, the Iberian notion of sorcery/witchcraft was generally confined to urban spaces. The tribunals of the Inquisition in Spanish America tried far more cases of sorcery (*hechicería*) than witchcraft (*brujería*). With the exception of the Basque country and some neighbouring regions of Aragon, where witches were believed to gather in assemblies and act collectively, early modern Spanish witches, who were usually old women living in rural areas, acted individually. As in Spain, witch-hunts rarely occurred in Spanish America. They took place only in Mexico and New Granada and were confined to short periods. Also as in Spain, sorcerers in Spanish America resembled Fernando de Rojas's literary figure of *La Celestina* (1499). An urban sorceress and procuress, Celestina conjured demons, prepared magic potions, and used spells to perform love magic at the request of her clients. In the urban centres of Spanish America numerous sorceresses (*hechiceras*) followed in Celestina's footsteps, offering their services as diviners, healers, and as specialists in love magic. Occasionally they also practised harmful magic, for example to remove a rival at their client's request. The Celestina-like sorceresses generally were poor, unmarried, or widowed women, and consequently lacked the protection and support of a husband or family. Sorcery provided them with income, and their supposed magical powers were a means of gaining respect, at least in their neighbourhood. Their mostly female clients, however, came from all levels of society.[19]

Techniques, spells, and incantations used in Spanish America were almost identical with those employed in Spain, which accounts for the existence of a magical culture with its own oral tradition. In love magic the most common incantations were made to St Martha, and these were often combined with conjurations of the Limping Devil (*el Diablo Cojuelo*). Both were considered to be specialists in love affairs. Additionally, other propitious saints or demons, especially Satan, Barabbas, and Lucifer would sometimes be conjured. Frequently used spells from the Spanish tradition were the so-called 'Prayer to Saint Sylvester', 'Prayer to the stars', or the 'Prayer to the palm leaves'. The latter was a divination performed at night in front of an image of the Virgin, holding two consecrated palm leaves and a lit candle. Seven knives had to be placed in front of the Virgin and the Lord's Prayer and Hail Marys had to be recited seven times. If the tips of the palm leaves converged and came into contact with each other it was a favourable sign and meant that everything would happen as expected. Doña Francisca de Maldonado, a thirty-year-old woman from Seville, confessed in 1597 to the inquisitors at Lima that she had learned most of her spells from sorceresses in her native town in Spain, and some from other women in Peru. She had lived in different parts of the viceroyalty and taught other women the art of love magic. Among the many incantations mentioned in Doña Francisca's confession, the so-called 'Prayer to the stars' was a rather wild conjuration of demons, including invocations of the

---

[19] Solange Alberro, *Inquisición y sociedad en México, 1571–1700* (Mexico City, 1988), 183–8, 296–304; Julio Caro Baroja, *Las brujas y su mundo* (Madrid, 1988), 135–9; Gareis, 'Spanish America', 1072.

Limping Devil, conjuring the teeth of Satan on the head of the victim to bind his free will and let him fall madly in love with the sorceress or her client. In a similar way the invocations of St Martha and other saints bore a stronger resemblance to conjurations of demons than to real prayers.[20] For this transmission of magic lore from the Spanish folk tradition to practitioners in colonial Spanish America, Gustav Henningsen coined the notion of 'black evangelization'. It accounts for the fact that by the end of the sixteenth century, incantations, spells, and techniques in divination, magical healing, or love magic, usually derived from the peninsular Celestina tradition. At the same time, there was considerable ethnic diversity among the defendants in sorcery cases. This suggests that within the lower levels of the colonial population, Spanish magical lore had been adopted and modified to conform to regional or ethnic magical lore, and thus was incorporated into a hybrid colonial magical culture.[21]

A great variety of materials were used in these practices, including hair, nail parings, or blood, and these were sometimes combined with indigenous materials, such as plants, seeds, or feathers of birds, and coca leaves in the Andes. Pieces from an altar stone, from a rope used to hang someone, or earth from a graveyard were equally considered to be propitious ingredients in magical potions or powders. Female magicians often practised at the request of their mostly female clients, whereas male sorcerers acted more often in their own interest.[22] Men frequently conjured demons to be lucky when gambling or to be successful in their love affairs. Magical treasure hunting was another domain of male magic in the Iberian Peninsula that was introduced into Spanish America. In Spain incantations were used to conjure the demons guarding treasures hidden at the time of the Moors. Magical treasure hunting in Spanish America aimed at gold and silver concealed by the Amerindians at the time of the conquest or buried in the tombs of pre-Columbian indigenous rulers. As in Spain, demons in Spanish America were conjured to reveal hidden treasures. Numerous male defendants—many of them members of religious orders—confessed to having made a pact with the devil in order to be successful in their magical endeavours. They submitted a written agreement to the devil, often composed in their own blood, in which they pledged their soul in return for the fulfilment of their wishes. Several of the men who had made a pact with the devil later denounced themselves to the Inquisition when they realized that their attempts had been completely fruitless. Some had been waiting at night in some solitary place where the devil was expected to appear, but in vain. Others were terribly frightened by the sudden appearance of a black dog and renounced their intentions. Finally, there were some who claimed to have seen the devil

---

[20] Archivo Histórico Nacional (Madrid), Inquisición, Libro 1028, fols 502^r–503^r.

[21] Gareis, 'Frauenkulturen', 187–8; Gustav Henningsen, 'La evangelización negra: difusión de la magia europea por la América colonial', *Revista de la Inquisición*, 3 (1994), 9–27.

[22] Paulino Castañeda Delgado and Pilar Hernández Aparicio, *La Inquisición de Lima*, i: (1570–1635) (Madrid, 1989), 374–6; Gareis, 'Spanish America', 1072; Noemí Quezada, *Amor y magia amorosa entre los aztecas: Supervivencia en el México colonial* (Mexico City, 1989), 72, 76–81, 100–4.

or various demons, but nonetheless were not successful in their plans.[23] Several male defendants confessed to having books on astrology and magical practices in their possession. Fernando de Cuevas, for instance, a priest tried by the Lima tribunal between 1581 and 1585, used a book on necromancy entitled *The Raven* (El Cuervo), which he himself had translated from Latin.[24]

In Brazil, as in Spanish America, European beliefs in witchcraft and sorcery, as well as magical practices, were soon blended with indigenous or African magic. Among other numerous divination techniques imported from the Iberian Peninsula to the Americas, the so-called *suerte del cedazo* (Spanish, the sortilege with the sieve) was particularly popular in Spanish and Portuguese America. A sieve, a basket, or a lady's slipper was raised into the air with a pair of scissors, while the frequently female diviner conjured specialized demons. The question was posed, and if the sieve or slipper moved, it meant that the answer was positive. In colonial Brazil, as early as the sixteenth century, indigenous people or practitioners of African descent also used this kind of divination.[25]

Magical treasure hunting, so widespread in Portugal, obviously did not become a common practice across the Atlantic. Laura de Mello e Souza argues that the colonial condition of Brazil was responsible for the lack of treasure because all the wealth was accumulated in the metropolis.[26] Additionally, magical treasure hunting made little sense in the first place, because the indigenous peoples of Brazil possessed neither gold nor silver nor precious stones, such as could be found, for example, in the tombs of pre-Columbian rulers in the viceroyalty of Peru. By contrast, the beliefs that illness was caused by *maleficium* were introduced to Portuguese America, probably by the first European settlers. Unlike most other magical practices, there were more male healers than female *curandeiras*. Indigenous and African healers were particularly valued in Brazil. They combined ideas and techniques from Portugal with their own beliefs and therapeutic procedures. Trial records against sorcerers from the eighteenth century show that the healing traditions of Portuguese, Africans, and Amerindians had merged into syncretistic forms. Shamanic healing procedures and the knowledge of curative properties of herbs and other materials were more often borrowed from indigenous and African traditions, while conjurations of demons, incantations, and prayers, as well as the specialized knowledge of curing some illnesses, such as sunstroke, were introduced by the Portuguese.[27]

In the seventeenth century, Portuguese witches and sorcerers were frequently banished to Brazil. Not surprisingly, some special features of Portuguese witchcraft flourished in the American colony. During the first two centuries of colonial

---

[23] Archivo Histórico Nacional (Madrid), Inquisición, Libro 1027, f. 16^v, 26^r; Castañeda Delgado and Hernández Aparicio, *La Inquisición*, 377–8.

[24] Castañeda Delgado and Hernández Aparicio, *La Inquisición*, 377; José Toribio Medina, *Historia del Tribunal de la Inquisición de Lima (1569–1820)*, 2 vols (Santiago de Chile, 1956), i, 178.

[25] Souza, *The Devil*, 93–6.

[26] Souza, *The Devil*, 97–8.

[27] Souza, *The Devil*, 99–109, 112.

occupation, several women and two men were accused of predicting the arrival of ships or of having magically altered their course, and even of having caused them to come into a Brazilian port. Another speciality of sixteenth-century Portuguese witchcraft was also linked to Brazil's colonial condition. Several sorceresses claimed to be able to fly, and even to take clients with them on nocturnal flights to Portugal. Dona Lianor, for instance, a resident in Bahia, boasted that she went to Lisbon in one night and that she could see and hear what was done and said there. Isabel Maria de Oliveira proudly declared that she had gone from north Brazilian Belém to Lisbon only to buy some ribbons, and offered to transport clients to any place they wished. Later she confessed that her flights to Lisbon were merely a joke. Others claimed that they had transformed themselves into animals for the witches' flight. In the town of Salvador (Bahia), Dona Mécia, a respectable lady, was nicknamed 'Goody Duckling', alluding to her flights in the shape of a duck.[28]

For Spanish America only few references exist regarding the witches' flight. Among Spanish creoles the most spectacular case of flying witches and report of the witches' sabbath comes from the Mexico Inquisition tribunal. In 1614, four years after the last witch-burnings in the Spanish Basque country, several Spanish creoles and a few mestizo women were accused of gathering at night to adore the devil in the form of a billy goat and kiss his back. Showing his satisfaction, the animal supplied each of the witches with a portion of dung. The devil's gift had special properties: used as an ointment, it transformed the witches into geese and enabled them to fly. At the trial, the witches prided themselves that they made nocturnal excursions by flying through the air and transporting other people to distant places. Eventually, the judge classified the stories of the witches' flight and sabbath merely as 'impertinencies' not deserving to be punished as witchcraft.[29]

Forced migration brought Africans from different regions, with different languages and cultures, to the Americas. Nominally they were baptised as Christians upon their arrival, but in practice the Africans had not received any instruction and, in general, knew almost nothing about the Catholic faith. Moreover, few slaveholders displayed any concern for the Africans' souls. As a consequence, many African slaves did not even know how to pray or make the sign of the cross.[30] On the other hand, Africans shared with early modern Europeans and Amerindians the belief that witchcraft was the cause of misfortune. Consequently, the notion of witchcraft provided a common ground in the interaction with other ethnic groups within colonial societies. Another feature of African belief systems was that magic was a key element in the constitution of authority. Gwendolyn Midlo Hall has highlighted the fact that belief in witchcraft and

[28] Souza, *The Devil*, 42, 112–18, 155.
[29] Alberro, *Inquisición*, 305–23.
[30] Iris Gareis, 'La evangelización de la población indígena y afro, y las haciendas jesuitas de la América española: logros y desencuentros', in Sandra Negro and Manuel M. Marzal, eds, *Esclavitud, economía y evangelización: Las haciendas jesuitas en la América virreinal* (Lima, 2005), 43–66, 58–9; Souza, *The Devil*, 49–50.

the important role of magical power in African religious systems inspired action to control one's fate and counteract the witches' spell.[31]

The great ethnic diversity of African slaves in Spanish and Portuguese America prevented a simple reproduction of local African belief in the New World. Instead of selecting some techniques or conjurations at random, Africans adopted specific elements of indigenous and Iberian magical lore, incorporating European or indigenous ideas on sorcery/witchcraft into their belief systems. In Mexico, for instance, several women of African descent claimed to possess a *nahual* or to have become themselves *nahuales*.[32] All over Spanish and Portuguese America African women acted in the Celestina tradition as specialists in love magic, curing, and divination, while African men often gained a reputation as healers or diviners. They used African techniques in combination with indigenous materials and pharmacopeia, or combined their herbal knowledge with the indigenous shamanic healing tradition.[33]

A substantial number of defendants in the sorcery or witchcraft cases of the Spanish and Portuguese inquisitions were of African descent. The majority of accusations revolved around magical healing, love magic, or divination. In Spanish America Africans were more often associated with witchcraft (*brujería*) and the witches' sabbath than other members of colonial society. In 1622, several African slaves working in the mining region of Antioquia in modern Columbia were accused of witchcraft and brought to the Inquisition's tribunal at Cartagena. An African slave named Lorenza denounced Leonor Zape of having inflicted harm on her and her owner. Eventually, Leonor Zape admitted she had caused the illness of Lorenza, but she claimed another slave, Guiomar, had forced her to cast the spell. Questioned under torture, Leonor and Guiomar declared they had attended a witches' assembly presided over by the devil. At times he appeared as a billy goat, at times as an African man, dressed in a loincloth with horns covered with a black scarf. Sometimes he transformed himself into a cat and transported the witches through the air to their meeting place. The witches' sabbath was conducted in the European tradition but was enriched with African elements. Auxiliary demons laid the rich table for the participants. A generous supply of wine was served with couscous, plantains, wild boar meat, and other dishes the Africans cherished. The devil informed his adherents that the whites held similar assemblies, in which the African witches should not take part. After having a meal, the African witches danced and played castanets to the sound of the drum beaten by an auxiliary demon. Then the women transformed themselves into chickens, the men into cats. Finally they adored the devil, kissing his hand and his back and concluding their assembly by having sexual intercourse with their friends. According to Guiomar about

[31] Gwendolyn Midlo Hall, *Social Control in Slave Plantation Societies: A Comparison of St. Domingue and Cuba* (Baltimore, MD, 1971), 34–7.

[32] Joan Cameron Bristol, *Christians, Blasphemers, and Witches: Afro-Mexican Ritual Practice in the Seventeenth Century* (Albuquerque, NM, 2007), 153–5; Laura A. Lewis, *Hall of Mirrors: Power, Witchcraft, and Caste in Colonial Mexico* (Durham, NC, 2003), 152–3.

[33] Gareis, 'Spanish America', 1070–1; Souza, *The Devil*, 98–103, 147–52, 218–22.

one hundred and fifty Africans attended such assemblies five days a week. The accused women confessed to having killed several slaves from rival African ethnic groups. Although, according to Leonor Zape's confession, she and Guiomar Bran would have been perfectly able to magically inflict harm, they killed their victims by suffocating them or by pulling down their houses and burying them under the debris. In spite of some African elements in the descriptions of these witches' assemblies, their resemblance to the Basque *aquelarre* or witches' sabbath is striking. Since the confessions were extracted under torture, it is likely that the inquisitors suggested considerable parts of the sabbath stories. Nevertheless, the African elements may reflect an adaptation of the European witchcraft model by New Granada's African slaves, while the European idea of the witches' sabbath might have appealed to the slaves because of its inherently rebellious character.[34]

In 1632 the Cartagena tribunal discovered another supposed witches' sect in the coastal town of Tolú. Again, the majority of defendants were of African descent; only some belonged to the mestizo population. Violently tortured, several of the supposed witches confessed to the well-known elements of the witches' sabbath, including flights to the assembly, transformation into animals, adoration of the devil, apostasy, harmful magic, and so forth. The witches' assembly was held under a great tree, while Lucifer, sitting on a black throne, presided at the meeting. Unlike the witches' assembly of Antioquia, the dishes served at Tolú were prepared without salt and had a stale taste. Also, the witches' partners appointed by the devil of Tolú were demons and not their friends, as was the case at the assembly of Antioquia.[35] On the whole, the witches' sabbath of Tolú showed more characteristics of the European popular and demonological traditions than the witches' assembly described by the Antioquia defendants. The depositions by African witnesses, however, reveal that at this time a modified version of the witches' sabbath had been incorporated into colonial popular tradition.

23.3 Converging Traditions and Regional Patterns

At the beginning of the eighteenth century, Cecilia Rosalía del Rosario Montenegro, a widowed tailor, descendant of Africans and Amerindians (*Zamba*), was charged by the

---

[34] Archivo Histórico Nacional (Madrid), Inquisición, Libro 1020, fols 208^v–226^v; Henry Charles Lea, *The Inquisition in the Spanish Dependencies: Sicily—Naples—Sardinia—Milan—The Canaries—Mexico—Peru—New Granada* (New York, 1922), 462–4; Adriana Maya Restrepo, 'Las brujas de Zaragoza: Resistencia y cimarronaje en las minas de Antioquia, Colombia 1619–1622', *América negra*, 4 (1992), 85–100; Heather Rachelle White, 'Between the Devil and the Inquisition: African Slaves and the Witchcraft Trials in Cartagena de Indies', *The North Star: A Journal of African American Religious History*, 8 (2005), 1–15.

[35] Archivo Histórico Nacional (Madrid), Inquisición, Libro 1020, fol. 313^r–320^v; Lea, *The Inquisition in the Spanish Dependencies*, 464–5.

Inquisition tribunal in Lima of gathering with other women on Thursday and Friday nights, where they transformed themselves into ducks for the witches' flight, and said: 'From joist to joist, without God and Holy Mary, Mondays, and Tuesdays, and Wednesdays three.'[36] A similar testimony appeared in an idolatry trial from northern Peru. In 1786 an indigenous woman was accused by her foster-daughter of assembling other villagers in her house, where, using a powder and reciting the same words as Cecilia had done eighty years earlier, they transformed themselves into ducks, then flew to a lake to take a bath and adore the devil. At the end of the trial, after the woman had spent two years in prison, it turned out that the accusation had been made up.[37] It is apparent that European ideas of the witches' flight and the witches' sabbath had become common lore among the different ethnic groups within the colonial population of Spanish America.

The colonial blend of magical traditions was not the outcome of a casual jumbling up of some rites and techniques, but rather resulted from transcultural processes of adoption, modification, and incorporation of selected elements that conformed to native belief systems. Each segment of the colonial population incorporated those elements of ethnic lore that made sense in their own belief systems. Europeans consulted indigenous and African healers because they all shared the same belief in magically inflicted illnesses. In the same way the indigenous and African population adopted only those aspects of European magical lore that were compatible with their own beliefs. As a universal phenomenon, the belief in witchcraft (harmful magic) provided a common ground for interethnic discourse. Therefore, especially at the lower strata of the colonial urban population, magical rituals, such as healing, divination, and counter-magic, offered a space for communication among members of different ethnic groups. The resulting synthesis of African, Amerindian, and European magical lore contributed to the emergence of different regional patterns that reflected different dominant ethnic traditions.

Only two major witch-hunts took place in Spanish America, and these occurred in the district that came under the jurisdiction of the tribunal at Cartagena. Although this tribunal was established forty years after the Lima tribunal, it heard more witchcraft and sorcery cases than either of the other two tribunals. During the sixteenth and seventeenth centuries, it adjudicated 169 sorcery and witchcraft cases. During the same period of time the Lima tribunal heard 136 sorcery cases, while the Inquisition in Mexico tried only seventy-four such cases over the course of two centuries. In the tribunals at Lima and in Mexico the number of sorcery and witchcraft cases increased during the eighteenth century. Although we don't have complete statistics for this last period in Mexico, there is evidence of twenty witchcraft cases and thirty-nine sorcery trials. None of the three Spanish American Inquisition tribunals sentenced an

---

[36] Medina, *Historia*, ii, 196; Monter, *Ritual*, 104.

[37] 'Expediente seguido contra María de la "O" Perfecta, del pueblo de San Pedro sobre supersticiones e irreligión', San Pedro de Lloc, 16 May 1786. Fs. 38, Archivo Arzobispal de Trujillo (Peru), Idolatrías, fols 2^v–3^r.

individual to death for sorcery or witchcraft during their period of existence or, in the case of the Cartagena tribunal, had the sentences commuted to less severe punishments.[38]

In Brazil there were different patterns of prosecution in the sixteenth and seventeenth centuries on the one hand, and in the eighteenth century on the other. The trials in the earlier period, most of which were individual prosecutions for witchcraft and sorcery, reflected the strong influence of Portuguese witchcraft beliefs. In the eighteenth century, Africans and Amerindians in northern Brazil became more prominent in witchcraft trials. In these prosecutions, witchcraft accusations were more often directed against groups of people, especially African slaves who were suspected of having conspired against their masters. Collectively performed propitiatory rituals, sometimes by Africans (*calundus*) and Amerindians (*catimbós*), were misinterpreted by the authorities as witches' assemblies and prosecuted by the Inquisition.[39]

In Spanish and Portuguese America witchcraft accusations, especially when they were combined with references to the witches' sabbath, reflected the relationships among the different ethnic groups in colonial society. Whereas slaveholders and colonial authorities feared witchcraft as a weapon of the powerless, Africans, Amerindians, and poor colonialists used it as a means of constituting authority and preventing the destruction of their cultures and belief systems.

FURTHER READING

Aguirre Beltrán, Gonzalo, *Medicina y magia: El proceso de aculturación en la estructura colonial* (Mexico City, 1992).

Alberro, Solange, *Inquisición y sociedad en México, 1571–1700* (Mexico City, 1988).

Behar, Ruth, 'Sex and Sin, Witchcraft and the Devil in Late Colonial Mexico', *American Ethnologist*, 14 (1987), 34–54.

Ceballos Gómez, Diana Luz, *Hechicería, brujería e Inquisición en el Nuevo Reino de Granada: Un duelo de imaginarios* (Bogotá, 1994).

Gareis, Iris, 'Brazil', in Richard M. Golden, ed., *Encyclopedia of Witchcraft: The Western Tradition*, vol. 1 (Santa Barbara, CA, 2006).

Gareis, Iris, 'Spanish America', in Richard M. Golden, ed., *Encyclopedia of Witchcraft: The Western Tradition*, vol. 4 (Santa Barbara, CA, 2006).

Henningsen, Gustav, 'The Diffusion of Magic in Colonial America', in J. C. V. Johansen, E. Ladevig Petersen, and Henrik Stevnsborg, eds, *Clashes of Culture: Essays in Honour of Niels Steensgaard* (Odense, 1992), 160–78.

Lea, Henry Charles, *The Inquisition in the Spanish Dependencies: Sicily—Naples—Sardinia—Milan—The Canaries—Mexico—Peru—New Granada* (New York, 1922).

Maya Restrepo, Luz Adriana, *Brujería y reconstrucción de identidades entre los Africanos y sus descendientes en la Nueva Granada, siglo XVII* (Bogotá, 2005).

---

[38] Aguirre Beltrán, *Medicina*, 333–76; Ronald Escobedo, 'América y la Inquisición', in *Los Inquisidores* (Vitoria-Gasteiz, 1993), 319–50, 348; Iris Gareis, 'Peru', in *Encyclopedia of Witchcraft*, iii, 894–6.

[39] Gareis, 'Brazil', 143–4; Souza, *The Devil*, 130–41, 167–75, 249–55.

Millar Carvacho, René, *Inquisición y sociedad en el virreinato peruano: Estudios sobre el Tribunal de la Inquisición de Lima* (Santiago de Chile, 1998).

Nutini, Hugo G. and Roberts, John M., *Bloodsucking Witchcraft: An Epistemological Study of Anthropomorphic Supernaturalism in Rural Tlaxcala* (Tucson, AZ, 1993).

Perry, Mary Elizabeth and Cruz, Anne J., eds, *Cultural Encounters: The Impact of the Inquisition in Spain and the New World* (Berkeley, CA, 1991).

Quezada, Noemí, *Enfermedad y maleficio: El curandero en el México colonial* (Mexico City, 1989).

Souza, Laura de Mello e, *The Devil and the Land of the Holy Cross: Witchcraft, Slavery, and Popular Religion in Colonial Brazil*, tr. Diane Grosklaus Whitty (Austin, TX, 2003).

Sweet, James H., *Recreating Africa: Culture, Kinship, and Religion in the African-Portuguese World, 1441–1770* (Chapel Hill, NC, 2003).

CHAPTER 24

THE DECLINE AND END OF WITCHCRAFT PROSECUTIONS

BRIAN P. LEVACK

DURING the seventeenth and eighteenth centuries, prosecutions and executions for the crime of witchcraft declined in number and eventually came to an end. The decline occurred in all European countries where witch-hunts had taken place, from Scotland to Transylvania and from Portugal to Finland. The same process took place in those colonial possessions of Spain, Portugal, and England where ecclesiastical or temporal authorities had brought witches to trial. The decline was marked by an increasing reluctance to prosecute witches, the acquittal of many who were tried, the reversal of convictions on appeal, and eventually the repeal of the laws that had authorized the prosecutions. By 1782 the last officially sanctioned witchcraft execution had taken place, and in many jurisdictions witchcraft, at least as it had been defined in the sixteenth and seventeenth centuries, had ceased to be a crime. Individuals continued to name their neighbours as witches, and occasional trials took place in areas that had not banned them. In some places villagers who had suffered physical harm or misfortune lynched witches whom they considered responsible, but they did so illegally and at the risk of being prosecuted themselves.

24.1 PATTERNS OF DECLINE

The reduction and eventual end of witch-hunting occurred at different times in the various kingdoms and territories of Europe, and its abandonment rarely followed a strictly linear trajectory. In some countries, such as the Dutch Republic, the decline in prosecutions became evident before the end of the sixteenth century, while in others, such as Poland and Hungary, it did not begin until the eighteenth century. The length of time that the entire process took also varied greatly from place to place. In Scotland, for example, a significant reduction in the number of prosecutions was followed by more than fifty years of trials, whereas in Franche-Comté and colonial Massachusetts witch-hunts came to a complete end only a few years after the courts started to discourage prosecutions. Even the legislation declaring that witchcraft was no longer a crime was passed at different stages of the process. In some kingdoms, such as Hungary and Prussia, the formal decriminalization of witchcraft preceded and was largely responsible for the end of witch-hunting, whereas in Great Britain and Denmark it did not occur until long after the trials had stopped.

The multiplicity of jurisdictions in many states and regions makes it difficult to establish a uniform chronology of decline within the boundaries of kingdoms, states, or even smaller territories. This was especially true in Spain, where a gross miscarriage of justice in the Basque country in 1609–14 led the Supreme Council of the Spanish Inquisition in Madrid to draft a new set of procedural rules that led to a sharp decline in prosecutions and the end of executions. These rules, however, did little to put an end to witchcraft prosecutions. The regional tribunals of the Inquisition at Barcelona and Valencia, for example, tried large numbers of witches between 1614 and 1690, although none of those resulted in executions.[1] Prosecutions in the secular courts were much more severe. Between 1614 and 1622 the local secular courts in Catalonia executed some four hundred witches.[2]

A similar situation prevailed in Italy, where witchcraft prosecutions tapered off after the Roman Inquisition issued new guidelines for trying witches in the 1620s. Executions had ended in Rome even earlier, but the Roman Inquisition was unable to stop prosecutions that continued in the municipal courts. Even more important, the Inquisition continued to try people accused of performing some of the spiritual offences that had formed part of the composite crime of witchcraft. The records of the Roman Inquisition in the late seventeenth and eighteenth centuries are replete with prosecutions for magical practices and making implicit pacts with the devil. Noticeably missing in these trials were charges of *maleficium*, which was essential to most definitions of witchcraft, as well as any charges of collective devil worship. In these cases, therefore witchcraft was reduced to practices that were deemed superstitious.

The definition of witchcraft was stretched even further when the Portuguese Inquisition prosecuted hundreds of people in the eighteenth century as witches for practising superstitious healing.[3] The crimes of which these people were accused can only be

---

[1] Between 1614 and 1690 the tribunal at Barcelona prosecuted 198 cases of witchcraft, and the tribunal at Valencia tried 281 cases. See Gunnar W. Knutson, *Servants of Satan and Masters of Demons: The Spanish Inquisition's Trials for Superstition, Valencia and Barcelona, 1478–1700* (Turnhout, 2009).

[2] For the large witch-hunt in Catalonia in 1622 see Augustí Alcoberro, 'Cacera de bruixes, justícia local i Inquisició a Catalunya, 1487–1643: alguns criteris metodològics', *Pedralbes: Revista d'Historia Moderna*, 28 (2008), 503.

[3] Timothy D. Walker, *Doctors, Folk Medicine and the Inquisition: The Repression of Magical Healing in Portugal during the Enlightenment* (Leiden, 2005).

considered witchcraft if we broaden the term to include benevolent or white witchcraft. Theologians who emphasized the demonic source of all magic, regardless of its purpose—especially Protestant demonologists such as the English divine William Perkins—often considered the white witch just as dangerous as her maleficent counterpart, but courts invariably treated the white witch more leniently.

An uneven pattern of prosecutions was also apparent in France, where criminal justice came under the authority of nine provincial parlements. The earliest noteworthy decline in prosecutions took place within the region governed by the Parlement of Paris, which exercised an appellate jurisdiction over about two-thirds of northern France. By a series of steps between 1590 and 1624 the Parlement established and enforced the rule that all capital witchcraft sentences had to be submitted to the Parlement for review. This practice, which resulted in the reversal of many convictions, led to an end of executions for witchcraft within the jurisdiction of the Parlement by 1625. It took longer, however, for other parlements to follow suit. A cluster of convictions in the 1660s and 1670s in Normandy, which fell within the jurisdiction of the Parlement of Rouen, and others within the jurisdiction of the parlements of Pau and Bordeaux were not overturned until the government of Louis XIV intervened and established a uniform procedure in witchcraft cases throughout France.

The pattern of decline in witchcraft prosecutions was even more uneven in the Holy Roman Empire, which consisted of more than four hundred separate jurisdictions, each of which had its own chronology of witchcraft trials. One reason for this diverse pattern was the absence of strict regulation and supervision of criminal justice. An imperial judicial institution, the *Reichskammergericht* at Speyer, could hear appeals of specific cases, but could not require the review of all sentences in the manner of French parlements. Without such control and supervision trials could continue to take place for years until the local princes, dukes, and prince-bishops realized that those who were accused had not committed any crimes. At that point the prosecutions ended.

The main institutions in the Holy Roman Empire that had the capacity to regulate the intensity of prosecutions were the law faculties of the German universities, which local governments were required to consult in cases of witchcraft. The law faculties acted as de facto courts of appeal, thus playing a role similar to the regional parlements in France. During most of the period of witch-hunting, consultation with the law faculties in cases of witchcraft did little to restrain witch-hunting. Indeed, the consultations often had the opposite effect, as jurists, being familiar with demonological theory and committed to the rigorous prosecution of the crime, probably did more to facilitate than restrain the prosecution of the accused.[4] In the late seventeenth century, however, the consultations began to have the opposite effect, as jurists started to advise the use of extreme caution in the prosecution of the crime, and to secure acquittals rather than

---

[4] Gerhard Schormann, *Hexenprozesse in Nordwestdeutschland* (Hildesheim, 1977), 9–44, 158; Sönke Lorenz, *Aktenversendung und Hexenprozess* (Frankfurt, 1982).

convictions.[5] This change was particularly evident at the University of Tübingen, which began to recommend against torturing witches and in favour of acquitting them in a majority of cases in the 1660s.[6] Consultations with the law faculty of the University of Helmstedt contributed to the striking decline in the percentage of witchcraft executions in the principality of Braunschweig-Wolfenbüttel in the second half of the seventeenth century. Not all law faculties demonstrated such scepticism. In the last witchcraft trial in the German town of Langenburg in 1672, consultations of municipal authorities with the law faculties of Altdorf and Strasbourg offered differing opinions, with the jurists at Strasbourg allowing the accused witch to be tortured a second time, a decision that led to her confession and execution.[7] Only in the last decade of the seventeenth century and the first decade of the eighteenth did the law faculties, especially at the University of Halle, where Christian Thomasius took a lead in ending prosecutions, collectively contribute to the end of witch-hunting.

In many European jurisdictions, prosecutions began to taper off in the wake of large witch-hunts, in which it became apparent that gross miscarriages of justice had taken place. The massive witch-hunts that took place at Ellwangen, Würzburg, and Bamberg in the early seventeenth century; the Basque witch-hunt of 1609–11; the cluster of trials in Denmark that followed the statutory definition of the crime in 1617; the witch-hunt conducted by Matthew Hopkins and John Stearne in England in 1645–7; the great Scottish witch-hunt of 1661–2; the Mora trials in Sweden in 1669–70; and the large witch-hunt at Salem, Massachusetts, in 1692 all led to a reduction in the number of trials in these states or regions in subsequent years. The witch panics and chain-reaction hunts in Germany in the 1620s led to what Erik Midelfort has called a 'crisis of confidence' in the criminal procedures used to prosecute witches, and in some of the beliefs regarding the nature of the crime, especially with regard to its collective nature. Other European regions experienced a similar crisis of confidence, although it is problematic to speak of a general European crisis of this sort between the 1620s and the 1680s.[8]

---

[5] The law faculties at Trier and Strasbourg also tended to recommend caution in witchcraft cases after 1650. These faculties exercised more influence over the criminal courts in the Saar region during the late seventeenth century, the period in which witchcraft prosecutions in that area declined. Eva Labouvie, 'Hexenspuk und Hexenabwehr: Volksmagie und volkstümlicher Hexenglaube', in R. van Dülmen, ed., *Hexenwelten: Magie und Imagination vom 16.–20. Jahrhundert* (Frankfurt, 1995), 70–1.

[6] Schormann, *Hexenprozesse in Nordwestdeutschland*, 20–1, 24, 57; Marianne Sauter, *Hexenprozess und Folter: Die strafrechtliche Spruchpraxis der Juristenfakultät Tübingen im 17. und beginnenden 18. Jahrhundert* (Bielefeld, 2010).

[7] Thomas Robisheaux, *The Last Witch of Langenburg: Murder in a German Village* (New York, 2009), 275–85.

[8] H. C. Erik Midelfort, *Witch-Hunting in Southwestern Germany, 1562–1684* (Stanford, CA, 1972), 121–63. For a broader application of this concept see Edward Bever, 'Witchcraft Prosecutions and the Decline of Magic', *Journal of Interdisciplinary History*, 40 (2009), 271–4.

24.2 DECRIMINALIZATION

Before the beginning of the nineteenth century witchcraft laws were repealed or significantly modified in only seven kingdoms: France in 1682, Prussia in 1714, Great Britain in 1736, the Austrian Habsburg monarchy in 1766, Russia in 1770, Poland in 1776, and Sweden in 1779. Only the last two kingdoms legislated a complete ban on witchcraft trials. The Polish statute, passed by the *Sejm*, the Polish parliament, a year after a witch-hunt in the village of Doruchów had claimed the lives of six women, forbade the prosecution of witches by all tribunals, including the court of the small town of Grabów, which had conducted the trials of the Doruchów witches. The Swedish National Code of 1779 simply omitted the clause regarding witchcraft that had been in the old Code of 1734, thus rendering prosecutions impossible.

The British statute of 1736 also bears most of the signs of a blanket prohibition of witchcraft prosecutions, since it repealed the English statute of 1604 and its Scottish counterpart of 1563. But, by making it an offence to 'pretend to exercise or use any kind of witchcraft, sorcery, enchantment or conjuration or undertake to tell fortunes' on the pain of imprisonment for one year, the British parliament failed to decriminalize all those activities that once marched under the broad banner of witchcraft. Prosecutions for conjuration under the statute of 1736 were rare, but they did take place, and the judges who charged grand juries continued to remind them that it was a crime to pretend to be a witch. This provision of the new witchcraft law was not repealed until 1951.[9]

The French royal edict of 1682 achieved even less than the British law of 1736. It is true that the edict, just like the later British statute, referred to magic as 'pretended', possibly to offer protection against impostors. But as far as witchcraft prosecutions were concerned, the law was far more qualified than the British statute. Designed in part to prevent a recurrence of the notorious 'Affair of the Poisons' that had scandalized Parisian society in 1679–81, it left intact the death penalty for forms of magic that were overtly sacrilegious, and it permitted some prosecutions for *maleficium* that continued in France during the following decade. France did not prohibit all witchcraft prosecutions until 1791. The same was true of the imperial Habsburg law of 1766, which was titled 'An Article on Sorcery, Witchcraft, Divination, and Similar Activities'. This piece of legislation, which was part of Maria Theresa's reform of criminal law, exhibited a fundamental scepticism regarding the reality of all magical phenomena. Nevertheless, the article continued to define as a crime the practice of 'true' or legitimate magical practices, as opposed to those arising from vulgar superstition, and it did not rule out the possibility of the death penalty (which would have to be determined by the sovereign) in cases of *maleficium* performed through the power of the devil. The decree eliminated prosecutions in cases arising from fraud and mental illness, but, like

---

[9] Brian P. Levack, ed., *The Witchcraft Sourcebook* (London, 2004), 171–2.

the statutes and ordinances of Great Britain and France, it did not completely decriminalize witchcraft.[10]

The least comprehensive of these laws was the Prussian edict of 1714, issued by King Frederick William I less than two years after his accession to the throne. This mandate was designed solely to reform the criminal procedures used in witchcraft trials so that innocent persons would no longer be tortured, forced to confess, and executed. Its concern with legal procedure reflects the influence of Christian Thomasius, the chancellor at the University of Halle, and indirectly that of Friedrich Spee von Langenfeld, upon whom Thomasius relied heavily in his published work. The edict, which was to be proclaimed in the local courts, demanded that all judicial decisions either to torture or execute witches be submitted to the king for confirmation before being implemented. This provision, which echoes French policy and anticipates that of the Habsburg monarchy, provides evidence of the role played by central authorities in restricting witchcraft prosecutions. The law did not, however, ban witchcraft trials or even executions, although it did require the removal of all the stakes from the public places where witches had been burned. In 1721 Prussia abolished the death penalty in all witchcraft trials.

The formal decriminalization of witchcraft had little bearing on the decline in prosecutions that had already begun. The blanket repeals that took place in Great Britain and Sweden had no effect whatsoever on witchcraft prosecutions in those countries because the last trials had long preceded the legislation effecting the change. The same could be said of the large number of states that repealed their laws only in the nineteenth century. Even in those countries that passed witchcraft statutes before the end of the trials, the new laws had only a limited effect on the volume of prosecutions. The first of these laws, the French edict of 1682, probably prevented prosecutions only in the few outlying regions of the country where trials were still taking place.[11] The same could be said of Frederick William I's edict of 1714, since prosecutions in Prussia had slackened considerably since the 1690s. The Polish law of 1776 affected only those isolated villages where there was still pressure to prosecute. Only Maria Theresa's law of 1766 seems to have led to a demonstrable curtailment in the number of trials and executions. Even then, however, witch-hunting was taking place only in certain parts of the Habsburg monarchy, mainly in Hungary, where authorities prosecuted 1,161 persons for magical crimes between 1690 and 1750, and executed 319 of those tried. In Austria trials had already ended before the promulgation of Maria Theresa's edict, with the last execution occurring in 1750.

---

[10] For a detailed analysis of Maria Theresa's legislation see Edmund M. Kern, 'An End to Witch Trials in Austria: Reconsidering the Enlightened State', *Austrian History Yearbook*, 39 (1999), 159–85. There is no evidence of any such prosecutions, much less executions in Austria. In Hungary, however, a number of prosecutions took place after the promulgation of the edict.

[11] For the effect it had in discouraging the prosecution of Marie-Catherine Cadiére for witchcraft at Aix in 1730 see B. Robert Kreiser, 'The Devils of Toulon: Demonic Possession and Religious Politics in Eighteenth-Century Provence', in Richard M. Golden, ed., *Church, State and Society under the Bourbon Kings of France* (Lawrence, KS, 1982), 187–200.

The more common pattern of decriminalization was the de facto cessation of trials, without any accompanying edict. This was achieved at different times in various jurisdictions, but in many cases the very last trials occurred long after the decline in prosecutions had begun. In Germany, for example, the decline in prosecutions had begun in the 1630s, but many German territories held prosecutions well into the eighteenth century. Würzburg had its last trial in 1749, Bavaria in 1792, and Württemberg in 1805. In Spain, where the decline in prosecutions began in the early years of the seventeenth century, occasional trials took place until 1820, while in Norway and Denmark, where trials had peaked in the mid-seventeenth century, prosecutions continued into the 1690s, when they stopped abruptly, without any official legislative action.[12]

24.3 HISTORIOGRAPHY

Historians of witchcraft have traditionally given much more thought to the question of why the trials began than why they came to an end. Those who have addressed the latter question have emphasized one of three explanations: changes in the witch beliefs of the educated classes, efforts of governments to control the administration of local justice, and changes in criminal procedure.

The first of these explanations, which dominated the historiography of witchcraft until the later decades of the twentieth century, focused on the witch beliefs of educated elites, especially theologians and philosophers. Those who adopted this approach attributed the decline and end of witch-hunting to the rise of modern rationalism, advances in science, and the triumph of the belief that the natural world was a machine that operated in accordance with natural laws, or a much vaguer rejection of ignorance and 'superstition'.[13] This interpretation of the decline of witchcraft prosecutions arose during the Enlightenment, and it became the backbone of late nineteenth- and early twentieth-century liberal and Whig historiography. Historians writing in this tradition focused mainly on the content of published witchcraft treatises and the theological and philosophical controversies to which those treatises contributed. The end of the trials thus became synonymous with the rejection of the demonological ideas that had provided the intellectual foundations of the witch-hunt.

During the past thirty years this explanation for the decline of witch-hunting based on the rejection of witch beliefs by educated elites has virtually collapsed. The main reason for this has been the recognition that the judges and magistrates who were

---

[12] Gunnar Knutsen, 'The End of the Witch Hunts in Scandinavia', *ARV: Nordic Yearbook of Folklore*, 62 (2006), 143–8. Swedish trials, however, continued into the 1770s and ended only with the decree of 1779. Only two of these trials in the eighteenth century resulted in executions.

[13] See, for example, William E. H. Lecky, *History of the Rise and Influence of the Spirit of Rationalism in Europe* (London, 1910), 102–54.

responsible for acquitting witches or refusing to prosecute them did not abandon their belief in the reality of witchcraft. The few sceptics who did deny that reality or came close to denying it in the late sixteenth and seventeenth centuries, such as Johann Weyer, Reginald Scot, Thomas Hobbes, Baruch Spinoza, and Bathalsar Bekker, did not attract a significant following. Not only did they fail to convince the majority of theologians, jurists, and demonologists who wrote treatises on the subject, but, more importantly, they failed to convince the magistrates and judges who controlled the judicial machinery used to prosecute witches.

When the tide of learned opinion did begin to turn in favour of scepticism if not disbelief in the reality of witchcraft, it failed to have a significant impact on the intensity of prosecutions for the simple reason that the decline had begun long before the sceptics could claim a majority of respectable demonological opinion. We have seen that the decline in prosecutions began in some jurisdictions as early as 1600 and in most others by 1670, with the exception of a few countries on the eastern and northern periphery of Europe. These were the years when the new mechanical philosophy of Descartes and Hobbes first made its appearance. The spread of the new philosophy, however, was a gradual process, and it was not uncontested. A few natural philosophers embraced the new ideas in the 1650s[14] but it took some time for mechanism to exercise a more pervasive influence within the universities, the legal profession, and the judicial bureaucracies of the state. It is unlikely that the judges and officials who applied the early brakes to witch-hunting during the first seventy years of the seventeenth century were even exposed to, let alone influenced by, the new ideas.

The critical period in that reception of these new ideas appears to have been the years between 1690 and 1720, the period of the early Enlightenment. Thus the new philosophy did not appreciably affect the mental outlook of the educated classes until well after prosecutions had begun to decline in number, and in some cases until after they had stopped altogether. In Geneva, for example, the first magistrate to profess an adherence to Cartesian ideas, Jean-Robert Chouet, wrote a critical commentary on Geneva's prosecution of witches in 1690, almost forty years after the last witch had been executed in that republic.[15] Even in France, where the new philosophy may have taken root somewhat earlier than in Geneva, Cartesianism probably did not have the negative influence on the level of prosecutions that scholars have often attributed to it.[16] Certainly, the members of the Parlement of Paris who played a decisive role in the decline of French witch-hunting could not have been influenced by Cartesianism or any other aspect of the 'intellectual revolution' until long after they had brought executions for witchcraft to an end within their jurisdiction in the early seventeenth

---

[14] See e.g. Brian Easlea, *Witch Hunting, Magic and the New Philosophy* (Brighton, 1980), 135.

[15] E. William Monter, *Witchcraft in France and Switzerland: The Borderlands during the Reformation* (Ithaca, NY, 1976), 38.

[16] See, for example, H. R. Trevor-Roper, *The European Witch-Craze of the Sixteenth and Seventeenth Centuries and Other Essays* (New York, 1969), 182.

century.[17] If the new philosophy played any role at all in the decline of witch-hunting, it was at the *end* of the process in the late seventeenth and early eighteenth centuries, when the last trials took place and witchcraft was decriminalized, not in the seventeenth century, when the initial and usually the most dramatic reduction in the number of trials occurred.[18]

When philosophical scepticism regarding witchcraft did take root among the magistracy and judiciary, it was not usually based on science, rationalism, or the mechanical philosophy. It is true that the mechanical philosophy articulated by Descartes, Hobbes, and others had the potential to destroy witch beliefs. It may have played a part in Bekker's rejection of the belief that the devil could not interfere in the natural world, but even when Cartesianism did enter the intellectual mainstream, such as at Geneva in the 1690s, it did not bring with it a rejection of the belief in witchcraft or of demonic intervention in the world. The main reason for this is that the mechanical philosophy, just like the science or natural philosophy that appealed to it as its intellectual foundation, had accommodated the devil as part of that natural world. One indication of this accommodation is that two English natural philosophers who were committed to the mechanical philosophy—Robert Boyle and Joseph Glanvill—believed in the reality of witchcraft, even at a time when prosecutions had begun to taper off in that kingdom. The critics of witchcraft for the most part came from the ranks of Neoplatonists, who accepted the reality of natural magic but opposed its demonic variant.

The only changes in witch beliefs among the educated that had a bearing on the decline of prosecutions were those rooted in theology and biblical studies. One such change was the gradual recognition that the execution of witches had no basis in scripture. By the late seventeenth century a clerical consensus gradually emerged that the apparent divine warrant to execute witches in Exodus 22:18, which was translated into English as 'Thou shall not suffer a witch to live', referred not to a maleficent magician who made a pact with the devil but to a figure identified in the original Hebrew as a poisoner or possibly a diviner. Johann Weyer, Reginald Scot, and others made this scriptural argument in the sixteenth century, but it found little support until the late seventeenth century, when new techniques of biblical scholarship began to find greater acceptance, especially in Anglican and Lutheran theological circles. A second religious belief that contributed to a decline in the number of prosecutions was that the devil, who was known to be a great trickster, could not be trusted when, for example, he identified witches by speaking through the mouths of demoniacs. This recognition was

---

[17] Alfred Soman, 'The Parlement of Paris and the Great Witch Hunt (1565–1640)', *Sixteenth Century Journal*, 9 (1978), 33, 39, 44. The last execution approved by the parlement took place in 1625.

[18] Even in the second half of the eighteenth century, Enlightenment thinkers did not completely reject the reality of witchcraft. Maria Theresa's legislation of 1766 that decriminalized witchcraft in the Austrian Habsburg monarchy, while admittedly reflecting the enlightened views of both the empress and Gerard van Swieten, did not reject the possibility of *maleficium* performed through the power of the devil. The enlightened character of their thought was limited to their disbelief in the superstitious beliefs of the uneducated. See Kern, 'An End to Witch Trials in Austria', 159–87. Their enlightenment had apparently nothing to do with the mechanical philosophy or science.

crucial to the end of witch-hunting in France in the second half of the seventeenth century and in New England in the wake of the witch-hunt at Salem. The third source was the belief expressed, mainly in Lutheran sources, that God would never allow the devil to give a human being the power to inflict harm by supernatural means. This belief helps to explain why prosecutions declined more rapidly in Protestant territories in Germany than in those under Catholic control. It also explains why the prosecution of witches for having caused demonic possessions came to an end, whereas cases of possession attributed to direct demonic invasion of human bodies continued to surface, although in reduced numbers, into the twentieth century.

When historians abandoned the theory that reason and science put an end to the trials, they replaced it with a political explanation that emphasized the efforts of governments to exercise control over the administration of local justice. This thesis was based on the recognition that the impulse to prosecute witches almost always came from the local community. The most severe witch-hunts in early modern Europe were conducted by local officials who operated with a certain amount of independence from central state control. These prosecutions therefore tended to take place where state power was relatively weak. Central governments only occasionally started witch-hunts, and when they did, it was with the intention of legitimizing new or challenged regimes. Central judicial authorities tended to treat witches with greater caution than local tribunals, both because central judges usually had more legal training than local judges and were therefore more committed to upholding due process, and because they were not members of the communities where witches were tried. Judges from central legal establishments tended to enforce stricter rules of criminal procedure, demand that all prosecutions be warranted by central authority, insist that death sentences in witchcraft cases be reviewed on appeal, and punish local officials who violated established procedural norms.

The classic illustration of this difference can be seen in contrasting the decline in witchcraft prosecutions in England and Scotland. In England, where almost all witch-craft cases were tried in circuit courts presided over by judges from the central courts at Westminster, prosecutions entered a period of decline in the early seventeenth century and spiked only once, during the 1640s, when central judges were unable either to superintend the trials properly or contain the zeal of local juries inspired by religious fervour at the time of the Civil War. In Scotland, however, where trained central judges were in much shorter supply, legally untrained local magistrates were granted permission by the Privy Council to conduct the trials themselves. This practice, which lasted at least in attenuated form until 1708, resulted in a higher rate of convictions and executions than when witches were brought to Edinburgh for trial before the court of justiciary, which was the highest criminal court in the kingdom; consequently, witch-craft trials and executions continued for a longer period of time, and in significantly larger numbers, than in England.[19]

---

[19] Brian P. Levack, *Witch-Hunting in Scotland: Law, Politics, and Religion* (London, 2008).

The tight regulation of local justice in England can also be contrasted with the virtual absence of such judicial oversight in Poland, where prosecutions peaked in the late seventeenth century but continued to take place in significant numbers until the edict of 1776 brought an end to the prosecutions. The main reason for this was the notorious weakness of the central judicial establishment, which allowed trials to be conducted in municipal courts. Without the threat of sanctions for violating due process, the judges of local courts in Poland continued to allow the trials to be held. The lack of judicial oversight from the centre also helps to explain the relatively large number of lynchings in Poland. After 1600, lynchings were relatively rare in most Western European countries, where the prospect that the government would prosecute the ringleaders of such displays of popular justice tended to keep the number of illegal executions at a minimum. Without the fear of prosecution by the government, local communities in Poland and other Eastern European countries were more inclined to take justice into their own hands.

The central governments of some of the larger states within the empire did play a role in reducing the incidence of witchcraft prosecutions in their own territories. In the duchy of Württemberg, a fairly large territory situated in south-western Germany, the central council or *Oberrat* of the duchy, situated in Stuttgart, took steps to regulate the justice administered by local magistrates. After a spate of prosecutions in the early 1660s, which took a heavy toll in lives, the *Oberrat* began to insist that local magistrates not accept testimony from children or from melancholic old women, and that they investigate whether allegedly supernatural acts of malefice might have been caused naturally. At the same time the government, faced with a swelling in the number of witchcraft accusations being brought before the courts, and aware that justice had miscarried in the past, took steps to prevent the process from getting out of control. The officers of the central courts stopped the practice of initiating proceedings themselves, used torture less frequently, followed the prescribed legal procedure with deliberate scrupulousness, and produced a large number of acquittals. In the 1670s and 1680s the number of trials began to plummet, so that by the 1690s at most only one trial was held each year. These very low levels of prosecution persisted into the eighteenth century, with the last execution taking place in 1749 and the last trial in 1805.[20]

The third major explanation for the decline in witchcraft prosecutions was that judicial authorities introduced fundamental changes in the conduct of witchcraft trials. Jurists almost always introduced these changes after they came to the realization that innocent people were being tried and executed for crimes they had not committed. This realization usually arose in response to the excesses of witch-hunting in certain localities. Criticisms of the way in which the trials were being conducted led in turn to the formulation and implementation of stricter procedural rules for the conduct of witchcraft trials, including greater restraint in the administration of torture, and the

[20] Edward Bever, 'Witchcraft in Early Modern Wuerttemberg', Ph.D. dissertation, Princeton University, New Jersey, 1983, 337–52; Midelfort, *Witch Hunting in Southwestern Germany*, 77–81.

application of more demanding standards of evidence. As a result of these changes in the judicial process, the trials of witches resulted in more acquittals, the mass panics in which scores of witches perished no longer recurred, and the courts became increasingly reluctant to initiate prosecutions in the first place. The judges who presided over these changes in judicial procedure did not, for the most part, deny the reality or possibility of witchcraft. They did, however, come to the realization that the crime was rarely performed and that most of the accused witches were innocent.

The main procedural critique of witch trials dealt with the torture of accused witches during their interrogation. This criticism led to a reduction in the frequency of torture and, ultimately, to its abolition. In the sixteenth century a few writers, including Anton Praetorius and Johann Weyer, objected to the torture of witches, but in the seventeenth century the critiques became more numerous and more passionate. Three of the most influential were written by Jesuits in German-speaking lands: Friedrich Spee, Adam Tanner, and Paul Laymann. All three of these men had been involved in, or had firsthand knowledge of, the trials themselves. From the Protestant side came works by Johann Meyfart, a Lutheran professor from Erfurt whose work betrayed a heavy reliance on Spee, and Johann Greve, a Dutch Arminian theologian who condemned the use of torture by Christians for any purpose whatsoever.[21]

This body of critical work on torture continued to grow in the late seventeenth century. Three of these later works achieved fairly widespread circulation. In 1682 the Burgundian judge Augustin Nicolas wrote a closely reasoned assault on the practice. The second work, a dissertation by Meint Johan Sassen, of the University of Halle, was published in 1697 and went into several printings, while the third, which also came from the law faculty at Halle, was a dissertation by Christian Thomasius. Thomasius drew heavily on the earlier works of Spee, Tanner, and Meyfart, but he also gave his treatise a distinctly Protestant flavour. A Pietist known for his anticlericalism, Thomasius argued in the manner of Greve that torture was an unchristian means of extorting the truth, that it was never mentioned in scripture, and that the papacy had used it to strike down its enemies under the pretext of heresy and witchcraft.

The decline and end of witch-hunting also resulted from the adherence of judges to new and more demanding standards of evidence. During the seventeenth century judges and legal writers throughout Europe showed themselves increasingly reluctant to accept the evidence that was presented to them to justify the conviction and execution of witches. This caution led to the realization that the crime of witchcraft was extremely difficult, if not impossible, to prove. This conclusion was of incalculable importance in bringing witchcraft trials to an end. It led directly to the increasing number of acquittals that occurred in virtually all jurisdictions, and it also contributed to the ultimate realization that witchcraft as a crime could no longer be effectively prosecuted.

---

[21] Johann Matthäus Meyfart, *Die Hochwichtige Hexen-Erinnerung* (Leipzig, 1664); Johannes Greve, *Tribunal reformatum* (Hamburg, 1624).

There had always been judges who demanded that proof of witchcraft be absolutely conclusive before proceeding to sentence. But whereas those early recommendations of caution were eventually ignored or contradicted, on the grounds that society needed to be protected, in the late seventeenth century they found more widespread and lasting acceptance. In this way an erratic pattern of witchcraft prosecution, in which courts oscillated between periods of intense prosecution and relative leniency, gave way to an enduring pattern of judicial caution and restraint.

This caution can be seen, first and foremost, in a growing reluctance among judges and legal writers to accept confessions, traditionally regarded as the queen of proofs, as sufficient proof of guilt. This scepticism was not restricted to those confessions that were adduced under torture. Judges and lawyers seemed just as unwilling to accept at face value those confessions that witches had allegedly made 'freely'. This scepticism arose mainly when the confessions had a high diabolical content, that is, when the witches had confessed to either a pact with the devil or attendance at the sabbath. By the late seventeenth century judges were willing to accept confessions to witchcraft (or any other crime) only if such confessions were in no way extorted, if they contained nothing that was impossible or improbable, and if the person confessing was not either melancholic or suicidal. The Danish jurist Laurits Nørregard, in urging the greatest possible caution in witchcraft cases, warned that the last thing an authority should do was believe the accused person's own confession.

A second and even more frequent expression of judicial caution in the interpretation of evidence was based on the possibility that events attributed to supernatural agency might have had natural causes. This was particularly relevant to charges of *maleficium*, in which it was claimed that witches had inflicted harm by supernatural, that is, diabolical means. The sceptical response to such allegations, frequently adopted when lawyers defended witches against such charges, was that the harm had natural causes, and that in order to convict a person of the crime, the possibility of natural causation had to be ruled out. Thus, in Spain, in the wake of the witch-hunt of 1609–14, inquisitors were instructed to inquire whether the maleficent deeds witches confessed to, such as having killed children or destroyed crops, might have had natural causes. Inquiries of this sort became more and more common in later seventeenth-century trials. In Italy legally trained officials who staffed the Roman Inquisition insisted that in cases of infanticide by witchcraft, the physicians who had treated the children should be examined to discover whether they could determine if the illness was or *could have been* natural. The burden of proof was on the prosecution; all that was necessary to secure acquittal was evidence that natural causation was *possible*. In a number of trials in Scotland in the late 1620s, advocates for the witches went to great lengths to prove that malefices, as they were referred to in that kingdom, might not have been the product of supernatural intervention. In securing the acquittal of a witch accused of murder by sorcery in 1662, Paul von Fuchs was content to show that the alleged supernatural cause of the disease that killed his victim could not be proved.

24.4 POPULAR ACCUSATIONS

Most explanations of the decline of witchcraft prosecutions focus on the actions of those persons who controlled the judicial machinery and the writers who apparently influenced them. But what about the members of middling and lower status groups, who were primarily responsible for bringing the initial accusations of *maleficium* against their neighbours, and for testifying against them in court? Without their support witch-hunting would not have been successful, at least not over a long period of time. Could these same people of inferior social rank have been at least partially responsible for the decline of witch-hunting? Did the number of trials decrease because fewer illiterate villagers were attributing their misfortunes to the magical powers of their neighbours? If that were the case, the lower number of accusations might very well be explained by social, economic, and demographic change.

There is little doubt that the dramatic changes in the fabric of European social life during the period 1550–1650 contributed to the great European witch-hunt. Overpopulation; an unprecedented rise in prices; a decline in real wages among the poor; chronic famine and dearth, especially during years of climatic severity; periodic outbreaks of the plague; extraordinarily high levels of infant mortality; migration of the poor from the countryside to the town; pestilence among men and beasts; and the social dislocations that resulted from widespread domestic and international warfare often lay at the root of those personal conflicts that found expression in witchcraft accusations.[22] The question for our purposes is whether there was a sufficient improvement in, or reversal of, these adverse economic and social conditions to bring about a reduction in the number of charges brought before the courts.

It is true that the demographic explosion of the sixteenth and seventeenth centuries came to an end around 1660, and inflation, which had been fuelled primarily by that demographic growth, began to level off. Real wages registered some improvement, and the effects of warfare on the civilian population were greatly reduced. Whether these improvements made daily village life more secure and personal tensions in small communities less acute is certainly problematic. One could argue that significant changes in the quality of rural life did not take place in most European countries until the end of the eighteenth century or the beginning of the nineteenth. The same might be said of the quality of medical care in those same communities; the country physician did not replace the wise woman in rural areas until long after the witch trials were over. The most that we can say with any degree of certainty is that communal provision for the poor became more systematic and effective in most European

---

[22] John Demos, *Entertaining Satan: Witchcraft and the Culture of Early New England* (New York, 1982), 368ff, argues that trials often did not coincide with periods of social conflict but that they could nonetheless have originated as delayed responses to such conflicts. On agrarian crises and witchcraft see Wolfgang Behringer, *Witchcraft Persecutions in Bavaria: Popular Magic, Religious Zealotry and Reason of State in Early Modern Europe* (Cambridge, 1997), 91–9.

countries after 1660, and that that development might very well have eliminated some of the social tension between the dependent members of the community and their more well-off neighbours.[23]

In the final analysis it remains impossible to determine to what extent the social and economic improvements and the changes in culture that did take place after 1660 helped to reduce the number of formal accusations made by non-elite members of society. It is difficult enough to identify the social and economic tensions that lay behind the specific quarrels leading to witchcraft accusations, but at least we have some tangible evidence, in the form of depositions taken from witnesses, with which to work. But when communities did *not* bring charges of witchcraft against their neighbours, at least not as frequently as they had in the past, they rarely left written evidence regarding the reasons for their inaction. A notation in the records of the Scottish justiciary court in 1671 that two witches were set free because 'there was no one to insist', that is, for lack of a formal accuser, still does not tell us why no one would take this judicial step.[24] We can only speculate, therefore, whether the decline in formal accusations reflects a real reduction in the number and gravity of personal conflicts at the village level or the more pragmatic calculation that judicial authorities would not be receptive to complaints brought before them.

There are, of course, other possibilities. One is that popular witch beliefs actually changed, following the same pattern that occurred first among the more highly educated members of society. One possible source of such a transformation would have been the sermons of sceptical and tolerant ministers, such as those delivered by Danish pastors trained in the providential tradition in the middle of the seventeenth century or the more admonitory one given in the next century by Joseph Juxon, the vicar of Twyford, Leicestershire, after a local witch-swimming.[25] Sermons served as one of the few vehicles for contact and interaction between popular and learned culture during this period. But there is little evidence that popular beliefs actually changed in response to such religious instruction, either before or after decriminalization, and there is much to suggest that they continued in their earlier form. Indeed, the frequency with which local communities took illegal counteraction against suspected witches suggests strongly that popular witch beliefs persisted for many generations after the trials had stopped.[26] One example of the vigour of such popular witch beliefs occurred in 1808, when a group of villagers violently assaulted Ann Izzard in Great Paxton, Cambridgeshire, because they believed she had caused several young women to

[23] Keith Thomas, *Religion and the Decline of Magic* (London, 1971), 581, makes this argument for England.

[24] S. Scott-Moncrieff, ed., *Proceedings of the Justiciary Court from 1661 to 1678*, Scottish History Society, 1905), ii, 56.

[25] J. Chr. V. Johansen, 'Witchcraft, Sin and Repentance: The Decline of Danish Witchcraft Trials', *Acta Ethnographica Hungarica*, 37 (1991–2), 415–18; Malcolm Gaskill, *Crime and Mentalities in Early Modern England* (Cambridge, 2000), 85.

[26] On popular beliefs in witchcraft in eighteenth- and nineteenth-century England see Owen Davies, *Witchcraft, Magic and Culture, 1736–1951* (Manchester, 1999), ch. 2.

experience convulsions by means of witchcraft. When prosecuted for assault, the defendants justified their violence, which included torturing and drawing blood from Izzard and dashing her head against large stones outside her cottage, on the grounds that it was the only remedy for witchcraft. In sentencing the members of the mob the judge revealed the gap between educated and popular witchcraft beliefs at the time, preaching that 'the power of witchcraft is only founded in delusion'.[27]

Another possibility is that people stopped bringing charges against witches because the prosecutions themselves became too costly. We know from isolated examples that the confinement and trial of witches could be expensive, even when the assets of the accused were used to defray the cost of incarceration and transportation. These financial burdens arising from the prosecution of witches fell on the entire community. In order to avoid further expenses a number of accused witches were actually released from gaol, and that result might easily have made villagers more reluctant to support further prosecutions.[28] It is unlikely, however, that the larger patterns of decline can be attributed to such financial considerations. It is more likely that residents of villages and small towns abandoned witch-hunting after experiencing the fear that gripped the entire community during the panics. The realization that no one was safe from the cycle of accusations and implications, coupled with the recognition that innocent people were being executed, was just as capable of affecting the members of the lower classes as those of the local ruling elite.

In any event, we still do not have any hard evidence showing why illiterate villagers and townspeople became reluctant to accuse and prosecute witches. Faced with a dearth of evidence from popular sources, we can only return to the sources we do have, which are: statistics showing a reduction in the number of trials and executions, the records of those trials that ended in acquittals, and the statements of those individuals who criticized the process of witch-hunting. These sources suggest that the main reason for the decline in prosecutions was the increasing reluctance of lay and clerical judicial authorities to convict persons of witchcraft, an attitude that was only occasionally and belatedly reinforced by a growing scepticism regarding the possibility of the crime.[29] It remains to be seen, however, how this reluctance to convict actually brought about a reduction of witchcraft prosecutions in different parts of Europe.

---

[27] Stephen Mitchell, 'A Case of Witchcraft Assault in Early Nineteenth-century England as Ostensive Action', in Willem de Blécourt and Owen Davies, eds, *Witchcraft Continued: Popular Magic in Modern Europe* (Manchester, 2004), 14–28.

[28] Brian P. Levack, *The Witch-Hunt in Early Modern Europe* (3rd edn, Harlow, 2006), 180–1; William Monter, *Frontiers of Heresy: The Spanish Inquisition from the Basque Lands to Sicily* (Cambridge, 1990), 273.

[29] See Bever, 'Witchcraft Prosecutions and the Decline of Magic', 281–3, for an analysis of the way in which changing elite views regarding magic led to a decline in the number of prosecutions.

24.5 FUTURE RESEARCH

The study of the decline and end of witch-hunting has seriously lagged behind that of its origins, despite the fact that the issues it raises are just as important and controversial. The same lack of balance is evident within the hundreds of case studies of witchcraft prosecution in particular states, regions, and jurisdictions. As a consequence of this imbalance, there is much work that has yet to be done on the subject. Besides testing theses advanced by others and discussed in this chapter, especially those concerning the role of central law courts, German law faculties, and the insistence on judicial caution, historians need to study whether changes in religious mentality might have influenced the decline in prosecutions.

This question is especially relevant in light of the widely held view, to which this chapter subscribes, that a fundamental philosophical scepticism based on or greatly influenced by the mechanical philosophy had little or no impact on the decline of prosecutions. But shifts in religious outlook, which profoundly influenced the views of sceptics throughout the period of the hunts and became widely accepted in the late seventeenth and early eighteenth centuries, had a more direct and immediate impact on the attitudes of both the educated and the uneducated. A systematic study of the sermons delivered not only at the time of witchcraft trials but at less critical times might help to illuminate these changes in popular mentality, if we assume that the messages delivered from the pulpit had an impact on the broader population. Sermons can also provide an indication of changing views regarding the devil among the clergy and, potentially at least, among those who heard them.

Sermons can also address the question of to what extent biblical commentary influenced both educated and uneducated views of witchcraft. The conventional wisdom is that the literal translation of Exodus 22:18 gave authorities a mandate to kill all the usual suspects. But Weyer and Scot in the sixteenth century and Bekker in the seventeenth century offered an alternate, sceptical interpretation of the original Hebrew text, and the declining number of executions suggests that judicial authorities no longer based their criminal proceedings on this biblical text.

A focus on the religious dimension of witch-hunting can also help to distinguish Protestant from Catholic patterns of decline. To be sure, Catholics had no monopoly of witchcraft prosecutions and executions, but there were fewer in both Lutheran and Calvinist communities, even when the relative size of the populations of those areas is taken into account. Even more striking is the fact that prosecutions and executions entered a period of decline earlier in predominantly Protestant regions. This was especially evident in Anglican England, Calvinist Geneva, the Dutch Republic, and many German Lutheran territories. Only in Calvinist Scotland did the intensity of witch-hunting begin to rival that of some Catholic German territories. Underlying this growing reluctance of Protestants to convict and execute witches was the Protestant belief that witches could not command demons to perform *maleficia*. This belief underlay this Lutheran canon *Episcopi* tradition that persisted throughout the period of witch-hunting.

One manifestation of this Protestant belief in the powerlessness of witches was that Protestants were more reluctant than Catholics to accept the possibility that witches could cause demonic possessions; in their view only the devil alone, acting with God's permission, could invade a person's body and take control of its physical movements and mental faculties. This belief, clearly expressed in the work of Johann Weyer and the English clergyman Samuel Harsnett, explains why, after 1620, relatively few Protestant witchcraft prosecutions were based on the accusations of demoniacs. The few Protestant cases that occurred after that date took place in Scotland and New England in the 1690s, and those prosecutions elicited challenges precisely on the grounds that the belief that witches caused demonic possessions denied the sovereignty of God. This theological argument helped to bring witchcraft prosecutions for having caused demonic possession to an end.

FURTHER READING

Bever, Edward, 'Witchcraft Prosecutions and the Decline of Magic', *Journal of Interdisciplinary History*, 40 (2009), 263–93.

Davies, Owen, 'Decriminalising the Witch: The Origin of and the Response to the 1736 Witchcraft Act', in John Newton and Jo Bath, eds, *Witchcraft and the Act of 1604* (Leiden, 2008), 207–32.

Henningsen, Gustav, *The Witches' Advocate: Basque Witchcraft and the Spanish Inquisition (1609–1614)* (Reno, NV, 1980).

Johansen, Jens Chr. V., 'Witchcraft, Sin and Repentance: the Decline of Danish Witchcraft Trials', *Acta Ethnographica*, 37 (1991–2), 413–23.

Kern, Edmund M., 'An End to Witch Trials in Austria: Reconsidering the Enlightened State', *Austrian History Yearbook*, 39 (1999), 159–85.

Klaits, Joseph, 'Witchcraft Trials and Absolute Monarchy in Alsace', in Richard Golden, ed., *Church, State and Society under the Bourbon Kings of France* (Lawrence, KS, 1982), 148–72.

Knutsen, Gunnar W., 'The End of the Witch Hunts in Scandinavia', *ARV: Nordic Yearbook of Folklore*, 62 (2006), 143–64.

Levack, Brian P., 'The Decline and End of Witchcraft Prosecutions', in Bengt Ankarloo and Stuart Clark, eds, *Witchcraft and Magic in Europe: The Eighteenth and Nineteenth Centuries* (London, 1999), 1–93.

Levack, Brian P., 'The Decline and End of Scottish Witch-Hunting', in Julian Goodare, ed., *The Scottish Witch-Hunt in Context* (Manchester, 2002), 166–81.

Lorenz, Sönke and Bauer, Dieter R., eds, *Das Ende der Hexenverfolgung* (Stuttgart, 1995).

Robisheaux, Thomas, *The Last Witch of Langenburg: Murder in a German Village* (New York, 2009).

Soman, Alfred, 'Decriminalizing Witchcraft: Does the French Experience Furnish a European Model?' *Criminal Justice History*, 10 (1989), 1–22.

Várkonyi, Agnes, 'Connections between the Cessation of Witch Trials and the Transformation of the Social Structure Related to Medicine', *Acta Ethnographica*, 37 (1991–2), 426–71.

Walker, Timothy D., *Doctors, Folk Medicine and the Inquisition: The Repression of Magical Healing in Portugal during the Enlightenment* (Leiden, 2005).

PART III

THEMES OF WITCHCRAFT RESEARCH

CHAPTER 25

WITCHCRAFT AND GENDER
IN EARLY MODERN EUROPE

ALISON ROWLANDS

THE French demonologist Jean Bodin noted in 1580 that women were fifty times more likely than men to succumb to the temptation of witchcraft,[1] while street urchins from the German city of Lemgo described the willingness of the authorities to hunt witches there in 1631 in terms of 'the building of a big fire, at which to warm [i.e. burn] the women'.[2] Shared by early modern people of such differing social status, the idea that witches were predominantly female is confirmed by modern statistical analysis, which shows that overall, 70 to 80 per cent of those tried for the crime of witchcraft in early modern Europe and New England were women.[3] There was, however, significant regional variation in the gendering of witch persecution. Women constituted 75 per cent or more of those accused of witchcraft in Norway, Sweden, Denmark, the northern Netherlands, England, Scotland, Hungary, Croatia, Piedmont, Siena, the Holy Roman Empire, Geneva, the bishopric of Basel, Neuchâtel, and Graubünden/Grisons, but men were in the majority in Iceland, Normandy, Estonia, and Russia; men and women were prosecuted in roughly even numbers in Finland, Burgundy, and those parts of France subject to the Parlement of Paris.[4]

---

[1] Claudia Opitz-Belakhal, *Das Universum des Jean Bodin: Staatsbildung, Macht und Geschlecht im 16. Jahrhundert* (Frankfurt, 2006), 136.

[2] Uschi Bender-Wittman, '*Gender* in der Hexenforschung: Ansätze und Perspektiven', in Ingrid Ahrendt-Schulte, Dieter R. Bauer, Sönke Lorenz, and Jürgen Michael Schmidt, eds, *Geschlecht, Magie und Hexenverfolgung* (Bielefeld, 2002), 13–37, 13.

[3] See Éva Pócs, 'Why Witches are Women', *Acta Ethnographica Hungarica*, 48/3–4 (2003), 367–83, 372 (*c.*78 per cent women); Lara Apps and Andrew Gow, *Male Witches in Early Modern Europe* (Manchester, 2003), 45 (*c.*66 per cent women); Brian P. Levack, *The Witch-Hunt in Early Modern Europe* (3rd edn, Harlow, 2006), 142 (*c.*69 per cent women); Rolf Schulte, *Man as Witch: Male Witches in Central Europe* (Basingstoke, 2009), 71–2 (*c.*69 per cent women).

[4] Schulte, *Man as Witch*, 71–2.

These data raise several questions. Why were the overall majority of those pros-ecuted for witchcraft in early modern Europe female? Was it because women were linked more readily than men with negative beliefs about the practice of harmful magic and association with the devil, or because systems of power in communities and courts worked against women rather than men? What sorts of women were accused and why, and did other factors—age or marital and socio-economic status—influence their vulnerability to accusation? Why did witch-hunting claim a significant proportion of male victims, and why did the gendering of witchcraft prosecutions vary geographic-ally? This chapter explores answers to these questions in the context of debates about witchcraft and gender, which have been shaped in particular by the influence of feminism on witchcraft historiography.

25.1 FEMINISM

Radical feminist accounts of witch-hunts portray them as a brutal means by which patriarchy exerted control over women and sought to curb the perceived threat posed to men's dominance of early modern society by women's allegedly rapacious sexuality; by the 'illicit' medical skills women supposedly exercised as wise women or midwives; by the power women supposedly possessed as the priestesses of surviving pre-Christian fertility cults; or by the challenge that women were deemed to pose to men in the economic sphere. Such accounts emphasize the horrors of the legal procedures used against accused women, especially the excessive use of torture and the burning of condemned witches at the stake. They also see misogyny, defined as a hatred of women and fear of women's sexuality, as the 'cause' of the hunts. These accounts often focus on the *Malleus maleficarum*, the demonological treatise written by the Dominican inquisi-tor Heinrich Kramer and published in 1486, as evidence of that misogyny among elites, who are seen as the driving force behind a 'top-down' persecution of witches. They point out, for example, that Kramer chose the term *maleficarum* (female evildoers) for the title of his work and that, in answering the question 'Why are there more workers of harmful magic found in the female sex . . . than among men?', Kramer replied: 'because of fleshly lust, which in [women] is never satisfied'.[5]

The most radical feminist interpretations of witch-hunting emerged in the context of feminist political activism outside academia, and were thus polemical and historically inaccurate. First-wave feminism produced one such account: *Woman, Church and State: A Historical Account of the Status of Woman through the Christian Ages,*

---

[5] P. G. Maxwell-Stuart, ed., *The Malleus Maleficarum* (Manchester, 2007), 74, 75, 77. For such use of the *Malleus* by radical feminists, see Matilda Joslyn Gage, *Woman, Church and State* (1893; Charleston, 2008), 122–69; Andrea Dworkin, 'Gynocide: The Witches', in *Woman Hating* (New York, 1974), 118–50; Mary Daly, 'European Witchburnings: Purifying the Body of Christ', in *Gyn/Ecology: The Metaethics of Radical Feminism* (Boston, 1978; London, 1979), 178–222.

published by the American suffragist Matilda Joslyn Gage in 1893. Gage asserted that nine million people—most of them women—were executed as witches, with old women, wise women, and the priestesses of anti-Christian cults the particular targets of a money-hungry Church, which taught that women were more likely to be witches than men because of their original sinful nature.[6] Radical second-wave feminists of the 1970s went further, claiming that witch-hunting was an egregious example, not just of patriarchal oppression, but also of 'gynocide'—the deliberate killing of women. In her 1974 essay entitled 'Gynocide: The Witches', Andrea Dworkin recycled many of Gage's ideas but placed greater emphasis on the Church's hatred and fear of women's sexuality, as shown in the 'frenzied and psychotic woman-hating' of the *Malleus maleficarum*, as the prime cause of witch-hunting.[7] A chapter on the 'gynocidal ritual' of 'witchburning' was also integral to Mary Daly's 1978 book *Gyn/Ecology*, in which the misogyny of the *Malleus*, allegedly directed towards wise women who possessed spiritual and medical knowledge that challenged the Church, was again central to the discussion.[8] The argument that early modern witch-hunters specifically targeted female healers, especially midwives, also found support in 1973 in the work of Barbara Ehrenreich and Deirdre English, who claimed that this had been done in order to eliminate the female rivals of male physicians and ensure a male dominance of the medical profession that continued to modern times.[9]

Radical feminist writing has had significant influence on perceptions of witchcraft outside academia: its emphasis on witches as wise women and pagan priestesses persecuted by the Church helped shape modern witches' perception of their craft's 'history', for example. It also continues to be taken seriously by publishers, with two major reworkings of the radical feminist line emerging in the early 1990s: *Lewd Women and Wicked Witches* by Marianne Hester, and *Witchcraze* by Anne Llewellyn Barstow. For both authors, men's sexual violence against women provided the key explanation for witch persecution.[10] Academic historians, however, are dismissive of such interpretations, criticizing radical feminists for their assumption that witch-hunting was 'woman-hunting', their over-reliance on the *Malleus*, their unwillingness to engage with manuscript records of witch trials, and their ahistorical use of the terms misogyny and patriarchy, which downplays the historical specificity of early modern culture and society.[11]

---

[6] Gage, *Woman, Church and State*, 122–69.

[7] Dworkin, 'Gynocide', 136.

[8] Daly, 'European Witchburnings'.

[9] Barbara Ehrenreich and Deirdre English, *Witches, Midwives and Nurses. A History of Women Healers* (New York, 1973).

[10] Marianne Hester, *Lewd Women and Wicked Witches. A Study of the Dynamics of Male Domination* (London, 1992); Anne Llewellyn Barstow, *Witchcraze: A New History of the European Witch Hunts* (San Francisco, 1994).

[11] Overviews of the criticisms usually levelled at feminists by academic historians are provided (and countered) by Elspeth Whitney, 'International Trends: The Witch "She"/The Historian "He": Gender and the Historiography of the European Witch-hunts', *Journal of Women's History*, 7 (1995), 77–101; and

Much of this criticism is entirely justified. Many elements of the radical feminist interpretation of witch-hunting stem from factually inaccurate myths created by nineteenth- and early twentieth-century writers on witchcraft, which feminists have adopted uncritically to suit their own agendas.[12] Archival research has shown that the total number of executions for witchcraft in early modern Europe was around 45–60,000, certainly not nine million,[13] and that there is no evidence for the survival of organized pagan cults into the early modern period, let alone priestesses who presided over them.[14] Historians have also disproved the idea that midwives and female healers were the specific targets of elite-orchestrated witch persecution.[15] Midwives were occasionally prosecuted for witchcraft, but they were far more likely to assist in the prosecution of infanticide than to find themselves accused of using witchcraft to kill the infants they delivered.

Female practitioners of healing or 'white' magic, such as Ursula Kemp of St Osyth in Essex, who was executed for witchcraft in 1582, were also potentially vulnerable to accusations of witchcraft.[16] Ordinary people, however, saw healers as a source of protection against misfortune, disease, and harmful magic, and were therefore reluctant to accuse them. Moreover, scholarly estimates suggest that a significant proportion (two-thirds, in England)[17] of all practitioners of white magic were men rather than women. Indeed, cunning men emerged as one of the distinct groups of men at risk of prosecution for witchcraft in some regions. The simplistic feminist representation of the witch as 'victimized wise woman' has thus been replaced by a more nuanced analysis of the gendered practice of white magic and popular medicine. This analysis suggests that, while early modern housewives made herbal remedies for household use, and while certain harmful female witches were also believed to be 'healing' witches (insofar as they were thought capable of lifting the spells they had inflicted), the semi-professional practice of 'good' magic was male dominated. More research is needed to establish the relative vulnerability of cunning men and women to accusations of harmful witchcraft at the regional level. Were cunning women dissuaded over time

---

Diane Purkiss, *The Witch in History: Early Modern and Twentieth-Century Representations* (London, 1996), 59–88; see also 7–29 for criticism of radical feminist accounts of witch persecution.

[12] See Christa Tuczay, 'The Nineteenth Century: Medievalism and Witchcraft', and Juliette Wood, 'The Reality of Witch-cults Reasserted: Fertility and Satanism', in Jonathan Barry and Owen Davies, eds, *Palgrave Advances in Witchcraft Historiography* (Basingstoke, 2007), 52–68 and 69–89.

[13] Levack, *Witch-Hunt*, 23.

[14] For scholarly refutation of these and other myths about witchcraft, see Rita Voltmer, *Hexen: Wissen was stimmt* (Freiburg, 2008).

[15] David Harley, 'Historians as Demonologists: The Myth of the Midwife-witch', *Social History of Medicine*, 3 (1990), 1–26.

[16] Kemp is listed among the forty-four men and eighteen women identified as cunning folk by Alan Macfarlane for Essex, 1560–1680; see *Witchcraft in Tudor and Stuart England* (1970; London, 1999), 117–18.

[17] Owen Davies, *Cunning-Folk: Popular Magic in English History* (London, 2003), 68–9.

from practising white magic because they were more likely to be accused of harmful magic than their male counterparts?

The antipathy many academic historians feel towards feminism in general and radical feminism in particular can be counterproductive, however, as it discourages them from engaging with any helpful insights feminism offers into the gendering of witchcraft prosecutions, particularly in relation to the analysis of patriarchy.[18] It is striking, for instance, how selectively many historians use the groundbreaking study of witch-hunting in early modern Scotland published by the feminist historian Christina Larner in 1981.[19] Larner's seminal conclusion that 'Witchcraft was not sex-specific but it was sex-related' is quoted frequently, because it undermines the assumption that witch-hunting was 'woman-hunting'. Her subsequent observation that 'The women who were accused were those who challenged the patriarchal view of the ideal woman' is cited much less often, however.[20] The workings of patriarchy, defined as historically specific ways of organizing and exercising political, legal, social, economic, and cultural power, which generally (but not exclusively) privilege men over women, need more analysis in order to establish how they shaped witchcraft belief, processes of accusation, and local trial episodes. As a starting point, we must accept the fact that the patriarchal organization of early modern society was not a 'cause' but a necessary precondition for witch-hunts that produced predominantly female victims. The role of patriarchy was particularly important in relation to the law, where patriarchy functioned to keep the making and implementation of law in the hands of men, to women's obvious disadvantage. Less plausible are feminist claims that witch trials were used against women as a strategic tool in a process of restructuring undertaken by a 'patriarchal system' that felt threatened during the upheavals of the early modern period,[21] or that witchcraft prosecutions were part of a long-term process of modernization, which resulted in the taming of women within the domestic sphere.[22] Such developments cannot be linked concretely to specific witch trials, and they also miss the point that witch-hunts were as likely to cause, as to resolve, anxieties about the stability of patriarchal social order.

[18] For further discussion, see Whitney, 'International Trends'; and Willem de Blécourt, 'The Making of the Female Witch', *Gender & History*, 12 (2000), 287–309, 291.

[19] See Blécourt, 'Making of the Female Witch', 289–91.

[20] Christina Larner, *Enemies of God: The Witch-hunt in Scotland* (London, 1981; Oxford, 1983), 92, 102.

[21] See Marianne Hester, 'Patriarchal Reconstruction and Witch Hunting', in Jonathan Barry, Marianne Hester, and Gareth Roberts, eds, *Witchcraft in Early Modern Europe* (Cambridge, 1996), 288–306.

[22] These ideas were argued by the 1970s feminists Silvia Bovenschen and Claudia Honegger; for criticism, see Claudia Opitz, 'Hexenverfolgung als Frauenverfolgung? Versuch einer vorläufigen Bilanz', in Opitz, ed., *Der Hexenstreit: Frauen in der frühneuzeitlichen Hexenverfolgung* (Freiburg, 1995), 248–9.

25.2 BELIEF

Was belief about witchcraft gendered in ways that made early modern people more likely to imagine witches as women than men? Scholars seeking to answer this question in relation to the educated male elites study demonologies and analyse the extent to which demonologists associated witchcraft (understood as the making of a pact with the devil) with women. Such scholars fall broadly into two categories: those who argue that demonologists asserted an overwhelmingly powerful conceptual link between women and demonic witchcraft, and those who argue that, while this link was of central importance in demonological thinking, it did not exclude the possibility of male witches.

The work of the feminist literary scholar Sigrid Brauner falls into the first category. Like radical feminists, Brauner focused on the *Malleus maleficarum* as the demonology that cemented the idea that witches were women. Unlike her radical foremothers, who simply plundered the *Malleus* for its most misogynistic quotations in order to give some historical gloss to their polemical claims that woman-hating 'caused' witch-hunts, Brauner published a much more subtle study. She compared the *Malleus* to earlier fifteenth-century demonologies, and argued that Kramer's emphases on women's greater susceptibility to the heresy of witchcraft because of their lust, and on the sexual nature of their pact with the devil, represented a significant departure from older traditions of thinking about heretical groups as male dominated. Brauner also argued that the *Malleus* was extremely influential, shaping subsequent demono-logical thinking about the 'sex-specificity' of witchcraft and the ways in which Martin Luther and key Lutheran playwrights wrote about 'good' and 'bad' women.[23]

In *Thinking with Demons*, his groundbreaking study of all published demonologies, Stuart Clark also argued that demonologists associated demonic witchcraft overwhelm-ingly with women. Clark, however, differed from Brauner in downplaying the novelty of this association and its links to the *Malleus*, suggesting instead that it drew on long-standing and widespread ideas about women's weakness, credulity, and carnality, all of which made them more open to demonic seduction. According to Clark, the association demonologists made between women and witchcraft was 'built on entirely unoriginal foundations; indeed, it was built on what, in the sixteenth and seventeenth centuries, had become the merest of clichés'.[24] Demonologists were not arch-misogyn-ists, then, but simply thought and wrote within a system of dual classification, within which they automatically associated women with the negative (evil/devil/witch) and men with the positive (good/God/not-witch) side of any pair of binary opposites. Clark

---

[23] Sigrid Brauner, *Fearless Wives and Frightened Shrews. The Construction of the Witch in Early Modern Germany* (Amherst, 1995), 29–49.

[24] Stuart Clark, *Thinking with Demons: The Idea of Witchcraft in Early Modern Europe* (Oxford, [1997] 1999), 106–33, quotation at 114.

concluded that, 'in the high culture of the age, the conceptual link between witchcraft and highly anomalous women was provided by the symmetries of inversion'.[25]

Unsurprisingly, historians interested in male witches suggest that the demonologists' gendering of ideas about witchcraft was more flexible and open to change over time than Brauner and Clark imply. Lara Apps and Andrew Gow tested Clark's argument that the male witch was 'literally unthinkable' for demonologists by means of the (admittedly relatively crude) method of taking ten key demonologies and counting the number of times that their authors used masculine and feminine terms for the word 'witch'. Their results showed a significant number of references to male witches in all, and a predominance of references to male witches in six of the demonologies studied.[26] They concluded that demonologists operated within 'a flexible linguistic and conceptual framework', rather than the straitjacket of binary oppositions suggested by Clark. According to Apps and Gow, demonologists thought that women were more likely than men to become witches, but this did not prevent them from imagining that men could also fall prey to the same temptation.[27]

Rolf Schulte reached similar conclusions in his study of male witches in the Holy Roman Empire, but offered a more nuanced comparison of demonological thinking along the lines of confessional difference. Schulte showed that the stereotype of the witch as woman remained dominant in Protestant demonology, while Catholic demonologists (with the exception of Kramer) were more willing to incorporate the male witch into their writings. This was partly because Protestants and Catholics had different ways of translating the all-important biblical exhortation 'Thou shalt not suffer a witch to live': Luther's translation referred specifically to 'female sorcerers', while the Catholic translation referred to 'sorcerers' who could be either female or male.[28] It was also because Catholic demonologists, unlike their Protestant counterparts, accepted and discussed at length the reality of the witches' sabbath: the collective gathering of witches to worship the devil. As the sabbath was imagined by Catholic demonologists as an event that both women and men could attend, this provided an important conceptual route by which male witches could enter the demonological picture. It also helps explain why the prosecution of men increased in the Holy Roman Empire during the seventeenth century.[29]

Rita Voltmer has shown how this shift occurred during the mass witch trials in the late sixteenth century in the Catholic Rhine-Meuse region, which centred on the German city of Trier. Here the idea of the dual-gendered sabbath first emerged as the result of the presence of a significant number of boy witches, who were pressured into confessing that they had played music at sabbaths. These imagined, gender-specific

---

[25] Clark, *Thinking with Demons*, 133.
[26] Apps and Gow, *Male Witches*, 104.
[27] Apps and Gow, *Male Witches*, 95–117, quotation at 107.
[28] Exodus 22:18 (King James Bible); Exodus 22:17 (Catholic Bible).
[29] Schulte, *Man as Witch*, 92–159, and 'Men as Accused Witches in the Holy Roman Empire', in Alison Rowlands, ed., *Witchcraft and Masculinities in Early Modern Europe* (Basingstoke, 2009), 52–73.

roles reflected the reality of village life, where men were the pipers and drummers at communal festivities. Subsequent trials against prominent local men who had been accused of witchcraft were both driven by, and helped to strengthen, the idea that men could attend sabbaths. This idea then spread to other Catholic parts of Germany by means of a demonological treatise, *Tractatus de confessionibus maleficorum et sagarum*, which the suffragan bishop of Trier, Peter Binsfeld, published in 1589, drawing on his first-hand experience of the Rhine-Meuse trials.[30] The presence of men as musicians and 'kings' of the sabbath was also confirmed in a finely detailed etching of the Trier witches' meeting, which was incorporated into a pamphlet published in three editions between 1593 and 1603.[31] The fact that men were portrayed as witches in printed images of the sabbath, while individual or small groups of women dominated the high art of the period that was concerned with witchcraft, points again to the importance of the concept of the sabbath in encouraging the incorporation of men into the imagined world of witchcraft.[32]

Demonologists were both deeply misogynistic and perfectly capable of imagining men as witches. How can these two, apparently contradictory, positions be reconciled? Thought-provoking answers to this question have been offered by Apps and Gow, and by Claudia Opitz-Belakhal. Apps and Gow suggest that demonologists understood weak-mindedness (meaning a lack of rational and intellectual strength, not mental illness in the modern sense) as the primary characteristic of the witch, as weakness of mind allowed the devil to seduce a person into witchcraft in the first place. Weak-mindedness was strongly, but not exclusively, associated with women in Western thinking; it was one of the 'web of assumptions' about gender (in this case, femaleness), which was 'not so rigidly polarised as to prevent "leakage" across the gender boundary'.[33] Some men, in other words, could plausibly be weak-minded too. Male witches were proof of this lamentable possibility; their 'weak-minded' pacts subordinated them to the devil and associated them with the female-connoted follies of witchcraft and irrationality. Apps and Gow conclude that demonologists accommodated male witches relatively unproblematically into their conceptual frame of reference by feminizing them, and that the 'feminized male witch' produced by such demonological thinking 'is an excellent example of the construction of difference

---

[30] Rita Voltmer, 'Witch-Finders, Witch-Hunters or Kings of the Sabbath? The Prominent Role of Men in the Mass Persecutions of the Rhine-Meuse Area (16th–17th Centuries)', in Rowlands, *Witchcraft and Masculinities*, 74–99.

[31] For discussion of the image of the Trier sabbath, see Rita Voltmer, '"Hört an neu schrecklich abentheuer/von den unholden ungeheuer"—Zur multimedialen Vermittlung des Fahndungsbildes "Hexerei" im Kontext konfessioneller Polemik', in Karl Härter, Gerhard Sälter, and Eva Wiebel, eds, *Repräsentationen von Kriminalität und öffentlicher Sicherheit. Bilder, Vorstellungen und Diskurse vom 16. bis zum 20. Jahrhundert* (Frankfurt, 2010), 89–163.

[32] For images of individual and small groups of women as witches, see, for example, Margaret A. Sullivan, 'The Witches of Dürer and Baldung Grien', *Renaissance Quarterly*, 53 (2000), 332–401; and Linda C. Hults, 'Baldung and the Witches of Freiburg: The Evidence of Images', *Journal of Interdisciplinary History*, 18 (1987), 249–76.

[33] Apps and Gow, *Male Witches*, 136.

within a gender category [i.e. maleness], and forces us to rethink the binary model of early modern gender'.[34] These ideas make a great deal of sense in the wider context of research into gender in early modern Europe, which has shown that, while there was an overarching gender hierarchy that placed men above women, the cultural category of masculinity was riven with divisions between men who had attained full patriarchal manhood and men who were deemed to have failed to do so.[35]

Opitz-Belakhal pursues a similar line of analysis in her study of Jean Bodin's 1580 demonology, *De la démonomanie des sorciers*. Women were fifty times more likely than men to be drawn to the devil, according to Bodin, because of the strength of their animal appetites and carnality. Bodin also portrayed women as strong of body and spirit, but only in order to stress that they were responsible for their actions before God and the law; this justified their merciless persecution as witches and lent credibility to their testimony against other 'witches'. Despite his emphasis on witchcraft as a predominantly female crime, anxiety about men whom he believed to be in league with the devil was a key theme of Bodin's work. He cited significantly more male than female witches by name and also reserved his greatest ire for educated men, most notably the German physician and witch-hunt critic, Johann Weyer, who did the devil's work by speaking out against witch-hunting. According to Bodin, such men were driven by their 'evil will' (their rationality corrupted by pride or the desire for power and knowledge) to make pacts with the devil, thereby associating themselves with the female-connoted sins of witchcraft and carnality. Opitz-Belakhal concludes that Bodin's misogynistic rhetoric could have fuelled a greater willingness to persecute not just women, but also men who were imagined to be 'like' women, as witches.

Opitz-Belakhal also reads Bodin's demonology as an exercise in masculine self-fashioning in which Bodin used strongly gendered language to represent himself as the virile, rational, and heroic defender of godly order and legal authority against witches and their defenders, while portraying his opponents (any men in positions of authority who disagreed with his call for more zealous witch-hunting) as cowardly, effeminate, stupid, and probably in league with the devil.[36] The extent to which the prosecution of witches was imagined, carried out, and justified as an expression of godly, dutiful, patriarchal manhood needs exploring in more depth in relation to other men who wrote in favour of witch-hunting or were particularly active in witchcraft prosecutions as judges, witchfinders, or witch-commissioners. Was there a code of 'merciful manhood' enabling witch-hunt critics and court officials who lacked enthusiasm for witch-hunts to justify their more moderate stance, and was declining elite enthusiasm for witch-hunts in the late seventeenth and eighteenth century linked to new ideas about 'enlightened' masculinity?

---

[34] Apps and Glow, *Male Witches*, 118–50, quotation at 136.

[35] See, for example, Alexandra Shepard, *Meanings of Manhood in Early Modern England* (Oxford, 2003).

[36] Opitz-Belakhal, *Das Universum des Jean Bodin*, 131–67.

At the elite level, then, women were more easily imagined as witches because they were believed to be more vulnerable to demonic temptation than men. Kramer's insistence on the witch's sexual seduction by the devil gave added emphasis to this belief in the late fifteenth century. But even this did not construct the witch as exclusively female, because it had always been possible for demonologists to imagine men having sexual intercourse with female demons. Popular beliefs about witchcraft were likewise gendered in ways that meant that women were, overall, associated more easily than men with harmful magic. In Tuscany, for example, only two of the 178 people tried for *maleficium* by the inquisitorial tribunal in Siena between 1580–1721 were men. Harmful male witches also appeared rarely before the courts in England, the Netherlands, and New England.[37] Eva Labouvie, furthermore, concluded that there was an overwhelming popular association between women and the practice of mysterious and harmful magic connected to childbirth, love, and death in the Saar region of Germany. Labouvie argued that this association resulted from long-standing popular beliefs that linked women with the world of spirits, night-flying, the mixing of poisons, and the casting of harmful spells. It was also rooted in the household division of labour that recognized women's power, as mothers and housewives, to create and sustain life—a power that harmful witchcraft, which attacked health, life, and fertility, inverted. Men in the Saar region were associated with positive, practical magical techniques aimed at preventing and curing illness and at ensuring the maintenance, recovery, or increase of property and goods.[38] Willem de Blécourt also argued that popular beliefs were strongly gendered, noting that 'Within a gendered society the idea of an un-gendered witch was unimaginable.' His work on rural communities in the Netherlands yielded two witch stereotypes similar to those identified by Labouvie: one male (the profit-making witch who favoured individual gain above the communal good), and one female (the worker of harmful magic).[39]

The association between women and harmful witchcraft was never exclusive, how-ever. Even in Tuscany the harmful male witch was not 'unthinkable'; at the other end of the spectrum of possibility lay Iceland, where men constituted the clear majority of those prosecuted (110 out of 120 trials) and executed (twenty-one out of twenty-two victims) for harmful witchcraft between 1604 and 1720.[40] Between these two extremes there was much regional variation in the gendering of belief about the practice of magic in general and harmful magic in particular. In her study of the German Duchy of Mecklenburg, for example, Katrin Moeller has shown that, while some magical practices were associated more strongly with one gender than the other, no magical

[37] On Tuscany, see Oscar Di Simplicio, 'Giandomenico Fei, the Only Male Witch: A Tuscan or an Italian Anomaly?', in Rowlands, *Witchcraft and Masculinities*, 121–48.

[38] Eva Labouvie, 'Men in Witchcraft Trials: Towards a Social Anthropology of "Male" Understandings of Magic and Witchcraft', in Ulinka Rublack, ed., *Gender in Early Modern German History* (Cambridge, 2002), 49–68.

[39] Blécourt, 'Making of the Female Witch', quotation at 298.

[40] Kirsten Hastrup, 'Iceland: Sorcerers and Paganism', in Bengt Ankarloo and Gustav Henningsen, eds, *Early Modern European Witchcraft: Centres and Peripheries* (Oxford, 1993), 383–401.

practices of either the harmful or the healing variety were imagined as exclusively male or female. Men could be accused of practising harmful magic, even in relation to the apparently quintessentially female area of childbirth, while women were believed to engage in the supposedly male activity of enrichment through magical means by using techniques (such as butter and milk magic) to improve their dairy yields.[41] Ordinary people may have imagined witchcraft in terms of gendered witch stereotypes, but this did not stop them applying such stereotypes flexibly in the context of everyday social interactions with neighbours whom they suspected of witchcraft. As de Blécourt noted for the rural Netherlands, men could be classified under the female stereotype as harmful witches, and women under the male stereotype as profit-seekers, while entire 'witch families' might be classified under either the male or female witch stereotype, regardless of the gender of individual family members.[42]

De Blécourt's ideas are important for our understanding of gender and witchcraft because—like those of Apps and Gow and Opitz-Belakahl—they encourage us to separate gender at the conceptual level from the sex of actual accused witches. De Blécourt, however, pays insufficient attention to the possibility that the flexible application of gendered witch stereotypes could, over time, blur their distinctiveness, thus allowing for the accusation of men for acts of harmful magic, especially in regions where the idea of the dual-gendered sabbath influenced popular beliefs. The idea of the sabbath was absent in Iceland: here, men were far more strongly associated than women with malevolent magical powers in local folkloric stereotypes that pre-dated, and then held firm during, the period of the witch trials.[43]

For all regions we need to know more about the gendering of popular magical beliefs, and especially beliefs about harmful magic, for the late medieval period. We also need to make beliefs about witch families—meaning groups of people related by blood or marriage among whom the ability to work witchcraft was imagined as being passed down from generation to generation—much more central to the analysis, in order to explore how they were gendered and what impact they had on patterns of prosecution. Finally, we need to analyse more systematically the extent to which the interactions between different social groups that occurred in the context of witch trials reconfigured gendered witch stereotypes among both the learned and the unlearned. Who were the key mediators in such processes of cultural exchange and what role did printed texts play in them?

25.3 ACCUSATION

Beliefs about witchcraft were one thing, but individuals only came to trial if they were formally accused of the crime. What sorts of women were particularly vulnerable to

---

[41] Katrin Moeller, *Dass Willkür über Recht ginge. Hexenverfolgung in Mecklenburg im 16. und 17. Jahrhundert* (Bielefeld, 2007), 224–31.

[42] De Blécourt, 'Making of the Female Witch', 298.

[43] Hastrup, 'Iceland'.

accusation? Historians agree that older women—those aged 50 and above—were over-represented among the accused in many regions, although they disagree about why this was so.[44] In the early 1970s Alan Macfarlane and Keith Thomas explained witchcraft accusations in English (and in Macfarlane's work, specifically Essex) communities in the context of requests for material assistance made by poorer villagers of their wealthier neighbours. Macfarlane and Thomas suggested that wealthier neighbours were increasingly likely to refuse such requests because of the economic pressures of the early modern period, but felt guilty about their behaviour because it contravened long-standing traditions of Christian charity. They thus assumed that their spurned neighbours would seek revenge against them and were encouraged to believe that any misfortune their household suffered subsequently was caused by the spurned neighbour's harmful magic. A witchcraft accusation against the latter offered the chance to resolve the tensions in the wealthier neighbour's favour. In this economic explanation of accusation, older women, who were often widows, were more vulnerable because they were most likely to be poor and dependent on neighbourly assistance.[45] This is the classic stereotype of witches as 'women which be commonly old, lame, bleare-eied, pale, fowle, and full of wrinkles', which took centre stage in the writings of witch-hunt critics seeking to generate sympathy for the victims of the persecution.[46]

Much work has been done since the early 1970s to complicate and criticize the Macfarlane/Thomas model. Lyndal Roper also concluded that old women were disproportionately represented among the victims of early modern German witch-hunts. This was not because of socio-economic tensions, however, but because post-menopausal women were feared and reviled in an age that revered fertility. In Roper's reading of trials and the emotional tensions that underpinned them, old women who were past childbearing were assumed to be jealous of—and to want to harm—younger women and their children. Roper also argued that post-menopausal women's bodies were viewed very negatively in early modern culture: as dried up and potentially poisonous, rather than flowing with the life-giving fluids of the maternal body (menstrual blood and breast milk). On both counts, old women were more easily imagined as witch-like by contemporaries. Roper's idea that anxieties about fertility were psychologically central to witchcraft fears is important, but she assumes too much about unlearned conceptions of the post-menopausal female body from elite artistic representations of it, and places too much emphasis on a handful of witch trials, like those in

---

[44] For further discussion, see Alison Rowlands, 'Witchcraft and Old Women in Early Modern Germany', *Past & Present*, 173 (2001), 50–89; and 'Stereotypes and Statistics: Old Women and Accusations of Witchcraft in Early Modern Europe', in Susannah R. Ottaway, L. A. Botelho, and Katharine Kittredge, eds, *Power and Poverty: Old Age in the Pre-Industrial Past* (Westport, CA, 2002), 167–86.

[45] Macfarlane, *Witchcraft in Tudor and Stuart England*; Keith Thomas, *Religion and the Decline of Magic* (London, 1971), 599–680.

[46] Quotation from the English critic Reginald Scot (1584), cited in Rowlands, 'Stereotypes and Statistics', 170.

Augsburg involving poor, post-menopausal lying-in maids, that best fit her explanatory model.[47]

Other historians posit links between aging and vulnerability to accusation that have much less to do with women's bodies and contemporaries' perceptions of them. Robin Briggs suggested that women were more likely to be accused of witchcraft between the ages of 40 and 60 because early modern people were imagined to attain the apex of their exercise of power at this stage of their lives. Witchcraft was understood as the exercise of magical power, so it was plausible to imagine witches as at the peak of their malevolent powers at this age, and to fear them accordingly. Moreover, in many parts of Europe women were formally accused of witchcraft years, and sometimes decades, after they had first gained a reputation as witches. Their age at trial thus resulted from the fact that communities could cope informally with reputed witches for lengthy periods before the final step of formal prosecution was contemplated.[48] This final step might have been shaped at some level by anxieties generated by a woman's menopause, but was more probably taken because the balance of power within a community had shifted in favour of the accusers and against the accused. This was particularly the case if a woman lost the protection of her husband: 36 per cent of women accused of witchcraft in the Jura region were widows, while the figure was 50 per cent in the Duchy of Lorraine and 64 per cent in the German Saar region (although most of these women had probably first gained their reputations for witchcraft while still married).[49]

Christina Larner described the stereotypical Scottish witch as 'a married middle-aged woman of the lower peasant class', with a 'sharp tongue and a filthy temper'.[50] This observation reminds us that socio-economic weakness alone did not render women vulnerable to accusation; what was important was how they managed their position of material dependence within a community. Society demanded that they be humble and grateful; women who quarrelled, cursed, and expressed anger in their dealings with neighbours were more likely to be imagined as witches who would use magic to gain revenge. Malcolm Gaskill's work on the English county of Kent,[51] and a number of studies of early modern German witchcraft, have also shown that the Macfarlane/Thomas model was never the only explanation for witchcraft accusations. Social conflicts of any sort were open to interpretation through the imaginative mesh offered by the belief that the witch was the archetypal 'bad neighbour', and thus that someone perceived as a 'bad neighbour' was potentially a witch. Women of relatively

---

[47] Lyndal Roper, 'Witchcraft and Fantasy in Early Modern Germany', in her *Oedipus and the Devil: Witchcraft, Sexuality and Religion in Early Modern Europe* (London, 1994), 199–225, and *Witchcraze: Terror and Fantasy in Baroque Germany* (New Haven, CT, 2004).

[48] Robin Briggs, *Witches and Neighbours: The Social and Cultural Context of European Witchcraft* (London, 1996), 257–86, and *The Witches of Lorraine* (Oxford, 2007), 153–79.

[49] See Rowlands, 'Witchcraft and Old Women', 61–9 for further discussion of the links between marital status and vulnerability to accusation.

[50] Larner, *Enemies of God*, 98.

[51] Malcolm Gaskill, 'Witchcraft in Early Modern Kent: Stereotypes and the Background to Accusations', in Jonathan Barry, et al., eds, *Witchcraft in Early Modern Europe*, 257–87.

high socio-economic standing could be accused of witchcraft by neighbours who were less well-off and jealous of them, and who believed that their economic success had been unfairly achieved by means of magic. In parts of western Germany where the witch-hunting initiative was seized from overlords by village witch-hunting committees, for example, it was often the case that the middle- to high-ranking village men who made up the committees attacked the wealth and influence of their more powerful neighbours by targeting the latter's wives as witches. Such accusations, like those of the wealthy against their poorer neighbours identified by Macfarlane for Essex, ran along generational lines, with younger villagers accusing neighbours who were a generation or two older of witchcraft.[52] This suggests that generational conflict over communal resources and power rather than a hatred of old women may have been at the heart of many accusations, even if women were the softest, and thus preferred, targets in these conflicts. How far such accusations were motivated by genuine fear of witchcraft and how far by the desire to gain economic and political advantage is hard to determine; a similarly inextricable tangle of motives was apparent in the New England witch trials analysed by Carol Karlsen, in which women who owned or stood to inherit land were vulnerable to accusations of witchcraft so that patriarchal control of property could be maintained.[53] Some women acquired a reputation for witchcraft simply by being born into a reputed witch family; for others, the roots of reputation lay in bad luck or bad timing. Crossing a household boundary just before its inhabitants suffered misfortune might be enough to arouse suspicions, for instance, although women who went in and out of neighbours' houses too often, even with good intentions, were more at risk in this context. Once a woman had gained such a reputation, anything she did or said could be reinterpreted by fearful neighbours as 'witch-like'.

Other scholars link women's vulnerability to accusation to their roles as mothers and housewives, and draw on psychoanalytic theory to explore what motivated people at the subconscious level to make accusations. The historian John Demos pioneered this approach in 1970, suggesting that accusations by adolescent girls against middle-aged women in the Salem witch trials of 1692 'masked deep problems stemming ultimately from the relationship of mother and daughter'.[54] The psychoanalyst Evelyn Heinemann reached more sweeping conclusions in 1986, claiming that the oppressive childrearing practices of early modern Europeans encouraged people to develop a split perception of the mother, which was divided into the good, providing mother (symbolized by the Virgin Mary) on the one hand, and the hated, depriving mother

---

[52] Walter Rummel, *Bauern, Herren und Hexen: Studien zur Sozialgeschichte sponheimischer und kurtrierischer Hexenprozesse, 1574–1664* (Göttingen, 1991). For more discussion, see Rowlands, 'Witchcraft and Old Women', 69–78.

[53] Carol F. Karlsen, *The Devil in the Shape of a Woman: Witchcraft in Colonial New England* (New York, 1987).

[54] John Demos, 'Underlying Themes in the Witchcraft of Seventeenth-century New England', *American Historical Review*, 75 (1970), 1311–26, quotation at 1324–5. For further discussion, see Katharine Hodgkin, 'Gender, Mind and Body: Feminism and Psychoanalysis', in Barry and Davies, eds, *Palgrave Advances in Witchcraft Historiography*, 182–202.

(symbolized by the witch) on the other.[55] Heinemann's idea that witchcraft accusations were essentially about the projection of this latter image by accusers onto women by whom they felt threatened was also central to Deborah Willis' book, *Malevolent Nurture*, in which she concluded that 'Witches were women . . . because women were mothers.'[56] Lyndal Roper also argued that 'deeply conflicted feelings about motherhood' were at the heart of witch trials from the German city of Augsburg. In Augsburg accusations were typically made by newly delivered mothers against the lying-in maids who cared for them and their babies, after some harm had befallen either mother or child. According to Roper, this was because the mother dealt with her anxieties about her baby's survival and her ability to feed it by projecting them onto the lying-in maid, who was imagined as the evil 'other' mother who sought to harm rather than nurture the infant.[57] Diane Purkiss suggested that concerns about housewifery as well as motherhood were central to the testimony of female accusers and witnesses from English witch trials, arguing that they projected anxieties about their own social identities, by means of witchcraft accusations, onto female neighbours who were perceived to threaten their domestic power. Here again 'the witch is the dark other of the early modern woman', an anti-housewife as well as an anti-mother.[58]

The work of Roper and Purkiss is important because it reminds us of the need to take accusers' concerns seriously in any analysis of the gendering of witchcraft prosecutions. Their work also suggests that allegations of witchcraft often emerged from disputes that developed around areas of responsibility that were socially and culturally defined as female in the early modern household, such as food production, childbirth, childcare, and the policing of household boundaries, and were thus more likely to target women than men. Such allegations were often made by women against other women in the context of a communal competition among them for status, which was fought by means of gossip, insult, and, ultimately perhaps, formal accusation.[59] This gave female accusers some power with which to fight for social position within their communities, but this was only because they did so according to patriarchal priorities. They helped uphold the ideal womanly roles of the good housewife and mother by vilifying other women as witches. Moreover, usually only married women had enough influence to spearhead such accusations, and then only against female and not male neighbours. Psychoanalytic approaches to the history of witchcraft have been generally valuable in

[55] Evelyn Heinemann, *Hexen und Hexenglauben—eine historisch-sozialpsychologische Studie über den europäischen Hexenwahn des 16. und 17. Jahrhunderts* (Frankfurt, 1986); an extended edition of this book is available in English: *Witches: A Psychoanalytical Exploration of the Killing of Women* (London, 2000).

[56] Deborah Willis, *Malevolent Nurture: Witch-Hunting and Maternal Power in Early Modern England* (Ithaca, NY, 1995), 6.

[57] Roper, 'Witchcraft and Fantasy', quotation at 217.

[58] Purkiss, *Witch in History*, 91–118, quotation at 100. Self-confession by women who felt they had failed as mothers and housewives can also be interpreted in this framework.

[59] See also J. A. Sharpe, 'Witchcraft and Women in Seventeenth-century England: Some Northern Evidence', *Continuity and Change*, 6 (1991), 179–99.

helping us theorize the role of emotions in explaining witchcraft accusations. Heinemann and Willis, however, are too reductive in their implication that psychic conflicts around the mother–child relationship 'caused' accusations. Mono-causal explanations for witch-hunts are never plausible, and this one has the added disadvantage of 'blaming' women, albeit unintentionally, for witch-hunting because of their 'bad' mothering. The work of Roper and Purkiss is more helpful because it embeds a psychoanalytic approach more firmly in the social and cultural realities of specific witchcraft cases, with the implication that certain accusations could be shaped, rather than explicitly 'caused', by the psychic legacies of infancy. Both works focus on the few cases that best fit their interpretative models, however, and both underplay the extent to which accusations could be motivated by strategic reasons as well as unconscious fears on the part of accusers.

All the theories for explaining accusation discussed above share one major flaw: they ignore or downplay the fact that men could be accused of witchcraft and thus fail to incorporate men adequately into their explanatory frameworks. This problem, which has its roots in the radical feminist refusal to acknowledge the persecution of male witches, is most marked among scholars using psychoanalytic theory who make motherhood and the maternal body central to their analysis, thus effacing men entirely. This sidelining of male witches has meant that sustained scholarly attention has only been paid to them since the late 1990s; the first monograph to deal explicitly with them was published in German by Rolf Schulte in 2000,[60] with the first English-language book following in 2003.[61] We now know that men made up 20–30 per cent of all those tried for witchcraft in early modern Europe, and constituted a majority in a few regions. We also know that men were prosecuted for witchcraft in all areas thus far researched, even if only in small numbers in some regions.[62] Various distinct groups of men have emerged among the accused, suggesting factors that rendered them vulnerable to accusation. Cunning men and other male purveyors of magical and illicit quasi-religious rituals—including clerics in some parts of Europe, the shamans of the Sami people of northern Norway, and the herdsmen identified as particularly vulnerable to accusation in Normandy—were recategorized as workers of witchcraft, particularly in the context of attempts by local elites to impose new standards of religious orthodoxy.[63] Male vagrants, feared for their mobility and magical aggression, were vulnerable to

---

[60] Rolf Schulte, *Hexenmeister: Die Verfolgung von Männern im Rahmen der Hexenverfolgung von 1530–1730 im Alten Reich* (2000; Frankfurt, 2001). This has been published in English as *Man as Witch. Male Witches in Central Europe*.

[61] Apps and Gow, *Male Witches*. The historiography on male witches is discussed further in Alison Rowlands, 'Not "The Usual Suspects"? Male Witches, Witchcraft, and Masculinities in Early Modern Europe', in *Witchcraft and Masculinities*, 1–30.

[62] See note 3 for statistics.

[63] See Voltmer, 'Witch-Finders', 88–90; William Monter, 'Toads and Eucharists: The Male Witches of Normandy, 1564–1660', *French Historical Studies*, 20 (1997), 563–95; Rune Hagen, 'Female Witches and Sami Sorcerers in the Witch Trials of Arctic Norway (1593–1695)', *ARV: Nordic Yearbook of Folklore*, 62 (2006), 123–42; Rowlands, 'Not "The Usual Suspects"', 13–19.

accusation in some areas, notably Carinthia and Salzburg, while itinerancy was also perceived as a threat to social order by the state and settled inhabitants of early modern Russia, a point which helps explain why men, who were more likely to be itinerant than women, were also more likely to be accused of witchcraft there.[64]

For men, as for women, simply being related to someone who had already been prosecuted for witchcraft increased the likelihood of accusation: this was one of the few common characteristics of male witchcraft suspects in the Duchy of Lorraine, where men made up 28 per cent of those prosecuted.[65] Like women, men who were deemed to have contravened patriarchal expectations about their social roles as good neighbours could find themselves vulnerable to accusation. This might be because they had committed adultery or indulged in criminal behaviour, or because they had failed markedly to live up to the standards of rational self-control and probity expected of the early modern household head.[66] In this context the male witch represented the inverse of the good husband and father in the same way that the female witch was imagined as the inverse of the good housewife and mother.

Men were also drawn into trials in greater numbers during large-scale witch panics, in which unrestrained torture forced suspects to denounce other people whom they had supposedly seen at witches' sabbaths. This process was identified, for the large witch-hunts of south-western Germany, in 1972 by Erik Midelfort, and was an import-ant feature of witch panics that occurred in several Catholic territories of the Holy Roman Empire.[67] In such episodes even men of the political and social elite, like Johannes Junius of Bamberg and Dietrich Flade of Trier, could be tried, tortured, and executed for witchcraft. Midelfort's idea that this process involved a breakdown of the stereotype of the witch as an older woman, which led to a crisis of confidence about witch-hunting that brought such panics to an end, needs refining, however. Such panics were fuelled by the emergence of new stereotypes, like that of the feminized male witch, in addition to existing ones, which justified the prosecution of increasing numbers of men without any discernible crisis of confidence among the judicial authorities.[68] This pattern was not universal, however. In Scotland the number of men prosecuted decreased during large-scale panics that were driven by state concerns about the threat posed to godly society by 'deviant' women. The degree to which a particular and strongly gendered stereotype of the witch was utilized by elites in the context of post-Reformation state-building also needs further exploration.

---

[64] On Carinthia, see Schulte, *Man as Witch*, 218–45; on Salzburg, Norbert Schindler, *Rebellion, Community and Custom in Early Modern Germany* (Cambridge, 2002), 236–92; on Russia, Valerie A. Kivelson, 'Male Witches and Gendered Categories in Seventeenth-century Russia', *Comparative Studies in Society and History*, 45 (2003), 606–31.

[65] Robin Briggs, 'Male Witches in the Duchy of Lorraine', in Rowlands, *Witchcraft and Masculinities*, 31–51.

[66] For further discussion, see E. J. Kent, 'Masculinity and Male Witches in Old and New England, 1593–1680', *History Workshop Journal*, 60 (2005), 69–92.

[67] H. C. Erik Midelfort, *Witch Hunting in Southwestern Germany, 1562–1684* (Stanford, CA, 1972).

[68] See Rowlands, 'Not "The Usual Suspects"', 5–7, for further discussion.

25.4 CONCLUSIONS

Gender shaped every aspect of early modern witchcraft and witch trials: beliefs about magic and witchcraft; the social and psychological tensions from which accusations emerged; the anxieties about their own gendered identities expressed by accusers and demonologists; the legal processes by which people were tried; and the degree of power that individuals had to defend themselves against formal prosecution. Historians of witchcraft must bear this in mind and think about gender in more nuanced ways: statistics on the numbers of men and women tried should be the starting point, not the conclusion, of analysis. Regional studies are crucial to enable us to identify similarities and differences in the gendering of belief and prosecution between individual European territories. A chronological dynamic is equally important: we need to delineate and explain the possibility of changes in gendered witch stereotypes and patterns of prosecution over time and in relation to specific trial episodes. We must, of course, be careful not to make gender, as a category of analysis, do too much work. Other factors, notably age and socio-economic status, affected an individual's vulnerability to accusation; we need to work harder to explain why some women (and some men) rather than others were accused, tried, and ultimately executed as witches. Work on male witches has enriched our understanding of early modern witchcraft (and gender) and shown clearly that male witches were both 'thinkable' and 'prosecutable'. Rather than focusing exclusively on either female or male witches, however, historians need to take their cue from early modern people and accept that they used concepts of witchcraft that could plausibly accommodate, or be adapted to accommodate, both. In this regard more work needs to be done on gender and witches' bodies. Was the concept of the threatening maternal body so powerful that it could be applied to male witches, who could be imagined as having unnatural teats and other, quasi-maternal characteristics, as a result? Or were the bodies of male witches imagined in the same way as those of men of the lower social orders—as disorderly and dangerous because of a lack of rational self-control on the part of the 'weak-minded' witch? The inclusion of male witches must not blind us to the fact that women were the main and easiest victims of witch-hunts, however. It is telling that even in parts of Germany where the notion of the dual-gendered sabbath was accepted and the authorities had lists of denounced male witches to work from, the overall proportion of male accused never spiralled out of control. Such was the power of patriarchy that even the witches' sabbath—supposedly the archetype of inversion—was imagined as governed by men: the male devil, assisted by male officials and kings of the sabbath. As long as the overall power of patriarchy remained firm, ruling male elites could countenance the executions of a minority of men, along with a much greater number of women, in their endeavour to rid society of witches.

Further Reading

Ahrendt-Schulte, Ingrid, Bauer, Dieter R., Lorenz, Sönke, and Schmidt, Jürgen Michael, eds, *Geschlecht, Magie und Hexenverfolgung* (Bielefeld, 2002).

Apps, Lara and Gow, Andrew, *Male Witches in Early Modern Europe* (Manchester and New York, 2003).

Blécourt, Willem de, 'The Making of the Female Witch: Reflections on Witchcraft and Gender in the Early Modern Period', *Gender & History*, 12 (2000), 287–309.

Durrant, Jonathan, *Witchcraft, Gender and Society in Early Modern Germany* (Leiden, 2007).

Karlsen, Carol F., *The Devil in the Shape of a Woman: Witchcraft in Colonial New England* (New York, 1987).

Purkiss, Diane, *The Witch in History: Early Modern and Twentieth-Century Representations* (London, 1996).

Reis, Elizabeth, *Damned Women: Sinners and Witches in Puritan New England* (Ithaca, NY, 1997).

Reis, Elizabeth, ed., *Spellbound: Women and Witchcraft in America* (Wilmington, DE, 1998).

Roper, Lyndal, *Witch Craze: Terror and Fantasy in Baroque Germany* (New Haven, CT, 2004).

Rowlands, Alison, 'Witchcraft and old Women in Early Modern Germany', *Past & Present*, 173 (November 2001), 50–89.

Rowlands, Alison, ed., *Witchcraft and Masculinities in Early Modern Europe* (Basingstoke, 2009).

Schulte, Rolf, *Man as Witch Male Witches in Central Europe* (Basingstoke, 2009).

CHAPTER 26

....

WITCHCRAFT AND THE LAW

....

BRIAN P. LEVACK

EVER since the beginning of the scholarly study of witchcraft prosecutions in the
nineteenth century, historians have recognized the central role played by the law
in what has become known as the great European witch-hunt. This should not be
surprising, since witch-hunting was primarily a judicial process. Suspicions and
accusations of witchcraft arose within village communities, but once witches had
been identified and informal countermeasures had proved ineffective, the witches'
fate was placed in the hands of law courts. Even when witches took their own lives,
they usually did so in order to avoid the often gruesome and apparently inevitable
processes of the law.[1] Occasionally, agitated villagers took justice into their own
hands and executed witches vigilante style, but even this type of extra-judicial activity
represented an effort to uphold community standards of justice. The law also
played a role in the development of the witch beliefs that provided the basis for
the prosecutions. Witch beliefs originated long before the prosecutions began in the
fifteenth century, but they did not have a demonstrable effect on witch-hunting until
judicial authorities defined the alleged activity of witches in statutes, edicts, or law
codes. Furthermore, many of these beliefs, especially those regarding the witch's
relationship to the devil, did not acquire legitimacy until prescribed criminal procedures, especially the use of torture in criminal trials, forced witches to confess to
diabolical activity.

---

[1] Marie-Sylvie Dupont-Bouchat, 'La Répression de la sorcellerie dans le duché de Luxembourg aux
XVIe et XVIIe siècles', in M.-S. Dupont-Bouchat, Willem Frijhoff, and Robert Muchembled, eds,
Prophètes et sorciers dans les Pays-Bas XVIe–XVIIIe siècles (Paris, 1978) 106; Christina Larner, *Enemies of
God: The Witch-Hunt in Scotland* (Baltimore, MD, 1981), 114, 116, 119; Hans Eyvind Naess, 'Norway: The
Criminological Context', in Bengt Ankarloo and Gustav Henningsen, eds, *Early Modern European
Witchcraft: Centres and Peripheries* (Oxford, 1990), 376. The French demonologist Nicolas Remy
interpreted suicides as attempts to escape the devil's powers. See Remy, *Demonolatry*, tr. E. Allen
Ashwin; ed. Montague Summers (London, 1929), 161.

Because witchcraft was considered a religious crime, and because many of the courts that prosecuted witches used torture to extort confessions from them, the law, as it applied to witchcraft, has often been thought of as a system of repression. The common reference to witchcraft prosecutions as persecutions reflects this view.[2] Without denying this coercive, repressive role of the law in the trial of witches, this chapter will study the role played by the law—both the written law and the officials who administered it—in restricting the number of prosecutions, curbing the use of torture in witchcraft cases, introducing new rules of evidence in witchcraft trials, and playing the leading role in ending the trials. By the mid-eighteenth century European courts devoted more energy to the prosecution of those who took illegal action against witches than those accused of this crime.

26.1 THE DEFINITION OF THE CRIME

The most fundamental way in which the law facilitated the prosecution of witches was the formal definition of the crime in both the secular and the ecclesiastical courts. Although there was some foundation for trying perpetrators of *maleficia* in the secular courts, on the grounds that such deeds involved physical harm, and in the ecclesiastical courts, on the grounds that they implied a pact with the devil, those who wished to proceed more vigorously against witches required a more specific definition of the crime. The definition of witchcraft as involving diabolism, especially the pact with the devil, which many demonologists considered the essence of the crime, required legislative action in all temporal jurisdictions, while papal bulls or demonological works by papal inquisitors were necessary to persuade episcopal authorities to take action against a new breed of heretics who differed from other, more familiar offenders in their practice of magic and their alleged ability to fly.

The identification of witchcraft as a crime that could be prosecuted in the church courts came about as a result of its gradual assimilation with the crime of heresy, on the basis of the belief that the witch made a pact with the devil. There was no clear statement of the crime of witchcraft in canon law. The only reference to activities and beliefs later interpreted as witchcraft was an eleventh-century restatement of a document drafted by Regino of Prüm in the ninth century known as the canon *Episcopi*. This canon warned bishops and their officials to punish those who practised the pernicious art of sorcery invented by the devil, but it did not call for their execution. It also condemned the beliefs of women who believed that they went out at night with

---

[2] The use of 'persecution' might be appropriate when courts considered witches to be members of a heretical sect, although even in those circumstances the fact that the accused were not, in fact, religious dissidents and did not hold heretical beliefs renders its usage problematic. But it is inappropriate to use the term when witches were tried for practising harmful magic.

the pagan goddess Diana and covered great distances, but the claim that these rides were illusory and the failure to call for the systematic prosecution of such offenders provided more support for early modern critics of the trials than those who called for their more vigorous prosecution. Without a clear statement in canon law, the assimilation of magic with the crime of heresy was brought about by a variety of means, including a decree by Pope Alexander IV in 1258, a handbook for inquisitors compiled by the Aragonese inquisitor Nicholas Eymeric in 1376, and an opinion by the theological faculty of the University of Paris under the leadership of Jean Gerson in 1398. When the trial of witches began in the early fifteenth century, two demonological treatises—Johann Nider's *Formicarus* (1437) and Heinrich Kramer's *Malleus maleficarum* (1487)—helped to define the new composite crime of witchcraft as a particularly heinous offence that involved both maleficent magic and diabolism.

The secular definition of witchcraft as a crime took place by means of legislation, such as the English statutes of 1542, 1563, and 1604, and the Scottish act of 1563; royal edicts or ordinances, such as the law passed by King Christian IV of Denmark in 1617; and the promulgation of law codes, such as the *Constitutio Criminalis Carolina*, the massive corpus of law published by the Holy Roman Emperor Charles V in 1532.[3] Treatises by jurists, such as Benedict Carpzov, which were recognized as authoritative in specific jurisdictions, also gave authoritative sanction to the prosecution of witches.[4]

Jurisdictions that defined witchcraft as diabolism witnessed far more intense prosecutions than those that restricted it to *maleficium*, mainly because diabolism was often thought of as a collective crime, in which witches allegedly gathered to worship the devil at the sabbath. The passage of such legislation was essential for the intensification of prosecutions in such jurisdictions as Denmark, Sweden, and Saxony.[5] By contrast, the almost exclusive attention given to harmful magic in the English witchcraft statutes of 1563 and 1604 helped to ensure that 95 per cent of English trials dealt exclusively with *maleficia*. The only diabolical activity prohibited by the act of 1604 was for covenanting with, feeding, or entertaining any evil spirit, a provision devised mainly to prevent witches from using demonic imps or familiars to help them perform their magical deeds.

---

[3] Territorial rulers within the empire subsequently passed additional ordinances that gave more specific definitions of the crime and provided guidelines for its prosecution. See Edmund M. Kern, 'An End to Witch Trials in Austria: Reconsidering the Enlightened State', *Austrian History Yearbook*, 30 (1999), 161–4.

[4] The Polish parliament, the *Sejm*, never defined witchcraft as a secular crime. A law of 1543 explicitly reserved jurisdiction over witchcraft to the ecclesiastical courts. See Michael Ostling, *Between the Devil and the Host: Imagining Witchcraft in Early Modern Poland* (Oxford, 2011), 47–8. Nevertheless, the secular courts gradually assumed jurisdiction over the crime.

[5] For the Danish ordinance on 1617, which made the pact with the devil the essence of the crime, see Louise Nyholm Kallestrup, 'Lay and Inquisitorial Witchcraft Prosecutions in Early Modern Italy and Denmark', *Scandinavian Journal of History*, 36 (2011), 266–8.

26.2 Criminal Procedure

Before the thirteenth century European courts used a system of criminal procedure that made all crimes, and especially concealed crimes, difficult to prosecute. This procedural system, which is generally referred to as accusatorial, existed in its purest form in the secular courts of north-western Europe, but it was also followed, with some significant modifications, in the secular courts of Mediterranean lands and in various tribunals of the Church.[6] According to the accusatorial system, a criminal action was both initiated and prosecuted by a private person, who was usually the injured party or his kin. The accusation was a formal, public, sworn statement that resulted in the trial of the accused before a judge. If the accused admitted his guilt, or if the private accuser could provide certain proof, then the judge would decide against the defendant. If there was any doubt, however, the court would appeal to God to provide some sign of the accused person's guilt or innocence. The most common way of doing this was the ordeal, a test that the accused party would have to take to gain acquittal. Either he would have to carry a hot iron a certain distance and then show, after his hand was bandaged for a few days, that God had miraculously healed the seared flesh; or he would have to put his arm into hot water and, in similar fashion, reveal a healed limb after bandaging; or he would be thrown into a body of blessed cold water and would be considered innocent only if he sank to the bottom; or he would be asked to swallow a morsel in one gulp without choking. As an alternative to the ordeal the accused or his champion might be asked to engage in a duel with the champion of the wronged party, his victory in this 'bilateral ordeal' or trial by combat being construed as a sign of his innocence. He also might be allowed, as an alternative to the ordeal, a trial by compurgation. In this case the accused would swear to his innocence and then obtain a certain number of 'oath-helpers' who would solemnly swear to the honesty (and indirectly, therefore, to the innocence) of the accused. During the trial, in whatever form it took, the judge would remain an impartial arbiter who regulated the procedure of the court but did not in any way prosecute the accused. The prosecutor was the accuser himself, and if the defendant proved his innocence of the charge, then the accuser became liable to criminal prosecution according to the old Roman tradition of the *lex talionis*.[7]

This medieval, accusatorial system of criminal procedure had two features that made it difficult for courts to serve the cause of justice. First, it did not allow for the determination of guilt or innocence by means of a rational inquiry into the facts of the case but by seeking guidance from the deity. In cases that were hard to prove it

---

[6] For a brief discussion of the differences between Germanic and Roman forms see G. Bader, *Die Hexenprozesse in der Schweiz* (Affolteren, 1945), 11–12.

[7] Henry Charles Lea, *The Ordeal* (Philadelphia, PA, 1973); Jean Gaudemet, 'Les ordalies au moyen âge: Doctrine, législation, et pratique canoniques', in *La Preuve* [Recueils de la Société Jean Bodin, 17] (Brussels, 1965), 99–136.

abdicated human responsibility for dealing with crime. Second, the system did not prove to be particularly successful in prosecuting crime. Not only did every prosecution require an accuser who was willing to risk the possibility of a countersuit on the basis of the *talion*, but the trial itself could be manipulated in favour of the accused. Calloused hands and proper breathing techniques could, for example, help one pass the ordeal, while men of high reputation (which admittedly many men accused of serious crimes were not) could usually secure acquittal by their mere oath or by compurgation. The system stands as a testament to human faith in God's immanence but not to human efforts to use the law as an effective instrument of social control.

Beginning in the thirteenth century, however, the ecclesiastical and secular courts of Western Europe abandoned this early medieval system of criminal procedure and adopted new techniques that assigned a much greater role to human judgement in the criminal process. The change from the old system to the new was stimulated to some extent by the revival of the formal study of Roman law in the eleventh and twelfth centuries,[8] but the main impetus came from the growing realization that crime—both ecclesiastical and secular—was increasing and had to be reduced. In bringing about this change, the Church, which was faced with the spread of heresy, took the lead. The Church also encouraged the new procedures in the secular courts by formally prohibiting clerics from participating in ordeals at the Fourth Lateran Council of 1215.[9] Since the ordeals, being appeals to divine guidance in judicial matters, required clerics to bless the entire operation, the action taken by the council signalled their end.[10]

The new system of criminal procedure that gradually took form during the thirteenth, fourteenth, and fifteenth centuries, and was employed in many parts of Continental Europe by the sixteenth century, is generally referred to as inquisitorial. Its adoption changed both the procedures by which criminal cases could be initiated and the procedures of the trials themselves. Regarding initiation, it is important to note that the adoption of inquisitorial procedure did not preclude the commencement of a legal action by private accusation.[11] Many crimes tried according to inquisitorial

---

[8] On this influence see Bruce Lenman and Geoffrey Parker, 'The State, the Community and the Criminal Law in Early Modern Europe', in V. Gatrell, B. Lenman, and G. Parker, eds, *Crime and the Law: The Social History of Crime in Western Europe since 1500* (London, 1980), 29–30.

[9] On the growth of clerical opposition to the ordeal and the crucial role played by the papacy in suppressing it see Robert Bartlett, *Trial by Fire and Water* (Oxford, 1986), 70–102.

[10] Some municipal jurisdictions nevertheless continued to use the ordeals into the seventeenth century. For the use of the hot water ordeal at Braunsberg in 1637 see Henry Charles Lea, *Materials toward a History of Witchcraft* (New York, 1957), iii, 1234.

[11] See John Langbein, *Prosecuting Crime in the Renaissance* (Cambridge, MA, 1974), 130–1. Until the early seventeenth century a person in the Netherlands could bring an accusation before the secular courts, but after 1600 the court only rarely entertained such accusations. See Hans de Waardt, 'Prosecution or Defense: Procedural Possibilities following a Witchcraft Accusation in the Province of Holland before 1800', in Marijke Gijswijt-Hofstra and Willem Frijhoff, eds, *Witchcraft in the Netherlands: From the Fourteenth to the Twentieth Century* (Rotterdam, 1991), 79–90.

procedure, including a large number of witchcraft cases, were initiated in this way.[12] The only difference between the new system and the old, when suits were begun by accusation, was that in an inquisitorial system the accuser was no longer responsible for the actual prosecution of the case, as shall be discussed below. In addition to the initiation of cases by accusation, however, the new procedure allowed the inhabitants of a community to denounce a suspected criminal before the judicial authorities, a procedure that the church courts had used in certain circumstances during episcopal visitations as early as the ninth century.[13] Even more importantly, the new system allowed an officer of the court—either the public prosecutor, who was sometimes known as the fiscal, or the judge himself—to cite a criminal on the basis of information he had obtained himself, often by rumour.[14] Once again, the Church had employed this procedure in certain cases as early as the ninth century, claiming that the *infamia* or ill-repute of the criminal was the legal equivalent of the private accusation.[15] During the late Middle Ages this practice became widespread both in the ecclesiastical and secular courts. The initiation of cases in this way led to a significant increase in the number of criminal prosecutions, but it also made individuals vulnerable to frivolous, malicious, politically motivated, or otherwise arbitrary prosecutions.

Even more important than the adoption of new modes of initiating criminal actions was the officialization of all stages of the judicial process once the charge had been made.[16] Instead of presiding over a contest between private parties in which the outcome was at least theoretically left to divine judgement, the officers of the court—judges and their subordinates—took it upon themselves to investigate the crime and to determine whether or not the defendant was guilty. This they did by conducting secret interrogations of the accused and witnesses, and recording their testimony in written depositions. In this way they established the facts of the case, which they then evaluated on the basis of carefully formulated rules of evidence, to determine whether or not the accused was guilty. The procedure, therefore, was not only completely officialized but also rationalized. Men were using their own judgement—which was informed by the rational rules of the law—to prosecute crime.

The introduction of inquisitorial procedure made possible the prosecution and conviction of witches on an unprecedented scale, especially in Germany, southern France, and Switzerland. But inquisitorial procedure was not essential to the successful

---

[12] Some of the witchcraft cases tried in Schleswig-Holstein were initiated by private accusation, but the early modern accusatory process was not the same as that which was used in the Middle Ages, and it often followed the same course as an inquisitorial process. See D. Unverhau, 'Akkusationsprozess-Inquisitionsprozess: Indikatoren für die Intensität der Hexenverfolgung in Schleswig-Holstein', in C. Degn, H. Lehmann, and D. Unverhau, eds, *Hexenprozesse: Deutsche und skandinavische Beitrage* (Neumünster, 1983), 59–143, esp. 116.

[13] On denunciation see *Malleus maleficarum*, pt. 3, qu. 1; Bader, *Die Hexenprozesse in der Schweiz*, 15.

[14] On the function of the fiscal see Friedrich Merzbacher, *Die Hexenprozesse in Franken* (Munich, 1957), 78–80.

[15] Henry Charles Lea, *Torture* (Philadelphia, PA, 1973), xiv.

[16] Langbein, *Prosecuting Crime in the Renaissance*, 130–1.

prosecution of witches. Kingdoms that had resisted its adoption, including England, Hungary, and Denmark, or had introduced only elements of it, such as Scotland and Sweden, were still able to convict witches using criminal procedures that were essentially accusatorial. English courts, which could not initiate prosecutions by themselves and which, after the abolition of the ordeals, assigned responsibility for determining guilt or innocence to lay juries, nevertheless managed to convict significant numbers of witches, although not on the same scale as in many German territories. As long as English villagers were willing to bring charges against individuals whom they believed had harmed them by magical means, and as long as trial juries were determined to convict them, the courts could prosecute witches without the involvement of the government, and in some cases without the approval of trial judges.[17] In Scotland, where juries also decided guilt or innocence (in some cases by majority votes), the courts participated in some of the most intense witch-hunting in all of Europe.[18]

On the other hand, some jurisdictions that had adopted inquisitorial procedure did not convict large numbers of witches. The *Carolina* had established strict rules regarding the use of inquisitorial procedure, and the degree to which courts in German territories followed those recommendations had a bearing on the number of witchcraft convictions and executions.[19] When jurists in the county of Hohenlohe in the 1660s and 1670s scrupulously adhered to those procedures, they slowed the momentum of witch-hunting.[20] The same was true in Iberia and Italy, where the adherence to strict procedural rules by the Spanish, Portuguese, and Roman inquisitions in the late sixteenth and early seventeenth centuries explains the relatively low incidence of executions in those jurisdictions.

26.3 TORTURE

More instrumental than the adoption of inquisitorial procedure in the conviction and execution of witches was the use of torture to extract confessions from the accused. Like

---

[17] In a witchcraft trial in Hertfordshire in 1712, the sceptical assize judge, Sir John Powell, could not prevent the jury's conviction of Jane Wenham, although he did reprieve her after the trial. See [Francis Bragge], *A Full and Impartial Account of the Discovery of Sorcery and Witchcraft* (London, 1712).

[18] The high execution rate in Scotland had little to do with the adoption of some features of inquisitorial procedure by Scottish courts. See Brian P. Levack, 'State-Building and Witch-Hunting in Early Modern Europe', in Jonathan Barry, Marianne Hester, and Gareth Roberts, eds, *Witchcraft in Early Modern Europe: Studies in Culture and Belief* (Cambridge, 1996), 96–115.

[19] On the *Carolina* and the controversy regarding the nature of inquisitorial procedure see Langbein, *Prosecuting Crime in the Renaissance*; Robert Zagolla, *Folter und Hexenprozess: Die strafrechtliche Spruchpraxis de Juristenfakultät Rostock im 17. Jahrhundert* (Bielefeld, 2007), 147–65.

[20] W. Trusen, 'Rechtliche Grundlagen der Hexenprozesse und ihrer Beendigung', in S. Lorenz and D. R. Bauer, eds, *Das Ende der Hexenverfolgung* (Stuttgart, 1995); Thomas Robisheaux, 'Zur Rezeption Benedict Carpzovs im 17. Jahrhundert', in Herbert Eiden and Rita Voltmer, eds, *Hexenprozesse und Gerichtspraxis* (Trier, 2002), 527–43.

inquisitorial procedure, with which it was closely associated, torture was reintroduced into European ecclesiastical and temporal jurisdictions (after its prohibition in the early Middle Ages) in the thirteenth century. The main reason for its adoption was the demanding rule of proof that accompanied the introduction of inquisitorial proced-ure.[21] The rule that capital punishments required either a confession or the testimony of two eyewitnesses made it difficult to convict those accused of secret crimes, such as heresy and witchcraft, since eyewitnesses could rarely be produced in such circum-stances. This placed a premium upon confessions, and when the accused refused to confess and judicial authorities were convinced of their guilt, they used a variety of instruments of torture to extract the desired confession.

The adoption of inquisitorial procedure cannot, however, explain the use of torture in all jurisdictions. In Scotland, for example, which had a primarily accusatorial system of procedure in which torture could be administered (as in England) only by special permission of the Privy Council, the procedure was employed in most cases by local magistrates under the pretext that they were using sharp instruments simply to find the devil's mark on the witch's body.[22] In Hungary, Norway, and Russia torture was used, even though those jurisdictions had not adopted the main features of inquisitorial procedure. In all these cases torture was administered for the practical reason that it was the only way to obtain evidence for a crime that authorities were convinced had been committed but which the accused denied.

The use of torture in witchcraft cases was the single most important factor in increasing the number of victims. Not only did it secure a large number of convictions, but the subsequent torture of confessing witches to force them to name their accom-plices accounted for hundreds of additional executions. The use of torture in witchcraft trials clearly had a bearing on the large witch-hunts in German territories, most notably in the area bordered by the Meuse, Rhine, and Moselle rivers. In these mass prosecu-tions, which numbered among the most brutal in Europe, the officials who conducted the trials often appealed to the definition of witchcraft as a *crimen exceptum*, a crime that was so heinous that the rules governing its prosecution did not apply. In other cases they simply proceeded in violation of due process.[23] There were, however, great disparities not only in the numbers of tortured witches from one jurisdiction to the next, but in the numbers of those who were able to survive its application. These

[21] On the difference between English and Continental practice in this regard see John Langbein, *Torture and the Law of Proof* (Chicago, 1977).

[22] Brian P. Levack, 'Judicial Torture in Scotland during the Age of Mackenzie', in Hector L. MacQueen, ed., *Stair Society Miscellany Four* (Edinburgh, 2002), 185–98. Many Scottish witches were apparently tortured illegally by local authorities but not in sufficient number to account for the intensity of Scottish witch-hunting.

[23] Rita Voltmer, 'Witch-Finders, Witch-Hunters or Kings of the Sabbath? The Prominent Role of Men in the Mass Persecutions of the Rhine-Meuse Area (Sixteenth-Seventeenth Centuries)', in Alison Rowlands, ed., *Witchcraft and Masculinities in Early Modern Europe* (Basingstoke, 2009), 77–9; Christina Larner, '"*Crimen Exceptum*"? The Crime of Witchcraft in Europe', in *Witchcraft and Religion: The Politics of Popular Belief* (Oxford, 1984), 35–67. Edward Peters, '*Crimen Exceptum*', in Richard M. Golden, ed., *Encyclopedia of Witchcraft: The Western Tradition* (Santa Barbara, CA, 2006), i, 232–3.

variations, which have been uncovered only through laborious archival research, depended mainly on the degree to which local jurisdictions adhered to the strict rules that accompanied the introduction of torture to ensure that the procedure be bearable and that suspects would not confess simply to stop the pain. In locations that observed these rules it was not at all uncommon for accused witches to withstand the torture and gain their freedom, however unwelcome such liberation might have been when they returned to their communities. William Monter has demonstrated that adherence to the strict rules regarding the administration of torture in the Jura region prevented the occurrence of large chain-reaction hunts such as those that took place in some German territories, while Alfred Soman has studied a pattern of even more remarkable restraint in the appellate review of witchcraft convictions by the Parlement of Paris.[24] Even within Germany, where torture was often applied without restraint, some jurisdictions followed a much more humane policy. The relatively low number of convictions and executions for witchcraft in Rothenburg ob der Tauber can be attributed at least in part to the reluctance of authorities in that city to torture those accused of witchcraft.[25] The severity and duration of torture administered to witches, and the rationales that authorities used to justify ignoring or violating the rules in the hundreds of jurisdictions, should be part of the agenda for future research in witchcraft studies.

The administration of torture and the confessions that it often adduced have also attracted the interest of scholars interested in the psychological dimensions of witch-hunting. Etienne Delcambre pioneered this approach in his psychological study of the judges as well as the witches in Lorraine,[26] while Lyndal Roper has proposed that witchcraft confessions were the product of collusion between the witch and the torturer.[27] Torture has attracted the attention of cultural historians interested in the history of the human body. Lisa Silverman has investigated how judges approving of the administration of torture in the parlements of Old Regime France based their decisions on theories regarding the location of truth in the body, while Elaine Scarry has explored both the effects of bodily pain on suffering and the political dimension of torture.[28] Scarry's work also fits into a large corpus of scholarship on confessions, many of which address the issue of the reliability of 'free' confessions.[29] Some of these

[24] William Monter, *Witchcraft in France and Switzerland* (Ithaca, NY, 1976); Alfred Soman, 'The Parlement of Paris and the Great Witch-Hunt (1565–1640)', *Sixteenth Century Journal*, 9 (1978), 31–44.

[25] Alison Rowlands, 'Eine Stadt ohne Hexenwahn: Hexenprozesse, Gerichtspraxis und Herrschaft in frühneuzeitlichen Rothenburg ob der Tauber', in Herbert Eiden and Rita Voltmer, eds, *Hexenprozesse und Gerichtspraxis* (Trier, 2002), 331–47.

[26] Etienne Delcambre, 'La Psychologie des inculpés Lorrains de sorcellerie', *Revue historique de droit français et étranger*, 4th ser., 32 (1954), 383–403, 508–26; Delcambre, 'Les procès de sorcellerie en Lorraine: Psychologie des juges', *Tijdschrift voor Rechtsgesciednenis*, 21 (1954), 389–419.

[27] Lyndal Roper, *Oedipus and the Devil: Witchcraft, Sexuality and Religion in Early Modern Europe* (London, 1994), 203–5.

[28] Lisa Silverman, *Tortured Subjects: Pain, Truth and the Body in Early Modern France* (Chicago, 2001); Elaine Scarry, *The Body and Pain* (Oxford, 1987).

[29] O. John Rogge, *Why Men Confess* (New York, 1975); Peter Brooks, *Troubling Confessions; Speaking Guilt in Law and Literature* (Chicago, 2000).

contributions say little about witchcraft per se, but they nonetheless have direct relevance to witchcraft studies.

26.4 LEGAL CAUTION AND DUE PROCESS

If the prosecution and execution of thousands of witches reveals the most repressive dimension of the law in early modern Europe, efforts by judges, inquisitors, jurists, and advocates to defend witches, secure their acquittal, and bring the trials to an end represent an often neglected side of 'the law' during the great witch-hunt. These judicial efforts dated from the earliest years of witch-hunting, but they increased in number in the late seventeenth and eighteenth centuries, and they contributed directly to the dramatic reduction in the number of witchcraft convictions and executions during those years. This insistence on adherence to due process was most evident in the implementation of new procedures in witchcraft cases, the adoption of more demanding standards of evidence and proof, and the prosecution of those who took illegal action against witches.

Most of the lawyers and judges who insisted upon due process in the prosecution of witches held positions as superior court justices or jurists who were otherwise not directly involved in the original prosecution of witches, and who therefore did not share the same fear of witchcraft as those who had participated in efforts to rid their communities of the devil's confederates. Superior court justices were also better trained in the law than the village and municipal judges who heard witchcraft cases in the first instance. Their demand for adherence to due process could not be separated from their condescending opinion of local judges, especially those who had little or no legal training, and their need to remedy the miscarriages of justice they believed such local officials had caused. The lawyers who staffed the Parlement of Paris, which acquired and enforced the right to review all witchcraft convictions in lower courts over which it exercised control in the early seventeenth century, fit this profile perfectly.[30] So too did the inquisitors who staffed *La Suprema*, the Supreme Council of the Spanish Inquisition, which published a new set of guidelines for the prosecution of witches in the wake of the massive witch-hunt of 1609–14 in the Basque country. Most of these instructions originated in the recommendations of the inquisitor Alonso de Salazar Frías, a university-trained lawyer who conducted a visitation of the afflicted region and concluded that none of the activities described in the witches' confessions had actually taken place.[31] In Italy the Roman Inquisition also insisted upon adherence to strict

---

[30] Robert Mandrou, *Magistrats et sorciers en France au XVIIe siècle* (Paris, 1968).

[31] Gustav Henningsen, *The Witches' Advocate: Basque Witchcraft and the Spanish Inquisition, 1609–1611* (Reno, NV, 1980). The new instructions issued by the Supreme Council are summarized on 371–6.

procedural rules in the conduct of witchcraft trials.[32] The instructions drafted by the inquisitor Cardinal Desiderio Scaglia in the 1620s, which circulated widely in manuscript until they were published as an appendix to the 1655 edition of Cesare Carena's manual for inquisitors, dealt with all aspects of criminal procedure, establishing strict rules for examining accused witches, calling for restraint in the administration of torture, and recommending particular care in the evaluation of witches' confessions.[33]

In the German territories, the lawyers who distinguished themselves as guardians of due process were the members of the law faculties of the German universities, who were regularly consulted by local jurisdictions when they conducted prosecutions of witches. Towards the end of the seventeenth century these law faculties often recommended procedural restraint, refused to sanction the use of torture, and recommended acquittals in witchcraft cases.[34] The consideration of the case of Barbara Labarentin by the law faculty of the University of Halle in 1694 was especially significant in this regard, since it led one member of that faculty, Christian Thomasius, to develop his ideas regarding the conduct of witchcraft trials. These ideas found their place in Thomasius' treatise on the crime of magic (1701), which argued that witchcraft prosecutions should end, and his dissertation on torture (1705), which condemned the procedure on legal and religious grounds.[35]

In Scotland Sir George Mackenzie, who received his education in Roman law at the University of Bourges in France, became the most vocal of those who called for the use of due process in the prosecution of witches. Mackenzie, who was responsible for the acquittal of a number of accused witches, published a treatise on the criminal law of Scotland in which he deplored the conviction of Scottish witches by 'country-men' who were not learned in the law. Mackenzie argued that the use of inquisitorial procedure, in which judges rather than ignorant juries would determine the guilt or innocence of the accused, would prevent the miscarriages of justice for which local Scottish magistrates and juries had been responsible.

The caution recommended by these judges, inquisitors, and advocates in witchcraft prosecutions contributed to a broader development in European jurisprudence regarding the admission and evaluation of evidence in criminal trials. Witchcraft

---

[32] John Tedeschi, 'Inquisitorial Law and the Witch', in Bengt Ankarloo and Gustav Henningsen, eds, *Early Modern European Witchcraft* (Oxford, 1990), 83–118; Tedeschi, *The Prosecution of Heresy* (Binghamton, NY, 1991).

[33] 'Instructio pro formandis processibus un causis strigum sortlegiorum et maleficiorum', in Cesare Carena, *Tranctatus de Officio Sanctissimae Inquisitionis et modo procedendi in causis fidei* (Cremona, 1655).

[34] Sönke Lorenz, *Aktenversendung und Hexenprozesz. Dargestellt am Beispiel der Juristfakultäten Rostock und Greifswald (1570/82–1630)*, 2 vols (Frankfurt, 1982–3); Lorenz, 'Die letzten Hexenprozesse in den Spruchakten der Juristfakultäten: Versuch einer Beschreibung', in Sönke Lorenz and D. R. Bauer, eds, *Das Ende der Hexenverfolgung* (Stuttgart, 1995), 227–47; Zagolla, *Folter und Hexenprozess*.

[35] Christian Thomasius, *De Crimine magiae* (Halle, 1701); Thomasius, *De Tortura ex foris Christianiorum proscribenda* (Halle, 1705).

provided the inspiration for much of this evidentiary revisionism because witchcraft was a capital crime that was, at the same time, notoriously difficult to prove. Moreover, because of the deep fear of witchcraft in all levels of society, traditional standards for the admission of testimony, the permissibility of torture, and the proof of guilt in witchcraft cases had often been relaxed, sometimes on the grounds that witchcraft was a *crimen exceptum*. These miscarriages of justice were especially evident in large witch-hunts, and it is no coincidence that demands for new procedural safeguards arose in the wake of these prosecutions. The new evidentiary standards that were recommended and eventually implemented in witchcraft trials were central, therefore, to the jurisprudential revolution of the late seventeenth and eighteenth centuries that established modern rules of evidence, the assignment of non-capital punishments in serious crimes, and the restriction and eventual abolition of torture.

The new procedural instructions and recommendations in witchcraft cases were mainly concerned with the evidentiary value of confessions, and in particular with the question of whether they were in any way coerced. Confessions had to be written down in the person's actual words, and the person had to be interrogated regarding his or her motivation for confessing. The new concern for reliable evidence also dealt with alleged acts of *maleficium*. The advocates of new standards of evidence and proof demanded that the crime had actually been committed (the corpus delicti in modern evidentiary law) and refused to accept the pronouncement of a curse followed by a misfortune suffered by the person cursed as evidence of maleficent magic. The refusal of courts to convict witches for having caused instances of demonic possession was based on the impossibility of proving that witches could command demons in this way. The argument of many physicians and some clergymen that the demoniacs' afflictions had natural causes gave further support to this judicial scepticism. The reluctance of courts to convict witches for causing demonic possession, first evident in the Parlement of Paris in the early seventeenth century, played a significant role in the decline of witchcraft prosecutions and convictions in the late seventeenth and early eighteenth centuries.

The evidentiary revolution of this period also had an English dimension, although the English prohibition of torture, the absence of any clearly defined law of proof in criminal trials, and the fact that the English rules of evidence were in their infancy during the early modern period meant that the revolution would take a different path from those Continental European jurisdictions that followed Roman–canonical criminal procedure. Many of the pressures for greater judicial caution in England came from critics of the witchcraft trials who were not judges or lawyers, a pattern that reflected the role of lay jurors in conducting pre-trial hearings, granting indictments, and determining the facts of the case. The scores of pamphlets that were written in response to the outcome of witchcraft trials nevertheless contributed to greater scepticism regarding the evidentiary value of confessions (which in England were still considered the most reliable indication of guilt, even if they were not required for conviction), the admissibility of certain types of evidence, and the qualifications of witnesses.[36] This literature contributed to the scepticism manifested by English assize judges both in the admissibility of witnesses and in their recommendations to lay juries regarding the sufficiency of evidence to convict. One indication of this increased judicial caution was the refusal to admit spectral evidence—the claim by a victim of witchcraft that she could see the spectre of her assailant in the courtroom—a claim that was rejected on the grounds that evidence allegedly produced by the devil himself was not admissible in court. Spectral evidence was not used in English criminal trials after 1662, and it was finally abandoned in colonial New England after it had led to the conviction and execution of nineteen witches at Salem, Massachusetts, in 1692.

The clearest indications of judges serving as the defenders of due process occurred when they took action against the lynching of witches. Lynching was a term coined in late eighteenth-century America to denote public executions without due process of law. A lynching bears the primary connotation of mob violence, but when applied to witchcraft it also describes the summary execution of witches by village or municipal judges who acted under pressure from the local community. Witches were lynched when it appeared that the regular judicial process would take too long, cost too much, or result in lenient punishments or acquittals.[37] The earliest known witch lynchings took place in Denmark in 1543, when fifty-two women were murdered for being witches in Jutland, while throughout the country peasants were reported to have hunted witches 'like wolves'.[38] Another fifty lynchings took place in the province of Champagne in north-eastern France in the 1580s, and isolated instances occurred in other parts of France in the early seventeenth century.[39]

Such manifestations of *Volksjustiz* became fairly common when prosecutions for witchcraft entered a period of decline, since it appeared to local communities that more guilty witches were being set free. Witchcraft scholars disagree whether the lynching of witches increased after decriminalization. It makes sense to assume that the number would rise considerably, since witch beliefs among the rural population showed few signs of abating, and since official judicial action was no longer an option. On the other hand, decriminalization was usually accompanied by an increase in state judicial power, and the prospect that central or superior judicial authorities might proceed against those who took illegal action against witches could easily have discouraged angry and frustrated villagers from taking justice into their own hands. This appears to have happened in Western and Central Europe, where central governments were able to uphold the rule of law and take swift, decisive judicial action against lynchers. In those places where the state had difficulty enforcing its judicial authority in the

---

[36] Orna Alyagon Darr, *Marks of an Absolute Witch: Evidentiary Dilemmas in Early Modern England* (Farnham, 2011).

[37] Brian P. Levack, 'Witch-Lynching Past and Present', in William D. Carrigan and Christopher Waldrep, eds, *Swift to Wrath: Lynching in Global Historical Perspective* (Charlottesville, VA, 2013), 49–67.

[38] Wolfgang Behringer, 'Lynching', *Encyclopedia of Witchcraft*, iii, 683–5.

[39] Alfred Soman, 'Le role des Ardennes dans la décriminalisation de la sorcellerie en France', in *Revue historique ardennaise*, 23 (1988), 30–1, 36; William Monter, 'Burgundy, Duchy of', *Encyclopedia of Witchcraft*, i, 152–3.

localities, most notably in Eastern Europe, lynchings either continued to take place in large numbers or, in some places, actually increased.[40]

26.5 WITCHCRAFT AND OTHER CRIMES

The legal revolution affected not only the prosecution of witchcraft but other crimes as well. Many of the regional and local studies of witchcraft prosecutions written in the past four decades might be viewed, at least to some extent, as contributions to the history of crime. A more distinct set of historical works, however, has specifically investigated the relationship between witchcraft and other crimes. Such an approach has challenged a long-standing tendency to consider witchcraft separately, as a crime that must be explained on its own special terms rather than as one crime among many. The special status of witchcraft as a crime stemmed mainly from the belief that it was the worst possible crime one could commit, a composite offence that entailed not only the infliction of physical harm and the abandonment of one's Christian faith but, in some cases, sexual promiscuity, cannibalism, and political conspiracy.

Some historians who have placed witchcraft in a broader criminal context have conducted comparative research in the records of a specific locality. Studies of this sort include Elisabeth Biesel's essay on witchcraft and other crimes in the city of Toul between 1570 and 1630, William Monter's work on the 'mixed crimes' of sodomy and witchcraft in Aragon, and Malcolm Gaskill's book on witchcraft, coining, and murder in early modern England.[41] Gaskill's study possesses considerable methodological interest, since it is concerned more with the cultural than the social context of crime, exploring the mentalities of the people who were involved in the prosecution of these offences. By investigating the social meaning of witchcraft, Gaskill reveals the way in which people from different social environments viewed the transgression of witchcraft.

Studies of witchcraft included in collections of essays on early modern European crime serve similar comparative purposes. A volume on female criminality in early modern Germany, for example, has revealed that witchcraft was not as central to the criminalization of women as Christina Larner and others have argued.[42] A collection of essays on women and the legal process in early modern England allows us to study the

---

[40] Aldona Christina Schiffmann, 'The Witch and Crime: The Persecution of Witches in Twentieth-century Poland', *ARV: Scandinavian Yearbook of Folklore*, 43 (1987), 147–67.

[41] Elisabeth Biesel, 'Hexerei und andere Verbrechen: Gerictspraxis in der Stadt Toul um 1570–160', in *Hexenprozesse und Gerichtspraxis*, 123–69; William Monter, *Frontiers of Heresy: The Spanish Inquisition from the Basque Lands to Sicily* (Cambridge, 1990), 255–99; Malcolm Gaskill, *Crime and Mentalities in Early Modern England* (Cambridge, 2000).

[42] O. Ulbricht, ed., *Von Huren und Rabenmüttern: weibliche Kriminalität in der Frühen Neuzeit* (Cologne, 1995).

role of women, both as witnesses and defendants, in the broader context of women accused of other crimes.[43]

The crime of witchcraft occasionally intersected or overlapped with political crimes, especially conspiracy and treason. In the Middle Ages, practitioners of ritual magic sometimes attempted to use their craft to inflict harm on high-ranking political or ecclesiastical figures, including popes and kings.[44] The main reason King James VI of Scotland became involved in witchcraft prosecutions in the 1590s was that he was convinced that witches were trying to kill him.[45] In the early eighteenth century the untimely death of Prince Vittorio of Piedmont led the Piedmont senate to investigate and try some seventy witches for using image magic to kill members of the royal family.[46]

Statistical studies of the criminal caseloads of various jurisdictions have also allowed us to assess the level of judicial concern with witchcraft at a particular time and place. Contemporaries may have believed that witchcraft was the most horrific crime one could commit, that its practitioners were legion, and that it presented a grave threat to society, but the actual records of criminal courts, especially the secular courts where most witches were tried, often present a picture of less urgent concern. Only during periods of intense prosecution, such as when large chain-reaction hunts took place, did witchcraft cases occupy a significant percentage of judicial time and effort. Even within the Mediterranean inquisitions, which tried only spiritual crimes, witchcraft was not the dominant concern, perhaps because strict procedural rules kept the number of cases fairly low.[47]

Investigations by historians into early modern European definitions of the crime of witchcraft have also raised the question of the relationship between witchcraft and other crimes. Witchcraft, as it was defined in the sixteenth and seventeenth centuries, was a composite crime. In its most elaborate form it combined the crime of maleficent magic with that of diabolism, although different social and professional groups tended to place different degrees of emphasis on one component or the other. More specifically, the crime of witchcraft encompassed a variety of activities that could be prosecuted as crimes in the ecclesiastical or secular courts. Witchcraft could denote heresy, apostasy, blasphemy, maiming, murder, poisoning, theft, the destruction of

[43] Jim Sharpe, 'Women, Witchcraft and the Legal Process', in Jenny Kermonde and Garthine Walker, eds, *Women, Crime and the Courts in Early Modern England* (Chapel Hill, NC, 1994), 113–30.

[44] Edward Peters, *The Magician, the Witch and the Law* (Philadelphia, PA, 1978), ch. 5; Richard Kieckhefer, *European Witch Trials: Their Foundations in Popular and Learned Culture, 1300–1500* (London, 1976), 52–3.

[45] Brian P. Levack, *Witch-hunting in Scotland: Law, Politics, and Religion* (London, 2008), ch. 3.

[46] Sabina Loriga, 'A Secret to Kill the King: Magic and Protection in Piedmont in the Early Eighteenth Century', in Edward Muir and Guido Ruggiero, eds, *History from Crime* (Baltimore, MD, 1994), 88–109.

[47] See, for example, E. W. Monter and J. A. Tedeschi, 'Toward a Statistical Profile of the Italian Inquisitions, Sixteenth to Eighteenth Centuries', in Gustav Henningsen and John Tedeschi, eds, *The Inquisition in Early Modern Europe* (Dekalb, IL, 1986), 130–57.

crops, the killing of livestock, arson, sodomy, fornication, adultery, infanticide, and conspiracy. In 1584 the English sceptic Reginald Scot identified fifteen different crimes attributed to witches.[48]

Most historical studies that deal with these definitions and relationships focus either on the late Middle Ages, when the definition of witchcraft was in the process of formation, or the late seventeenth and early eighteenth centuries, when the concept was disintegrating. In the formative period, the crimes that eventually became identified with witchcraft were magic and heresy, although separate prosecutions for both crimes continued throughout the period of witch trials. In the period of decline and disintegration, persons accused of witchcraft were often prosecuted for committing some of the more specific acts encompassed in the composite notion of witchcraft. The most common of these was the crime of poisoning, which could be interpreted in either a natural or supernatural terms.[49] Less common were trials for making pacts with the devil—such as those prosecuted in Sweden between 1680 and 1789—the trials for sacrilege in late seventeenth- and eighteenth-century France, and the trials for magic that took place in Finland when witchcraft trials began to wane.[50]

A further dimension of this study of witchcraft and its relationship to other crimes was the legal situation caused by the repeal of witchcraft statutes or edicts. The two legislative acts that have received the greatest historical attention are the French edict of Louis XIV in 1682 and the British statute of 1736. The French edict, the product of the 'Affair of the Poisons' that rocked Parisian high society, as well as a series of miscarriages of justice in the provincial parlements, in effect reclassified witchcraft as fraud while reserving the severest penalties for the crimes of poisoning and blasphemy.[51] One effect of this legislation was the pursuit of 'false sorcerers' by the Paris police in the eighteenth century.[52] The criminality of these people, who were versed in various occult practices, including fortune-telling, alchemy, and the sale of talismans and philters, represented a transformation rather than an elimination of the crime of witchcraft.

---

[48] Reginald Scot, *The Discoverie of Witchcraft* (London, 1584), 32–9.

[49] Giovanna Fiume, 'The Old Vinegar Lady, or the Judicial Modernization of the Crime of Witchcraft', in *History from Crime*, 65–87.

[50] Soili-Maria Olli, 'The Devil's Pact: A Male Strategy', in Owen Davies and Willem de Blécourt, eds, *Beyond The Witch Trials: Witchcraft and Magic in Enlightenment Europe* (Manchester, 2004), 100–16; Mandrou, *Magistrats et sorciers*; Marko Nenonen, *Noituus, taikuus ja noitavainot: Ala-Satakunnan, Pohjois-Pohjanmaan ja Viipurin Karjalan maaseudulla vuosina 1620–1700* [*Witchcraft, Magic and Witch Trials in Rural Lower Satakunta, Northern Ostrobothnia and Viipuri Carelia, 1620–1700*] (Helsinki, 1992).

[51] Ian Bostridge, *Witchcraft and Its Transformations, c.1650–c.1750* (Oxford, 1997), 203–31.

[52] Ulrike Krampl, 'When Witches Became False: Séducteurs and Crédules Confront the Paris Police in at the Beginning of the Eighteenth Century', in K. A. Edwards, ed., *Werewolves, Witches and Wandering Spirits: Traditional Belief and Folklore in Early Modern Europe* (Kirksville, MO, 2002), 137–54.

FURTHER READING

Darr, Orna Alyagon, *Marks of an Absolute Witch: Evidentiary Dilemmas in Early Modern England* (Farnham, 2011).

Eiden, Herbert and Voltmer, Rita, eds, *Hexenprozesse und Gerichtspraxis* (Trier, 2002).

Henningsen, Gustav, *The Witches' Advocate: Basque Witchcraft and the Spanish Inquisition (1609-1614)* (Reno, NV, 1980).

Kallestrup, Louise Nyholm, 'Lay and Inquisitorial Witchcraft Prosecutions in Early Modern Italy and Denmark', *Scandinavian Journal of History*, 36 (2011), 265–78.

Langbein, John, *Torture and the Law of Proof* (Chicago, 1976).

Larner, Christina, '"*Crimen exceptum*"? The Crime of Witchcraft in Europe', in *Witchcraft and Religion: The Politics of Popular Belief* (Oxford, 1984), 35–67.

Levack, Brian P., 'Judicial Torture in Scotland during the Age of Mackenzie', in Hector MacQueen, ed., *Stair Society Miscellany Four* (Edinburgh, 2002), 185–98.

Levack, Brian P., 'Crime and the Law', in Owen Davies and Jonathan Barry, eds, *Palgrave Advances in Witchcraft Historiography* (Basingstoke, 2007), 146–63.

Midelfort, H. C. E., 'Johann Weyer and the Transformation of the Insanity Defense', in R. Po-Chia Hsia, ed., *The German People and the Reformation* (Ithaca, NY, 1988), 234–61.

Peters, Edward, *The Magician, the Witch and the Law* (Philadelphia, PA, 1978).

Robisheaux, Thomas, '"The Queen of Evidence": The Witchcraft Confession in the Age of Confessionalism', in John M. Headley, et al., eds, *Confessionalization in Europe, 1555–1700: Essays in Honor and Memory of Nodo Nischan* (Aldershot, 2004), 175–206.

Sharpe, Jim, 'Women, Witchcraft and the Legal Process', in Jenny Kermonde and Garthine Walker, eds, *Women, Crime and the Courts in Early Modern England* (Chapel Hill, NC, 1994), 106–24.

Stokes, Laura, *Demons of Urban Reform: Early European Witch Trials and Criminal Justice, 1430–1530* (Basingstoke, 2011).

Tedeschi, John, 'Inquisitorial Law and the Witch', in Bengt Ankarloo and Gustav Henningsen, eds, *Early Modern European Witchcraft: Centres and Peripheries* (Oxford, 1990), 83–118.

Unsworth, C. R., 'Witchcraft Beliefs and Criminal Procedure in Early Modern England', in Thomas G. Watkin, ed., *Legal Record and Historical Reality* (London, 1989), 71–98.

Zagolla, Robert, *Folter und Hexenprozess: Die strafrechtliche Spruchpraxis de Juristenfakultät Rostock im 17. Jahrhundert* (Bielefeld, 2007).

CHAPTER 27

SIXTEENTH-CENTURY RELIGIOUS REFORM AND THE WITCH-HUNTS

GARY K. WAITE

Was there an association between the Protestant and Catholic Reformations and the revival of intense witch-hunting in the late sixteenth century? While the wars of religion of the late sixteenth and seventeenth centuries tended to suppress witch-hunting, the tensions that gave rise to the persecution of religious dissidents and the religious wars were similar if not identical to those that fuelled the witch-hunts. There was, however, no direct causal connection between confessional conflict and the burning of witches. This chapter will therefore discuss the role of religious reform, zeal, and conflict, polemical sermonizing, demonizing rhetoric, and changing views of women in the intensification of witch-hunting. It will highlight the relationship between the prosecution of witches and that of other heretics, and discuss the relevance of both spiritualism and Biblicism to the rise and fall of prosecutions.

27.1 THE SCHOLARLY DEBATE

Ever since social historians exposed the inadequacy of Hugh Trevor-Roper's 1967 argument that the Protestant and Catholic Reformations were directly responsible for the intense witch-hunting that began in the 1560s, few scholars have revisited the subject. Historical attention has turned instead to identifying local social pressures to prosecute witchcraft.[1] Nevertheless, since the demonological construct that turned

---

[1] H. R. Trevor-Roper, *The European Witch-Craze of the Sixteenth and Seventeenth Centuries* (Harmondsworth, 1969); see also Alan Macfarlane, *Witchcraft in Tudor and Stuart England: A Regional*

practitioners of maleficent magic into members of a diabolical sect was essentially religious in nature, several scholars have noted ways in which the Reformation shaped this template.[2] Other scholars have challenged any such causal connection. Robert Thurston, for example, argues that since trials for witchcraft pre-dated the Reformation, religious reform had little to do with early modern witch panics.[3] This argument is flawed in two respects. First, witchcraft prosecutions did increase during the first four decades of the Reformation, especially in the Holy Roman Empire, where the number of prosecutions had entered a period of decline before the turn of the sixteenth century. Between 1520 and 1560 most secular and ecclesiastical authorities were more concerned with real heretical sects than with witches, but a significant number of witch trials did take place across Europe during these decades. Second and more important, witchcraft trials intensified greatly after 1560, precisely at the time when confessional divisions throughout Europe hardened. During these years many new witch beliefs, including that of a more terrifying devil, and a more fully elaborated concept of the witches' sabbath, changed the nature of the fifteenth-century stereotype. At the same time scientific discourse made the definition of the nature, power, and limitations of demons an issue of prime importance.[4] Religious preoccupations, persecution, and conflict must be considered, therefore, as immediate and important triggers in the resurgence of witch-hunting, especially major panics, after 1562.

Only a few surveys of the Reformation era discuss the relationship between Reformation theology, polemics, and witch-hunting. Diarmaid MacCulloch argues that the Reformers' preoccupation with fighting the Antichrist in the Last Days inflamed concerns about diabolical witchcraft.[5] Peter G. Wallace suggests that since 'all religious parties dichotomized confessional struggles' as part of the apocalyptical battle between God and the devil, it was natural that theologians and prosecutors 'believed that the

and Comparative Study (2nd edn, London, 1999); Robin Briggs, Witches and Neighbours (London, 1996), and '"Many Reasons Why": Witchcraft and the Problem of Multiple Explanation', in Jonathan Barry, Marianne Hester, and Gareth Roberts, eds, Witchcraft in Early Modern Europe: Studies in Culture and Belief (Cambridge 1996), 49–63.

2 See, for example, Joseph Klaits, Servants of Satan: The Age of the Witch Hunts (Bloomington, IN, 1985); William Monter, 'Witchcraft', in Hans J. Hillerbrand, ed., The Oxford Encyclopedia of the Reformation (Oxford, 1996), iv, 276–82; Brian P. Levack, The Witch-Hunt in Early Modern Europe (3rd edn, Harlow, 2006); Stuart Clark, 'Witchcraft and Magic in Early Modern Culture', in Bengt Ankarloo and Stuart Clark, eds, Witchcraft and Magic in Europe: The Period of the Witch Trials (London, 2002), 97–169; Gary K. Waite, Heresy, Magic, and Witchcraft in Early Modern Europe (Basingstoke, 2003), and 'Irrelevant Interruption or Precipitating Cause?: The Sixteenth-Century Reformation and the Revival of the European Witch Hunts', in Georg Modestin, Martine Ostorero, and Kathrin Utz Tremp, eds, Chasses aux sorcières et démonologie: Entre discours et pratiques (XIVᵉ–XVIIᵉ siècles) (Florence, 2010), 223–42; and Wolfgang Behringer, Witches and Witch-Hunts: A Global History (Cambridge, 2004).

3 Robert W. Thurston, The Witch Hunts: A History of the Witch Persecutions in Europe and North America (Harlow, 2007), 143–4.

4 Stuart Clark, Thinking with Demons: The Idea of Witchcraft in Early Modern Europe (Oxford, 1997).

5 Diarmaid MacCulloch, The Reformation: A History (New York, 2004), 560–83.

magic-laced religiosity of the people grew out of explicit or implicit negotiations with the devil'.[6] Other scholars see the witch-hunts as products of the efforts of Reformers to cleanse communities of godlessness and the pollution of false worship that made them liable to God's wrath.[7] This fear of God fed the demonizing polemic of the Reformation era, and explains why so many reform-minded individuals risked life and limb to publish forbidden books or preach illicit sermons or destroy religious images, and why Catholics were willing to kill so many for the sake of their faith. Much work remains, however, to explicate the relationship between religious reform and the trial of witches.

The elaboration of the diabolical witch stereotype in the century before the Reformation reveals something of this complex relationship. Witchcraft prosecutions began in the early fifteenth century—another important period for ecclesiastical reform— after inquisitors fused the image they had developed of mostly male Waldensians with that of devil-worshipping Luciferians and practitioners of magic.[8] Several decades of prosecution of groups of witches who were now believed to be members of a large diabolical sect followed, although considerable scepticism towards the sabbath conspiracy remained. For example, in 1486 the German Dominican inquisitor Heinrich Kramer (Institoris) published his witch-hunter's manual *Malleus maleficarum* in a spirit of frustration with his ecclesiastical and secular superiors who, disgusted with Kramer's extreme interrogation techniques, had just ordered an end to the witch trials he had been conducting in Innsbruck. When further efforts to inspire witch-hunting likewise failed, Kramer returned to prosecuting male religious heretics in Bohemia and defending Catholic sacramental miracles against the anti-sacramental teachings of 'Waldensians'. For Kramer, religious dissidence and witchcraft were related as distinct wings of the devil's assault on the Catholic faith, the former dominated by men and the latter by women. He therefore helped pull apart the fusion of Waldensian heresy and maleficent magic that had preoccupied courts and inquisitions earlier in the century.[9] This 'gendered' depiction of heresy also helped set the stage for the distinctive pattern of heresy prosecution that followed in the wake of the sixteenth-century Protestant Reformation.

   [6] Peter G. Wallace, *The Long European Reformation: Religion, Political Conflict, and the Search for Conformity, 1350–1750* (Basingstoke, 2004), 214.

   [7] James D. Tracy, *Europe's Reformations, 1450–1650: Doctrine, Politics, and Community* (2nd edn, Lanham, MD, 2006), 265.

   [8] Kathryn Utz Tremp, *Von der Häresie zur Hexerei: 'Wirkliche' und imaginäre Sekten im Spätmittelalter* (Hanover, 2008); and Wolfgang Behringer, 'Detecting the Ultimate Conspiracy, or How Waldensians Became Witches', in B. Coward and J. Swann, eds, *Conspiracies and Conspiracy Theory in Early Modern Europe: From the Waldensians to the French Revolution* (Aldershot, 2004), 13–34.

   [9] Tamar Herzig, 'Flies, Heretics, and the Gendering of Witchcraft', *Magic, Ritual and Witchcraft*, 5 (2010), 51–80, and *Christ Transformed into a Virgin Woman: Lucia Brocadelli, Heinrich Institoris, and the Defense of Faith* (Rome, 2013).

27.2 THE REFORMATION AND
RELIGIOUS CONFLICT

Martin Luther and the other major Reformers had not intended to alter beliefs about witchcraft; instead, their concern was to improve the relationship between humans and God, revive religious fervour, and reintroduce biblical norms for behaviour. Challenging the medieval church's strict control over biblical interpretation, Luther wanted everyone to read the Bible, his sole religious authority, but was shocked at the variety in interpretation that resulted. Anabaptists, for example, who first appeared in Zurich in January 1525, made Jesus' teaching their core, thereby advocating the baptism of believers instead of infant baptism and refusing to swear oaths or bear arms. They also affirmed free will in salvation, while Luther and Calvin, appealing to St Paul, proclaimed the bondage of the will as a means of emphasizing the sovereignty of God. All Protestants rejected five of the seven Catholic sacraments—confirmation, last rites, holy orders, marriage, and confession—leaving only baptism and the Lord's Supper (Eucharist) as the sacramental signs of divine grace or favour. They also rejected the Catholic ecclesiastical hierarchy and the special status of the priesthood, promoting a simpler model of ecclesiastical organization, and declaring the priesthood of all believers. Protestants won the support of many princes and magistrates hoping to profit from the sale of church property.

Luther's message appealed greatly to laypeople; his slogans of the 'priesthood of all believers' and the 'freedom of the Christian' were widely used by commoners during the German Peasants' War of 1524-6. While the rebels principally sought social and economic amelioration, Reformation propaganda depicting the papacy as the Antichrist and the devout peasant as the carrier of the gospel offered commoners biblical justification to oppose their masters. Some preachers, such as Thomas Müntzer, encouraged the peasants to destroy the godless lords and clergy on the eve of Christ's return. In reaction, a shocked Luther advised the princes to hunt down the rebels like dogs, advice that lost him popular support.

Luther was angered also by his fellow Reformers' take on the Eucharist. In the Catholic Mass priests transformed the communion wine and wafer into the real body of Christ in a miraculous process called transubstantiation. Reformed Protestants such as Ulrich Zwingli and Calvin interpreted Jesus' phrase 'this is my body' metaphorically. For his part, Luther took Jesus' words literally, affirming the Real Presence of Christ along with the sacramental bread and wine (consubstantiation), but as a miracle based solely on Christ's promise to his disciples during the Last Supper. Despite their intense disagreement over the nature of the Eucharistic elements, all Reformers rejected the priest's ability to 'conjure' Christ's body. They also affirmed the right of laypeople to partake of the wine during the Eucharist, something that had been denied them by the medieval church. By the fifteenth century, many laypeople had become fed up with what they saw as the depreciation of their spiritual maturity, evident by their mass participation in the Bohemian religious revolt sparked by the burning of the popular preacher of reform Jan Hus in 1415. By 1436 most Bohemians had been granted the right to the chalice. Luther's opponents accused him of following Hus on his critique of the priesthood and advocacy of utraquist communion (in both kinds) and threatened him with the same end. Luther stood firm against both Catholic transubstantiation and the Reformed symbolic interpretation, making a Protestant political and military union against the Catholic Habsburg Emperor Charles V impossible.

The emperor was an implacable foe of Protestant heresy, especially its Calvinist and Anabaptist variants. Regardless, Calvin's followers established Reformed communities in France, Germany, England, Scotland, the Low Countries, Hungary, and Switzerland. Calvin's repudiation of Catholic idolatry and sacramental 'magic' was unequivocal, leading to intense purification efforts and iconoclasm, while the Habsburgs feared the divine wrath that such apostasy would bring. In 1529 Charles V therefore made rebaptism a capital offence and in 1532 oversaw the reform of imperial law, the *Constitutio Criminalis Carolina*, which made heresy a secular offence. While harsh for Anabaptism, this legislation treated witchcraft mildly by reserving capital punishment for cases of undoubted harmful magic. By granting secular courts the jurisdiction over both heresy and witchcraft, the *Carolina* excluded inquisitions from Germany, in stark contrast to Habsburg Spain and the Low Countries. Without any effective central court, heresy and witch persecution could now easily run out of control in the empire.

For Luther, the cosmic war between Christ and the devil was escalating with the approach of the Last Days. In such an atmosphere, religious compromise was demonized and confessional lines politicized. In 1555 the Peace of Augsburg divided the Holy Roman Empire between Lutheran and Catholic territories, but excluded Calvinists and other sects. What followed were religious civil wars across northern Europe, a partially successful counteroffensive by the new Jesuit order, and the creation of a new Roman Inquisition in 1542. Everywhere political conflict was sharpened by religious hatred, division, persecution of dissidents, and fear of divine wrath and diabolical plots.

27.3 THE REFORMATION AND WITCHCRAFT: GENERAL INTERSECTIONS

The Reformation inaugurated a severe crisis in religious belief that, combined with social and economic crises, created an environment favourable to scapegoating. While the Protestants' emphasis on divine providence should have led to scepticism about the diabolical elements of the witches' sabbath, it also escalated concern over false religion, idolatry, 'superstition', and apostasy. All clergy sought to reform popular religiosity by depriving ordinary folk of the preternatural weapons they had traditionally used against magical and demonic assault in favour of approved religious practices. Reformers also raised religious expectations for laypeople, since they were to be as godly as the clergy, whatever their vocation. These expectations took, in Brian Levack's words, a 'heavy psychological toll' on parishioners, relief for which was sought by projecting guilt onto the community's 'outsiders' and by recourse to judicial processes.[10] Witch-hunting was thus neither Protestant nor Catholic, but arose where rulers were motivated by an intense reform agenda combined with anxiety over demonic agency and divine displeasure.

27.4 BIBLICISM

Since all Reformers emphasized obedience to the scriptures, the gospel record of Jesus' miracles, especially the exorcism of demons, encouraged preachers to emphasize the reality of demonic beings and their nefarious interaction with humans. Biblical injunctions such as Exodus 22:18, 'Thou shalt not suffer a witch to live', also seemed to sanction witch-hunting, although sceptics of the witch stereotype, such as the Dutch physician Johann Weyer (Wier), chief surgeon to the Duke of Cleves and author of the 1563 *De praestigiis daemonum* (The Trickery of Demons), pointed out that the Hebrew term for 'witch' here should really have been translated as 'poisoner'.[11] Such efforts fell largely on deaf ears. Similarly, those wishing to deny that witches could do anything preternatural had to contend with the account in 1 Samuel 28:3–25 of King Saul's visit to the witch of Endor, during which she obligingly raised the deceased prophet Samuel. Most interpreters, not wishing to grant witches such preternatural authority, argued that a demon in disguise had appeared to Saul. If so, the demon's prediction of Saul's demise was also a knotty problem.

It all came down to which biblical passages to interpret literally; Luther's general position was that whatever was not explicitly forbidden in scripture was permissible, while Reformed and Anabaptist leaders argued that whatever was not explicitly approved in scripture was forbidden, including religious images and organs.[12] Reformed preachers therefore castigated a wide array of popular ritual and magical practices as non-Christian or proto-Catholic. Faith, prayer, and the Bible remained Luther's weapons against demonic temptation, since the proper protection of the soul was more important than warding off magical assaults on the body. In 1535 Luther interpreted Paul's question in Galatians 3:1, 'who hath bewitched you, that ye should not obey the truth', affirming,

> we, too, must labor with the Word of God against the fanatical opinions of the Anabaptists and the Sacramentarians . . . For we have recalled many whom they had

[10] Levack, *The Witch-Hunt*, 115.

[11] Johann Weyer, *De Praestigiis Daemonum*, in George Mora, ed., *Witches, Devils, and Doctors in the Renaissance* (Binghamton, NY, 1991), 93–8.

[12] Susan Karant-Nunn, *The Reformation of Ritual: An Interpretation of Early Modern Germany* (London, 1997).

bewitched, and we have set them free from their bewitchment, from which they could never have been untangled by their own powers if they had not been admonished by us and recalled through the Word of God . . . So great is the efficacy of this satanic illusion in those who have been deluded this way that they would boast and swear that they have the most certain truth.

For Luther, spiritual bewitchment was a diabolical act in which a 'false opinion' opposed to Christ overwhelmed the reason and senses.[13] Those only mildly afflicted could be redeemed, but harsh judicial action was required for recalcitrant Anabaptists. Even though the spiritually possessed were mad, Luther still held them responsible for their evil acts.

Luther distinguished between the ravings of misguided zealots and the malice of diabolical witches, but many others did not. Over the decades parishioners listened to sermons expounding the present fulfillment of the apocalypse. For example, in his 1596 published collection of fifty sermons on the book of Revelation, the English Puritan George Gifford commented that he had preached these sermons twice through for his congregation. Regarded as a moderate on the question of witchcraft prosecution, Gifford's Revelation sermons depicted the pope as the Antichrist, with his allies the Anabaptists, Libertines, Familists, and other such 'filthy monsters'. Since the papacy could no longer legally interfere in the religious life of the English common-wealth, these secret agents of Satan were spreading immorality and atheism from within.[14] Seeking to divert his parishioners' eyes away from vain fears of witchcraft, Gifford affirmed divine providence and denied the devil's ability to create storms or spread disease. Do not be so foolish to imagine, he fumed, that the mighty devil, transformed into a small familiar, 'lyeth at the witches house' to be fed by the unfortunate old hag.[15] More dangerous for Gifford were Catholics and religious dissent-ers, who were members of an apocalyptical conspiracy of frightening proportions.

While increasing anxiety over diabolical agents, such providentialists eventually undermined the intellectual basis underpinning the stereotype of diabolical witchcraft. Those governments that renounced enforced confessional conformity, such as the officially Reformed Dutch Republic, conducted few if any witch-hunts. As Alexandra Walsham explains, to 'live alongside dissenters without an angry God striking one dead for tolerating falsehood was to see the transparent and comforting polarities of truth

---

[13] Martin Luther, *Lectures on Galatians*, in Jaroslav Pelikan, gen. ed., *Luther's Works*, American edn, vol. 26 (St Louis, MO, 1955–86), 194–7. See also H. C. Erik Midelfort, *A History of Madness in Sixteenth-Century Germany* (Stanford, CA, 1999), 92–7; and Heiko A. Oberman, *Luther: Man between God and the Devil* (New Haven, CT, 1989).

[14] George Gifford, *Sermons vpon the Whole Booke of the Revelation* (London, 1596). See also Andrew Cunningham and Ole Peter Grell, *The Four Horsemen of the Apocalypse: Religion, War, Famine and Death in Reformation Europe* (Cambridge, 2000); Robin Barnes, *Prophecy and Gnosis: Apocalypticism in the Wake of the Lutheran Reformation* (Stanford, CA, 1988); and Clark, *Thinking with Demons*, 321–74.

[15] George Gifford, *A Discourse of the Subtill Practises of Devilles by Vvitches and Sorcerers* (London, 1587), fol. G3r–v. Gifford's obsession with the devil is seen in his innocuously entitled *A Godly and comfortable treatise . . .* (London, 1585).

and falsehood, good and evil, that underpinned persecution dissolve and evaporate'.[16] Increasing confessionalization, however, delayed the full development of this attitude.

As confessional lines hardened around mid-century, the need for church leaders to prove the verity of their faith and enforce parishioners' proper moral conduct increased; Lutherans conducted clerical visitations to monitor their parishioners' attitudes and behaviour; Calvinist consistories prosecuted members of their congregations for moral offences; and Catholic inquisitors investigated a growing list of spiritual crimes, including blasphemy, love magic, and divination. The presumption was that full civic obedience required submission to the one true faith; tolerating alternate confessions was risky business. Moral policing became the norm, not just of blasphemy and magical offences, but also all forms of previously tolerated sexual misconduct. Associating non-approved beliefs with the devil was one technique to suppress dissidence.

27.5 SPIRITUALISM

Religious persecution tends to drive unapproved beliefs underground; Jesus' secret disciple Nicodemus (John 19:39) provided the justification for those wishing to hide unorthodox beliefs from public view in the Renaissance. Deciding against martyrdom or exile, many persecuted dissidents adopted spiritualism, thereby depreciating doctrinal confessions and rites in favour of a religion of the heart; pretending public orthodoxy for them was no sin. Prominent spiritualists such as the German Sebastian Franck and Caspar von Schwenckfeld, and the Dutch David Joris, Hendrik Niclaes (founder of the Family of Love), Matthias Wier—brother to Johann Weyer—and the playwright and secretary Dirck Volckertsz Coornhert, saw Jesus' prescription to love God and one's neighbour as the core of true religion. Their spirit/flesh dualism depreciated physical aspects of religion, leading Calvin to label them libertines, that is, those wishing to live without laws altogether.[17] Some joined the Neoplatonic quest for inherent unity in all religions, seeking true, spiritual meaning in the occult sciences. Among these were Theophrastus Bombastus von Hohenheim, more commonly known

---

[16] Alexandra Walsham, 'The Reformation and "The Disenchantment of the World" Reassessed', *The Historical Journal*, 51 (2008), 497–528, quotation at 508. See also Gary K. Waite, 'Demonizing Rhetoric, Reformation Heretics and the Witch Sabbaths: Anabaptists and Witches in Elite Discourse', in Richard Raiswell and Peter Dendle, eds, *The Devil in Society in the Premodern World* (Toronto, 2012), 195–219; and Gary K. Waite, *Eradicating the Devil's Minions: Anabaptists and Witches in Reformation Europe* (Toronto, 2007), 34–62, 133–44.

[17] Perez Zagorin, *Ways of Lying: Dissimulation, Persecution, and Conformity in Early Modern Europe* (Cambridge, MA, 1990). On spiritualism, see also G. K. Mirjam van Veen, 'Spiritualism in the Netherlands: From David Joris to Dirck Volckertsz Coornhert', *Sixteenth Century Journal*, 33 (2002), 129–50; and Benjamin Kaplan, *Calvinists and Libertines: Confession and Community in Utrecht, 1578–1620* (Oxford, 1995).

as Paracelsus, the medical reformer and alchemist whose religious reform ideas were as radical as his medical ones.[18]

In the 1570s Coornhert helped persuade Prince William of Orange to make religious toleration a principle for the Dutch Republic, which established a public Reformed church without requiring membership for all citizens. While opposing the more narcissistic claims of his predecessors, Niclaes and Joris, Coornhert supported their condemnation of theological dogmatism, intolerance, and sectarianism. Like them, he identified persecution and confessional strife as the devil's true work.[19] Several key players in Holland's renunciation of witch-hunting were influenced by such arguments, as were anti-witch-hunting authors Weyer and the Englishman Reginald Scot.[20] Not bound to a literal reading, spiritualists' biblical interpretation could be quite creative; Joris argued that scriptural references to the devil were merely figurative representations of the inner evil desires of an individual's fallen nature, a view that quickly became infamous.[21]

For orthodox polemicists, the spiritualists' depreciation of a personal devil was diabolical and proto-atheistic. Many jurists made belief in the devil's powers 'a criterion of sound religion, since doubt on this point might reveal scepticism, unwillingness to accept the authority of scripture, or "atheism"'.[22] Hence, efforts to dispute spiritualism's tolerance and depreciation of diabolical interference led, in the short term, to increased fear of satanic plots. Ultimately, however, spiritualism's ethos eventually undercut belief in diabolical conspiracies.

27.6 RELIGIOUS PROPAGANDA AND THE EXORCISM OF DEMONS

Many Catholic clergy sought to neutralize both the Protestant challenge and their own parishioners' doubts about orthodox dogma by proving their control over the supernatural through staged exorcisms, something Calvinists avoided as a remnant of Catholic superstition. Luther took the middle ground, exorcizing infants as part of

---

[18] Charles Webster, *Paracelsus: Medicine, Magic and Mission at the End of Time* (New Haven, CT, 2008).

[19] Dirck Volckertsz Coornhert, *Wercken* (Amsterdam, 1630/1), i, 89r.

[20] Hans de Waardt, 'Religie, duivelspact en toverij', *Tijdschrift voor geschiedenis*, 118 (2005), 400–15; and David Wootton, 'Reginald Scot/Abraham Fleming/The Family of Love', in Stuart Clark, ed., *Languages of Witchcraft: Narrative, Ideology and Meaning in Early Modern Culture* (Basingstoke, 2001), 119–38.

[21] Gary K. Waite, '"Man is a Devil to Himself": David Joris and the Rise of a Sceptical Tradition towards the Devil in the Early Modern Netherlands, 1540–1600', *Nederlands Archief voor Kerkgeschiedenis/Dutch Review of Church History*, 75 (1995), 1–30.

[22] H. C. Erik Midelfort, *Witch Hunting in Southwestern Germany 1562–1684: The Social and Intellectual Foundations* (Stanford, CA, 1972), 27.

the baptismal rite, although by mid-century some Lutheran ministers were also doing away with this. Fearing association with Anabaptists, orthodox Lutherans assured parents that their children and foetuses were not possessed; as the pastor Adam Crato warned, removing paedo-exorcism would imply that 'Christian children prior to holy baptism are not heathens, nor under the authority of Satan, nor physically nor spiritually possessed', as demons sought 'to establish their dwelling in the children'.[23]

This dispute was merely part of the growing Lutheran obsession with the diabolical, evidenced best in the series of 'devil books' (*Teufelbücher*) linking particular vices to their corresponding demons.[24] In a major compendium of these published in 1569, Sigmund Feyerabend attacked those who propagated the proverb: 'Hell is not as hot as the priests make it and the devil is not as black as the artists paint him', or who taught that sermons about demons were 'vain falsehood . . . to frighten the people and bring the priests money'. He was especially concerned about suggestions that the devil existed merely as the evil thoughts of humans.[25] Just as Heinrich Kramer had compelled witches to confess to impeding sacramental marriage,[26] Feyerabend explained the failure of Luther's gospel to transform human relations by blaming Satan's machinations. These arguments about exorcism clearly raised interest in the subject, sparking a rise in demonic possession cases in Lutheran Germany, some of them including 'revival sermons and angelic visions'.[27] Some possessions led to accusations of bewitchment.

Propagandistic exorcisms were particularly important in France, where zealous Catholic polemicists sought to prove the power of their sacraments against Protestant scepticism. The famous staged exorcisms of the teenager Nicole Obry (Aubrey) in 1565–6 in Laon enthralled thousands. Consecrated hosts were the principal weapon in the exorcists' arsenal, while Beelzebub, speaking through Obry, agreeably identified the Protestants as his servants, encouraging them to desecrate hosts.[28] Nervous Huguenots called the possession a hoax, yet when, on 8 February 1566, Beelzebub finally abandoned Nicole's body in a cloud of smoke and thunder, many Protestants converted. The Crown immediately suppressed further public exorcisms, but once the Edict of Nantes ended the religious warfare in 1598, the propagandistic exorcisms returned, culminating in the infamous possession of several Ursuline convents in the seventeenth century. Exorcists used these opportunities to inculcate greater zeal among Catholics.

---

[23] Adam Crato, *Rettung Des Christlichen Tauffbuchleins Heern D. Martini Lutheri* (n.p., 1591), 3, 8–10; Bodo Nischan, 'The Exorcism Controversy and Baptism in the Late Reformation', *The Sixteenth Century Journal*, 18 (1987), 31–51.

[24] Bob Scribner, 'The Reformation, Popular Magic and the "Disenchantment of the World",' *Journal of Interdisciplinary History*, 23 (1992–3), 475–94, esp. 487.

[25] Sigmund Feyerabend, *Theatrvm Diabolorum* (Frankfurt, 1569), Ir.

[26] Walter E. Stephens, *Demon Lovers: Witchcraft, Sex, and Belief* (Chicago, 2002).

[27] H. C. Erik Midelfort, 'The Devil and the German People: Reflections on the Popularity of Demon Possession in Sixteenth-Century Germany', in Steven Ozment, ed., *Religion and Culture in the Renaissance and Reformation* (Kirksville, MO, 1989), 99–119, at 111.

[28] Jonathan L. Pearl, *The Crime of Crimes: Demonology and Politics in France, 1560–1620* (Waterloo, 1998), 43–5. On possession, see Sarah Ferber, *Demonic Possession and Exorcism in Early Modern France* (London, 2004).

In three of these group possessions, a controversial priest was executed for allegedly causing the bewitchment of the nuns, most notably the burning of the Jesuit-educated priest and anti-celibacy writer Urbain Grandier at Loudun in 1634.

The Calvinists' response was to demonstrate that Catholic sacred images and objects were devoid of supernatural power. In France, Protestant iconoclasm was repaid by Catholic mobs seeking instead to purify the realm of the sacrilegious iconoclasts, replicating on Huguenot corpses the desecration the victims had performed on Catholic saints.[29] In the Low Countries, the iconoclastic fury of 1566 was as elaborately staged as Obry's exorcisms. As iconoclasts publicly stabbed and smashed saints' images and vessels containing consecrated hosts, they revealed the impotence of these sacred objects.[30] Such counter-propaganda had limited success, as by 1600 in Calvinist Geneva the single most common act of *maleficium* was causing the demonic possession of another, while many citizens frequented Catholic exorcists.[31]

27.7 THE REFORMATION AND WOMEN

The Reformation profoundly changed religion, but it also affected other areas of human relationship, including those between women and men. The Reformers did little to alter the traditional, negative views of women, leaving in place Aristotle's polarity system whereby women were seen as dominated by the cooler, baser humours and men by the hot humours, which promoted intellect. Protestants, furthermore, removed any option of a religious vocation for women, closing convents, sometimes after years of struggle, and insisting that the normal vocation for woman was marriage and motherhood. In this they sought to promote married life, rather than celibacy, as the ideal state for Christians, alleviating the sense of inferiority that married laypeople had long endured.[32] Options for single women were generally bleak. Even within Catholic territories, the reforms of the Council of Trent (1545–63) restricted the freedom of religious women, as convents were more strictly cloistered and their inmates more closely supervised, contributing to the oppressive atmosphere of the Ursuline convents that made them susceptible to claims of demonic possession and to the manipulation of male exorcists pursuing their own agendas.[33]

---

[29] Natalie Zemon Davis, 'The Rites of Violence', in *Society and Culture in Early Modern France* (Stanford, CA, 1975), 152–88.

[30] Waite, *Heresy*, 143–4.

[31] William Monter, *Witchcraft in France and Switzerland: The Borderlands during the Reformation* (Ithaca, NY, 1976), 76.

[32] Merry Wiesner-Hanks, 'Society and the Sexes Revisited', in David M. Whitford, *Reformation and Early Modern Europe: A Guide to Research* (Kirksville, MO, 2008), 396–414.

[33] Robert Rapley, *A Case of Witchcraft: The Trial of Urbain Grandier* (Montreal, 1998); and Merry E. Wiesner-Hanks, 'Women', in *Oxford Encyclopedia of the Reformation*, iv, 290–8, esp. 295.

Catholic and Protestant leaders were both reacting to the infamous actions of some women in the early Reformation era. Many women interpreted Luther's 'priesthood of all believers' as tacit permission to preach the gospel, despite St Paul's proscription against women teachers in I Timothy 2:12. Some women were inspired by radical preachers to participate in the Peasants' War or to protect evangelical preachers, such as the group of women who, in 1522, sprang Hendrik van Zutphen from his Antwerp prison. Even here the perpetrators were only mildly punished since it was assumed they must have been misled by men.[34] In 1529 some women preachers of Zwickau were exiled, while Memmingen's magistrates forbade servant women from discussing religion when drawing water from wells. An English statute of 1543 outlawed women from reading the Bible; all authorities remained suspicious of women who discussed the scriptures.[35]

Anabaptist women, however, at times asserted a greater level of religious leadership as prophets, informal teachers, and martyrs. The visions of the Strasbourg prophetesses Barbara Rebstock and Ursula Jost convinced the Anabaptist leader Melchior Hoffman to become the prophet of the Last Days. Despite the tendency of jurists to excuse Anabaptist women as victims of men, hundreds of Anabaptist women were arrested, tortured, and executed. Male Anabaptist leaders also sought to limit their women's leadership aspirations. For example, in 1534 when the Anabaptist-controlled city of Münster was under siege, women greatly outnumbered men, presenting a problem for the newly crowned king Jan van Leiden. On 16 June, Hille Feicken, inspired by stories of the biblical Judith who had delivered Israel from a Babylonian siege by slipping into the Babylonians' camp and beheading Holofernes, snuck out of Münster to assassinate the besieger, Bishop Franz von Waldeck. Although caught before fulfilling her mission, her attempt shocked van Leiden, who shortly afterward mandated polygamy, so that every woman would be under the control of a husband.[36] In such ways Anabaptist women inspired parallels with earlier Waldensian women preachers.

Catholic and Protestant leaders therefore reinforced patriarchalism to impose tighter control over all women, whom they believed were easily tempted by the devil. In the process, the image of the potential witch was broadened to include any non-submissive woman; the polar opposite of the young, obedient, and sexually passive wife and mother, the witch was so assertive and sexually ravenous that she could be satiated only by demon lovers. Such an image heightened anxiety over female sexuality,

[34] Waite, *Heresy*, 71; see also Natalie Zemon Davis, 'Women on Top', in *Society and Culture*, 124–51.

[35] Merry E. Wiesner, 'Nuns, Wives, and Mothers: Women and the Reformation in Germany', in Sherrin Marshall, ed., *Women in Reformation and Counter-Reformation Europe: Private and Public Lives* (Bloomington, IN, 1989), 15.

[36] Sigrun Haude, *In the Shadow of 'Savage Wolves': Anabaptist Münster and the German Reformation during the 1530s* (Leiden, 2000), 14, and 'Anabaptist Women—Radical Women?' in Max Reinhart, ed., *Infinite Boundaries: Order, Disorder, and Reorder in Early Modern German Culture* (Kirksville, MO, 1998), 313–28.

inspiring powerful fears of the witch, and focusing the idea of the witch increasingly on women as the gender most susceptible to the charms of Satan.[37]

27.8 ANABAPTISTS AND WITCHES

Between 1525 and 1540, the number of Anabaptists persecuted was comparable to moderate witch-hunts, with one notable exception: roughly two-thirds of Anabaptists executed were men, while roughly three-quarters of accused witches were women. By 1570 at least two thousand Anabaptists had been executed, and thousands more arrested and interrogated. Execution of Anabaptists preceded or alternated with the punishment of witches, and almost never occurred in the same year. Both persecutions were motivated by the need to purify realms of blasphemous heresy in the Last Days. Claims to piety by Anabaptists were ignored, as orthodox preachers, stinging from Anabaptist anticlerical rebukes, described Anabaptist 'hyper-piety' as a cover for diabolical deception.[38] Protestant and Catholic theologians saw heresy and witchcraft as distinct arms of the devil's plot, and Anabaptists were not normally charged with performing magic. Lower clergy and parishioners, however, often interpreted Anabaptist activity in a magical direction, as when, in Schwäbisch-Gmünd, 'witch dances were said to take place at the same location that served in "1529 as the secret meeting place of Gmünd's Anabaptists"'.[39] Inquisitors ascribed Anabaptist women's literacy to magical agency, while some jurists applied preternatural techniques to extract confessions from Anabaptists.

Yet there were key differences between the persecution of Anabaptists and witches: for one thing, many Anabaptists happily confessed their beliefs as a form of witnessing, while witches were surely innocent of diabolism, if not of *maleficium*. As efforts to inculcate commoners with anti-Anabaptist fervour failed, the clergy's demonizing rhetoric was transferred by the people onto witches. Court officials learned how to extract confessions from Anabaptists, and applied their experience to interrogations of witches. Since some Anabaptists actually desecrated sacraments, including hosts, it became easier, at least for demonologists, to imagine witches performing such sacrilege. Similarly, the idea that witches were rebaptized into the devil's sect only became prominent in the literature after the advent of Anabaptism.[40]

---

[37] See Ulinka Rublack, *Reformation Europe* (Cambridge, 2005), 188. Also Sigrid Brauner, *Fearless Wives and Frightened Shrews: The Construction of the Witch in Early Modern Germany*, ed. Robert H. Brown (Amherst, MA, 1995).

[38] On excessive piety as an indication of witchcraft, see Friedrich Spee von Langenfeld, *Cautio Criminalis, or a Book on Witch Trials*, ed. and tr. M. Hellyer (Charlottesville, VA, 2003), 24.

[39] Edward Bever, *The Realities of Witchcraft and Popular Magic in Early Modern Europe: Culture, Cognition, and Everyday Life* (Basingstoke, 2008), 96. See also Waite, *Eradicating*, esp. 41–51, 66–71, 174–85.

[40] Gary K. Waite, 'Naked Harlots or Devout Maidens? Images of Anabaptist Women in the Context of the Iconography of Witches in Europe, 1525–1650', in Gary K. Waite, Els Kloek, Marion Kobelt-Groch,

A central difference between Anabaptists and witches is gender, and this helps explain why Anabaptists were not demonized successfully, as the Waldensians had been in the fifteenth century. Anabaptist women were treated with mildness relative to their male compatriots because most jurists and inquisitors followed Kramer's gendered heresy perspective, by which women were mentally incapable of participating actively in intellectual heresy and were instead the pawns of male leaders. For a 'dumb' woman to be misled by a man to follow a heresy she could not truly comprehend was perhaps excusable, but to make a willing pact with the devil in a quest for wealth, power, sexual fulfillment, or revenge was another matter entirely. In these cases, there could be no excuse, and, for many jurists, no leniency.

27.9 WITCH TRIALS DURING THE EARLY REFORMATION, 1520–60

Even during the tumultuous decades of the Reformation, there were a number of witch trials across Europe, especially in Italy, northern Spain, parts of France and Switzerland, and the Low Countries. The worst seem to have been areas suffering from the plague, including northern Italy, where the Inquisition at Como alone possibly executed hundreds. That said, mass prosecutions had already petered out before the Reformation in most areas of the Holy Roman Empire.[41]

Both Luther and Calvin supported witch-hunting, with Luther approving the execution of four witches at Wittenberg in 1541 and Calvin, a few years, later advising Geneva to 'extirpate the race of witches', resulting in the city's infamous plague-spreading trials.[42] Yet, until 1560, most jurisdictions were reluctant to treat witchcraft as a criminal conspiracy involving large groups of suspects. Similarly, few publications appeared on the subject, and there were no known printings of the *Malleus maleficarum* between 1521 and 1569. Witchcraft remained a concern within the local community, and people continued to counteract evil magic by a variety of means.[43] Most accusations of witchcraft involved maleficent magic, such as the cursing of agricultural implements and livestock, the brewing of crop-destroying storms, arson, love magic, or the discovery of stolen objects. In the Netherlands, there were some trials of groups of witches, such as in Namur, where judges tried traditional Waldensian witches, largely because they did not have to deal with large numbers of Anabaptists.[44] The eastern province of Groningen

---

Mirjam van Veen, Anna Voolstra, and Piet Visser, eds, *Sisters: Myth and Reality of Anabaptist, Mennonite, and Doopsgezind Women, ca. 1525–1900* (Leiden, 2014), 17–51.

[41] Behringer, *Witches and Witch Hunts*, 76–81.

[42] Monter, 'Witchcraft', 277–8.

[43] Bob Scribner, 'Witchcraft and Judgement in Reformation Germany', *History Today*, 40 (1990), 12–19.

[44] Waite, *Eradicating*, 76–7.

also saw a significant number of trials. Twenty accused witches were executed there in 1547, and five more in 1562. Both of these witch-hunts were sparked by news of witch trials in the neighbouring portions of the western Holy Roman Empire.

27.10 JOHANN WEYER (WIER)

It was, in fact, these particular cases that caused the Dutch court surgeon for the duchy of Cleves, Johann Weyer (Wier) to publish his famous treatise opposing the prosecution of witches, in 1563. Weyer's book provoked both admiration and anger—the latter especially from Jean Bodin, who responded in 1580 with his defence of witch-hunting, *Demonomania (On the Demon-Mania of Witches)*.[45] Weyer explained witch confessions as caused by diabolical delusions on the minds of old women already mentally disturbed by the humoral imbalance of melancholia. He admitted that some 'deluded old women are convinced . . . that crimes of this sort are perpetrated by them', but argued that this is merely 'phantasms' arising from unbelief. Hence, when subjected to torture 'they confess to crimes which are purely imaginary on their part, and which truly proceed from Satan, with God's permission'.[46] For their delusion, Weyer prescribed medical and spiritual treatment. Based on correspondence with his brother Matthias and David Joris, it seems Weyer's religiosity was spiritualistic rather than orthodox Lutheranism, and his affirmation of the reality of a powerful devil was likely a spiritualist's cover for the depreciation of corporality in religious matters. Reginald Scot's similarly sceptical treatise was heavily indebted to Weyer's work, and it was very clearly spiritualistic in approach.[47] Weyer also called inquisitors and persecutors of witches 'the special slaves of the Devil; some may call them diviners, but for me they shall stand as the real evildoers'.[48]

27.11 WIESENSTEIG: WITCH-HUNTING REVIVED

Unfortunately the 1560s witnessed 'the last gasp of the "third way"' of a moderate, compromising approach to reform that Weyer's prince, the Duke of Cleves, had

---

[45] Jean Bodin, *On the Demon-Mania of Witches*, tr. Randy A. Scott; ed. Jonathan Pearl (Toronto, 1995).

[46] Mora, *Witches, Devils, and Doctors in the Renaissance*, 285; see also 498–9 and 521.

[47] Wooton, 'Reginald Scot'.

[48] See Hans de Waardt, 'Witchcraft, Spiritualism and Medicine: The Religious Convictions of Johan Wier', *Sixteenth Century Journal*, 42 (2011), 369–91; and Gary K. Waite, 'Radical Religion and the Medical Profession: The Spiritualist David Joris and the Brothers Weyer (Wier)', in Hans-Jürgen Goertz and James M. Stayer, eds, *Radikalität und Dissent im 16. Jahrhundert/Radicalism and Dissent in the Sixteenth Century* (Berlin, 2002), 167–85.

pursued.[49] By 1563 confessional lines were hardening, as evidenced by new doctrinal statements, most notably the Heidelberg Catechism for the Reformed, the Thirty-Nine Articles for the English Church, and the conclusions of the Council of Trent. At the same time new, tougher witchcraft statutes were passed in England and Scotland in 1563. Moreover, as Weyer was finishing his manuscript, Count Ulrich von Helfenstein, ruler of the region around the south-western German city of Wiesensteig, was directing a witch-hunt that ultimately destroyed over sixty witches for causing a destructive hailstorm in August 1562, robbing children of their 'holy baptism', and infanticide. The count's decision to pursue a diabolical sect of witches, rather than the more typical few individuals, set a new precedent.[50] At that very moment Ulrich was debating whether to adhere to the Lutheranism of his powerful neighbour, Duke Christoph of Württemberg, or return to Catholicism at the urging of his family. Until he made his decision in favour of the latter a few years later, Ulrich was considering a variety of religious positions, including that of the spiritualist Schwenckfeld, and attended the interrogations of arrested sectarians.

Why did the count, in the midst of this religious turmoil, suddenly decide to attack a sect of witches? Witches were traditionally blamed for hailstorms, yet other recent storms had resulted in trials of only a few individual witches. Three factors relating to the Reformation were involved in expanding the alleged conspiracy. First, the demonizing invective of polemicists aggravated religious confusion and fear. Second, all confessions believed that the devil was running amok during the Last Days. Finally, the decades-long attack on the Anabaptists had made credible a belief in the existence of an underground, diabolical, heretical sect, even though most people no longer feared the Anabaptists.

Just weeks before the 1562 hailstorm, an Anabaptist nocturnal meeting was discovered in a mountain forest near Esslingen, Württemberg and twenty-eight individuals were arrested. Several of the suspects had travelled many kilometres to participate in this worship meeting. The authorities, however, quickly released seven women suspects, leading one bailiff to complain that one of these women had been misled by 'Satan's true minister', an Anabaptist preacher. When these same officials were required to oversee accusations of witchcraft the following month, they immediately thought of women witches, whom they now imagined worked in a large group. Since witches were believed to fly long distances to their sabbaths, news of the Anabaptists' arrests further inflamed the popular imagination about secretive nocturnal gatherings. Duke Christoph, however, was convinced by his Lutheran preacher Johannes Brenz that witches could not alter the weather. Count Ulrich, for his part, followed the approach of the Esslingen Lutheran preacher Thomas Naogeorgus, who was subsequently sacked by the city council for his provocative witch-hunting sermons.[51] While

[49] MacCulloch, *The Reformation*, 570.
[50] William Monter, 'Witch Trials in Continental Europe, 1560–1660', in Ankarloo and Clark, *Witchcraft and Magic in Europe*, 1–51, esp. 20–1.
[51] Waite, *Eradicating*, 144–53.

Count Ulrich's example was not immediately followed by other princes, the precedent was set, so that when similar storms struck in the 1580s and 1590s, the people automatically assumed a sect of witches was responsible.

27.12 CONSPIRATORIAL ARSON

Added to this 'sectarianizing' of witchcraft were growing fears of arson gangs in the crucial two decades before Wiesensteig. The government associated several such groups with the Anabaptists, such as the Batenburgers and the 'children of Emlichheim', who killed livestock and set haystacks aflame in the eastern Netherlands in revenge for the Anabaptist persecution. Unable to catch the perpetrators, magistrates were forced to calm fears of plots to set entire cities alight.[52] The crimes of these quasireligious groups were analogous to those of alleged witches: destruction of crops and livestock, arson, and murder.

These conspiracies were comparable also to the plague-spreading panics that gripped Geneva in 1530, 1545, and 1568–71. The first two of these saw plague workers accused of profiting from the epidemic by smearing plague essence on door handles and then stealing from the homes of the deceased. Interrogations therefore focused on the suspects' accomplices, the oath of secrecy they had apparently made to each other, and how they made the plague grease they used to commit their crimes; few confessions related these actions to witchcraft. In the third outbreak, however, such practical issues receded into the background as investigators pursued diabolical elements to explain the perpetrators' motivation. Here too the image of the accused switched from a conspiracy led primarily by male plague workers, to a witch sect made up almost entirely of women, working under Satan.[53] This shift coincided neatly with the turn from persecuting real sectarian Anabaptists in south-western Germany up to August 1562, to hunting demonic witches thereafter. In the process, spreading plague, arson, and the large-scale destruction of crops and livestock were now more strongly emphasized in portrayals of sectarian witchcraft.[54]

[52] Gary K. Waite, 'Apocalyptical Terrorists or a Figment of Governmental Paranoia? Re-evaluating the Religious Terrorism of Sixteenth-Century Anabaptists in the Netherlands and Holy Roman Empire, 1535–1570', in Anselm Schubert, Astrid von Schlachta, and Michael Driedger, eds, *Grenzen des Täufertums/Boundaries of Anabaptism: Neue Forschungen* (Gütersloh, 2009), 105–25; Penny Roberts, 'Arson, Conspiracy and Rumour in Early Modern Europe', *Continuity and Change*, 12 (1997), 9–29; and J. Dillinger, 'Terrorists and Witches: Popular Ideas of Evil in the Early Modern Period', *History of European Ideas*, 30 (2004), 167–82.

[53] William G. Naphy, *Plagues, Poisons and Potions: Plague-Spreading Conspiracies in the Western Alps, c. 1530–1640* (Manchester, 2002), 199.

[54] Rita Voltmer, '"Hört an neu schrecklich abentheuer/von den unholden ungeheuer"—Zur multimedialen Vermittlung des Fahndungsbildes "Hexerei" im Kontext konfessioneller Polemik', in Karl Härter, Gerhard Sälter, and Eva Wiebel, eds, *Sicherheitsdiskurse—Kriminalität, Sicherheit und Strafe in der Repräsentation öffentlicher Diskurse (15.-20. Jahrhundert)* (Frankfurt, 2009), 89–163.

27.13 RELIGIOUS FEATURES OF WITCH PROSECUTION, 1560–1630

Shortly after Bodin's rejoinder to Weyer in 1580, another set of devastating storms and crises helped spark a new, more terrifying wave of persecution, engulfing the Holy Roman Empire, the southern Netherlands, Switzerland, Burgundy, and elsewhere from the late 1580s to the 1630s. Here we will highlight some aspects of the witch panics that can be linked to the Reformation.

Diabolical sabbaths were inversions of Christian ritual, as witches were alleged to venerate Satan in physically and sexually perverse ways, rather than the spiritual veneration required in Christian worship. They were allegedly rebaptized by the devil himself; said prayers backwards; gorged themselves on tasteless food blessed in the name of Beelzebub in a mockery of the Eucharist; desecrated Christian ritual objects; used consecrated hosts in their magical potions; and murdered and boiled down unbaptized infants, in a disturbing revival of ritual murder charges that had for centuries hounded the Jews.

The most infamous panics occurred in the heartland of the religious conflict between Lutheran, Calvinist, and Catholic territories and cities. Only rarely was the confessional polemic front and centre in the witch trials, such as when the prince-bishop of Würzburg, Julius Echter von Mespelbrunn, accused Protestants of witchcraft as part of his re-Catholicization campaign.[55] Instead, the fear of witchcraft prosecution was used to warn the populace away from heresy and superstition in general, and to reinforce the veracity of their ruler's faith, especially in the small Catholic bishoprics. For example, between 1581 and 1595 Archbishop Johann VII von Schönenberg oversaw a frightening panic in Trier involving hundreds of accused. Surrounded by larger Protestant territories, the archbishop used popular demands for witch trials to drive out any residual doubts about the verity of Catholic dogma. He was ably assisted by the Jesuits and his suffragan bishop, Peter Binsfeld, whose *Treatise on the Confession of Witches and Sorcerers* (1589), detailed how witches profaned the sacraments, threatened to bring down the wrath of God, and destroyed crops and livestock. To hesitate in the task of eradication merited divine punishment. For this reason, the mildly sceptical treatise *The True and False Magic* by the Dutch priest Cornelius Loos, which argued that witch-hunting was a distraction from the real dangers of Protestant heresy, led to Loos' own trial, since only those in league with Satan doubted his own danger. In 1593 Loos saved his skin by renouncing his book.[56]

---

[55] Midelfort, *Witch Hunting in Southwestern Germany*, 138.
[56] P. C. Van der Eerden, 'Cornelius Loos und die magia falsa', in Hartmut Lehmann and Otto Ulbricht, eds, *Vom Unfug des Hexen-Processes: Gegner der Hexen verfolgungen von Johann Weyer bis Friedrich Spee* (Wiesbaden, 1992), 139–60.

While most witch accusations arose out of the complex neighbourly dynamics of village life and conflict, major witch prosecution required officially approved belief in a sectarian conspiracy of witches in league with the devil. Although there were sceptics among them, such as Friedrich Spee and Adam Tanner, Jesuits often took the lead in promoting witch persecution, as they did in Trier and Ellwangen. The Ellwangen witch confessions focused on the renunciation of God, the Church, and baptism, submission to diabolical versions of the sacraments, and desecration of Eucharistic hosts, as well as *maleficium* and infanticide. Witch confessions, like exorcisms, thus became a weapon in the Catholic arsenal to reassert theological hegemony, reassure the faithful, and counteract Protestant and Anabaptist challenges to the reality of sacramental power.

27.14 CONCLUSION

In the 1560s, as jurists and inquisitors switched their focus from heretics and conspirators to demonic witchcraft, the gender of suspects changed abruptly from men to women. Once revived, witch panics took on lives of their own, spreading to realms that had either long suppressed their religious dissidents or had never had to deal with them. The fusion of elite-demonizing rhetoric against anticlerical heretics with popular anxiety over militant conspiracies, fear of divine anger, and intensified suspicion of assertive women, were significant features in the revival of witch-hunting in the 1560s in Germany. Thanks to anti-Anabaptist rhetoric, rebaptism was added to the diabolical sabbath, which became more credible thanks to rumours about Anabaptist nocturnal meetings and fears of arson gangs. The orthodox also sought to suppress the alleged atheism of spiritualists. At the same time, increasing pressure from the people to identify and punish those believed responsible for disasters and disease, presented desperate rulers with a ready-made tool to enforce religious conformity. Although many Reformers remained sceptical, the Reformation on the whole made the diabolical and conspiratorial aspects of witchcraft more credible in the short term, at least until the logic of providentialism could take hold. It had done so by 1600 in Protestant realms, as rulers and jurists now tended to see witchcraft accusations as specifically Catholic. Where rulers gave up on efforts to create the spiritually pure kingdom of God, major witch trials could now begin to collapse under their own illogical weight.

These insights into the interrelatedness of the religious reform movements and the revival of witch-hunting require further testing and deeper analysis, both at the elite and popular levels. While preachers frequently bemoaned their lack of success in reforming popular religiosity,[57] we know that clerical visitations, sermonizing, and confessional advising were powerful means of shaping popular opinions. We therefore require further study of the role of clergy, both Protestant and Catholic, in encouraging

---

[57] See Gerald Strauss, *Luther's House of Learning: Indoctrination of the Young in the German Reformation* (Baltimore, MD, 1978).

or discouraging fear of the devil and the religious opponent in the local community. While we know that the publication of demonological treatises such as Binsfeld's followed rather than preceded witch trials, it is likely that sermons on the subject were preached to local citizens long before the trials began. Closer analysis of these sermons, both printed and manuscript, could reveal much about the shaping of attitudes in the local community that made it more or less conducive to conspiratorial thinking. The correspondence between the delivery of sermons promoting or opposing baptismal exorcism in Lutheran Germany and the rise of mass possession cases on the eve of the witch-hunts provides one intriguing possibility. Following on Walter Stephens' insights into the mentality of demonologists, research into sermonic literature should further illuminate the doubts and anxieties that preachers felt and expressed, which may help explain why they projected those fears onto others. On this score their efforts to rebuff anticlerical sentiment presents a valuable starting point.[58]

Second, the relationship among demonic possession, diabolical witchcraft, and religious propaganda needs closer attention in regions outside of France, such as the German cases cited above or Brian Levack's intriguing study of demonic possession cases in Scotland.[59] Third, the dynamics of the Reformation and Counter-Reformation movements need to be more fully integrated into the witch-hunts narrative. Some of this has been done for the Holy Roman Empire, the Netherlands, Scotland, and England, for example, but other regions need further study.[60] The transition from the persecution of 'real' heretics to 'imagined' witches in the fifteenth century, so richly documented by Kathrin Utz Tremp, should be pursued more closely for the sixteenth century.[61] And how did these changing views of heretics and witches relate to the always problematical beliefs about Jews? There was, in the late Middle Ages, a great deal of cross-fertilization among stereotypes of heretics, Jews, and witches, and pursuing these through the sixteenth and seventeenth centuries could bear much fruit. For example, the rich source material relating to the persecution of Anabaptists in the Swiss territories has yet to be compared to the region's significant witch trials.[62] Local lore

---

[58] See especially Kevin C. Robbins, 'Magical Emasculation, Popular Anticlericalism, and the Limits of the Reformation in Western France circa 1590', *Journal of Social History*, 31 (1997), 61–83.

[59] Brian P. Levack, 'Demonic Possession in Early Modern Scotland', in Julian Goodare, Lauren Martin, and Joyce Miller, eds, *Witchcraft and Belief in Early Modern Scotland* (Basingstoke, 2008), 166–84.

[60] For the Netherlands and Holy Roman Empire, see Waite, *Eradicating*. For Scotland, see esp. Brian P. Levack, *Witch Hunting in Scotland: Law, Politics and Religion* (London, 2008); and P. G. Maxwell-Stuart's *Satan's Conspiracy: Magic and Witchcraft in Sixteenth-Century Scotland* (East Linton, 2001) and *An Abundance of Witches: The Great Scottish Witch-Hunt* (Stroud, 2005). For England, see Darren Oldridge, *The Devil in Early Modern England* (Stroud, 2000); and James Sharpe, *Instruments of Darkness: Witchcraft in England, 1550–1750* (London, 1996). For New England, Richard Godbeer, *The Devil's Dominion: Magic and Religion in Early New England* (Cambridge, 1994).

[61] Utz Tremp, *Von der Häresie zur Hexerei*; see also Waite, *Eradicating*.

[62] A region not covered in Waite, *Eradicating*, but see Sydney Penner, 'Swiss Anabaptists and the Miraculous', *Mennonite Quarterly Review*, 80 (2006), 207–28.

about radical dissidents such as Anabaptists on the eve of the witch-hunts could also bear closer scrutiny, especially as these relate to women.[63]

Fourth, the significant variations in attitude towards the prosecution of witchcraft within particular reform camps need greater clarity. For example, why could Dutch Reformed theologians and ministers generally oppose or ignore pressure to justify witch trials when their counterparts in Geneva, England, Scotland, and New England were at times vigorous proponents? What interpretive strategies did anti-witch-hunting preachers adopt in their efforts to explain the problematic scripture passages? Fifth, while the intersection between religious reform movements and conflict and the rise of the witch-hunts is becoming clearer for the sixteenth century, the ongoing relationship among these various features in the seventeenth century needs further analysis. Finally, the question of how changing notions of religious toleration and accommodation with the religious other influenced (or not) waning fears of diabolical conspiracies is worth exploring across Europe, as is the significant impact of spiritual-ism on the pulling apart of the demonologists' construct. The picture on this score is becoming clear for the Dutch Republic, but spiritualism was not restricted to this realm, and its impact on the development of proto-Enlightenment ideas of toleration and reason is the subject of exciting new research.[64] The depreciation of the role of the devil in human affairs, including the possibility that he did not exist outside of the human imagination, was not merely a response to the devastations of the witch-hunts, but was an integral element of early spiritualism.[65]

FURTHER READING

Ankarloo, Bengt, and Stuart Clark, eds, *Witchcraft and Magic in Europe: The Period of the Witch Trials* (London, 2002).

Behringer, Wolfgang, *Witches and Witch-Hunts: A Global History* (Cambridge, 2004).

Cameron, Euan, *Enchanted Europe: Superstition, Reason, and Religion 1250–1750* (Oxford, 2010).

Clark, Stuart, *Thinking with Demons: The Idea of Witchcraft in Early Modern Europe* (Oxford, 1997).

Ferber, Sarah, *Demonic Possession and Exorcism in Early Modern France* (London, 2004).

Levack, Brian P., *The Witch-Hunt in Early Modern Europe* (3rd edn, Harlow, 2006).

MacCulloch, Diarmaid, *The Reformation: A History* (New York, 2004).

---

[63] Waite, 'Naked Harlots'.

[64] See Andrew C. Fix, *Fallen Angels: Balthasar Bekker, Spirit Belief, and Confessionalism in the Seventeenth Century Dutch Republic* (Dordrecht, 1999), and *Prophecy and Reason: The Dutch Collegiants in the Early Enlightenment* (Princeton, 1991), as well as Jonathan Israel, *Radical Enlightenment: Philosophy and the Making of Modernity 1650–1750* (Oxford, 2001).

[65] Gary K. Waite, 'From David Joris to Balthasar Bekker? The Radical Reformation and Scepticism towards the Devil in the Early Modern Netherlands', *Fides et Histori*, 28 (1996), 5–26; Hans de Waardt, 'Religie, duivelspact en toverij', *Tijdschrift voor geschiedenis*, 118 (2005), 400–15.

Naphy, William G., *Plagues, Poisons and Potions: Plague-Spreading Conspiracies in the Western Alps, c. 1530–1640* (Manchester, 2002).

Tracy, James D., *Europe's Reformations, 1450–1650: Doctrine, Politics, and Community* (2nd edn, Lanham, MD, 2006).

Waite, Gary K., *Heresy, Magic, and Witchcraft in Early Modern Europe* (Basingstoke, 2003).

Waite, Gary K., *Eradicating the Devil's Minions: Anabaptists and Witches in Reformation Europe* (Toronto, 2007).

Wallace, Peter G., *The Long European Reformation: Religion, Political Conflict, and the Search for Conformity, 1350–1750* (Basingstoke, 2004).

Walsham, Alexandra, 'The Reformation and "The Disenchantment of the World" Reassessed', *The Historical Journal*, 51 (2008), 497–528.

CHAPTER 28

....

ON THE NEUROPSYCHOLOGICAL ORIGINS OF WITCHCRAFT COGNITION: THE GEOGRAPHIC AND ECONOMIC VARIABLE

....

OSCAR DI SIMPLICIO

DID economic change foster witchcraft accusations and prosecutions? Historical research during the past three decades has not offered conclusive answers. On the one hand, intense witch-hunting coincided with a number of significant economic developments, such as the price revolution, during the late sixteenth and seventeenth centuries. On the other hand, it is often difficult to establish a direct causal connection between such economic developments and individual witchcraft prosecutions. However, if we think in terms of extended, epochal economic transformations we realize that witchcraft belief has gone through phases of adaptation to different physical and human environments, and these developments have changed people's attitudes towards the nature of the crime.

This chapter will provide: 1) a hypothesis regarding the neuropsychological origins of witchcraft cognition, accounting for its persistence over long periods of time; 2) a theoretical framework concerning the appearance of a new 'socio-economic grammar' in the early modern period and its relevance to human behaviour; 3) a study of local and regional variations in witchcraft prosecutions to determine the extent to which they may have been affected by geographic and ecological factors; and 4) a reappraisal of witchcraft cognition in light of the *nature* through *nurture* dynamic.

28.1 WHY WITCHCRAFT PERSISTS

The traditional world of village community was fading away. The *villain* of the story, the 'long sixteenth century', made a fledgling agrarian capitalism emerge. The religious and political complexities of the period overlapped with socio-economic factors. The turmoil of the age unleashed a century of erratic witch-hunting that eventually came to an end in the late seventeenth and eighteenth centuries. But witchcraft cognition is still with us in Europe, and prosecutions based on such ideas occur on other continents as well. This persistence of witch belief and its appalling contemporary manifestations, reminiscent of early modern European witch-hunts, far from indulging in 'a meta-commentary on the ill-doings of capitalism and globalisation',[1] seem to indicate that witch belief, linked as it is to socio-economic developments, doesn't remain immutable but adapts to such developments. This persistence and adaptation has led some scientists, sociologists, and historians to consider two assumptions that illustrate a nature/nurture dynamic: 'human beings are machines for the creation of beliefs', and they show an innate 'propensity to truck, barter, and exchange'.[2] A man's inbuilt neural network is confronted by the developmental components of socio-economic reality.

28.1.1 The Brain and Deep History

More than half century ago Bronisław Malinowski argued that the origins of magic and witchcraft had to be sought in anxious reactions of oppressive emotions or obsessive desires based on a universal psycho-physiological mechanism. Some decades later, Edward E. Evans-Pritchard remarked that it is not possible to look inside the head of a man as easily as inside a large-plaited basket.[3] In a way recent neurosciences are trying to do just that by using empirical research (mostly through functional magnetic resonance imaging) to address such questions. An understanding of the origins, rationale, and persistence of magic and religion would today remain elusive without taking into consideration the 'revolution of the brain' of the past few decades. Neuro-sciences have enhanced our knowledge of the evolution of human behaviour, proving the existence of some hard-wired propensities of our psyche to direct attention to what is counter-intuitive. From this perspective, beliefs are seen as 'a consequence or

---

[1] Peter Geschiere, *The Modernity of Witchcraft: Politics and the Occult in Postcolonial Africa* (Charlottesville, VA, 2000), 223.

[2] Michael S. Gazzaniga, *The Ethical Brain: The Science of Our Moral Dilemmas* (New York, 2005), 157; Adam Smith, *Inquiry into the Nature and Causes of the Wealth of Nations* (New York, 1937), 13.

[3] Some decades later, another eminent anthropologist, analysing witch belief, attempted to find out a term valid for both an individual and a group and referred to the 'brain'. But he admitted that the current knowledge of the organ was 'superficial and partial'; see Rodney Needham, *Primordial Characters* (Charlottesville, VA, 1978), 60.

side-effect of having the brains human beings have',[4] which were formed in distant prehistory, when scattered groups of humans were shrouded in an atmosphere of awe and fear. Some thirteen thousand years ago, when the first agrarian civilizations emerged, societies determined that the performance of harmful magic was incompatible with religious belief and practice, and magic/religious cognitions parted ways, the dividing line between them being the *evil*. In monotheist religions faith was incompatible with the performance of evil, while harmful deeds featured as a possible or intrinsic reality of witchcraft cognition. There is no way of knowing how our prehistorical ancestors coped with occasional, non-cooperative, maleficent people. Some rudimentary, crude solutions, from ostracism to lynching, have persisted throughout history. With the development of agrarian, stable, literate societies, however, law codes were formulated to prohibit harmful magical activities. There is evidence of such measures from the law code of Hammurabi to the customs of many Italian and German communities in the Middle Ages.

Evidence of occasional ancient and medieval witch-hunts show that these societies had the legal capacity to punish harmful magic.[5] Nevertheless, the enforcement of the law must have been perfunctory and erratic, proving that, very likely, judicial action was a secondary option. In fact, between cooperative and cheating individuals a homeostatic equilibrium, essential to the survival of communities, had established a 'natural method of control' of harmful witchcraft to avoid traumatic repressions.[6] This informal *system* implied the presence in the village of magical practitioners (cunning folks, *indovini, curanderos, devins-guérisseurs, toverdokters, Hexenmeisters*) whose powers counterbalanced those of the witch. Historical research has largely overlooked this natural control of witchcraft, hampering a deeper understanding of the belief system. Consequently, a geographical study of witch-hunts should consider the following: first, they were concentrated in few territories and were rare or absent in most regions; second, in persecution-free areas the witchcraft system was operative; and third, even in the affected areas the absence of long-standing hunts strongly points to an alternative method of dealing with the crime. This natural way to cope with non-altruistic people that show intentions of acting maliciously had already developed over thousands of years, and had been present in ancient and medieval societies. Occasional witch-hunting was dysfunctional to human societies. Evolved within agrarian civilizations, the system remained operative even when the concept of evil had undergone an abstract, metaphysical transformation under the influence of monotheist religious thinking. There is no room here to dwell on cultural factors that might have found in Stoic and Christian values a firmer footing to strengthen the civilizing process. Yet

---

[4] Pascal Boyer, *Religion Explained: The Human Instincts that Fashion Gods, Spirits and Ancestors* (London, 2001), 379. The paragraph's heading refers to Daniel Lord Smail, *On Deep History and the Brain* (Berkeley, CA, 2008).

[5] Compare Wolfgang Behringer, *Witches and Witch-hunts: A Global History* (Cambridge, 2004), 56; and Norman Cohn, *Europe's Inner Demons: The Demonization of Christians in Medieval Christendom* (Chicago, 2001).

[6] Christina Larner, *Witchcraft and Religion: The Politics of Popular Beliefs* (Oxford, 1984), 127–39.

the outcome of the nature/nurture dynamic is clear: it eventually engineered a 'non-automatic evaluative step between causative objects and emotional responses' to stop primary intense reactions involving those cruder violent means that must have been rife in the infancy of humankind to respond to primal forms of harmful magic.[7]

Witchcraft cognition, when studied from the perspective of a nature-via-nurture interpretive criterion, shows that the system had reached its zenith sometimes near the end of the Middle Ages. Then, supposedly, something went wrong.[8] Economic developments during the long sixteenth century—most notably the introduction of agrarian capitalism—destabilized European society, unintentionally fuelling modern witch-hunts, which received inspiration from a religious ideology, epitomized by Heinrich Kramer's *Malleus Maleficarum*, to fight the enemies of God. This development created the preconditions of a new nature/nurture balance, in which more civilized, non-violent methods of controlling witchcraft belief could emerge. Shakespeare's reference to Caliban, 'whose nature nurture can never stick',[9] provides a metaphor to characterize his tormented age. If 'witch trials belong to the modern era as they belong to no other',[10] then the protagonists of 'historical witch-hunts' appeared at times reluctant to be nurtured and lacked coherent intellectual resources to stop the prosecutions.[11]

28.2 A New Socio-Economic Grammar

During the 'long sixteenth century' a series of decisive transformations that engendered new socio-economic attitudes and new 'ends of life' eventually led to the development of *possessive individualism*.[12] In the age of witchcraft prosecutions, no less than 80 per cent of the population were peasants, a very heterogeneous group practising diversified kinds of farming in extremely different agricultural areas. The toil on the land that fed some 70 million inhabitants was on the verge of an epochal transformation. It is rather pointless to observe that something of the new was present in the old, since in previous centuries those elements did not affect the social grammar of the period. Then, due to the interplay of natural and human factors, some regions developed an economic advantage over others. Economists and economic historians agree that if a critical combination of events makes this competitive edge of 'central importance in terms of determining social action, then the slight edge is converted in large disparity and the

---

[7] Antonio Damasio, *Looking for Spinoza: Joy, Sorrow, and the Feeling Brain* (Orlando, FL, 2003), 54.

[8] See Theodore Rabb, *The Struggle for Stability in Early Modern Europe* (New York, 1975).

[9] William Shakespeare, *The Tempest*, IV.I.188–9.

[10] Bengt Ankarloo and Stuart Clark, eds, *Witchcraft and Magic in Europe*, iv: *The Period of the Trials* (London, 2002), vii.

[11] I have anticipated a neuropsychological approach to the study of witchcraft cognition in my *Luxuria: Eros e violenza nel Seicento* (Naples, 2011), 66–85.

[12] Keith Thomas, *The Ends of Life: Roads to Fulfilment in Early Modern England* (Oxford, 2009).

advantage holds'.[13] In fact, under the influence of different patterns of landownership some farming regions developed while others stagnated or declined, and the driving force of these changes was the growth of urban markets. An economic leadership was passing to north-western European cities, as can be seen below in Table 28.1. Though the commercialization of agriculture was not an innovation in highly urbanized areas, in the long sixteenth century it spread, developing most strongly in England and the Netherlands. Historians have not made clear how or if witch-hunts were linked to the diverse patterns of the European economy. But this chapter, using the English and Dutch cases as paradigmatic, purports to follow a different course, and suggest that their peculiar economic change had a momentous impact on witchcraft belief.

28.2.1 England

In the early 1970s Alan Macfarlane and Keith Thomas argued that witchcraft accusations were caused by social tensions among the peasantry.[14] The anxieties and antitheses of early sixteenth-century England were grounded in the economic policies and social legislation emblemized by two words: 'covetousness' and 'commonweal'.[15] Macfarlane's research, which focused on Essex, showed that the county's farming, stimulated by the growing London market, had become increasingly capitalist. This reorganization of English agriculture took a heavy human toll but was profitable. An island roughly self-sufficient in grain at the end of the sixteenth century would become a grain exporter a century later. Unlike almost all the other Western European countries, England's population more than doubled between 1500 and 1700, and almost quadrupled between 1500 and 1800. The pressure of the market broke down the old values of mutual support within the village community: 'A real regrouping of social forces going on, and a rearrangement . . . of economic and political ideas' followed.[16] An ethic hiatus corroded the moral duty of the rich to give alms to the poor and the moral right of the poor to ask for them. At the time of this socio-economic change a pattern of witchcraft accusation was discovered: a poor villager (mostly a woman) begging at the door of a richer one is refused alms and goes away mumbling some threat, sometime later a misfortune occurs in the house of the uncharitable neighbour, who now accuses the woman of witchcraft. The psychological mechanism of witchcraft

---

[13] Jan de Vries, *The Economy of Europe in an Age of Crisis 1600–1750s* (Cambridge, 1978); Emmanuel Wallerstein, *The Modern World-System*, i: *Capitalist Agriculture and the Origins of the European World-Economy in the Sixteenth Century* (New York, 1976), 98.

[14] Keith Thomas, *Religion and the Decline of Magic: Studies in Popular Beliefs in Sixteenth- and Seventeenth-Century England* (Harmondsworth, 1971); Alan Macfarlane, *Witchcraft in Tudor and Stuart England: A Regional and Comparative Study* (London, 1970).

[15] Joan Thirsk, *Economic Policy and Projects: The Development of a Consumer Society in Early Modern England* (Oxford, 1978).

[16] Richard H. Tawney, *The Agrarian Problem in the Sixteenth Century* (Oxford, 1967), 231.

accusations transferred the guilt of the transgressor of community norms back to the alms-seeker.

The charity-refused model of accusation cannot be generalized to apply to the whole of England, but the impact of economic change on the old agrarian ethos has led some historians to abandon the concept of a 'decline' of witchcraft belief and to refer instead to its adaptation. A reviewer of Thomas' book has argued that quantifying belief is an intractable problem and that it cannot be proved whether it 'increased or diminished by comparison with the Middle Ages'.[17] More recently Macfarlane claimed that the process of the decline of belief 'was already well advanced before the sixteenth century'.[18] Be that as it may, European statistics on witch-hunting denote an unquestionable though puzzling link. In England and Holland, the two areas where agriculture performed best and engineered an inverted city–countryside relation (the countryside affected by the city), the working out of the well-oiled witchcraft system came to a halt, lost its peculiarities, and adapted to better fit the emerging urban civilization. By the 1630s English witchcraft trials declined rapidly, except for the massive East Anglian witch-hunt of 1645–7, which was due in part to the temporary suspension of normal legal procedures.

True, as the *Merry Wives* remind us, traditional witchcraft did not disappear in the countryside or in small-town domestic life. Yet the relevant drift of people into cities marked the beginning of another epochal mutation of the belief: a phase comparable in its civilizing implication to that which had taken place during the transition from a society of hunters/gatherers to one of villagers in the Neolithic period. Far from declining, the traditional cognition would adapt its shape to the new social grammar generated by economic change. During the shift of population from rural to urban areas the socio-economic machinery of a self-sufficient peasantry, hothouse of the 'natural control' of witchcraft, began to give way to a dependent culture; this was a centuries-long drift, slowly but steadily reliant for its survival on an socio-economic urban development. Urban growth implied not only a geographical process but one involving modes of thought and types of activity that may be considered as 'behavioural urbanisation',[19] as we will see after considering the Dutch case.

28.2.2 The Netherlands

The Dutch Republic was the other European state that enjoyed the coincidence of a social economic primacy with an early decline of witch-hunting. In Holland the

---

[17] Lawrence Stone, *The Past and the Present Revisited* (London, 1987), 195.
[18] Alan Macfarlane, 'Civility and the Decline of Magic', in P. Burke, B. Harrison, and P. Slack, eds, *Civil Histories: Essays Presented to Sir Keith Thomas* (Oxford, 2000), 152, 159.
[19] Jan de Vries, *European Urbanization 1500–1800* (Cambridge, MA, 1984), 11–12.

chrysalis of agrarian capitalism burst through a feudal order that had never played a larger role in the region. Agriculture underwent a reorientation to take advantage of growing urban markets, specialized production, and new opportunities opened by international trade. The dominance of crop cultivation disappeared because of the Republic's ability to import grain produced in Eastern Europe. The socio-economic circle promoting the Dutch Republic's golden age was not brought about by the mammoth pressure of a capital city such as London. To the contrary, a thick net of clusters of medium cities promoted Holland's economic boom. This integrated urban area, the *Randstad* as it has come to be identified, included Amsterdam, Leiden, and The Hague, among several others: a new urban environment, which no other region possessed to a comparable degree, and which was quite different from the closed, corporative medieval culture that it replaced. The cities became, legally, physically, and economically, more open: social centres stimulated cultural functions, a variety of consumptions, and, most significantly, developed an integrated system. Consequently, the peasant economy of the region was rapidly transformed. Extensive historical research in the 1980s proved the impact of such 'behavioural urbanisation' on witchcraft prosecutions, revealing a trend similar to that which occurred in England. In Holland the last witch trial took place in 1659, in a rural area, some forty years after the last death sentence had been carried out.

The argument that Holland's seventeenth-century prosperity, and especially the predominance of its towns over the countryside and the ascendancy of an urban culture, were crucial in bringing an end to Dutch witchcraft trials has not been immune to criticism. Nevertheless, historians have suggested that various socio-cultural groups in the towns became more sceptical of witchcraft accusations. For instance, sources from seven Dutch towns have shown that university-trained doctors and lawyers in the cities, while admitting that witchcraft was possible, became less inclined to recognize it as a cause of illness. The same social groups no longer attributed occasional disturbances concerning food production to *maleficium*, a change related to economic development. What is more, there are no indications in most Dutch provinces that witchcraft accusations were preceded by conflicts such as those that underlay witch trials in Essex. Most revealing of all, the Netherlands displayed a connection between a decline in witchcraft accusations and a rise in slander cases brought by those who were called a witch.[20]

[20] Willem de Blécourt, *Termen van toverij: De veranderende betekenis van toverij in Noor-doost-Nederland ussen de 16de en 20ste eeuw* (Nijmegen, 1990); Marijke Gijswijt-Hofstra, 'Six Centuries of Witchcraft in the Netherlands: Themes, Outlines, and Interpretations', in M. Gijswijt-Hofstra and Willem Frijhoff, eds, *Witchcraft in the Netherlands from the Fourteenth to the Twentieth Century* (Rotterdam, 1991), 9; Hans de Waardt, 'Prosecution or Defence: Procedural Possibilities following a Witchcraft Accusation in the Province of Holland before 1800', in Gijswijt-Hofstra and Frijhoff, *Witchcraft in the Netherlands*, 79–90.

28.2.3 Towards a New Phase of Witchcraft Belief

Before focusing on the adaptation of witchcraft beliefs in an urban civilization, it is necessary to identify the novel features of early modern cities. In medieval times, cities were defined mainly by the possession of specific political and economic privileges. In the early modern period the size of the population was probably the single most important factor. Demographic growth had the greatest impact on attitudes towards witchcraft, because the progressive anonymity of larger populations created circumstances in which accusations of *maleficium* were less likely to occur than in small-scale villages.

On the Continent and in the British Isles, towns of only two thousand to three thousand inhabitants predominated. Still, a significant demographic change was occurring, with larger cities growing at the expense of smaller ones. The result was that in the late seventeenth century Western and Central Europe had some two hundred cities with more than ten thousand inhabitants. Also, the number of metropolitan centres with more than 100,000 inhabitants increased from eight to thirteen. Aggregate figures for all of Europe can, of course, be misleading. Both Spain and Italy experienced a marked decline in their urban populations, in contrast to the pattern of growth that prevailed in north-western Europe.

In spite of these hard demographic facts urban witchcraft has not been a specific object of historical research, and we do not know whether the still half-hidden agrarian roots of early modern urban centres weakened the impact induced by population density. To what extent did the sudden effect of a new urban way of life overcome the patterns of traditional agrarian societies, namely, bonds of kinship, god-parentage, and neighbourhood? 'On what pretext—remarked a twentieth-century French peasant—would city-dwellers mutually bewitch each other, since there is no

Table 28.1 Urban Shares of the Population in Europe, 1500–1850 (%)

	1500	1600	1700	1800	1850
England & Wales	3.1	5.8	13.3	20.3	40.8
Netherlands	15.8	24.3	33.6	28.8	29.5
Belgium	21.1	18.8	24.3	18.9	20.5
France	4.2	5.9	9.2	8.8	14.5
Spain	6.1	11.4	9.0	11.1	17.3
Italy	12.4	15.1	13.2	14.6	20.3
Poland	0.0	0.4	0.5	2.4	9.3
Austria/Bohemia	1.7	2.1	3.9	5.2	6.7
Germany	3.2	4.1	4.8	5.5	10.8

Source: Adapted from de Vries, *European Urbanization*, 30, 36, 45.

real contact . . . or acquaintanceship'?[21] Or did weekly markets linking the countryside with towns help maintain significant contact between migrants and their home villagers' moods and minds?

Yet, notwithstanding all these uncertainties, the trend seems unmistakable: large urban populations were becoming sufficiently mobile and anonymous to discourage the long build-up of hostility characteristic of witchcraft accusations in close-knit communities. The English and Dutch cases support the hypothesis that European urbanization initiated a fundamental change in beliefs regarding witchcraft and magic. The discontinuities inducted by the 'long sixteenth century', the predominance of towns over the countryside, and the blossoming of an urban culture are markers of a modernization of witchcraft beliefs and prosecutions described as 'witchcraft after the witch-burning', a formula implying the millennial persistence of witchcraft cognition well beyond the end of persecution.[22] Historians should start thinking of urban witchcraft as a separate category and address some critical issues in this context. First, they should reconsider the entire notion of a witchcraft decline and retreat. Determining such changes in the cities is, at the same time, methodologically impracticable and theoretically misleading. Impracticable, because, due to the scarcity of sources, no comparison can be made between the periods before and after the age of witch trials; misleading, because this approach distracts historians' attention from the deep-seated neuropsychological reality of witchcraft cognition that was closely linked to geographical, environmental parameters that distinguish a world populated by hunters/gatherers from that of peasants/villagers and that of town dwellers. Second, a city had a constructed landscape, and the larger the city, the deeper the physical separation from the rural world. This might enhance people's anxiety on the basis of such conditions as weather disturbances, the adequacy of the food supply, the availability of medical facilities, and the fear of darkness. Third, the culture of 'civic rationalism' fostered moderation among judicial authorities and contributed to an already long-existing scepticism in the cities.[23] The argument of the 'rational city' might indirectly feed the unproven assumption that peasant scepticism did not exist. Quite the contrary. Though next to nothing is known regarding its strength in the past, scholars acquainted with village-based witchcraft trials have repeatedly come across cases of an unlearned peasant unbelief rooted in the centuries-long protracted observation of natural facts.[24]

[21] Jeanne Favret-Saada, *Deadly Words: Witchcraft in the Bocage* (Cambridge and Paris, 1980), 81.
[22] Marijke Gijswijt-Hofstra, 'Witchcraft after the Witch Trials', in Bengt Ankarloo and Stuart Clark, eds, *Witchcraft and Magic in Europe*, v: *The Eighteenth and Nineteenth Centuries* (London, 1999), 95–190.
[23] Behringer, *Witches and Witch-Hunts*, 82.
[24] See Oscar Di Simplicio, *Autunno della stregoneria: Maleficio e magia nell'Italia moderna* (Bologna, 2005), 369–71.

28.3 LOCAL AND REGIONAL VARIATIONS

A focus on short-term expanding or declining economies helps to shed light on the problem of the origins, diffusion, and transformation of witchcraft. In fact, urban and rural socio-economic structures in many areas of the Continent and the British Isles that did not experience witch-hunting were not substantially different from those that did. A history of places that did not experience witch-hunts is badly needed. The geographical diffusion of the phenomenon makes it difficult to distinguish between areas of growth and areas of stagnation or decline.

28.3.1 Rural Witchcraft

England. Let's take the case of a commercial, capitalist-oriented agrarian structure first. It is theoretically undeniable that a new mode of production would possibly lead to contrasting interests, values, and expectations; nevertheless, the charity-refused model witnessed in Essex does not seem to emerge in regions that experienced a similar agrarian reorganization. In England, for instance, it is 'uncertain why Kent, Hertfordshire, Middlesex and Surrey, counties undergoing the same type of socioeconomic change as Essex, had far lower level of witchcraft prosecutions'.[25] In Lancashire recent research on the outbreaks of witchcraft accusations in 1612 and 1633 have empirically tested the Thomas–Macfarlane hypothesis, concluding that conflicts over begging weren't the key factor. Similarly, evidence from Yorkshire, the Midlands (Belvoir and Northamptonshire), and the south (Royston and Milton) shows that demographic pressure and socio-economic disturbances, while providing a context in which prosecutions took place, cannot give a complete explanation for those prosecutions and do not support a particular sociological model.

The Continent. Economic life on the European Continent manifested few signs of peasant exploitation. The only agrarian transformation along capitalist lines barely comparable to the English one was taking place in the French region of Île-de-France. There, under the opportunities given by a growing metropolitan urban market, the nobility was investing considerable sums in land, anticipating a sort of physiocratic organization of farming.[26] There, as in England, the mechanisms of an early agrarian capitalism were beginning to result in the eviction of the peasantry. In France, however, there is no evidence of witchcraft accusations by prosperous neighbours against their poor neighbours to whom they had denied alms. Aside from the strong pressure exerted by the Parisian Basin on the whole, the peasant world was little altered. All

---

[25] James Sharpe, *Instruments of Darkness: Witchcraft in England 1550–1750* (London, 1996), 63.
[26] Emmanuel Le Roy Ladurie, 'Peasants', in Peter Burke, ed., *The New Cambridge Modern History*, viii: *Companion Volume* (Cambridge, 1979), 131–2.

in all, the socio-economic profile of the peasantry on the Continent remained substantially unchanged for the period of witchcraft prosecutions, and the limited food supply kept most of regions operating along Malthusian lines. Despite these economic realities, almost all historical investigations of the past three decades have attempted to test the Thomas–Macfarlane denial of charity syndrome on their local and regional sources.

Germany. Extensive witchcraft research carried out in the 1980s and 1990s has confirmed that basic economic conflicts and social tensions between neighbours were also a feature of small German communities. From microhistorical studies we know that most village animosity pivoted on economic matters, that conflict was an accepted part of competitive local strategies, and that people employed a range of means that included verbal abuse, gossip, physical violence, and legal action to win their case. Certainly the economy of the countryside was not stagnant, and in certain localities disputes resulted from more individualistic methods of farming. But no local economic developments were sufficiently extensive or long-lasting to force a reconfiguration of the agrarian social order.[27]

In the Saarland, accused female witches were predominantly poor: 43 per cent of them owned no property or were beggars; the rest were evenly divided between villagers of very slender means and lower-middle-class households possessing only a small income. However, in the nearby village of Winningen almost 40 per cent of accused witches between 1640 and 1660 came from the top social stratum. The begging paradigm, therefore, is not applicable in this context, and we cannot distinguish any particular emerging or declining social or occupational group.[28] In Protestant northern Germany, a social analysis of the pattern of accusations made by village committees in the county of Lippe has demonstrated that members of middling status brought most accusations of witchcraft against community members of relatively high local status, in order to resolve internal village conflicts.[29] As for England, witchcraft accusations could arise between households of relatively equal social and economic status out of competition for resources and influence within their communities. Whenever local elites got deeply involved in witchcraft accusations, their actions seem motivated by vested interests; therefore, they could be seen as witches endangering traditional communal norms.

In other areas the Thomas–Macfarlane model is even more difficult to apply. During the period of witch-hunting in Eichstätt between 1617 and 1631 a possible decline of charity did not provide the driving force for accusations, and both interpersonal

[27] 'Probably micro-sociological models are more promising for the explanation of suspicions of witchcraft'; see Wolfgang Behringer, *Witchcraft Persecutions in Bavaria: Popular Magic, Religious Zealotry and Reason of State in Early Modern Europe* (Cambridge, 1997), 412.

[28] Éva Labouvie, *Zauberei und Hexenwerk: Ländlicher Hexenglaube in der frühen Neuzeit* (Frankfurt, 1991).

[29] Rainer Walz, *Hexenglaube und Magische Kommunikation im Dorf der Frühen Neuzeit: Die Verfolgungen in der Grafschaft Lippe* (Paderborn, 1993).

conflicts and agrarian crises fail to account for the prosecutions.[30] In Württemberg, where prosecutions originated in accusations of *maleficium* that centred on economic issues, anger and violence between prosperous commoners and less fortunate neighbours did take place, but the dominant pattern of village animosity occurred most frequently between people who were relatively equal in station.[31]

Francophone Europe. Several thousand trials and a few hundred executions took place in the regions ruled by the Valois and Bourbon kings between 1570 and 1670. The poor preservation of local judicial archives only allows us to surmise a very loose correlation between the judicial evidence scattered over a wide geographical area and the economic disturbances associated with Malthusian crises. The scanty surviving sources hamper the historical research and forbid the individuation of a particular pattern of accusations. And no different conclusions can be drawn from border regions, such as the famous hunt of 1609–10 in the Pays du Labourd, which spilled over into the Basque region of northern Spain. But the records of witch trials abound for Lorraine. There, grass-roots prosecutions lasting for decades and producing a large number of victims sharply contrast with the German witch-hunts. In Lorraine economic and demographic developments in the late sixteenth century did not produce a major disruption of the social order, and tensions between the relatively prosperous and the poor increased. 'A fair number of changes did involve more prosperous households that had refused alms or assistance to the poor, but this seems to have been the dominant theme even when the accused were regular beggars. Social antagonisms play a fairly muted role in the vast majority of trials, with the typical accusations coming from neighbours who were hardly distinguishable, in economic terms, from those who were blamed for their misfortunes.'[32]

Mediterranean Countries. In order to spur economic growth, a self-sufficient peasantry had to be transformed in a mass of potential consumers, but this did not occur in Spain or Italy. Mediterranean agrarian economies remained long-term poor performers, with significant growing differentiations within the rural population causing the collapse of peasant communities and accentuating the differences between rich and poor. Of course, there are exceptions, and we know that landowners in the north Italian plain of Venetia, Lombardy, and Piedmont introduced intensive agriculture to avoid Malthusian crises. Unfortunately, we lack specific research to verify whether the improving agricultural productivity engendered the model of witchcraft accusation that was typical of areas in which agrarian capitalism was taking shape. Where regional investigations are available, as for Tuscany and Emily, witchcraft trials between 1580 and 1680 were endemic but not epidemic. There was, moreover, no evidence that these accusations reflected changing attitudes towards indigence. On the whole, the involvement of Italian and Spanish peasants in witch-hunting was no different from those in

---

[30] Jonathan B. Durrant, *Witchcraft, Gender and Society in Early Modern Germany* (Leiden, 2007).
[31] Edward Bever, *The Realities of Witchcraft and Popular Magic in Early Modern Europe: Culture, Cognition, and Everyday Life* (Basingstoke, 2008), 45.
[32] Robin Briggs, *The Witches of Lorraine* (Oxford, 2008), 376.

many other areas of Europe where *maleficium* provided the driving force behind accusations and prosecutions.

At the Margins of Europe. If we move from the southern to the northern margins of Europe, the connection between class differentiation and socio-economic change on the one hand, and witchcraft prosecutions on the other, becomes more problematic. The Swedish case epitomizes this northern European pattern. In cases of *malefic* witchcraft, Swedish accusations were 'to some extent divorced from social context'; they were not directly connected to any concrete conflicts between the parties.[33]

Scotland. Studies of witch-hunting in Scotland offer a perceptive, balanced appreciation of the Thomas–Macfarlane paradigm. Although 'the early seventeenth century appears as a period of a significant rural transformation and the more commercialized areas such as the Lothians and Fife experimented the heaviest witch hunting',[34] recent witchcraft research indicates that quarrels leading to witchcraft accusations took place mostly between social equals, not between neighbours of higher and lower status.[35] This research tends to support the argument of the late Christina Larner, which can be extended to apply to the whole of Europe. Larner maintained that the interplay of relationships between accusers and accused cannot always be linked to agriculturally advanced areas where the destruction of a peasantry involved the collapse of village solidarity. Witchcraft accusations were often related to human problems that occurred, if not universally, certainly more widely than only during the transition to a commercial economy. Circumstances that eventually led to witchcraft accusations in Scotland cannot be attributed to economic instability, even if the reaction to the cost of living appears to be the one factor common to all periods of witch-hunts.[36] Admittedly, exceptions abound. Individual cases in which the accused had lost social status, and the accusers had benefited from economic change can be found everywhere. But nowhere outside England did this pattern of witchcraft accusation predominate over a long period of time.

28.3.2 Urban Witchcraft

The vast majority of European witchcraft trials began in the countryside, but a not insignificant number originated in towns and cities. Does this pattern contradict the

---

[33] Per Sorlin, 'Sweden', in Richard M. Golden, ed., *The Encyclopedia of Witchcraft: The Western Tradition*, 4 vols (Santa Barbara, CA, 2006), iv, 1096.

[34] Julian Goodare, ed., *The Scottish Witch-hunt in Context* (Manchester, 2002).

[35] Lauren Martin, 'The Devil and the Domestic: Witchcraft, Quarrels and Women's Work in Scotland', in *The Scottish Witch-hunt in Context*, 75.

[36] Christina Larner, *Enemies of God: The Witch Hunt in Scotland* (London, 1981). In fact 'we cannot demonstrate that those individuals who were accused were those who had been displaced or were about to be displaced, and their accusers were the new single unit owners', 52.

argument presented above: that English and Dutch urbanization was a watershed in the history of witchcraft belief?

Again, the crucial question seems to be at what point early modern cities became centres of innovation and creativity, and their size and 'culture' impacted everyday life strongly enough to transform the attitudes of their inhabitants towards such basic issues as health, love, and reproduction. The answer depends on the size of the urban units. On the one hand, there is no evidence of large-scale witchcraft prosecutions in big cities like Amsterdam, Hamburg, London, Vienna, Venice, Paris, or Madrid. These cities were early modern sociological 'monsters', where traditional ways of living and thinking were likely to be quickly altered. On the other hand, towns of less than five thousand inhabitants often created the same *malefic* atmosphere of envy, backbiting, and calumny that were typical of small-scale village communities. In large cities people inhabited a milieu where available opportunities for better worship, schooling, medical care, and policing influenced their worldview. Such modernizing factors contributed to shaping an entirely different frame of mind, eventually undermining a system pivoting around the 'natural control' of *maleficium*.

Pandemics of witchcraft prosecutions that occurred in some German towns, such as Furld, Ellwangen, Bamberg, and Würzburg, provide a major test case for this argument regarding urban witchcraft prosecutions. Witchcraft in early modern Germany was an unstable mixture of maleficent magic and devil worship. The roles played by these two components differed, and it is unlikely that any particularly urban trends can be extracted from studies unconcerned with the civilizing role of cities. For instance, the cumulative demonological concept of witchcraft was debated in south-western German and Bavarian areas, but 'was [it] after all, principally a construction which was (or could be) called upon during judicial interrogations, but which did not play a significant role in the context of daily life?'[37] We know that many of Germany's numerous free cities, such as Nördlingenand Rottweil, conducted relatively frequent witch trials, and that some of the largest and most important among them, such as Augsburg and Strasbourg, continued to execute witches long after 1650. Still, we lack any specific indication about the possible impact of those modernizing factors or whether they definitely affected German urban milieus sooner and more strongly than rural zones. For example, granted that witchcraft accusations for killing livestock or raising hailstorms are less likely to recur in larger cities, it could be meaningful to compare data linking charges of witchcraft with infanticide in urban and rural settings. It has been shown that the judicial reclassification of charges against accused witches 'involved the judicial abandonment of the general word for witchcraft (such as *hexerei, sorcellerie, brujeria, stregoneria*, etc.) and its replacement with more specific terms'.[38] A clear hint to this lexical 'modernization' of witchcraft might concern the case of infant mortality. Between 1550 and 1750, did a greater proportion of town dwellers view it as

---

[37] Gijswijt-Hofstra, 'Witchcraft after the Witch Trials', 164.

[38] Brian P. Levack, 'The Decline and End of Witchcraft Prosecutions', in *Witchcraft and Magic in Europe: The Eighteenth and Nineteenth Centuries*, 81.

unreasonable to charge a suspected person with *maleficium* for the sudden and strange death of a baby? We note that, from 'the central government of Württemberg in the eighteenth century . . . infanticide came to be detached from its association with witch-craft'.[39] But was such a trend more relevant in an urban milieu, where, admittedly, infant mortality was higher?

The southern Netherlands, an exceptionally urbanized region that suffered from severe economic dislocations during the early modern period, offers another challenge to the hypothesis of 'behavioural urbanisation'. In this region, as in Germany, the cumulative concept of witchcraft became a central feature of witchcraft prosecutions, which spread to small cities, and to larger ones with populations of more than ten thousands inhabitants, including Bruges, Malines, Ghent, Louvain, and, of course, Lille and Antwerp.

In France, a full study of the geographical distribution of witchcraft prosecutions is not yet available, but the relevance of the phenomenon of urban demoniacs is beyond question. It is important to understand that 'the normative configuration of possession in the period did not assume a *maleficium* [and] only very few cases developed into accusation of witchcraft'.[40] Cases of collective possession took place mostly in nunner-ies and hospitals. Demoniacs, mostly women and children, blamed witches as the cause of their possession, and their exorcisms attracted large crowds of spectators. Collective possessions of nuns such as took place at Loudun or Aix also occurred in many other French cities, and became the source of intellectual debate. Although the impact of such widely publicized urban exorcisms on the broader population is difficult to assess, in the short run these episodes probably served as strong antidotes to urban 'modern-ization'. The actual dissemination of information about French exorcisms is difficult to determine because, unlike witchcraft trials, they rarely left written traces. This remark applies equally to seventeenth-century Italy, where many collective possessions also took place, but where it is difficult to determine their urban, as opposed to rural, intensity.

In Mediterranean cities, revealing the future, telling fortunes, finding lost objects, and attracting lovers were common. Love magic was a typically urban phenomenon in Castile and southern Spain, as in larger Italian towns. Unfortunately, except for Venice,

---

[39] H. C. Erik Midelfort, *Witch Hunting in Southwestern Germany, 1562–1684* (Stanford, CA, 1972), 82–3. Seventeenth-century German cities show a growing number of people found guilty of casting charms, fortune-telling, and magical treasure hunting rather than being accused of devil worship, a trend already noted in Geneva. In Augsburg, one of Germany's largest imperial free cities, a place where trials for witchcraft remained sporadic, we know that a tycoon like Jacob Fugger dabbled in crystal ball gazing, but we have no idea how widespread this recourse to supernatural economic information was among his fellow urban merchants.

[40] Moshe Sluhovsky, *Believe Not Every Spirit: Possession, Misticism, Discernment in Early Modern Catholicism* (Chicago, 2007), 26–7. In 'Geneva, as in many other places, witchcraft was not static but dynamic. The typical form of this crime changed considerably between 1527 and 1652, [mostly] in the form of the witch's *maleficia*.' The changes consisted mostly in elimination of details such as as orgies at sabbaths. Geneva's most common *maleficium* after 1605 became demonic possession: William Monter, *Witchcraft in France and Switzerland: The Borderlands during the Reformation* (Ithaca, NY, 1976), 56.

no thorough research on urban witchcraft in these towns has been done to date. To generalize from a single example is always a risky procedure, and in the case of Venice these dangers multiply, because the city was so enormous (some 139,000 inhabitants, early the seventeenth century) and cosmopolitan. Venetian incantations were motivated by love and gain. Infant deaths and deliberately diabolical forms of witchcraft attracted scant attention here. Instead, Venetian witchcraft activity centred on money. Necromancy concentrated on treasure hunting, while conjuration, divination, and many charms and incantations were employed in gambling. Though the city must be seen as a sprawling collection of smaller communities likely to reproduce neighbourhood crimes common in any rural environment, the extent to which superstitious remedies were allowed to prevail was perhaps limited because of the concentration in the city of opportunities (worship, medical care) and agencies of control (Inquisition, police), which might have provided alternatives to, or brakes upon, prosecutions for maleficent witchcraft. How far this possible Venetian pattern could be extended to other Italian cities remains an open question; the lack of information makes it impossible to say anything with certainty about long-term changes. A similar profile of illicit magic probably prevailed in every major Italian city between 1580 and 1660. Wherever witchcraft trial records have survived, comparisons may be ventured. The Venetian model seems to apply to the cities of Siena and Modena, where a long series of trials suggest that town dwellers stopped accusing witches of causing strange illnesses or the deaths of infants a half century earlier than in the *contado* (countryside). Did these patterns exist in all Mediterranean cities during the early modern period? From the case of Aragon we could extend this pattern to many Mediterranean cities.[41] No doubt, 'there was more than one "world of the witches" in early modern Europe',[42] but the urban world remains one area where further research is greatly needed.

28.4 THE WEIGHT OF GEOGRAPHY

The behavioural reactions of the generations of Europeans who lived in the age of historical witch-hunts are not to be simplified and measured according to the divergent paths of expanding or declining economic zones. And, if instead of focusing on economic growth we want to establish a connection between witchcraft prosecutions and short Malthusian crises, the attempt looks even more set for failure, because within each area the coincidence between the impact of economic variations and a witch-hunt appears erratic or non-existent.

In Germany it has been suggested that 'practically every great witch hunt had it root in a time of agrarian crises, while only minor witch trials can be found in the cheap

---

[41] See María Tausiet, *Abracadabra Omnipotens: Magia urbana en Zaragoza en la Edad Moderna* (Madrid, 2007).

[42] Brian P. Levack, *The Witch-Hunt in Early Modern Europe* (3rd edn, Harlow, 2006), 140.

years [of prices] between 1560 and 1630'. The greatest waves of persecution corresponded with the four greatest agrarian crises of the region. But notwithstanding the
hunger, disease, and death to which people were exposed in times of crisis, 'not all the
accusations of bewitchment have a recognisable connection with the agrarian crisis . . .
and we also find countless accusations of witchcraft which cannot be seen as either
direct or indirect consequences of crises in agriculture'.[43] In some German areas this
connection seems even more dubious. In Eichstätt agrarian crises do not seem to have
affected the course of witch trials at all, and agrarian crises did not feature prominently
in the witches' confession narratives.

In places where the pattern of witch-hunting drastically differs from the German
one, as in Lorraine, a correlation between agrarian crises and witch trials cannot be
proved, and recent research has shown that 'an unfavourable economic context does
not produce witch trial in particular'.[44]

In order to provide a more persuasive causal connection between Malthusian crises
and witchcraft prosecutions throughout Europe, historians have introduced a thesis
that combines economic and climatic change. The long sixteenth century experienced a
'little ice age' in which severe winters and extreme climatic events aggravated recurrent
subsistence crises. The Little Ice Age hypothesis, however, fails to provide a comprehensive explanation of witch-hunting throughout Europe. The climate-change hypothesis is based on: a) the temporal coincidence of accusations and prosecutions with
catastrophic meteorological events; b) the supra-regional and transnational character
of the severe climatic change; and c) the demonological literature that recognizes the
influence of weather on intense witch-hunting, such as Remy's and Binsfeld's references to witch trials in Lorraine and Trier.

A general congruence of the Little Ice Age with the age of witch-hunting cannot be
denied, but the thesis is a flawed insight. One problem is that the most important
charges brought against suspected witches in some areas involve accusations of the
witch's magical manipulation of weather conditions. In the northern Alpine regions
and in many parts of Central Europe witches were blamed for meteorological disasters
(hail, storms, frost, prolonged rains, drought). But there were many regions, even in
Central Europe, where they were not charged with the manipulation of the weather. In
Eichstätt witches were apparently not concerned with weather magic. In the duchy of
Württemberg manipulation of the weather was not included with other forms of
maleficium. In Lorraine and Alsace the association between climate and witchcraft
cannot be clearly established. Individual witches in this region were unlikely to have
been blamed for causing hail or frost. In fact only a tiny proportion of the natural
disasters associated with the witches' sabbath seem to have given rise to direct
witchcraft accusations. Suspicions about weather magic do appear in the trials, but
they usually played a secondary role, the one exception being the major witch-hunt that

[43] Behringer, *Witchcraft Persecutions in Bavaria*, 97, 98.
[44] Maryse Simon, *Les affaires de sorcellerie dans le Val de Lièpvre (XVIe et XVIIe siècles)* (Bar le Duc,
2006), 252.

took place in Germany in the late 1620s. If we widen the viewpoint to look to the whole European scene, the infrequency of charges of weather magic makes the assertion that witchcraft was the characteristic crime of the Little Ice Age, at the very least, problematic.

Outside the Holy Roman Empire the climatic hypothesis is based on very few chronological coincidences. England, Scotland, Spain, and sub-Alpine Italy were agrarian societies that experienced colder winters, subsistence crises, and occasional meteorological disasters, but human reactions to these economic hardships appear to have been different from those within the empire, and villagers very rarely connected unusually severe storms with witchcraft. In England, 'the storm at sea which affected a single ship might sometimes be attributed to witchcraft, but on land the action of a tempest was usually too indiscriminate for such an interpretation ... Witch belief, in other words, did not explain misfortune in general, but only in particular.'[45] In Scotland, witchcraft was blamed 'occasionally for storm raising; it was rarely held to be responsible for large-scale disasters in which the suffering might be random'; and in coastal communities only occasional accusations of weather magic causing the sinking of ships were reported.[46] In sixteenth- and seventeenth-century Spain, Aragonese mountains were considered to shelter witches, but there is no trace that those witches engaged in weather magic. During the Basque witch-hunt of 1609–14 the conjuring of storms was only a marginal activity of the accused. In Italy, south of the Alpine valleys, no witches were reported to have caused damaging meteorological events, although in the middle regions of Italy agriculture suffered from many cold winters and wet summers.

A peste, fame, bello ... Early modern European populations had to deal not only with colder winters and subsistence crises but also with recurrent plagues. There is, however, even less evidence that witches were accused of causing epidemic diseases than harsh weather conditions. There is no doubt, for instance, that even when such a disaster occurred before or during a witch-hunt, as in Scotland between 1590 and 1597, it caused greater social instability and deepened people's anxiety. But in Scotland, as in the rest of Europe, 'explicit charges of spreading plague were largely absent from witchcraft accusations'.[47]

Historians have already debated the link between geography and witch-hunts; such as the association of witchcraft and mountainous areas in Old Regime Europe. In a controversial essay the late Hugh Trevor-Roper maintained that 'mountains are the home not only of sorcery and witchcraft, but also of primitive religious forms and resistance to new orthodoxies'.[48] No wonder that Europe's many large witch-hunts took place in the Swiss and French Alps or other mountainous zones, such as the Jura,

---

[45] Thomas, *Religion and the Decline of Magic*, 668.

[46] Larner, *Enemies of God*, 82.

[47] William G. Naphy, *Plagues, Poisons, and Potions: Plague-spreading Conspiracies in the Western Alps, c.1530–1640* (Manchester, 2002).

[48] Hugh Trevor-Roper, 'The European Witch-craze of the Sixteenth and Seventeenth Centuries', in *Religion, the Reformation and Social Change* (London, 1967), 106.

the Vosges, the Pyrenees, Franche-Comté, Alsace, Lorraine, the Valtelline, Tyrol, and Bavaria. The 'mountain theory' of the origin of witch-hunting has been rightly discredited, but we might reconsider its broader spatial, environmental implications. Witchcraft, magic, and religious beliefs, being a function of man's brain, took shape in concrete natural settings. Witchcraft ideas preserved the spatial context in which they originated, where vegetation, woods, rivers, mountains, light, and darkness greatly mattered. 'The divide between town and countryside stands out as the most striking geographical feature' of the origins of this cognition.[49] In the long run, witchcraft has been conditioned by an environmental psychotropic mechanism, resulting in changes in perception, mood, consciousness, practices, norms, and institutions. The things peasants and mountain folks see, hear, and do are different from those experienced by urban dwellers. This spatial imprinting affects personal experiences and feeds man's innate predisposition towards counter-intuitive beliefs.

28.5 A REAPPRAISAL OF
WITCHCRAFT COGNITION

Why, then, the early modern systematic witch-hunting? Other contributions to this book analyse the late medieval development of demonological ideas, the impact of religious reform on the intensity of prosecutions, and the efforts of ruling elites to consolidate their control of potentially rebellious subjects. This complex mixture of religious and political developments coincided with the socio-economic difficulties of the time, which were possibly worsened by regional climatic developments. Although historians sometimes seek general causes for the many witch-hunts that occurred during the early modern period, and occasionally speculate on the development of a European-wide psychological atmosphere, they nevertheless prefer to consider the phenomenon as primarily the result of local, individual circumstances.

The aim of this chapter has been to suggest a different perspective. Instead of trying to link witch-hunts to an expanding or declining economy, it has redirected the focus towards the basic elements of witchcraft cognition. Magic ideas are the product of the human brain that took shape in societies of hunters/gatherers who faced specific prehistorical constraints, especially the difficulty of coping with predation and the adverse forces of nature. In later millennia the operations of the human mind had to be adapted to the new living conditions of a population of peasants. And when European villagers became permanent settlers in urban areas, the preconditions for a further

---

[49] Willem de Blécourt, 'The Witch, Her Victim, the Unwitcher and the Researcher: The Continued Existence of Traditional Witchcraft', in Bengt Ankarloo and Stuart Clark, eds, *Witchcraft and Magic in Europe*, vi: *The Twentieth Century* (London, 1999), 202.

adaptation of the belief arose. If the insights derived from neuropsychological studies of the human mind are valid, asking whether the decrease of witchcraft accusations resulted from a decline of witch belief or the other way round is barking up the wrong tree. Not only because it is difficult to measure beliefs, but mostly because the machinery of the human brain has remained unchanged and moulds people's reactions to newly developed spatial and environmental settings. The prosecution of witches during the long sixteenth century thus marked the end of a traditional witchcraft paradigm rooted in the village and contemporary forms of neighbourhood. The new basic social cosmology that replaced it was influenced by the constant influx of people into cities and the gradual transition to the psychological practices of possessive individualism.[50]

The fear of *malefic* dangers still operates in human minds. In contemporary urban civilization new witch-hunts still take place. This scaremongering phenomenon rests on the same neuropsychological premises as have always operated, and in spite of a more sophisticated legal environment and enhanced non-automatic evaluation stages, its aftermath—though most often bloodless—is no less dangerous.[51]

FURTHER READING

Behringer, Wolfgang, *Witches and Witch-hunts: A Global History* (Cambridge, 2004).

Bever, Edward, *The Realities of Witchcraft and Popular Magic in Early Modern Europe: Culture, Cognition, and Everyday Life* (Basingstoke, 2008).

Boyer, Pascal, *Religion Explained: The Human Instincts that Fashion Gods, Spirits and Ancestors* (London, 2002).

Briggs, Robin, *Witches and Neighbours: The Social and Cultural Context of European Witch-craft* (Oxford, 2002).

Damasio, Antonio, *Looking for Spinoza: Joy, Sorrow, and the Feeling Brain* (Orlando, FL, 2003).

Di Simplicio, Oscar, *Autunno della stregoneria: Maleficio e magia nell'Italia moderna* (Bologna, 2005).

Durrant, Jonathan, *Witchcraft, Gender and Society in Early Modern Germany* (Leiden, 2007).

Gijswijt-Hofstra, Marijke, 'Six Centuries of Witchcraft in the Netherlands: Themes, Outlines, and Interpretations', in Marijke Gijswijt-Hofstra and Willem Frijhoff, eds, *Witchcraft in the Netherlands from the Fourteenth to the Twentieth Century* (Rotterdam, 1991), 1–36.

Larner, Christina, *Enemies of God: The Witch-Hunt in Scotland* (London, 1981).

---

[50] Johan Galtung, Eric Rudeng, and Tore Heiestad, 'On the Last 2,500 years in Western History, and Some Remarks on the Coming 500', in Peter Burke, ed., *The New Companion Cambridge Modern History*, 318–61.

[51] In my *Dentro la stregoneria* (forthcoming), I deal with the 'political' role of fear.

Levack, Brian, *The Witch-Hunt in Early Modern Europe* (3rd edn, Harlow, 2006).

Macfarlane, Alan, *Witchcraft in Tudor and Stuart England: A Regional and Comparative Study* (London, 1970).

Thomas, Keith, *Religion and the Decline of Magic: Studies in Popular Beliefs in Sixteenth-and Seventeenth-Century England* (London, 1971).

de Vries, Jan, *European Urbanization 1500–1800* (Cambridge, MA, 1984).

CHAPTER 29

....

POLITICS, STATE-BUILDING, AND WITCH-HUNTING

....

JOHANNES DILLINGER

MOST witch trials took place before secular courts. This simple fact begs a number of questions. As secular courts were part and parcel of the state administrations of early modern Europe (including Britain) we must ask in what way different administrative patterns influenced the witch trials. It is impossible to understand the working and meaning of administrative patterns without taking into consideration the political structures that shaped and were upheld by them. Thus, the political system of the state, its changing distribution of power, and its inherent tensions must be regarded as one of the many factors which influenced witch-hunting. Evidently, what exactly 'the state' could mean, should mean, and finally did mean in the early modern period is a question that plagued contemporaries and still plagues scholars today.

The early modern period witnessed the slow and often erratic rise of bureaucracies run, as a rule, by salaried office holders with some expert knowledge. These bureaucracies mostly served emerging government centres, usually under the, at least nominal, guidance of a monarch, which increasingly managed to control countries with ever more clearly defined borders. It goes almost without saying that these processes of state formation were highly prone to conflict. State formation needed the erection of borders between states, which led in turn to a long series of military conflicts. In order to ascertain his power and that of the office holders within his country, the monarch had, in some way, to come to terms with the old elites of the estates, as a rule the Church, the nobility, and the oligarchy of the most influential towns. Without the cooperation of these elites taxation and administration on the regional and local levels would have been impossible. In addition to that, all state apparatuses needed the population to know and respect their authority. This could be a serious challenge: the villages and country towns of the early modern period tended to insist on what they considered

their rights and privileges. They often followed their own agenda, using the opportunities the emerging state offered as they saw fit.

Of course, all these conflicts produced a huge amount of literature in the early
modern period. From the late Middle Ages onwards the questions regarding what a
prince or a government should do and was entitled to do, and in what ways the
'subjects' were allowed to react, became hotly debated issues. The ongoing discussion
not so much about the virtues of the prince but rather about the role of the state and the
right to resist is one of the hallmarks of rising modernity. With the Reformation and
the increasing control princes exercised over ecclesiastical organizations, the early
modern state conquered new territory and had to face new challenges. It would be
foolish to assume that state formation was just an incessant struggle without winners or
losers. In many cases, by the late seventeenth century the centralized governments of
the monarchs had managed to 'tame' the competing powers and to integrate them into
their own administrative system. The new administrations, run by professionals, were
more effective than ever. Most communities acknowledged the princely government's
rule. The princes controlled well-trained standing armies. The governments of the
eighteenth century enjoyed levels of power far beyond the possibilities of their predecessors in the sixteenth and early seventeenth centuries. They felt confident enough to
actively 'reform' their apparatus and to plan new bureaucracies as they planned new
towns. Nevertheless, their power was largely based on compromise and cooperation.
Indeed, central governments ruling over individuals with more or less equal political
rights in more or less unified states with more or less undisputed borders was
principally a product of the long nineteenth century. Early modern state formation is
best seen as a torturous process leading to bitterly contested and often unstable
compromises between monarchs, elites, and so-called commoners, at times punctuated
by outbursts of popular unrest and violent suppression.[1]

State formation and witch-hunting are clearly two of the 'big' topics for the historians of the early modern period. Strangely enough, there is still not much overlap
between these two subjects. Early studies of witchcraft, especially German ones,
were fascinated with the role the churches had supposedly played in witch-hunts.
The state(s) disappeared in the background. In the late 1960s, the new witchcraft
research emerged from a number of different areas, among others: gender history
and the discussion between history and anthropology. Political history was quite alien
to those new sub-fields. Nevertheless, Alfred Soman and others were quick to point out
the influence of the judicial system on the persecutions.[2] Administrative history and
thus the history of political organizations crept into witchcraft research with each new
regional study. Erik Midelfort's work on the widely different patterns of witch-hunting

---

[1] Henri J. M. Claessen and Peter Skalník, eds, *The Early State* (The Hague, 1978); Wolfgang Reinhard,
Geschichte der Staatsgewalt (2nd edn, Munich, 2000); Wim Blockmans and J.-Ph. Genet, eds, *The
Origins of the Modern State in Europe, 13th to 18th Centuries*, 7 vols (Oxford 1995–2000).

[2] Alfred Soman, 'The Parliament of Paris and the Great Witch Hunt', *Sixteenth Century Journal*,
9 (1978), 32–44.

in the various principalities of south-western Germany made it obvious that the leadership and the political structures of these principalities needed to be taken into account in order to understand the rise and the decline of witch trials. Wolfgang Behringer and I wrote very 'political' regional studies of witchcraft that presented witch-hunting as part and parcel of wider political conflicts, in which tensions within the princely administration or quarrels between the emerging bureaucracy and local elites played crucial roles. Brian Levack was the first to suggest a coherent theory of witch-hunting and state formation, suggesting that the growth of the modern state apparatus marginalized witch-hunts. In 2002 a major international conference explored this avenue of research further.[3]

29.1 DEMONOLOGY AND POLITICS

One of the most important points Kramer made in the *Malleus maleficarum* was that the princes and the secular courts, that is, the early embodiments of the state, had the responsibility to prosecute witches actively. Coming from an inquisitor, this might seem like a major concession. However, Kramer simply accepted a long established fact: temporal rulers had always punished harmful magic. Some of the earliest witch trials took place before secular courts. Demonologists, whether they were theologians or jurists, never questioned the authority of secular courts and legislators. Rather, they declared that unfailing zeal in the prosecution of witches was the hallmark of the good and godly ruler. Unsurprisingly, the theory of divine right helped to drive that message home. If the monarch was God's vicegerent on earth, he was under a special obligation to do God's will. For the demonologists this, of course, included the extermination of witchcraft.[4]

Bodin, the political theorist and radical demonologist came close to constructing two entirely parallel and completely antithetical hierarchies, with Satan, the demons, and the witches on one side, and God, the angels, the king, and his judges on the other. If the king failed to live up to his distinctive role in the eschatological fight against evil, God would punish him, possibly even with insurrections by his subjects.[5] Coming from

---

[3] H. C. Erik Midelfort, *Witch Hunting in Southwestern Germany* (Stanford, CA, 1972); Wolfgang Behringer, *Witchcraft Persecutions in Bavaria: Popular Magic, Religious Zealotry and Reason of State in Early Modern Europe* (Cambridge, 1997); Johannes Dillinger, *'Evil People': A Comparative Study of Witch-Hunts in Swabian Austria and the Electorate of Trier*, tr. Laura Stokes (Charlottesville, VA, 2009); Brian P. Levack, 'The Decline and End of Witchcraft Prosecutions', in Bengt Ankarloo and Stuart Clark, eds, *Witchcraft and Magic in Europe: The Eighteenth and Nineteenth Centuries* (London 1999), 7–33; Johannes Dillinger, Jürgen Michael Schmidt, and Dieter R. Bauer, eds, *Hexenprozess und Staatsbildung: Witch-Trials and State-Building* (Bielefeld, 2008).

[4] Johannes Dillinger, *Hexen und Magie* (Frankfurt am Main, 2007), 43–55; Stuart Clark, *Thinking with Demons* (Oxford, 1997), 547–682.

[5] Jean Bodin, *De la démonomanie des sorciers* (Paris, 1580), fol. 166r–167r.

so ardent a champion of royal prerogatives as Bodin, this was indeed a formidable threat. It was undisputed among the authors of the witchcraft doctrine that all office holders fighting witches operated under God's special protection. After James VI of Scotland narrowly escaped a misfortune at sea that was believed to have been caused by witchcraft, one of the 'terrorist' witches explained, probably after sufficient prompting, that she had been unable to harm the king because he was 'un homme de Dieu'.[6] Some demonologists like Peter Binsfeld even argued that God would not only prevent the witches from harming court officials, but would also prevent the courts from making any mistakes while they prosecuted witches. Faced with the embarrassing example of Didier Finance, the magistrate from Saint-Dié who had confessed to being a witch, the judge and demonologist Nicolas Remy suggested that Finance had been unable to converse with demons while he was in office.[7]

However, what did the concept of divine right and the idea of the godly state really mean? First of all, the theory of divine right must not be confused with absolutism. Today, most expert historians agree that absolutism was a theory rather than a political fact. We will not use the label 'absolutism' in this text. Regimes that propagated the theory of divine right and accepted the Ten Commandments as the inspiration of legislation and judicial practice were under some pressure to prosecute witches—at least in theory. However, such theoretical predispositions explain very little about the actual development of witch-hunts. The doctrine of the divine right of kings flourished in late seventeenth-century France, but France prosecuted very few witches during that period. The godly states of New England appealed to the Bible as the basis of their criminal code, but these states held relatively few witchcraft trials, especially when compared to the mass prosecutions in Scotland or Franconia. In order to understand the political realities of witch-hunting, we need to turn to organizational matters and administrative affairs.

29.2 WITCHFINDER INSTITUTIONS: SPECIAL ADMINISTRATIONS

Generally speaking, in witch-hunting, all legal administrations that allowed individuals or very small groups to acquire power without effective control were extremely dangerous. If the administrative structure gave radical individuals the chance to occupy key positions, they could spark major witch-hunts. In the late seventeenth and eighteenth centuries, the *Bannrichter* (district judges) Georg Pickhl and Georg Wolfgang

---

[6] James I, *Daemonologie*, in *Minor Prose Works of King James VI and I*, ed. James Craige (Edinburgh 1982), 35. Case file quoted in Stuart Clark, 'King James's Daemonology: Witchcraft and Kingship', in Sydney Anglo, ed., *The Damned Art: Essays in the Literature of Witchcraft* (London, 1977), 156–81, 164–7.

[7] Peter Binsfeld, *Tractat von Bekantnuß der Zauberer vnd Hexen* (Trier 1590), fols 144v–148r; Nicolas Remy, *Demonolatry*, tr. E. Allen Ashwin, ed. Montague Summers (London, 1930), 2–5, 188.

von Tschabueschnig were alone responsible for criminal trials in all of Carinthia. Both were responsible for a number of comparatively late witch trials, as they saw fit to use torture indiscriminately in a way reminiscent of the worst prosecutions of the sixteenth century. The best examples of office holders who used their exceptional positions of power to promote witch-hunts are Nicolas Remy, the demonological hardliner notorious for his treatise *Démonolâtrie*, and his son Claude. Both enjoyed the trust of Duke Charles III of Lorraine. Nicolas Remy served as a judge of the Change, Lorraine's central court, between 1576 and 1591. Afterwards, he worked as *procureur général* until his son Claude succeeded him in 1606. Together they controlled this office for forty years. With the support of the duke, the Remys managed to exercise considerable influence on Lorraine's most powerful court. They were at least partially responsible for keeping the number of witch trials in Lorraine at a consistently high level. The Remys' forty years in office marked the period of most severe witch-hunting in Lorraine.[8]

Officials like von Tschabueschnig and Remy exploited, or even abused, their powerful positions within the state apparatus. However, their positions were not out of the ordinary. More dangerous was any kind of policy that created special positions in the administration or the judiciary or even established new institutions that served the sole purpose of prosecuting witches. Office holders or institutions that had witch-hunting as their only raison d'être were typical elements of witch-hunts that originated 'from above; that is, prosecutions organized according to the will, and with the power, of the prince. In many cases, such witch-hunts, sponsored by a prince and run by a special administration, developed into persecutions of catastrophic scale. Because these offices and courts had been established to hunt witches in the first place, the individuals who staffed them usually strove to do exactly that, often with no regard for due process. Any hesitation on their part could be seen as a lack of determination or reliability.

A number of German princes appointed special witch commissioners whose sole function was to organize witch-hunts. Some princes made such appointments with the ultimate goal of reducing the number of trials and eventually letting them die out. The witch commissioner Dr Leonhard Neusesser, who virtually ended the witch-hunt in the Habsburg territories in modern-day Bavaria is a case in point.[9] But most princes apparently employed witch commissioners with special powers to promote witch-hunts. For example, the prince-elector of Cologne authorized Dr Heinrich von Schultheiß to superintend the witch trials in Westphalia. Dr Wolfgang Kolb worked as a witchfinder for the prince-bishop of Eichstätt, the count of Oettingen-Wallerstein, and the duke of Bavaria, who gave him the title of 'Rat von Haus aus' (councillor with special commission). His appointment to these positions illustrates the high demand for specialist bureaucrats during the early modern period.[10] Even some towns granted

---

[8] Gerhard Sarman, 'Kärntens letzter Hexenrichter', in Heide Dienst, ed., *Hexenforschung aus österreichischen Ländern* (Vienna 2009), 143–61; Elisabeth Biesel, *Hexenjagd, Volksmagie und soziale Konflikte im lothringischen Raum* (Trier, 1997).

[9] Johannes Dillinger, *'Evil People'*, 172–3.

[10] Wolfgang Behringer, *Hexenverfolgung in Bayern* (3rd edn, Munich, 1997), 238–41, 314–17; Tanja Gawlich, 'Der Hexenkommissar Heinrich von Schultheiß und die Hexenverfolgungen im Herzogtum

additional powers to clerks who were supposed to investigate rumours of witchcraft. In the Imperial Free City of Esslingen, the town council empowered the attorney Daniel Hauff to prepare all charges against witches. Hauff used his assignment to rise to the position of town councillor. Hermann Cothmann, the notorious 'witch burgomaster' of Lemgo in Westphalia, began his career, which would lead him to the very top of the town's hierarchy, as Lemgo's 'director of criminal trials against sorcerers and witches'.[11]

Special courts set up to prosecute witches were even more instrumental than witch commissioners in increasing the number of trials. Since these courts operated outside of the ordinary judicial system, they had considerable independence. A special witch-hunting institution was at least in part responsible for the outbreaks of witch-hunting in Sweden between 1669 and 1676. Local courts of the Dalarna region had traditionally tried witchcraft suspects. When the Royal Court of Appeal at Stockholm repealed some of the death sentences passed by these courts, considerable dissatisfaction arose in the countryside. The village of Mora sent delegates to Stockholm to demand the establishment of a special court to try the witches in summary fashion. The government obliged by appointing a witchcraft commission under Councillor Lorentz Creutz in 1669. No other courts were to interfere with the work of the commission, there would be no appeals, and the commission was entitled to have its sentences implemented immediately. Evidently, the commission regarded it as its duty to eradicate witchcraft, not to examine the depositions of witnesses and the evidence critically. The commissioners interrogated no fewer than sixty suspects, and passed twenty-three death sentences within two weeks. The speedy 'justice' of the Dalarna witchcraft commission provoked widespread demands for further investigations along the same administrative lines in other parts of Sweden that the government found difficult to ignore. Even though the other witchcraft commissions proceeded more cautiously than the one established in 1669, and in some instances even tried to stop the prosecutions, the spectacular trials of Dalarna had sparked a witch-hunt that would last for seven years.[12] A similar special court facilitated the witch-hunts of late seventeenth-century Bohemia.[13]

The best-known example of a witch-finding institution was the Court of Oyer and Terminer established at Salem, Massachusetts, in 1692. This court was given only one

---

Westfalen', in Harm Klueting, ed., *Das kurkölnische Herzogtum Westfalen von den Anfängen der kölnischen Herrschaft im südlichen Westfalen bis zur Säkularisation 1803* (Münster, 2009), 279–320.

[11] Günter Jerouschek, *Die Hexen und ihr Prozeß: Die Hexenverfolgung in der Reichsstadt Esslingen* (Esslingen, 1992). Nicolas Rügge, 'Cothmann, Hermann', in *Lexikon zur Geschichte der Hexenverfolgung.* <http://www.historicum.net/no_cache/persistent/artikel/1587/> (accessed 20 August 2012).

[12] Birgitta Lagerlöf-Génetay, *De svenska häxprocessernas utbrottsskede 1668–1671* (Stockholm, 1990); Marie Lennersand, 'Androm till sky och skräck: Den rättsliga behandlingen av trolldomsprocesserna i Älvdalen och Mora 1668–1669', in Linda Oja, ed., *Vägen till Blåkulla* (Uppsala, 1997), 23–44; Bengt Ankarloo, 'Witch Trials in Northern Europe, 1450–1700', in Bengt Ankarloo and Stuart Clark, eds, *Witchcraft and Magic in Europe*, iv: *The Period of the Witch Trials* (London, 2002), 53–95.

[13] Petr Kreuz, 'Der Einfluss des Rechtssystems und der Gerichtsorganisation auf Entwicklung, Dynamik und Formen der Hexenprozesse in den böhmischen Ländern', in Heide Dienst, ed., *Hexenforschung aus österreichischen Ländern* (Vienna, 2009), 231–60.

task, and it exercised it exclusively: the trial of the Salem witches. It was largely immune from the interference of other courts or government agencies. The Salem court certainly made the most of these privileges. Within the structure of this special court, William Stoughton was, at least temporarily, the leading figure. Cotton Mather included a rather self-gratulatory introduction written by Stoughton to his book on witchcraft.[14] The new governor of Massachusetts dissolved the court after serious doubts were voiced, principally by a group of ministers, regarding the sufficiency of the evidence against the accused. Even though Stoughton also headed the new Superior Court of Judicature, this court, under the influence of the governor, dispatched the remaining cases without executing any more accused witches.[15]

The ecclesiastical lands of the prince-bishops of Eichstätt, Würzburg, Bamberg, the prince-abbot of Fulda, and the prince-provost of Ellwangen witnessed some of the most intense witch-hunts in early modern Europe. The ecclesiastical princes of these territories saw themselves as the leaders of a battle between Tridentine Catholicism and the devil. All of these prince prelates set up special courts or small special committees of administrators that were intended to eradicate witchcraft. These institutions were either completely new or represented a thorough restructuring of older ones. They had few officers, and their inner structure was simple. The princes gave them special powers that placed them outside the ordinary legal system and beyond the control of other government agencies. Thus freed from administrative restraints, the witchfinder institutions became independent bureaucracies whose main concern was efficiency rather than adherence to due process. They 'processed' a great number of suspects in short order. We might say their records resembled modern fill-in forms: the only entries that really changed were the names of the suspects and the date. It was characteristic of such prosecutions 'from above' that they relied heavily on denunciations and on the use of torture.[16]

The witchfinder institutions were originally meant to remedy the administrative shortcomings of the states in which they arose. The logistical and organizational problems early modern Sweden faced are obvious: the country was huge, the infrastructure poorly developed, and regional office holders of the king were virtually powerless without the active support of the peasants who organized themselves in

---

[14] Cotton Mather, *The Wonders of the Invisible World* (Boston, MA, 1693), 3–5.

[15] Peter Charles Hoffer, *The Devil's Disciples: Makers of the Salem Witchcraft Trials* (Baltimore, MD, 1996); Kai Erikson, *Wayward Puritans* (New York, 1966), 137–53.

[16] Andrea Renczes, *Wie löscht man eine Familie aus? Eine Analyse Bamberger Hexenprozesse* (Pfaffenweiler, 1990), 38–42; Wolfgang Mährle, ' "O wehe der der armen seelen": Hexenverfolgungen in der Früstpropstei Ellwangen', in Johannes Dillinger, Thomas Fritz, and Wolfgang Mährle, eds, *Zum Feuer verdammt* (Stuttgart, 1998), 325–500, 383–92; Harald Schwillus, *Die Hexenprozesse gegen Würzburger Geistliche unter Fürstbischof Philipp Adolf von Ehrenberg* (Würzburg, 1989); Jonathan Durrant, *Witchcraft, Gender and Society in Early Modern Germany* (Leiden, 2007); Robert Walinski-Kiehl, 'Witch-Hunting and State Building in the Bishoprics of Bamberg und Würzburg', in Dillinger, Schmidt, and Bauer, eds, *Hexenprozess und Staatsbildung*, 245–64.

regional assemblies. Massachusetts was far removed from the government of the mother country, and when the Salem witch-hunt started, the colony had not yet recovered from the severe political and military crisis of the late 1680s. It was, moreover, still waiting for a new governor to arrive with a new charter that would guarantee the fundamental rights of the colony. Relatively weak administrations were characteristic of the German ecclesiastical territories. Due to the lack of a ruling dynasty they often found it difficult to establish clear patterns of power and obedience. The witch-hunting institutions expanded the prince's jurisdiction dramatically in all his lands.[17] Thus, the witch-hunting institutions contributed directly to the process of state formation. They clearly helped to centralize the country and to focus attention on the government. However, their 'success' and their 'usefulness' was short-lived. The mounting death toll began to damage the very fabric of society and the state itself. Observers in neighbouring territories and officials in the state bureaucracy viewed the growing power of the witchfinder institutions with grave suspicion.

29.3 WITCHFINDER INSTITUTIONS: COMMUNAL STRUCTURES

Some of the most aggressive witch-hunts were not orchestrated by some prince's specialized court or administrative unit. As a matter of fact, they seem to have worked quite independently of the princely sovereign.

In early modern Scotland, the court of justiciary in Edinburgh had the highest judicial authority in the kingdom, but the court was often unable or unwilling to bring suspects to Edinburgh for trial. The more usual practice was for Scotland's Privy Council—or occasionally the Scottish parliament—to appoint ad hoc commissioners from the local elites to conduct the trials themselves. The main reason for this delegation of central power to the localities was that the government did not have the resources to support a large judicial establishment capable of presiding over witchcraft trials on the circuit, as was the custom in England. This practice prevented the government from exercising direct control over the trials and from guaranteeing that the courts followed due process. This meant, in effect, that the local elites who had taken the lead in requesting a commission to try a witch from the Privy Council also determined the witch's fate.[18]

Once they received their commissions, the local elites were essentially left to their own devices. They were even able to use torture to force suspected witches to confess,

[17] Johannes Dillinger, 'The Political Aspects of the German Witch-Hunts', *Magic, Ritual, and Witchcraft* (2008), iii, 62–81.

[18] Brian P. Levack, 'State-Building and Witch-Hunting in Early Modern Scotland', in Dillinger, Schmidt, and Bauer, eds, *Hexenprozess und Staatsbildung*, 77–96.

despite the prohibition of torture in Scotland except when approved by the Privy Council. With biased and frightened local communities and untrained judges in charge of the trials, witch-hunting in Scotland became far more intense than in England. With a population of only about one-quarter of that of England, Scotland executed at least three times as many witches.

When Scotland was forced into a union with England during the Interregnum, the number of witch trials declined significantly. The English managed to exercise some control over the judicial system of their northern neighbours by sending their own commissioners to preside at Scottish witchcraft trials. The English judges—outsiders par excellence—had no reason to cater to the demands of local communities. Shortly after the English withdrew from Scotland in 1660, the traditional local elites returned to power, and the country experienced the worst witch-hunt in its history. Intense witch-hunting did not end until the late seventeenth century, when the Privy Council began to exercise tighter control over the prosecutions.[19]

One of the reasons why about half of all executions for witchcraft took place in the Holy Roman Empire of the German Nation is that many of its principalities offered people without any legal training whatsoever the chance to critically influence criminal procedures. The peasants and people from small towns made their voices heard during the witch-hunts. Numerous communities managed to usurp parts of the legal adminis-tration. Various German principalities witnessed severe witch prosecutions 'from below', that is, prosecutions initiated and organized by the so-called subjects without the approval, or even against the will, of the respective lord. Some of these grass-roots witch-hunts numbered among the most ferocious ever.

In the Rhine-Moselle-Saar region, communal self-government was traditionally strong. The peasant communities elected village committees to redress local grievances. As a rule, the basis of their power was an ad hoc village covenant that acknowledged the committee as acting on behalf of the whole community. The respective lord had, at best, nominal control over these institutions of village self-government. A committee might, for example, reform the local tax system or act as the legal representatives of the village in court. However, a village might also elect a committee for the sole purpose of witch-hunting. Such witch-hunting committees established their own investigative organization. They collected evidence, heard witnesses, and contacted the official courts in order to find out who had been denounced as a witch. Some committees even employed their own scribes and lawyers. The committees brought charges against witchcraft suspects collectively. Of course, the activities of the witch-hunting commit-tees were costly. As a rule, the accused or their relatives had to pay not only the expenses of the trial proper but also those of the—strictly speaking extra-legal—investigations of the committee. If confiscations did not cover all the costs, the village community itself had to pay. Some villages introduced a 'witch tax' in order to finance the committees. The local and regional courts of the princes and their judicial officers

---

[19] Dillinger, Schmidt, and Bauer, eds, *Hexenprozess und Staatsbildung*, 79–80.

found it difficult, or indeed impossible, not to cooperate with the committees, let alone to reject charges brought by them. With the authority of the community behind them and office holders of the prince usually willing to accept them as partners, the witch committees enjoyed a uniquely strong position.[20]

Villages committees were part of the communal self-government apparatus in a number of West German principalities. In other regions, the town councils and traditional peasant assemblies initiated and organized witch-hunts. In the Black Forest–Neckar River area town councils that were dominated by the middle ranks of society organized exceptionally severe persecutions. Their aggressiveness was a match for that of the witch committees. The town of Rottenburg am Neckar empowered the two youngest and least experienced members of the town council to preside over witch trials. In 1596, these two lay judges, with the help of only one clerk, managed to try ten suspects in less than a month without any outside intervention. Of course, all suspects were found guilty. In 1602 in the county of Wertheim, the village population tried to force their somewhat reluctant lord into witch-hunting: villagers carried a wooden staff through the community, and everyone willing to support the witch-hunt was supposed to cut a notch in the staff. Thus, the communities not only made their decisions collectively, but they demonstrated to outsiders (and would-be opponents) how numerous and determined they were. The Wertheim government became very apprehensive when it learned about this witch-hunting organization: traditionally, peasant rebels had used the same method to recruit supporters and to organize. The notorious persecutions in the ecclesiastical territory of Marchtal were in fact orchestrated by the village of Alleshausen. The isolated village of Alleshausen had effectively managed to resist the Marchtal prince-abbot's control. In 1745, members of the local elite of Alleshausen even succeeded in gaining influence on the central court of Marchtal. They ignored expert opinions from learned jurists until the court reached decisions that suited their witch-hunting zeal. The result was a severe persecution in the 1750s, one of Germany's last witch-hunts.[21] The region of Prättigau in the eastern Alps witnessed a somewhat similar development. Originally, Prättigau had belonged to the Habsburgs. However, the Prättigau communities managed to become independent of the Habsburg lordship and join the Swiss Confederation in 1652. Free from the control of the Habsburg officials and courts, the Prättigau indulged in a witch-hunting frenzy, later known as 'Groos Häxatöödi' (Swiss German: Big Witch Killing). These prosecutions bore a close resemblance to the Scottish witch-hunts of 1661/2.[22]

[20] Dillinger, 'Evil People', 126–42, 185–90.

[21] Constanze Störk, "Mithin die natürliche Vernunfft selbst dictiert, das es Hexen gebe" in Hexenverfolgung in der Reichsabtei Marchtal, 1586–1757', Ph.D. thesis, University of Tübingen, Germany 2003, <http://www.historicum.net/themen/hexenforschung/thementexte/magisterarbeiten/art/MITHIN_DIE_NAT/html/ca/405e118fcf/#3.5/ (accessed 20 August 2012); Dillinger, 'Evil People', 109–26.

[22] Dillinger, 'Political Aspects of the German Witch Trials', 83–4; Constanze Störk, '"Mithin die natürliche Vernunfft"'; Manfred Tschaikner, Damit das Böse ausgerottet werde' Hexenverfolgungen in Vorarlberg (Bregenz, 1992), 227–9.

Witchcraft trials in the numerous dwarf states within the Holy Roman Empire offered a variant of communal witch-hunting. In these territories the imperial knights, that is, petty nobles or the prince-abbots of minor ecclesiastical lands who were nominally in charge of their miniscule principalities, had to cooperate with the population. These miniature states—often only a handful of hamlets spread over a few square miles—had hardly any legal administration to speak of but could still pass death sentences. If a community in a dwarf state demanded the prosecution of witches, it would have been political suicide for the petty lord not to comply with its wishes.[23] Agatha von Sontheim, the sovereign ruler of the tiny principality of Nellingsheim in Swabia, was herself under suspicion of witchcraft. In 1590, her peasant subjects kidnapped her and imprisoned her in a larger neighbouring state. This unprecedented case kept various lawyers busy for years, and the emperor had to intervene personally to avoid a war.[24]

The princely governments of larger states and their officials in the communities also proved incapable of controlling the communal agents of witch-hunting. Even if many local officials were willing to cooperate with communal witch-hunters, their respective governments were reluctant to endorse their activities. Some witch-hunting organizations openly ignored the direct orders of the princely administration. Even if they did not, communal witch-hunting groups always questioned the authority of the emerging state apparatuses. They claimed that they could handle a central element of law enforcement—investigation and accusation—more efficiently than the prince's office holders. The very existence of local witch-hunting organizations as a form of criminal justice lying outside the state apparatus called into question the authority of the state itself. Explicitly or implicitly these grass-roots witch-hunts claimed that criminal justice was not exclusively a prerogative of the sovereign. Authority over criminal courts was the hallmark of lordship in the emerging states of early modern Germany. All princes and the councils of autonomous towns either strove to achieve this authority or, after successfully monopolizing it, tried to defend it against any encroachment. The witch-hunting agencies of the subjects can be regarded as aggressive forms of communalism. Communalism was a form of voluntary local organization. It was based on periodical meetings of householders resident in the community, who claimed a right to define local norms and appoint non-professionals to office.[25] Communalism was not a form of institutionalized resistance of the peasantry against the aristocracy. In practice, the princely administration and the communities interacted and cooperated in many ways. Nevertheless, in the process of state-building, tensions between the territorial states and communalist systems were unavoidable. Local structures, based on traditional

[23] Rolf Schulte, *Hexenverfolgung in Schleswig-Holstein* (Heide, 2001); Rita Voltmer, 'Hexenverfolgungen im Maas-Rhein-Mosel-Raum', in Franz Irsigler, ed., *Zwischen Maas und Rhein* (Trier, 2006), 153–87.
[24] Dillinger, *'Evil People'*, 74–5, 157–8.
[25] Peter Blickle, *Kommunalismus: Skizzen einer gesellschaftlichen Organisationsform*, 2 vols (Munich, 2000), ii, 374.

corporations, attempted to defy the larger, territorial state organizations that were about to absorb them into their own structure.

The witch-hunts show the dark side of communalism. Villages and small towns turned witch-hunting into a means to achieve autonomy or into an outward sign to demonstrate their independence of the hierarchical institutions of the princely state. The communalist structure is especially obvious in the case of the witch-hunting committees and their attempts to finance the prosecutions. They established their own quasi-legal rules and aimed at creating an administrative apparatus of their own, including a nascent system of taxation. The reason for the eventual failure of witch-hunting committees was that they never fully achieved that aim. Eventually, witch-hunting committees broke down because they lacked adequate financial resources. The communalist set-up of these organizations prevented them from forming larger structures with better access to sources of revenue. Grass-roots witch-hunts organized by the councils of small towns proved to be less prone to financial difficulties than the witch-hunting committees of villages in the western territories of the empire.[26]

29.4 COMPLEX ORGANIZATIONS, DISCUSSION, AND CONTROL

Witch-hunting institutions of the princes and the grass-roots witch-hunting organizations of the communities both had a simple structure that allowed the witch trials to progress swiftly from initial accusation to execution. The reason for this procedural similarity was the fact that both systems lacked internal controls or 'checks and balances'. States that subjected their criminal courts to administrative control were less prone to witch-hunting. The further removed the controlling agency was from the local milieu in which the suspicion of witchcraft had arisen, the less likely it was to find the suspect guilty. Central high courts or courts of appeal that had the power, or indeed the regular duty, to supervise local criminal courts tended to slow down the progress of witch-hunts or quash them altogether.

The French parlements were good examples of this general trend. The parlements were courts of appeal that exercised criminal jurisdiction over the country's provinces. The most prominent and important of these was the Parlement of Paris, which had authority over about two-thirds of northern France. Beginning in the late sixteenth century, this parlement required that all capital sentences in witchcraft cases be appealed. Only one out of five death sentences between 1550 and 1625 was upheld on appeal. The parlement enforced the automatic appeal of all witchcraft verdicts in its vast jurisdiction, and consistently refused to sentence anyone to death for this crime.

---

[26] Dillinger, 'Evil People', 109–48.

Thus, long before Louis XIV's edict of 1682, which in effect decriminalized witchcraft, legal executions for witchcraft became relatively rare occurrences in France.

The other eight provincial French parlements generally followed the example of the Parlement of Paris. Although each of these appellate courts upheld some witchcraft sentences during the sixteenth and seventeenth centuries, only the Parlement of Rouen, which had jurisdiction over Normandy, condemned more than one hundred witches to death during this period. The Parlement of Bordeaux had considerable difficulty controlling the excesses of local witch-hunting when the king appointed a commission, including one of the members of the Parlement, to eradicate witchcraft in the Basque borderlands in 1609. At the request of local communities, the commissioners, led by the demonologist hardliner Pierre de Lancre, were granted full powers to investigate and punish witchcraft. In this witch-hunt at least two dozen suspects were executed. The rampage was finally stopped by de Lancre's own colleagues, the judges of the Parlement of Bordeaux. It might well be that Bodin's radical stance on witchcraft finished his surprisingly mediocre career in the French legal system for good.[27]

Outside of France, we find similar patterns. Very much like the Paris Parlement, the High Court of Flanders helped to curb witch-hunting.[28] Some of the larger and better organized German principalities boasted powerful central institutions that were capable of controlling witch-hunts. A good example was the duchy of Württemberg. After 1572, the local criminal courts of Württemberg had to report every criminal trial to the *Oberrat* (superior council). This administrative institution, which was dominated by trained lawyers, superintended all criminal procedures, including the decision whether and when to apply torture. The Oberrat cooperated closely with the law faculty of Tübingen University. Electoral Saxony more or less followed the Württemberg pattern. There, the High Court of Leipzig controlled the progress of witch trials. Brandenburg-Prussia adopted a similar judicial structure. In all of these territories, only about one-third of all accused witches suffered capital punishment.[29] The Palatinate had a similar organizational structure. Here, however, the government agencies were influenced by the sceptical views of Hermann Witekind. This territory did not execute any witches at all.[30]

The highest courts of the empire, the *Reichskammergericht* (Imperial Chamber Court) and the *Reichshofrat* (Imperial Aulic Court), were also responsible for reducing the intensity of German witch-hunting. The highly qualified judges of the Imperial Chamber Court set and raised the tone of the legal discussion of the cases brought

---

[27] Alfred Soman, *Sorcellerie et justice criminelle: le Parlement de Paris* (Basingstoke, 1992).

[28] Jos Monballyu, 'Staatsbildung und Hexenprozesse in Flandern: die Rolle des Provinzialjustizrates Rat von Flandern', in Dillinger, Schmidt, and Bauer, eds, *Hexenprozess und Staatsbildung*, 117–34.

[29] Marianne Sauter, *Hexenprozess und Folter. Die strafrechtliche Spruchpraxis der Juristenfakultät Tübingen im 17. und beginnenden 18. Jahrhundert* (Bielefeld, 2010); Dillinger, 'Political Aspects of the German Witch-Hunts', 77–9.

[30] Jürgen Michael Schmidt, 'Die Kurpfalz', in Sönke Lorenz and Jürgen Michael Schmidt, eds, *Wider alle Hexerei und Teufelswerk: Die europäische Hexenverfolgung und ihre Auswirkungen auf Südwestdeutschland* (Ostfildern, 2004), 237–52, esp. 239–42.

before them. Suspects who were sufficiently knowledgeable and well-off to have the judges hear their appeals were, at the very least, able to extend the length of the judicial proceedings. The imperial judges' often harsh criticism of miscarriages of justice helped to end a number of witch-hunts. The individual German principalities could hardly ignore a decision of one of these imperial courts, despite the fact they lacked the power to enforce their sentences.[31]

Even though England's criminal justice had a rather different structure, it provides another case in point. Until the reign of William III, England did not have a large administrative apparatus, but royal judges exercised considerable control over criminal justice. Most English witches were tried at the assizes, county courts that met twice each year to decide criminal as well as civil cases. The royal government sent out two judges from the central common law courts into each of the country's six circuits to preside at the assizes. These circuit judges were usually senior jurists, well-trained and experienced, whose function was to uphold the common law of the kingdom. They were, therefore, instruments of royal power.

The assize judges were meant to be immune from interference by local or regional magistrates. This immunity explains why the assize courts helped to keep the number of persons executed for witchcraft in England at a remarkably low level. In contrast to many judges in the small-town courts of the German principalities, the assize judges did not belong to local networks and power structures that might try to influence the outcome of the trials. As the judges of the assizes were outsiders, any gossip that had damaged the suspects' reputation before the trial meant little to them. In contrast to the county justices of the peace, they heard the evidence with an open mind. In their instructions to the juries that decided the outcome of the cases, the assize judges demanded high standards of proof.[32] At first glance, the circuit judges of the assizes might look like the witch-hunting commissions of de Lancre or Creutz. However, the assizes were no exceptional courts with special assignments; they were part of England's regular judicial structure. No monarch ever gave special authority to these circuit judges to exterminate witchcraft.

Only when the assize system suffered a temporary breakdown during the Civil War did a major witch-hunt develop in East Anglia, where the king was weakest and Puritans exercised considerable influence. Matthew Hopkins was thus able to launch a short-lived career as a witchfinder. It seems that Hopkins was not so much an active agent of the witch-hunt but a catalyst: he gave his expert support to communities that demanded to be rid of alleged witches. Whereas the judges of the assizes kept their distance from local rumours and prosecutorial zeal, Hopkins helped to transform

[31] Dillinger, 'Political Aspects of the German Witch-Hunts', 62–3.
[32] James Sharpe, 'State Formation and Witch-Hunting in Early Modern England', in Dillinger, Schmidt, and Bauer, eds, *Hexenprozess und Staatsbildung*, 59–75; Sharpe, *Witchcraft in Early Modern England* (Harlow, 2001); Alan Harding, *Medieval Law and the Formation of the State* (Oxford, 2002).

such elements into actual trials. It was only after the English central authority had broken down that the local communities could take criminal justice in their own hands.[33]

If there were no central controlling agencies, open discussions within the court system were a good way to keep witch-hunting at a low level. Germany's largest cities and towns experienced remarkably few witch trials. Cologne witnessed the execution of fewer than forty witches, Augsburg sixteen, Hamburg fourteen, Vienna one. Frankfurt and Nuremberg seem not to have executed any witches at all. All of these cities had more than 30,000 inhabitants around 1600. In other words, they were metropolises by early modern German standards. The main reason why big cities hosted comparatively few witch trials is that their political elites were simply not part of the communicative circles of the lower strata of urban society. In order to preserve its political power, the well-established council elites of big cities kept themselves informed about rumours in the town but, for the same reason, were sceptical of such popular gossip. The city councils themselves, at least in the larger cities, were relatively complicated political structures. They were often divided into competing factions and staffed by self-assured members of powerful families or guilds. The very structure of those councils made it unlikely that they would arrive at rash or radical decisions. The discussions and critical appraisals that character-ized the legal administration of a well-ordered principality existed *in nuce* in the councils of big towns.[34]

Whereas even Germany's more powerful towns could not directly influence the legislation of major territories, the towns in the complicated anti-structure of the highly urbanized Netherlands did just that. Especially in Holland and Zeeland, the critical stance of the big towns apparently set the tone for the provincial governments. As early as 1593/4 the highest courts of Holland passed laws that made it exceedingly difficult to convict witches.[35]

These various examples suggest that any debate about the validity of witchcraft accusations sowed the seeds of scepticism regarding their validity. If the government itself demanded or provoked such debates, a verdict of 'guilty' became less likely. Intense witch-hunting depended on the ability to proceed summarily against witches. The more complicated and critical the legal system, the longer the way to the stake, and the less likely it became for the accused to actually have to go there.

---

[33] Sharpe, *Witchcraft in Early Modern England*, 70–2, 123–5; Malcolm Gaskill, *Witchfinders: A Seventeenth-Century English Tragedy* (London, 2005).

[34] Johannes Dillinger, 'Hexenverfolgungen in Städten', in Gunther Franz and Franz Irsigler, eds, *Methoden und Konzepte der historischen Hexenforschung* (Trier, 1998), 129–65.

[35] Hans de Waardt, 'Staat, Kirche und lokale Kultur: Die Zaubereiverfolgungen im Burgundischen Kreis', in Heide Dienst, ed., *Hexenforschung aus österreichischen Ländern* (Vienna, 2009), 17–34.

29.5 STATECRAFT AND WITCHCRAFT: WITCH TRIALS AND POLITICAL CONTROVERSIES

Witch-hunts were shaped by certain administrative structures and political tensions. However, they also helped to shape administrative structures and provoked political tensions. Indeed, the witch trials helped to shape the map of Europe. In 1679/80 the county of Vaduz witnessed a number of witch trials. The driving force behind the trials was the lord of this principality, Count Ferdinand Karl von Hohenems. Complaints against the gross injustice of the prosecutions reached the emperor, Leopold I, who authorized a thorough investigation. Leopold subordinated Count Ferdinand to the authority of his most powerful neighbour, the prince-abbot of Kempten, whom he appointed to serve as an imperial commissioner. In the course of the investigation, which unearthed serious miscarriages of justice, the prince-abbot eventually deprived the count of his lordship of Schellenberg and the county of Vaduz. With the emperor's backing, the Liechtenstein dynasty gained possession of these territories, which they have kept as an independent monarchy until the present day.[36]

Even in comparatively well-organized states, witch-hunts could become a controversial political issue. The debate about witch-hunts that took place early in the seventeenth century in the duchy of Bavaria is a good example. The severe witch-hunts of the 1580s had provoked the formation of two opposing parties at the duke's court. The 'Zelanti' or zealots advocated tough laws against witchcraft and demanded more witch trials. The mindset of the Zelanti was comparable to that of the witch-bishops. They came from a background of well-to-do but provincial families that still fought for a secure foothold in the upper strata of the duke's administration. On the other side stood the 'Politici', the advocates of *raison d'état*. They were a faction of influential and well-established office holders with an urban background who were very reluctant to allow witch-hunts. Some of the Politici were related to witchcraft suspects. Whenever the Zelanti managed to goad the ducal administration into another wave of persecutions in the Bavarian province, the Politici opposed them vehemently. They demanded expert opinions and threatened the local witch-hunters with dire consequences should they not observe due process. In 1612, Bavaria passed one of the most severe laws against witchcraft in German history. The Zelanti seemed to have won the day. However, their opponents managed to stop the publication of the mandate. The law was watered down and finally rendered inconsequential. One year later, the Politici had a witch-hunter executed for the miscarriage of justice. The Zelanti faction never recovered from that blow.[37]

---

[36] Manfred Tschaikner, '"Der Teufel und die Hexen müssen aus dem Land..." Frühneuzeitliche Hexenverfolgungen in Liechtenstein', *Jahrbuch des Historischen Vereins für das Fürstentum Liechtenstein*, 96 (1998), 1–197.

[37] Behringer, *Hexenverfolgung in Bayern*, 241–320.

Conflicts about witch-hunts could play a major role in community politics. In the Imperial Free City of Reutlingen witch-hunting had become an integral part of the struggle for political power between the 1590s and the 1660s. Whenever the ruling clique of the town council retired, the would-be successors fought among each other. Some of them sought the support of the public by calling for decisive action against the witches. Populist demands for 'tougher criminal justice' were certain to meet with a favourable response from the general public. Thus, Reutlingen temporarily deviated from the urban pattern. As soon as the new power elite of the city council had established its position, witch-hunting ceased. The new leaders sometimes even made a positive effort to end the prosecutions they had helped to initiate.[38]

The highly conflict-ridden fields of witch-hunting and political decision-making intermingled in another, fundamentally different, way. Political conflicts made witches. It is best to consider witchcraft accusations as a way to express any kind of deep distrust and severe hostility. As a rule, accusations of witchcraft had a background of long tension within a local community or a family. When people of the early modern period searched for witches, they did not, of course, suspect their beloved children or partners, their best friends, or the most popular people in the village. People with a bad reputation, 'evil' persons were the more likely suspects. Contemporaries considered all kinds of undesirable behaviour as clues in the search for witches, provided this behaviour had inspired deep and lasting tensions between the accuser and the accused.[39] At times, political behaviour created just that kind of enduring and entrenched aversion. In the villages, the adherents of competing aristocrats could express their ill feeling in the form of witchcraft accusations. For example, around 1620 the followers of the influential Waldburg dynasty in southern Germany accused their political enemies, whether they were adherents of the Habsburgs or of local nobles, of witchcraft.[40]

It was part and parcel of the prosecutions from below that some of their victims belonged to the political clientele of the territorial lords. In some territories, we even find a disproportional number of officials of the prince among the accused. One of these witch officials was arguably the most prominent alleged witch of sixteenth-century Germany, Diederich Flade from Trier. Flade was a careerist who had risen quickly in the service of the prince-elector, helping to bring the old self-assured city of Trier permanently under the prince-elector's thumb. Moreover, Flade had a reputation—deservedly—for corruption and usury. In 1589 Flade was executed for witchcraft after the whole town, including the town councillors, had pressured the prince-elector to drop his old servant. Such witch trials with political overtones were no pretexts for cynically eliminating adversaries. Political factionalism did indeed create

---

[38] Thomas Fritz, 'Hexenverfolgungen in der Reichsstadt Reutlingen', in Dillinger, Fritz, and Mährle, eds, *Zum Feuer verdammt*, 63–327.

[39] Dillinger, *'Evil People'*, 79–97.

[40] Dillinger, *'Evil People'*, 89; Martin Zürn, 'Abseits und verfolgt? Die Hexen vom Bussen', in Otto Borst, ed., *Minderheiten im deutschen Südwesten* (Tübingen, 1996), 35–72, 56–67.

animosity strong enough to erode social trust. The political opponent could begin to appear like a truly evil person who might even be in league with the devil.[41]

29.6 THE MATURING STATE AND THE END OF THE PROSECUTIONS

The end of the witch-hunts came when a complex and flexible state apparatus controlled by responsible professionals replaced the overtly simple systems that had given too much unchecked power to special administrations or communal agencies. Of course, this was the general trend of the early modern state-building process. Nevertheless, the witch-hunts played an active role in this process. After the Thirty Years' War, a number of German principalities finally found enough strength to bring the devastated countryside under their control. Excessive witch-hunts, especially those 'from below' justified decisive measures taken by the central government to weaken or to destroy whatever was left of local autonomy. In Electoral Trier prince-archbishop Karl Kaspar von der Leyen simply banned witch trials as part of a reform programme designed to increase the government's authority after the Thirty Years' War.[42] The Württemberg government sent armed forces to end the last serious outbreak of witch-hunting orchestrated by a rural town. In Brandenburg and annexed Pomerania, King Friedrich Wilhelm I of Prussia overcame local resistance against his rule during the last prosecutions in the early eighteenth century. As if to express their newfound authority, some monarchs reserved the ultimate verdict in all witch trials for themselves. Louis XIV was already able to do so in 1682. Friedrich Wilhelm I of Prussia and Empress Maria Theresa followed suit in 1714 and 1766 respectively. This ultimate complication of the trials ended witch-hunting effectively. As witch-hunters could not afford to ignore the will of the monarch any more, they would have had to run the gauntlet through a long line of legal appraisals till they finally reached the monarch personally. Even though the state still did not deny the existence of witches, actual witch trials became a merely theoretical option.[43]

On a more abstract level, it seems obvious that the two most aggressive types of witch-hunting agencies, the communal groups of the subjects and the special witch-finding institutions of the princes, were both eventually doomed to failure. Both were small and simple systems. Both were largely isolated from the rest of the administrative

---

[41] Dillinger, 'Evil People', 84–5, 87–94.
[42] Dillinger, 'Evil People', 183–7.
[43] Wolfgang Behringer, *Witches and Witch-Hunts: A Global History* (Cambridge, 2004), 187, 191; Brian P. Levack, 'The Decline and End of Witchcraft Prosecutions', in Bengt Ankarloo and Stuart Clark, eds, *Witchcraft and Magic in Europe*, v: *The Eighteenth and Nineteenth Centuries* (London, 1999), 7–33; Edmund Kern, 'An End to Witch Trials in Austria: Reconsidering the Enlightened State', *Austrian History Yearbook*, 30 (1999), 159–85; Dillinger, 'Political Aspects of the German Witch-Hunts', 80–1.

system. Both attempted to monopolize legal decisions and to avoid critical discussions as well as outside control. Thus, both systems, the grass-roots witch-hunters' groups and the witchfinders' special institutions, ran contrary to the general trend of state formation. State-building processes diversified courts and administrations and brought them into more hierarchical structures. They often even created new administrative units. In any case, the maturing state apparatus established links between existing branches of the administration and required them to cooperate. This cooperation implied control, and was designed to serve the purposes of the monarchical centre. A well-organized bureaucracy that employed experts for law and administration and allowed them to arrive at decisions in a discourse that was not totally predetermined by partisan opinions ended the witch-hunts. Such sophisticated state machinery was greatly superior to the small and rigid systems that relied on isolated accumulations of power, no matter whether they were based on communal structures or on exceptional princely privileges. Thus, severe witch-hunts were inescapably linked with administrative patterns that proved to be dead ends or short-lived anomalies in the state-building process. Even though they might thrive for a certain period of time in a particular region, they had no future. Superior political organization would eventually marginalize them. And, with a view to the mounting death toll, many contemporaries would agree that it was best to marginalize or to abolish them. The prosecution of witches was a symptom of the failure of state formation rather than a source of its success.

The political aspects of the witch trials suggest a number of new avenues of research; it will suffice to name only the most urgent ones. We still need a comprehensive comparative study of laws against witchcraft, that is, a thorough examination of the origins of these laws and the debates in the governments that surrounded them. The alleged crime of the witches was just a tiny fraction of a huge magical culture. We need to know more about the way the legislators, the courts, and the administrations dealt with magic other than witchcraft, for example treasure hunting or soothsaying. So far, historiography has only scratched the surface of the magical qualities of the early modern state itself. The state emerged in, and into, a thoroughly magical culture. We still need to find out what exactly that meant for political thought and the representation of the state. A deeper understanding of witch-hunting and failures in state-building in Europe, together with careful political and anthropological comparisons, might help to see the persecutions that go on in the 'failing states' of twenty-first century Africa more clearly.

FURTHER READING

Blockmans, Wim, ed., *The Origins of the Modern State Europe*, 7 vols (Oxford 1995–2000).
Dienst, Heide, ed., *Hexenforschung aus österreichischen Ländern* (Vienna, 2009).
Dillinger, Johannes, 'Hexenverfolgungen in Städten', in Gunther Franz and Franz Irsigler, eds, *Methoden und Konzepte der historischen Hexenforschung* (Trier, 1998), 129–65.

Dillinger, Johannes, 'The Political Aspects of the German Witch-Hunts', *Magic, Ritual, and Witchcraft*, 3 (2008), 62–81.

Dillinger, Johannes, *'Evil People': A Comparative Study of Witch-Hunts in Swabian Austria and the Electorate of Trier*, tr. Laura Stokes (Charlottesville, VA, 2009).

Dillinger, Johannes, Schmidt, Jürgen Michael, and Bauer, Dieter, eds, *Hexenprozess und Staatsbildung: Witch-Trials and State-Building* (Bielefeld, 2008).

Levack, Brian P., 'The Decline and End of Witchcraft Prosecutions', in Bengt Ankarloo and Stuart Clark, eds, *Witchcraft and Magic in Europe: The Eighteenth and Nineteenth Centuries* (London, 1999), 1–93.

Sharpe, James, *Witchcraft in Early Modern England* (Harlow, 2001).

Soman, Alfred, *Sorcellerie et justice criminelle: Le Parlement de Paris* (Basingstoke, 1992).

CHAPTER 30

···

SCIENCE AND WITCHCRAFT

···

PETER ELMER

IN 1713 the English scholar and cleric Richard Bentley (1662–1742) asked 'What then has lessen'd in England your stories of sorceries?' His reply, an attempt to undermine the pretensions of his deist adversary Anthony Collins (1676–1729), was stark and to the point. Belief in witchcraft had not been undermined and fatally wounded by the atheistical labours of freethinkers like Collins, but was rather the product of recent advances in natural philosophy and medicine conducted by men such as Robert Boyle (1627–1691), Isaac Newton (1642–1727), and Thomas Sydenham (1624–1689), and promulgated through the auspices of institutions such as the Royal Society and Royal College of Physicians in London. In short, Bentley was arguing, and others were soon to follow suit, that the delusory belief in witchcraft had succumbed to the new spirit of rational, empirical enquiry, which was the hallmark of the Scientific Revolution of the seventeenth century.[1] For almost two hundred and fifty years, the idea that the march of modern science was responsible for bringing to an end the era of the witch trials has held sway in academic and popular writing on the subject. At the same time, it has become equally axiomatic that the belief system that underpinned the legal persecution of witches was itself the product of faulty scientific thinking that was widely rejected as backward-looking, medieval, or superstitious.[2]

In time, as we shall see, this overly simplistic account of the demise of witchcraft would be challenged by a later generation of scholars, paving the way for a new consensus that has greatly diminished the role of science in this historical process. It

---

[1] Phileleutherus Lipsiensis [Richard Bentley], *Remarks upon a Late Discourse of Free-Thinking* (London, 1713), 33.

[2] I discuss these and related historiographical developments more fully in my 'Science, Medicine and Witchcraft', in Jonathan Barry and Owen Davies, eds, *Palgrave Advances in Witchcraft Historiography* (Basingstoke, 2007), 33–51.

would be a mistake, however, to conclude that such thinking has altogether disappeared from contemporary writing on the subject (discussed further below). In part, this clearly reflects the enormous shadow cast by the principles of the Enlightenment over European culture and learning in the period since the eighteenth century. Faith in reason constituted the hallmark of Enlightenment thinking, and, as such, was greatly indebted to, and supportive of, new approaches to science and the natural world. The Scientific Revolution itself was the product of two key intellectual developments. In the first place, it was made possible by the growing popularity of the empirical methodology pioneered by the English philosopher Francis Bacon (1561–1626), which encouraged experiment at the expense of theory. Equally important, however, were the insights of the French philosopher René Descartes (1596–1650), whose mechanical philosophy postulated the idea that the world, and all matter in it, operated like a machine and thus followed regular and immutable laws of nature. Operating together, it isn't difficult to understand why scholars of witchcraft became wedded to the idea that it was science in general, and Cartesianism in particular, that was chiefly responsible for fatally undermining belief in witches, spirits, and devils.

Extensively promoted by the *philosophes* of the Enlightenment, such ideas would help to lay the foundations for modern, industrial society. At the same time they fostered a 'triumphalist' approach to the past in which social, economic, cultural, and intellectual backwardness were forever associated with former times, while progress and reason dominated the present. In the nineteenth century, in particular, such attitudes shaped the approach of a new generation of historians of witchcraft, whose faith in progress and science led them to denounce the corrupt and superstitious practices of the clergy and to blame them, rather than 'bad science' per se, for the excesses of the 'witch craze'. Consequently, scholars in England, France, Germany, and the United States of America, all of whom were committed to a deep-seated anticlericalism, found themselves attracted to the study of witchcraft, the history of which provided a devastating critique of institutionalized religion, both in its ancient and present forms.[3]

Typical of this approach was the work of the liberal American scholar Andrew Dickson White (1832–1918), the first president of Cornell University. In his *History of the Warfare of Science with Theology in Christendom* of 1896, he included a section on the witch craze, which he not surprisingly attributed to the religious dogmatism of the age. Its demise was firmly ascribed to scientific progress. The legacy of this liberal, rational, and secular tradition is most apparent today in the vast collection of witchcraft tracts now held at Cornell, the achievement of White's colleague and the college's first librarian, George Lincoln Burr (1857–1938), whose published writings on the subject betray the prejudices of his own liberal and anticlerical outlook.[4] Such thinking was

---

[3] Elmer, 'Science, Medicine and Witchcraft', 34–5.

[4] Elmer, 'Science, Medicine and Witchcraft', 35, 47n. Burr's views on the subject of witchcraft were shared by his colleague and fellow librarian at the University of Pennsylvania, Henry Charles Lea (1825–1909); George Lincoln Burr, ed., *Narratives of the Witchcraft Cases, 1648–1706* (New York, 1914);

also mirrored in the groundbreaking work of the German scholars Wilhelm Gottfried Soldan (1803–1869) and Joseph Hansen (1862–1943), both of whom blamed the witch-hunts on the overweening power of the Roman Catholic Church and saw the demise of witch trials as a natural corollary of the progress of reason and science.[5]

The first evidence of a crack in this edifice came with the publication, from the 1920s onwards, of a slow trickle of works dedicated in the first instance to promoting a much more positive view of the relationship between religion and science in late medieval and early modern Europe. Particularly important in terms of its long-term impact was the work of the American sociologist Robert K. Merton (1910–2003), who in 1938 proposed that the emergence of the new science of the seventeenth century was linked to the values and ethos of puritanism. In the decades that followed, as the confidence of the West in science and reason began to wane in the face of the Holocaust, the Cold War, and the threat of global nuclear destruction, academic scholarship looked again at the relationship between religion and science in earlier eras, often concluding that the former helped to shape many of the key concepts of modern scientific thought. Now, the emphasis in scholarly discussions about the origins and nature of early modern science was frequently placed on the creative tension and interaction between religion and science, though the impact of such thinking on witchcraft itself was slow to bear fruit.[6] Initially at least, few scholars who wrote on witchcraft were able to see beyond the commonplace that equated belief in witches with the backward-looking state of knowledge in general, and science in particular, in the period before 1650. The dominance of Aristotelian scholasticism in the universities, which were themselves under the control of the clergy, was widely perceived as a stumbling block to funda-mental intellectual change. Other strains of scientific thinking such as the 'occult sciences' of alchemy, astrology, and natural magic, which had experienced a revival in the late medieval and early Renaissance period, were considered even more likely to promote belief in spirits, devils, and witches.

It was not until the publication of the groundbreaking research in the 1960s of the English scholar Frances Yates (1899–1981) that a more nuanced and historically acute picture of the nature of early modern science began to emerge. She, above all, was responsible for turning on its head all previous assumptions about the origins of modern science by demonstrating the critical role played by the Renaissance revival

---

Henry Charles Lea, *Materials Toward a History of Witchcraft*, ed., A. C. Howland, 3 vols (New York, 1957).

[5] Wilhelm Gottfried Soldan, *Geschichte der Hexenprozesse aus dem Quellen Dargestellt* (Stuttgart, 1843); Joseph Hansen, *Zauberwahn, Inquisition und Hexenprozess in Mittelalter und die Entstehung der Grossen Hexenverfolgung* (Leipzig, 1900); Hansen, *Quellen und Untersuchungen zur Geschichte des Hexenwahns unter der Hexenverfolgung im Mittelalter* (Bonn, 1901).

[6] For a good overview of these developments, see Andrew Fix, *Fallen Angels: Balthassar Bekker, Spirit Belief, and Confessionalism in the Seventeenth-Century Dutch Republic* (Dordrecht, 1999), 6–7. Among those scholars working to reconcile religion and science in this period, Fix highlights the work of Reijer Hookyaas, J. R. and Margaret Jacob, Paul Kocher, Margaret Osler, Theodore Raab, Barbara Shapiro, and Richard Westfall.

of Neoplatonism, hermeticism, and the 'occult sciences' in encouraging new ways of investigating and understanding the natural world.[7] Scholars of witchcraft were not slow to pick up on the ramifications of Yates' work, which suggested that ideas previously derided and ignored as unscientific were in fact inherently rational and thus capable of eroding faith in ideas such as witchcraft. In particular, the publication in 1967 of a pioneering essay on the witch craze by the English historian Hugh Trevor-Roper (1914–2003) led to a major reassessment of intellectual change in early modern Europe and its impact upon those who wrote for and against belief in devils, demons, and witches. While remaining committed to the idea that belief in witchcraft was ultimately undermined and argued away by the onset of the Scientific Revolution and the acceptance of Newtonianism, Trevor-Roper nonetheless made a strong case for an interim role in this process, that is, for occult or hermetic philosophy encouraging demonological scepticism. Consequently, natural magicians and alchemists like Cornelius Agrippa (1486–1535), Girolamo Cardano (1501–1576), and Paracelsus (1493–1541) now assumed the role of champions in the early struggle to discredit witchcraft, while their rivals in mainstream academia, trained up in the traditional scholastic and Aristotelian curriculum of the universities, were largely blamed for promoting demonological speculation and witch-hunting.[8]

Trevor-Roper's pioneering work radically disturbed the traditional, 'whiggish', picture of intellectual change in early modern Europe, arguing against a present-centred view of the past and for the idea that 'mental structures differ with social structures', so that the 'superstition' of one age might become the 'rationalism' of another. Others were quick to follow in his footsteps. Keith Thomas, for example, incorporated Trevor-Roper's views on science and witchcraft into his groundbreaking study of religion and the decline of magic in 1971.[9] At the same time, scholars such as Brian Easlea and Thomas Jobe offered variant readings on the same theme, though both expressed important reservations about the role played by specific aspects of the 'new science', and its debt to Cartesian mechanism (discussed more fully below), in subverting belief in witchcraft. Increasingly, the focus of scholarly argument centred on England and the role played there by its forward-thinking scientists and natural philosophers within new scientific institutions such as the Royal Society. The latter, founded at the Restoration by Charles II (r. 1660–1685), was widely perceived by historians at this time as representing the high watermark of European science. And yet, as Easlea and Jobe pointed out, many of its members, including prominent figures like Robert Boyle and Joseph Glanvill (1636–1680), were lined up on the side of the 'credulous', in stark contrast to 'sceptics' such as John Webster (1611–1682), whose science was firmly embedded in a worldview that accentuated the place and role of hidden or 'occult' magical forces in creation. Ultimately, the paradox could only be resolved by arguing

    [7] See especially Frances Yates, *Giordano Bruno and the Hermetic Tradition* (London, 1964).
    [8] Hugh Trevor-Roper, 'The European Witch-Craze of the Sixteenth and Seventeenth Centuries', in *Religion, the Reformation and Social Change* (London, 1967), 90–192.
    [9] Keith Thomas, *Religion and the Decline of Magic* (London, 1971), 578–9, 643–4.

that the stance of prominent and outspoken figures like Boyle and Glanvill was primarily a product of their religious, rather than their scientific, beliefs. As representatives of the religious and political status quo in Restoration England, they and their colleagues were duty-bound to uphold belief in witches and to reject the subversive and atheistic implications of the sceptical position. The fact that Webster, whose *Displaying of Supposed Witchcraft* (1677) has been seen as making a major contribution to the sceptical case, was a former religious extremist, simply provided further evidence to support the underlying contention that it was religion rather than science that was the chief influence on the debate over witchcraft in late seventeenth-century England.[10]

Throughout much of the 1980s, as interest in witchcraft mushroomed in academic circles and numerous new general studies appeared on the subject, a consensus emerged that helped to perpetuate the idea that the demise of witchcraft remained inextricably linked to the ultimate victory of the new science over the various forces of intellectual superstition. Such developments, moreover, were not restricted to England. Joseph Klaits, for example, citing extensively from the pioneering work of the French witchcraft scholar Robert Mandrou (1921–1984), argued in 1985 that it was 'the new ways of thinking inspired by science and Cartesian philosophy' that informed the judgements of the French judicial elite in their campaign to bring the witch trials to an end.[11] Eventually, however, this rather comfortable view of witchcraft's decline was radically challenged by various new approaches to the subject, which focused critically on what it meant for historians to talk about 'science' in this period. Firstly, the rather neat narrative of scientific progress in which scholastic Aristotelianism was supplanted by the occult sciences, only to fall victim to the mechanistic worldview, underwent radical reappraisal by a new generation of historians of science. There were various strands to this process. On the one hand, scholars such as Charles Schmitt (1933–1986) were eager to confirm the continuing vitality and significance of Aristotelianism in scientific circles throughout the sixteenth and seventeenth centuries.[12] Others have dissected the life and thought of early modern scientists to discover that the most common feature of their approach to nature was a widespread philosophical eclecticism. Thus, iconic figures such as Boyle and Newton now stand revealed as men of science, who appear to have imbibed a range of approaches to natural investigation and speculation. Both, for example, were keen adepts or students of alchemy who were reticent to expose their private speculations on such realms of thought to public scrutiny.[13] Other studies have demonstrated similar eclecticism among those lesser

---

[10] Brian Easlea, *Witch-Hunting, Magic and the New Philosophy: An Introduction to Debates of the Scientific Revolution 1450–1750* (Brighton, 1980); Thomas Harmon Jobe, 'The Devil in Restoration Science: The Glanvill-Webster Debate', *Isis*, 72 (1981), 343–56.

[11] Joseph Klaits, *Servants of Satan: The Age of the Witch-Hunts* (Bloomington, 1985), 161–8; Robert Mandrou, *Magistrats et sorciers en France aux XVIIᵉ siècle: Un analyse de psychologie historique* (Paris, 1968), 539–64.

[12] Charles Schmitt, *Aristotle and the Renaissance* (Cambridge, MA, 1983).

[13] For Newton, see Betty Jo Dobbs, *The Janus Face of Genius: The Role of Alchemy in Newton's Thought* (Cambridge, 1991). For Boyle, see Lawrence M. Principe, *The Aspiring Adept: Robert Boyle and*

members and virtuosi who attended the meetings of nascent scientific institutions such as the Royal Society of London and the Academy of the Lincei in Italy.[14] There now exists a vast literature on this subject, which unequivocally suggests that it is no longer possible to categorize early modern scientific practitioners into simple, ideological pigeonholes. On the contrary, the scientific scene of the period is characteristically defined as 'one of radical epistemological instability', which requires a new, more nuanced terminology to describe the activities of those engaged in scientific experiment and speculation.[15]

Out of this new approach has arisen a second, critical development, that it is no longer de rigueur to speak of science in this period, but rather to use the contemporary tag of natural philosophy to describe more accurately what it was that men like Boyle, Newton, and their associates were doing. The term 'science' itself is now increasingly seen as an anachronism by historians of science and others working in this period. Natural philosophy, on the other hand, allows scholars to reflect more accurately the way in which contemporary commentators on the natural world incorporated theological and other concerns into their investigations into the natural world. In this way, science is no longer seen as distinct from, or antithetical to, religion, but rather as part of a broader intellectual endeavour whose chief goal was to explain the marvellous workings of God's creation.[16] This radical reinterpretation of science in the age of the Scientific Revolution has had a profound effect on witchcraft studies. Instead of attempting to excuse or explain away the commitment of eminent scientific figures like Robert Boyle to belief in an active devil, spirits, and witches, historians of science are now far more likely to stress the extent to which men like Boyle, Glanvill, and Henry More (1614–1687) invoked witchcraft as an integral element of their natural theology—an attempt to synthesize religious and scientific beliefs in such a way as to preserve orthodox belief from the growing threat posed by atheistical wits and subversive 'enthusiasts'.[17] Nowhere, however, is the impact of these developments on

His Alchemical Quest (Princeton, 1998). For a general overview of the place of alchemy in early modern science that incorporates much of the recent work on this subject, see Bruce T. Moran, Distilling Knowledge: Alchemy, Chemistry, and the Scientific Revolution (Cambridge, MA, 2005).

[14] For England and the Royal Society, see especially the groundbreaking work of Michael Hunter, Science and Society in Restoration England (Cambridge, 1981). For Italy and the Lincean Society, see David Freedberg, The Eye of the Lynx: Galileo, His Friends, and the Beginnings of Modern Natural History (Chicago, 2002).

[15] Stuart Clark, Thinking With Demons: The Idea of Witchcraft in Early Modern Europe (Oxford, 1997), 257. I discuss Clark's major contribution to the wider debate surrounding science and witchcraft below.

[16] It is impossible to do justice here to the vast and growing literature that has adopted this approach to the history of early modern science. For a broad overview of these developments, and their incorporation into general textbooks on the subject, see especially Simon Shapin, The Scientific Revolution (Chicago, 1996); Margaret J. Osler, 'The Canonical Imperative: Rethinking the Scientific Revolution', in Osler, Rethinking the Scientific Revolution (Cambridge, 2000), 3–22; John Henry, The Scientific Revolution and the Origins of Modern Science (1st edn, 1997; Basingstoke, 2008).

[17] See, for example, Shapin, The Scientific Revolution, 153–5; Michael Hunter, 'Alchemy, Magic and Moralism in the Thought of Robert Boyle', British Journal for the History of Science, 23 (1990),

our understanding of the relationship between science and witchcraft more evident than in the groundbreaking work of Stuart Clark, whose *Thinking With Demons* (1997) has revolutionized the way in which we now think about the place of witchcraft belief in early modern thought.

Clark devoted a large section of his *magnum opus* to science and its relationship to early modern demonology, providing in the process an invaluable guide to much previous work on the subject. At the same time, he proposed an entirely new way of envisaging that relationship, arguing, against all former assumptions, for the complete compatibility of early modern science with other studies focused on unravelling the means by which demons and devils acted on the sublunary world. Demonology itself was reclaimed as a sub-branch of scientific investigation, its focus on preternatural activity (that is, natural events that had as yet defied understanding and thus remained unexplained or 'occult') acting as a magnet to natural philosophers of various schools of thought. Demonologists and others thus sought to investigate the preternatural activity of the devil and his minions precisely because such study promised to yield vital new knowledge about the workings of nature. This was not the pursuit of the esoteric for its own sake, but rather a form of cutting-edge science in which investigation of the powers attributed to witches and demons was understood to offer, in the words of the great prophet of modern science Francis Bacon, 'prerogative instances' or peculiar insights into the workings of nature.[18]

Clark's analysis of the relationship between early modern science and demonology has not only helped to explain why contemporary natural philosophers were drawn to investigate witches and witchcraft, but also reaffirms the conclusions of other scholars like Michael Hunter and Allison Coudert, who have sought to demonstrate that the witchcraft preoccupations of men such as Boyle and More were perfectly in accord with their wider natural philosophical concerns. Citing the work of historians of science such as John Henry and Keith Hutchison, Clark thus affirms that mechanism, one of the core tenets of the Scientific Revolution, was a 'radically supernaturalist philosophy' that was perfectly capable of accommodating belief in witches and spirits.[19] It also retained a place for 'occult' causation, exemplified by Newton's concept of gravity, and thus, not surprisingly, encouraged speculation as to the nature of spirits and their manner of working on material substance. It was for this reason, argues Clark, that witchcraft was designated as a suitable subject of investigation by certain members of the new experimental community in post-Restoration England, who were eager to

387–410; Allison Coudert, 'Henry More and Witchcraft', in Sarah Hutton, ed., *Henry More (1614–1687): Tercentenary Studies* (Dordrecht, 1990), 115–36.

[18] Clark, *Thinking With Demons*, 252–5. For earlier discussion of these themes, see Stuart Clark, 'The Scientific Status of Demonology', in Brian Vickers, ed., *Occult and Scientific Mentalities in the Renaissance* (Cambridge, 1984), 351–74.

[19] See especially John Henry, 'Occult Qualities and the Experimental Philosophy: Active Principles in Pre-Newtonian Matter Theory', *History of Science*, 24 (1986), 335–81; Keith Hutchison, 'What Happened to Occult Qualities in the Scientific Revolution?', *Isis*, 73 (1982), 233–54; Hutchison, 'Supernaturalism and the Mechanical Philosophy', *History of Science*, 21 (1983), 297–33.

apply Baconian methods to the creation of a databank of 'matters of fact' verifying the reality of witchcraft. Collaborative and empirical in approach, schemes such as those proposed by Joseph Glanvill were thus perceived by Clark as perfectly in keeping with other 'experimental' projects undertaken by the nascent Royal Society. If belief in witchcraft, as traditionalists asserted, was fatally eroded by the new science, then all the evidence would appear to suggest that this particular process began much later than previously thought.[20]

Recent research concerned with unravelling the relationship between science and witchcraft suggests the merits of a more nuanced and balanced approach to the subject. Future studies will undoubtedly seek to build on these foundations and to explore more closely some of the fundamental concepts that inform the groundbreaking work of a new generation of historians of science. Two in particular would appear to offer potential riches: the preternatural and natural theology. In recent years, there has been an outpouring of research concerned with exploring the place of preternatural or 'prodigious' phenomena in early modern Europe, culminating in the establishment in 2010 of a new journal, entitled *Preternature*, devoted exclusively to discussion of such matters. For early modern natural philosophers such as Joseph Glanvill, following in the footsteps of men like Francis Bacon, nature itself was 'a constant Prodigy'. Situated on the contested border between the natural and the supernatural, knowledge of the prodigious promised to overhaul early modern understanding of causation in the natural world and, in the phrase of Allison Coudert, to place demonology and related fields of study, such as pneumatology, on a 'scientific basis'. More recently, John Henry has invoked the concept of 'boundary work', itself a variant form of what Clark had identified as 'cutting edge science', in order to account for the decline of magic in Europe. According to Henry, magic, and related realms of thought such as alchemy and witchcraft, were not so much argued out of existence by the new science but fell into gradual disrepute as part of a much wider and elongated process, in which some elements of the magical tradition were integrated into mainstream science (e.g. occult forces such as gravity) while others were slowly rejected and abandoned. The traditional depiction of this process as one-sided and inherently rational is thus dismissed as historical fiction, the product of Enlightenment apologists for the new science in an 'Age of Reason'.[21]

Exploration of the place of, and fascination for, the preternatural in early modern Europe remains in its infancy. Scholars working in this field, however, have already performed an invaluable service by stressing the extent to which contemporary interest in the prodigious was stimulated by broader political concerns. In England, such work has tended to focus on the role played by the Royal Society, and like-minded supporters of the new science, in naturalizing prodigies and so neutralizing the threat that they

---

[20] Clark, *Thinking With Demons*, 294–311.

[21] Joseph Glanvill, *A Philosophical Endeavour Towards the Defence of the Being of Witches and Apparitions* (London, 1666), 2; Coudert, 'Henry More and Witchcraft', 119–20; John Henry, 'The Fragmentation of Renaissance Occultism and the Decline of Magic', *History of Science*, 46 (2008), 1–48.

posed to the religious and political status quo.[22] While this may represent something of an oversimplified approach to a complex issue, the implicit suggestion that knowledge of nature in the early modern period cannot be divorced from wider theological and political concerns is surely significant for scholars of witchcraft. The concept of natural theology itself assumes as much, though the majority of historians of science who have written on this subject have tended more often than not to perceive natural theology as inimical to ideas such as witchcraft. Within an English context, this is principally evident in the tendency of such writers to equate early support for natural theology with the latitudinarian wing of the restored Anglican Church after 1660. Others, such as Scott Mandelbrote, have argued for two related but distinct conceptions of natural theology, both concerned in the first instance with combating the twin dangers of atheistic materialism and sectarian enthusiasm, but divided on the manner and extent to which God intervened on a regular basis in the world of man and nature.[23] In both cases, the victory of 'right reason' and empiricism over excessive credulity is seen as the principal agent in undermining beliefs such as witchcraft, while the partisan and highly charged political atmosphere in which these ideas were debated is largely ignored. Here, I suggest, is one avenue worthy of further exploration. Science, as most historians would now happily accept, does not exist or evolve in a vacuum. In England, in the crucial period after 1660—crucial, that is, for both science and witchcraft—ideas were debated within a context of growing sectarian and partisan conflict. Moreover, the nature and outcome of these debates was both volatile and difficult to predict. This was particularly true in the early years of the Restoration, when various groups vied for religious and political authority while others sought accommodation with the powers that be. In this context, it wasn't just the boundaries between the natural and supernatural realms that were contested, but those relating to order in the social and political world. As my own work on the Irish miracle healer and witchfinder Valentine Greatrakes suggests, the outcome of this debate was neither inevitable nor clear-cut, leastwise in the early years of the Restoration.[24]

The sensitivity of scholars to developments such as these, whereby the pursuit of scientific knowledge in early modern Europe is now widely perceived as part of, and immersed in, a much wider programme of religious renewal and political change, thus promises to fundamentally reshape our understanding of the relationship between science and witchcraft in this period. In particular, it provides a crucial key to

---

[22] See, for example, William E. Burns, *An Age of Wonders: Prodigies, Politics and Providence in England, 1657–1727* (Manchester, 2002); Christopher Carter, '"A Constant Prodigy": Empirical Views of an Unordinary Nature', *The Seventeenth Century*, 33 (2008), 266–89.

[23] Scott Mandelbrote, 'The Uses of Natural Theology in Seventeenth-Century England', *Science in Context*, 20 (2007), 451–80.

[24] Peter Elmer, *The Miraculous Conformist: Valentine Greatrakes, the Body Politic, and the Politics of Healing in Early Modern Britain* (Oxford, 2012). For another example of the politically charged nature of such 'boundary work', see Simon Schaffer, 'Piety, Physic and Prodigious Abstinence', in Ole Peter Grell and Andrew Cunningham, eds, Religio Medici: *Medicine and Religion in Seventeenth-Century England* (Aldershot, 1996), 171–203.

unlocking what many historians of witchcraft have seen as one of the most obdurate aspects of their subject, namely the role of science in the decline of educated belief in witches, demons, and devils. There is little doubt that the general impact of such thinking has led to a gradual undermining of the old orthodoxy that assumed a causal link between scientific progress and scepticism. Even in those cases where the connection would seem most apposite and obvious, current research strongly suggests that factors other than scientific orientation were responsible for promoting attitudes that were inimical to belief in witchcraft. This is evident, for example, in recent attempts to reappraise the origin of Isaac Newton's denial of witchcraft and evil spirits, one in which it is now argued that Newton's thinking on the subject owed more to his immersion in radical, heterodox, and mystical strains of Protestantism than it did to his mathematical conception of the natural world.[25] In a similar vein, scholars of the Dutch sceptic and theologian Balthasar Bekker (1634–1698) have long suspected that his attempt to disenchant the world and purge it of the influence of witches, devils, and demons was primarily shaped by religious and political motives rather than his attachment to the mechanical philosophy of Descartes. Moreover, the reception of his ideas is now widely understood to have followed a similar trajectory.[26]

As the examples of Newton and Bekker suggest, historians need to tread carefully in exploring the influence of science, or more properly natural philosophy, on attitudes to witches, devils, and the supernatural in this period. The fusion of science and religion evident in the thinking of Newton, Bekker, and others, remained a factor in the debate over witchcraft well into the eighteenth century. Recent interest in Bekker himself, and his place in what Jonathan Israel has termed the 'radical enlightenment', would appear to offer one important new avenue of research for those interested in tracing the impact of science upon the decline of witchcraft.[27] Israel's work, in particular, strongly hints at the need to revisit the late seventeenth and early eighteenth centuries in order to understand this process better. For too long scholars have tended to accept at face value the comments of sceptics like Richard Bentley, cited in the opening paragraph, or those of the Anglican bishop Francis Hutchinson (1660–1739), to the effect that educated belief in witchcraft had largely been eradicated by the early eighteenth century because of the pioneering work of scientific bodies such as the Royal Society in the previous century. Recent research, however, suggests that such men were rewriting Restoration intellectual history to fit their own ends, which were often highly political

[25] Stephen Snobelen, 'Lust, Pride and Ambition: Isaac Newton and the Devil', in James E. Force and Sarah Hutton, eds, *Newton and Newtonianism: New Studies* (Dordrecht, 2004), 155–81.

[26] Fix, *Fallen Angels*; Jo Spaans, 'Censorship, Satire and Religion: A Seventeenth-Century Satirical Print on the Condemnation of Balthasar Bekker's *The Enchanted World*', in J. A. C. van Ophem and C. H. E. Verhaar, eds, *On the Mysteries of Research: Essays in Various Fields of Humaniora* (Leeuwarden, 2007), 273–87.

[27] Jonathan Israel, *Radical Enlightenment: Philosophy and the Making of Modernity, 1650–1750* (Oxford, 2001), esp. 375–405.

and partisan in nature.[28] Clearly, we need to explore more fully the complex web of religious and scientific attitudes to witchcraft and related phenomena that shaped such discourse in a period in which it is now apparent that demonology itself remained contentious and open to continued debate.

The shift of historical focus among historians of witchcraft to the eighteenth century in part reflects a growing belief among scholars of the period that the age of the Enlightenment, and the philosophical changes ushered in by the movement of the same name, was not a straightforward, smooth, or uniform process. Not only did the pace of change vary across Europe, but the process itself was uneven and often contentious. Moreover, recent scholarship has also suggested that the assumption of a growing divide between 'popular' and 'elite' views on controversial topics such as witchcraft—a staple theme of earlier accounts—is no longer tenable. Ignorance and 'superstition' was not the preserve of the masses, no more than faith in reason and science was the monopoly of ruling elites. The problematizing of the Enlightenment, evident in recent approaches to witchcraft, remains in its infancy. It nonetheless promises to open up important new areas of research, especially with regard to the precise role played by the new science in both undermining and upholding belief in witchcraft and related phenomena.[29] At the same time, however, it is important to acknowledge that there remains a strong resistance in both historical and philosophical circles to the idea that demonology was not inherently inimical to the rational and empirical temper of the Scientific Revolution and Enlightenment. Michael Wasser, for example, has recently attempted to resuscitate a link between the reception of Cartesian mechanism and the demise of witch trials and witch beliefs in late seventeenth-century Scotland.[30] Others, such as Jacqueline Broad, have chosen to take mechanical philosophers, such as Joseph Glanvill, to task for 'practising bad science by the light of his own principles'. Echoing the approach of fellow philosopher Robin Attfield, Broad thus reproves Glanvill for failing to follow to its logical conclusions the inherently rational

---

[28] See, for example, Michael Winship, *Seers of God: Puritan Providentialism in the Restoration and Early Enlightenment* (Baltimore, MD, 1996), 132; Michael Hunter, 'The Royal Society and the Decline of Magic', *Notes and Records of the Royal Society*, 65 (2011), 103–19; Andrew Sneddon, *Witchcraft and Whigs: The Life of Bishop Francis Hutchinson, 1660–1739* (Manchester, 2008).

[29] For the impact of these developments on witchcraft across Europe in this period, see especially Owen Davies and Willem de Blécourt, eds, *Beyond the Witch Trials: Witchcraft and Magic in Enlightenment Europe* (Manchester, 2004). This collection of essays is, to a large extent, a conscious attempt to build upon the seminal work of scholars such as Brian Levack, Marijke Gijswijt-Hofstra, and Roy Porter, for which see their respective essays in Bengt Ankarloo and Stuart Clark, eds, *The Athlone History of Witchcraft and Magic in Europe*, v: *The Eighteenth and Nineteenth Centuries* (London, 1999).

[30] Michael Wasser, 'The Mechanical World-View and the Decline of Witch Beliefs in Scotland', in Julian Goodare, Lauren Martin and Joyce Miller, eds, *Witchcraft and Belief in Early Modern Scotland* (Basingstoke, 2008), 206–26. Personally, I remain unconvinced by Wasser's arguments. Not only does his essay seem to lack a thorough understanding of recent developments in the history of science (as outlined above), but it contains few documented cases that help to prove his hypothesis. Just because the Scots, like other Europeans, were increasingly exposed to Cartesian mechanism, either through study at home or abroad, this does not mean that they necessarily applied such ideas in order to undermine witch-hunting, witch trials, and witch beliefs.

and materialist implications of his scientific credo. She also, not surprisingly perhaps, goes on to locate the source of Glanvill's failure in his 'uncritical prejudice' or 'uncritical religious ideology', demonstrating in the process an ahistorical and present-centred approach to Glanvill's demonological views that few historians of witchcraft and science would happily condone today.[31]

It is clear from these examples, frequently replicated in popular and non-academic literature on the subject, that much of the agenda of the new history of science—one predicated on a need to fully contextualize the origins and nature of early modern science—continues to be ignored, misunderstood, or challenged to various degrees by those writing on the subject of witchcraft. Clark's view of demonology as inherently reasonable by the logical standards of early modern science and philosophy may constitute a new orthodoxy in some circles, but it remains controversial for others. Perhaps the most original attempt to subvert Clark's construct of the 'rational witch-finder' is to be found in the work of Edward Bever, who, in utilizing a vast range of modern-day scientific evidence and insights taken from a bewildering array of disciplines, including neurophysiology and parapsychology, has attempted to demonstrate the 'reality' of witchcraft and diabolical possession. If science failed to destroy belief in witchcraft, then perhaps, so Bever argues, science can be utilized to explain why our early modern forbears (in this case drawn from a case study of the duchy of Württemberg in Germany) truly believed they were bewitched.[32] Is it possible, one might ask, in any future research agenda to square this particular circle, or to find common ground between those who veer towards a social constructionist view of all knowledge, including science, and others who place their faith in the objectivity of scientists and their ability to account for witchcraft as either delusion or reality? On the surface the two approaches appear implacably opposed and may well remain so as each turns a deaf ear to the other. On the other hand, attempts to apply insights drawn from various branches of psychology to a fuller appreciation of the social and personal dynamics of witch accusations may point the way to a new accommodation—one that I discuss more fully in the following chapter, which is concerned with the specific role played by

---

[31] Jacqueline Broad, 'Margaret Cavendish and Joseph Glanvill: Science, Religion and Witchcraft', *Studies in History and Philosophy of Science*, 38 (2007), 493–505; cf. Robin Attfield, 'Balthasar Bekker and the Decline of the Witch-Craze: The Old Demonology and the New Philosophy', *Annals of Science*, 42 (1985), 393–4. Broad's article, I feel, is based on a misreading of Stuart Clark, in particular by seeking to suggest that interest in the new science inevitably encouraged witch-hunting (he argues, on the contrary, that it inevitably led to greater discussion of these and related issues, without assuming that it might provoke the search for actual witches). Its wider aim would appear to rest in an attempt to vindicate modern science from the charge of aiding and abetting criminal acts against women in general and witches in particular, as suggested by her citation of Karen Green and John Bigelow, 'Does Science Persecute Women? The Case of the 16th–17th Century Witch-Hunts', *Philosophy*, 73 (1998), 195–217.

[32] Edward Bever, *The Realities of Witchcraft and Popular Magic in Early Modern Europe: Culture, Cognition and Everyday Life* (Basingstoke, 2008). Despite the monumental scale of Bever's thesis, I find its arguments, predicated upon constant recourse to 'may' and 'might', as ultimately unconvincing. For a fuller analysis and critique, see my review essay in *Social History of Medicine*, 22 (2009), 398–400.

medicine and the medical sciences in shaping and making sense of early modern witchcraft.

FURTHER READING

Bever, Edward, *The Realities of Witchcraft and Popular Magic in Early Modern Europe: Culture, Cognition and Everyday Life* (Basingstoke, 2008).

Clark, Stuart, *Thinking With Demons: The Idea of Witchcraft in Early Modern Europe* (Oxford, 1997).

Davies, Owen and Blécourt, Willem de, eds, *Beyond the Witch Trials: Witchcraft and Magic in Enlightenment Europe* (Manchester, 2004).

Easlea, Brian, *Witch-Hunting, Magic and the New Philosophy: An Introduction to Debates of the Scientific Revolution 1450–1750* (Brighton, 1980).

Elmer, Peter, 'Science, Medicine and Witchcraft', in Jonathan Barry and Owen Davies, eds, *Palgrave Advances in Witchcraft Historiography* (Basingstoke, 2007), 33–51.

Fix, Andrew, *Fallen Angels: Balthasar Bekker, Spirit Belief, and Confessionalism in the Seventeenth-Century Dutch Republic* (Dordrecht, 1999).

Israel, Jonathan, *Radical Enlightenment: Philosophy and the Making of Modernity, 1650–1750* (Oxford, 2001).

Jobe, Thomas Harmon, 'The Devil in Restoration Science: The Glanvill-Webster Debate', *Isis*, 72 (1981), 343–56.

Shapin, Simon, *The Scientific Revolution* (Chicago, 1996).

Trevor-Roper, Hugh, 'The European Witch-Craze of the Sixteenth and Seventeenth Centuries', in *Religion, the Reformation and Social Change* (London, 1967), 90–192.

CHAPTER 31

MEDICINE AND WITCHCRAFT

PETER ELMER

IN addition to constituting a sin and a crime, witchcraft was widely perceived as an instrument to inflict physical harm and ill health upon those who fell out with their diabolically inspired neighbours. As such, it often fell under the peculiar purview of the physician or healer, who frequently worked alongside those other demonological experts involved in witchcraft cases: the cleric and the magistrate. Like the latter, medical experts gained first-hand experience of witchcraft trials through providing testimony to courts of law, and in the process built up a substantial body of knowledge in relation to illnesses purportedly caused by witches and demons. Some were subsequently motivated to publish their thoughts on the subject, though the extant literature fails to suggest any clear-cut preference either in favour of, or against, the reality of diseases attributed to witchcraft. Other practitioners of the healing arts, particularly those who lay outside the tripartite hierarchy of the early modern medical profession—that is, physicians, surgeons, and apothecaries—might find themselves the object of suspicion as their application of 'unlearned' folk medicine was the equivalent in some circles of a species of black magic or witchcraft. Despite the obvious interest of members of the healing arts in witchcraft, and their engagement in both practical and theoretical aspects of the subject, major historical studies of the relationship between medicine and witchcraft are thin on the ground. With one exception, discussed in more detail below, there have been few case studies of individual physicians in this respect, and only fleeting accounts of the attitude of medical practitioners as a whole to the phenomenon of witchcraft. Why should this be so? In all probability the answer lies in the tendency of historians to conflate the contribution of doctors to the witchcraft debate with that of scientists or natural philosophers, given that the former, particularly those trained at universities, frequently shared a similar education and approach to nature, and were themselves often to be found at the forefront of scientific advance in the early modern period.

There is little doubt, however, that because of the practical nature of the work of the physician, healers generally occupied a privileged position with regard to understanding the causes and cure of illnesses produced by witchcraft, particularly diabolical possession, and as a result their engagement with such matters has attracted the sporadic interest of historians and others. From the age of the Enlightenment through to the twentieth century, two linked assumptions have tended to prevail in historical discussion of this subject, both echoing similar assumptions about the role played by science generally with regard to witchcraft and its eventual decline in early modern times. In the first place, there was a widespread consensus that the attribution of a range of ailments and afflictions to witchcraft in medieval and early modern times was a manifestation of the 'superstitious' and backward character of contemporary medical practice and thought. Secondly, much writing on the subject has been predicated on the idea that those who claimed to suffer at the hands of witches and the devil were in reality suffering from various forms of physical and mental illness that early modern medical practitioners were incapable of diagnosing with any degree of accuracy or consensus. Moreover, the problem for doctors faced with patients who claimed to be either bewitched or possessed was further compounded by the widespread belief in the idea that the devil was able to use his superior knowledge to manipulate natural causes in order to produce a wide range of ill effects, including diseases, that to all intents and purposes were indistinguishable from those that occurred naturally. It was thus possible to conjecture—as some did— that the devil, either with or without the assistance of human confederates such as witches, was the cause of all disease and ill health.

This overwhelmingly negative appraisal of early modern medicine and its practitioners continues to permeate discussions of the medical aspects of witchcraft and demonology to the present day. In many respects, its intellectual origins lie in the nineteenth century and the rise of a new branch of the medical profession— psychiatry—whose exponents were eager to expose some of the more egregious errors of their predecessors in falsely diagnosing diabolical possession, either with or without the assistance of the witch, as a disease of demonic origins rather than a by-product of mental illness. This movement first gained pre-eminence in France under the supervision of the innovative neurologist Jean-Martin Charcot (1825–1893), who initiated a large-scale project designed to demonstrate that historical accounts of possession and other ecstatic states shared much in common with contemporary descriptions of hysteria. Employing the concept of 'retrospective medicine', a term first coined by the radical republican Émile Littré (1801–1881) in 1869, Charcot and his colleagues at the Salpêtrière asylum in Paris thus set about compiling and publishing a series of tracts, including original works on witchcraft, designed to demonstrate the value of the new psychiatry in explaining the historical myth of the witch. Between 1882 and 1897, eight early modern tracts concerned with possession, and to a lesser extent witchcraft, were republished under the supervision of the neurologist Désiré-Magloire Bourneville (1840–1909)—pride of place being reserved for the work of the sixteenth-century

Dutch physician, Johann Weyer (1515–1588), who was now credited with almost single-handedly exploding the witchcraft superstition.[1]

The French translation, with commentary, of Weyer's groundbreaking work, *De Praestigiis Daemonum* (On the Tricks of Demons), first published in 1563, appeared in 1885. Prior to this date, Weyer's work, in which he cited a wide range of medical and other explanations for the behaviour of alleged witches, was little known among physicians or historians. Weyer, in particular, had highlighted the role played by melancholy—a humoral condition that particularly affected the aged—in encouraging suspected witches, usually old women, to confess to a range of crimes, including the imposition of physical harm on their neighbours, which they were in fact powerless to commit. The republication of Weyer's treatise on witchcraft at this time—probably inspired by a series of lectures given to the Paris Faculty of Medicine by another eminent neurologist, Alexandre Axenfeld (1825–1876), in 1865—was destined to elevate Weyer to a position of unique prominence, indeed hero status, in the eyes of those who applauded his rational scepticism in the face of his contemporary detractors and witch-hunting opponents. From this point on, Weyer was routinely depicted as the lone voice of enlightenment in a world steeped in superstition and bigotry, and his progressive views favourably compared to those of the clergy, who were widely held as responsible for introducing witch-hunting into early modern Europe. Weyer thus stood out, for the rationalist Charcot and his anticlerical colleagues, as a beacon for his profession—a model practitioner who embodied the virtues of progressive physicians in late nineteenth-century Europe.[2]

During the course of the following century, Weyer's reputation as an enlightened witchcraft sceptic became an integral element in a wider discourse aimed at elucidating the origins of a new branch of the medical profession: psychiatry. Such an approach was largely indebted to the pioneering research and writings of the Russian-born psychoanalyst and early historian of psychiatry, Gregory Zilboorg (1890–1959), who was eager to appropriate Weyer for the cause of medical and psychiatric progress in his own day. In particular, Zilboorg's early essay, *The Medical Man and the Witch* (1935), championed Weyer as the 'founder of modern psychiatry', emphasizing the originality of his thinking ('one gains the impression that a new man, a new type of individual, has entered upon the scene of medicine'), and the methodical and systematic nature of his practice, which betrayed all the features of the modern-day psychiatrist. Zilboorg also lauded Weyer as a great clinician, whose case studies were so prescient and acute that it

---

[1] For a good general account of the background to these developments, see Sarah Ferber, 'Charcot's Demons: Retrospective Medicine and Historical Diagnosis in the Writings of the Salpêtrière School', in Marijke Gijswijt-Hofstra, Hilary Marland, and Hans de Waardt, eds, *Illness and Healing Alternatives in Western Europe* (London, 1997), 120–40.

[2] For the rationalist and anticlerical circle of Charcot, and the relation of their work on hysteria and witchcraft to contemporary religious and political debates in France, see especially Jan Goldstein, 'The Hysteria Diagnosis and the Politics of Anticlericalism in Late Nineteenth-Century France', *Journal of Modern History*, 54 (1982), 209–39; Goldstein, *Console and Classify: The French Psychiatric Profession in the Nineteenth Century* (Cambridge, 1987), 322–84.

was possible to detect in them a whole host of recognizable mental states and illnesses, including depression, megalomania, and schizophrenia. In short, Zilboorg credits Weyer with the capacity to anticipate future developments in psychiatry, garlanding him for his achievements, despite the fact that he himself was almost certainly unaware of their revolutionary significance for the profession. Thus, according to Zilboorg:

> [Weyer] knew that the answer to the problem was to be found in medicine; he knew that the doctors were woefully inadequate; he knew also that medicine itself was not yet ready to meet the problem. He felt that a psychiatry must be created, and he sensed that if it was to be created, it would be brought about by medicine and not by theology, philosophy or jurisprudence . . . Thus, although he left us no system, no well-rounded theory—in fact no theory at all—he actually viewed the psychopathological problems of his day with an empirical matter of factness which proved revolutionary in the history of medical psychology.[3]

With the privilege of hindsight it is apparent that Zilboorg's hagiographic and 'present-centred' approach to Weyer says more about Zilboorg's anxieties for his own nascent profession, psychiatry, than it does about the reality of Weyer's practice and his attitudes to witchcraft. Writing in the 1930s, Zilboorg was acutely aware of the uncertain and disputed status of his profession and the ridicule that it evoked in large sections of the population. Unlike mainstream medicine, where physicians had been able to promote the wider benefits of the new medical sciences of the nineteenth and twentieth centuries with ease, the trade of the early psychiatrist was beset with problems. Weyer himself had faced an uphill struggle in attempting to persuade the 'insane' that they were ill and so create the specialism of psychiatry 'uninvited and against the terrible odds, against the will of the public, against the will of the established legal authority and against the will of a variety of established religious faiths'.[4] Despite, then, his claim to write with 'detachment' and to shun the 'undercurrent of condescending admiration' that he believed characterized the history of medicine, Zilboorg, in eulogizing the achievements of Weyer, was clearly working to his own agenda. It is a measure of his success that the claims he made for Weyer as a pioneer in the field of psychiatric medicine were rapidly assimilated by academic colleagues across the disciplines, and soon took on the status of undisputed fact.[5]

It is difficult to exaggerate the extent of Zilboorg's influence on subsequent generations of historians of medicine, psychiatry, and witchcraft. The 'foundation myth' that

---

[3] Gregory Zilboorg, *The Medical Man and the Witch During the Renaissance* (Baltimore, MD, 1935); Gregory Zilboorg and George W. Henry, *A History of Medical Psychology* (New York, 1941), 207, 211, 221.

[4] Zilboorg laid bare his own professional insecurity when he lamented the fact that his embryonic profession abounded in 'quacks' and other 'nonmedical amateurs, lay and clerical', who 'are more readily accepted by patients and their relatives than are psychiatrists, and mental hospitals'; Zilboorg and Henry, *A History of Medical Psychology*, 24–5.

[5] Zilboorg and Henry, *A History of Medical Psychology*, 17–18, 20.

focused on the role of Weyer in the early modern origins of psychiatry was endlessly repeated and recycled, particularly in manuals of abnormal psychology.[6] It also became a standard feature of general histories of early modern medicine and science, where Weyer's heroic stand against the theologians and demonologists dovetailed neatly with the whiggish 'great man' approach that characterized so much writing on this subject both before and after the Second World War. George Sarton (1884–1956), for example, one of the pioneers of the new history of science, heralded the work of Weyer as one of the first to adopt a truly 'medical point of view' in the treatment of witchcraft, adding that it was 'thanks to him and his followers, [that] "witches" are now considered mental cases and treated as such'. Typically, Sarton portrayed Weyer as a pioneer and an iconoclast, keen to explore new ways of treating the mentally ill.[7] Later writers working in this historical tradition went in search of Weyer's supporters and disciples in an attempt to trace the legacy of Weyer's scepticism through subsequent generations of physicians down to the age of the Enlightenment. In England, for example, Hunter and Macalpine uncovered an English Weyer in the shape of the early seventeenth-century physician Edward Jorden (1569–1633), whose published account of a witchcraft trial they acclaimed as 'the first book by an English physician which reclaimed the demoniacally possessed for medicine'.[8] The American psychiatrist and historian Oskar Diethelm (1897–1993) was yet more ambitious. In 1970, he attempted to demonstrate the gradual and corrosive influence of Weyer's ideas on the medical profession in general through the analysis of published medical dissertations at European universities, which, by 1700, he depicted as broadly questioning of, and antagonistic towards, witchcraft and witch-hunting. Moreover, Diethelm, unlike Zilboorg, was happy to extend the medical roll call of honour to other 'sceptical' physicians such as Jean Fernel, Felix Platter, Daniel Sennert, and Thomas Willis—a move that may well have encouraged a more open approach to the subject of medical influence upon the witchcraft debate.[9]

---

[6] For examples of this hagiographic tradition in the writings of post-war historians of psychiatry, see Dennis Leigh, 'Recurrent Themes in the History of Psychiatry', *Medical History*, 1 (1957), 237–48; Abraham A. Roback, *History of Psychology and Psychiatry* (London, 1962), 244–8; Joost A. M. Meerloo, 'Four Hundred Years of "Witchcraft", "Projection" and "Delusion"', *The American Journal of Psychiatry*, 120 (1963), 83–6; George Mora, 'On the 400th Anniversary of Johann Weyer's *De Praestigiis Daemonum*: Its Significance for Today's Psychiatry', *The American Journal of Psychiatry*, 120 (1963), 417–28; Franz Alexander and Sheldon T. Selesnick, *The History of Psychiatry* (New York, 1966). For the self-confirmatory and circular manner in which these texts were cited by the authors of textbooks on abnormal psychology and historians of psychiatry, see Nicholas P. Spanos, 'Witchcraft in Histories of Psychiatry: A Critical Analysis and an Alternative Conceptualization', *Psychological Bulletin*, 85 (1978), 419, 434.

[7] George Sarton, *Six Wings: Men of Science in the Renaissance* (London, [1957] 1958), 212–18.

[8] Richard Hunter and Ida Macalpine, *Three Hundred Years of Psychiatry, 1535–1860* (London, 1963), 68. The influence of their own work on the profession is evident in Robert E. Hemphill, 'Historical Witchcraft and Psychiatric Illness in Western Europe', *Proceedings of the Royal Society of Medicine*, 59 (1966), 891–902.

[9] Oskar Diethelm, 'The Medical Teaching of Demonology in the 17th and 18th Centuries', *Journal of the History of the Behavioral Sciences*, 6 (1970), 3–15. In contrast to Diethelm, Zilboorg was scathing in his

It was not until the 1970s that new approaches to the relationship between medicine and witchcraft began to emerge, following a growing disenchantment in historical circles with the older whiggish approach to understanding the processes of change in the past. Increasingly, historians were voicing concern with the dangers of an anachronistic, present-centred methodology that tended to label early modern physicians as either heroes or villains depending upon the apparent progressiveness of their views. This was especially the case with regard to Weyer, who, as we have seen, was widely lauded in medical and psychiatric circles as a lone advocate for the 'mad' witch. The challenge to the older orthodoxy with regard to Weyer came from two directions. In the first instance, it arose among a new generation of historians of witchcraft who, imbued with a more nuanced and relativist approach to the past, sought to recontextualize Weyer's life and ideas and subject them to detailed analysis. Seen in this way, a new view began to emerge of Weyer that was radically at odds with his former image. In contrast to Zilboorg's portrait of the man as a confirmed sceptic, Weyer was now depicted as a medical conservative, whose views on demonology and medicine were neither radical nor convincing, and whose approach to witchcraft differed little from that of his supposedly 'credulous' opponents. Particularly damaging to his reputation was the emphasis that some now placed on his deep-seated belief in the existence of the devil and his ability to perform evil in the world through the intercession of willing accomplices in the shape of various sorcerers and magicians. Weyer may have shifted the blame for witchcraft away from innocent old women by invoking various medical explanations for their confessions of guilt, but he nonetheless remained wedded to a system of ideas that retained a central role in the sublunary world for the devil, demons, and sorcerers.[10]

At roughly the same time as these developments, Weyer's role as exemplary sceptic came under fire from the same sub-discipline, the history of psychiatry, which had done so much to elevate the Dutch physician to prominence in the first place. Psychiatry as a branch of medicine was itself increasingly exposed to criticism both from within and outside the nascent profession. During the course of the 1960s, for example, the emergence of the 'anti-psychiatry' movement, spearheaded by prominent figures such as Thomas Szasz (1920–2012), encouraged members of the profession to reexamine their past as well as their present. Szasz himself was eager to expose some of

assessment of the contribution of physicians like Willis to the development of medical psychology; Zilboorg and Henry, *A History of Medical Psychology*, 247–53, 256, 263, 277. In all probability, Zilboorg's antipathy towards the neurological approach of iatromechanists like Willis is best explained by his commitment to an autonomous psychiatric profession based on Freudian psychotherapeutic methods, which steadfastly shunned neurological explanations for mental illness and a therapeutic regime based on drugs.

[10] Sidney Anglo, 'Melancholia and Witchcraft', in Aloïs Gerlo, ed., *Folie et Déraison à la Renaissance* (Brussels, 1976), 209–22, esp. 210–12. More recently Erik Midelfort has argued that Weyer's legacy was more profound in the field of early modern forensic medicine, where he helped to pioneer the insanity defence; H. C. Erik Midelfort, 'Johann Weyer and the Transformation of the Insanity Defense', in Ronnie Po-Chia Hsia, ed., *The German People and the Reformation* (Ithaca, NY, 1988), 234–61.

the many myths attached to the origins of psychiatric practice, focusing in particular on the creation of an elaborate chain of great men and thinkers, from Pinel in the late eighteenth century through to Charcot, Freud, and Zilboorg in the nineteenth and twentieth centuries. Among the many untruths peddled by some of these figures, he specifically alluded to the role played by the latter in perpetuating the idea of the witch as mentally ill.[11] At about the same time that Szasz was composing his broadsides against the psychiatric profession, which he accused of being engaged in a form of social and political control, the French philosopher and historian Michel Foucault (1926–1984) was leading a revisionist onslaught against traditional Whig historiography by proposing, among other things, that eighteenth-century Europe had witnessed a 'great confinement' in which the mentally ill were now stigmatized as antisocial outcasts and deviants.[12] Others soon followed in the footsteps of Szasz and Foucault. In 1977, for example, the clinical psychologist Thomas Schoeneman adopted Szasz's stance, backed up this time by much of the most recent research produced by a new generation of historians of witchcraft, in order to demolish Zilboorg's central thesis that all witches were mad. In its place, he suggested a far more nuanced and historically sensitive approach to the whole question of what it meant to be mentally ill, or perceived as such, in early modern Europe. A year later much the same approach was taken by Schoeneman's colleague, Nicholas Spanos, who launched a scathing attack on the 'present-centeredness' of Zilboorg's methodology, rejecting, among other things, the claim of Zilboorg and his followers that it was possible to apply modern psychiatric diagnostic labels retrospectively to those ailments suffered by earlier generations of men and women who claimed to be bewitched and possessed.[13]

An important by-product of the debate surrounding Zilboorg and the role allocated to Weyer in the history of psychiatry was the growing tendency of historians to question many of the aprioristic assumptions about madness and witchcraft that had featured so prominently in the work of an earlier generation of scholars. During the 1980s, a number of pioneering studies suggested a radically new approach to these issues. Foremost among these was the work of the American scholar Michael MacDonald, whose detailed and intricate study of the casebooks of a provincial doctor, Richard Napier (1559–1634), demonstrated the varied nature of responses to the diagnosis and treatment of the mentally ill in early modern England.[14] MacDonald's work was

---

[11] Thomas Szasz, *The Manufacture of Madness* (New York, 1970), 75.

[12] Michel Foucault, *Madness and Civilization*, tr. Richard Howard (New York, 1965).

[13] Thomas J. Schoeneman, 'The Role of Mental Illness in the European Witch Hunts of the Sixteenth and Seventeenth Centuries', *Journal of the History of the Behavioral Sciences*, 13 (1977), 337–51; Nicholas Spanos, 'Witchcraft in Histories of Psychiatry: A Critical Analysis and an Alternative Conceptualization', *Psychological Bulletin*, 85 (1978), 417–39. For a further attempt to trace the origins of the myth of the early modern foundations of psychiatry and to post-date such developments to the period after the French Revolution, see Patrick Vandermeersch, 'The Victory of Psychiatry over Demonology: The Origin of the Nineteenth-Century Myth', *History of Psychiatry*, 2 (1991), 351–63.

[14] Michael MacDonald, *Mystical Bedlam: Madness, Anxiety, and Healing in Seventeenth-Century England* (Cambridge, 1981).

notable on numerous fronts, particularly in relation to the eclectic methodology—combining ethnographic, anthropological, and historical approaches— which he opted to apply to Napier's casebooks, as well as his avoidance of anachronistic psychological jargon. In addition, for the first time perhaps, one was allowed to hear the afflicted describe in their own terms and language what they believed lay at the root of their mental afflictions. MacDonald's study provides fascinating insights into the nature of early modern madness. More specifically, with respect to witchcraft and its relationship to insanity, it is readily apparent from the evidence unearthed in this study that the two concepts were not synonymous in the eyes of practitioners like Napier and his patients. On the contrary, MacDonald was able to demonstrate that early modern English men and women possessed a rich vocabulary of terms for medical symptoms, through which they were able to articulate and understand their daily fears and anxieties. In short, MacDonald had produced the first evidence-based study of the social and cultural construction of madness in pre-industrial Europe.[15]

The idea that mental illness was socially constructed and constituted the product of a specific time and place was to prove of great significance for scholars of witchcraft. Rather than seeking to 'explain away' the abnormal behaviour traditionally ascribed to witches and their victims, historians of witchcraft, under the influence of such approaches, have become increasingly sensitive to the idea that such afflictions are, in the words of Erik Midelfort, 'too idiosyncratic and culture-bound to fit well into our secular and psycho-pharmacological notions of neurosis and psychosis'.[16] The religio-centric nature of witchcraft in particular would appear to defy the logic of applying the reductivist categories of mental illness favoured by modern psychiatrists to the mental habits and ailments of our early modern predecessors. It also provides a rich explanatory framework for understanding the motives of men like Weyer and Jorden, whose scepticism on the subject of witchcraft, it has been argued, was more likely to have been shaped by religious factors rather than medical orientation. Midelfort, for example, while playing down the originality of Weyer's psychological insights, has identified his commitment to Erasmianism as a central plank in his sceptical outlook.[17] In a similar

---

[15] See also Michael MacDonald, 'Insanity and the Realities of History in Early Modern England', *Psychological Medicine*, 11 (1981), 11–25; MacDonald, 'Religion, Social Change, and Psychological Healing in England, 1600–1800', in William J. Shiels, ed., *The Church and Healing* (Oxford, 1982), 101–25. For another important attempt to apply the same criteria to the study of medicine, madness, and witchcraft see David Harley, 'Mental Illness, Magical Medicine and the Devil in Northern England, 1650–1700', in Roger French and Andrew Wear, eds, *The Medical Revolution of the Seventeenth Century* (Cambridge, 1989), 114–44.

[16] H. C. Erik Midelfort, *A History of Madness in Sixteenth-Century Germany* (Stanford, CA, 1999), 49. For a good overview of these developments and the application of social constructivist approaches to the history of madness, see Roy Porter, *Mind-Forg'd Manacles: A History of Madness in England from the Restoration to the Regency* (Cambridge, MA, 1987), 1–18.

[17] Midelfort, *A History of Madness*, 205. For the author's earlier attempt to summarize the benefits of a social constructivist approach to madness, see Midelfort, 'Madness and the Problems of Psychological History in the Sixteenth Century', *Sixteenth Century Journal*, 12 (1981), 5–12; Midelfort, 'Sin, Melancholy, Obsession: Insanity and Culture in Sixteenth-Century Germany', in Steven L. Kaplan, ed.,

vein, MacDonald has opted to downplay the significance of Jorden's diagnosis of hysteria in a case of witchcraft in 1603, arguing instead that his attempt to vindicate the suspected witch in print was largely 'a work of religious propaganda' and, as such, part of a wider debate in English society over the nature and direction of the Church of England.[18]

Despite the growing acceptance in historical circles of the validity of this new methodology, both in relation to medicine and science, it is nonetheless probably fair to conclude that medicine's role in the witch-hunts of early modern Europe remains contested, controversial, and open to further exploration. Scholarly consensus has proved elusive for a number of reasons. For many seeking to understand why witches were prosecuted in early modern Europe, the inclination to lay much of the blame at the door of contemporary medicine and its 'superstitious' and impotent practitioners continues to appeal. Following the lead of historians such as Garfield Tourney and Leland Estes, new generations of writers on witchcraft continue to echo their complaints that witchcraft itself lay beyond the competence of contemporary doctors who, according to Estes, simply gave up and left the field to persecuting clerics. Writing in 1983, Estes even went so far as to speculate that it was the failure of medical practitioners to diagnose a range of new diseases that led to a widespread 'witch-disease complex' in the period, which in turn provided the essential spark for subsequent bouts of mass witch-hunting.[19] The mixed reception afforded to social constructivist attempts to understand madness in early modern Europe is particularly evident in the continuing debate surrounding the talismanic Weyer. In general texts on witchcraft, for example, Weyer continues to be lauded as the 'father of modern psychiatry' and, while there is now general agreement concerning the limitations of his scepticism, he remains a pivotal and inspired figure, a man before his time whose 'remarkable insights' often anticipate later developments in the field of twentieth-century psychopathology.[20] Moreover, further evidence of the failure of the social constructivist approach to acquire general acceptance is readily apparent in the continuing attempt by some witchcraft scholars to explain, or rather explain away, the symptoms of bewitchment and possession by recourse to modern psychiatric and medical labels. Accordingly, conversion and trance disorder, hysteria, epilepsy, psychotic episodes, and a range of other conditions continue to be widely invoked in order to account for the abnormal

Understanding Popular Culture: Europe from the Middle Ages to the Nineteenth Century (Berlin, 1984), 113–45.

[18] Michael MacDonald, *Witchcraft and Hysteria in Elizabethan London: Edward Jorden and the Mary Glover Case* (London, 1991), viii–ix.

[19] Garfield Tourney, 'The Physician and Witchcraft in Restoration England', *Medical History*, 16 (1972), 143–55; Leland L. Estes, 'The Medical Origins of the Witch Craze: A Hypothesis', *Journal of Social History*, 17 (1983), 271–84.

[20] Brian P. Levack, *The Witch-Hunt in Early Modern Europe* (London, 1987), 56–7; George Mora, ed., *Witches, Devils, and Doctors in the Renaissance: Johann Weyer*, De Praestigiis Daemonum (Binghamton, NY, 1991), lxiii–lxxix.

behaviour of those who claimed to be possessed.[21] Others, citing developments in the field of pharmacology, have sought to establish a link between the witch-hunts and the spread of ergotism and widespread use of hallucinogenic plants in early modern Europe.[22] Edward Bever's most recent attempt to resuscitate retrodiagnosis and to incorporate recent developments from a variety of medical fields, including neurophysiology, parapsychology, and the physiological function of dream states and out-of-body experiences, thus represents a deeply engrained tradition in the historiography of witchcraft.[23]

In a survey of English witchcraft written in 1996, the historian Jim Sharpe opined that '[t]he medical dimensions of the history of witchcraft still remain one of its great uncharted areas'.[24] Given the patchy and controversial nature of so much that has been written on this particular aspect of the subject, both before and since, it is difficult to dissent from this view. Despite a growing acceptance among historians of social constructivist approaches to medicine, madness, and witchcraft in the period, non-specialists and others continue to investigate the medical origins of the 'witch craze' by recourse to more traditional models that have become increasingly discredited in academic, historical circles. There is evidence, however, that a radical reappraisal of the relationship between medicine and witchcraft may bear fruit in the years ahead. One strand in this process is suggested by the pioneering work of Lyndal Roper on the psycho-social dynamics of German witchcraft, which combines insights drawn from modern psychology with a sensitive cultural relativism. In her most recent work on the subject, and building on the work of scholars such as Stuart Clark, she has made the case for seeing the demonologist as embodying many of the virtues of the modern psychiatrist, particularly in relation to his work in exploring the uncertain boundary between soul and body, and the role of the imagination in witch beliefs. In short, she concludes that 'the science of demonology had always been a science of psychology, for witch-hunting required the interrogator to probe the witch's motivations and gain her trust in order to provide an account of her life history and her deepest truths'.[25]

In a twist on the 'foundation myth' concerned with the origins of modern psychiatry in the work of sceptics such as Johann Weyer, Roper alludes to the seminal role of the later eighteenth-century exorcist Johann Joseph Gassner in promoting psychoanalytical

---

[21] For two examples, among many, of this kind of approach applied to specific witchcraft cases, see S. W. McDonald, A. Thom and A. Thom, 'The Bargarran Witchcraft Trial: A Psychiatric Assessment', *Scottish Medical Journal*, 41 (1996), 152–8; Gilbert Geis and Ivan Bunn, *A Trial of Witches: A Seventeenth-Century Witchcraft Prosecution* (London, 1997), esp. 129–34.

[22] Michael J. Harner, 'The Role of Hallucinogenic Plants in European Witchcraft', in *Hallucinogens and Shamanism* (New York, 1973), 125–50; Linnda R. Caporael, 'Ergotism: The Satan Loosed in Salem?', *Science*, 192 (1976), 21–6.

[23] Edward Bever, *The Realities of Witchcraft and Popular Magic in Early Modern Europe: Culture, Cognition, and Everyday Life* (Basingstoke, 2008).

[24] James Sharpe, *Instruments of Darkness: Witchcraft in England 1550–1750* (London, 1996), 271.

[25] Lyndal Roper, *Oedipus and the Devil: Witchcraft, Sexuality and Religion in Early Modern Europe* (London, 1994); Roper, *Witch Craze: Terror and Fantasy in Baroque Germany* (New Haven, CT, 2004), 106, 243.

techniques, suggesting a direct lineage between Gassner and later writers and exponents of the art such as Mesmer, Charcot, and Freud. Others, moreover, such as Erik Midelfort, have rightly pointed to the case of Gassner as an important reminder to scholars of the fragile, tenuous, and often controversial nature of scientific and medical progress in the Enlightenment—a corrective, as it were, to the triumphalism of an older orthodoxy in witchcraft studies.[26] Here surely lies rich terrain for further exploration and study. By and large, historians of witchcraft have largely assumed that the decline of witchcraft followed inexorably on the heels of medical and scientific progress in the eighteenth century. However, as the work of Roper and Midelfort on Gassner, and the intriguing research of scholars such as Rhodri Hayward on Edwardian Britain suggests, the path to modernity, and with it the disappearance of 'irrational' systems of thought such as demonology, was neither smooth nor straight.[27] To some extent, this kind of approach has been prefigured in the work of an earlier generation of witchcraft scholars, who sought to link scepticism with specific schools of medical thought, such as Paracelsism. Hugh Trevor-Roper, for example, was the first to suggest a central role for the Swiss physician Paracelsus (1493–1541) and his followers in debunking established witchcraft beliefs despite the seemingly irrational and unscientific nature of the hermetic tradition to which such thinkers belonged.[28]

Generally speaking, however, and with a few notable exceptions, recent work in this field has tended to shy away from attempts to link specific medical or natural philo-sophical systems of thought to either sceptical or credulous approaches to witchcraft. In 1981, Thomas Jobe suggested a novel approach to the problem when he argued that it was the broader religious positions and beliefs that underpinned medical and scientific ideas, and that their propagation was ultimately critical in fostering specific attitudes to witchcraft.[29] While his solution may have been overly simplistic in equating hermetic

[26] Roper, *Witch Craze*, 242–3; H. C. Erik Midelfort, *Exorcism and Enlightenment: Johann Joseph Gassner and the Demons of Eighteenth-Century Germany* (New Haven, CT, 2005).

[27] Rhodri Hayward, 'Demonology, Neurology, and Medicine in Edwardian Britain', *Bulletin of the History of Medicine*, 78 (2004), 37–58. In a fascinating account of the widespread revival of interest in important aspects of demonological belief, including possession and spirits, Hayward is at pains to observe that medical men were not immune from these developments. He cites the case of Sir James Risdon Bennett (1809–1891), nonconformist president of the Royal College of Physicians of London, who in 1889 defended the biblical veracity of demon possession and claimed that it could still be found in Britain's asylums; Hayward, 'Demonology, Neurology, and Medicine', 44.

[28] Hugh Trevor-Roper, 'The European Witch-Craze of the Sixteenth and Seventeenth Centuries', in *Religion, the Reformation and Social Change* (London, 1967), 132–3. Trevor-Roper's views were later echoed, among others, by Keith Thomas and Charles Webster; Keith Thomas, *Religion and the Decline of Magic* (London, 1971), 578–9; Charles Webster, *From Paracelsus to Newton: Magic and the Making of Modern Science* (Cambridge, 1982), 80–6. For an early attempt to enlist Paracelsus as a pioneering psychiatrist in the mould of Weyer, see Iago Galdston, 'The Psychiatry of Paracelsus', *Bulletin of the History of Medicine*, 24 (1950), 205–18; repr. in E. Ashworth Underwood, ed., *Science, Medicine and History: Essays on the Evolution of Scientific Thought and Medical Practice Written in Honour of Charles Singer*, 2 vols (London and New York, 1953), i, 408–17.

[29] Thomas Harmon Jobe, 'The Devil in Restoration Science: The Glanvill–Webster Witchcraft Debate', *Isis*, 72 (1981), 343–56. For a recent attempt to provide a revisionist account of the supposed witchcraft scepticism of the eminent English physician William Harvey (1578–1657) see Cathy Gere,

and occult strains of thought with radical Protestantism and scepticism, and linking advocates of witchcraft with the new mechanical philosophy and orthodox Anglicanism or latitudinarianism, it nonetheless provides a more realistic assessment of the way in which medical and scientific ideas were elaborated and disseminated in Restoration Britain. Jobe's research focused on the work of a specific medical sceptic John Webster (1610–1682). There have, however, been few other attempts to delve deeper into the lives of those medical practitioners who wrote on the subject of witchcraft. This, surely, is a major omission, for until we know more about such men—their religious, political, and intellectual preoccupations—it is virtually impossible to speak with certainty of underlying patterns that might explain changing attitudes to witchcraft and demonology in the early modern period. Thus, in the case of England, we know little of the lives and careers of two important medical authors on witchcraft, John Cotta (c.1575–1628 or 1629) and Thomas Ady (d.1672), and precious little about the kind of networks to which such men belonged.[30] Outside of England, the picture is even bleaker.

Writing as one with a profound interest in both the wider religious and political context in which early modern medical practitioners plied their trade, as well as the contribution that such men made to controversial topics such as witchcraft, I strongly feel that the time has come for more detailed studies of those who engaged in such debates. Only then will it be possible to speak with more certainty of overarching trends linking healers and physicians with specific positions on a range of issues, including demonology, possession, and the existence of witches. To some extent, I have tried to initiate this process in a recent essay, exploring the educational, religious, and political associations of nonconformist medical practitioners in post-Restoration England, and how these may have helped to shape a uniform and coherent approach among dissenters to issues such as witchcraft and associated beliefs.[31] There is clearly a great deal of further work to be done here, particularly in relation to developments elsewhere in Europe, before comparative studies can allow broader, all-encompassing judgements to be made as to the impact of medicine on demonological speculation and the wider debate on the existence of witchcraft. Again, the signs are positive. The work of Jonathan Israel on the Dutch 'Radical Enlightenment', for example, has suggested strong links between the spread of Spinozistic atheism and witchcraft scepticism. He also provides some very useful case studies of Dutch physicians indebted to this tradition, including the important sceptic Anthonie van Dale (1638–1708).[32] In a similar

'William Harvey's Weak Experiment: The Archaeology of an Anecdote', *History Workshop Journal*, 51 (2001), 19–36.

[30] For Cotta, see my article in the *Oxford Dictionary of National Biography*. I am currently compiling a detailed life of Ady, and his puritan connections in East Anglia, as part of a much larger project to create a comprehensive database of medical practitioners in early modern Britain (excluding Scotland).

[31] Peter Elmer, 'Medicine, Witchcraft and the Politics of Healing in Late Seventeenth-Century England', in Ole Peter Grell and Andrew Cunningham, eds, *Medicine and Religion in Enlightenment Europe* (Aldershot, 2007), 223–41.

[32] Jonathan Israel, *Radical Enlightenment: Philosophy and the Making of Modernity 1650–1750* (Oxford, 2001). For van Dale, see especially 361–5. Following Israel, I discuss the disproportionate

vein, Ann Thomson has recently reminded us of the vibrant debate in European academic circles at this time with regard to the boundary between matter and spirit, and body and soul, in which contemporary medical writers such as Francis Glisson, Thomas Willis, and William Coward played such a crucial role.[33] It would be helpful, to say the least, to understand more about how, and the extent to which, such debates informed popular and judicial understanding of witchcraft, and their role, if any, in the decline of prosecutions.

Elsewhere, the search for broader, overarching explanations for the decline of witchcraft, most notably in relation to political change and the emergence of a pluralist society, has produced important studies linking developments in medicine and healing to these wider processes. Both David Lederer's case study of the demise of 'spiritual physic' in seventeenth-century Bavaria, and, to a lesser extent, Gary Waite's wide-ranging study linking the demise of witchcraft with an emergent plural religious culture, suggest important ways in which future studies of medicine's impact on witchcraft may take into account broader, non-medical factors.[34] These are all themes upon which I hope to publish in due course. In the meantime, it is to be hoped that the continuing emergence of the history of medicine as a distinct and popular sub-discipline within historical study will continue to foster a growing awareness and detailed understanding of the role of medical practitioners in the wider culture of early modern Europe, including its preoccupation with all matters demonological.

FURTHER READING

Diethelm, Oskar, 'The Medical Teaching of Demonology in the 17th and 18th Centuries', *Journal of the History of the Behavioral Sciences*, 6 (1970), 3–15.

Elmer, Peter, 'Medicine, Witchcraft and the Politics of Healing in Late Seventeenth-Century England', in Ole Peter Grell and Andrew Cunningham, eds, *Medicine and Religion in Enlightenment Europe* (Basingstoke, 2007), 223–41.

Estes, Leland L., 'The Medical Origins of the Witch Craze: A Hypothesis', *Journal of Social History*, 17 (1983), 271–84.

Jobe, Thomas Harmon, 'The Devil in Restoration Science: The Glanvill–Webster Witchcraft Debate', *Isis*, 72 (1981), 343–56.

Lederer, David, *Madness, Religion and the State in Early Modern Europe: A Bavarian Beacon* (Cambridge, 2006).

MacDonald, Michael, *Mystical Bedlam: Madness, Anxiety, and Healing in Seventeenth-Century England* (Cambridge, 1981).

influence of medical friends and associates on Spinoza in my 'Medicine, Witchcraft and the Politics of Healing', 223–5.

[33] Ann Thomson, *Bodies of Thought: Science, Religion, and the Soul in the Early Enlightenment* (Oxford, 2008).

[34] David Lederer, *Madness, Religion and the State in Early Modern Europe: A Bavarian Beacon* (Cambridge, 2006); Gary K. Waite, *Heresy, Magic, and Witchcraft in Early Modern Europe* (Basingstoke, 2003).

MacDonald, Michael, *Witchcraft and Hysteria in Elizabethan London: Edward Jorden and the Mary Glover Case* (London, 1991).

Midelfort, H. C. Erik, *A History of Madness in Sixteenth-Century Germany* (Stanford, CA, 1999).

Roper, Lyndal, *Witch Craze: Terror and Fantasy in Baroque Germany* (New Haven, CT, 2004).

Schoeneman, Thomas J., 'The Role of Mental Illness in the European Witch Hunts of the Sixteenth and Seventeenth Centuries', *Journal of the History of the Behavioral Sciences*, 13 (1977), 337–51.

Zilboorg, Gregory, *The Medical Man and the Witch during the Renaissance* (Baltimore, MD, 1935).

CHAPTER 32

....

DEMONIC POSSESSION, EXORCISM, AND WITCHCRAFT

....

SARAH FERBER

THE affliction of demonic possession and its treatment through the rite of exorcism took on new significance in the peak period of witch trials (*c*.1430–*c*.1750). This was a consequence of heightened attention to the perceived agency—and imagined human agents—of the devil in the world. The most dramatic aspect of this development was the performance of exorcism on persons believed to have become possessed because of another's evil acts, leading to witch trials. In these cases, exorcism was a direct spiritual cure for the possessed person, the rite itself acting on the possessing demon, as well as a wider social 'cure' in the exposure of a member of the newly imagined witch sect. Such cases were, however, only one of the ways that possession, exorcism, and witchcraft came to be connected in this period; they were the most potent manifestation of a wider sensitivity to the possibility of diabolical intervention in worldly affairs.

In this unique epoch in the history of demonic possession and exorcism in Western Christianity, several new or newly accentuated phenomena arose. The idea that a demonically possessed person could be seen as somewhat akin to a holy prophet(ess), which had arisen in the thirteenth century, became almost mundane, while holy people themselves were more likely to be suspected of being secretly under the devil's sway, sometimes undergoing tests by exorcism to prove their good faith. And, in the confessional struggles and religious wars of the sixteenth and seventeenth centuries, exorcists were energetic advocates for the rival confessions—particularly Catholic, but also Reformed—demonstrating publicly the willingness of the devil to yield to their own approved rituals. Because the rite of exorcism dealt with 'demons' face-to-face, many religious reformers from the later Middle Ages feared that such displays gave rise to a reliance on demons which could draw in credulous viewers. Regarded in this light as little better than magicians, many exorcists became subject to condemnation, derision, and regulation. Thus, the histories of possession, exorcism, and witchcraft intersected in sometimes complex ways. As David Lederer observes for early modern Bavaria, 'The diachronic conjunctures of demonic possessions and witch-hunting . . . are many, including the danger that complaints of possession might spill over into accusations of witchcraft. Nevertheless, despite many parallels, the exact relationship between the two remains a significant historiographical problem.'[1]

The aim of this chapter is to profile the distinctive features of possession and exorcism in this historical period, then to give some thought to the problem identified by Lederer: in what ways did the beliefs about possession, exorcism, and witchcraft intersect? It will begin by providing an overview of the characteristic developments of the period: the rise of the exorcist; the significance of the role model of the medieval holy woman; and the emergence of the demoniac as both witchcraft victim and prophetess (but also as possible witch). To analyse these trends it will then explore just one link between the three phenomena: the primacy given to vigilance in guarding against devil worship in cases of possession, exorcism, and witchcraft. Just as the spectre of human frailty in the face of diabolical temptation framed suspicion of witchcraft, it framed suspicion of the motives of exorcists, the possessed, and even holy persons. Historians have identified 'demoniza-tion' as a distinctive feature of the religious mindset of this period, showing the ways in which it generated an increasingly monochromatic view of the moral world. But the social expression of this development was nonetheless characterized by sometimes seemingly contradictory developments, for the need to oppose the power of the devil formed part of the interpretative armoury of those who displayed religious zeal and persecutory behaviours, as well as those arguing for moderation.

The discourse of demonology, meaning both scholarly readings of demonic action as well as its social manifestations, expanded dramatically in this period. It appeared in a large array of written, oral, and performative forms: statutes, tracts, medical literature, trial records, theological texts, manuals of ritual, and in ritual itself. Its presence was felt in different degrees at a range of social flashpoints, including witch trials, scrutiny of the behaviour of churchmen and women, religious wars, and confessional conflict, as well as in many forums, such as villages, universities, churches, private homes, religious houses, and law courts. Politics were always at work, and there were always insti-tutional and judicial intrigues in which 'thinking with demons' could point to a variety of outcomes. For example, Martín de Castañega's 1529 treatise on superstition and witchcraft clearly targeted not only the practices of errant Christians but was deeply absorbed in the campaigns of the reconquest of Spain against the rival religions of Judaism and Islam, which he saw as belonging ultimately to one of only two churches in the world, 'the Catholic and the diabolical'.[2] The force of demonological thinking

---

[1] *Madness, Religion and the State in Early Modern Europe: The Bavarian Beacon* (Cambridge 2006), 201. Thanks are due to Kerry Ross for her assistance in the preparation of this chapter and Leigh Dale for her comments.

[2] David Darst, ed., 'Witchcraft in Spain. The Testimony of Martín De Castañega's Treatise on Superstition and Witchcraft (1529)', *Proceedings of the American Philosophical Society*, 123 (1979), 302.

was its capacity to both undermine and radically recreate identities and social align-ments. Such a reading permits the resolution of a number of what (to modern eyes) might seem paradoxes: why was exorcism sometimes seen as a form of witchcraft and at others as the singular cure for it? Why were holy women likely to be suspected as witches? Why were demon-possessed women seen to be holy?

32.1 THE RISE OF THE EXORCIST

Ritual exorcism in the Christian Church dates from the miracles of Christ himself: he was a successful exorcist in a time when many healers used the expulsion of 'unclean spirits' in response to a range of conditions, such as blindness, deaf-mutism, and psychological torment.[3] Christ was the only person to expel demons on his own authority, but invoking his name was one of the signal healing gifts he bestowed on his disciples and on holy men in the early Christian Church. Peter Brown has documented the use of exorcism in antiquity: people with seemingly incurable afflic-tions who responded only to the presence of a saint, either in person or in the form of holy relics, gave proof of the healing power of the Christian Church.[4] In the increas-ingly Christianized Europe of the Middle Ages, exorcism became part of the folklore of the saintly history of Christianity, retailed in stories such as those in the thirteenth-century *Golden Legend* by Jacobus of Voragine. It also became an important part of the local Christian healing practices, which were one of the means whereby the Roman Church maintained its foothold at the local level.

Exorcists did not have the same standing in the Catholic Church as ordained clergy. Unlike the official seven sacraments, which could only be performed by an ordained priest, there could be no theological guarantee that the exorcist's rite was efficacious.[5] Perhaps ironically, this proved at times to be a positive. As a portable rite that could be performed outside the bounds of the liturgical calendar and even away from churches, administered by a larger number of clergy than those who could administer the sacraments, exorcisms could play a part in the healing of sickness of all kinds, including outright possession. Other forms of rite, also known as exorcisms, performed a service to communities in the ritual removal of perceived devil-infested obstacles to communal well-being, such as bad weather and pestilence. The spoken formulae of exorcism derived from a variety of sources, and usages varied from place to place. The fact that individual exorcists cultivated their own reputations as healers proliferated the forms of

---

[3] See: Matt. 12:22; Mark 5:3–4; Mark 9:17–22, 25–9; Luke 8:29. Graham H. Twelftree, *Jesus the Exorcist: A Contribution to the Study of the Historical Jesus* (Peabody, MA, 1993); Twelftree, *In the name of Jesus: Exorcism among Early Christians* (Grand Rapids, MI, 2007).

[4] Peter Brown, *Relics and Social Status in the Age of Gregory of Tours* (Reading, 1977); Brown, *Society and the Holy in Late Antiquity* (Berkeley, CA, 1989), 18–19.

[5] R. W. Scribner, 'Ritual and Popular Religion in Catholic Germany at the Time of the Reformation', *Journal of Ecclesiastical History*, 35 (1984), 69–71.

ritual further: they assembled elements of liturgy, para-liturgy, magical tradition, and invention to face off against the devil, as well as urging him to reveal his name, and using blessings and curses to free the possessed.[6] Exorcism notably appropriated the routine expulsion of the devil used on the newborn child in the sacrament of baptism. Jewish traditions (or their medieval appropriations) also seem to have been a characteristic influence.[7]

Because exorcists often worked in public spaces, such as chapels, interrogating demons in the bodies of the possessed, the exorcist's potential pact with the devil was there for all to see—at least, for those with the inclination to see. By the later Middle Ages, not only had the work of exorcism as an antidote to paganism become largely redundant, but the tables had begun to turn. In reaction to Renaissance 'new paganism', exorcism became caught up in critiques of learned, male magicians, and Catholic reformers saw exorcism more as a symptom of paganism than its opposite.

Medieval theology increasingly condemned male magicians for having made a pact with the devil in order to obtain the knowledge they sought to work magic.[8] The exorcist, in this light, could be seen as little different from a witch, a servant of the devil, of which he purported to be the master. The line tended to blur between exorcists' (often home-grown) altruistic healing rites, and those used for the conjuration of demons for the selfish purpose of attaining magical powers. In 1398 the faculty of theology at the University of Paris, under the influence of its chancellor Jean Gerson (1363–1429), condemned illicit exorcisms amid its wider critique of the conjuring demons to gain power over the natural world. Item 13 of the twenty-eight-point 'Condemnation of Magic' objects specifically to exorcism, stating that it is 'an error and a blasphemy' to believe that by magical arts 'the holy prophets and other saints... performed miracles or expelled demons'.[9] In Spain in the early sixteenth century, the reforming priests Pedro Ciruelo (1470–1560) and Martín de Castañega (1485?–1551?) singled out fraudulent exorcists as the embodiment of all the problems the Church faced. Ciruelo referred to priests who claimed to have special powers to exorcise as 'certainly aligned with the devil',[10] while Castañega saw exorcists who used magical rituals such as describing 'circles on the ground, with certain letters and signs inside' for public exorcism as 'ministers and disciples of the devil and

---

[6] Richard Kieckhefer, *Forbidden Rites: A Necromancer's Manual of the Fifteenth Century* (University Park, PA, 1997).

[7] Kieckhefer, *Forbidden Rites*, 116, 161. On Jewish elements see also: Armando Maggi, *Satan's Rhetoric: A Study of Renaissance Demonology* (Chicago, 2001), 101–2.

[8] Richard Kieckhefer, *Magic in the Middle Ages* (2nd edn, Cambridge, 2000), 196–7; Edward Peters, *The Magician, the Witch, and the Law* (Philadelphia, PA, 1982), *passim*.

[9] 'The University of Paris: A Condemnation of Magic, 1398', in Brian P. Levack, ed., *The Witchcraft Sourcebook* (New York, 2004), 47–50, quote at 49.

[10] *Pedro Ciruelo's A Treatise Reproving all Superstitions and Forms of Witchcraft: Very Necessary and Useful for all Good Christians Zealous for Their Salvation (c. 1530)*, tr. Eugene A. Maio and D'Orsay W. Pearson; ed. D'Orsay W. Pearson (London, 1977), 272.

deceived by him'.[11] Ciruelo complained that a 'fraudulent exorcist . . . exchanges many words with the devil, wastes much time in questions and answers, and performs all this in the presence of a large audience'.[12] Rapid dispatch was the most frequent plea.

Both Ciruelo and Castañega saw the need to distinguish between licit and illicit rituals as a necessary response to the apparent efflorescence of exorcist practice in communities. They urged prelates not to allow specialist exorcists into their dioceses. In a light mode, but with no less intent, the 1524 colloquy of Erasmus of Rotterdam (1466–1536), entitled *Exorcism*, elevated the role of learned clergy and pilloried as a fool the exorcist who 'looked upon himself as uncommonly wise, especially in divinity'.[13] Such works expressed the view that only the truly learned could ensure that the devil did not sneak in under the guard of the Church by mimicking its rites. A rhetoric of discernment, however, did not mean that an instant uniformity was at hand to be imposed by the Church. Erasmus, for example, parodied one of the rites approved by Ciruelo, and different authorities had very different interpretations of where the line should be drawn between licit and illicit. Systematization nonetheless became one of the tasks of the later sixteenth century: at the level of ritual it led to the publication of a papally approved exorcism ritual in the *Rituale romanum* in 1614. In administrative terms, reforming bishops such as Carlo and Federigo Borromeo in Milan tightened control of exorcisms by their city clergy, while inquisitors pressed rural clergy to explain what they thought they were doing when they used unapproved rituals to heal the bewitched.[14]

Notwithstanding the suspicion that surrounded their rites—and, indeed, perhaps as a defensive response to it—there were also educated promoters of exorcism. These clerics and authors, most of whom belonged to the regular clergy, positioned themselves as legitimate sources of moral and ritual leadership in the Church. Notably, members of the Franciscan, Dominican, and Jesuit orders saw themselves as the vanguard against the new menaces to true religion, in the form of both witches and heretics—the latter being the new Evangelical and Reformed churches. Girolamo Menghi (1529–1609), an Italian Franciscan, was chief among these proponents of the rite. He produced several books in Italian and Latin, most notably the best-selling *Flagellum daemonum* (*Flail of Demons*) of 1576, which exorcists across Europe brandished to show their own legitimacy. In systematizing the rite he also sought to defend it against the 'elevated intellects' who held it as suspect.[15]

Though not noted as a major witch-hunter, Menghi referred to the value of exorcism in identifying the work of witches.[16] In Provence, the Dominican Prior Sébastien

[11] Darst, ed., 'Witchcraft in Spain,' 317.

[12] Ciruelo, *A Treatise Reproving all Superstitions*, 275.

[13] Desiderius Erasmus, 'Exorcism', in *Ten Colloquies*, tr. Craig R. Thompson (New York, 1957), 37–46, quote at 39.

[14] Mary R. O'Neil, '"Sacerdote ovvero strione": Ecclesiastical and Superstitious Remedies in Sixteenth-century Italy', in Steven L. Kaplan, ed., *Understanding Popular Culture* (Berlin, 1984), 53–83, quote at 74; Moshe Sluhovsky, *Believe Not Every Spirit: Possession, Mysticism, and Discernment in Early Modern Catholicism* (Chicago, 2007), 76–7.

[15] O'Neil, '"Sacerdote ovvero strione"', 54.

[16] Sluhovsky, *Believe Not Every Spirit*, 79.

Michaëlis (1543–1618) began his public career as a witch-hunter and later emerged as something of an innovator by combining the vigorous use of exorcism to elicit 'demonic' evidence from the possessed to secure a witchcraft prosecution against a fellow priest, Louis Gaufridy, at an Ursuline convent in Aix-en-Provence (1609–11). He later moved north to Lille to attempt the same success in another convent. However, the faculty of theology at Louvain placed his co-authored book about the Provence case under interdict, underscoring the suspicion attendant on activist exorcists.[17]

Both Catholic and Protestant clerics used exorcism to discover the work of witches through the ritual of exorcism. It was a widely held view that the identity of someone who had caused witchcraft (of any kind) needed to be established before the spell could be lifted. In cases involving exorcism, this took on a new and problematic aspect when the exorcist called on the supposed special powers of demons to reveal how and through whose ill will they had come to enter the body of the possessed. Exorcists permitted, indeed encouraged, the possessed to name supposed witches in order to make healing possible. The idea that witches could send demons directly into the body of the possessed was somewhat controversial; it was not assumed that witches could direct demons. In most of the cases in which possession occurred as a result of witchcraft, the use of magic charms either hidden or given in food was the more common attribution, bridging the divide between common bewitchment and the direct command of devils.

Early modern rituals seem distinctive in the history of Christian exorcisms for their formidable duration, involving hours, days, even months during which exorcists interrogated demons of the possessed but were unable to expel them, seemingly justifying endless conversations with humanity's mortal enemy. A decisive feature of the rite of exorcism was its quasi-judicial character, which permitted the direct interrogation of resistant demons. This pointed to exploitation of the rite for the purposes of proselytism and controversy, and it was a feature which both resonated with and became a 'value-added' element in the context of actual trials for witchcraft, whether ecclesiastical or secular. In *Unclean Spirits* (1984) D. P. Walker countered a common assumption that exorcism refers, at base, to the expulsion of the demon. He noted that the word exorcism derived from the Greek (*exorkisein*), that is, to place on oath. Successful exorcism hinged on the capacity of the exorcist to place the possessing demon on oath, in order to ascertain, for example, its name (as a prelude to expelling it) and, often most controversially, the reason for its presence.[18] Many exorcists of all kinds—regulars, secular priests, even bishops—took an active role in public exorcisms and worked to root out the witches who they believed had caused the possession.

---

[17] Alain Lottin, *Lille, citadelle de la contre-réforme?: 1598–1668* (Dunkirk, 1984), 176–7.

[18] Armando Maggi, *In the Company of Demons: Unnatural Beings, Love, and Identity in the Italian Renaissance* (Chicago, 2008), 64.

In several witch trials the power of this judicial feature was entrenched further when, in the process of exorcism, the exorcists spiritually tortured the possessing demon to reveal 'under oath' evidence of activity at the witches' sabbath. Thus, the torture used in witch trials worked in counterpoint with exorcism to fuel, often literally, the fires of persecution. This was one of the reasons that notorious legal cases of possession became as dramatic as they did. In at least two cases—at Aix-en-Provence and at Louviers in the 1640s—the bodies of possessed nuns were the medium for accessing the stories of the sabbath, which then transited into the legal forum, with lethal consequences. That the devil was, according to John 8:44, also the Father of Lies did not significantly impede these heavily politicized trials. The frequent affirmation of exorcists that 'he' must be believed if the exorcism is successful provided sufficient, if circular, logic to act on the basis of what the devil said. Most notorious, perhaps, were the several cases in France in which the possessed, speaking under exorcism, accused males, several of them priests, of having caused the possession through witchcraft. These cases generated vituperative pamphlet wars that extended across decades, each case referencing the ones before. In the end, however, the most lethal of the possession/witch trials were not related to internecine struggles in the Church. Rather they were trials involving lay possessed accusers, which ended in multiple executions, such as those in *carroi* de Marlou in France (1582–3), and in Paderborn (1656–9).[19]

Later, in England particularly, Puritan exorcists used prayer and fasting to heal the possessed and to expose witchcraft.[20] In New Spanish colonies there were several cases of demonic possession among religious women.[21] It is sometimes suggested that the witch trials at Salem were possession cases, but this does not really hold true. They included features that had, by that time, become recognized as part of the public religious repertoire, such as the affliction of young women, malicious witchcraft accusations, and self-aggrandizing clergy. But this series of trials were not strictly cases of possession, and the work of the witch-hunters was not strictly a form of ritual exorcism.

From the mid-sixteenth century, in the wake of the early successes of the Evangelical and later Reformed Christian churches, exorcism provided Catholic priests with a significant platform in their battles against their confessional opponents. For the Jesuit Louis Richeome (1544–1625), the Catholic Church's historical strength could be traced

---

[19] Nicole Jacques-Chaquin and Maxime Préaud, *Les Sorciers du carroi de Marlou: un procès de sorcellerie en Berry, 1582–1583* (Grenoble, 1996); Rainer Decker, *Witchcraft and the Papacy: An Account Drawing on the Formerly Secret Records of the Roman Inquisition*, tr. H. C. Erik Midelfort (Charlottesville, VA, 2008), 157–73. See also E. William Monter, *A Bewitched Duchy: Lorraine and its Dukes, 1477–1736* (Geneva, 2007), 112–23, which refers to the mass possession of 85 people at Mattaincourt, which led to two executions for witchcraft. There is yet to be an overview study of the phenomenon of mass possessions.

[20] D. P. Walker, *Unclean Spirits: Possession and Exorcism in France and England in the Late Sixteenth and Early Seventeenth Centuries* (London, 1981), 49–73.

[21] Fernando Cervantes, *The Devil in the New World: The Impact of Diabolism in New Spain* (New Haven, CT, 1994), 115–24.

directly to the continued historical lineage of its successful exorcisms.[22] In Germany and France, in particular, exorcists used the Host as well as saints' relics and other sacramental paraphernalia to display the power of the Catholic Church to constrain demons. Pushing the limits of licit ritual to extremes, they interrogated the demons in the bodies of the possessed: usually women or girls; rarely married; sometimes nuns; of all ages, but mostly young. Exorcists sought to force the demon's 'reluctant' endorsement of the power of the Catholic Church against the heretics. Because, as exorcists reasoned, the devil was, of necessity, on the side of the heretics, 'his' submission in the face of exorcism showed the greater power of the Church. These rituals thus brought forth verbal testimony from demons on the power of exorcism and drew attention to the rite of exorcism as one of the most uncompromising features of Catholic revival.[23] They also elicited scepticism: endless speeches, devils who announced their own scheduled departure times, and communally divisive exorcisms gave weight to fears that the devil was on the loose, in the most elusive form, beguiling and confusing, in the pursuit of fraudulent holiness.

32.2 THE MEDIEVAL HOLY WOMAN AS ROLE MODEL FOR THE POSSESSED

One of the most striking features of demonic possession in the period of the witch trials is the emergence of the demoniac as someone who might resemble a saint. The phenomenon of 'positive possession' was not without historical, biblical, or mythic precedent. However, the scale on which it arose in the early modern era seems to be distinctive, as a new accretion on the widespread affective religiosity of the later medieval period. It would be impossible to make sense of this new, if bleak, 'career option' for women, without some appreciation of the significance of the holy women of the later Middle Ages as role models for many of the possessed in early modern era.[24] Extensively documented in modern historiography, these saintly women, many of whom were officially canonized, provided inspiration to young Catholic women, both to those who resisted the religious life, and those who embraced its exigencies.[25] As religious houses multiplied in the era of Catholic revival from the mid-sixteenth

---

[22] Louis Richeome, *Trois discours pour la religion Catholique: des miracles, des saincts et des images* (Bordeaux, 1598), 38.

[23] See, for example, Lyndal Roper, 'Exorcism and the Theology of the Body', in *Oedipus and the Devil* (London, 1994), 171–98; Sarah Ferber, *Demonic Possession and Exorcism in Early Modern France* (London, 2004); Lederer, *Madness, Religion and the State*, 206–14.

[24] Adult male possessions were few but not unknown. See: Sarah Ferber, 'Possession and the Sexes', in Alison Rowlands, ed., *Witchcraft and Masculinities in Early Modern Europe* (Basingstoke, 2009), 214–38.

[25] See, for example, the numerous studies by Alison Weber, Anne Jacobson-Schutte, Gabriella Zarri, Jodi Bilinkoff, John W. Coakley, Dyan Elliott, and Nancy Caciola, among others.

century, women such as Bl. Angela of Foligno (1248–1309), St Catherine of Sienna (1347–1480), St Brigid of Sweden (1303–1373), as well as the modern examples of St Magdalena de' Pazzi (1566–1607) and St Teresa of Avila (1515–1582), showed ways to be holy without absolute retreat from the world. Many of these women came to achieve prominence as the recipients of divine favour in the form of direct communications from God, as well as the gifts of special spiritual insight, clairvoyance, raptures, and ecstasies. Beyond the well-known figures there was a large number of would-be holy people, most of them women, whose proliferation gave rise to anxiety among clerical authorities, male and female.

Visionaries, models of self-sacrifice, champions of the Roman Church, and, crucially, models of resistance to the torments imposed by demons (in forms other than possession) were the types of women to whom some of the most prominent demoniacs of the early modern era referred when they came to reflect on their lives. From the ecstasies of the holy woman learning of the state of souls in purgatory to the demoniac 'falling as if dead' under the sway of demons, learning the secrets of the witches' sabbath, or indeed also of purgatory, was quite a short step. People who saw the possessed did not always differentiate in their reading of what the possessed or the local lay saint, for example, could offer them. They sought the same kind of clairvoyant advice that they would have from a holy woman, or indeed in some cases, from a witch. It was a short step, too, between the torment external demons imposed on the saints in their struggle for holiness in the medieval era, and the inwardly tormented demoniac of the early modern era. A premium on martyrdom in the early modern Catholic Church added value to the torment of possession: suffering or the status of a victim purchased an additional portion of credibility for potentially dubious pretensions to sanctity.

Yet the very potential for worldly prominence in this life or beyond bore with it the risk that these women would be seen as either the direct agents or the deluded victims of the Prince of the World, the devil. In the view, once again, of the inestimably influential Jean Gerson, unchecked manifestations of affective spirituality had the capacity to undermine the currency of holiness, responding to or even embodying demons disguised as 'angels of light', the classic trope of the expanding discernment literature.[26] As brokers in the marketplace of this powerful spiritual currency, the exorcist often played a special role: any signs or claims for holiness could be tested by the use of 'probative' exorcisms, and the exorcist was, in many cases, a sensor (and censor) in relation to claims of female holiness. The bodies of enraptured holy women were, in the words of Alison Weber, 'mysteriously polyvalent texts' for which exorcism provided a path to accurate perception.[27]

---

[26] Jean Gerson, *De distinctione verarum visionum a falsis*, in *The Concept of Discretio Spirituum in John Gerson's "De probatione spirituum" and "De distinctione verarum visionum a falsis"*, ed. and tr. Pascal Boland (Washington, DC, 1959), 80; Alison Weber, 'Between Ecstasy and Exorcism', *Journal of Medieval and Renaissance Studies*, 23 (1993), 222.

[27] Weber, 'Between Ecstasy and Exorcism', 230.

The exorcism of a holy woman provided the opportunity for a diagnosis that the signs of rapture were signs of possession by demons. Therefore, the behaviour lay somewhere on a continuum with witchcraft, that is, a woman was either merely deluded by demons, or worse, had consciously accorded them her will in exchange for a reputation of holiness. Again, in its judicial nature, exorcism both enacted and echoed the interrogatory work of inquisitions, notably in Spain, which sought to mitigate popular reliance on the holiness of women operating outside the bounds of Church hierarchy.[28] St Teresa of Avila's own confessors were 'prepared to have her exorcised' although she became in the end a triumphant example of Catholic reform.[29] In stark contrast Magdalena de la Cruz, an abbess reputed for her holiness, underwent investigation by the Inquisition and admitted that she was a fraud. She said that she made a pact with the devil, who gave her a lover in the form of a Moor. She was not convicted of witchcraft, interestingly, but condemned to live out her life in religion with the lowliest rank in the convent.[30] Such a dramatic fall served as a cautionary tale against the too-eager embrace of claims to holiness by women and, later, the holy possessed.

32.3 THE EARLY MODERN MEANINGS OF POSSESSION

Demonic possession is generally understood as the invasion of a person's body by one or more demons in ways that, if left untreated, can pose a threat to the fate of their eternal soul by leading the person to sin and/or (in Catholicism at least) preventing participation in the sacraments. Its symptoms are extremely varied: the classic manifestations are those described in the gospels, but early modern sources elaborated on these, with Francesco Maria Guazzo's *Compendium maleficarum* identifying around fifty.[31] D. P. Walker isolated four as the most significant for the early modern era: extreme physical strength, ability to understand foreign languages, knowledge of secrets and distant things, and revulsion when confronted by holy objects.[32] As a condition with an irreducible spiritual element, possession itself was not strictly identifiable other than by reference to the rite of exorcism: not only did exorcism bring out the devils masked behind a show of holiness, it served to discern possession from natural physical or mental illnesses. A physician might diagnose possession by a

---

[28] Sluhovsky, *Believe not Every Spirit*, 181.

[29] Weber, 'Between Ecstasy and Exorcism', 230, n. 28.

[30] Gillian T. W. Ahlgren, 'Negotiating Sanctity: Holy Women in Sixteenth-Century Spain', *Church History*, 64 (1995), 373–88, at 383.

[31] Francesco Maria Guazzo, *Compendium Maleficarum*, tr. E. A. Ashwin, ed. Montague Summers (New York, 1988), 167–9.

[32] Walker, *Unclean Spirits*, 12.

process of elimination once he was satisfied his own knowledge or healing power had reached its limits, but he was not qualified to treat it.

A full typology of possession would be vast (if not endless): from the single case swiftly cured; through group possessions, among both laity and in religious houses; to the notion espoused by the exorcist Giovan Battista Chiesa, that all illness was a form of possession— meaning for him that nine thousand of every ten thousand people were possessed.[33] There is sufficient evidence to suggest that thousands of people in the medieval and early modern era experienced possession as a terrible imposition; thus we must pause on their plight before going onto analysis. Setting aside the often polemical or strategic uses of descriptions of the suffering occasioned by possession, and the idea that it was predomin- antly discussed for some promotional end, there remains a credible case for evidence of emotional devastation on a grand scale, which came to be designated as possession and was sometimes expressed merely as an intense personal or collective affliction.

What counts in *stories* of possession (as distinct from the *experience* of the condition) is that it is legible, ultimately and exclusively, on a moral register. Possession might be punishment for another's sin; the result of another's malicious causing of the possession; a sign of something like holiness, elevated through suffering; or a consequence of the practice of evil itself, including the practice of magic. The diverse historical forms that stories of possession took led to a widely accepted view of its multiple possible causes.[34] Martín de Castañega identified three ways in which a person might be possessed by the devil: 'First, as his subject and prisoner; second, as his disciple, by an express or occult pact; and third, as an innocent object of his torment.'[35] The physician Barthélemy Pardoux, writing in 1639, referred to negatives such as 'infidelity, vexatious arguments, abuse of sacred things, the persecution of good people, contempt of religion, mistreat- ment of parents, horrible curses . . . the impiety of magicians'. But he conceded that God also permits the possession of people of 'good and holy life and of irreproachable appearance . . . in order to avenge the sins of parents on their children or for some other incomprehensible effect of His providence'.[36] In practice, the final twist was suspicion attendant on the latter—of a person whose possession had been a sign of their innocence or even holiness. Thus, in Paderborn during the possession epidemic of 1656–9, one laywoman was first diagnosed as possessed, but in the end was executed for witchcraft, and at Aix-en-Provence in 1653, Madeleine de Demandols was prosecuted for witchcraft nearly forty years after testifying as a young nun–demoniac in the trial of the alleged witch-priest, Louis Gaufridy.[37]

[33] Giovanni Levi, *Inheriting Power: The Story of an Exorcist*, tr. Lydia Cochrane (Chicago, 1988), 4.

[34] See also the discussion in H. C. Erik Midelfort, 'The Devil and the German People: Reflections on the Popularity of Demon Possession in Sixteenth-Century Germany', in Steven Ozment, ed., *Religion and Reformation* (Kirksville, MO, 1989), 99–119.

[35] Darst, ed., 'Witchcraft in Spain', 319.

[36] Paraphrased in Congnard, *Histoire de Marthe Brossier pretendue possedee* (Rouen, 1652), 22–3.

[37] Decker, *Witchcraft and the Papacy*, 172; Anita Walker and Edmund Dickerman, 'A Notorious Woman: Possession, Witchcraft and Sexuality in Seventeenth-century Provence', *Historical Reflections*, 27 (2001), 1–26.

For the possessed who were victims two principal explanatory schemes were at work: possession as a result of bewitchment (especially of children by older people), a common allegation in witch trials; and possession as a result of some kind of cursing, particularly adults cursing children. The first was malicious and intentional, the second more like a sin of abandon, something with dire consequences that could have been avoided had the person who uttered the curse considered the serious implications of their blasphemy. In cases of possession as a result of deliberate witchcraft, alleged use of love magic by a male suitor on a female was a significant cause.[38] Magic charms, possibly delivered without the woman's knowledge, threatened the elevated status of virginity inside religious houses and among 'lay saints'. Even when the woman was in some way an agent of this misfortune—by having felt sexual attraction in spite of herself, for example—insistence on a rhetoric of martyrdom could serve to counterbalance any sense of a culpable, self-serving state of possession.

To modern sentiment, the idea that possession could be both credible and something like a 'life choice' does not ring true: surely these people were frauds? Moreover, from a feminist perspective it could be argued in a functionalist way that the role of the female demoniac—which might entail lengthy 'diabolical' discourses on religious themes in a manner only suitable for a male preacher—was one in which women could take on a spiritually significant role. What needs to be borne in mind, before imputing modern secular motives to the possessed, is that they worked within a system which widely accepted the possibility that such demonic incursions were often real. Just as admissions of fraud usually only came when the person was under some kind of duress, perhaps sending modernizing interpreters off on a false scent, it also tended to be only when the stakes were high that scepticism intensified. These assertions of the 'cultural reality' of possession are by now something of nostrum of recent historiography, having arisen in reaction to the materialist and psychologizing views of earlier scholarly work. It is nonetheless worth being mindful that, even among believers such as the abbot Caesarius of Heisterbach, as early as the thirteenth century the possibility of actual fraud (however hard to define) was not discounted.[39]

32.4 DEVIL WORSHIP

Witchcraft historiography has retreated from generalization at perhaps an even faster rate than studies of other historical phenomena. Historians long ago abandoned the attempt to interpret the diverse manifestations of beliefs about witchcraft in the light of a single interpretative schema. Yet narrative still requires some kind of exploratory if

[38] Witch-priests causing possession to gratify their lust were also known in the medieval era. See P. G. Maxwell-Stuart, ed. and tr., *The Occult in Mediaeval Europe* (Basingstoke, 2005), 56–8.

[39] Caesarius of Heisterbach, *The Dialogue on Miracles*, tr. H. von E. Scott and C. C. Swinton Bland, with introduction by G. C. Coulton (London, 1929), i, 333.

not wholly explanatory framework. An analysis that considers the fears of devil worship characteristic of the later medieval and early modern era lays stress on the question of human beings' relationship and duty to God, and their presumed interactions with the devil. Religion mediated relations between people, but it is important to contemplate that the actors themselves were, in many cases, experiencing their relations with *God* as the primary or only relationship to matter. Relations with human beings were secondary in every respect and potentially an impediment to the first.

The historian of European reform John Bossy, reading in this vein in 1988, brought to light a crucial development, in the context of his interest in the history of pastoral care.[40] The essay 'Moral Arithmetic: Seven Sins into Ten Commandments' argued that Catholic moral teaching of the later Middle Ages underwent a shift in emphasis from the seven deadly sins—anger, greed, sloth, pride, lust, envy, and gluttony—to an emphasis on the need for the populace and the clergy to adhere to the Ten Commandments. Citing a new emphasis 'more on worship than on love', Bossy referred to the first two commandments: 'Thou shalt have no other gods before me; and Thou shalt not make unto thee any graven image.'[41] Focused against pagans, this theology pictured one god against many idols of other faiths. By the later Middle Ages, the injunction had come to point more narrowly to the threat posed by the idea of devil worship. Fear of demonolatry seems to have added a powerful accelerant to concerns about sins against God. Bossy singles out changes in attitudes to witchcraft, therefore, as a prime example of the shift in focus to the Ten Commandments.[42]

Bossy's observation is especially important for the purpose of the present chapter, as he underlines the significance of ritual in the second commandment. He argues: 'The rationale of the Decalogue was the prohibition of idolatry; it was a ritual as well as moral code; its purpose was to keep the people of Israel in holiness, and thereby ensure the perpetuity of their alliance with God; its strategy was the fear of the Lord.' The classic text in the history of demonology, Stuart Clark's 1997 *Thinking with Demons*, underscored Bossy's observations in relation to the sin of superstition as that which most violated the first commandment.[43] The etymology of the word 'superstition' pertains to the idea of superfluous or inappropriate rituals. As one authority wrote in 1643: '[S]uperstition is defective worship in which either a creature is honoured with

---

[40] John Bossy, 'Moral Arithmetic: Seven Sins into Ten Commandments', in Edmund Leites, ed., *Conscience and Casuistry in Early Modern Europe* (Cambridge, 1988), 222.

[41] Bossy, 'Moral Arithmetic', 223. This chapter follows Bossy in using the Calvinist/Anglican system in which the graven images are number two and the two commandments against coveting (neighbour's ox, neighbour's wife) are under the tenth.

[42] Bossy's chronology holds well in terms of the critical mass of materials written and their overall emphasis. However, the theme of devil worship was articulated throughout the Middle Ages, in imputations of both paganism and heresy, some of which also touched on later witchcraft beliefs.

[43] Modern readers will be more familiar with 'superstition' as a term that refers to a ritualized and wholly faulty understanding of the natural operations that occur to link physical cause and effect. See Peter Burke, *Popular Culture in Early Modern Europe* (3rd edn, Farnham, 2009), 331.

divine worship or God in worshipped in a way He should not be . . .'[44] Trivial in modern parlance, the early modern view of superstition encompassed all unapproved healing and magical practices as devil worship. One of the great delusions of witches, in the eyes of reformers, was a mistaken belief that their ritual actions could bring about effects on their own account, rather than with the help of the devil. In cases of witchcraft, by definition, but also in the ritual of exorcism, illicit ritual was the invoking of demons for the purpose of attaining magical powers.

Devil worship could be understood as any form of 'sacrifice' made with any expectation of help from the devil. It could emerge in cases of alleged witchcraft, of holy possession, of more traditional holiness, and exorcism. This line of thinking linked alleged witches to the suspect holy woman, the suspect holy possessed, or the apparently holy exorcist.[45] Worldly benefits included admiration of other people, 'living' sanctity or canonization after death, wealth, or false illumination. Thus, the magician offers his soul in return for magical powers; an exorcist brings forth demons who (he believes) bend to his will; the ecstatic consigns her virginity to the devil (rather than to Christ); the possessed woman seems holy because she is suffering at the hands of the devil; the witch receives from the devil the ability to go out at night and fly through the air. Any of these implies the possibility of becoming beholden to the devil for worldly benefits.

Receiving the devil's help always came at the highest cost for even the slightest service, for seemingly small sacrifices meant the devil held the person captive. The surrender of the witch's body in diabolical seduction represented the unwitting surrender of the soul through the medium of the unthinking flesh. The giving of a locket of hair, the formal legal surrender of the soul in a written pact, the surrender of the soul evidenced by a demonic mark were all, ultimately, evidence that the sacrifice was willingly made. This surrender was expressed in the identification of a wide spectrum of self-seeking and worldly acts associated with ecstatic spirituality, witchcraft, and exorcism.

Active worship of devils by witches at the sabbath was the extreme point of imagined behaviour of witches, but trivial actions were morally equivalent. When accused witches said (most often under torture or some other duress) that they had renounced their baptism, taken the devil as master, surrendered sexually to demons, or performed the obscene kiss on the devil, they were describing several versions of 'worship'. Acceptance of the devil's mark or the signing of a pact provided clear evidence of devil worship. This mark served in many trials, in effect, as evidence of the illiterate person's pact. A mark given by the devil implicitly pointed to the devil having gained access to the soul of the person, via his or her body; consent was visible in the devil's tattoo.

---

[44] From Carolus de Baucius, *Modus interrogandi daemonum ab exorcista* (1643), excerpted in Maxwell-Stuart, *The Occult in Early Modern Europe*, 60–1.

[45] The Paris faculty's twelfth item states that demon worship through misplaced sacrifice is to be found in the practice even of good works (such as prayer, fasting, and the celebration of the Mass), which are intended to cleanse the magician prior to performing a magical act. Thus, the fact that the next item on the list refers specifically to exorcism underscores the fact that the faculty had in mind clerical magicians, as well as lay ones.

Nor was outright seduction by the devil necessary. Witchcraft narratives tell of demons who tempt with promises of love, food, or money, while the holy possessed and the holy woman by their very prominence are suspect because of the enduring value attached in religious life to resisting the sin of pride. The jurist Jean Bodin and Jesuit Martín Del Rio, for example, tell of a claimed visionary, a young girl from Saragossa, who ultimately revealed the demonic source of her powers when she admitted that she had provided a hair to him.[46] For the would-be holy person, even fame through suffering apparent torture by demons or acts of extreme, eye-catching, self-mortification could be re-read as service to the devil.

A sin against divine majesty was perceptible in the most trivial act of popular magic, describing the supposedly unmistakable arc which was held to link uneducated use of (usually) Christian ritual and objects to obtain worldly ends to the extremes of renunciation of baptism. This kind of conflation of individual behaviours with cosmic-ally and socially corrosive ones was characteristic of the way in which demonology operated in the early modern era. Demonization narrowed the explanatory boundaries and cut a deep ideological path from the activities recommended for communities to the heart of individual psychology. If the Ten Commandments were originally laws that bound a community to its god, repudiating the threat of other competing religions, the demonology of the early modern era linked the most extreme imagined exaltation of the devil to the most common human foible.

Commission and omission, in this light, became conflated. Most poignant of these 'sins' against the first commandment was perhaps that of despair. The late medieval *ars moriendi* depicted despair of God's mercy at the point of death as one of the risks to the soul's chance of eternal life.[47] By the sixteenth century, despair took its place among the causes of both demonic possession and the sin of witchcraft. In sixteenth-century exorcism manuals, as Moshe Sluhovsky notes, one of the key causes of possession was the person's despair. Clark, similarly, identifies the crime of witchcraft and recourse to superstitious practices as the consequence of despair of God's mercy. The use of illicit magic as a consequence of despair thus amounted to the very same despair that led to possession. In both, the person risks the fate of the soul through turning away (if unknowingly) from God. Ignorance is no excuse for giving offence.

Modern historians have characterized the overarching social, institutional, and theological drives of the period by reference to such developments as the separation of sacred from profane, the intellectualization and interiorization of religiosity, the demonization of popular belief (or 'demonization of the world' as it has also been called[48]), and the clericalization of religious practice. The discourse of demonology contemplated exhaustively the vagaries of the devil, a wilful being appropriating the worst of human will to its own evil ends. A script about human cooperation with the

---

[46] Ferber, *Demonic Possession*, 118.

[47] Austra Reinis, *Reforming the Art of Dying: The ars moriendi in the German Reformation (1519–1528)* (Aldershot, 2007), 23.

[48] Midelfort, 'The Devil and the German People', 99.

devil fed into an interpretation of the alleged behaviours of witches, the possessed, holy persons, and exorcists. New meaning was created, new assumptions generated, and fear and excitement spread. Demonization both gratified and nourished previously held prejudices, while the campaign against superstition was accompanied by a substantial social agenda. The distance and difference that reform sought to place between God and humanity, between material and spiritual, was enacted in a social imperative of distancing of educated from uneducated, clergy from laity, and, in many cases, men from women. The priority given to the first two commandments therefore participates in multiple related processes of social distinction—around class and gender, for example— and arguments for a change of practice. Local factors played a role, too. As noted above, the politics of Christian reconquest of the Iberian Peninsula led Martín de Castañega to see the fight against ignorant exorcists, and that against other representatives of the 'devil's church' in the form of Jews and Muslims, as the same battle. A characteristic if not a defining feature of all of these trends was a concern about devil worship.

32.5 DECLINE

Explaining why an established phenomenon ceases to occur remains a challenge for any historian; it always seems easier to claim to know how or why something *starts*. For the historiography of witchcraft, again, the reasons for the decline in prosecution has been strongly debated, not least because traditional assumptions about the triumph of Enlightenment sensibility and the rise of science have been found wanting. By the eighteenth century witchcraft prosecutions overall, and with them confessions and accusations about the witches' sabbath, had declined. It has been suggested that disbelief about the sabbath was one of the factors that led to a decline in witch trials. One door—the use of exorcism to 'see' into the sabbath—closed between the practice of exorcism and the goal of witch prosecution.

If one subscribes to the view that societies that have suffered several disruptions will naturally gravitate towards a state of equilibrium, it would be easy to suggest that the socially divisive character of witch trials in general and those generated by exorcism cases in particular gave grounds to wariness in communities where such cases occurred. In 1968 Robert Mandrou speculated that dramatic French cases of demonic possession and witch trials induced such shock in official opinion as to influence the history of witch trials in that country. His view has some validity, as these cases did lead to sharp lines being drawn between powerful opposing views, but, as Briggs notes, other evidence shows that no automatic decline in witch trials can be attributed solely to the effect of a handful of controversial cases, even in France.[49] Nonetheless,

---

[49] Robert Mandrou, *Magistrats et sorciers en France au XVIIe siècle* (Paris, 1968), 197–312; Robin Briggs, *Witches and Neighbours: The Social and Cultural Context of European Witchcraft* (Oxford, 2002), 112–23.

Erik Midelfort's account of the most successful exorcist of the eighteenth century, the German Joseph Gassner, shows that one reason that Gassner's numerous public exorcisms gave rise to anxiety was a continuing fear that they would lead to accusations of witchcraft.

What became of the links between exorcism and affective spirituality after the period of the witch trials? The high-water mark of affective spirituality was the prolonged period from the late Middle Ages to the eighteenth century. Historians of Catholic spirituality have claimed something of an anti-mystic backlash in the early modern era, starting perhaps as early as the mid-sixteenth century, and best exemplified in the late seventeenth-century suppression of 'Quietism'.[50] Against this view, however, is a strong case that a 'backlash' mindset works historically alongside depth of belief, rather than in cycles. It is thus still not wholly clear why the link between exorcism and positive possession came to have less prominence, but certainly its value in promoting inter-confessional disharmony would have been less after the end of the Thirty Years' War. And as witch trials gradually diminished in number across Europe, the value of the exorcist as an interrogator of the devil would have likewise reduced. Affective spirituality was still a feature of Catholic practice in the nineteenth century, however, and claimed miracles became the subject of scientistic condemnation by secularizing physicians.[51] The elements that have changed the most are the diminished legal status of witch trials, the decline in outright religious war between Christian groups, and the significance of and openness to affective spirituality in the Catholic Church. 'Positive possession' seems to have vanished entirely from the map of holiness. Exorcism remains a part of the armoury of many modern Christian churches, however, and the diagnosis of demonic possession is probably not very much less common now than it was in the early modern era. Exorcism of the possessed occurs on a massive scale, in Christian churches of all kinds, worldwide, but without the development of cults around the possessed. And modern sainthood is less often linked to the practice of mystical spirituality. The risk associated now with exorcism is related to the injuries inflicted on the possessed themselves, rather than on secondary parties such as alleged witches. And routine exorcism continues to feature in baptisms, which in most confessions still contain some kind of more or less explicit acknowledgment that the godparent's role is to protect the newborn from the powers of the devil.

FURTHER READING

Ahlgren, Gillian T. W., 'Negotiating Sanctity: Holy Women in Sixteenth-Century Spain', *Church History*, 64 (1995), 373–88.
Behringer, Wolfgang, *Witches and Witch-Hunts: A Global History* (Cambridge, 2004).

---

[50] See Sluhovsky, *Believe Not Every Spirit*, 97–136.

[51] On medical readings of the Belgian visionary Louise Lateau see Jan Goldstein, *Console and Classify: The French Psychiatric Profession in the Nineteenth Century* (Cambridge, 1990), 371.

Clark, Stuart, *Thinking with Demons: The Idea of Witchcraft in Early Modern Europe* (Oxford, 1997).

Elliott, Dyan, *Proving Woman: Female Spirituality and Inquisitional Culture in Later Middle Ages* (Princeton, 2004).

Ferber, Sarah, *Demonic Possession and Exorcism in Early Modern France* (London, 2004).

Lederer, David, *Madness, Religion and the State in Early Modern Europe: The Bavarian Beacon* (Cambridge, 2006).

Levi, Giovanni, *Inheriting Power: The Story of an Exorcist* (Chicago, 1988).

Midelfort, H. C. Erik, 'The Devil and the German People: Reflections on the Popularity of Demon Possession in Sixteenth-Century Germany', in Steven Ozment, ed., *Religion and Reformation* (Kirksville, MO, 1989), 99–119.

Midelfort, H. C. Erik, *Exorcism and Enlightenment: Johann Joseph Gassner and the Demons of Eighteenth-Century Germany* (New Haven, CT, 2005).

O'Neil, Mary R., '"Sacerdote ovvero strione": Ecclesiastical and Superstitious Remedies in Sixteenth-Century Italy', in Steven L. Kaplan, ed., *Understanding Popular Culture* (Berlin, 1984), 53–83.

Scaraffia, Lucetta, and Gabriella Zarri, eds, *Women and Faith: Catholic Religious Life in Italy from Late Antiquity to the Present* (Cambridge, MA, 1999).

Schutte, Anne, *Aspiring Saints: Pretense of Holiness, Inquisition, and Gender in the Republic of Venice, 1618–1750* (Baltimore, MD, 2001).

Sluhovsky, Moshe, *Believe Not Every Spirit: Possession, Mysticism, and Discernment in Early Modern Catholicism* (Chicago, 2007).

Walker, D. P., *Unclean Spirits: Possession and Exorcism in France and England in the Late Sixteenth and Early Seventeenth Centuries* (London, 1981).

Weber, Alison, 'Between Ecstasy and Exorcism', *Journal of Medieval and Renaissance Studies*, 23 (1993), 221–34.

INDEX

Riis, Thomas 304
ritual: Christian 52; cleansing 132; counter-
magic 56; magic 4, 13, 26; murder 331;
traditional 52
rivalries, magical 350–1
Roberts, Gareth 304
Roermond, Netherlands 245
Roesch, Gottofried: *Exercitatio historico
philologica de cultu Simonis Magi* 342
Rojas, Fernando de: *La Celestina* 420, 421
Roman de la Rose 90–1
Romania 335, 337, 340, 343, 345
Roman Inquisition 253–8, 261–3, 264, 265–6,
270, 275, 277, 280, 383, 384, 430, 441, 474, 477–8
Roman law 35, 192, 194, 229, 236, 237; *lex
talionis* 471–2; revival in study of 472
romanticism 59, 66
Rome 250, 251, 252, 254, 258
Romeo, Giovanni 255, 261, 263
Roper, Lyndal 88–9, 143, 150–1, 315, 320, 460–1,
463, 464, 476, 570–1
Rosa, Salvator 145, 151, 152
Rose, Antonia 164–5
Rosenblatt, Jósef 327
Rosselló, Spain 272
Rostock, University of 195
Rothair, King of the Lombards 102
Rothenburg ob der Tauber, Franconia
183, 191, 476
Rottenburg am Neckar, Germany 186, 537
Rouen, Normandy 221; Parlement of 220,
222, 223, 225, 227–8, 431, 540
Rowley, William 138
Royal Society 297, 548, 551, 553, 555–6, 557
Rubens, Peter Paul 126
Rummel, Walter 215
runamicuc 418–19
rural areas: Amerindians in 414; disasters lead
to witchcraft accusations 181–2; influence
of physical geography 524–5; relationship
with towns 169, 173; socio-economic
factors 516–19; *see also* communities, local
Russell, Jeffrey 166
Russia 355–74; characteristics of the
accused 360–1; conceptions of
witchcraft 359–60; decriminalization 433;
law and legal process 356–9; male majority

as accused 356, 361, 362–4, 449, 465;
medieval 358; records 365–6; relationship
with, and comparison to Europe 365–6;
scholarship 364–72; Soviet 365, 366–7, 369;
torture 356, 357, 359, 360, 366, 475; Western
scholarship on 368, 370–1
Russian Orthodox Church 356–7, 364,
365, 372
Ruthenia 328–9, 332
Ryan, Will 371
Ryzhei, Ivan 355–6, 359, 362

Saarland 199, 201, 211, 517
Saar region 458, 461, 536–7
sabbaths 5, 33, 41, 84–100; African slaves
and 424–5; Alpine 'nocturnal meetings' 39;
Basque 425; birthplace of 220; Calvinist
view of 341; Catholicism and 455–6;
composite nature of 3; confessions on 169,
170; as 'dance' 86; de Lancre's description
of 80; development of concept 84–5, 486;
and devil worship 588; dissemination of
accounts of 96–8; diversity in descriptions
of 85–6; as dream experiences 215; earlier
terms for 93; early instances 90–3, 259;
evidence produced under torture 84, 85,
88–9; as fixed notion 159; France 220,
230–1; and gender 455–6, 466; Grillando's
description of 78–9; historiography 86–90;
Hungary 343, 345; Iberia 270, 274, 278–9,
280; as illusions 87; illustrations of 75,
85–6, 97, 149, 150; influence of classical texts
on concept 8; interrogations on 94;
intruder stories 88, 91, 95–6, 97–8; as
inversion of Christianity 86, 502; Italian
version of 260, 261; lack of witness
evidence 89, 95; later accounts of 93–6;
learned demonology on 45, 46, 71, 85, 87,
88, 89–90, 93, 95–6, 97; locations of 51;
Mexico 423; Norway 390; not mentioned
at some trials 174; origins of term 93;
Peru 425–6; as pre-Christian shamanistic
tradition 66; religious context 98–9;
scepticism about 112–13, 263, 487; sexual
aspect 87; similar descriptions of heretical
gatherings 103; Spanish America 417–18; as
stories 88, 90

Printed and bound by CPI Group (UK) Ltd, Croydon, CR0 4YY